Humanitarian Law in Action within Africa

HUMANITARIAN LAW IN ACTION WITHIN AFRICA

Jennifer Moore

Oxford University Press, Inc., publishes works that further Oxford University's objective of excellence in research, scholarship, and education.

Oxford   New York
Auckland   Cape Town   Dar es Salaam   Hong Kong   Karachi   Kuala Lumpur   Madrid   Melbourne
Mexico City   Nairobi   New Delhi   Shanghai   Taipei   Toronto

With offices in
Argentina   Austria   Brazil   Chile   Czech Republic   France   Greece   Guatemala   Hungary   Italy
Japan   Poland   Portugal   Singapore   South Korea   Switzerland   Thailand   Turkey   Ukraine
Vietnam

Copyright © 2012 by Oxford University Press, Inc.

Published by Oxford University Press, Inc.
198 Madison Avenue, New York, New York 10016

Oxford is a registered trademark of Oxford University Press
Oxford University Press is a registered trademark of Oxford University Press, Inc.

All rights reserved. No part of this publication may be reproduced, stored in a retrieval system, or transmitted, in any form or by any means, electronic, mechanical, photocopying, recording, or otherwise, without the prior permission of Oxford University Press, Inc.

Library of Congress Cataloging-in-Publication Data

Moore, Jennifer, 1961-
  Humanitarian law in action within Africa / Jennifer Moore.
     p. cm.
  Includes bibliographical references and index.
  ISBN 978-0-19-985696-1 (hardback: alk. paper)
  1. Humanitarian law. 2. Humanitarian law—Africa. I. Title.
  KZ6471.M66 2012
  341.6'7096—dc23   2011042322

---

9 8 7 6 5 4 3 2 1

Printed in the United States of America on acid-free paper

Note to Readers
This publication is designed to provide accurate and authoritative information in regard to the subject matter covered. It is based upon sources believed to be accurate and reliable and is intended to be current as of the time it was written. It is sold with the understanding that the publisher is not engaged in rendering legal, accounting, or other professional services. If legal advice or other expert assistance is required, the services of a competent professional person should be sought. Also, to confirm that the information has not been affected or changed by recent developments, traditional legal research techniques should be used, including checking primary sources where appropriate.

(Based on the Declaration of Principles jointly adopted by a Committee of the American Bar Association and a Committee of Publishers and Associations.)

You may order this or any other Oxford University Press publication by
visiting the Oxford University Press website at www.oup.com

To my parents
Jonathan and Katherine A. Moore

CONTENTS

Acknowledgments   ix

Introduction   1

PART I: International Legal Rules for Conflict Resolution
  1. The Human Fundamentals of International Law   13
  2. Humanitarian Law: The Law of Armed Conflict   45
  3. Human Rights Law: The Law of Human Dignity   75
  4. International Criminal Law: Accountability for Crimes of War and Crimes Against Humanity   123
  5. International Refugee Law: Protection for Individuals Fleeing Persecution and Armed Conflict   153

PART II: Humanitarian Law and Post-conflict Reconstruction in Africa
  6. Tools for Implementing Humanitarian Law: Courts, Troops, the Media, Development, and Communities   177
  7. Beyond Juba in Uganda: Reconciling Restorative and Retributive Justice   209
  8. After Lomé in Sierra Leone: The Special Court and National Reconciliation   241
  9. After Arusha in Burundi: Disarming the Heart to Disarm the Body   283

Conclusion   323

Index   335

ACKNOWLEDGMENTS

This book is a kind of tapestry woven from threads that bind me to fellow travelers and kindred spirits on both sides of the Atlantic Ocean. I am particularly grateful for the support of my colleagues and students at the University of New Mexico School of Law, the scholars and human rights defenders I met and interviewed in Uganda, Burundi and Sierra Leone, my editing team at Oxford University Press, and my home team of family and friends. Back in 2008, Kevin Pendergast, OUP Senior Acquisitions Editor, encouraged me to spin an idea about the relationship between punitive and restorative justice in post-conflict African countries into a book proposal. His enthusiasm, flexibility and expertise launched the book and helped me keep it afloat throughout the research and writing process. Without Kevin, this project would never have been started.

Thanks first to my UNM colleagues: to my students Heba Atwa, Brianne Bigej, Greg Cole, Kameron Kramer, and Sophia Lane, who provided inspiration, sounding boards and research assistance, as needed; to Ernesto Longa, law librarian par excellence, for his zeal in locating essential books and articles, peace accords and national constitutions; to Nancy Harbert and Carolyn Gonzales, our in-house journalists, for reporting on the project; to my Dean Kevin Washburn, for supporting not one but two research trips to Africa in one year; to my fellow law profs Jim Ellis, Chris Fritz, Laura Gomez, Fred Hart, Nathalie Martin and Liz Rapaport, for talking me through the various stages of writing process; to Prof. Norman Bay, for sharing his expertise on international criminal law and critiquing Chapter 4; to Dr. Steve Bishop in Africana Studies for introducing me to child soldier narratives and reviewing the chapter on Sierra Leone; and to Dr. Felipe Gonzales in Sociology for helping me think about humanitarian law as a tool of social change and for editing the entire manuscript.

I owe a great intellectual and moral debt to the Ugandans, Burundians and Sierra Leoneans working in the field of humanitarian action and transformative justice in their countries. This book is meant to honor their commitment, their insights and their perseverance. For their efforts during my trip to Kampala in March of 2010, I would like to thank especially Rachel Odoi-Musoke, of the Ugandan Government's Justice, Law and Order Sector; Dr. Joseph Oloka-Onyango, Zahara Nampewo and Busingye Kabumba of the Human Rights and Peace Centre at Makerere University School of Law; and Moses Okello of the Beyond Juba Project. For their time and counsel during my visit to Burundi in 2010, thanks, merci and murakoze to Pie Ntakarutimana and Alexis Sinduhije, human rights defenders and pro-democracy activists; and Charles Ndayiziga of the Centre d'Alerte et Prévention de Conflits. For teaching me about Sierra Leone's political development, thanks to Dr. Jimmy Kandeh of the University of Richmond. For sharing their musical narratives of flight and exile, and for allowing me to use their song lyrics as chapter introductions, thanks to the Sierra Leone Refugee All Stars. For broadening my experience in Sierra Leone in October of 2010, thanks to Thomas Mark Turay, Mary Turay, Francis Massaquoi, Agnes Jattu Carew-Bah, Mohamed Kamara and all their colleagues at the Centre for Development and Peace Education in Mayagba, Bombali District; Joseph Sesay of the Centre for Accountability and the Rule of Law; John Caulker and Sheku Koroma of Fambul Tok; and Binta Mansaray, Registrar, and her staff at the Special Court for Sierra Leone. Special appreciation to Ibrahim George, Officer-in-Charge of the Freetown office of the International Committee of the Red Cross, for his dedication to humanitarian action as a global movement.

Throughout my research and during my trips to Kampala, Bujumbura and Freetown, I also met with members of the international community, who shared their insights on post-conflict reconstruction in Africa. I am especially grateful to Maud Roure, Burundi desk officer for Interpeace, who welcomed me to a peace conference supported by her organization in Bujumbura; Prof. Joel Samuels, who invited me to participate in a conference on Sierra Leone at the University of South Carolina; and Kassie McIlvaine, who connected me to her colleagues in Burundi. Thanks also to the United Nations Peacebuilding Office in Freetown, led by Michael von der Schulenburg; the Sierra Leone delegation of United Nations High Commissioner for Refugees; Anne-Marie Callan, the Irish Chargé d'Affaires in Sierra Leone; Aitor Sanchez Lacomba, head of the Freetown delegation of the International Rescue Committee; and the Kampala, Bujumbura and Freetown delegations of the International Committee of the Red Cross. Geoff Loane, ICRC Delegate in London, deserves special mention for linking me to the ICRC offices in all three countries. ICRC kindled my interest in humanitarian law back in law school, and continues to inspire my engagement in the field of transitional justice.

My family members and dear friends all contributed to the writing of this book, intellectually and emotionally. My gratefulness to them goes beyond words. My godfathers Thomas Thornton and Dismas Mdachi form a bridge between the land of my birth and the land of my work. My daughter Kyra accompanied me to Sierra Leone and with my father and sister Joan read drafts of individual chapters. My friends Dana Bell, Janet Buck and Jim Vogele reviewed portions of the text. My mother, sister Joss, brother Charley and my daughter Tessa sent me off to Africa and welcomed me home, as they have many times. Felipe read every word of the manuscript, and without him this book would never have been finished.

Introduction

Humanitarian law, strictly speaking, is the branch of international law that regulates the conduct of warfare. In broader conception, international humanitarian law (IHL) establishes a framework for the enduring resolution of armed conflicts through the cultivation of more healthy societies. In seeking to realize the full potential of IHL, scholars and practitioners of humanitarian law borrow and incorporate the principles and methods of other legal fields that share its central preoccupation with human integrity, agency, and well-being. This book is dedicated to the articulation and application of a transformative vision of humanitarian law, inspired and tested by the experiences of individual countries emerging from civil wars on the African continent.

In emphasizing the *resolution* of armed conflict in a particular country, it is a given that force has been resorted to, with all the human costs that this entails. Chief among these casualties of war are the loss of life and health; destruction of the environment, socioeconomic infrastructure and means of sustenance; violations of human integrity, liberty, and equality; individual and social trauma; and the forced displacement of populations. International humanitarian law is concerned with preventing and remedying all these consequences of war, whether such acts are committed by states or non-state actors, and regardless of whether they are defined as persecution, international crimes, human rights abuses, or "collateral damage."

Africa has engendered resilient and pluralistic democratic traditions in such countries as Botswana, Ghana, Tanzania, and Senegal, which have enjoyed sustained periods of peace and security since they attained independence in the late 1950s and early 1960s.[1] Yet over the past two decades, the continent has endured some of the world's gravest humanitarian emergencies, including wars and genocides in Burundi, the Democratic Republic of the Congo, Liberia, Rwanda, Sierra Leone, Somalia, Sudan, and Uganda.[2]

Given that sixteen African countries were at war around the turn of the twenty-first century,[3] Africa is a vital stage on which to test the content and value of humanitarian law.[4] International law provides standards and mechanisms to exchange diplomats, regulate trade, alleviate poverty, fight repression, resolve conflicts, and much more. Africa has as much need for and openness to these international norms and institutions as any other region.[5]

Extreme forms of violence are not unique to Africa. The crime rate in Caracas, Venezuela rivals that of Johannesburg, South Africa.[6] Violence against women is epidemic in Guatemala as well as the Democratic Republic of the Congo.[7] More child soldiers have been conscripted by the Karen insurgency in Myanmar than have participated in the Lord's Resistance Army in Uganda.[8] Genocide and ethnic cleansing have ravaged Bosnia and Croatia as well as Rwanda and Darfur, Sudan. For all these reasons, the study of armed conflicts and peace movements in Africa is of vital significance to conflict resolution and reconstruction efforts throughout the world.

The final chapters of this book will examine humanitarian law in action in three African states currently emerging from periods of protracted civil war. Uganda, Sierra Leone, and Burundi illustrate the possibilities and challenges in translating international law into practical solutions for deep-rooted conflict resolution at the national and regional levels. The experiences of these African countries offer guidance to other nations emerging from armed conflict in diverse settings throughout the world from Kosovo and Afghanistan to Sri Lanka and Colombia. But in order to fully appreciate the lessons that these countries have to teach, we need to start with a broad and nuanced understanding of the rules and tools of international law—the legal norms and institutions, as well as the mechanisms and arenas for implementing those legal principles in societies transitioning from war to peace.

PART I: INTERNATIONAL LEGAL RULES FOR CONFLICT RESOLUTION

Part I, "International Legal Rules for Conflict Resolution," presents a legal primer of the core principles of international law, starting with an overview of public international law generally. Individual chapters explore the four branches of international law mutually concerned with preventing, alleviating, and remedying armed conflict: humanitarian law, human rights law, criminal law, and refugee law. Humanitarian law is the first among equals given its essential concern with alleviating the brutality of war. Nevertheless, IHL relies upon and collaborates with the other branches in its broader project of rebuilding societies torn by war. These interconnections are emphasized throughout the text.

Chapter 1, "The Human Fundamentals of International Law," establishes the basic vocabulary of international law, including its essential purposes, primary sources, and lawmakers, while also portraying the relationship between international and national legal systems. The distillation of the fundamentals of public international law provides the platform for a deeper exploration of the four specialized areas of international law that are most inherently responsive to the phenomenon of armed conflict.

Chapter 2, "Humanitarian Law: The Law of Armed Conflict," sets forth the tenets of international humanitarian law, also known as the law of armed conflict. IHL governs internal conflicts and wars between states and non-state agents, as well conflicts between states. Particular attention is devoted to the customary norms of humanity, distinction, necessity, and proportionality. These principles underlie the more technical provisions of the Geneva Conventions and dramatically illustrate the driving purpose of humanitarian law to lessen the shattering impact of war on human beings and their communities.

The remaining three chapters of Part I concern areas of law that apply in time of peace as well as war. Like humanitarian law, they are fundamentally concerned with affirming human dignity in the face of violence in all its physical, social, and symbolic forms. Chapter 3, "Human Rights Law: The Law of Human Dignity," stresses the symbiotic relationship between civil-political rights and socioeconomic rights, while exploring the creative tension between individual and collective rights, and comparing the regional human rights frameworks established in Europe, the Americas, Africa, and the Middle East. Chapter 4, "International Criminal Law: Accountability for Crimes of War and Crimes against Humanity," surveys the various international criminal tribunals for the former Yugoslavia, Rwanda, and Sierra Leone, as well as the International Criminal Court (ICC). This chapter suggests that restorative and reconciliative justice mechanisms are also components of criminal justice, at times undercutting but often complementing its predominantly retributive approach. Finally, Chapter 5, "International Refugee Law: Protection for Individuals Fleeing Persecution and Armed Conflict," highlights nonreturn to persecution as the heart of refugee protection, while also confronting the reality of second-class legal status for many civil war refugees and internally displaced persons.

Part I covers much theoretical terrain, in order to lay the foundation for the country studies in Part II, "Humanitarian Law and Post-conflict Reconstruction in Africa." The attempt is to balance precision regarding essential legal principles with creativity in addressing conceptual nuances and unanswered questions from each of the four fields of international law. While the aim is to ground theory in practice, we should not shy away from the aspirational reach of IHL, recognizing that the law of armed conflict has a hopeful heart. Through a deep examination of the visionary aspects of humanitarian law, we may better judge which of its goals are most worthy and capable of implementation.

PART II: HUMANITARIAN LAW AND POST-CONFLICT RECONSTRUCTION IN AFRICA

Part II is dedicated to the practical implementation of international humanitarian law in the context of post-conflict transition in particular African countries. Individual chapters are devoted to the experiences of three countries emerging from prolonged civil wars: Uganda, Sierra Leone, and Burundi. As a foundation for the country studies, specific tools are identified for engaging the rules of international law in the realities of armed conflict.

Chapter 6, "Tools for Implementing Humanitarian Law: Courts, Troops, the Media, Development, and Communities," sets forth five important mechanisms or arenas within which humanitarian norms respond to armed conflict and systemic repression, beginning with the judicial and military realms most often considered in international legal and policy discussions. The first entails international and domestic criminal prosecutions against individuals implicated in war crimes and crimes against humanity. The second comprises military incursions, humanitarian interventions, and peacekeeping operations in regions of armed conflict. Alongside the judicial and military frameworks, international law also operates in the domains of public opinion, social welfare, and local communities. Thus, three additional mechanisms for the application of humanitarian law are: human rights education and advocacy, including "naming and shaming;" development programs, chiefly focused on the alleviation of poverty; and, finally, social healing efforts, from national truth commissions to local reconciliation ceremonies. In short, implementation occurs when humanitarian law engages with some combination of the following five institutions or actors: courts, troops, the media, development, and communities.

Three country studies are presented in succession in Chapter 7, "Beyond Juba in Uganda: Reconciling Restorative and Retributive Justice;" Chapter 8, "After Lomé in Sierra Leone: The Special Court and National Reconciliation;" and Chapter 9, "After Arusha in Burundi: Disarming the Heart to Disarm the Body." Uganda, Sierra Leone, and Burundi have utilized the five mechanisms of conflict resolution in various combinations, according them differing degrees of priority. Moreover, in adapting the available tools of international humanitarian law to their particular purposes, each country has shed its own light on the meaning of peace and justice. Collectively, all three countries demonstrate that transitional justice has three fundamental components: criminal, social, and historical. While criminal justice aims to bring individual war offenders to account, social justice seeks to improve the material conditions of life for members of the society, and historical justice works to reconcile community members traumatized by the violence of the past. The interdependence of these three facets of justice plays itself out in the experiences of all three countries.

Uganda in East Africa comes first. In addition to hosting refugees from Burundi, Rwanda, Congo, the Sudan, Chad, and Somalia, Uganda has experienced more than twenty years of civil conflict between the Lord's Resistance Army (LRA) and the Ugandan People's Defense Forces (UPDF). As of 2011, military engagements between the LRA and the UPDF on Ugandan territory are infrequent, as most LRA troops are now operating in the territories of the Democratic Republic of the Congo, the Central African Republic, and the Darfur region of the Sudan, or moving between the three.[9]

Five leaders of the LRA have been indicted in the International Criminal Court in The Hague, and although none are yet in custody,[10] their prospective trials have resulted in a fascinating and often fraught debate within Ugandan civil society regarding whether and how international war crimes prosecutions deepen conflict, contribute to its resolution, or both.[11] In particular, demands from some quarters for a withdrawal of the ICC's indictments have inspired a deeper consideration of the relationships between international proceedings and the various judicial mechanisms operating at the national and local levels.[12] Ugandan civil society organizations have firmly and consistently called for accountability on all sides of the conflict, in addition to meaningful reforms of Uganda's legal and political systems.[13] In 2010, the Ugandan Parliament passed legislation implementing the Rome Statute of the ICC and paving the way for domestic war crimes trials.[14]

In 2002, the West African nation of Sierra Leone began to emerge from a decade-long civil war with links to the Liberian civil conflict. The experience of Sierra Leone, somewhat parallel to that of Uganda, may suggest that the apparent opposition between criminal justice and restorative justice—accountability and forgiveness—is a creative tension rather than a zero-sum game.[15] Sierra Leone's nuanced peace process has extended amnesty to some combatants, while prosecuting top commanders of rebel and pro-government forces alike, as well as Charles Taylor, the former President of Liberia, for his alleged support for the rebels of Sierra Leone's Revolutionary United Front (RUF).

The 1999 Lomé Peace Agreement between the Government of Sierra Leone and the RUF called for the creation of a national Truth and Reconciliation Commission (TRC). The TRC later operated alongside a hybrid tribunal, the Special Court for Sierra Leone, established by the Government of Sierra Leone and the United Nations in 2002. The Lomé Agreement mandated that at the conclusion of the TRC's work, its recommendations for essential political and legal reforms must be implemented by the Government of Sierra Leone.[16] That implementation process remains a work in progress.

Burundi is a Central African nation in the process of national reconciliation. Throughout its twelve-year civil war, it did not garner the international attention of its northern neighbor Rwanda. Other than a regional peacekeeping mission, the international community has mounted no large-scale military, economic, or prosecutorial interventions in Burundi.[17] This third country study draws on the common heritage of Burundi and Rwanda, while appreciating their distinct histories and their divergent approaches to post-conflict reconstruction.

In the spirit of the Arusha Peace and Reconciliation Agreement, and outside the glare of sustained media attention or international war crimes procedures, Burundians are struggling to create an ethnically inclusive society and political process from the ground up. Burundi demonstrates that civilians and combatants must be willing to disarm themselves in both psychic and physical terms if humanitarian law in action is to have any meaning.

MOVING FROM ARMED CONFLICT TO DURABLE PEACE: REDEFINING NONVIOLENCE

Chapter 2 will define *armed conflict* more precisely, drawing on the relevant provisions of the governing humanitarian law treaties. For the moment, a common-sense understanding of armed conflict entails a destructive physical contest between organized forces wielding guns, bombs, mortars, machetes, or other weapons of war. Armed conflict encompasses military engagements between opposing forces, whether they are two or more state-sponsored armies, the armed forces of a state versus local or transnational militant groups, or two or more insurgencies. This book puts a greater emphasis on non-international conflict, as civil wars now constitute 95 percent of all armed conflicts throughout the world.[18]

This text will regularly employ the terms *violence, repression,* and *peace,* principally referring to the most brutal forms of violence associated with war; physical repression such as torture, arbitrary detention, disappearance and extrajudicial execution; and peace in the form of a durable end to the suffering of war and widespread political repression. In addition, the discussion draws from the teachings of peace and conflict studies, acknowledging that violence occurs in time of war and peace, and emphasizing that violence is committed and propagated on social and symbolic as well as individual levels.[19] Although rape and inhumane treatment are first experienced as physical violence, within or outside the context of armed conflict, they have political and ideological dimensions as well, reflecting the social status or identity of the victims and survivors. Similarly, poverty and illiteracy are forms of violence that have both personal and social aspects, which may feed armed conflict or be exacerbated by it. Finally, sexism and racism are expressed in concrete experiences as well as abstract ideologies, and may serve as powerful symbolic weapons of war in their own right.

In the same way that violence and repression exist on at least three planes—the physical, the social, and the ideological—conflict resolution or *peace* has kindred dimensions. Peace is the absence of war and the prevention of rape, but it is also expressed in the alleviation of poverty, the spreading of literacy, the growth of accountable political institutions, and the reconciliation of social factions. Likewise, deep-seated and enduring conflict resolution requires the growth and flourishing of alternative world views such as humanism, feminism, tolerance, and pluralism.

Also central to the successful resolution of conflicts is the exercise of self-restraint. At a fundamental level, self-restraint creates space and time for dialogue, compromise, and agreement. Moreover, self-restraint is closely related to the concept of sovereign integrity, signifying a responsible sovereign, faithful to the rule of law. Thus, in speaking of international humanitarian law as a set of rules and tools for building durable peace, we should not forget that the rule of law is fundamentally concerned with the appropriate use of power by states, communities, and individuals alike. This multi-tiered approach to the rule of law may also help resolve some of the tensions between the rights of individuals, groups, and states. At the very least, a comprehensive vision of power, restraint, rights, duties, violence, and peace will further illuminate humanitarian law in action within and beyond Africa, and help us reach a fuller appreciation of the essential components of justice at the individual, national, and community levels.

NOTES

1. Ghana attained its independence from Great Britain in 1957. Tanganyika ended its status as a British protectorate in 1961, and unified with Zanzibar as the independent Republic of Tanzania in 1964. Botswana attained its independence from Great Britain

in 1966, and Senegal broke away from France in 1960. In 1983, a low-intensity civil war broke out between the Senegalese armed forces and the Mouvement des Forces Democratiques de la Casamance (MFDC) in the Casamance region of Southern Senegal. In 2005, a peace accord was formalized between the Government of Senegal and MFDC. See Ernest Harsch, *Peace Pact Raises Hope in Senegal*, AFRICA RENEWAL, v19, 1: 14, http://www.un.org/ecosocdev/geninfo/afrec/vol19no1/191senegal.htm.

2. According to the medical relief agency Doctors Without Borders, of the ten most serious humanitarian emergencies in 2008, five were situated in the African countries of Somalia, the Democratic Republic of the Congo, the Sudan, Zimbabwe, and Ethiopia. See Doctors Without Borders, "2008 Top Ted Humanitarian Crises," www.doctorswithoutborders.com.

3. *See* Chris Huggins and Jenny Clover, *From the Ground Up: Land Rights, Conflict and Peace in Sub-Saharan Africa*, a Joint Project of the Institute for Security Studies and the African Centre for Technology Studies, published by the Southern African Regional Poverty Network, June 2002, http://www.sarpn.org.za/documents/d0001337/index.php. The high incidence of armed conflict in Africa at least correlates with underdevelopment, given that all 22 of the world's least developed nations are in Africa. *See* United Nations Development Programme, HUMAN DEVELOPMENT REPORT 2007–08, *infra*, Table 1, at 244–47. The relationship between poverty and war will be further explored in Chapter 3.

4. *See* Paul Collier, *Natural Resources and Conflict in Africa*, CRIMES OF WAR PROJECT: WAR IN AFRICA, THE MAGAZINE, October 2004. Collier explains that the increasing incidence of civil war in Africa since the mid 1970s, compared to opposite trends elsewhere in the world, is a reflection of relatively low gross national product (GDP) per capita figures, downward growth trends, and economies skewed towards exports of natural resources: " . . . the big brute fact is that civil war is heavily concentrated in countries with low income, in economic decline, and dependent upon natural resources." *Id.*, http://www.crimesofwar.org/africa-mag/afr_04_collier.html.

5. *See generally*, Kathy L. Powers, *Dispute Initiation and Alliance Obligations in Regional Economic Institutions*, J. PEACE RESEARCH 43, 4: 453–71 (July 2006) (Powers' quantitative research suggests that the proliferation of regional economic institutions in Africa lessens the likelihood of armed aggression between member states.).

6. *See, e.g.,* Professor Alan Gilbert (University College, London), testimony to United Kingdom (UK Parliament, Aug. 7, 2009, http://www.publications.parliament.uk/pa/cm200809/cmselect/cmintdev/memo/poverty/ucm0102.htm.

7. *See generally*, "Guatemala's Femicides and the Ongoing Struggle for Women's Human Rights: Update to CGRS's 2005 Report *Getting Away with Murder*," Hastings College of the Law, Center for Gender and Refugee Studies, September 2006, *available at* http://cgrs.uchastings.edu/documents/cgrs/cgrs_guatemala_femicides.pdf. *See also*, Judith Wanga, *Why Congo is the World's Most Dangerous Place for Women*, THE GUARDIAN [UK], Mar. 28, 2010, *available at* http://www.guardian.co.uk/lifeandstyle/2010/mar/28/congo-women-danger-war-judith-wanga.

8. Anna Sussman, *Child's View of Burma's Civil War*, CHRISTIAN SCIENCE MONITOR, June 22, 2005, http://www.csmonitor.com/2005/0622/p15s01-wosc.html.

9. In January of 2010, Ugandan troops killed a top commander of the Lord's Resistance Army (LRA), Bok Abudema, in the Central African Republic. In September of 2008, Joseph Kony's bodyguard was captured, and, in November, members of the Ugandan armed forces killed another top LRA commander. *See Ugandan Army Kills LRA Commander*, N.Y. TIMES, Jan. 2, 2010.

10. Joseph Kony, the LRA leader, and four senior LRA officers were originally indicted. Two of Kony's deputies have subsequently died and arrest warrants are outstanding against the other three individuals.

11. *See generally*, Refugee Law Project, Makerere University Faculty of Law, Report of Stakeholders' Dialogue, "Beyond Juba: Building Consensus on a Sustainable Peace Process for Uganda," Dec. 1–3, 2006, Kampala, Uganda (February 2007). *See also*, Internal Displacement Monitoring Centre, Norwegian Refugee Council, Press Release, *NGOs Unite in Call for Patience & Persistence to Salvage Northern Uganda's Peace Process* (May 7, 2008, Washington, DC).
12. *See*, Refugee Law Project, *op. cit.*, p. 11 (referencing comments by individuals representing Ugandan civil society organizations "express[ing] considerable resistance/hostility to the ICC, and suggest[ing] the need for an emphasis on more restorative forms of justice that reconcile and restore social order"). *See generally*, Linda M. Keller, *Achieving Peace With Justice: The International Criminal Court and Ugandan Alternative Justice Mechanisms*, 23 CONN. J. INT'L L. 209–79 (2008).
13. *See*, Chris Dolan, "Whatever happened to comprehensive justice?" (Beyond Juba Project, Refugee Law Project, Faculty of Law, Makerere University, June 2007), paras. 2 and 7 (stressing Uganda's need for "justice which has both retributive and restorative elements and which considers the various wrongs committed by all parties to the conflict," and the potential for "justice [to serve] as the handmaiden of sustainable peace."). *See also*, Internal Displacement Monitoring Centre, Norwegian Refugee Council, *op. cit.*, para. 5 (statement released by more than thirty humanitarian and civil society organizations from within and outside of Uganda, stressing the need to "promote reconciliation across Ugandan society and establish accountability for crimes committed during the war"). *See also*, Amy Ross and Chandra Lekha Siram, *Catch-22 in Uganda: the LRA, the ICC and the Peace Process* (JURIST LEGAL NEWS & RESEARCH, University of Pittsburgh School of Law, July 17, 2006), para. 10 (citing a "recent UN report not[ing] that more than 90% of the fatalities in Northern Uganda are the result of the policy of forced displacement [by the Ugandan military] with 9% attributed to attacks by the LRA"). *See also* William Schabas, *Prosecutorial Discretion v. Judicial Activism at the International Criminal Court*, 6 J. INT'L. CRIM. JUST. 731, 747–48 (Sept. 2008) (even a lesser number of direct civilian deaths at the hands of the Ugandan People's Defense Forces, as compared to the LRA, arguably represents a "classic impunity paradigm," given that the killers were "acting on behalf of a state that shelters them from its own courts.").
14. Bill Oketch, *Uganda Set for First War Crimes Trial*, ACR Issue 264, Institute for War and Peace Reporting, June 16, 2010, *available at* http://www.iwpr.net/report-news/uganda-set-first-war-crimes-trial.
15. *See*, William A. Schabas, *Conjoined Twins of Transitional Justice? The Sierra Leone Truth and Reconciliation Commission and the Special Court*, J. INT'L. CRIM. JUST. 2, 1082–99 (Oxford University Press, 2004) at 1091 (concluding that "'synergy' may well be the better term [rather than "complementarity"] to describe the relationship between international trials and domestic truth and reconciliation commissions"). *See also, generally*, Linda M. Keller, *The False Dichotomy of Peace versus Justice and the International Criminal Court*, 3 HAGUE JUST. J. 12–53 (2008). Prof. Keller expanded upon the themes in this essay in a later article, also published in 2008, referenced above. *See*, Keller, *Achieving Peace With Justice: The International Criminal Court and Ugandan Alternative Justice Mechanisms, op. cit.*
16. Schabas, *op. cit.*, pp. 1082–83.
17. The African Union Mission in Burundi (AMIB) was deployed in late 2001. AMIB was the first peacekeeping mission organized under the auspices of the African Union. Its mandate to implement the 2000 Arusha Accords and the 2003 Pretoria Protocol (signed by the Government of Burundi and the FDD rebel forces) did not extend to the protection of civilians. *See* HUMAN RIGHTS WATCH, *Everyday Victims: Civilians in the Burundian War*, Dec. 2003, 15:20(A), 2, 9–10.

18. *See Human Security Report 2005*, Fact Sheet on "Wars and Political Violence," Human Security Centre, LIU Institute for Global Issues, the University of British Columbia, Armed-Conflict-Factsheet.pdf.
19. *See, generally,* works of Johan Galtung, the Norwegian sociologist credited with founding the field of peace and conflict studies, *inter alia, Transcend and Transform: An Introduction to Conflict Work* (2004); and *Peace by Peaceful Means: Peace and Conflict, Development and Civilization* (International Peace Research Institute, Oslo [PRIO], 1996). Galtung is credited with distinguishing between "negative peace" (i.e., the absence of war) and "positive peace" (the establishment of a healthy international society). *See* PETER LAWLER, A QUESTION OF VALUES: JOHAN GALTUNG'S PEACE RESEARCH (Lynne Rienner Publisher, Inc. 1995) at 52.

PART I

International Legal Rules for Conflict Resolution

CHAPTER 1
The Human Fundamentals of International Law

We the Peoples of the United Nations

Determined to save succeeding generations from the scourge of war, which twice in a lifetime has brought untold sorrow to mankind, and to reaffirm faith in fundamental human rights, in the dignity and worth of the human person, in the equal rights of men and women and of nations large and small, and to establish conditions under which justice and respect for the obligations arising from treaties and other sources of international law can be maintained, and to promote social progress and better standards of life in larger freedom, [...]

Have resolved to combine our efforts to accomplish these aims.
                    Charter of the United Nations[1]

A. THE ESSENCE AND PURPOSES OF INTERNATIONAL LAW

Classical international law was chiefly concerned with relations between so-called nation-states, according to one scholarly view prevalent in Europe from the seventeenth century until the founding of the United Nations (UN).[2] This state-centric vision of classical international law, itself subject to considerable historical debate,[3] no longer accurately describes the reach or grasp of this transnational legal discipline. Today, international law[4] is widely understood to govern the appropriate use of power among states, but also to encompass norms recognizing the dignity of human beings and imposing limits on the exercise of state power against individuals and members of communities, variously defined. Like municipal or domestic law,[5] international law embraces numerous subfields, from the *jus ad bellum*,[6] or norms defining the legality of resort to military force, to rules governing copyrights and trademarks in the international commercial realm. In between the law of war and the law of intellectual property, international law seeks to regulate a broad spectrum of human relations, including international business transactions and telecommunications, the law of the sea and international environmental law, diplomatic relations between states, state responsibility to immigrants and citizens, and individual rights and responsibilities.

Teachers often approach the vast body of international law by way of sources and actors. They start by identifying where the law is found and who makes it. An equally apparent entry point is to ask what purposes international law serves. While this second question may seem the more contentious, a partial resolution of the tensions that exist between the various objectives of international law will help clarify the essential content and principal makers of international law.

Thus, before delving into the sources and subjects of international law, it will help to openly identify the most urgent and essential goals of international law. This is not a simple project. A diverse group of scholars and practitioners would not easily reach agreement on the central purposes of international law beyond a fairly basic level of generality. Given the primary project of analyzing how legal rules and mechanisms work to alleviate or resolve armed conflict and repression, part of the task in selecting a fundamental goal for international law is accomplished at the outset. It makes sense for conflict resolution to be the focus in addressing armed conflict from the standpoint of international law. Nevertheless, there are various ways to approach conflict resolution. One common approach focuses on the state, another on the individual, and still another on the community, defined in familial, ethnic, political, geographic, or other terms. For this reason, there may be no way to talk meaningfully about conflict resolution as a fundamental goal without confronting an essential tension between state-centric and polycentric views of international law.[7]

The UN is an international organization composed of states and dedicated to human rights and social progress. Its very structure suggests that state sovereignty and individual integrity are not mutually exclusive. Its founding instrument is an appropriate place to start in framing the central project of international law. A widely endorsed vision of the essential goals of international law is set forth in the Preamble and Articles 1 and 2 of the Charter of the United Nations (Charter).[8] The Charter's linking of friendly relations between states to the fundamental rights of individuals is also reflected in the founding instruments of several regional international organizations, including the Constitutive Act of the African Union (AU).[9]

The objectives of the United Nations set forth in its Charter include the prevention of war and the practice of peace among nations,[10] the general prohibition against the use of military force,[11] the promotion of human rights and social development,[12] and the realization of equality and self-determination among nations and peoples.[13] While many of these goals are in accord, in the abstract especially, others are not, particularly when one state is at war with another, or a conflict exists between armies or militias affiliated with a government and militants unaffiliated with any state.

In a pitched contest between state interests, on the one hand, and individual or collective rights, on the other, the international community increasingly favors protecting the integrity of individuals and peoples over maintaining a state's territorial sovereignty.[14] By the same token, the importance of state integrity cannot be denied, philosophically or pragmatically, not least because it is to healthy states that individuals and communities most often look to vindicate their rights, claims, and needs, both legal and material. One way to help reconcile state and nonstate interests is to define state legitimacy in terms of the capacity to protect instead of the power to coerce. A central purpose of the UN and the international rule of law, then, is to further this modern vision of statehood, in which sovereignty entails the ability and willingness to enhance human dignity.

B. SOURCES OF INTERNATIONAL LAW

1. Primary Sources Set Forth in the UN Charter

The three primary sources of international law are treaties, customary norms, and general principles of law, according to the Statute of the International Court of Justice (ICJ Statute), the judicial organ of the United Nations.[15] Treaties, as defined by the Vienna Convention on the Law of Treaties (VCLOT), are international agreements governed by international law.[16] There are various synonyms for *treaties* as binding international instruments, including conventions, covenants, pacts, and statutes.[17] Treaties tend to be written, but need not be.[18] They are normally between states, less often between states and international organizations.[19] When states enter into treaties with indigenous nations, such agreements are the product of state-to-state negotiations.[20] States may seek to alter treaty obligations by entering a reservation at the time of signing, amending the treaty after ratification, or adopting a subsequent treaty,[21] so long as the amendments do not violate certain critical norms (so-called *jus cogens*).[22]

Customary norms, in contrast, are practices widely and consistently followed by states, accompanied by a sense of legal obligation, or *opinio juris vel necessitatis*.[23] Customary international law is unwritten, although specific norms may be evidenced through various writings, including international treaties, national legislation and constitutions, diplomatic communiqués, and the resolutions of international organizations. The obligation to follow a customary norm can be avoided through persistent objection at the time that the norm is coming into existence, unless that norm is regarded to be *jus cogens* or nonderogable.[24]

General principles of law are common to many of the world's national or international legal systems. Examples are respect for treaty obligations; basic due process and fundamental human rights; and restitution for unjust enrichment.[25]

Treaties are sometimes the preferred form of international law given their typical written form and the fact that states and other parties are bound through signature and a formal process of ratification.[26] Nevertheless, customary norms have their own efficacy, unburdened by the need for treaty ratification, let alone implementation through domestic legislation. General principles of law constitute primary sources of international law in a de jure or formal sense as provided in the ICJ Statute, which is an annex to the UN Charter. Nevertheless, general principles of law are listed third among those sources that Article 38 instructs the ICJ to consult in deciding cases under its jurisdiction. Perhaps for this reason, some scholars and jurists relegate general principles to a de facto secondary status behind treaties and customary norms.[27]

2. Jus cogens and Security Council Resolutions as Binding International Law

a. Jus cogens

Jus cogens norms are primary sources of international law, although the term is not enumerated in Article 38 of the ICJ Statute. They are peremptory rules from which states may not derogate even through treaty enactment or persistent objection to an emergent customary norm.[28] In this sense, *jus cogens* rules of international law are "super-norms" with some roots in natural law or the concept of inalienable rights. As such, they constitute an overlapping subset of the three other discrete categories of binding international law.

First, *jus cogens* norms include treaty provisions that are identified as nonderogable, normally through a specific provision of the treaty itself. To illustrate this idea, consider a human rights treaty such as the International Covenant on Civil and Political Rights (ICCPR). The ICCPR, while allowing states to derogate from certain enumerated provisions in times of national emergency, explicitly identifies specific provisions that are binding at all times and in all situations. The prohibition against torture is an example.[29]

Customary norms can also have *jus cogens* status, although they need not. Before the norm against torture was codified in the ICCPR and the Convention Against Torture (CAT and Torture Convention), it was regarded as a nonderogable customary norm.[30] In contrast, the protection of free expression, or freedom of speech, is regarded as a customary norm, but it does not have the character of *jus cogens*. The nonperemptory nature of freedom of expression is reflected in the fact that customary international law tolerates certain state restrictions on free expression in time of war or other so-called national emergency.[31]

Finally, *jus cogens* general principles of international law are seldom referred to, but could be postulated. For example, the presumption of innocence in criminal prosecutions is a general principle of law, included in the constitutions, judicial decisions, and legislative enactments of many countries. The presumption of innocence is also *jus cogens* because it cannot be suspended in time of war or national crisis, whether as a function of the federal law of the United States or under international law.[32]

b. UN Security Council Resolutions

Like *jus cogens* norms, pronouncements by the UN Security Council do not initially appear to fall under the UN Charter's "big three" primary sources of international law. Nevertheless, resolutions of the Security Council, when it acts under Chapter VII of the Charter, indeed have a "hard law" character, despite the general rule that declarations and resolutions by international organizations are secondary instruments. The special force of these resolutions stems from their goal of maintaining or reestablishing international peace and security. Their obligatory character is rooted in Articles 24, 25, and 39 of the UN Charter.[33] In essence, Chapter VII Security Council resolutions are extensions of the Charter and binding instruments because the constitutional treaty of the United Nations makes them so.

3. Domestic Law Metaphors for International Law

Teachers of international law in the United States often seek metaphors for international law in US constitutional or common law, but international law could just as well be the frame of reference for domestic or national law. Students of international law often appreciate the refreshing historical fact that, in declaring their independence, the former British colonies appealed to the international community to support and legitimize their claim to collective statehood.[34] Similar respect for international law is articulated in the United States Constitution.[35]

In terms of domestic analogs for international law, treaties are sometimes compared to legislation because of their common written form and use of provisions. Nevertheless, the treaty-as-statute metaphor is a limited one. After all, legislative enactments are not one of the primary sources of international law. Alternative analogs for international law are found in commercial law. The closest counterpart to the treaty in domestic law is likely the contract. For just as treaties are agreements governed by international law, contracts are agreements governed by domestic law. Moreover, like contracts, treaties flow from requisites of promise and consent, and bind the parties under the common notion of *pacta sunt servanda*.[36] As for state practices deemed obligatory, if international customary norms are to be compared to a component of the common law of contracts, a domestic cousin might be the notion of "terms of trade" or common practices among merchants,[37] which include such notions as good faith and fair dealing. Finally, general principles of law also have their parallel within the law of contracts. The utilization of certain widespread domestic legal principles by the International Court Justice might be compared to a US federal court in a contract dispute applying a rule of contract interpretation that was followed by a majority of state courts throughout the United States.

4. Secondary Sources

The Statute of the ICJ lists only two secondary sources of international law. In addition to judicial decisions, Article 38 mentions the "opinions of publicists," normally signifying the scholarship of legal academics.[38] Other secondary sources not enumerated in Article 38 are often lumped together under the somewhat unhelpful term, soft law. *Soft law* denotes norms that are not "hard" or primary sources of law. Such secondary sources include declarations, resolutions, conclusions, and codes of conduct promulgated by international organizations; guidelines and recommendations from both international and nongovernmental organizations (NGOs); and laws enacted by national legislatures.

It is worthy of reinforcement that according to the Statute of the ICJ, legislative enactments by national parliaments (which are not mentioned in Article 38) and judicial decisions (which are) must be treated as secondary sources of international law, in contrast to their status as primary sources under national law.[39] To bring this point home regarding judicial rulings, the Statute of the ICJ clarifies that even ICJ decisions do not have precedential impact.[40]

In this sense, the international legal system is not a classic common law system—judges do not make law as they do in the United States and in many other common law countries. Rather, jurists deciding international law cases decide the disputes in front of them. In this context, they may provide useful guidance on the proper way to interpret treaties or to apply general principles, and their decisions may serve as persuasive evidence of the existence of one or more customary norms. Nevertheless, while jurists' opinions provide a lens through which to view primary sources of international law, judges do not have the capacity, under international law, to make new international rules through their judicial pronouncements. For students from common law countries, such as the United States, this can be a difficult concept to swallow. The rule that all judicial decisions are merely persuasive as a matter of international law is an important reminder that the global legal system is modeled upon a diversity of national legal cultures.

5. The Porous Border Between Primary and Secondary Sources

Secondary sources of law are inherently dynamic. Hence, soft law sometimes hardens or matures into binding rules of international law as when a declaration or resolution promulgated by the UN General Assembly gives way to a subsequent convention or rule of customary international law. The declaration may have been merely persuasive or aspirational in nature and tone, but the convention is binding on its parties under the principle of *pacta sunt servanda*. An example of the soft-to-hard law evolution is represented by the progression from the Declaration against Torture, promulgated by the UN General Assembly in 1975, to the Convention Against Torture, adopted in 1984.[41]

Another example of the dynamism of soft law is offered by the Universal Declaration on Human Rights (UDHR or Universal Declaration).[42] The UDHR was adopted by the UN General Assembly in 1948 without a dissenting vote. Although it was an eloquent and broadly endorsed document, the UDHR was not promulgated as a treaty. Like most resolutions of the General Assembly, it was a secondary source of international law at the time of its adoption. Nevertheless, over the decades since 1948, many scholars and jurists have come to regard the UDHR as binding international law, at least with regard to certain provisions, which are now seen to evidence rules of customary human rights law.[43] Thus, just as secondary instruments can spawn treaties, soft law can evolve into custom. For this to happen, however, the definition of a customary norm must be satisfied, namely, a widespread state practice accompanied by the sense of legal obligation, or *opinio juris*.

Many of the human rights norms enumerated in the UDHR have been incorporated into the national constitutions and bills of rights of particular states that achieved their independence after 1948.[44] This domestic law incorporation of specific UDHR provisions constitutes evidence of their customary status, or at least constitutes state practice. As for *opinio juris*, official pronouncements imply the obligatory character of certain aspects of the UDHR. The strongest indications of *opinio juris* emanate from official acknowledgment of the *jus cogens* status of particular provisions of the UDHR, particularly the norms against torture, arbitrary detention, and extrajudicial execution.[45]

C. SUBJECTS OR MAKERS OF INTERNATIONAL LAW

1. States and Beyond

The year 1618 marked the beginning of Europe's Thirty Years War, initially a conflict between Protestant Germans from Bohemia and Catholic Germans allied with Austria. The war eventually involved the armies of France, Sweden, and other European nations seeking to challenge the hegemony of the Hapsburg Empire. Half the population of Germany is thought to have perished in this conflict, whether by force of arms, starvation, or disease.[46] In 1648, the former belligerents concluded a treaty that conceded territory to France and Sweden, and recognized the independence of a number of states, including Switzerland, the Netherlands, and the sovereign states of the German Empire. International law scholar Mark Janis describes the Peace of Westphalia as "a great property settlement for Europe, a quieting of title across the continent."[47] In addition to redrawing the map of Europe, the treaty is credited with articulating a new organizing principle for political power, signifying the birth of the nation-state.

In the generation after the Peace of Westphalia, most European scholars, statesmen, soldiers, and merchants would likely have agreed that the nation-state was the essential if not sole subject of international law. If we define international law as the law governing relations between states (*internation*), this conclusion appears the product of simple if circular reasoning. Indeed, the customary law definition of a subject of international law, evidenced in the 1933 Montevideo Convention on the Rights and Duties of States (Montevideo Convention), entails a government with authority over a territory and its resident human population, plus the capacity to engage in international relations.[48] But the fact that states, by definition, have the capacity to enter into treaties with one another does not signify that nonstate entities cannot engage in international relations, create international law, or otherwise serve as international actors.

Alternatively, if *international* is understood as transnational or global, rather than strictly interstate, possibilities open up to recognize numerous other subjects of international law. The Peace of Westphalia did more than recognize the independence of particular states governed by individual sovereigns or political leaders. The treaty anticipated the exchange of diplomats between European nation-states and required signatories to respect the principles of diplomatic immunity and freedom of religious expression. To this extent, Westphalia was an early precursor to modern human rights law.

Despite this individual-centered view of history, most scholars would agree that, until the mid-twentieth century, the conferring of first-class international legal personality was confined largely to members of the fraternity of European states. Beginning in 1945, however, the birth of the United Nations, and the founding of regional bodies in the Middle East, the Americas, Europe, Africa, and Southeast Asia inaugurated a series of expansions in the cast of characters on the global stage.[49] In the first wave, international organizations and newly independent states were recognized as subjects. In subsequent waves, international legal personality was gradually conferred on NGOs, individuals, indigenous peoples, and a variety of other nonstate actors. Today, international scholars increasingly refer to states and international organizations as *traditional* subjects of international law, and individuals, NGOs, and other actors as *modern* subjects.[50]

The gradual expansion in recognized subjects of international law since 1945 could not have occurred without an evolution in the concept of statehood itself. While the Peace of Westphalia and the Montevideo Convention inspired a remarkably enduring vision of the state as an entity with *power over* territory and people, that view is now challenged and complemented by a definition of statehood that entails the *duty to protect* the rights of individuals and communities. The *Responsibility to Protect* (R2P), addressed in Chapter 2,[51] is more than a green light for states to intervene in situations of mass atrocities in other countries. The foundational principle of R2P is the state's core responsibility to prevent, prosecute, and remedy human rights abuses occurring on its territory. Burundian journalist and political activist Alexis Sinduhije's vision of responsible sovereignty, set forth in Chapter 9, is consonant with this principle of protection.

Even if we adopt the most inclusive definition of international subjects, it is clear that not all actors are considered equal in terms of their capacities on the global stage. Perhaps the most dramatic example is the contrast between the international legal personality of a state, which may govern a population on a particular territory, regulate domestic commerce, appoint ambassadors, enter into treaties, and bring and respond to claims before international tribunals, and that of an individual, who has a more limited capacity to engage in international relations.

2. Individuals

While individuals can bring claims before certain regional human rights and other tribunals, individuals cannot become parties to treaties. Moreover, although individuals can be prosecuted or sued for criminal or civil violations of international law, unlike states, they cannot bring criminal charges against other individuals or state actors. Nevertheless, individuals have increasingly become subjects of international law, quite literally. Since 1945, dozens of human rights treaties have been adopted whose object and purpose are the protection of the rights of individuals and communities. While these rights are often honored in the breach, they also evidence an evolution in international law from the distribution and regulation of power between states, to the imposition of legal limits on the exercise of state power over individuals. Illustrating the growing status of individuals under international law, an increasing number of treaties create and empower judicial and quasi-judicial bodies to hear claims brought by individuals alleging human rights violations by state actors, in addition to claims brought by states against other states (so-called interstate petitions).[52] In a similar vein, the constitutional treaty of the International Criminal Court (ICC) allows individual victims to observe or give testimony in proceedings against accused individuals.[53]

3. The United Nations as a Model for International Organizations

International organizations (IOs) are composed of states. They take organic form through treaties, which define their constituent parts, powers, and purposes. IOs are distinct from NGOs, as discussed below. IOs, like national governments, often have legislative, judicial, and executive organs. They may be global or regional in scope, and interdisciplinary or more specialized in the issues they address. The UN, universal in both geography and subject matter, provides a useful template for understanding IOs of various stripes. Founded in 1945, its primary goals were and remain the prevention of war, the protection of human rights, the advancement of socioeconomic development, and the promotion of equality and self-determination among nations and peoples. The five primary organs of the UN were created to focus upon one or more of these fundamental purposes.[54] They are the UN

General Assembly, the UN Security Council, the International Court of Justice, the UN Secretariat, and the Economic and Social Council (ECOSOC).

a. The UN General Assembly

The UN General Assembly (General Assembly), with ambassadorial representation by each of the now 194 member nations, is the plenary legislative body of the Organization. The General Assembly may debate and pass resolutions on any issue encompassed by the UN Charter, from budgetary rules, to human rights and matters of war and peace. With the exception of decisions related to its internal administrative functioning, General Assembly resolutions are not binding, and lack the status of primary sources of international law.

The Universal Declaration of Human Rights, discussed above, helps illustrate the role of the General Assembly. When adopted by the Assembly in 1948 without a dissenting vote, the UDHR was soft law and aspirational in tone. However, through the subsequent practice of states, and their frequent invocation of the instrument as the gold standard in drafting domestic bills of rights, the UDHR has attained the status of customary international law. Thus, what the General Assembly lacks in formal legal authority, it compensates for in rhetorical power, the breadth of its mandate and representation, and its success in spurring states and sister UN organs to take further action.

b. The UN Security Council

The UN Security Council (Security Council) is the other legislative organ of the United Nations. Its mandate to maintain international peace and security is more limited than that of the General Assembly, but its resolutions to remove "threats and breaches of the peace" are binding on all nations, and, through Chapter VII of the UN Charter, constitute primary sources of international law as discussed above. The fifteen members of the Security Council include five permanent seats and ten that rotate among the other members of the Organization. Each of the five permanent members—China, France, Russia, the United Kingdom (UK), and the United States—has veto power over substantive resolutions, meaning that binding decisions of the Council cannot be reached without either the assent or silence of those five countries.[55]

Beginning in the 1950s, the General Assembly passed a series of resolutions condemning the systemic racial discrimination of apartheid in South

Africa and recommending economic sanctions against its government. Mounting testimonies to pervasive violations of the norm of equality led the Security Council to impose a mandatory arms embargo against South Africa in 1977.[56] To justify invoking its lawmaking power, and guard against charges of overreaching, the Security Council needed to connect the dots between human rights abuses and "threats to the peace." It identified brute force by South African security forces as the heart of apartheid, and the only means by which the repression of the nonwhite majority could be maintained. The Security Council concluded that a militarized South Africa was a threat to peace and security throughout the African continent and, on that basis, acted to shut down the flow of weapons, ammunition, military vehicles, and equipment into the country.[57]

In 1990, African National Congress leader Nelson Mandela was released after twenty-seven years of imprisonment, including eighteen years on Robben Island. He was elected president of South Africa in its first nonracial election in 1994. In his inauguration speech, Mandela credited the solidarity of civil rights activists throughout the world for strengthening popular resistance to apartheid, and helping pave the way for a nonviolent transition to a democratic system of government based upon universal suffrage.[58]

The slow and inexorable dismantling of apartheid was the product of peaceful protest and armed resistance in South Africa, encouraged by international civil society and supported by the formal institutions of the United Nations. The UN Security Council played an essential role in this historical drama. As a matter of legal precedent, the Council acknowledged that apartheid violated the founding principles of the UN, threatening its very legitimacy. In blocking the flow of arms to a racist government, the Council affirmed the principle of equality set forth in the UN Charter, and the symbiotic relationship between human rights and peace.

c. The International Court of Justice

The ICJ is the judicial branch of the UN. The ICJ can hear "contentious" cases between two states that have accepted its jurisdiction, or issue advisory opinions at the request of states, the General Assembly, or NGOs. The ICJ rules on a broad range of issues from boundary disputes between states, to the interpretation of international humanitarian law. In *US v. Iran*, the ICJ determined that Iran was obliged to pay reparations to the United States for the seizing of American hostages and the destruction of the US Embassy in 1979, during the early days of the Iranian Revolution.[59] In 1986, the ICJ found that the United States violated international law in funding insurgents and mining the port of Managua during the civil war between the Sandinista government and the Contras.[60]

Unlike judicial decisions by many national courts throughout the world, rulings by the International Court of Justice are not "precedential," meaning they only serve to resolve the specific dispute between the two parties that voluntarily submit to the Court's jurisdiction. The nonlawmaking character of ICJ decisions reflects the fact that the primary sources of international law are limited to treaties, customary norms, and general principles of law. Nevertheless, decisions by the Court are cited widely, and their formal soft-law status may belie their force as persuasive interpretations of international law.

d. The UN Secretariat

The UN Secretariat is the executive branch of the UN and represents both the diplomatic arm and the human face of the Organization. The Secretary General is appointed by the General Assembly after a recommendation by the Security Council.[61] The Secretariat serves to galvanize public concern and mobilize resources in response to conflicts and emergencies throughout the world. During his tenure from 1997–2006, former Secretary General Kofi Annan of Ghana focused on poverty alleviation and socioeconomic development as essential tools for international peace and security. He also promoted the concept of a "responsibility to protect" civilian victims of genocide and other crimes against humanity. Current Secretary General Ban Ki-moon of Korea is heavily immersed in alleviating the tragedy of Darfur, Sudan, and efforts to protect civilians from attacks by government-funded Janjaweed rebels; as well as raising global awareness about the linkages between climate change, competition for scarce resources, and armed conflict.

e. The Economic and Social Council

The Economic and Social Council is the fifth and final primary organ of the UN, concentrating on the promotion of human rights, socioeconomic development, and the protection of the environment. ECOSOC has given birth to a variety of suborgans and offices, including the UN High Commissioner for Human Rights.[62] ECOSOC also consults with NGOs working in the field of human rights advocacy,[63] and collaborates with the specialized agencies of the United Nations (including the UN Development Programme, the World Health Organization, the UN Environmental

Program and the World Food Program), as well as semiautonomous IOs affiliated with the United Nations, such as the UN High Commissioner for Refugees.[64]

ECOSOC is the parent organ of the Human Rights Council, a secondary body of the UN that investigates widespread human rights abuses in individual countries. In January 2009, the Human Rights Council called for an independent fact-finding mission to evaluate claims of war crimes by Israel and Hamas during Israel's three-week military incursion into Gaza in December 2008 and January 2009.[65] In September 2009, the mission, led by South African jurist Richard Goldstone, released its findings of violations on both sides, and called on the UN Security Council to require the parties to investigate and prosecute individuals responsible for targeting civilians, in order to avoid a potential Security Council referral to the ICC.[66]

f. Assessing International Organizations as Subjects of International Law

In addition to their de facto power in convening and cajoling states to act on the global stage, international organizations play a direct role in generating international law and making claims regarding breaches of international law. International organizations are sometimes parties to international agreements, as demonstrated by the treaty creating the Special Court for Sierra Leone between the United Nations and the Government of Sierra Leone, discussed extensively in Chapter 8. International organizations may also seek redress before the ICJ, as in UN reparations claims against governments, such as the Bernadotte case.[67] Representatives of international organizations can also participate in the drafting of treaties, convene treaty negotiation conferences, and lobby government representatives to amend, sign, or ratify such agreements.

4. NGOs, Indigenous Peoples, Corporations, Insurgencies, and Terrorist Organizations

NGOs cannot formally enter into treaties, but they may apply for consultative status before international organizations,[68] and, like international organizations, their representatives often have profound influence over the drafting, conclusion, and interpretation of treaties. The International Committee of the Red Cross (ICRC) played a central role in creating the four 1949 Geneva Conventions and their two 1977 Protocols,[69] humanitarian law treaties that collectively establish a legal framework for the conduct of armed conflict. On the African continent, the Refugee Law Project at Makerere University has helped to ensure a role for local communities in the implementation of the Juba Peace Accords between the Government of Uganda and the rebels of the Lord's Resistance Army.[70] NGOs also may encourage international organizations to bring claims or seek advisory opinions from international tribunals, as the World Court Project was instrumental in getting the ICJ to consider the legality of the use of nuclear weapons.[71]

For their part, indigenous nations have long engaged in international relations with other states, particularly through the treaty-making process. However, the history of genocide against native peoples and the abrogation of aboriginal treaty claims by European colonial powers and modern states alike suggests the limited significance of de jure recognition of such indigenous nations as subjects of international law. The early twenty-first century has brought some progress in the de facto recognition, if not full enjoyment, of group rights on the part of indigenous peoples, particularly in the areas of cultural autonomy and collective land ownership. These advances were reflected recently in the adoption by the UN General Assembly of the United Nations Declaration on the Rights of Indigenous Peoples (UNDRIP) in 2007.[72] Although the UNDRIP is not a treaty, it is evidence of evolving customary norms regarding the rights of indigenous communities.

Corporations also have significant capacity under international law. While they cannot sign and ratify treaties, through their economic power, they may influence states in their treaty-making, or encourage them to bring or respond to international judicial claims. Corporations also may be served as defendants in tort actions based on their alleged involvement in human rights violations, as in the case against Royal Dutch Shell for its conduct in Nigeria. Shell agreed, in June 2009, to pay a $15.5 million settlement in an Alien Tort Claims Act case brought by the Center for Constitutional Rights, an NGO incorporated in the United States, and based in New York City. CCR claimed that Shell was complicit in the 1995 arbitrary execution of Nigerian Ken Saro-Wiwa, an Ogoni community leader who protested the environmental degradation caused by Shell's oil extraction activities in the Niger River Delta, the traditional homeland of the Ogoni people.

To a limited extent, international law accords quasi-state status to certain nonstate militant groups. Protocol I to the 1949 Geneva Conventions was adopted in 1977, to further regulate and limit the suffering caused by international armed conflicts. Protocol I recognizes the legal personality of certain so-called movements of national liberation. Moreover, both Common Article 3 of the four 1949 Conventions and Protocol II recognize certain insurgent groups in the context of non-international armed conflict.[73]

International law is currently grappling with the status of transnational entities involved in racketeering, trafficking,[74] and/or terrorist activities. A particularly troubling question is the status of decentralized global organizations such as al Qaeda, which target civilians in large-scale catastrophic acts of violence. To what extent al Qaeda is subject to the law of armed conflict and whether its members are combatants entitled to prisoner of war (POW) status are questions that will be more fully addressed in Chapter 2. The fact remains that from 2001 to 2008, it was official US policy to detain without charge hundreds of individuals on suspicion of involvement in acts of terror, depriving them of a formal judicial process under criminal or humanitarian law to determine their guilt, innocence or eligibility for POW status.

US federal courts have pushed back and begun to recognize the legal personality of all individuals implicated in the so-called War on Terror, culminating in the US Supreme Court's recognition of the right to habeas corpus on the part of individuals detained as enemy combatants in the US Naval Station at Guantánamo Bay, Cuba.[75] This fragile, yet enduring recognition of terrorist suspects' rights to humane treatment in captivity and due process at trial bears witness to a gradual elevation in the status of individuals under international law in the four and a half centuries since the Peace of Westphalia.

If international legal personality is a "bundle of sticks," it is clear that not all actors need have the entire, or even the same, bundle. Arguably, only states and international organizations carry the largest bundles—particularly the capacities to make treaties and to bring and respond to international claims and criminal prosecutions. Nevertheless, other actors, particularly NGOs and individuals, possess a significant share of the sticks.

5. Rights and Responsibilities

A number of international human rights treaties include sections devoted to individual responsibilities, particularly the African Charter on Human and Peoples' Rights (the Banjul Charter)[76], adopted under the auspices of the Organization of African Unity, the precursor to the African Union. A section of Chapter 3 devoted to regional human rights treaties examines the advantages and liabilities (for the state and the society) of an emphasis on "duties." While there is a genuine risk that treaty provisions devoted to individual responsibilities will serve as window dressing for the abuse of state power, the pairing of rights and duties has much to recommend itself. This is particularly the case if a broad swath of civil society insists on interlocking rights and duties at all levels of human society, from the individual and the local community to the state and the international community. This approach helps guard against the tendency to spotlight the abuse of power by certain entities, while overlooking such abuses by others.

It might be agreed, in the abstract, that international law abhors a vacuum, and rejects the very concept of a "black hole" devoid of accountability or restraint. Yet that is precisely the term that has been used to critique the US government's detention and interrogation of suspected terrorists in Cuba, Iraq, Afghanistan, and elsewhere, since 2001.[77] Human history is rife with narratives of persecuted groups becoming persecutors and victims victimizers. Also common are instances of human rights abusers suffering persecution, and victimizers becoming victims, through arbitrary policies that threaten the very integrity of a system of justice. Thus, a sense of urgency animates our efforts to define the international rule of law in terms of self-restraint and the appropriate use of power by states, communities, organizations, and individuals alike.

D. DUELING SOVEREIGNTIES: THE RELATIONSHIP BETWEEN INTERNATIONAL AND DOMESTIC LAW

As suggested above, sovereignty and integrity do not constitute the unique province of states, but are also essential components of individual and group identity. This section will explore aspects of the complex relationships between multiple levels of sovereignty and law, in particular, the principal mechanisms through which international law expresses itself at the national level, and the various rules limiting the reach of national law on the international plane.

1. International Law at Home

Two dominant theories describe the impact of international law on the domestic or national plane. *Monism* describes an integrated framework in which international law is automatically incorporated into domestic, or municipal, law. The two areas of law are part of one larger system in which international law is supreme. *Dualism,* on the other hand, is the view that international law and domestic law are separate domains, such that international law must be explicitly incorporated into national law to take effect, normally through the enactment of implementing legislation.

The European Union (EU) is a monist system par excellence. EU treaties once ratified are binding on all EU members, as are policy directives promulgated by the EU Commissioners.[78] In this sense, the EU is a confederated system with EU law supreme over municipal law, in the same way that the US Constitution makes federal law supreme over the laws of the fifty states. In contrast, most member states do not regard the UN as a monist global system. Treaties adopted under the auspices of the UN may be deemed self-executing or not, depending on the constitutional, statutory, or common law structure of the individual member state. Although the US Constitution regards treaties as part of federal law, US courts have seldom concluded that specific treaties are self-executing, in most instances requiring domestic legislation before giving them domestic effect. Other UN member states take a more monist approach, through constitutional provisions that rank ratified treaties above domestic legislation. In such instances, statutes may be deemed unconstitutional when they compromise treaty obligations.[79]

Most states find themselves somewhere along the spectrum between pure monism and absolute dualism. In the United States, for example, customary norms are apparently self-executing, despite the fact that most treaties are deemed not to be.[80] The US Constitution identifies duly ratified treaties as part of federal law, under the Article VI Supremacy Clause. However, if otherwise binding treaty provisions are followed by inconsistent federal legislation, the US statute will normally prevail under the "last-in-time" rule.[81] In contrast, the supremacy clause of the Constitution of the Republic of Uganda does not mention international law, and states simply that the "Constitution is the supreme law of Uganda.... If any other law or any custom is inconsistent with any of the provisions of this Constitution, the Constitution shall prevail...."[82]

2. Domestic Law Abroad

If monism and dualism describe the impact of international law "at home" within domestic legal systems, international jurisdictional rules circumscribe the impact of domestic law "abroad." There are two classic situations in which an individual state prosecutes transnationally without reproach: (1) when the state accuses a nonnational of criminal conduct that occurred within the state's territorial boundaries; or (2) when the state charges its "own" national with criminal conduct committed in another country. The two principles that rationalize these exercises of jurisdiction are the territorial and nationality principles, respectively. If we are operating within a territorial sovereignty mind-set, the idea is that the state can protect its own territory, while the nationality principle allows a country to control its own nationals, even if they are outside the territory.

There are two other jurisdictional principles that involve slight extensions of this state-centric perspective: the protective principle and the passive nationality principle. Under the *protective principle*, the state can define conduct as criminal if it threatens the national security of the state. This principle has been used to justify federal statutes that criminalize the offense of airline hijacking, or certain acts of terrorism that occur overseas. Under the *passive nationality principle*, the state may prosecute nonnationals for criminal conduct abroad when the victims are its own nationals. More important, both protection and passive nationality are principles that extend the concept of the state's territory and the state's nationals to additional contexts and roles.

The fifth international jurisdictional principle is unique in that it does not depend upon traditional state prerogatives. Under the universality principle, any state can criminalize, prosecute, and punish particularly egregious conduct, regardless of the nationality of the offender or the specific location or impact of the offense. On occasion, states have joined together to empower an international tribunal to exercise jurisdiction over *universal crimes*, encompassing conduct that the principle of universal jurisdiction would permit any state to criminalize and prosecute at the domestic level. But in classic usage, *universality jurisdiction* is exercised by the political and judicial organs of individual states, whether national legislatures or courts.[83]

Universality suggests that certain acts of war and violence, regardless of circumstances, threaten our common humanity and hence the international community as a whole. Nevertheless, universality jurisdiction likely poses as many challenges as it solves, particularly concerning who exercises such power, and over whom. These issues are more fully addressed, in Chapter 5, on international criminal law; and, in Chapter 6, on courts, troops, the media, development, and communities as interlocking arenas for conflict resolution. Just two of the challenges of universal jurisdiction bear mention here.

First, the availability of universal jurisdiction for heinous crimes begs the question of which courts should exercise such jurisdiction in specific instances. While a tribunal such as the ICC may exercise universal jurisdiction, so may national courts. In fact, it was the exercise of transnational judicial power by national courts that prompted the development of international legal limitations on jurisdiction in the first place. Validating jurisdiction should be much more than a legalistic exercise. If criminal prosecutions of alleged enemies of mankind are to serve as mechanisms of conflict resolution, and not merely expressions of coercive power, there may be reason to favor national courts over international courts in certain instances.

Second, just as there are vital choices to be made regarding proper and optimal venues for criminal trials, there are equally critical choices regarding whom to prosecute. In a conflict involving state and nonstate actors, one-sided prosecutions are likely to be counterproductive. The use of universal jurisdiction solely or even predominantly against certain types of offenders imperils both the legitimacy of the prosecutions and the authenticity of post-conflict reconciliation.

As this first chapter on the fundamentals of international law concludes, it is clear that the mere availability of universal jurisdiction is not proof that human society has progressed since the Peace of Westphalia. Universality is least contested when the requisite offenses are limited to gross violations of human rights and humanitarian law, but the exercise of universal jurisdiction does not guarantee that we will reach a higher legal or moral ground after the outrages of war and persecution. Like other aspects of international law in the twenty-first century, universal jurisdiction needs to be applied with a judicious touch, to ensure that it is part of a restrained and even-handed reassertion of the rule of law in societies emerging from conflict.

E. INTERNATIONAL HUMANITARIAN LAW AND ITS SISTER FIELDS OF INTERNATIONAL LAW

The next four chapters address in turn the four subfields of international law most concerned with problems of armed conflict, violence, and repression, and whose collective *raison d'être* is the protection of human dignity, both individual and collective. These fields are international humanitarian law, human rights law, international criminal law, and international refugee law. By way of introduction and transition to the individual chapters devoted to the vocabulary, core doctrines, and central challenges of each field, it may be useful to provide concise overviews of the four disciplines, emphasizing some of their distinct aspects, as well as certain commonalities.

International humanitarian law applies in wartime and seeks to lessen the suffering caused by armed conflict, building upon the customary norms of humanity, distinction, necessity, and proportionality, and prioritizing the protection of wounded combatants, POWs, occupied populations, and civilians.[84] International human rights law applies in time of peace and war, and encompasses the promotion and protection of a wide spectrum of civil, political, economic, cultural, and social rights—from humane treatment, liberty, and free expression to cultural integrity, health care, and education. International criminal law legitimizes and regulates national and international judicial mechanisms to prevent, prosecute, and punish individuals for offenses against international civil society, and sometimes works in tandem with traditional and reconciliative mechanisms to support and compensate victims. International refugee law responds to the urgency of fear-motivated flight, calling on states to protect and assist individuals who flee persecution and armed conflict across international frontiers, while increasingly recognizing the rights of internally displaced persons.

Visually, we can think of these four areas of international law as a constellation of legal fields or as a set of overlapping circles. Each field shares terrain with each of the others and, in some areas, three or all four are concentrated. Starting with international humanitarian law and human rights law, the area of common purpose would be human rights violations in time of war. Adding a third element of commonality, international criminal law overlaps with human rights and humanitarian law on a foundation of universal jurisdiction, with respect to crimes that violate *jus cogens* norms of human rights law, principally wartime genocide, and other attacks on civilian populations. International refugee law is a subset of human rights law, and also intersects with the other two fields when individuals are forced to flee war crimes and crimes against humanity. Chapter 2 begins with the fundamentals of international humanitarian law.

NOTES

1. *See* Charter of the United Nations (UN Charter), *signed* June 26, 1945, *entered into force* Oct. 24, 1945, 59 Stat. 1031, TS No. 993, 3 Bevans 1153 (1969), Preamble.
2. It was Jeremy Bentham who apparently coined the phrase *international law* in 1789, deeming it to be "that branch of jurisprudence" exclusively concerned with "mutual transactions between sovereigns as such." *See* JEREMY BENTHAM, AN INTRODUCTION TO THE PRINCIPLES OF MORALS AND LEGISLATION (1789) (Burns and Hart, eds. 1970) at 296, cited in MARK W. JANIS, AN INTRODUCTION TO INTERNATIONAL LAW (4th Edition, Aspen Publishers) at 242.
3. According to Sir William Blackstone, the *law of nations* was not limited to interstate relations, but encompassed individuals as well, governing "that intercourse which must frequently occur between two or more independent states, and the individuals belonging to each." *See* W. BLACKSTONE, 4 COMMENTARIES ON THE LAWS OF ENGLAND 66 (1st ed. 1765–1769), cited in Janis, *op. cit.* at 240.

    A century before Bentham and Blackstone, the Dutch jurist Hugo Grotius, widely viewed as a founding father of classical international law, helped to define the early contours of the "common law among nations." *See* HUGO GROTIUS, DE JURE BELLI AC PACIS (1625), translated by Francis Kelsey (Cambridge edition, 1925), Prologue, section 28. Like Blackstone, Grotius' scholarly treatment of the "law of nations" also touched upon the dignity, rights, and responsibilities of individuals. In addressing the law of war, Grotius was preoccupied with the protection of noncombatants. *See id.*, Prol., sec. 28. Similarly, in proclaiming the freedom of the seas, and the principle of free maritime trade, Grotius condemned the practice of piracy as perpetrated against individual ship captains and crew members. *See generally* GROTIUS, MARE LIBERUM (The Free Sea, 1609).

4. The term public international law is sometimes although not always coherently defined in opposition to the term private international law, despite the considerable overlap between the two realms, and the various uses of the two terms. Essentially, *public international law* is synonymous with the more common term *international law*, and encompasses international treaties and customary norms on a broad range of topics of interest to states and individuals, as well as international organizations, nongovernmental organizations (NGOs), and other international actors. In contrast, the term *private international law* is sometimes used to refer to the regulation of international business transactions. But at other times, and somewhat confusingly, private international law also refers to rules governing conflicts of law and choice of law, in disputes involving two or more states or individuals from different states.

   This author suggests that the domain of *conflicts of law* is more usefully approached as a subset of public international law, rather than a separate branch of the tree of international law, since courts often need to consult competing national rules in interpreting international treaties and customs. Moreover, even in seeking to resolve disputes arising in the context of international business transactions, courts apply classic international principles. In order to ascertain whether transnational agreements have been breached, and what damages may be due, courts are required to interpret relevant treaties governing transnational commercial relations, which are primary sources of international law. *See, e.g.,* JANIS, *op. cit.* at 2 ("[international law] is sometimes conceived to be divided into public and private parts, the first concerning the legal relations of states, the second involving the law governing the foreign transactions of individual and corporations. However, the public-private division of international law can be misleading.")

5. *Domestic law* is one term for the law of an individual state within the international community of states, typically used within United States (US) legal and diplomatic circles. Other countries, including common law states from the United Kingdom (UK) to Tanzania, prefer the term *municipal law*.

6. The *jus ad bellum*, or law of going to war, refers to those international norms regulating the "use of [military] force" or the decision to initiate armed conflict. This term is often contrasted with the *jus in bello*, or "law within war," comprising the contemporary norms of international humanitarian law (IHL) or "the law of armed conflict." IHL rules impose international legal restraints on the conduct of war, once initiated. These rules limit the ways in which war may be waged, and seek to lessen its destructive impact on human beings and communities.

7. The concept of *polycentricity*, namely, the idea of multiple cultural frameworks characterized by autonomy and integrity, but also dynamism and interdependence, is articulated and explored by Moroccan scholar Anouar Majid in UNVEILING TRADITIONS: POSTCOLONIAL ISLAM IN A POLYCENTRIC WORLD (Duke University Press 2000) at 132–56.

8. *See* UN Charter, *op. cit.*, art. 1 and art. 2.

9. *See* Constitutive Act of the African Union (AU), *adopted* July 11, 2000, *entered into force* May 26, 2001, OAU Doc. CAB/LEG/23.15, Article 3 ("Objectives"); Charter of the Organization of American States, *signed* April 30, 1948, *entered into force* December 31, 1951, Organization of American States (OAS) Treaty Series No. 1-D; OAS Doc. OEA/Ser. A/2 (English) Rev. 2, art. 2 (including "peace and security," "pacific settlement of disputes" and "economic, social, and cultural development" among "essential purposes") and art. 3 (mentioning "the fundamental rights of the individual"); Statute of the Council of Europe, *adopted* May 5, 1949, *entered into force*, Aug. 3, 1949, 87 UNTS 103, Europ. TS No. 1, Preamble.

10. UN Charter, Preamble ("to save succeeding generations from the scourge of war" and "to practice tolerance and live together in peace with one another as good neighbors").

11. UN Charter, art. 1(1) ("[t]o maintain international peace and security . . ."); and UN Charter, art. 2(4) ("[a]ll Members shall refrain . . . from the threat or use of force against the territorial integrity or political independence of any state").
12. UN Charter, Preamble ("to reaffirm faith in fundamental human rights [and] . . . to promote social progress"); and art. 1(3) ("[t]o achieve international co-operation in solving international problems of an economic, social, cultural or humanitarian character, and in promoting and encouraging respect for human rights . . .")
13. UN Charter, Preamble ("faith . . . in the equal rights . . . of nations large and small") and art. 1(2) ("friendly relations among nations based on respect for the principle of equal rights and self-determination of peoples").
14. *See* "The Responsibility to Protect," a report prepared by the International Commission on Intervention and State Sovereignty, December 2001, *available at* http://www.iciss.ca/pdf/Commission-Report.pdf. The responsibility to protect (R2P) is further discussed in Chapter 2, Section B.2.

    Scholars have also criticized the very concept of state *sovereignty* as a distraction from the more essential attributes of statehood. Professor Louis Henkin speaks of sovereignty as "a conception deriving from the relations between a prince and his/her subjects," urging that, "[f]or legal purposes at least, we might do well to relegate the term sovereignty to the shelf of history as a relic from an earlier age." LOUIS HENKIN, INTERNATIONAL LAW: POLITICS AND VALUES, 9 and 10 (1995). The characteristics of state authority and legitimacy that Henkin counts as fundamental include "independence, equality, autonomy, 'personhood,' territorial authority, integrity and inviolability, impermeability and 'privacy.'" *Id.* at 10. It is noteworthy that at least some of these central characteristics of statehood, particularly equality, autonomy, and integrity, are attributes shared with other subjects of international law, including international organizations, indigenous peoples, and individuals.
15. UN Charter, Statute of the International Court of Justice (ICJ Statute), art. 38.
16. Vienna Convention on the Law of Treaties (VCLOT), *adopted* May 23, 1969, *entered into force* Jan. 27, 1980, UN Doc. A/CONF. 39/27 (1969), 8 ILM 679 (1969), art. 2(1)(a).
17. We need to distinguish between statutes as international agreements and statutes as enactments of state legislatures. Legislative enactments by national congresses and parliaments are secondary sources of international law to the extent that they merely provide evidence of certain primary sources of law, particularly customary norms or general principles. In contrast, the ICJ Statute is a portion of the UN Charter, and hence a primary source of international law. Normally, use of the term *statute*—rather than other synonyms for treaty, such as convention, covenant, or pact—signifies that the instrument is a constitutional treaty serving to create and define the organs, powers, and distribution of functions of an international organization.
18. VCLOT, art. 3 ("[t]he fact that the present Convention does not apply . . . to international agreements not in written form shall not affect: (a) the legal force of such agreements . . ."); *see also* Janis, *op. cit.,* at 15–16 (VCLOT art. 2(1)(a) defines treaties as written agreements, but "general international law," which also encompasses the customary law of treaties, does not impose a writing requirement).
19. *See generally,* Vienna Convention on the Law of Treaties between States and International Organizations or between International Organizations, *adopted,* March 21, 1986, *not yet in force,* UN pub., Sales No. E.94.V.5.
20. *See* Worcester v. Georgia, 31 US (6 Pet.) 515 (1832).
21. VCLOT, art. 30(3) ([concerning "successive treaties relating to the same subject manner,"] "[w]hen all the parties of the earlier treaty are parties also to the later treaty . . . the earlier treaty applies only to the extent that its provisions are compatible with those of the later treaty.")

22. The concept of *jus cogens* or nonderogable norms, and their relationship to our understanding of inalienable rights, will be explored below.
23. "Opinion of law or necessity," Janis, *op. cit.*, at 46 and n. 17 (citing the RESTATEMENT (THIRD) OF THE FOREIGN RELATIONS LAW OF THE UNITED STATES, sec. 102(2) (1987), which defines *opinio juris* as the sense of legal obligation); *see also* AMERICAN LAW INSTITUTE RESTATEMENT (THIRD) OF THE FOREIGN RELATIONS LAW OF THE UNITED STATES, sec. 102(2) (1987); *see also*, The Paquete Habana, 175 US 677, 686 (USSC 1900) (defining a customary norm as "an ancient usage among civilized nations . . . gradually ripening into a rule of international law") and 711, citing The Scotia, 14 Wall. 170, 187, 188, *sub nom.* Sears v. the Scotia, 20 L. Ed. 822, 825, 826, (emphasizing the requirement that "by common consent of mankind these [customary] rules have been acquiesced in as of general obligation.").
24. *See* Janis, *op.cit.* at 54 (referencing the ICJ finding in the Fisheries Jurisdiction Cases that "Norway was not obliged to follow the ordinary customary rules about the drawing of maritime baselines because it had long enforced a contrary principle"). *See also* RESTATEMENT OF THE LAW, THIRD, FOREIGN RELATIONS LAW OF THE UNITED STATES (THIRD RESTATEMENT ON FOREIGN RELATIONS LAW), Section 102, Sources of International Law, Comment d (re: "Dissenting views": "in principle a state that indicates dissent while the law is still in the process of development is not bound by that rule even after it matures") and Comment k (re: "Peremptory norms of international law": "peremptory . . . rules prevail over and invalidate international agreements and other rules of international law in conflict with them.").
25. *See* Hermann Mosler (1984), 2 ENCYCLOPEDIA OF PUBLIC INTERNATIONAL LAW 511, 520 (re: prohibitions against "unjust enrichment" and "denial of Justice" as general principles of national law), and 524–5 (re: "[e]lementary considerations of humanity" as a general principle of international law; and *pacta sunt servanda* ("treaties are binding"), "equity" and "[r]espect of basic human rights" as "General Principles Applicable to all Kinds of Legal Relations") (Rudolfo Bernhardt, ed. 1995). *See also* Janis, *op. cit.* at 58 (pointing to the principle of *res judicata* as a general principle of law).
26. *See* VCLOT, art. 11 (providing list of potential "means of expressing consent to be bound by a treaty").
27. *But see*, Mosler, *op. cit.* at 518. Mosler states that general principles are equal to treaties and customary norms in "their legal quality." Nevertheless, he concedes that not all scholars agree, and explains that the "difference of opinion as to whether general principles . . . possess only a subsidiary character" stems from the order in which the three primary sources are listed in the ICJ Statute, art. 38. Mosler cautions that the order in which the ICJ is directed to consider the specific primary sources of international law should not be confused with a hierarchical relationship between the three.
28. VCLOT, art. 53 ("[a] treaty is void if, at the time of its conclusion, it conflicts with a peremptory norm of general international law.").
29. *See* International Covenant on Civil and Political Rights (ICCPR or Civil and Political Covenant), *adopted*, Dec. 19, 1966, *entered into force*, Mar. 23, 1976, 999 UNTS 171, art. 4(2) ("[n]o derogations may be made from articles 6 [right to life], 7 [prohibition against torture], 8 (paragraphs 1 and 2) [prohibition against slavery], 11 [prohibition against debtor's prison], 15 [prohibition against ex post facto prosecutions], 16 [personhood before the law], 18 [freedom of thought, conscience and religion]. . . .") *See also* RESTATEMENT (THIRD) ON FOREIGN RELATIONS LAW OF THE UNITED STATES (RESTATEMENT ON FOREIGN RELATIONS), Section 102, Reporters Notes, 6 ("Peremptory norms: . . . Such norms must include rules prohibiting genocide, slave trade and slavery, apartheid and other gross violations of human rights. . . .").

30. *See* Filartiga v. Peña-Irala, 630 F. 2d 876, 883 (2nd Cir. 1980) ("[t]urning to the act of torture, we have little difficulty discerning its universal renunciation in the modern usage and practice of nations.") *See also* RESTATEMENT (THIRD) OF FOREIGN RELATIONS LAW OF THE UNITED STATES, Section 702 (1987), regarding the "Customary International Law of Human Rights." Section 702 of the Third Restatement on Foreign Relations Law lists seven human rights violations which are prohibited by customary international human rights law: "(a) genocide, (b) slavery or slave trade, (c) murder or disappearance ... (d) torture or other cruel, inhuman or degrading treatment or punishment, (e) prolonged arbitrary detention, (f) systematic racial discrimination, or (g) a consistent pattern of gross violations of internationally recognized human rights." Comment n following Section 702 indicates that the first six of these customary human rights prohibitions are peremptory in nature, meaning that they are accorded the status of *jus cogens*, and hence that "an international agreement that violates them is void." *See id.*, sec. 702, Comment n, citing sec. 331(2).
31. *See* THIRD RESTATEMENT ON FOREIGN RELATIONS LAW, *supra*, section 703 (free expression is not listed among the customary norms that have *jus* cogens status). *See also* ICCPR, art. 4 (article 19, re: free expression, is not among those listed as nonderogable in article 4(2)).
32. There is a close kinship between *jus cogens* human rights norms on the international plane and the idea of inalienable rights on the domestic civil rights plane. To the peremptory or nonderogable aspect of *jus cogens* is added the natural law element of inalienable rights. Although certain political philosophers would distinguish between *jus cogens* and inalienability, there are also those who refer to *jus cogens* as the modern form of natural law. *See* MARK W. JANIS, AN INTRODUCTION TO INTERNATIONAL LAW 63 (2nd Edition, Little, Brown & Company, 1993).
33. UN Charter, Chapter V, art. 24 ("... Members confer on the Security Council primary responsibility for the maintenance of peace and security") and art. 25 ("[t]he Members of the United Nations agree to accept and carry out the decisions of the Security Council ..."); and Chapter VII, art. 39 ("[t]he Security Council shall determine the existence of any threat to the peace ... and shall make recommendations, or decide what measures shall be taken. ...").
34. In Congress, July 4, 1776, The Unanimous Declaration of the Thirteen United States of America (American Declaration of Independence), para. 1 ("When in the Course of human events, it becomes necessary for one people to dissolve the political bonds that have connected them with another, ..., a decent respect to the opinions of mankind requires that they should declare the causes which impel them to the separation.").
35. The Constitution of the United States, adopted by the Constitutional Congress, Philadelphia, Pennsylvania, Sept. 17, 1787, art. VI, cl. 2 ("This Constitution, and the Laws of the United States which shall be made in Pursuance thereof; and all Treaties made, or which shall be made under the Authority of the United States, shall be the supreme Law of the Land...").
36. "Agreements [or promises] must be kept." VCLOT, art. 26 (Article 26 is entitled "Pacta sunt servanda" and reads: "[e]very treaty is binding upon the parties to it and must be performed by them in good faith.") *See also* American Law Institute Restatement (2nd) of Contracts, sec. 205 (1978) ("[e]very contract imposes upon each party a duty of good faith and fair dealing in its performance and its enforcement.").
37. *See* Uniform Commercial Code (UCC), Section 1-205(3) (pre-2000 version) ("[a] course of dealing between parties and any usage of trade in the vocation or trade in which they are engaged or of which they are or should be aware give particular meaning to and supplement or qualify terms of an agreement.").
38. UN Charter, ICJ Statute, art. 38(1)(d).

39. *Id.*, art. 38(1)(d) ("[t]he Court ... shall apply: ... judicial decisions and the teachings of the most highly qualified publicists of the various nations, as subsidiary means for the determination of rules of law").
40. *Id.*, art. 59 ("[t]he decision of the Court has no binding force except between the parties and in respect of that particular case.").
41. *See* Declaration on the Protection of all Persons from Being Subjected to Torture, General Assembly Resolution 3452, 30 UN GAOR Supp. (No. 34) 91, UN Doc. A/1034 (1975). *See also* Convention Against Torture and Other Cruel, Inhuman or Degrading Treatment or Punishment (CAT or Torture Convention), *adopted*, Dec. 10, 1984, *entered into force*, June 26, 1987, GA Res. 39/46, 39 UN GAOR Supp. (No. 51) at 197, UN Doc. A/39/51 (1984).
42. Universal Declaration of Human Rights (UDHR or Universal Declaration), GA Res. 217A (III), UN Doc. A/810 at 71 (1948).
43. *See Filartiga*, 630 F.2d at 883 ("several commentators have concluded that the Universal Declaration has become, in toto, a part of binding, customary international law,") citing, *inter alia*, Wadlock [1965] at 15.
44. *See* The Constitution of Sierra Leone, 1991 (Act No. 6 of 1991), Chapter III (entitled "[t]he Recognition and Protection of Fundamental Human Rights and Freedoms of the Individual"), articles 15–30. Chapter III enumerates most of the substantive civil and political rights set forth in Articles 2–21 of the UDHR, with the exception of the right to nationality (UDHR, art. 15) and the right to seek and enjoy asylum (UDHR, art. 14). However, Sierra Leone's constitution lacks specific provisions relating to those economic, social, and cultural rights set forth in Articles 22–28 of the UDHR. Like the antidiscrimination language of Article 2 of the UDHR, Article 27 of Sierra Leone's constitution prohibits discrimination on account of race, color, gender, political opinion, and religion. Whereas the UDHR mentions "language" as an impermissible basis for discrimination, the Constitution of Sierra Leone cites "tribe." Socioeconomic status is the only distinct attribute identified in the UDHR, which is not enumerated in the nondiscrimination provisions of Sierra Leone's constitution.

    See also The Constitution of the Republic of Uganda, 1995, Chapter Four ("[t]he Protection and Promotion of Fundamental and Other Human Rights and Freedoms"), articles 20–58. Chapter Four enumerates most of the substantive civil, political, economic, social, and cultural rights found in Articles 2–28 of the UDHR. Furthermore, the Constitution of Uganda encompasses human rights protections not included in the UDHR, with specific articles devoted to the rights of women, children, persons with disabilities, and minorities, respectively. Finally, it expands upon Article 2 of the UDHR to include disability as an impermissible ground upon which to discriminate.

    See also La Constitution de La Republic du Burundi, Loi No. 1/010 du 18 Mars 2005, Titre II ("De la Charte des Droits et des Devoirs Fondamentaux, de L'Individu et du Citoyen") [The Constitution of the Republic of Burundi, Law No. 1/0101 of March 18, 2005, Title II ("Concerning the Charter of Fundamental Rights and Duties of the Individual and Citizen")], articles 19–74. The Preamble of Title II specifically mentions the Universal Declaration of Human Rights, and articles 19–58 encompass the full gamut of individual rights proclaimed in the UDHR. Unlike the UDHR, the Constitution of Burundi contains a separate section (articles 62–74) on the "Fundamental Duties of the Individual and Citizen."
45. *See Filartiga*, 630 F.2d at 884 (stating that "United States diplomatic contacts confirm the universal abhorrence with which torture is viewed ..."). *See also* RESTATEMENT ON FOREIGN RELATIONS, Section 702 and Comment n (1987).
46. JANIS, AN INTRODUCTION TO INTERNATIONAL LAW at 154.
47. *Id.*

48. Montevideo Convention on the Rights and Duties of States, *adopted*, Dec. 26, 1933, *entered into force*, Dec. 26, 1934, art. 1 ("[t]he state as a person of international law should possess the following qualifications: (a) a permanent population; (b) a defined territory; (c) government; and (d) capacity to enter relations with the other states.").
49. *See* Arab League Pact, March 22, 1945, *available at* http://avalon.law.yale.edu/20th_century/arableag.asp; Charter of the Organization of American States (OAS) (1948), *available at* http://www.oas.org/dil/treaties.htm; Statute of the Council of Europe, May 5, 1949, *available at* http://conventions.coe.int/treaty/en/Treaties/Html/001.htm; Organization of African Unity Charter (OAU Charter), May 25, 1963, *available at* http://www.au2002.gov.za/docs/key_oau/oau_charter.htm; Treaty of Amity and Cooperation in Southeast Asia, Feb. 24, 1976, *available at* http://www.aseansec.org/1217.htm.
50. *See* DUNOFF, RATNER, AND WIPPMAN, INTERNATIONAL LAW NORMS, ACTORS, PROCESS: A PROBLEM-ORIENTED APPROACH (2nd Ed., Aspen, 2006), at 111 ("[o]rthodox international law doctrine has regarded states as the primary, even sole, actors in international law") and 201 ("[a]ctors unaffiliated with governments have long played a role in the prescription, invocation, and application of international norms.").
51. *See* related discussion in Chapter 2, Section B.2. *See also* "The Responsibility to Protect," a report prepared by the International Commission on Intervention and State Sovereignty, Dec. 2001, *available at* http://www.iciss.ca/pdf/Commission-Report.pdf.
52. *See* American Convention on Human Rights (American Convention), *signed*, Nov. 22, 1969, *entered into force*, July 18, 1978, OAS Treaty Series No. 36, at 1, OAS Off. Rec. OEA/Ser. L/V/II.23 doc. rev. 2, art. 44 ("[a]ny person or group of persons, or any nongovernmental entity ... may lodge petitions with the [Inter-American] Commission [on Human Rights] containing denunciations or complaints of violation of this Convention by a State Party"); art. 61 (if the Commission is unable to reach friendly settlement in a case, the State Party or the Commission itself may submit the case to the Inter-American Court of Human Rights for a ruling); and art. 63 ("[i]f the Court finds that there has been a violation of a right or freedom protected by [the American] Convention, the Court shall rule that the injured party be ensured the enjoyment of his right or freedom that was violated").

It is worthy of note that while states that have signed and ratified the American Convention "automatically" recognize the competence of the Commission to hear individual petitions against them, only states that have made special declarations under art. 45 need recognize the competence of the commission to hear interstate petitions. *Compare* American Convention, arts. 44 (re: individual petitions) and 45 (re: interstate petitions). At the time that the American Convention entered into force in 1976, the opposite presumption applied in another regional human rights system, that of the Council of Europe.

At the inception of the European system, while interstate petitions were a matter of course, individual petitions required a declaration by the state alleged to have violated the European Convention on Human Rights and Fundamental Freedoms, which recognized the competence of the European Court of Human Rights to hear such complaints. *See* [European] Convention for the Protection of Human Rights and Fundamental Freedoms, *signed* Nov. 4, 1950, *entered into force*, Sept. 3, 1953, UNTS 222, Europ. TS No. 5, arts. 24 ("[a]ny ... Party may refer to the [European] Commission [on Human Rights] ... any alleged breach of the provisions of the [European] Convention by another ... Party") and 25 ("[t] Commission may receive petitions ... from any person, nongovernmental organization or group of individuals claiming to be a victim of a violation by one of the ... Parties of the rights set forth in this Convention, provided that the ... Party against which the complaint has been lodged has declared that it recognizes the competence of the Commission to receive such petitions"). In 1994, the European Convention was amended through Protocol 11 to the European Convention, *adopted*,

May 11, 1994, *entered into force,* Nov. 1, 1998, 2061 UNTS 7, Europ. TS No. 155. By the terms of Protocol 11, all parties to the European Convention accept the jurisdiction of the European Court of Human Rights over both interstate and individual petitions. *See* Protocol 11, arts. 33 (re: interstates cases) and 34 (re: individual applications).

In the African system, the African Commission on Human and Peoples' Rights is competent to hear both interstate and individual petitions. Nevertheless, in the case of interstate petitions, once local remedies have been exhausted, and assuming no friendly settlement, the Commission must ("shall") prepare a report of its findings regarding any alleged violations of the African Charter of Human and Peoples' Rights. In contrast, communications brought by nonstate petitioners require a majority vote by the members of the Commission in favor of consideration. *Compare* African [Banjul] Charter of Human and Peoples' Rights, *adopted,* June 27, 1981, *entered into force,* Oct. 21, 1986, OAU Doc. CAB/LEG/77/3 Rev. 5 (1981), arts. 48 (in the case of interstate petitions "either State shall have the right to submit the matter to the Commission") and 55 ("communications other than those of States Parties . . . shall be considered by the Commission if a simple majority of its members so decide").

53. As discussed in Chapter 4, only states parties, the ICC Prosecutor or the Security Council may initiate prosecutions by the ICC. *See* Rome Statute of the International Criminal Court (Rome Statute or ICC Statute), UN Doc. A/CONF. 183/9; 37 ILM 1002 (1998); 2187 UNTS 90, art. 13. Nevertheless, victims are permitted to observe the proceedings and to give testimony. *Id.* at art. 68.

54. The UN Charter provides for a sixth primary organ, the Trusteeship Council, mandated to help usher "non-self-governing territories" or colonies toward statehood, in accord with the norm of self-determination of peoples. *See* UN Charter, art. 1(2). After World War I, the colonies of the defeated powers were "mandated" to individual Allied nations to administer until independence. In 1945, Tanganyika, a former German colony, became a British mandate during that period, attained its independence in 1961, and united with the island of Zanzibar to create the modern Republic of Tanzania in 1964. The mandate system was originally administered by the League of Nations, which collapsed upon the outbreak of World War II. In 1945, the UN inherited the continuing mandates, and the UN Charter created a similar system of "trusteeships" with regard to former colonies of the defeated Axis powers at the end of World War II. When Palau attained its independence in 1994, the Trusteeship Council suspended operations, its work completed. Palau had been administered by the United States as the Pacific Islands Trusteeship.

55. UN Charter, art. 27 ("[d]ecisions of the Security Council [on nonprocedural matters] shall be made by an affirmative vote of nine members including the concurring votes of the permanent members . . .").

56. UN Security Council Resolution 418, 32 UN SCOR, Res. and Dec. at 5 (1977).

57. *Id.,* paras. 1 and 2 ("strongly condemning the South African Government for its resort to massive violence against and killing of the African people, including schoolchildren and students and others opposing racial discrimination" and "[r]ecognizing that the military build-up and persistent acts of aggression by South Africa against neighbouring States seriously disturb the security of those States").

58. *See, generally,* NELSON MANDELA, LONG WALK TO FREEDOM (Little Brown and Co., 1995).

59. Case Concerning United States Diplomatic and Consular Staff in Tehran (U.S. v. Iran), 1980 ICJ Reports (May 24).

60. Military and Paramilitary Activities in and against Nicaragua (Nicaragua v. United States), 1986 ICJ Reports (June 27), 14, 134–35.

61. UN Charter, art. 97.

62. UN Charter, art. 68 ("[t]he Economic and Social Council shall set up commissions in economic and social fields and for the promotion of human rights").
63. UN Charter, art. 71 ("[t]he Economic and Social Council may make suitable arrangements for consultation with nongovernmental organizations").
64. UN Charter, art. 57 ("[t]he various specialized agencies, established by intergovernmental agreement . . . in economic, social, cultural, educational, health, and related fields, shall be brought into relationship with the United Nations").
65. *See* Human Rights Council, S-9/1, "The grave violations of human rights in the occupied Palestinian Territory, particularly due to the recent military attacks against the occupied Gaza Strip," A/HRC/S-9/L.1, Jan. 12, 2009.
66. Richard Goldstone, former Chief Prosecutor of the International Criminal Tribunals for the former Yugoslavia and Rwanda, released the delegation's findings on September 16, 2009. The mission found credible evidence of war crimes by Israeli forces and Hamas militants, as well as crimes against humanity by Israeli forces. *See* www.nytimes.com/2009/09/16/world/middleeast/16gaza.html. After the publication of the 2009 Goldstone mission report, the UN appointed a committee of independent experts, chaired by former judge Mary McGowan Davis, which evaluated follow-up efforts by Israel to investigate the allegations of international law violations by members of its armed forces contained in the Goldstone report. On April 1, 2011, after the publication of the McGowan Davis report, Goldstone published an opinion piece in *The Washington Post* "welcome[ing] Israel's investigations into [the] allegations" against it and expressing "concerns . . . that few of Israel's inquiries have been concluded and . . . that the proceedings should have been held in a public hearing." Nonetheless, Goldstone notes that the McGowan Davis report findings "indicate that civilians were not intentionally targeted as a matter of [Israeli] policy." *See* Richard Goldstone, "Reconsidering the Goldstone Report on Israel and War Crimes," Wash. Post, Apr. 1, 2011, http://www.washingtonpost.com/opinions/reconsidering-the-goldstone-report-on-israel-and-war-crimes/2011/04/01/AFg111JC_story.html.
67. *See* Reparation for Injuries Suffered in the Service of the United Nations ["the Bernadotte Case"], 1949 ICJ Reports 174, 178–179 (the ICJ concluded that "the Organization [the United Nations] is an international person. That is not the same thing as saying it is a State. . . . What it does mean is that it is a subject of international law and capable of possessing international rights and duties, and that it has the capacity to maintain its rights by bringing international claims.").
68. UN Charter, art. 71 ("[t]he Economic and Social Council [of the United Nations] may make suitable arrangements for consultation with non-governmental organizations which are concerned with matters within its competence.").
69. *See* Janis, *op. cit.* at 174; *see also* International Committee of the Red Cross (ICRC), Preliminary Remarks, [prefacing] the Geneva Conventions of August 12, 1949, at 1 (published by ICRC, *available at* http://www.icrc.org/Web/Eng/siteeng0.nsf/htmlall/p0173/$File/ICRC_002_0173.PDF) ("[t]he International Committee of the Red Cross has, from the outset, been the sponsor of the Geneva Convention for the protection of wounded military personnel, and of the humanitarian Conventions which supplement it.").
70. *See* website of the Beyond Juba Project, http://www.beyondjuba.org/project_info.html.
71. *See generally*, Legality of the Threat or Use Of Nuclear Weapons, 1996 ICJ 226 (July 8); *see also* Dunoff *et al., op. cit.* at 539 (referencing the role of the World Court Project, a consortium of NGOs, in inspiring the ICJ to issue an advisory opinion on the legality of the threat or use of nuclear weapons under international law).
72. *See* United Nations Declaration on the Rights of Indigenous Peoples, *adopted* by the General Assembly, 13 September., 2007, A/RES/61/295.

73. *See* Protocol Additional to the Geneva Conventions of 12 August, 1949, and Relating to the Protection of Victims of International Armed Conflicts (Protocol I), of 8 June, 1977, 1125 UNTS 3, art. 1(4) ("[this Protocol ... shall apply in] armed conflicts in which peoples are fighting against colonial domination and alien occupation and against racist regimes in the exercise of their right of self-determination ...") and art. 96 ("[t]he authority representing a people engaged against a High Contracting Party in an armed conflict of the type referred to in Article 1, paragraph 4, may undertake to apply the Conventions and this Protocol in relation to that conflict by means of a unilateral declaration ..."); *see also*, Protocol Additional to the Geneva Conventions of 12 August, 1949, and Relating to the Protection of Victims of Non-International Armed Conflicts (Protocol II), of 8 June, 1977, 1125 UNTS 609, art. 1(1) ("[t]his Protocol ... shall apply to all armed conflicts ... which take place in the territory of a High Contracting Party between its armed forces and dissident armed forces or other organized armed groups which, under responsible command, exercise such control over a part of its territory as to enable them to carry out sustained and concerted military operations and to implement this Protocol").
74. Trafficking entails transnational trade in prohibited goods, including the sale of illegal narcotics or weapons transactions in violation of arms embargoes or disarmament conventions. Human trafficking involves transnational commerce in human beings, involving elements of coercion and exploitation. *See* Protocol to Prevent, Suppress and Punish Trafficking in Persons especially Women and Children, *adopted*, Nov. 15, 2000, *entry into force*, Dec. 25, 2003, 2237 UNTS 319, Doc. A/55/383, art. 3 ("'[t]rafficking in persons' shall mean the ... transportation ... of persons, by means of the threat or use of force or other forms of coercion ... for the purposes of exploitation ...").
75. Boumediene v. Bush, 553 US 723 (2008).
76. African [Banjul] Charter on Human and Peoples' Rights, *adopted* June 27, 1981, *entered into force* Oct. 21, 1986, OAU Doc. CAB/LEG/67/3 Rev. 5 (1981).
77. Lord Johan Steyn of the United Kingdom (UK) House of Lords delivered the 27th annual Mann Lecture on November 25, 2003, stating that "[t]he most powerful democracy is detaining hundreds of suspected foot soldiers of the Taliban in a legal black hole at the U.S. naval base at Guantánamo Bay, where they await trial on capital charges by military tribunals." *See* Johan Steyn, "A Monstrous Failure of Justice: Guantánamo," INT'L HERALD TRIB., Nov. 27, 2003. N.B.: At the time of Lord Steyn's address in 2003, the vast majority of the approximately 750 individuals within US custody in Guantánamo were being detained without charge. *See* Jennifer Moore, "Practicing What We Preach: Humane Treatment for Detainees in the War on Terror," 37 DENVER J. INT'L L. POL'Y, 33–61 at 44 and n. 37.
78. *See generally,* Van Gend en Loos v. Nederlandse Administratie Der Belastingen, [1963] ECR 3 (the European Court of Justice, the judicial organ of the European Union (EU), held that EU treaty provisions take "direct effect" in the national legal systems of EU member states); *see also* Costa v. Ente Nazionale per l'Energia Ellettrica, [1964] ECR 585 ("[t]he precedence of Community law is confirmed by Article 189 [of the Rome Treaty establishing the EU], whereby a regulation 'shall be binding' and 'directly applicable in all Member States.'").
79. *See* Constitution of the Fifth Republic [of France], Oct. 4, 1958, art. 55 ("[t]reaties or agreements duly ratified or approved upon publication, prevail over Acts of Parliament, subject, in regard to each agreement or treaty, to its application by the other party").
80. *See* The Paquete Habana, at 700 ("[i]nternational law is part of our law, and must be ascertained and administered by the courts of justice of appropriate jurisdiction. . . . For this purpose, where there is no treaty and no controlling executive or legislative or judicial decision, resort must be had to the customs and usages of civilized nations.").
81. *See* Whitney v. Robertson, 124 US 190, 194 (1888) ("[b]y the Constitution a treaty is placed on the same footing, and made of like obligation, with an act of legislation. . . .

When the two relate to the same subject . . . if the two are inconsistent, the one last in date will control the other, provided always the stipulation of the treaty on the subject is self-executing.").

82. *See* Constitution of the Republic of Uganda, 1995, Chapter One, art. 2 (re: "Supremacy of the Constitution").

83. This occurred in 1945, in the Charter of the International Military Tribunal at Nuremburg (IMT or Nuremberg Tribunal), and more recently in 2002, with the creation of the ICC. The Statute of the ICC limits the exercise of universal jurisdiction by the court to three enumerated offenses or broader categories of offenses: genocide, other crimes against humanity, and war crimes. Rome Statute of the ICC, *adopted*, July 17, 1998, *entered into force*, July 1, 2002, A/CONF./83/9, art. 5 ("Crimes within the jurisdiction of the Court: (a) The crime of genocide; (b) Crimes against humanity; (c) War crimes; (d) The crime of aggression."). Despite the theoretical scope of universal jurisdiction, in fact the ICC is not constitutionally mandated to try all alleged perpetrators of war crimes and crimes against humanity. The Statute of the ICC limits the scope of potential prosecutions under the rubric of "admissibility," with prerequisites that somewhat ironically mirror the two classic jurisdictional principles of territoriality and nationality: before a case is admissible, either the state in which the offense occurred or the offender's state of nationality must be a party to the Statute. *See* Rome Statute, art. 12(2) ("Preconditions to the exercise of jurisdiction").

84. This text focuses on international humanitarian law, or the *jus in bello*, meaning rules regarding the conduct of war. A close cousin to IHL is the law governing "the use of force," or the *jus ad bellum*, regulating the decision to go to war. One simple way to distinguish between IHL and use of force law is to contrast the rules governing "the going to war" and those limiting "the conduct of war." Although regarded as fairly distinct, in fact IHL and use of force law overlap, as discussed in Chapter 2 of our text, particularly Sections B, on the use of force, and C, on the essential principles of humanitarian law. In essence, both IHL and use of force law rely on the principles of necessity and proportionality, i.e., war should neither be initiated nor prosecuted in such a manner that the use of firepower, so to speak, overwhelms the purported threat by "the other side." The complex and fascinating interrelationship between humanitarian law and the rules governing the use of force will be further explored in Chapter 2.

CHAPTER 2

Humanitarian Law

The Law of Armed Conflict

When two elephants are fighting, the grass will suffer.
Which is the position of the civilians.
They have no mercy for the vulnerable, have no mercy for the old ones,
have no mercy for the children, have no mercy for the women.
Why should the civilians pay the wages of the corrupt?
Oh, you mighty men, no sympathy for the little ones.

Reuben M. Koroma[1]

A. THE MORALITY OF WAR AND THE LAW OF WAR

In recent centuries, numerous philosophers and religious leaders have taught that war is inherently immoral. Others have objected to armed conflict because, as a matter of historical fact, it consistently and predictably leads to the targeting of civilians and the suffering of innocents. Influential pacifists from a diversity of religious and secular traditions across the globe include Russian philosopher Leo Tolstoy,[2] American Catholic Dorothy Day,[3] Indian Hindu Mohandas Gandhi,[4] Palestinian Sufi Nafez Assaily,[5] South African Anglican Archbishop Desmond Tutu,[6] and eighteenth-century American Quaker John Woolman.[7] An earlier school of thought differentiated between military campaigns on moral grounds. The just war theory is seen to have originated in the work of philosopher-theologians Augustine and Thomas Aquinas, writing in the fifth and thirteenth centuries, respectively.[8]

The law of war has developed over many centuries against this philosophical, religious, and historical backdrop. Since the time of Hugo Grotius, a founder of the field of international law that flowered in Europe beginning in the seventeenth century, the *jus ad bellum* has concerned the initiation of war—when it is lawful to go to war, whereas the *jus in bello* or humanitarian law has regulated the conduct of war—how war may be waged lawfully. One of the essential principles espoused by Grotius was that the *jus in bello* must apply to so-called just wars and not merely to unjust wars.[9] Grotius rejected the supposition that the ends justify the means in wartime. He posed two questions of every armed conflict: Is the war justified? Are the methods justified? Although for several centuries after Grotius the law of war concerned clashes between states, today, rules regulating military force also apply to armed conflicts between states and certain nonstate entities.[10] Despite the evolution in the practitioners and technology of war, one of Grotius' greatest legacies remains his insistence that humanitarian law applies to all sorts of armed conflicts.

Although the *jus in bello*—humanitarian law—seeks to lessen the brutality and human suffering experienced in war, the essence of the *jus ad bellum* is to prohibit war except in extraordinary circumstances. In more modern parlance, the *jus ad bellum* has given way to rules governing the *use of force*, which attempt to regulate the resort to military force by states against other states or by states against nonstate agents.[11]

Thus, since the seventeenth century, the law of war has encompassed rules governing both the *whether* and the *how* of war: whether under international law it is lawful to resort to military force in the first instance; and how, once initiated, an armed conflict may be waged lawfully. When a state *decides* to go to war unlawfully, resorting to military force without legal justification, it has committed an act of aggression. In contrast, when a state or nonstate agent wages war in an unlawful *manner*, such conduct amounts to a violation of humanitarian law, meaning a war crime.

This chapter ultimately focuses on the *how* of war—humanitarian law and its specific rules aimed at alleviating the suffering caused by war.[12] Nevertheless, the rules regarding whether war is justified are closely linked to the rules regulating the methodology of war. Thus, Section B will summarize the principal rules regarding the resort to the use of military force, and Sections C–F will provide deeper discussions of the essential principles and rules of humanitarian law. Section B begins with the general prohibition against the use of force and then analyzes its various exceptions.

B. RULES REGARDING THE USE OF FORCE

1. The General Prohibition Against Force and the Concept of Aggression

Use of force norms are grounded in the customary preference for peaceful settlement of disputes between states. The international community attempted to codify these rules in the mid-twentieth century, after earlier attempts to abolish war utterly failed to prevent Nazi aggression and the World War II.[13] The United Nations (UN) was born on the ashes of the Holocaust, and avoiding resort to military attack by one state against another is one of its defining purposes, along with the protection of human rights, the promotion of socioeconomic development, and progress toward the self-determination of peoples.

Conflict prevention is a cornerstone of the UN. The Preamble to the Charter of the United Nations (Charter) speaks of the motivation of the founders of the UN "to save succeeding generations from the scourge of war" and "to ensure... that armed force shall not be used, save in the common interest."[14] The founding purposes of the United Nations set forth in Article 1 of the Charter include "maintain[ing] international peace and security."[15] The essential principles of the UN instruct "all members [to]... settle their international disputes by peaceful means," in Article 2(3), and to "refrain in their international relations from the threat or use of force against the territorial integrity or political independence of any state," in Article 2(4).[16] Most importantly, Article 2(4) of the UN Charter is the source of the "general prohibition against the use of force."

In the common parlance of international lawyers, aggression is a state's unlawful use of military force in violation of Article 2(4). An individual in control of the state's military in such circumstances would have to answer for the *crime* of aggression. But despite widespread usage of the term *aggression*, it is only recently that acts or crimes of aggression have been defined by treaty. In 1945, the Nuremburg Charter set forth "crimes against peace" as offenses for which individual Nazi defendants were charged and convicted[17] without elaborating on the meaning of "waging a war of aggression." Likewise, the 1998 Rome Statute of the International Criminal Court (Rome Statute or ICC Statute) established subject matter jurisdiction over the crime of aggression alongside war crimes, crimes against humanity, and genocide, but deferred the issuance of indictments for the crime of aggression until the International Criminal Court (ICC) parties agreed upon a precise definition.[18]

At the 2010 ICC Review Conference held in Kampala, Uganda, the attendees agreed by consensus to amend the Statute to define an *act* of aggression as "[t]he invasion or attack by the armed forces of a State of the territory of another State, or any military occupation, however temporary, resulting from such invasion or attack, or any annexation by the use of the territory of another state."[19] To be guilty of the *crime* of aggression, the accused individual must have been in control of the state's armed forces, and have planned or carried out an act of aggression of sufficient gravity to constitute a violation of the UN Charter.[20] Thus, according to the ICC

Statute, the crime of aggression signifies that a state actor has perpetrated a cross-border military attack, occupation, or annexation without justification, in violation of Article 2(4) of the UN Charter. Nevertheless, this new definition is still not operational, because the Kampala Conference attendees agreed in a separate amendment that the ICC would not exercise jurisdiction over the crime of aggression until at least 2017.[21]

2. Exceptions to the General Prohibition

Despite its dedication to the peaceful settlement of international disputes, the UN Charter expresses considerable ambivalence towards military action. Whether a principled stance or an acceptance of human realities, the Charter offers a limited endorsement of the use of force in response to the unlawful use of force. For example, in referencing "armed force... in the common interest"[22] and in calling for "collective measures for the prevention and removal of threats to the peace,"[23] the Charter suggests that some forms of military intervention may be legitimate in response to certain military attacks or invasions. Once the door to military countermeasures is opened, however, new challenges emerge.

Alongside its widespread condemnation of acts of aggression, international law provides several important exceptions to the general prohibition against the use of force. Starting with UN Security Council resolutions explicitly authorizing military actions, our text proceeds to the customary law principles of self-defense and humanitarian intervention. Humanitarian intervention is analogous to the common law defense of others principle, as well as the newer *responsibility to protect* (R2P) concept under international law. We also consider the problematic application of use of force rules to wars of national liberation and so-called wars against terrorism.

UN Security Council Enforcement

In large part, the Security Council was created first to contemplate and then to regulate collective economic and military responses to unlawful military actions. The leading role of the Security Council in responding to threats to international peace and security is defined in Chapter VII of the UN Charter.[24] Article 39 permits the Security Council to identify a "threat to the peace" (*i.e.,* Iraq's annexation of Kuwait in 1990); Article 40 enables the Security Council to take preliminary steps to reestablish peaceful conditions (*i.e.,* entreaties to Iraq to withdraw from Kuwait);[25] and Article 41 empowers it to impose economic sanctions (*i.e.,* a Security Council-mandated trade embargo against goods from Iraq and Kuwait).[26] Only pursuant to Article 42 may the Security Council authorize or require member states to launch military countermeasures aimed at reestablishing conditions of peace and security (*i.e.*, UN Security Council Resolution 678 in 1990 authorizing military attacks against Iraq).[27]

The Claim of Self-Defense

It would be simpler, and perhaps more coherent, for the UN Charter to recognize one clear exception to the general prohibition against the use of military force by member nations, namely a resolution by the Security Council authorizing military countermeasures under Article 42, Chapter VII of the Charter. However, the drafters of the treaty charted a less clear course for the international community. In Article 51, the Charter acknowledges a preexisting norm of customary international law relating to the self-defensive use of force, stating that "[n]othing in the present Charter shall impair the inherent right of individual or collective self-defense in an armed attack against a Member of the United Nations, until the Security Council has taken measures necessary to maintain international peace and security."[28]

Article 51 requires an "armed attack" before the use of force in self-defense is justified. It also mandates that such self-help measures should end in response to Security Council action. However, Article 51 does not specify what states must do if the Security Council fails to take action under Chapter VII. Nor does the Charter interpret the significance of a debate in the Security Council regarding a draft resolution contemplating military countermeasures that is never adopted. The fact that force is not authorized might be taken to mean either that self-defense is foreclosed or that it is permitted. Article 51's limited endorsement of self-defense at best compels states to conduct a difficult balancing act; at worst, it creates a gaping hole in the general prohibition against the use of force.

Despite the open language of the UN Charter, customary law and secondary sources of international law provide some constraints against the unbridled use of violence in the name of self-defense. In what has come to be called the *Caroline* Incident of 1837, a group of Americans, supportive of Canadian separatists fighting the British during the Upper Canadian Rebellion of the 1830s, armed and provisioned a steamboat called the *SS Caroline* on the US side of the Niagara River. In response, Canadian militia forces under British Royal Navy command seized, burned, and launched the boat over Niagara Falls, leading to the death of one American, Amos Durfee. After an initial claim of self-defense, the British government ultimately apologized for the incident in the context of the successful negotiation of the 1842 Webster-Ashburton Treaty.[29] This bilateral accord was the brainchild of US Secretary of State Daniel Webster and British Foreign Secretary Lord Ashburton.

The resolution of the *Caroline* imbroglio was the genesis of the "*Caroline* principles," now regarded as part of customary international law regulating the use of force in self-defense. In a colorful illustration of the genesis of soft law, these norms were first articulated in a letter dated April 24, 1841, from Webster to Henry Stephen Fox, the British Ambassador to the United States, which Webster appended to his subsequent correspondence to Lord Ashburton dated July 27, 1842. Webster famously wrote:

> "[If] the destruction of the *Caroline* is to be defended, [i]t will be for that Government to show a necessity of self-defense, instant, overwhelming, leaving no choice of means and no moment for deliberation. It will be for it to show, also, that the local authorities ... did nothing unreasonable or excessive; since the act justified by the necessity of self-defense, must be limited by that necessity, and kept clearly within it.[30]

Webster's analysis is often cited in the context of a discussion of anticipatory or preemptive self-defense. Nevertheless, by their own terms, the *Caroline* principles apply to self-defense more generally, limiting the lawful use of military force to conditions of immediacy, necessity, and proportionality.[31]

The Challenge of Humanitarian Intervention

There is an additional customary basis for the lawful use of military force that is not explicitly mentioned in the UN Charter, namely, a so-called *humanitarian intervention,* or the use of force by one state to stop widespread human rights abuses within the territory of another state. Two cases are often cited, both from 1978: Vietnam's invasion of Cambodia, motivated in part to stop the killing fields of the Khmer Rouge, and Tanzania's invasion of Uganda, predicated by Idi Amin's repression and killing of more than one-hundred thousand ethnic minorities and political opponents. Humanitarian intervention is a tricky rationale for the use of military force in part because there are bound to be mixed motives, including territorial acquisitiveness. Moreover, even if the defense of others is the primary motivating cause, humanitarian intervention runs counter to the norm of nonintervention in the internal affairs of a state, also enshrined in the UN Charter.[32] Finally, the motivation of ending human rights abuses does not protect civilians from being harmed in pursuit of that goal. Human rights abuses against civilians flowing from the intervention may rival those that motivated a military response in the first place.[33]

The Responsibility to Protect

In recent years, international paralysis in the face of recurring and enduring humanitarian tragedies from Bosnia to Rwanda to Darfur have prompted some human rights advocates to call for a more effective principle of state accountability for massive human rights violations. One emergent concept is known as the responsibility to protect (R2P). Arguably more ambitious than humanitarian intervention, which purports to *justify* a state's military action to stop abuses in another state, R2P implies state *obligation* to end such abuses. "The Responsibility to Protect" was the title of a document published in December 2001 by the International Commission on Intervention and State Sovereignty, established by the Government of Canada, whose authors called for rules and procedures for "intervention on human protection grounds."[34] The commission presented its recommendations to then UN Secretary General Kofi Annan and inspired a 2005 report he presented to the General Assembly entitled, "In Larger Freedom." The concept of R2P was in turn endorsed by 150 members of the General Assembly during the 2005 session.[35]

As a source of international law, the responsibility to protect is still in the throes of "progressive development." Without a treaty or UN Security Council resolution to codify it, and in the absence of widespread state practice accompanied by a sense of legal obligation evidencing its status as a customary norm, R2P is still an aspiration. Recognizing its emergent character, Secretary General Annan challenged the international community to give the fledgling principle greater life:

> As to genocide, ethnic cleansing and other such crimes against humanity, are they not also threats against international peace and security, against which humanity should be able to look to the Security Council for protection?[36]

Annan responded to his own rhetorical question by deferring to the Security Council and its prerogative to specifically define the parameters of the responsibility to protect. His report recommended "that the Security Council adopt a resolution setting out these principles and expressing its intention to be guided by them when deciding whether to authorize or mandate the use of force."[37] To date the Security Council has not acted to formalize R2P.

In 2009, during the term of Annan's successor, Secretary General Ban Ki-moon, the General Assembly reevaluated the responsibility to protect, inviting the testimony of Edward Luck, Ban's special advisor on R2P. Luck recommended a three-stage approach: first, calling upon the state of origin to fulfill its primary responsibility to protect the people residing on its territory from massive human rights abuses; second, encouraging the state of origin to call on other states for help in the event it is unable to stop violations on its own; and third, requiring the international community to intervene to provide life-saving assistance not otherwise forthcoming, with military action a last resort.[38] During the debate regarding implementation of R2P, several state representatives and invited experts challenged the wisdom of the principle, most notably and eloquently the General Assembly President himself, Rev. Miguel D'Escoto Brockmann of Nicaragua. D'Escoto cautioned that R2P was ripe for abuse by powerful countries. He challenged that "R2I"—the right to *intervene*—was a more candid moniker.[39]

The potential corruption of the responsibility to protect in the cynical service of national self-interest is dramatically illustrated by the US rationalization for launching the Iraq war in 2003 and Russia's characterization of its invasion of South Ossetia in 2008. But the prevailing critique of R2P may also obscure two competing and compelling realities. First, the more long-standing norm of humanitarian intervention already tolerates military intervention by another state in extreme human rights emergencies. Thus, the risk of a superpower overreaching is not a new one. Second, the most challenging aspect of R2P is not that it permits military intervention, but that, in extreme cases, it will require states to provide assistance to other states facing humanitarian crises, including the provision of food, shelter, sanitation, and medical care.[40] Thus, the bigger impediment to implementing the responsibility to protect may be the economic burden it requires developed states to assume, rather than the military liberties it allows them to take. In any event, without stronger consensus from the General Assembly, and in the absence of a Security Council Resolution implementing R2P, the responsibility to protect remains in the realm of soft law.

The Twilight Zone: Wars of National Liberation and Wars against Terrorism

Movements of national liberation (MNLs) are accorded considerable symbolic legitimacy, especially when they are supported by major world powers. In such cases, the claim to statehood is justified by the norm of self-determination.[41] Indeed, the Palestinian Liberation Organization (PLO) and the African National Congress (ANC) are notable examples of dissident political organizations seeking political independence that enjoyed MNL observer status in the UN General Assembly during the 1970s and 1980s. Nevertheless, rhetorical support for a movement of national liberation is quite distinct from sanctioning a war of national liberation, and the international community has rarely endorsed the call to arms by such entities.[42]

A perhaps more difficult question is whether states may initiate military force against acts of terrorism, defined as catastrophic, politically motivated, and targeted attacks on civilians.[43] Some scholars argue that if nonstate agents launch military attacks against a state's nationals, the self-defensive use of force is justified so long as it is necessary and proportionate, according to the *Caroline* principles discussed above.[44] Other international law experts insist that criminal law enforcement is the better mechanism for pursuing terrorism suspects.[45]

Despite the shaky legal foundation for wars of national liberation and wars against terror, the tendency, once such campaigns are initiated, is to bring them under the protective embrace of the *jus in bello*, in order to regulate their methods and lessen their brutality. Whether wars between states, civil wars, wars to bring about independence, or wars to stop terrorism, the pervasive human cost of armed conflict is undeniable. Thus, there is a palpable sense of urgency in the international community to ensure that all wars, lawful or not according to the *jus ad bellum*, result in the least amount of destruction and human suffering possible. This is the heart of humanitarian law.

C. THE ESSENCE OF HUMANITARIAN LAW

International humanitarian law (IHL) is agnostic as to the rationales for armed conflict and unimpressed by its purported justifications. Rather than struggling to differentiate between lawful and unlawful conflicts, IHL strives to ensure that all conflicts are less brutal. The universal application of humanitarian law means that no conflict may be relegated to a lawless zone.

Practitioners of humanitarian law push confidence in the rule of law to its very limits, descending proverbially, if not literally into the jaws of death in order to regulate war. This gritty aspect of humanitarian law is both its strength and its vulnerability.[46] Legal norms calling for humanity in war are singular in their capacity to confront the bloody realities of armed conflict. At the same time, such rules may be criticized for reinforcing the idea that war is an acceptable or unavoidable aspect of human relations.

The remaining four sections of this chapter delve into the nuances of international humanitarian law. IHL is codified by a family of treaties, most notably the four 1949 Geneva Conventions and their two 1977 Protocols.[47] Like the law governing the use of force, IHL builds upon a foundation in customary law. This section begins with a discussion of these customary principles, and then proceeds to the substantive provisions of the treaties themselves.

1. The Four Foundational Principles of Customary Humanitarian Law

The human essence of the *jus in bello* is to protect civilians, wounded combatants, and prisoners of war from the violence, destruction, and suffering of combat. IHL also defends the humanity of soldiers in combat. In order to shield all persons from the worst ravages of war, four interrelated customary norms have been articulated, beginning with the principle of *distinction*, which prohibits the targeting of civilians and civilian areas, including homes; hospitals; schools; and places of recreation, work, and worship. The three companion principles are humanity, necessity, and proportionality. *Humanity* insists upon concern for human welfare in all instances. *Necessity* requires that violent measures be taken only in response to actual or threatened violence. *Proportionality* prohibits a response more intense than the provocation.[48] In all cases, humanitarian law signifies that the military response to a military attack must be restrained, although the provocation itself was not. Thus, a corollary principle to the four pillars of humanitarian law is that reciprocal violations are forbidden.[49]

Necessity and proportionality are also customary principles relating to the use of force, highlighting the close kinship between the *jus in bello* and the *jus ad bellum*. Just as a state is not justified in launching a war in the absence of a macrolevel military attack, an army is prohibited from targeting a particular group of combatants, installation, or geographical location unless part of a proportional response to a microlevel attack.[50] As with self-defense under the *jus ad bellum*, the humanitarian rule of proportionality will often arise in a situation in which the other side has acted without regard for any legal rules whatsoever. Thus, humanitarian law in action is both idealistic and tough-minded. It appeals to the capacity for self-restraint on the part of each party to the conflict *and* repeatedly invokes the rule against reciprocal violations.

2. The International Committee of the Red Cross as Champion and Drafter of Humanitarian Law

The International Committee of the Red Cross (ICRC), a Swiss nongovernmental agency, was founded in 1863 by Henri Dumont. Dumont had been a horrified observer of the suffering and deaths of wounded soldiers in the 1859 Battle of Solferino, decisive in Italy's Second War of Independence. Upwards of two-hundred thousand troops fought over nine hours in the streets and fields in and around San Marino and Solferino, until the Franco-Italian forces finally prevailed over the Austrian fighters. More than five thousand combatants died, including many soldiers on both sides who were shot or bayoneted after being wounded.[51] One year after its founding, the ICRC drafted and opened for signature the 1864 Geneva Convention, the first treaty of international humanitarian law, obligating state parties to provide medical care and protection for sick and wounded soldiers.[52]

Between the 1864 Geneva Convention and the four Geneva Conventions of 1949, several intermediate humanitarian instruments were adopted. Hague Declaration IV of 1899 is notable for outlawing bombardments from the air, chemical weapons, and exploding or "hollow-point" bullets.[53] Hague Convention IV of 1907 on the Laws and Customs of War sought to protect additional groups of persons, incorporating the protections of wounded combatants from the 1864 Geneva Convention, adding protections for prisoners of war, and explicitly limiting the "Means of Injuring the Enemy, Sieges and Bombardments" in Chapter 1.[54] In particular, Hague Convention IV laid the foundation for the Fourth Geneva Convention of 1949 by declaring that "[t]he right of belligerents to adopt means of injuring the enemy is not unlimited" and prohibiting attacks on undefended towns and dwelling places.[55] Later, the Geneva Protocol of 1925 outlawed the use of poison gas and biological ("bacteriological") weapons[56] and the 1929 Geneva Convention further amplified the protection of prisoners of war.[57]

In 1949, four new Geneva Conventions were opened for signature, and in the ensuing fifty years, all 194 members of the UN have become parties.[58] With their two 1977 Protocols, the 1949 Geneva Conventions remain the most authoritative codification of international humanitarian law in the twenty-first century. They build on the earlier Hague and Geneva Conventions to amplify protections of wounded combatants, POWs, and civilians.

The International Committee of the Red Cross is not a party to the four 1949 Geneva Conventions, but as with the earlier Hague and Geneva Conventions, ICRC played a central role in their drafting, adoption, and entry into force. Moreover, ICRC is mentioned in each of the four 1949 Geneva Conventions. Article 9 of the respective treaties[59] recognizes ICRC's prerogative to conduct "humanitarian activities," with the consent of the parties to the conflict. Article 8[60] provides that "Protecting [and non-warring] Powers" will be designated in a given conflict to "safeguard the interests of the [warring] Parties" and Article 10[61] allows such a role to be played by a neutral organization, rather than a state, with ICRC mentioned as the default entity to serve in this humanitarian capacity. Finally, the ICRC plays a continuing role in promoting respect for the Geneva Conventions through its eighty diplomatic missions worldwide, in coordinating with national Red Cross and Red Crescent societies the distribution of humanitarian relief supplies to populations affected by war; offering training programs for members of the armed forces and civilians alike; making visits to detained combatants; and helping to reunify families separated by conflict, occupation, and detention.

As discussed in Chapter 1, nongovernmental agencies (NGOs) are subjects of international law, which, like international organizations, can be instrumental in the creation of international law, whether treaties or customary norms. NGOs may also encourage states to bring legal claims before international and national tribunals. In promoting respect for international norms, NGOs "speak truth to power," inspiring, challenging, and cajoling states to following through on their treaty and customary obligations.

The ICRC plays all these roles in the field of humanitarian law. Formally speaking, it is properly characterized as an NGO, insofar as it is incorporated under the domestic laws of Switzerland. Nevertheless, it shares some of the attributes of an international organization, predating the UN by nearly a century, operating diplomatic missions in some eighty countries worldwide, convening conferences, and drafting multilateral conventions. As an operational humanitarian agency working directly with governments, individuals, and communities affected by armed conflict, ICRC is perhaps better thought of as a hybrid subject of international law, a transnational actor *sui generis*.

D. UNDERSTANDING ARMED CONFLICT THROUGH THE 1949 GENEVA CONVENTIONS AND THE 1977 PROTOCOLS

The four humanitarian Geneva Conventions of 1949 have 194 parties, including all members of the United Nations.[62] The two 1977 Protocols have 170 and 165 parties, respectively, comprising roughly 86 percent of all states. Sierra Leone, Uganda, and Burundi, our three country studies, have each signed and ratified the Geneva Conventions and their Protocols.[63] These treaties remain the bedrock of international humanitarian law, and provide us with greater insight into the meaning of armed conflict and the content of the rules that constrain it.

1. Defining Armed Conflict Through the Lens of the 1949 Geneva Conventions

In the Introduction, armed conflict was defined as "a destructive physical contest between organized forces armed with guns, tanks, bombs and other weapons of war." Although this working definition deserves considerable legal elaboration, we should not lose sight of the common-sense approach, in part because the international law definition of armed conflict has itself been contested.[64] Nevertheless, just as the 1949 Geneva Conventions supply the core treaty-based norms of international humanitarian law, Common Article 2 of those four Conventions gives us a starting point for a more precise definition of armed conflict, starting with wars between states.

Common Article 2 of all four Geneva Conventions of August 12, 1949 defines the scope of application of the Conventions, and thus sheds some light on the definition of armed conflict: "the present Convention shall apply to all cases of declared war or of any other armed conflict which may arise between two or more of the High Contracting Parties, even if the state of war is not recognized by one of them."[65] Common Article 2 emphasizes that interstate conflicts were the central concern in 1949, while clarifying that armed conflicts are not limited to officially declared wars. Nonetheless, Article 2 does not delve into the substantive nature of armed conflict itself, perhaps by design. We need to look elsewhere for this elaboration.

Common Article 3 of the 1949 Geneva Conventions was included to insure basic standards of humanity in non-international armed conflicts, prohibiting the murder, torture, mutilation, cruel treatment, hostage-taking, humiliation, and extra-judicial executions of any and all "[p]ersons taking no active part in the hostilities and those placed *hors de combat* (outside of combat)."[66] This provision suggests an inclusive definition of *armed conflict* through use of the descriptive term *hostilities*. More significantly, by applying the most fundamental humanitarian protections to non-international conflicts, the Geneva Conventions serve as primary international legal authority that armed conflicts are not limited to military contests between states and extend to "conflicts occurring in the territory of one of the High Contracting Parties."[67] Article 3 has become increasingly relevant in the twenty-first century, given that 95 percent of today's wars are civil or non-international armed conflicts, in which the vast majority of the victims are civilians.[68]

Since the end of the cold war, the typical structure of civil wars has changed, attributable to, among other reasons, ebbing levels of superpower patronage. Without sufficient outside funding, insurgent armies need to exploit local resources on the territory they occupy, often by operating mines and other extractive industries to facilitate the procurement of weapons, while preying upon the local population to sustain their troops. This entrepreneurial form of insurgency tends to prolong conflict and foster the splintering of insurgent groups as new aspiring leaders seek a piece of the action in economic, territorial, and military terms. This phenomenon is particularly well illustrated in what anthropologist Joseph Opala has described as the "competitive banditry" of the various factions in Sierra Leone's rebel war.[69] The wildly disproportionate burden of brutality that civilians bear in entrepreneurial civil wars is yet another reason why the fundamental protections of Common Article 3 remain essential.[70]

2. Counterterrorism as Armed Conflict Governed by Humanitarian Law

As discussed earlier in this chapter, political analysts and international lawyers continue to debate whether acts of terrorism are acts of war and whether a military campaign of counterterrorism is a lawful use of force. Without conceding the wisdom of fighting terrorist crimes on the battlefield rather than through the criminal justice system, once military force is used, the rules of humanitarian law come into play.[71]

After the terrorist attacks on the World Trade Center and the Pentagon on September 11, 2001, the United States made a concerted decision to mount a military response under the rubric of its self-proclaimed War on Terror. It is thus ironic that the US government maintained, throughout the administration of President George W. Bush, that the suspected terrorists who were held at the US Naval Base in Guantánamo Bay, Cuba, were not entitled to POW status, even though many were subject to detention without charge or to a long-delayed trial by military commission.[72] As a result, such detainees were effectively cut off from both the due process protections of US criminal law and the humanitarian protections of the Geneva Conventions.

Increasingly, US courts have recognized the rights of suspected terrorists to the protections of both US and international law.[73] The US Supreme Court's application of international humanitarian law to the War on Terror, since 2006, is consistent with the dominant approach among international law scholars outside the United States. As early as 1999, the Institute of International Law resolved that "[a]ll parties to armed conflicts in which non-state entities are parties, irrespective of their legal status. . . have the obligation to respect international humanitarian law, as well as fundamental human rights."[74]

From the most basic and common-sense standpoint of international law, if the means and metaphors of war are used to combat terrorism, the rules of humanitarian law must apply. Under the Third Geneva Convention relative to the Treatment of Prisoners of War, the POW Convention, if suspected terrorists are pursued, captured, and detained by soldiers in uniform, they are presumed to be POWs, until proven otherwise by a "competent tribunal."[75] Moreover, even if a war against suspected terrorists were deemed a non-international armed conflict, the fundamental protections of Common Article 3 would apply.[76] Finally, all persons are entitled to humane conditions of detention, regardless of their formal or extraordinary status, under both humanitarian law[77] and human rights law.[78]

3. Defining Armed Conflict Through the Lens of the Additional Protocols

In 1977, two additional Protocols to the Geneva Conventions were adopted, which are not as widely ratified as the four 1949 Geneva Conventions. Although the two Protocols are primary sources of international law only for the states that have ratified them, or to the extent that they evidence customary norms, they do constitute at least secondary or persuasive authority regarding the definition and scope of the term *armed conflict*. Protocol I relates to international armed conflicts,[79] and by its own terms applies to "the situations referred to in Article 2 common to those [1949 Geneva] Conventions."[80] The treaty clarifies that international armed conflicts include those "in which peoples are fighting against colonial domination and alien occupation and against racist regimes in the exercise of their right of self-determination. . ."[81] Though the inclusion of so-called movements of national liberation within the scope of Protocol I is thought to be one reason that the United States and other countries are not parties to the treaty,[82] the language of the treaty suggests that the international legal definition of armed conflict is evolving and expanding.

Protocol II, for its part, relates to non-international armed conflicts.[83] By its own terms, it "develops and supplements Article 3 common to the [1949] Geneva Conventions." In defining its scope of application, Protocol II sheds considerable light on the definitions of both *non-international armed conflicts*, and *armed conflicts* more generally. It states: "[t]his Protocol. . . shall apply to all armed conflicts. . . which take place in the territory of a High Contracting Party between its armed forces and dissident armed forces or other organized armed groups which, under responsible command, exercise such control over a part of its territory as to enable them to carry out sustained and concerted military operations and to implement this Protocol."[84] More enlightening still is the language of Protocol II regarding what does *not* constitute armed conflict: "[t]his Protocol shall not apply to situations of internal disturbances and tensions, such as riots, isolated and sporadic acts of violence and other acts of a similar nature, as not being armed conflicts."[85] Like Common Article 3, Protocol II is increasingly consulted today, given the much greater incidence of non-international armed conflicts as compared to traditional wars between states.

Collectively, the 1949 Geneva Conventions and their two 1977 Protocols signify that the term armed conflict is no longer limited to a war between two states. *Armed conflicts* now encompass anticolonial wars of independence as well as interstate conflicts. The term also applies to civil conflicts between state armies and insurgent movements, assuming those insurgencies constitute "forces to be reckoned with," and are not merely involved in staging isolated violent actions such as urban riots.[86] Finally, the US Supreme Court and international law scholars alike conclude that military campaigns by states against terrorist organizations are subject to the protections of international humanitarian law.[87] With this basic understanding of armed conflict, we can now turn to the substantive norms and protections of international humanitarian law.

E. LIMITING THE METHODS OF ARMED CONFLICT: THE HUMANITARIAN PROTECTIONS WITHIN THE 1949 GENEVA CONVENTIONS AND THE 1977 PROTOCOLS

1. Common Article 3

Before addressing the Geneva Conventions separately, let us start with a provision reiterated in all four humanitarian Conventions. So-called Common Article 3 applies by its own terms to non-international armed conflicts. Nevertheless, it is now regarded, as a matter of customary law, to apply to international armed conflicts as well:[88]

> . . . the following acts are and shall remain prohibited at any time and in any place whatsoever: (a) violence to life and person, in particular murder of all kinds, mutilation, cruel treatment and torture; (b) taking of hostages; (c) outrages upon personal dignity, in particular humiliating and degrading treatment; [and] (d) the passing of sentences and the carrying out of executions without previous judgment pronounced by a regularly constituted court, affording all the judicial guarantees which are recognized as indispensable by civilized peoples.[89]

Common Article 3 is significant in another regard, for codifying, in a humanitarian law treaty, a number of nonderogable human rights norms, including the prohibitions against torture, inhuman treatment, and arbitrary execution. In this sense, Common Article 3 operates as a miniature human rights treaty for wartime and, as such, represents one of the areas in which international humanitarian law and human rights law overlap and mutually reinforce one another. The common ground shared by humanitarian and human rights law is particularly evident in the domain of customary law, in which the technicalities of treaties do not distract from the underlying purposes of these norms.

2. The Four Geneva Conventions of 1949

The First Geneva Convention of 1949 was dedicated to the protection of wounded and sick soldiers "in the field."[90] As stated above, the First Geneva Convention, like all four of the 1949 Conventions, has been universally ratified. Article 12 provides that such members of the armed forces "shall be respected and protected in all circumstances." In addition to their rights to medical assistance without discrimination, the treaty provides that "they shall not be murdered or exterminated [or] subjected to torture or to biological experiments."[91] The Second Geneva Convention, the Maritime Convention, extends the full protections accorded wounded soldiers under the First Geneva Convention to wounded and shipwrecked sailors.[92]

The Third Geneva Convention of 1949, the POW Convention, protects prisoners of war. Although POWs were embraced in the Hague Regulations of 1929, those provisions were much less extensive. The ICRC's Commentary on the 1949 Conventions sheds light on this development: "[t]his extension is no doubt due, in part, to the fact that, in modern warfare, prisoners are held in very large numbers, but it also interprets the desire of the 1949 Conference, representing all nations, to submit all aspects of captivity to humane regulation by International Law."[93] The ICRC commentators go on to make explicit the distinction between POWs and persons accused or convicted of crimes: "[t]he civilized world finally accepted the principle that the prisoner of war is not a criminal, but merely an enemy no longer able to bear arms, who should be liberated at the close of hostilities, and be respected and humanely treated while in captivity."[94] Article 13 of Geneva Convention III states that "[p]risoners of war must at all times be humanely treated... [and] must at all times be protected, particularly against acts of violence or intimidation and against insults and public curiosity."[95]

One specific aspect of the POW Convention is particularly relevant to the detention of suspected terrorists in the so-called War on Terror at the US Naval Base at Guantánamo Bay, Cuba, and in other official and clandestine facilities throughout the world. Article 4 clarifies that POWs include members of a state's armed forces, militia members, and "members of other volunteer corps, including those of organized resistance movements," so long as they are commanded by a responsible superior, have "a fixed distinctive sign," openly carry their weapons, and operate "in accordance with the laws and customs of war."[96] Although actual members of terrorist organizations such as al Qaeda might not meet these requirements, in case of doubt, the treaty provides that "such persons shall enjoy the protection of the present Convention until such time as their status has been determined by a competent tribunal."[97]

The Fourth Geneva Convention of 1949, the Civilian Convention, protects civilians, and is universally ratified like the others. Though the Hague Convention IV of 1907 prohibited the targeting of undefended towns and dwellings, specific protections for civilians as individuals were very limited under prior instruments. Referring to the Holocaust as "this tragic period... of deportations, mass exterminations, taking and killing of hostages, and pillage," the ICRC Commentary emphasized the need for a separate and extensive treaty for civilians, who "were certainly 'in the war,' and exposed to the same dangers as the combatants–and sometimes worse."[98]

Common Article 3 of all four 1949 Geneva Conventions prohibits "murder of all kinds, mutilation, cruel treatment and torture" of civilians, POWs, and all others *hors de combat*. In addition, the Fourth Geneva Convention specifically provides for the economic and social welfare of civilians. Various provisions prohibit the destruction of civilian property, and, in the case of military occupation, obligate the occupying power to provide adequate food and medical supplies and maintain public health, "with particular reference to the adoption and application of the... preventive measures necessary to combat the spread of contagious diseases and epidemics."[99]

Finally, the Civilian Convention provides additional protections for detained persons who may not enjoy the protection of the POW Convention. Article 37 of the Civilian Convention states that "persons who are confined pending proceedings or [who are] serving a sentence involving loss of liberty, shall during their confinement be humanely treated."[100] If military detainees, including suspected terrorists, are deemed not to be POWs, their civilian status brings them under the Fourth Geneva Convention. The Civilian Convention provides essential protections for individuals detained without charge in the War on Terror, and helps to ensure that there is no lawless zone between the due process protections of criminal law and the special humanitarian protections accorded to POWs.

3. The Enhanced Humanitarian Protections Within the 1977 Protocols

Additional Protocol I to the 1949 Geneva Conventions relates to international armed conflicts and Protocol II relates to non-international armed conflicts. Only 170 of the 194 state parties to the 1949 Geneva Conventions have joined Protocol I, some states abstaining on account of its application to certain wars of national liberation.[101] Protocol II is also somewhat controversial, with 165 parties, perhaps because it is the first treaty specifically regulating the conduct of a state's armed forces on its own territory, as opposed to the territory of another state. The approximately 75 percent of states that are party to the additional Protocols, while significant, contrasts with the universal acceptance of the Geneva Conventions of 1949.[102]

Beyond the type of conflicts they regulate, the most significant aspects of Protocols I and II are the additional and more precise limitations they impose upon military forces, particularly in selecting targets for aerial bombardment or ground attack. Although the customary norm of distinction has long proclaimed that civilian persons and places should not be military targets, the 1977 Protocols seek to give some teeth to these protections.

Article 13 of Protocol II regarding non-international armed conflicts states that "[t]he civilian population as such, as well as individual civilians, shall not be the object of attack." Article 14 prohibits "[s]tarvation of civilians as a method of combat" as well as destroying "foodstuffs, agricultural areas..., crops, livestock, drinking water installations and supplies..." Article 16 protects "historical monuments, works of art or places of worship..." Finally, Article 17 prohibits "displacement of the civilian population" not related to their security.[103] Although Protocol II cut substantial new ground in carving out protections in the context of so-called civil wars, its 28 provisions are much less extensive than the 102 articles of its companion treaty.

The drafters of Protocol I took on the substantial challenge of translating the customary norm of distinction into more meaningful and pragmatic protections for civilians in international armed conflicts, particularly against aerial bombardment. Like Article 13 of the non-international Protocol, Article 51 of Protocol I states that "[t]he civilian population as such, as well as individual civilians, shall not be the object of attack." But unlike its companion treaty, Article 51 goes on to prohibit "indiscriminate attacks," including "an attack which may be expected to cause incidental loss of civilian life... excessive in relation to the... military advantage anticipated," and Article 52 defines legitimate military targets as "those objects which... make an effective contribution to military action." For objects of doubtful purpose, Article 52 establishes the presumption that they lack a military function, putting them off limits unless proven otherwise.[104] Furthermore, Article 57 requires the taking of precautionary measures before and during military strikes, including the suspension and cancellation of attacks, to ensure that the principle of distinction is honored in practice.[105] Finally, Article 54, similar to Article 14 of Protocol II, prohibits the destruction of food supplies, as well as agricultural and food distribution systems.[106]

4. Reflecting on the Law of Geneva at 60

On the occasion of the sixtieth anniversary of the Geneva Conventions, the International Committee of the Red Cross published the results of a global survey finding that close to half the participants from war-affected countries were not familiar with the humanitarian treaties. Even among those generally familiar, only half were specifically aware that humanitarian law attempts to shield civilians from the worst ravages of war. Nevertheless, 75 percent of the participants believed that international law should indeed limit the conduct of war. Moreover, in certain countries, such as Liberia, a majority of those polled believed that the treaties had a positive impact on the behavior of combatants.[107] ICRC is calling for revisions to the Geneva Conventions, "to reflect the fact that most conflicts now take place inside states rather than between them."[108]

F. HUMANITARIAN LAW ON THE CONTINENT OF AFRICA

All fifty-four African countries are parties to the four 1949 Geneva Conventions. The ICRC has a presence in thirty-five of these countries, including delegations in Uganda, Sierra Leone, and Burundi,[109] and works in collaboration with national Red Cross chapters in almost every country.[110] As in other parts of the world, ICRC trainings on humanitarian law incorporate an appreciation of regional customary humanitarian norms. Whether in Africa, the Americas, Asia, Europe, or the Middle East, the law of Geneva resonates with much older rules regarding the protection of innocents in time of war.

In his digest of African customary humanitarian law, Emmanuel Bello cites certain tribal norms and practices that presaged the Geneva Conventions. In particular, he points to the practice in which women of the Tallensi tribe of Ghana carried water to combatants and recovered the bodies of fallen warriors;[111] the practice among the Ngoni of Central Africa of granting captives and prisoners the protection of tribal law;[112] and the strict prohibition among the Nuer people of Kenya against warrior abuse of women and children.[113]

Nobel laureate Wole Soyinka of Nigeria wrote eloquently in 1999 of the danger of reciting platitudes about "that generous earth of Africa's humanity... with Rwanda hardly a memory beat away...."[114] As Soyinka suggests, humanitarian norms, like human rights norms, are too often honored in the breach. This is a problem in all regions of the world. The gap between law and practice is illustrated by tragic conflicts throughout the world: whether in Darfur or Gaza, Sierra Leone or Kosovo, Burundi or Guatemala, Uganda or Sri Lanka. Nevertheless, our efforts to craft better mechanisms for bringing humanitarian and human rights law to life in and outside of Africa will be strengthened by drawing upon the local traditions and practices adopted throughout the world to lessen the suffering of war.

Utilizing a variety of treaty-based and customary humanitarian principles, the modern Red Cross movement continues to intervene on behalf of the victims of war, focusing on their physical and psychosocial well-being. Alongside the 150-year evolution of the law of Geneva, humanitarian workers in regions of conflict do not insist on legal technicalities or artificial boundaries between humanitarian and human rights law. In the words of one advocate for people displaced by the civil war in northern Uganda, "it is in the interests of civilians to appeal to *any* law that protects their basic rights." Her colleague agreed, affirming that "humanitarian need is the focus of our work."[115]

Chapter 3 turns to international human rights law and the additional norms it provides to empower members of societies emerging from armed conflict and repression.

NOTES

1. "Weapon Conflict" is track 3 on Disc One of the Sierra Leone Refugee All Stars' *Living Like a Refugee* album (a two-disc CD set). *Living Like a Refugee* is a Sodasoap Production, 2005, recorded at Island Studios, Freetown, Sierra Leone (Anti Records 2006).
2. *See* Leo Tolstoy, "Letter to Ernest Howard Crosby," January 12, 1896, in WRITINGS ON CIVIL DISOBEDIENCE AND NONVIOLENCE, trans. Aylmer Maude (New Society Publishers, 1987). Reading Tolstoy's 1894 work, *The Kingdom of God Is Within You,* inspired the young lawyer Mohandas Gandhi to embrace nonviolent resistance to apartheid in South Africa. *See*, ALL MEN ARE BROTHERS: LIFE AND THOUGHT OF MAHATMA GANDHI AS TOLD IN HIS OWN WORDS, cited below. Gandhi considered that "Tolstoy was the best and brightest (modern) exponent of the doctrine [of passive resistance]." *Id.* at 99.
3. *See generally* DOROTHY DAY, THE LONG LONELINESS: THE AUTOBIOGRAPHY OF DOROTHY DAY (Harper & Row, 1952). Day was a social activist who founded an influential journal called *The Catholic Worker*.
4. *See generally* MOHANDAS GANDHI, "Ahimsa, or the Way of Nonviolence," from ALL MEN ARE BROTHERS: LIFE AND THOUGHT OF MAHATMA GANDHI AS TOLD IN HIS OWN WORDS at 85–107 (UNESCO and Columbia University Press, 1958). Gandhi wrote that "non-violence is not passivity in any shape or form.... [It] is the most active force in the

world [and] ... the supreme law." *Id.* at 97. Gandhi's principled rejection of war extended to the use of force by state and non-state agents alike: "If I can have nothing to do with the organized violence of the government, I can have less to do with the unorganized violence of the people. I would prefer to be crushed between the two." *Id.* at 96.

5. *See* ANDREW RIGAND AND NAFEZ ASSAILY, "The Intifada," in NONVIOLENT STRUGGLE AND SOCIAL DEFENSE (WRI, London, 1991). Nafez Assaily is a Palestinian who advocates nonviolent forms of resistance to Israeli occupation.
6. *See generally* DESMOND TUTU, NO FUTURE WITHOUT FORGIVENESS (Doubleday, 1999).
7. *See generally* JANET PAYNE WHITNEY, JOHN WOOLMAN, AMERICAN QUAKER (Little, Brown and Company 1942). Until his death in 1772, Woolman spoke out against slavery, poverty, and war. *See also* FERGUS M. BORDEWICH, BOUND FOR FREEDOM: THE UNDERGROUND RAILROAD AND THE WAR FOR THE SOUL OF AMERICAN (HarperCollins 2005) at 54 (quoting Woolman's statement that "[t]he Colour of a Man avails nothing, in Matters of Right and Equity"). *See also* "Quaker Declaration of Pacifism," presented to King Charles II of England in 1660, *available at* http://www2.gol.com/users/quakers/quaker_declaration_of_pacifism.hlm. ("We utterly deny all outward wars and strife ... for any end, or under any pretense whatever; ... we certainly know, and testify to the world, that the Spirit of Christ, which leads us into all truth, will never move us to fight and war against any man with outward weapons, neither for the kingdom of Christ, nor for the kingdoms of this world.").
8. *See* WILLIAM V. O'BRIEN, "The Conduct of Just and Limited War," from APPROACHES TO PEACE: A READER IN PEACE STUDIES (ed. David P. Barash, Oxford University Press, 2000) at 80.
9. *See* HUGO GROTIUS, DE JURE BELLI AC PACIS LIBRI TRES (1625) (Kelsey trans. 1913) at 18 ("war ought not to be undertaken except for the enforcement of rights; when once undertaken, it should be carried on only within the bounds of law and good faith."), as cited in MARK W. JANIS, AN INTRODUCTION TO INTERNATIONAL LAW (2nd Edition, Little Brown and Company, 1993) at 161.
10. As discussed in Sections D and E below, not all insurgencies are equally regulated by humanitarian law. For example, to fall within a 1977 treaty governing non-international armed conflicts, the dissident group must be capable of "sustained . . . military operations and ... [be] able to implement its own responsibilities under humanitarian law." *See* Second Additional Protocol to the 1949 Geneva Conventions, art. 1(1), *infra*. In essence, an insurgency must control territory and maintain discipline over its forces before it assumes obligations and privileges under the Second Protocol. Nevertheless, certain minimal humanitarian protections apply to all non-international conflicts. *See* Geneva Conventions, Common Article 3, *infra*. Moreover, international human rights law applies in all situations, and becomes particularly relevant in "low-intensity" conflicts without formally constituted dissident armies. *See* Civil and Political Covenant, *infra*, art. 4.
11. One reason for the evolution toward the more modern "use of force" language is that by the nineteenth century, the just war theory had fallen into considerable disrepute. Just war theory had come to be associated with a double standard whereby the targeting of civilians was tolerated if committed by an army deemed to have the just cause, and condemned when committed by the army deemed to be the aggressor. The same inconsistent treatment of humanitarian law violations was prevalent during both World Wars I and II. The use of mustard gas during World War I, and the massive bombing runs over Dresden, Tokyo, and London during World War II are cases in point. The late Robert McNamara, former US Secretary of Defense, reflected 60 years later on the firebombing of Japan's cities by the Allied forces during World War II, at which time McNamara was conducting a statistical analysis for General Curtis LeMay of the Army's Air Force. McNamara declared: "We burned to death 100,000 Japanese civilians in Tokyo—men,

women and children.... LeMay said, 'If we'd lost the war, we'd all have been prosecuted as war criminals.' And I think he's right. He—and I'd say I—were behaving as war criminals.... What makes it immoral if you lose and moral if you win?" *See* Tim Weiner, *Robert S. McNamara, Architect of a Futile War, Dies at 93*, N.Y. TIMES, July 6, 2009, *available at* http://www.nytimes.com/2009/07/07/us/07mcnamara.html.

12. It is important to point out that in regulating the conduct of war, international humanitarian law governs both the treatment of victims of war and the designation of lawful and unlawful weaponry. Our text focuses on the first subset of humanitarian law, Geneva Law, or those treaties and principles that protect victims of war, encompassing civilians, wounded soldiers and sailors, and prisoners of war (POWs). Hague Law, the branch of international humanitarian law that outlaws certain types of weapons, is barely touched upon in this text, although it is the subject of important advances in international law, from early twentieth-century conventions outlawing the use of exploding bullets, mustard gas, and other chemical weapons, to the more recent treaty abolishing the use of land mines. *See* Protocol for the Prohibition of the Use in War of Asphyxiating, Poisonous or other Gases, and of Bacteriological Methods of Warfare, Geneva, June 17, 1925; Convention on the Prohibition of the Use, Stockpiling, Production and Transfer of Anti-Personnel Mines and on their Destruction, *signed* Sept. 18, 1997, *entered into force*, Mar. 1, 1999.

13. *See, e.g.*, Kellogg-Briand Pact (Pact of Paris, General Treaty for the Renunciation of War), Aug. 27, 1928; Covenant of the League of Nations, Apr. 28, 1919.

14. UN Charter, Preamble.

15. *Id.*, art. 1.

16. *Id.*, art. 2 (3) and (4).

17. In Article 6, the Nuremberg Statute provided precise definitions of the crimes within its jurisdiction. "Crimes Against Peace" encompassed "planning, preparation, initiation or waging of a war of aggression, or a war in violation of international treaties..." Agreement for the Prosecution and Punishment of the Major War Criminals of the European Axis of Aug. 8, 1945 (London Agreement), art. 6(a), 59 Stat. 1544, 1547–1548.

18. Rome Statute of the International Criminal Court (Rome Statute or ICC Statute), 2187 UNTS 90, *entered into force*, July 1, 2002, art. 5(2).

19. *See* Amendments to the Rome Statute of the International Criminal Court on the crime of aggression (2010 Amendments to the ICC Statute), art. 8 *bis* [Crime of Aggression], Resolution RC/Res. 6, adopted at the 13th plenary meeting [of the parties to the ICC Statute] on 11 June 2010, by consensus, *available at* http://www.icc-cpi.int/iccdocs/asp_docs/Resolutions/RC-Res.6-ENG.pdf. *Act of aggression* is defined in ICC Statute, art. 8(2) *bis*.

20. *Crime of aggression* is defined in ICC Statute, art. 8(1) *bis*: "[f]or the purpose of this Statute, 'crime of aggression' means the planning, preparation, initiation or execution, by a person in a position effectively to exercise control over or to direct the political or military action of a State, of an act of aggression which, by its character, gravity and scale, constitutes a manifest violation of the Charter of the United Nations."

21. *See* 2010 Amendments to the ICC Statute, art. 15 *bis* ["Exercise of jurisdiction over the crime of aggression"]. Article 15 *bis* provides that jurisdiction over the crime of aggression may not be exercised until 30 or more state parties have ratified the amendments, and in any case no earlier than January 1, 2017, subject to a specific decision by 30 or more state parties to initiate the exercise of jurisdiction. *See id.*, art. 15(2) and (3) *bis*, *available at* http://www.icc-cpi.int/iccdocs/asp_docs/Resolutions/RC-Res.6-ENG.pdf.

22. UN Charter, Preamble.

23. *Id.*, art. 1(1).

24. *Id.*, arts. 39–50.

25. *See* UNSC Res. 660 of Aug. 2, 1990, S/RES/0660 (1990), in which the Security Council, citing both Articles 39 and 40 of the Charter, "condemns" the invasion, "demands" withdrawal and "calls upon" Iraq and Kuwait "to begin immediately intensive negotiations for the resolution of their differences..."; *see also* UN Charter, arts. 39 and 40.
26. *See* UNSC Res. 661 of Aug. 6, 1990, S/RES/0661 (1990), in which the Council "decides that all States shall prevent: (a) the import into their territories of all commodities and products originating in Iraq or Kuwait...."; *see also* UN Charter, art. 41.
27. *See* UNSC Res. 678, S/RES/0678 (1990), in which the Council "[a]cting under Chapter VII of the Charter.... [a]uthorizes Member States cooperating with the Government of Kuwait to use all necessary means to restore international peace and security in the area"; *see also* UN Charter, art. 42.
28. *Id.*, art. 51.
29. *See* A Treaty to settle and define the Boundaries between the Territories of the United States and the possessions of Her Britannic Majesty, in North America; For the final Suppression of the African Slave Trade; and For the giving up of Criminals fugitive from justice, in certain cases (Webster-Ashburton Treaty of 1842), art. VIII, http://avalon.law.yale.edu/19th_century/br-1842.asp#art8. In addition to establishing the border between the United States (US) and the "British Dominions in North America," the Webster-Ashburton Treaty also touched on international criminal and human rights law, specifically requiring each party to maintain a naval force off the coast of Africa to suppress the slave trade.
30. *See* correspondence from Mr. Webster to Lord Ashburton, Department of State, Washington, July 27, 1842, *available at* http://avalon.law.yale.edu/19th_century/br-1842d.asp#web1.
31. *See* T.D. Gill, *The Temporal Dimension of Self-Defense: Anticipation, Pre-emption, Prevention and Immediacy*, J. CONFLICT SEC. L., Winter 2006; 11: 361–69.
We will encounter the customary norms of necessity and proportionality again in our discussion of the fundamental principles of international humanitarian law, or the *jus in bello*, which regulates the conduct of armed conflict once military force has been initiated. *See* Section C.1 below.
32. *See* UN Charter, art. 2(7): "[n]othing contained in the present Charter shall authorize the United Nations to intervene in matters which are essentially within the domestic jurisdiction of any state..."
33. Professor Richard Falk analyses one of the prevailing rationales for the 1999 North Atlantic Treaty Organization (NATO) bombing of Kosovo, namely, that it was a humanitarian intervention in response to President Milosevic's campaign of ethnic cleansing against the Kosovar Albanians. He cautions that "[g]enocidal behavior cannot be shielded by claims of sovereignty, but neither can these claims be overridden by unauthorized uses of force delivered in an excessive and inappropriate manner." Richard Falk, *Humanitarian Intervention after Kosovo*, HUMAN RIGHTS AND CONFLICT: EXPLORING THE LINKS BETWEEN RIGHTS, LAW AND PEACEBUILDING (ed. Julie Mertus and Jeffrey Helsing, United States Institute of Peace Press, 2006) at 187. Falk also cites critics of the NATO bombings who "regard the Serbs' massive resort to ethnic cleansing by the most brutal means as largely an *effect* of the bombing" or who believe that "the severity of NATO's strategy,... has produced... a second cycle of ethnic cleansing in Kosovo... by Kosovar Albanians against Serbs and Roma..." *Id.* at 193.
34. *See* "The Responsibility to Protect," International Commission on Intervention and State Sovereignty, Dec. 2001, *available at* http://www.iciss.ca/pdf/Commission-Report.pdf.
35. *See* UNGA Res. 60/1 of Oct. 24, 2005, A/RES/60/1 (2005); *see also* Neil MacFarquhar, "When to Step in to Stop War Crimes Causes Fissures," N.Y. TIMES, July 23, 2009.

36. Kofi Annan, *In Larger Freedom: Towards Development, Security and Human Rights for All* (Mar. 21, 2005), Chapter III, Section E, para. 125, *available at* http://www.un.org/largerfreedom/chap3.htm.
37. *Id.*, para. 126.
38. "An idea whose time has come—and gone?" THE ECONOMIST, July 23, 2009, *available at* http://www.economist.com/research/articlesBySubject/displaystory.cfm?subjectid=348951&story_id=E1_TQDRSSRR.
39. *Id.*
40. *See generally*, Jonathan Moore, *Morality and Inter-Dependence* (The Nelson A. Rockefeller Center for the Social Sciences at Dartmouth College, Occasional Paper Series, No. 4, 1994).
41. *See* UN Charter, art. 1(2) ("respect for the principle of equal rights and self-determination of peoples"). *See also* International Covenant on Civil and Political Rights, *infra*, art. 1(1) and International Covenant on Economic, Social and Cultural Rights, *infra*, art. 1(1).
42. *See* CHRISTINE GRAY, INTERNATIONAL LAW AND THE USE OF FORCE 53 (2nd Edition, Oxford University Press 2004). Gray discusses the purported "legal right ... for national liberation movements to use force under international law" and cautions that "[t]he colonial powers and western states have resisted such claims." *Id.*
43. In 1994, the UN General Assembly denounced all acts of terrorism, defined as "[c]riminal acts intended or calculated to provoke a state of terror in the general public, a group of persons or particular persons for political purposes." *See* UNGA Res. 49/60 of Dec. 9, 1994, A/RES/49/60 (1994). Though the UN definition would encompass attacks by both state and nonstate actors, the more narrow US statutory definition, found in Title 22 of the US Code, is limited to "premeditated, politically motivated violence perpetrated against noncombatant targets by subnational groups or clandestine agents." *See* 22 USC 2656f(d)(2).
44. *See* THOMAS M. FRANCK, RECOURSE TO FORCE: STATE ACTION AGAINST THREATS AND ARMED ATTACKS 96 (Cambridge University Press 2002). Franck states that "the concept of self-defense, under Article 51, ... include[s] a right to use force in response to an attack against nationals, providing there is clear evidence of extreme necessity and the means chosen are appropriate." *Id.*
45. *See* Kenneth Roth, *The Rule of Law in the War on Terror: Washington's Abuse of "Enemy Combatants"*, 83 FOREIGN AFFAIRS 2, 7 (No. 1, Jan.–Feb. 2004). Roth states that "Washington should never resort to war rules away from a traditional battlefield if local authorities can and are willing to arrest and deliver a suspect to an independent tribunal..." *Id.*
46. *See, e.g.,* Dennis King, *Paying the Ultimate Price: Analysis of the deaths of humanitarian aid workers (1997–2001)* (UN Office for the Coordination of Humanitarian Affairs, January 15, 2002), *available at* http://www.reliefweb.int/symposium/2002_symposium/PayingUltimatePrice97-01.html.
47. As mentioned in endnote 12, Hague Law is also a branch of international humanitarian law, alongside Geneva Law. In addition to the treaties outlawing the use of exploding bullets, mustard gas, and land mines, international humanitarian law scholars and activists are struggling with the use of unmanned drones in the wars in Iraq and Afghanistan. In a recent report to the United Nations Human Rights Council, a UN expert cautioned that the use of drones was particularly problematic because of the heightened limitations in human intelligence given the distance between launching points and target sites. *See Report of the Special Rapporteur on Extrajudicial, Summary or Arbitrary Executions*, Philip Alston, Human Rights Council, 14th Session, Agenda Item 3, A/HRC/14/24/Add.6 (May 28, 2010), *generally*, and at para. 84 (" ... because operators are based thousands of miles away from the battlefield, and undertake

operations entirely through computer screens and remote audiofeed, there is a risk of developing a 'Playstation' mentality to killing. States must ensure that training programs for drone operators who have never been subjected to the risks and rigors of battle instill respect for IHL and adequate safeguards for compliance with it"), *available at* http://www2.ohchr.org/english/bodies/hrcouncil/docs/14session/A.HRC.14.24.Add6.pdf.

48. The principle of proportionality is also at play in the Hague Law principles governing the lawful and unlawful use of particular weapons. The employment of unmanned drones raises particular concerns regarding proportionality, given the physical and mental distance between the individual launching the device and the individuals in the vicinity of the intended and actual target sites. *See* Philip Alston, *op. cit.*, para. 84.

49. As is true under human rights law, violations of IHL treaties by one party do not release other parties from their obligations. For example, if one side attacks civilians, the other side must still refrain from targeting civilians. *See* First Protocol Additional to the 1949 Geneva Conventions, art. 51(8), *infra* (regarding "protection of the civilian population," "[a]ny violation of these prohibitions shall not release the Parties . . . from their legal obligations with respect to civilian populations and civilians, including the obligation to take . . . precautionary measures . . .").

50. *See* earlier discussion of the Caroline principles and Daniel Webster, *op. cit. See also* Second Protocol Additional to the 1949 Geneva Conventions, art. 51(5)(b), *infra* ("an attack . . . which would be excessive in relation to the concrete and direct military advantage anticipated" is considered indiscriminate and hence prohibited.).

51. *See generally* HENRI DUNANT, MEMORY OF SOLFERINO (ICRC, 1986; originally published in 1862; translated from the French and published by the American Red Cross in 1959).

52. *See* Convention for the Amelioration of the Condition of the Wounded in Armies in the Field, Geneva, Aug. 22, 1864, http://www.icrc.org/ihl/FULL/120?OpenDocument.

53. *See* 1899 Hague Declaration IV Prohibiting Launching of Projectiles and Explosives from Balloons, July 29, 1899, http://avalon.law.yale.edu/19th_century/hague994.asp.

54. *See* 1907 Hague Convention IV Respecting the Laws and Customs of War on Land, Oct. 18, 1907, http://avalon.law.yale.edu/20th_century/hague04.asp.

55. *See id.*, arts. 22 and 25.

56. *See* Protocol for the Prohibition of the Use in War of Asphyxiating, Poisonous or Other Gases, and of Bacteriological Methods of Warfare, *opened for signature*, June 17, 1925, *entered into force*, Feb. 8, 1928, http://www.fas.harvard.edu/~hsp/1925.html.

57. *See* Convention relative to the Treatment of Prisoners of War, Geneva, July 27, 1929, http://www.icrc.org/ihl.nsf/FULL/305?OpenDocument.

58. *See* ICRC, "States Parties to the Following International Humanitarian Law and Other Related Treaties as of 2 Dec. 2, 2010," *available at* http://www.icrc.org/IHL.nsf/(SPF)/party_main_treaties/$File/IHL_and_other_related_Treaties.pdf.

59. The relevant provision is Article 10 in the case of the Fourth Geneva Convention.

60. The relevant provision is Article 9 of the Fourth Geneva Convention.

61. The relevant provision is Article 11 of the Fourth Geneva Convention.

62. *See* ICRC, *States Parties to the Following International Humanitarian Law and Other Related Treaties as of 2 December 2010*, *available at* http://www.icrc.org/IHL.nsf/(SPF)/party_main_treaties/$File/IHL_and_other_related_Treaties.pdf.

63. Sierra Leone ratified the 1949 Geneva Conventions in 1965, and ratified the two Additional Protocols of 1977 in 1984. Uganda ratified the Geneva Conventions in 1964 and the Protocols in 1991. Burundi ratified the Geneva Conventions in 1971 and the Protocols in 1993. *See* ICRC, *op. cit.*

64. *See* Natasha Balendra, *Defining Armed Conflict*, New York University Public Law and Legal Theory Working Papers, Paper 63 (2007) ("[c]urrently there is no authoritative definition of armed conflict in international law").
65. *See* Common Article 2, Geneva Conventions of August 12, 1949.
66. *Id.*, Common Article 3. *Hors de combat* means "outside of combat." The text of Article 3 clarifies that the term refers to combatants who have laid down their arms or been injured, as well as all detained persons and civilians. *Id.*
67. *Id.*
68. *See Human Security Report 2005*, Fact Sheet on "Wars and Political Violence," *op. cit.*
69. The assessment by Sierra Leone's Truth and Reconciliation Commission (TRC) of the conduct of the various factions in the civil war is referenced in Chapter 8, Section B, and further discussed in Section C.2 on the TRC's Final Report. *See* Joseph Opala, "What the West Failed to See in Sierra Leone," WASH. POST, May 2, 14, 2000, cited in Chapter 8, endnote 6.
70. *See* JEAN-CHRISTOPHE RUFIN, *The Economics of War: A New Theory for Armed Conflicts*, in FORUM: WAR, MONEY AND SURVIVAL (ed., International Committee of the Red Cross, 2000).
71. *See* Grotius, *op. cit.* at 18 ("once undertaken, [war] should be carried on only within the bounds of law and good faith"). *See also*, Jennifer Moore, *Practicing What We Preach: Humane Treatment for Detainees in the War on Terror*, 34 DENV. J. INT'L L. & POL'Y 33–61 (2006) (concluding that suspected terrorists detained in military facilities should enjoy a presumption of POW status).
72. As early as January of 2002, then US Defense Secretary Donald Rumsfeld declared that suspected terrorists detained at Guantánamo Bay Cuba were not eligible for POW status. *See No POW rights for Cuba prisoner*, BBC NEWS, January 27, 2002, *available at* http://news.bbc.co.uk/2/hi/americas/1784700.stm.
73. See Hamdan v. Rumsfeld, 548 US 557 (2006); *see also* Boumediene v. Bush, 553 US 723 (2008).
74. *See* Andrew Clapham, *Human Rights Obligations of Non-State Actors in Conflict Situations*, 863 INT. REV. RED CROSS 491 (2006), at 503, *citing* resolution adopted by the Institute of International Law at its Berlin conference in 1999.
75. *See* Third Geneva Convention, art. 5. *See also* Jennifer Moore, *op. cit.*
76. Hamdan, 548 U.S. 557 at 562 (holding that the due process protections of Common Article 3 apply to an individual "captured during the war with al Qaeda, given that it constitutes 'a conflict not of an international character'"), citing Common Article 3, Geneva Conventions of August 12, 1949.
77. *See* Fourth Geneva Convention, art. 37 ("protected persons who are confined pending proceedings or serving a sentence involving loss of liberty, shall during their confinement be humanely treated").
78. *See* International Covenant on Civil and Political Rights, *infra*, art. 9 ("[n]o one shall be subjected to arbitrary arrest or detention").
79. *See* Protocol Additional to the Geneva Conventions of August 12, 1949, and Relating to the Protection of Victims of International Armed Conflicts (Protocol I).
80. *See* Protocol I, art. 1(3).
81. *Id.*, art. 1(4).
82. According to R.R. Baxter, "[t]he United States was concerned that a provision on wars of national liberation might introduce a subjective and judgmental element in the law of war, which had hitherto rested on a foundation of neutrality and equality of application to all belligerents, without regard to the legality of their resort to hostilities." *See* R.R. Baxter, *Modernizing the Law of War*, 78 MIL. L. REV. 165, 173 (1978). *See also*, Guy Roberts,

26 Va. J. Intl. L. 109, 126 (1985) (documenting the US abstention from the vote on art. 1(4) at the drafting conference of Protocol I).
83. *See* Protocol Additional to the Geneva Conventions of August 12, 1949, and Relating to the Protection of Victims of Non-international Armed Conflicts (Protocol II).
84. *Id.,* art. 1(1).
85. *Id.,* art. 1(2). Although *internal disturbances* may not be regulated by humanitarian law, they do fall within the protective ambit of human rights law, which applies in all times and places. Because of the limited scope of humanitarian law, there is a particularly crucial role for human rights law in so-called states of emergency, in which some states use security forces to threaten or eliminate perceived or actual political opponents in the absence of a well-organized insurgent movement. It is ironic that that humanitarian law does not apply to the "dirtiest" wars—those in which potential insurgencies are figuratively or literally wiped out before they can constitute a military threat, and all the more reason for these two fields of law to work in consort. *See* ICCPR, *infra,* art. 4 (specifying those specific human rights, especially the rights to life, humane treatment, and due process, which are absolute, even "[i]n time of public emergency which threatens the life of the nation").
86. What we do not get from the Geneva Conventions and their Protocols is much substantive guidance regarding the physical reality of armed conflict. Protocol II tells us that we need more than "sporadic acts of violence," but not the nature of non-sporadic violence itself. For this we need to turn to secondary sources of international law, and there is considerable debate in scholarly circles on this score. One such definition focuses on the use of destructive weapons and the deaths they cause: "[a]n armed conflict is a contested incompatibility which concerns governments and/or territory where the use of armed force [defined as 'any material means, e.g. manufactured weapons but also sticks, stones, fire, water, etc.'] between two parties, of which at least one is the government of a state, results in at least 25 battle-related deaths." *See* Uppsala Conflict Data Program, Department of Peace and Conflict Research, Uppsala University (*date of retrieval* July 4, 2009 [09/07/04]), "Definition of armed conflict," http://www.pcr.uu.se/research/ucdp/definitions/definition_of_armed_conflict/.
87. *See* Hamdan, 548 US at 562 (applying Common Article 3 of the 1949 Geneva Conventions to the conflict against al Qaeda, by interpreting *non-international armed conflict* to include wars between states and non-state agents); *see also* Geneva Convention III, art. 5 (re: presumption of POW status for individuals under military detention). *See also* Geneva Convention IV, art. 37 (re: humane conditions for all civilian detainees). *See also* 1999 Berlin resolution of the International Law Institute, cited in Clapham, *op. cit.* at 503.
88. *See* Jean-Marie Henckaerts, *Study on customary international humanitarian law: A contribution to the understanding and respect for the rule of law in armed conflict,* Int'l Rev. Red Cross, Vol. 87, No. 857 (March 2005) at 187, n. 33, citing Case concerning Military and Paramilitary Activities in and against Nicaragua (Nicaragua v. United States), Merits, Judgment, June 27, 1986, ICJ Reports 1986, p. 114, para. 218.
89. *See* Geneva Conventions of August 12, 1949, Article 3, Common.
90. *See* Geneva Convention for the Amelioration of the Condition of the Wounded and Sick in Armed Forces in the Field of August 12, 1949.
91. *Id.,* art. 12.
92. *See* Geneva Convention for the Amelioration of the Condition of Wounded, Sick and Shipwrecked Members of Armed Forces at Sea of August 12, 1949, art. 12.
93. *See* ICRC Preliminary Remarks to the 1949 Geneva Conventions, *op. cit.,* at 12.
94. *Id.*

95. Geneva Convention Relative to the Treatment of Prisoners of War of August 12, 1949, art. 13.
96. *Id.*, art. 4.
97. *Id.*, art. 5. Rather than applying the POW Convention to suspected terrorists detained by the US military in Guantánamo Bay, Cuba, the US Supreme Court has applied Common Article 3 of the Geneva Conventions. The Supreme Court, among other authorities, has concluded that the military commissions and "Combatant Status Review Tribunals" established in Guantánamo Bay to detain suspected terrorists pursuant to the US Military Commissions Act do not satisfy the requirements for a "regularly constituted court" under Common Article 3, nor do they meet basic standards of due process. *See* Hamdan v. Rumsfeld, 548 US 563 ("Common Article 3's requirements are general, crafted to accommodate a wide variety of legal systems.... The commission convened to try Hamdan does not meet them."). *See also* Boumediene v. Bush, 553 US 557, 128 S. Ct. 2229 at 2274 ("the Government has not established that the detainees' access to the statutory review provisions at issue is an adequate substitute for the writ of habeas corpus.").
98. ICRC Preliminary Remarks to the 1949 Geneva Conventions, *op. cit.*, at 18 and 17.
99. *See* Geneva Convention Relative to the Protection of Civilian Persons in Time of War of August 12, 1949, arts. 53, 55, and 56.
100. *Id.*, art. 37.
101. *See* Baxter, *op. cit.*
102. *See* ICRC, *States Parties to the Following International Humanitarian Law and Other Related Treaties as of 2 December 2010,"* available at http://www.icrc.org/IHL.nsf/(SPF)/party_main_treaties/$File/IHL_and_other_related_Treaties.pdf. Notably, the United States is not a party to either of the additional Protocols of 1977. *Id.*
103. Protocol II, arts. 13, 14, 16, and 17.
104. *See* Protocol I, art. 52(3): "[i]n case of doubt whether an object which is normally dedicated to civilian purposes, such as a place of worship, a house or other dwelling or a school, is being used to make an effective contribution to military action, it shall be presumed not to be so used."
105. According to Protocol I, Article 57(2)(a)(i), military planners must "do everything feasible to verify that the objectives to be attacked are neither civilians nor civilian objects...." Article 57(2)(a)(ii) mandates similar "precautions in the choice of means and methods of attack with a view to avoiding, and in any event to minimizing, incidental loss of civilian life, injury to civilians and damage to civilian objects...." Most ambitiously, Article 57(2)(b) requires that "an attack shall be cancelled or suspended if it becomes apparent that the objective is not a military one ... or that the attack may be expected to cause incidental loss of civilian life, injury ... [or] damage to civilian objects ... which would be excessive in relation to the concrete and direct military advantage anticipated."
106. *See* Protocol I, art. 54(2): "[i]t is prohibited to attack, destroy, remove or render useless objects indispensable to the survival of the civilian population, such as foodstuffs, agricultural areas ..., drinking water installations ..., whether in order to starve out civilians, to cause them to move away, or for any other motive."
107. ICRC, The Geneva Conventions at 60: Learning from the past to better face the future, ICRC News Release No. 90/152, Aug. 6, 2009, http://www.reliefweb.int.rw/rwb.nsf/db900SID/LSGZ-7UNHKX?OpenDocument.
108. Olesya Dmitracova, Geneva Conventions are obscure or ineffective–poll, Aug. 6, 2009, http://www.alertnet.org/thenews/newsdesk/L6422096.htm.
109. ICRC, ICRC in Africa: A long-term commitment, Sept. 2009, *available at* http://www.icrc.org/Web/eng/siteeng0.nsf/htmlall/africa-newsletter-021009/$File/Africa-newsletter-09-eng.pdf.

110. Information about Red Cross and Red Crescent Societies in Africa is available on the website of the International Federation of Red Cross and Red Crescent Societies, http://www.ifrc.org/where/africa.asp?navid=05_02.
111. EMMANUEL G. BELLO, AFRICAN CUSTOMARY HUMANITARIAN LAW (Oyez Publishing Limited, International Committee of the Red Cross, 1980) at 51.
112. *Id.* at 53.
113. *Id.* at 54.
114. *See* WOLE SOYINKA, THE BURDEN OF MEMORY, THE MUSE OF FORGIVENESS (Oxford University Press, 1999) at 32.
115. *See* notes from interview with humanitarian workers in Kampala, Uganda, Mar. 23, 2010, from p. 11(a) of author's field notebook.

CHAPTER 3

Human Rights Law

The Law of Human Dignity

All human beings are born free and equal in dignity and rights. They are endowed with reason and conscience and should act towards one another in a spirit of brotherhood.
Universal Declaration of Human Rights[1]

The African States members of the Organization of African Unity . . . [proclaim] that it is henceforth essential to pay particular attention to the right to development and that civil and political rights cannot be dissociated from economic, social and cultural rights in their conception as well as universality. . .
African Charter on Human and Peoples' Rights[2]

Human rights law is the most comprehensive of the four fields of international law concerned with conflict resolution. Humanitarian law applies in time of war and its aftermath; international criminal law focuses on individual accountability for war crimes and other offenses against the world community; and refugee law seeks protection for individuals displaced by conflict and repression. In contrast, human rights law operates in all times and places. In addition to recognizing the liberty, equality, and material needs of human beings, international human rights law imposes responsibilities on states, individuals, and communities alike. Despite their distinct mandates and modes of operation, these four sister fields of transnational law share much common ground in defining violations of human dignity and in responding to such violations. Studying the resonances between human rights and humanitarian law is particularly relevant in the context of war, when acts of inhumanity are commonplace. Moreover, human rights violations, whether political or socioeconomic, are often at the root of armed conflict in the first place.

The essence of human rights law recognizes the integrity, vulnerability, and vast potential of human beings, as individuals and members of communities. Echoing the French Revolution's rallying cry of *liberté, egalité, fraternité*, human rights law encompasses political liberties, basic equality, and social well-being. Despite differences in orientation—the traditional emphasis on civil-political rights in the Western and Northern worlds, and the predominant concern with socioeconomic rights in countries of the East and South—the indivisible quality of human rights is widely acknowledged.[3] The Kenyan national anthem's appeal to *undugu, amani na uhuru* (unity, peace, and liberty)[4] suggests an appreciation for the interdependence between individual rights and concern for the collective good even at the level of political rhetoric. Likewise, the quintessential American vision of "life, liberty, and the pursuit of happiness" encompasses the fullness of human life, from basic survival and self-expression to the quality of our existence.

It is fashionable to talk about generations of human rights, particularly first-generation civil and political rights, and second-generation economic and social rights. In fact, these two categories of rights are interdependent rather than consecutive, and both play a role in preventing armed conflict. One cannot meaningfully exercise the rights to free expression and political participation without adequate health care and education, and one cannot enjoy social security without a government that serves and is accountable to the people.[5] Moreover, the protection of political liberty and the promotion of social welfare are equally fundamental attributes of deep-rooted and enduring peace within a society.

The United Nations General Assembly declared in 1948 that "recognition of the inherent dignity and of the equal and inalienable rights of all members of the human family is the foundation of freedom, justice and peace in the world."[6] This symbiotic relationship between human rights and peace has been reiterated by the world community in the text of numerous human rights instruments formalized in the sixty-five years since the birth of the UN.[7]

Human rights activists also speak of a third generation of human rights, most often a reference to "group rights" including self-determination, cultural survival, the collective development of economic and cultural resources, and the protection of the environment. Increasingly, international law recognizes that human beings are entitled to protection both as individuals and members of communities.[8] Guarantees of individual rights cannot provide the sustenance that group identity and membership in indigenous and other communities provide, yet communities at times discourage individual dissent from prevailing norms. Thus, all dimensions of human rights are essential, the individual and the collective, the political and the social, the guarantee of justice, and the making of peace.

A. MEASURING SOCIOECONOMIC SECURITY AND HUMAN LIBERTY

It is a difficult task to evaluate countries in terms of the levels of welfare, freedom, and security that their citizens and residents enjoy. Nevertheless, in reading and analyzing legal instruments that obligate states and other actors to respect human dignity in very concrete ways, it is essential to acknowledge the vast divide between human rights standards and realities on the ground in specific societies. In assessing the social and political conditions of life in individual countries, the interrelationships between poverty, repression, and the incidence of armed conflict are exposed. Confronting the realities of poverty, political violence, and war is the first step towards a fuller implementation of the principles of human rights and humanitarian law. This section starts by considering ways to define human security in socioeconomic terms and then explores indicators of human liberty in the political realm. First to consider is the concept of human development.

1. Socioeconomic Security

Human development and *human security* are terms of art increasingly utilized by the international community to emphasize and enhance the material or socioeconomic dimension of human rights. The United Nations has labored to develop and refine terms and indicators that meaningfully reflect the quality of life for individuals in particular countries. Illustrative of this trend, the contemporary global conversation about human security is occurring against the backdrop of the Millennium Development Goals, in which the General Assembly pledged to cut extreme poverty in half by the year 2015.[9]

Despite an increasing emphasis on the material conditions of life at the household level in the assessment of human rights standards around the world, the modern rhetorical focus on poverty and human security has not displaced deeply entrenched macroeconomic benchmarks for social progress at the global level that have been utilized since the founding of the UN. For nearly half a century, UN officials, humanitarian workers in the field, academics, and lay people alike have loosely applied the labels "developing" and "least developed" to countries with relatively less economic, political, and military power at the global level. Many such developing countries in the global South are former colonies of major industrial nations, located in Africa, South America, and parts of Asia and the Middle East. Others are newly independent states formed by the breakup of the former Soviet Union and other states in Eastern Europe.

As of 2010, the UN Development Programme (UNDP) classifies 86 of the 194 member states of the UN as "developing countries."[10] Within that group of 86, the UN identifies 49 as "the least developed countries."[11] Thus, the UN considers nearly one-half the countries of the world to be developing, and classifies one-quarter as the least developed. The downside of using the terms developing and least developed to refer generally to poorer or less powerful countries is that the terms, by themselves, do not shed much light on the actual living conditions for most people living in such nations. Indeed, some developing countries devote more resources to social services in relative terms than do major industrial countries, particularly in the health sector.[12]

Recognizing the disconnect between gross indicators of economic growth at the national level and the particular experiences of material deprivation within families and communities in various countries around the world, the UN and its partners in the nongovernmental sector have endeavored to formulate, in recent years, a more precise and multidimensional definition of underdevelopment, particularly with respect to countries at the extreme margins of the global economy. For the UNDP and other agencies, the term *least developing country* now corresponds to a cluster of social and economic attributes, chief among these a very modest gross domestic product (GDP) per capita, a low level of adult literacy, and a high level of insecurity in the agricultural and food production sectors.[13] Uganda, Sierra Leone, and Burundi, the three countries profiled in Chapters 7, 8, and 9, are all characterized as least developed countries.[14]

In an attempt to better measure the quality of life for people residing in developing and least developed countries, the UNDP formulated a new calculus, optimistically dubbed the human development index (HDI). Rather than ranking countries in terms of GDP alone, the HDI focuses instead on "three basic dimensions of human development—a long and healthy life, knowledge, and a decent standard of living."[15] As conceptualized by UNDP, the top HDI score would be 1.0. According to statistics compiled by UNDP in 2010, the world HDI average was .624, and for the least developed countries, the average HDI was .386.[16] Of the 169 countries with sufficient data to be ranked in 2010, HDI scores ranged from .938 for Norway, in first place, to .140 for Zimbabwe, in last place.[17] Uganda, Sierra Leone, and Burundi, from our three country studies, are ranked 143th, 158th and 166th, with HDIs of .422, .317 and .282, respectively.[18]

The United Nations compiles separate statistics[19] on the three aspects of material well-being used in computing the human development index—life expectancy at birth, mean years of schooling, and gross national income (GNI) per capita.[20] On average globally, life expectancy at birth is 69.3 years, years of schooling are 7.4, and GNI per capita is $10,631,

[78] *International Legal Rules for Conflict Resolution*

corresponding to the global average HDI of .624.[21] For the least developed countries, life expectancy is 57.7 years, years of schooling are 3.7, and $1,393 is the average GNI per capita, with an HDI of .386.[22] Data from our three case studies help complete the picture: for Uganda, life expectancy is 54.1 years, with years of schooling at 4.7, and a GNI per capita of $1224 (HDI .422); for Sierra Leone, life expectancy is 48.2 years, years of schooling 2.9, and GNI per capita $809 (HDI .317); and for Burundi, life expectancy is 51.4 years, years of schooling are 2.7, and the GNI per capita is $402 (HDI .282).[23]

An essential dimension of human development is the status of women in both legal and material terms. Countries with low HDI tend to have relatively low levels of literacy among women and lower female life expectancy, and this trend plays itself out in our three country studies. According to the UNDP *Human Development Report* for 2010, the maternal mortality rate for women in the United States between 2003 and 2008 was 11 out of one-hundred thousand live births, whereas it was 550 for women in Uganda, 2,100 for women in Sierra Leone, and 1,100 for women in Burundi. Data for women who had achieved at least secondary education by 2010 was 9.1 percent for Uganda, 9.5 percent for Sierra Leone, and 5.2 percent for Burundi. Overall, 2010 statistics for women reaching the secondary level of education or higher was 17.8 percent for least developed countries overall. In the United States, in 2010, 95.3 percent of women had achieved secondary education or higher.[24]

2. Human Insecurity in the Context of Armed Conflict

There is a powerful correlation between entrenched poverty and war, reflected in the higher rates of armed conflict in countries with relatively low levels of human security as compared to the more developed countries of the world. Based on statistics for the decade between 1997 and 2006, the likelihood of armed conflict in the countries with the highest human development indicators was 1.6 percent, whereas it was 30.1 percent in the middle range of countries, and 38.7 percent in the least developed countries.[25] Uganda, Burundi, and Sierra Leone are examples of countries with very low human development indicators that are emerging from prolonged periods of armed conflict: over ten years, in the case of Burundi and Sierra Leone, and upwards of twenty years for Uganda.

A causal relationship between armed conflict and underdevelopment is easy to posit but more difficult to prove. Social scientists, humanitarian workers, and journalists alike report widely that competition for scarce economic resources fuels armed conflict, and that conflict exacerbates underdevelopment. Certainly war torn societies experience frequent food, public health, and sanitation emergencies; increased levels of unemployment; and decreased access to education. In exploring the causes of war, researchers on conflict in Africa have identified food insecurity as the most significant contributing cause of civil strife.[26] War tends to break out in African countries with the highest levels of hunger and malnutrition. Enhancing access to food throughout a population promotes conflict resolution while serving as a powerful engine for conflict prevention in the first place.

At the start of the civil war in 1991, Sierra Leone ranked at the very bottom of the UN's ranking of developing countries in terms of its human development index. In 1991, Burundi and Uganda were both ahead of Sierra Leone in terms of human development rankings, but still in the lowest 20 percent of all developing countries.[27] In 2007, five years after the official end of hostilities, Sierra Leone still found itself in last place in terms of its HDI. For its part, by 2007, Uganda had moved into the middle tier of human development as defined by the United Nations, shortly after the Juba peace process had begun to bear fruit. That same year, Burundi was also emerging from armed conflict—still situated in the lowest tier of human development, with an HDI even closer to that of Sierra Leone than had been the case in 1991.[28] Recent modest gains for Ugandans, and the prolonged socioeconomic insecurity of most Sierra Leoneans and Burundians highlight the fragility of long-term peace processes in countries emerging from armed conflict.

3. Political Liberty

Linked to the experience of human security in socioeconomic terms is the enjoyment of civil and political rights—the freedom from inhuman or arbitrary treatment, freedom of expression, and freedom to participate freely in the political process. Compared to its quantitative data analysis in the area of human material security, the UN does not have a precise methodology for measuring civil liberties. Nevertheless, a number of nongovernmental agencies specialize in measuring relative experiences of political pluralism in individual states. One prominent research institute, the Freedom House, issues yearly surveys of countries throughout the world, utilizing a particular index of civil and political freedoms.

Beginning in the 1950s, Freedom House began publishing an annual *Balance Sheet of Freedom,* which evolved into its current yearly report entitled *Freedom in the World.* The organization maintains that its perspective is not culture-bound, but rather based upon broad standards set forth in the Universal Declaration of Human Rights (UDHR or Universal Declaration). Nevertheless, Freedom House is forthright about its "assumption that freedom for all peoples is best achieved in liberal democratic societies." Its data collection considers the conduct of public officials as well as nonstate actors in the enjoyment or denial of civil and political rights.[29]

Freedom House's index assigns each of the 193 countries surveyed a number between 1 and 7 in both of two categories corresponding to political rights and civil liberties. In each case, the continuum between 1 and 7 reflects an assessment ranging from the highest to the lowest levels of freedom. The assessment of political rights considers the development of the electoral process, the degree of political pluralism, and the extent of individual participation in the political process. The evaluation of civil liberties takes into account freedom of expression, "associational and organizational rights," the development of the rule of law, and "personal autonomy and individual rights."[30] A state with an average composite score between 1.0 and 2.5 is defined as "free," one with a composite between 3.0 and 5.0 as "partly free," and one between 5.5 and 7.0 as "not free."

In 2009, based on Freedom House's methodology and typology, 89 countries, nearly one-half, were deemed "free." Another 62 nearly one-third were considered "partly free." The remaining 42 countries, something over one-quarter, were labeled "not free." The US received a composite score of 1, the gold standard on Freedom House's freedom continuum, illustrating the institute's positive bias towards liberal democratic systems. For the three African case studies, all three were determined to be "partly free:" Uganda and Burundi with a score of 4.5 and Sierra Leone with a score of 3.[31]

Freedom House's assigned index values reflect an analysis of prevailing political and social conditions, reported in the yearly report for each country. *Freedom in the World 2008* notes that in Uganda, opposition political parties were prohibited until 2005. In 2008, Uganda experienced ongoing conflict between its armed forces and the Lord's Resistance Army (LRA), as well as social tensions associated with hosting increased numbers of refugees from the Democratic Republic of the Congo (DRC).[32] In Sierra Leone, Freedom House noted recent progress in efforts to combat a high level of official corruption, as well as the holding of local elections, in 2008, following free and fair presidential and parliamentary elections, in 2007. *Freedom in the World* also reported on de facto restrictions on press freedoms in Sierra Leone despite constitutional guarantees.[33] In the case of Burundi, Freedom House reported progress in peace negotiations in 2008, but expressed concern about a recent crackdown on the political opposition and the government's failure to establish either a special tribunal or a national truth commission to confront war crimes committed during the prolonged civil war.[34] These concerns played out in the elections of 2010, in which allegations of fraud by the ruling party in communal elections were followed by repression of opposition parties, whose candidates subsequently boycotted the presidential election.

On this foundation of the realities of socioeconomic suffering and political repression in countries emerging from armed conflict, we now turn to the various sources of human rights law enacted to enhance human security and political expression. Although most human rights instruments are treaties, the best-known source of human rights law started as a nonbinding resolution of the UN General Assembly, adopted in 1948. This early UN resolution is notable for its integration of civil and political rights with socioeconomic and cultural rights.

B. THE UNIVERSAL DECLARATION OF HUMAN RIGHTS AND THE INTERDEPENDENCE OF FUNDAMENTAL RIGHTS AND FREEDOMS

In consulting the sources of international human rights law in the form of treaties and nonbinding resolutions, the 1948 Universal Declaration of Human Rights is a fitting place to start. It was adopted without dissenting vote by the UN General Assembly, and what started as soft law has attained the status of customary law.[35] Its provisions span the full spectrum of individual rights from the prohibition of state-sponsored violence to the provision of health care and education. The Universal Declaration also affirms that people should claim their rights with an awareness of the impact that their actions have on the life and dignity of others. Finally, the UDHR set a precedent for future treaties by identifying the symbiotic relationship between human rights and peace. Its Preamble states that "recognition of the inherent dignity and of the equal and inalienable rights of all members of the human family is the foundation of freedom, justice and peace in the world..."[36]

1. The Norm of Equality

Articles 1 and 2 of the UDHR set forth the norm of equality from multiple perspectives. Article 2 is the most cited in its articulation of the principle of "nondistinction" and its enumeration of ten nonexclusive grounds on which discrimination should not occur: "race, colour, sex, language, political or other opinion, national or social origin, property, birth or other status."[37] Sexual orientation is notably absent. Article 1 is also important, in emphasizing that people "are born free in dignity and rights" and in exhorting people to "act towards one another in a spirit of brotherhood." Thus, although the UDHR is fundamentally a bill of rights, it acknowledges the responsibilities that come with community life.

2. Basic Liberties

Articles 3–21 of the UDHR proclaim what are generally regarded as civil and political liberties: the right to life (Article 3); freedom from slavery (Article 4); the prohibition against torture (Article 5); the right to basic legal personality or personhood in the eyes of the law (Article 6); equal protection of the law (Article 7); the right to an effective legal remedy (Article 8); freedom from arbitrary arrest and detention (Article 9); the right to a public and impartial hearing on criminal charges (Article 10); the presumption of innocence (Article 11); the right to privacy (Article 12); freedom of movement (Article 13); the right to seek and enjoy asylum from persecution (Article 14); the right to a nationality (Article 15); the right to marry and create a family (Article 16); the right to own property individually and collectively (Article 17); freedom of thought, conscience, and religion (Article 18); freedom of opinion and expression (Article 19); freedom of assembly (Article 20); and the right to participate in government (Article 21).

Political and civil rights are sometimes referred to as negative rights, or "hands-off" rights, insofar as they emphasize freedom *from* the abuse of power, often by the state, but also by other individuals. The idea is that if individuals are given free rein, they may form their own beliefs, speak their minds, worship freely, found a family, choose their place of residence, and defend themselves in court if accused of a crime. Another component of the concept of negative rights is the claim that fewer state resources are implicated in the guarantee of civil and political rights than in the enjoyment of economic and social rights, based on the presumption that it costs governments less to leave their denizens alone than it does to grant them various forms of material assistance.

Despite its rhetorical appeal, the negative or hands-off metaphor for civil and political rights is imperfect at best. Even if we focus on the freedom from torture and arbitrary arrest, state resources and proactive measures are needed, in addition to a forbearance from abusive conduct, if individuals are to enjoy such protections. Adequate police stations, courts, and prisons must be built and maintained; police officers and prison guards need to be hired in sufficient numbers and trained in lawful and humane forms of arrest, interrogation, and detention; and prosecutors, defense counsel, judges, and magistrates require effective schooling in constitutional, legislative, and common law rules regarding criminal justice. Furthermore, with regard to freedom of thought, expression and participation, individuals need access to primary, secondary, and ideally postsecondary education in order to more fully develop the political, philosophical and religious beliefs and opinions that they may then seek to express through participation in political and cultural life.

Civil and political rights embody a free society and a government accountable to the rule of law. But governmental restraint alone will not guarantee these liberties for all people. To strengthen civil and political rights, the state must put its money where its mouth is, investing the financial and human resources necessary to cultivate the rule of law at all levels of society.

3. Fundamental Material Needs

Articles 22–27 of the Universal Declaration emphasize social and economic rights: the right to social security (Article 22); freedom of choice in employment, the right to form trade unions, and guarantees of fair wages and safe working conditions (Article 23); the right to reasonable working hours and periodic holidays (Article 24); the right to an adequate standard of living, including food, shelter, medical care, and assistance for the elderly and disabled (Article 25); the right to free primary education, and fair access to secondary education (Article 26); and finally rights to share in the artistic and scientific advancements of the community, and to enjoy the protection of one's own intellectual property (Article 27).

Economic and social rights are often referred to as "positive" rights, reflecting the reality that enjoyment of such rights will require significant state resources, policies, and programs. As with the "negative" vision of civil-political rights, the "positive" conception of economic-social rights is oversimplified. Certainly the provision of free public education, adequate nourishment, universal health care, and security in retirement is costly to the state and, indeed, in the case of many developing countries, difficult if not impossible to pay for without international assistance. The same is true of humanitarian relief for individuals who flee conflict, repression, and natural disaster. Nevertheless, there is a hands-off element to socioeconomic rights as well, in poor and rich countries alike. In many societies, individuals and groups are arbitrarily denied access to employment or education, or forcibly displaced from their land and means of sustenance. In such situations, the problem is not simply a lack of adequate state expenditures, but also the abuse of power by the state and the failure of the state to allocate its resources equitably.

Economic and social rights embody a decent society, with a government accountable for the welfare of its citizens. But government largesse alone will not secure the safety net. To guarantee economic and social rights the state must police itself, providing human services to political compatriots and adversaries alike, weaving the principle of equity into the social fabric.

It thus appears that both families of individual rights recognized in the Universal Declaration—the civil-political and the economic-social—have negative and positive dimensions. All human rights along the spectrum from freedom of speech to affordable health care require both self-restraint and affirmative measures on the part of the state and members of society if they are to be effectively enjoyed.

4. Collective Life—The UDHR, the Banjul Charter, and the UN Declaration on the Rights of Indigenous Peoples

Articles 28–30 of the UDHR focus on collective rights and responsibilities to the collective: the individual's right to an international system or "order" dedicated to the enjoyment of human rights (Article 28); and the individual's duty to exercise her rights in such a way that others' rights are protected as well (Articles 29 and 30). Article 29 specifically mentions the UN, and prohibits the exercise of particular rights in a manner "contrary to [its] purposes and principles." In reference to Article 1 of the Charter of the United Nations (Charter), the text of UDHR Article 29 cautions that human rights should not be exercised so as to endanger international peace and security, or discourage friendly relations among nations.[38]

Despite references to "others" and the need to consider the interests of the community of nations, there are no explicit references to the rights of groups as such in the Universal Declaration, nor in the majority of the human rights instruments that have been adopted subsequently. A notable exception is one of the four regional human rights conventions, the aptly named African Charter on Human and Peoples' Rights (Banjul Charter). This treaty recognizes the rights of peoples to equality, self-determination, development, and peace.[39] Although the international community has yet to draft a treaty of universal application specifically dedicated to collective human rights, there are emerging norms on this issue, especially regarding the communal rights of first nations and all aboriginal communities.

Nearly sixty years after the UDHR, the General Assembly adopted another comprehensive resolution with global reach: the 2007 UN Declaration on the Rights of Indigenous Peoples (UNDRIP).[40] Although

Article 28 of the UDHR recognizes the individual's right to an international order in which human rights may flourish, the UNDRIP concerns the rights of indigenous communities *as* collectives, proclaiming that "*peoples*," and not only *people*, have rights. UNDRIP encompasses the protection of indigenous languages, religions, and cultures; and recognizes and promotes collective land ownership and collective management of natural resources.[41] Because it is a resolution and not a treaty, UNDRIP currently has the status of soft law. It remains to be seen whether UNDRIP will lead to a convention on the rights of indigenous peoples, or whether the provisions of UNDRIP and the Banjul Charter will evolve into norms of customary international law regarding the rights of peoples more generally.

5. The Impact of the Universal Declaration of Human Rights

The customary status attained by the Universal Declaration in the sixty years since its adoption is widely recognized, as discussed more fully in Chapter 1. The UDHR is significant not just for its enumerated provisions and principles, but for the treaties and national constitutions that it has inspired. Moreover, the Universal Declaration remains "cutting edge" in its insistence that no "State, group or person" may "engage in any activity . . . aimed at the destruction of the rights and freedoms set forth"[42] in the Universal Declaration. Hence, although the UDHR is a universal bill of rights, it goes further than most national constitutions in prohibiting violations of human rights by "private" individuals and communities as well as abuses by state actors.[43]

Nevertheless, as a written instrument of international law, the UDHR is a resolution, not a treaty, and therefore lacks the formal enforcement bodies typically created by human rights treaties. In reviewing the most significant treaties that have entered into force since the birth of the UN, it is essential to consider both the substance of the human rights obligations imposed on states and other actors, as well as the specific treaty-based mechanisms for challenging those actors when they fail in their obligations to respect human dignity.

C. HUMAN RIGHTS TREATIES

There are numerous international treaties dedicated to the protection and promotion of human liberty, equality, well-being, and security. One organizing principle is whether the treaty has a global or a regional reach, contrasting the International Covenant on Economic, Social and Cultural

Rights (ICESCR or Economic and Social Covenant), for example, with a regional human rights treaty such as the Banjul Charter. Some treaties with global reach are more comprehensive, such as the two international covenants dealing collectively with the two predominant "families" of individual rights. Other treaties are focused on defining and preventing a specific human rights violation, such as torture or genocide. Below, we will discuss the essential provisions of ten major human rights treaties, starting with the Convention on the Prevention and Punishment of the Crime of Genocide (Genocide Convention), and ending with the Arab Charter on Human Rights.

1. Treaties to Combat Institutionalized Human Rights Abuses

a. The Genocide Convention

It is not an accident that genocide was the subject of the first human rights treaty adopted after World War II and the birth of the UN. Shamed into action by the extermination of over six million Jews and other minorities including gays and Roma people, the international community was compelled to condemn the very idea of a "final solution," and all campaigns of ethnic annihilation. Thus, in the aftermath of the Holocaust, and one year before the 1949 Geneva Conventions laid the foundation for modern humanitarian law, the General Assembly adopted the Convention on the Prevention and Punishment of the Crime of Genocide.[44] As of December 2008, its sixtieth anniversary, 140 states had ratified the Genocide Convention, out of 194 members of the UN.[45] The United States ratified the treaty in 1988. Although Burundi and Uganda acceded to the Genocide Convention in 1997 and 1995, respectively,[46] Sierra Leone is not a party, although it has signed and ratified the Rome Statute of the International Criminal Court (Rome Statute or ICC Statute).[47]

Genocide is defined in the Genocide Convention as certain "acts committed with intent to destroy, in whole or in part, a national, ethnical, racial or religious group, as such."[48] While the definition of genocide does not require a certain number of persons killed, it does require proof of intent to destroy the group, partially if not completely. In addition to the challenge of proof, the treaty limits genocide to the attempted destruction of certain kinds of groups, essentially defined in terms of ethnicity or religion. Political and other social categories are not included in the treaty's definition. Nevertheless, some human rights advocates and scholars have argued that the attempted extermination of political opposition groups also constitutes genocide, particularly in the case of Cambodia's "killing fields," in which over 1.5 million people were murdered as counter-revolutionaries by the Khmer Rouge in the 1970s.[49]

The treaty-based definition is also significant because it does not limit genocide to the killing of group members. Also included are acts that cause "serious bodily or mental harm" and the infliction of "conditions of life calculated to bring about [the group's] physical destruction."[50]

The Genocide Convention requires state parties to punish genocide as well as certain acts related to genocide, including attempted genocide and conspiracy and incitement to commit genocide.[51] Accountability for acts of genocide is not limited to "private" individuals, but also extends to "constitutionally responsible" public officials.[52]

Article VIII allows parties to request action by the UN to prevent and suppress acts of genocide.[53] Although to date no state has invoked Article VIII, the treaty has played an important role in bringing the norm against genocide into the domain of customary law as well as into the popular imagination. Moreover, the Genocide Convention is referenced in other instruments, including the International Covenant on Civil and Political Rights (ICCPR or Civil and Political Covenant) and the ICC Statute.[54]

b. Genocide and Other Crimes Against Humanity

Genocide shares certain attributes with other human rights abuses that typically target entire communities. Apart from the Genocide Convention, the international community has concluded other major treaties defining and combating specific institutionalized human rights crimes. Two of these crimes, slavery and apartheid, are addressed below. In 1956, the Supplementary Convention on the Abolition of Slavery, the Slave Trade, and Institutions and Practices Similar to Slavery, was concluded, building on the foundation of an earlier treaty adopted in 1926. In 1976, the International Convention on the Suppression and Punishment of the Crime of Apartheid was concluded.[55]

Genocide, like institutionalized slavery and systemic racial discrimination, is an offense against human dignity that operates on a wholesale or metalevel. Essentially, genocidists attack individuals in order to destroy the community in which they are members. In the same vein, historically, members of certain slave-owning elites have claimed ownership over other individuals by asserting that the social or ethnic group to which they belong is subservient by nature. Such was the case for the institution of black chattel slavery established and practiced in the American colonies and the United States between the seventeenth and nineteenth centuries. Similarly, *apartheid* marginalizes members of particular ethnicities in multiple sectors of life, entrenching their collective "separateness" by discriminating against group members in eligibility for housing and employment, as well as access to public amenities, education, health care, the court system, and the political process itself.

Meta abuses, such as genocide, are both human rights violations and crimes against humanity that implicate international criminal law, which is the focus of Chapter 4. Just as common crimes are deemed offenses against the national community, international crimes are deemed offenses against global society because they degrade and endanger our common humanity. Crimes against humanity, including genocide, slavery, and apartheid, differ from other international crimes insofar as t they attack communities per se as well as individuals. These offenses may also constitute war crimes under international humanitarian law if they occur in time of armed conflict.

Genocide, slavery, and apartheid are wholesale abuses because they attack communities or whole social categories, but also because they take myriad forms. Thus, genocide constitutes a compound human rights violation, wrapping together multiple instances and forms of abuse, ranging from dislocation, detention, and deportation, to rape, torture, and extermination. Although institutionalized slavery incorporates many of the same abusive methods as genocide, its primary purpose is the economic exploitation of the group, which requires its preservation rather than its physical destruction. For its part, apartheid strings together multiple acts of discrimination. Although abuses will not always rise to the level of physical attack or servitude, the marginalized group remains extremely vulnerable to both violence and economic exploitation.

All three of the major crimes against humanity—the wholesale patterns of abuse, as well as the specific human rights violations through which they are implemented—violate *jus cogens* rules. This means that genocide, slavery, and apartheid, on the one hand, and murder, torture, servitude, and discrimination, on the other, each violate peremptory or nonderogable norms of international law. To this extent, these acts would violate international customary law, even if there were not treaties in force prohibiting them.[56] The treaties are important in defining the specific crimes against humanity with greater precision, and establishing institutional mechanisms to prevent and punish such abuses.

The Genocide Convention did not create its own commission or court to prevent or punish acts of genocide, relying instead on states to prosecute genocide domestically or request intervention by the UN. Indeed, until the establishment of the ICC in 2002, there was no treaty-based international tribunal of global reach created for the specific purpose of prosecuting prospective crimes against humanity. But as we shall see in Chapter 4, there have been numerous criminal tribunals of more limited geographic and temporal jurisdiction, including the Nuremburg Tribunal; ad hoc courts for the former Yugoslavia and Rwanda; and hybrid courts for Sierra Leone, Cambodia, and East Timor. Nevertheless, criminal prosecutions are but one judicial mechanism for protecting human dignity. Human rights violations may also result in civil actions, building upon the concepts of tort law, and seeking damages for the injured person, rather than criminal fines or imprisonment for the author of a crime.

The human rights treaties adopted after 1948 are notable for establishing new bodies to evaluate and improve human rights conditions in particular states. In some cases, these entities adjudicate specific claims of human rights violations. However, unlike criminal tribunals that convict and incarcerate individuals, the goal of human rights commissions is for states to make reparations for human rights abuses and change legal and economic structures so that such abuses do not occur in the future. Increasingly, international criminal law, the subject of Chapter 4, is also exploring the use of restorative justice mechanisms at the community level in combination with prosecutions that impose criminal liability on individuals.

2. The 1966 International Covenants

It took nearly twenty years from the adoption of the Universal Declaration in 1948, before comprehensive human rights treaties were drafted and opened for signature to all members of the UN. Work began immediately on regional human rights treaties, and indeed Europe's Convention for the Protection of Human Rights and Fundamental Freedoms (European Convention on Human Rights or European Convention) entered into force in 1953. Nevertheless, at the international level, it took more time to codify the provisions of the Universal Declaration in treaty form. Part of the delay was due to the rhetorical tension between civil-political and economic-social rights described above. Although Eleanor Roosevelt and other proponents of the UDHR had advocated one comprehensive treaty, other voices insisted on a bifurcated approach with express language that economic and social rights were contingent upon state resources.[57] The bifurcated approach won the day, and two covenants with global reach were adopted on December 19, 1966. Uganda, Burundi, and Sierra Leone have each acceded to both the ICESCR and the ICCPR.[58]

a. The International Covenant on Economic, Social, and Cultural Rights

The Preamble of the International Covenant on Economic, Social and Cultural Rights[59] explicitly recognizes the interconnections between economic and social rights, on the one hand, and civil and political rights, on the other.[60] Moreover, like the Universal Declaration, it states that "recognition of the inherent dignity and of the equal and inalienable rights of all members of the human family is the foundation of freedom, justice and peace in the world."[61]

The ICESCR contains 31 articles, the first fifteen codifying, amplifying and, in some cases, adding to the provisions in Articles 22–27 of the Universal Declaration. Article 1 cuts new ground in articulating and defining the principle of self-determination as the right of all peoples "to freely determine their political status and freely pursue their economic, social and cultural development." Many of the provisions to follow incorporate the text of the UDHR, especially regarding: the principle of nondiscrimination (Articles 2(2) and 3); freedom of choice in employment and the rights to enjoy fair wages, hours, and working conditions and form trade unions (Articles 6–8); the right to social security (Article 9); the right to marry and create a family (Article 10); and the right to an adequate standard of living, including food, shelter, and "the highest attainable standard of physical and mental health" (Articles 11 and 12).

Although the ICESCR does not include the UDHR's specific language on social security in time of disability and old age,[62] it goes farther than the Universal Declaration in elaborating that the "right of everyone to be free from hunger" will require improved methods of food production and equitable distribution.[63] Like the UDHR, the ICESCR recognizes the rights to free primary education and fair access to secondary education (Article 13), but the treaty also obligates signatories to implement "a detailed plan of action for the progressive implementation. . . of the principle of compulsory education free of charge for all" (Article 14). Finally, the treaty codifies the references in the UDHR regarding the right to share in the artistic and scientific advancements of the community, and enjoy the protection of one's own intellectual property (Article 15).

Because the ICESCR is a treaty, it introduces language regarding state obligations and mechanisms for state participation and implementation not contained in the Universal Declaration. The language of Article 2 is notable for allowing states time to implement their obligations and for implicitly recognizing the severe resource limitations faced by individual countries:

> [e]ach State Party. . . undertakes to take steps, individually and through international assistance and co-operation, especially economic and technical, to the maximum of its available resources, with a view to achieving progressively the full realization of the rights recognized in the present Covenant by all appropriate means, particularly the adoption of legislative measures.[64]

The *progressive realization* component of the ICESCR is distinct from the language of many human rights treaties and is a likely product, if not a casualty, of the decision to draft two separate international covenants in 1966. Articles 16–24 establish procedures for signatories to submit reports to the UN Secretary General regarding the progress they have made in realizing the rights enumerated in the treaty, and mechanisms for states to collaborate with the Economic and Social Council, the Human Rights Commission,[65] specialized agencies,[66] and the UN General Assembly. However, the covenant does not create and empower a specific body to hear complaints by states or individuals that specific provisions of the treaty have been violated, in contrast to other treaties that we will explore below.

b. The International Covenant on Civil and Political Rights

The International Covenant on Civil and Political Rights[67] echoes the language of the Economic and Social Covenant in the text of its Preamble, acknowledging the interlocking nature of civil-political and socioeconomic rights, as well as the familiar text from the Universal Declaration regarding the interdependence of human rights and peace.[68] The ICCPR contains 53 articles to the ICESCR's 31. Like the ICESCR, the Civil and Political Covenant begins with an initial article articulating the norm of self-determination of peoples. The Civil and Political Covenant also includes almost verbatim the nondiscrimination clause contained in the ICESCR.[69] The ICCPR subtly parts company with the Economic and Social Covenant in the language of obligation used in Article 2. In contrast to the references in the Economic and Social Covenant to "progressive achievement" and "available resources," the Civil and Political Covenant reads simply that "[e]ach State Party... undertakes to respect and to ensure to all individuals" the rights enumerated in the treaty.[70]

Like the Economic and Social Covenant, the ICCPR builds upon specific provisions of the Universal Declaration. Articles 3–27 correspond quite closely to Articles 3–21 of the UDHR. In addition to the nondiscrimination language in Article 2 of both instruments, the Civil and Political Covenant includes, in Article 3, a separate provision focusing on "the equal rights of men and women."[71] The ICCPR then echoes much of the substance of the Universal Declaration in recognizing the right to life (Article 6); the prohibitions against torture and slavery (Articles 7 and 8); the rights to liberty and security, including due process for individuals accused of crimes and dignified treatment for detained persons (Articles 9, 10, 14, and 15); the right to freedom of movement (Article 12); the rights to legal personality and privacy (Articles 16 and 17); freedom of conscience and religion and freedom of expression (Articles 18 and 19); the rights of assembly, association, and political participation (Articles 21, 22, and 25); and the principle of equal protection of the law (Article 26).

The Civil and Political Covenant amplifies the rights set forth in the Universal Declaration in several regards, including the right of juveniles accused of crimes to be detained separately from adults (Article 10) and the prohibition against the imprisonment of debtors (Article 11). However, one right recognized in the Universal Declaration that did not make it into the ICCPR is the "right to seek and to enjoy in other countries asylum from persecution."[72] The Civil and Political Covenant does include certain protections against arbitrary deportation, but only for "[a]n alien lawfully in the territory" who "may be expelled therefrom only in pursuance of a decision reached in accordance with law."[73] Even this protection is qualified "where compelling reasons of national security otherwise require."[74]

The lack of a right to asylum in the Civil and Political Covenant has additional relevance in the field of refugee law, the subject of Chapter 5. Although the 1951 Convention relating to the Status of Refugees (Refugee Convention) accords *states* the right to grant asylum, there is no right on the part of the *individual* to seek and enjoy asylum.[75] Nevertheless, as we shall see in Chapter 5, both the Refugee Convention and customary international law recognize the essential if more limited right to *non-refoulement*, or the right not to be sent back to a situation of likely persecution.[76] Thus, although refugees cannot rely on the more durable status of asylum, states are absolutely prohibited from forcibly returning them to the place they fled in fear of persecution. Refugees are entitled to protection in the form of *non-refoulement*, which has attained the status of a nonderogable or *jus cogens* norm.[77]

Like other human rights treaties, the Civil and Political Covenant includes a derogation provision, which permits state parties to avoid their obligations under the treaty in certain situations. Unlike some other treaties, the ICCPR sets forth detailed limitations on the extent to which states may derogate from their obligations under Article 4 of the treaty:

1. In time of public emergency which threatens the life of the nation and the existence of which is officially proclaimed, the States Parties to the present Covenant may take measures derogating from their obligations under the present Covenant to the extent strictly required by the exigencies of the situation, provided that such measures are not inconsistent with their other obligations under international law and do not involve discrimination solely on the ground of race, colour, sex, language, religion or social origin.

2. No derogation from articles 6, 7, 8 (paragraphs 1 and 2), 11, 15, 16 and 18 may be made under this provision.

Article 4 is notable because, while it recognizes certain national emergencies as potential justification for what would otherwise be violations of human rights, such an emergency must be sufficiently serious to "threaten the life of the nation," and the state must make an official declaration before taking emergency measures. Moreover, the derogations must be closely tailored to respond to the specific exigencies facing the nation. Most significantly, Article 4(2) identifies certain rights as nonderogable, or peremptory, meaning they must be respected in all situations, including states of emergency.

The eight rights enumerated as immune from derogation in Article 4 of the Civil and Political Covenant are the norm against discrimination (Article 2); the right to life (Article 6); the prohibition against torture (Article 7); the ban on slavery and servitude (Articles 8, paragraphs 1 and 2); the protection against imprisonment for debt (Article 11); the prohibition against retroactive criminal prosecution (Article 15); the right to legal personality (Article 16); and the right to freedom of thought, conscience, and religion (Article 18). There is substantial overlap between those norms recognized as *jus cogens* or peremptory under customary international law and those rights immunized against derogation under Article 4 of the Civil and Political Covenant.[78]

Article 4 has a special relevance in time of war, whether foreign invasion or civil conflict within the society. An armed conflict may inherently "threaten the life of the nation" or be claimed to do so by the state, and hence provides an opportunity or pretext for the derogation of human rights. Article 4(2) signifies that even in time of war, states may not torture, enslave, disappear, or arbitrarily execute individuals. In this sense, Article 4 of the Civil and Political Covenant is the counterpart of Common Article 3 of the 1949 Geneva Conventions, which sets minimum standards of humanity for non-international armed conflict. Using kindred language, Common Article 3 also prohibits torture, "outrages upon personal dignity," and extrajudicial execution.[79] Thus, ICCPR Article 4 and Common Article 3 of the Geneva Conventions provide a vivid illustration of the shared terrain of human rights and humanitarian law.

It is also enlightening to consider those rights that are *not* listed as immune from derogation during a legitimate state of emergency under Article 4: the right to liberty and security (Article 9); the right of detained persons to be treated with humanity (Article 10); freedom of movement (Article 12); freedom from arbitrary deportation (Article 13); the right to a public trial (Article 14); the right to privacy (Article 17); the right to freedom of expression (Article 19); the ban on war propaganda (Article 20); the rights to freedom of assembly and association (Articles 21 and 22); protections for families and children (Articles 23 and 24); the right to participate in the political process (Article 25); the right to equal protection (Article 26); and the cultural, religious, and linguistic rights of minorities (Article 27). Some of these rights are implicitly or partially immunized by the nonderogable provisions themselves, including the right of detainees to treatment with humanity, presumably covered by the norm against torture; and equal protection and minority rights, buttressed by the norm against discrimination. Nevertheless, important civil and political liberties are not immunized from at least partial derogation during states of emergency, particularly the rights to personal security, political expression, and political participation.

The remaining aspect of the Civil and Political Covenant that was not present in the UDHR is the section devoted to enforcement mechanisms. Part IV establishes a Human Rights Committee that not only evaluates self-assessments by state parties of their own successes and failures in meeting their obligations under the treaty, but also acts as a quasi-court in adjudicating alleged violations of the treaty under certain circumstances. A state may "sue" another state under the treaty only if that other state has made a specific declaration under Article 41 empowering the committee to hear interstate claims. Individual complaints of human rights violations by states are not contemplated in the treaty itself, but are allowed if the offending state has ratified the First Optional Protocol to the ICCPR.[80]

In one such case, the Human Rights Committee heard a petition brought against the Government of Sierra Leone on October 13, 1993, by Gilbert Samuth Kandu-Bo and eleven other former members of the armed forces of Sierra Leone who were awaiting execution. In defiance of the committee's request for interim measures of protection, the men were executed by firing squad on October 19. The committee condemned the executions and demanded that the government report on its efforts to ensure respect for the rights to life and humane treatment under Articles 6 and 7 of the Civil and Political Covenant.[81]

In addition to the Genocide Convention of 1948, a number of treaties have been adopted by members of the UN in order to spotlight a particular norm inscribed in the Civil and Political Covenant. Three of these treaties are particularly relevant insofar as they elaborate upon specific nonderogable rights enumerated in the ICCPR. These three treaties seek to combat racial discrimination, discrimination against women, and torture, respectively.

3. The Specialized Human Rights Treaties

a. The 1966 Convention on the Elimination of All Forms of Racial Discrimination

The Preamble of the Convention on the Elimination of All Forms of Racial Discrimination (CERD or the Racial Convention) "reaffirm[s] that discrimination between human beings on the grounds of race, colour or ethnic origin is an obstacle to friendly and peaceful relations among nations and is capable of disturbing peace and security among peoples..."[82] Article 1 of the treaty then states:

> (1) racial discrimination shall mean any distinction, exclusion, restriction or preference based on race, colour, descent, or national or ethnic origin which has the purpose or effect of nullifying or impairing the recognition, enjoyment or exercise on an equal footing, of human rights or fundamental freedoms in the political, economic, social, cultural or any other field of public life.
>
> (2) This Convention shall not apply to distinctions . . . between citizens and non-citizens.
>
> . . .
>
> (4) Special measures taken for the sole purpose of securing adequate advancement of certain racial or ethnic groups or individuals requiring such protection as may be necessary in order to ensure such groups or individuals equal enjoyment or exercise of human rights and fundamental freedoms shall not be deemed racial discrimination, provided, however, that such measures do not, as a consequence, lead to the maintenance of separate rights for different racial groups and that they shall not be continued after the objectives for which they were taken have been achieved.[83]

The Racial Convention's definition of racial discrimination starts by recognizing that racial identity, ethnicity, and national origin are related and equally impermissible motivations for differential treatment. Moreover, racial inequality by design and disparate impact on members of a particular racial community are equal dimensions of discrimination according to the treaty. At the same time, the CERD does not prohibit differential treatment in a particular state based on an individual's lack of that state's citizenship. Likewise, the treaty's definition of discrimination does not include affirmative measures (sometimes called *affirmative action*) specifically designed to remedy historical discrimination by promoting the advancement of victims of past inequality, so long as such measures do not entrench racial disparities in the future.

Under the Racial Convention, state parties commit to embrace concrete policies to eliminate racial discrimination (Article 2), by state officials and nonstate actors alike (Article 2(1)(a) and (b)), particularly in the context of court proceedings, elections, and the criminal justice system (Article 5). Signatories also must condemn racial segregation and apartheid (Article 3), and must criminalize the distribution of propaganda asserting the superiority of a given racial community or promoting racial hatred (Article 4).

In terms of enforcement mechanisms, the CERD created a Committee on the Elimination of Racial Discrimination that contemplates both interstate and individual "communications" claiming violations of the treaty. Article 11 clarifies that by ratifying the CERD parties automatically make themselves amenable to challenges by another state. In contrast, a state party must make an explicit declaration under Article 14 before it empowers the CERD committee to hear claims by individuals that they have been victims of that state's racial discrimination.

Uganda, Burundi, and Sierra Leone are all parties to the International Convention on the Elimination of all Forms of Racial Discrimination. Uganda acceded to the CERD on November 21, 1980, Burundi ratified the Convention on October 27, 1977, and Sierra Leone ratified on August 2, 1967.[84]

b. The 1979 Convention on the Elimination of All Forms of Discrimination Against Women

The Convention on the Elimination of All Forms of Discrimination Against Women (CEDAW or Women's Convention) defines its central concern as:

> any distinction, exclusion or restriction made on the basis of sex which has the effect or purpose of impairing or nullifying the recognition, enjoyment or exercise by women, irrespective of their marital status, on a basis of equality of men and women, of human rights and fundamental freedoms in the political, economic, social, cultural, civil or any other field.[85]

In addition to requiring state parties to take steps through legislation and otherwise to promote "the full development and advancement of women,"[86] signatories also pledge to take steps toward:

> modify[ing] the social and cultural patterns of conduct of men and women, with a view to achieving the elimination of prejudices and customary and other practices which are based on the idea of the inferiority or the superiority of either of the sexes or on stereotyped roles for men and women...[87]

CEDAW has 186 parties, even more than the Civil and Political and Economic and Social Covenants, and more than the Racial Convention, with 166, 160, and 173 state parties respectively. Uganda, Burundi, and Sierra Leone have all ratified CEDAW.[88] Nevertheless, although the treaty establishes a Committee on the Elimination of Discrimination Against Women, this body is only mandated to receive and consider reports from state parties regarding action they have taken under the treaty. Unlike its sister bodies under CERD and the international covenants, the CEDAW committee is not empowered to consider interstate or individual petitions alleging violations of the terms of the treaty.[89] In its yearly reporting to the General Assembly, the committee may make specific recommendations based on its evaluation of the state reports, and the UN Secretary General is required to pass on this information to the UN Commission on the Status of Women (CSW). Nevertheless, no particular action is required on the part of the General Assembly, the Secretary General, or the CSW in response to the CEDAW committee's recommendations.[90]

Despite its relative lack of enforcement mechanisms, CEDAW is significant for its rhetorical power. Like other human rights treaties, CEDAW recognizes and celebrates the close kinship between human equality and global peace. Specifically, the Preamble to CEDAW instructs that gender equality is a prerequisite of global security, and cautions that gender roles will need to change in order for such equality to be possible:

> ... the full and complete development of a country, the welfare of the world and the cause of peace require the maximum participation of women on equal terms with men in all fields... [;] a change in the traditional role of men as well as the role of women in society and in the family is needed to achieve full equality between men and women...'[91]

Finally, CEDAW is increasingly referred to as a standard for defining violations of human rights under other treaties. In a case involving the largely unsolved femicides in Juarez, Mexico, further discussed below, the Inter-American Court of Human Rights considered Mexico's report to the CEDAW committee in January of 2005.[92] In addressing the failure to end the pattern of violence against women in Juarez, the Government of Mexico reported to CEDAW that a "culture of discrimination" helped explain why "the murders were not perceived at the outset as a significant problem requiring immediate and forceful action on the part of the relevant authorities."[93] The report went on to state that this culture of discrimination against women was "based on the erroneous idea that women are inferior."[94]

Data from our three country studies powerfully illustrate the correlation between armed conflict and the debased status and treatment of women in particular societies: in Uganda, there are no laws criminalizing domestic violence; in Burundi, only 5 percent of eligible young women are enrolled in secondary school; and in Sierra Leone, despite de jure constitutional protections and new legislation enhancing women's marriage and inheritance rights,[95] women's customary legal status is on a par with minors.[96]

c. The 1984 Convention Against Torture and Other Cruel, Inhuman, or Degrading Treatment

The Preamble of the Convention Against Torture (CAT or Torture Convention) starts with the now familiar invocation of the Universal Declaration, recognizing that human rights are the foundation of a peaceful society. The opening passages also acknowledge that in prohibiting torture, the CAT stands on the shoulders of both the UDHR and the Civil and Political Covenant.[97]

Article 1 of the treaty defines torture as:

> any act by which severe pain or suffering, whether physical or mental, is intentionally inflicted on a person for such purposes as obtaining from him or a third person information or a confession, punishing him for an act he or a third person has committed or is suspected of having committed, or intimidating or coercing him or a third person, or for any reason based on discrimination of any kind, when pain or suffering is inflicted by or at the instigation of or with the consent or acquiescence of a public official or other person acting in an official capacity."[98]

The essence of the CAT definition is that torture is the purposeful infliction of suffering on an individual by a state official. The infliction of suffering is not gratuitous or an end in itself, but rather is calculated to serve a particular purpose. Suffering may be inflicted to coerce a confession from the victim, but not always. The torture also may serve to intimidate, punish, or discriminate against the individual, or be utilized as a tool for frightening or harming someone close to the victim.

Article 2 clarifies that the prohibition of torture is a nonderogable obligation. The norm against torture has this same status under customary law as a *jus cogens* norm, and under Article 4 of the Civil and Political Covenant. The Torture Convention's nonderogation clause is even broader than that of the earlier treaty, and clarifies that "[n]o exceptional circumstances whatsoever, whether a state of war or a threat of war, internal political instability or any other public emergency, may be invoked as a justification of torture." In explicitly mentioning the state of war, Article 2 of the CAT dovetails with Common Article 3 of the Geneva Conventions.

The Convention Against Torture is notable in several other respects: It obligates signatories to use their domestic legal systems to prevent torture, including criminalizing torture and excluding tortured testimony from legal proceedings;[99] it prohibits the forced return of an individual to a country where he or she is likely to face torture;[100] and it requires state parties to ensure that their law enforcement, medical and other personnel undergo trainings that include an understanding of the prohibition against torture.[101] Signatories are also required to prevent "other acts of cruel, inhuman or degrading treatment or punishment which do not amount to torture."[102]

In prohibiting the forced return (*refoulement*) of an individual to a torture-prone situation, the Convention Against Torture also dovetails with international refugee law. As noted above with regard to the non-entitlement to asylum under the Civil and Political Covenant, the Refugee Convention and customary international law provide an essential if more limited form of protection by prohibiting *refoulement* to countries in which an individual risks persecution. Persecution is defined as a serious human rights violation, and therefore can take various forms, including but not limited to torture.[103]

Like the Civil and Political Covenant, the Racial Convention, and the Women's Convention, the Convention Against Torture creates a committee to receive and review periodic reports from state parties evaluating and attesting to their conduct under the treaty. And unlike CEDAW, but like the others, the CAT committee can sometimes serve as a quasi-court in receiving and adjudicating alleged treaty violations by a state, but only if that state has empowered it to do so. Article 21 requires a specific declaration for the state to make itself amenable to challenges by another state; and Article 22 clarifies that a separate declaration is necessary before the state opens itself up to challenges by an individual that it has violated the CAT.[104]

Thus, in terms of supranational enforcement mechanisms, the Convention Against Torture is more robust than the Women's Convention and roughly on a par with the Civil and Political Covenant, and the Racial Convention.[105] But in terms of substance, the CAT stands together with all the major human rights, humanitarian, and refugee instruments in prohibiting torture and other forms of inhuman treatment. The Convention Against Torture has 147 parties, including Uganda, Burundi, and Sierra Leone.[106]

4. The Regional Human Rights Treaties

a. The 1950 European Convention for the Protection of Human Rights and Fundamental Freedoms

Europe was the first region to write its own human rights treaty. Adopted under the auspices of the Council of Europe, a regional international organization, the 1950 Convention for the Protection of Human Rights and Fundamental Freedoms[107] reads very much like the ICCPR. As such, the treaty recognizes individual legal personality, liberty and security, and freedom from torture, slavery, arbitrary detention and execution, as well as freedom of expression, religion, assembly, and participation; but not the typical socioeconomic rights, such as those related to labor, social security, health care, education, science, and culture. Unlike the Civil and Political Covenant, the European Convention has no provision regarding freedom of movement, let alone the rights to seek and enjoy asylum, and no explicit protection against *refoulement* to persecution, although *non-refoulement* can arguably be implied from the Article 1 obligation of states to "secure" the rights and freedoms enumerated in the treaty.[108] Also analogous to the Civil and Political Covenant, the European Convention includes a public emergency clause that clearly immunizes the right to life, as well as the freedoms from torture, slavery and retroactive criminal prosecution, from any derogation.[109]

The European Convention started a trend under regional human rights treaties of establishing a more formal structure for vindicating the individual rights enumerated under the treaty. In 1950, rather than merely creating a "committee" to receive periodic state reports, the European Convention established a European Commission and Court of Human Rights, the commission operating as a kind of trial court to the quasi-appellate court, and both empowered to adjudicate petitions brought by one state party against another.[110] Various protocols followed amending the treaty in various ways, until nearly fifty years later, Protocol 11 entered into force, eliminating the commission, expanding the court, and allowing individuals as well as states to bring direct claims of treaty violations.[111]

The European Court of Human Rights (European Court), the most productive human rights court in the world, has delivered over fifteen hundred judgments in contentious cases in its 50 years of operation.[112] In 1978, in its first decision in an interstate case, brought by the Republic of Ireland against the United Kingdom (UK), the European Court found that UK officials in Northern Ireland violated the norm against humane treatment in their detention and interrogation of suspected Irish Republican Army operatives.[113] In 2006, the European Court held Russia responsible for the disappearance of a Chechen man, and in 2005, it upheld Turkish legislation prohibiting the wearing of headscarves by women at public universities.[114]

b. The 1969 American Convention on Human Rights and the 1988 Protocol of San Salvador

Almost 20 years after the Council of Europe drafted its regional treaty, the Organization of American States (OAS) adopted the text of the American Convention on Human Rights (ACHR or American Convention) in 1969.[115] Like the European Convention, the American Convention is a treaty that concentrates on civil and political rights and that limits the power of the state to derogate in time of public emergency.[116] The American Convention, unlike the European, recognizes a qualified right to asylum.[117] Moreover, under Article 26, state parties also pledge to take measures toward the "progressive development" of economic, social, and cultural rights.[118]

Analogous to the original vision of the European Convention, the American Convention created an Inter-American Commission and Court of Human Rights, empowered to hear both interstate and individuals' allegations of human rights abuses by state parties.[119] In the case of the American Convention, individual petitions are "automatic," while interstate petitions require a special declaration by the state charged with violating the treaty that it is amenable to such a claim.[120] In its first decision in the 1986 *Velasquez-Rodriguez Case*,[121] the Inter-American Court found Honduras responsible for the disappearance and presumed killing of a university student at the hands of a government-affiliated death squad.[122] Over the twenty-three years since, the Inter-American Court has rendered judgment in 110 cases,[123] compared to the over fifteen hundred decisions issued by the European Court in its fifty years of operation.

The OAS drafted a second treaty in 1988, expanding the "progressive development" clause in Article 26 of the American Convention.[124] Known as the Protocol of San Salvador, the Additional Protocol to the American Convention on Human Rights in the Area of Economic, Social and Cultural Rights[125] includes provisions roughly paralleling those of the Economic and Social Covenant, encompassing the rights to work, social security, health, food, and education.[126] Surpassing the ICESCR, the Protocol of San Salvador also includes a provision recognizing the right to a healthy environment, as well as separate articles devoted to the protection of families, children, the elderly, and the handicapped.[127]

There are important distinctions between the American Convention on Human Rights and the Protocol of San Salvador that concern the language of obligation used, as well as the enforcement mechanisms established, in each treaty. Article 1 of the American Convention obligates state parties to "undertake to respect the rights and freedoms recognized herein and to ensure to all persons subject to their jurisdiction the free and full exercise of those rights and freedoms . . ."[128] In contrast, Article 1 of the Protocol requires that parties:

> undertake to adopt the necessary measures, both domestically and through international cooperation. . ., to the extent allowed by their available resources, and taking into account their degree of development, for the purpose of achieving progressively . . . the full observance of the rights recognized. . .[129]

The more qualified obligation clause of the Protocol of San Salvador is similar to that of the Economic and Social Covenant, whereas the "respect and ensure" language of the American Convention resembles that of the Civil and Political Covenant.

In terms of enforcement mechanisms, the Protocol of San Salvador does not contemplate a commission or court to adjudicate alleged violations of economic and social rights. Rather, state parties are required to submit to the Secretary General of the OAS period reports of the progressive measures they have taken toward full observance of these rights.[130]

The Inter-American Court Speaks Out against Juarez Femicides in the "Cotton Field Case"

Illustrating the more robust nature of the obligations of states parties under Article 1 of the American Convention, in December 2009, the Inter-American Court of Human Rights found Mexico responsible for the kidnapping, mistreatment, and murder of three individuals whose bodies were found in a cotton field in the city of Juarez on November 6, 2001.[131] The deceased were two girls, named Laura Berenice Ramos Monarrez and Esmeralda Herrera Monreal, and one young woman, Claudia Ivette González. In its final ruling in the *González Case*, the court required the Government of Mexico to conduct investigations and trials of suspected perpetrators of the young women's disappearances and murders, to publically acknowledge its responsibility for their mistreatment and death, and to construct a monument to commemorate all the victims of gender-based murders in Ciudad Juarez.[132]

The "Cotton Field Case" is a significant decision in many respects, including its response to the ongoing pattern of unsolved murders of women in Juarez, Mexico, since the early 1990s. In finding the Government of Mexico responsible for their disappearance and deaths, the Inter-American Court found it significant that Ramos, Herrera, and González were kidnapped eight years after the first femicides were reported in Juarez. In addition to finding that these young women suffered deprivations of their rights to life, personal integrity, and personal liberty under Articles 4, 5, and 7 of the American Convention,[133] the court found that Mexico had the obligation "to adopt special measures of protection" to ensure these rights.[134]

In reaching its judgment in *González*, the Inter-American Court carefully analyzed the text of Article 1 of the American Convention and concluded that although Mexico did not violate its obligation to "respect" the rights of the three young women, it did violate its obligation to "ensure" their rights.[135] In essence, the court determined that the Government of Mexico lacked the overt participation in the young women's murders to have direct responsibility for the violations of their rights to life, personal integrity, and personal liberty. Nevertheless, by failing to take measures to prevent their kidnapping, mistreatment and deaths, and neglecting to vigorously investigate their deaths, Mexico was ultimately responsible for the violations of their human rights.

In late 2010, the Mexican Congress established a reparations fund for victims of human rights violations, including the next of kin of the three women disappeared in the Cotton Field Case. Despite the significance of the Inter-American Court's ruling in *González*, as of 2011, the Government of Mexico had failed to charge, convict, or censure anyone for the disappearance and murder of the three women, nor had it enacted policy reforms to improve the prevention and investigation of disappearances as ordered by the court in its judgment.[136]

c. The Banjul Charter

The African Charter on Human and Peoples' Rights, known as the Banjul Charter, was adopted by the Organization of African Unity (OAU) in 1981, and came into force in 1986.[137] It was the first among the regional human rights treaties to enumerate specific economic and social rights alongside civil and political rights. It also has separate articles devoted to group rights, and a chapter on individual duties. Burundi, Sierra Leone, and Uganda have each ratified or acceded to the Banjul Charter.[138]

Articles 1–18 of the Banjul Charter cover substantially the same individual rights as those enumerated in Articles 1–27 of the Universal Declaration of Human Rights, and the corresponding provisions of the Civil and Political Covenant, as well as the American and European Human Rights Conventions. Comparing the Banjul Charter to the UDHR, there is just one specific difference in terms of coverage: the Banjul Charter does not have an article devoted to the right to privacy, enumerated in Article 12 of the UDHR. On the other hand, it does include, in Article 12(3), "the right, when persecuted, to seek and obtain asylum." As stated above, the right to asylum is inscribed in the Universal Declaration, but not in the Civil and Political Covenant, nor in the European Convention, although it is recognized to a limited extent in the American Convention.[139]

Articles 19–24 of the Banjul Charter concern collective rights, namely, the rights of *peoples* to: equality and freedom from domination (Article 19); existence and self-determination, including freeing themselves "from the bonds of domination by resorting to any means recognized by the international community" (Article 20); free utilization of wealth and natural resources, including the right of dispossessed people whose land has been "despoiled... to the lawful recovery of its property as well as to an adequate compensation" (Article 21); economic, cultural, and social development (Article 22); "national and international peace and security" (Article 23); and "a general satisfactory environment favourable to their development" (Article 24).

The Banjul Charter includes a separate Chapter II entitled "Duties," with three articles devoted to the individual's duties to family, community, society, state, and the international community.[140] In addition to these broad provisions, individual articles of Chapter I of the Banjul Charter include what some commentators have evocatively termed "clawback" clauses, apparently providing state signatories considerable room to limit specific human rights obligations in imprecisely defined circumstances.[141] Article 6, for example, recognizes that "[e]very individual shall have the rights to liberty and to the security of his person. No one may be deprived of his freedom except for reasons and conditions previously laid down by law." Similar "subject-to-law" provisions are peppered throughout the provisions of the treaty,[142] and risk swallowing up the very rights that they proclaim.

The Banjul Charter creates an African Commission on Human and Peoples' Rights (African Commission),[143] empowered to gather documentation on human rights, investigate human rights problems, organize educational conferences, and evaluate "communications" from states and other entities alleging human rights violations by particular parties to the treaty.[144] Both interstate and individual communications are within the mandate of the commission, without the need for a special declaration by the state involved.[145] However, in the case of "other communications," Article 56 enumerates several filtering requirements that apply only to petitions from individuals, including non-anonymity, compatibility with the Banjul Charter, lack of "disparaging or insulting language" towards the state involved, and exhaustion of domestic remedies.[146]

Between 1988 and 2006, the African Commission ruled on 322 communications brought by individuals or states against other member states, including several communications concerning Uganda, Burundi, and Sierra Leone.[147] In a case involving the use of force, the commission found that Uganda and other neighboring countries had not violated the Banjul Charter when they imposed an economic embargo on Burundi in response to a 1996 military coup in which Major Pierre Buyoya was installed as president.[148] In a communication concerning the 1993 ethnic massacres in Burundi, the commission found that the Government of Burundi had violated Gaetan Bwampamye's right to a fair trial when it sentenced him to death for incitement and organizing mass atrocities without allowing him access to defense counsel or leave to appeal his conviction.[149] In a communication relating to the civil war in Sierra Leone, the commission found that the Government of Sierra Leone had violated the rights to life and fair trial in the arbitrary executions of 24 soldiers for their alleged role in a coup overthrowing President Ahmed Kabbah in 1998.[150]

In 1998, the OAU adopted a Protocol to the Banjul Charter (Banjul Protocol), for the purpose of creating an African Court on Human and Peoples' Rights (ACHPR).[151] The ACHPR was designed to act as a quasi-appellate body to the African Commission, analogous to the relationship between the Inter-American Commission and Court of Human Rights created under the auspices of the OAS. Jurisdictionally, things began to get complicated in 2001 when the OAU was converted into the African Union (AU), complete with its own primary judicial organ, the African Court of Justice, and then subsequently the Banjul Protocol entered into force in 2004. For the next four years, the ACHPR worked to harmonize its procedures with those of the African Commission, in preparation for adjudicating its first cases concerning alleged violations of human and peoples' rights inscribed in the Banjul Charter. At the same time, discussions were underway to merge the ACHPR with the African Court of Justice.

The efforts of the member states of the African Union to create a consolidated court with broad subject matter jurisdiction came to fruition in 2008 with the adoption of the Protocol on the Statute of the African Court of Justice and Human Rights (ACJHR).[152] On December 15, 2009, this new African tribunal published its first ruling, denying the admissibility of a claim brought by Senegal. Two years later, the ACJHR rendered its first judgment on the merits, in a claim brought by the African Commission alleging massive violations of the human rights of civilians in Libya's Arab Spring uprising. On March 25, 2011, the ACJHR issued provisional measures, ordering Libya to "immediately refrain from any action that would result in loss of life or violation of physical integrity of persons" and to report on steps taken to implement its order within fifteen days.[153] The two-week deadline expired without compliance by the Government of Libya.

d. The Arab Charter on Human Rights

In 1994, the League of Arab States, an international organization composed of Arabic-speaking countries, adopted the Arab Charter on Human Rights (Arab Charter).[154] In its Preamble, the Arab Charter reaffirms the principles of the UN Charter, the Universal Declaration, the two International Covenants and the Cairo Declaration on Human Rights in Islam. The Preamble also "[a]cknowledg[es] the close interrelationship between human rights and world peace," and affirms that "the eternal principles of brotherhood and equality... were firmly established by the Islamic Shari'a and the other divinely-revealed religions...."[155] With respect to Articles 1–39, state parties "ensure" to all individuals within their territories enjoyment of a spectrum of individual civil and political as well as economic and social rights roughly equivalent to those set forth in the Universal Declaration as well as the Banjul Charter, "without any distinction on grounds of race, colour, sex, language, religion, political opinion, national or social origin, property, birth or other status and without any discrimination between men and women."[156]

Like Article 4 of the Civil and Political Covenant, Article 4 of the Arab Charter allows for limited derogations of human rights obligations "in time of public emergency which threatens the life of the nation." The specific rights that are nonderogable are "the prohibition of torture and degrading treatment, return to one's country, political asylum, trial, the inadmissibility of retrial for the same act, and the legal status of crime and punishment."[157] The Arab Charter is unique among human rights treaties in enumerating the right to asylum as a peremptory norm. Although the Arab Charter does not include articles specifically devoted to peoples' rights as in the Banjul Charter, it does include a provision on the right of minorities "to enjoy their culture or to follow the teachings of their religion."[158]

Like the Banjul Charter, the Arab Charter includes claw-back measures, starting with broad language that any restrictions on rights are legitimate only "where such is provided by law and deemed necessary to protect the national security and economy, public order, health or morals or the rights and freedoms of others."[159] There are also individual subject-to-law clauses with respect to freedom of religion and the right to form trade unions.[160]

Finally, the Arab Charter establishes a Committee of Experts on Human Rights, empowered to receive and evaluate reports from state parties regarding fulfillment of their treaty obligations.[161] Although the Committee of Experts is required to submit its assessment of these reports to the Standing Committee on Human Rights at the Arab League, it is not empowered to receive interstate or individual petitions alleging human rights violations under the Arab Charter.[162] Thus, among the four regional or common language-based international organizations that we have surveyed, the Arab League is the only one that as of 2011 lacks a quasi-judicial mechanism for the enforcement of human rights norms.

D. HUMAN RIGHTS PROVISIONS IN NATIONAL CONSTITUTIONS

Human rights protections are also laid out in the constitutions of individual states. Those of our three case studies are particularly illuminating in the differing approaches they take to the type of rights enumerated, the mechanisms for enforcement, and the presence or absence of provisions respecting duties.

1. The Constitution of Uganda

Uganda's constitution incorporates both civil-political rights and economic, social, and cultural rights, like the UDHR, the Banjul Charter, and the Constitution of Burundi.[163] Chapter Four of the constitution enumerates most of the substantive civil, political, economic, social, and cultural rights found in Articles 2–28 of the UDHR. Moreover, in addition to provisions devoted to the rights to education, a healthy environment, a safe workplace, and cultural expression, the Constitution of Uganda includes additional human rights protections not envisioned in the UDHR. The Constitution of Uganda has separate articles devoted to the rights of women, children, persons with disabilities, and minorities. It expands upon the UDHR's impermissible grounds for discrimination to include disability, in addition to gender, ethnicity, social standing, and political opinion. It defines affirmative action as a lawful mechanism for remedying past discrimination.

Finally, like Article 4 of the Civil and Political Covenant, Articles 43 and 44 of Uganda's constitution specifically define and limit the scope of governmental emergency powers utilized in time of national crisis. In Article 44, the Ugandan constitution enumerates those rights deemed to be nonderogable, including the rights to humane treatment, freedom from slavery, fair trial, and habeas corpus.[164] Perhaps more significant than the rights specified in Article 44 is the qualified language utilized in Article 43 with respect to the government's prerogative to invoke "national security" as a justification for suspending individual rights. Article 43(b)(2) makes it crystal-clear that security concerns are never a valid basis for arbitrary detention. The preclusion of special administrative measures for extrajudicial detention is notable, and, in this respect, the Ugandan constitution accords states less discretion in responding to self-declared states of emergency than the ICCPR.[165]

2. The Constitution of Sierra Leone

To begin with, the Constitution of Sierra Leone is notable for its focus on civil and political rights to the exclusion of most of the economic, social, and cultural rights referenced in Articles 22–28 of the Universal Declaration of Human Rights.[166] This approach parallels that of the Civil and Political Covenant, as well as the European and American Conventions. In contrast, the Banjul Charter and both the Ugandan and Burundian Constitutions encompass a broader spectrum of human rights.

Chapter III of Sierra Leone's Constitution enumerates most of the substantive civil and political rights set forth in Articles 2-21 of the Universal Declaration of Human Rights. Notably absent are the right to a nationality (UDHR, Article 15) and the right to seek and enjoy asylum (UDHR, Article 14). In accord with Article 2 of the UDHR, Article 27 of Sierra Leone's constitution prohibits discrimination on account of race, color, creed, gender, and political opinion. However, socioeconomic status, also included in the UDHR (referenced as "social origin, property, [or] birth"), is not identified as an impermissible basis for discrimination in Sierra Leone's constitution.

3. The Constitution of Burundi

Burundi's Constitution contains provisions devoted to the two typical "families" of individual rights, but, unlike the other two states' charters and like the Banjul Charter, also includes a subsection devoted to individual duties.[167] The Preamble of Title II specifically mentions the Universal Declaration of Human Rights, as well as the African Charter on Human and Peoples' Rights (the Banjul Charter), the Convention on the Elimination of all Forms of Discrimination Against Women, and the Convention on the Rights of the Child. Articles 19–51 proclaim civil and political rights similar to those enumerated in the Ugandan and Sierra Leonean Constitutions. Articles 52–58 concern economic and social rights along the lines of those contained in the Ugandan Constitution and the Banjul Charter.

Burundi's Constitution has broader de jure human rights protections than those of either Sierra Leone or Uganda in several respects. In the context of several articles relating to children, Article 45 prohibits a child from being "directly utilized in an armed conflict;" Article 50 recognizes the right of asylum "in conditions defined by law;" and Article 58 protects intellectual property rights.

Nevertheless, the Constitution of Burundi also employs the kind of clawback or subject-to-law language seen in the Banjul Charter. For example, with regard to administrative detention, Article 42 reads that "no one may be subjected to security measures unless in cases and forms provided by the law [and] notably for reasons of public order or State security."[168] More broadly, Article 61 provides that "no one may abuse rights recognized by the Constitution or the law in order to compromise national unity, peace, democracy, [or] Burundian independence. . ."[169] Finally, unlike Uganda's Constitution, the Constitution of Burundi does not enumerate those rights that are nonderogable even in declared states of emergency.

Like the Banjul Charter, but unlike the Constitutions of Sierra Leone and Uganda, Title II of the Constitution of Burundi contains a separate section (Articles 62–74) on the "Fundamental Duties of the Individual and the Citizen." A few notable examples are the duty not to discriminate against one's fellow citizens (Article 62) and general duties toward family and society (Article 63). There are also other provisions expressing deference to so-called national interests, which may serve to justify state-imposed limitations on the full enjoyment of individual human rights in circumstances the government deems extraordinary. These interests include the duty to "preserve and reinforce national unity . . ." (Article 64), the duty to "safeguard and reinforce respect and harmony" (Article 67) and the duty to "preserve and reinforce Burundian cultural values" (Article 68).

At the same time, appeals to "national unity" and "respect and harmony" in Burundi's constitution have the potential to strengthen a more pluralistic culture in that country in the aftermath of its civil war. References to "ethnic balance" in Burundi's constitution as well as "cultural values" in its Arusha peace accords are further discussed in Chapter 9.

CONCLUSION

It is fitting to conclude this digest of international human rights law with a consideration of how individual countries weigh human rights protections in times of national crisis. Armed conflict, particularly civil war, throws the nation into an existential crisis in cultural, economic, political, and constitutional terms. Countries with a strong tradition of the rule of law, and the expectation that power will be exercised with restraint, have more judicial resources at their disposal in charting a course towards durable peace and post-conflict reconciliation. In the following chapter, we consider international criminal law as a normative framework for seeking individual accountability for war criminals and perpetrators of crimes against humanity.

NOTES

1. Universal Declaration of Human Rights (UDHR or Universal Declaration), GA Res. 217A (III), U.N. Doc. A/810 at 71 (1948), art. 1.
2. African [Banjul] Charter on Human and Peoples' Rights, *adopted*, June 27, 1981, *entered into force*, Oct. 21, 1986, OAU Doc. CAB/LEG/67/3 Rev. 5 (1981), Preamble.
3. An alternative view of human rights is presented by Dean Makau Mutua of SUNY Buffalo Law School. Mutua suggests that the deep Western roots of the human rights movement limit its liberating potential. He points out that the very language of human rights, with its emphasis on individual liberties, reinforces the ideological and economic dominance of the major industrial powers. For the human rights movement to more fully realize its pluralistic and universal potential, he argues, it must incorporate deeper linkages with the value systems of local cultures of the North and South. *See generally*, MAKAU MUTUA, HUMAN RIGHTS: A POLITICAL AND CULTURAL CRITIQUE (University of Pennsylvania Press, 2008).
4. *See* Kenyan National Anthem, lyrics, *available at* http://www.statehousekenya.go.ke/anthem.htm.
5. In 1941, President Franklin Delano Roosevelt made his famous "Four Freedoms" speech, in which he stressed the importance and interdependence of freedom of speech, freedom of worship, freedom from want, and freedom from fear. *See* President Franklin D. Roosevelt, Message to Congress, Jan. 6, 1941.
6. *See*, UDHR, *op. cit.*, Preamble, para. 1.
7. *See, e.g.*, International Covenant on Economic, Social and Cultural Rights (ICECSR or Economic and Social Covenant), *infra*, Preamble, para. 1 (verbatim text from the Preamble of the Universal Declaration ["recognition of the ... equal and inalienable rights of all members of the human family is the foundation of freedom, justice and peace in the world"]); *see also* International Covenant on Civil and Political Rights (ICCPR), *infra*, Preamble, para. 1 (identical passage from the Universal Declaration); and International Convention on the Elimination of All Forms of Racial Discrimination (CERD), *infra*, Preamble, para. 7 (recognizing that "discrimination ... is capable of disturbing peace and security among peoples ...").
8. *See*, United Nations Declaration on the Rights of Indigenous Peoples (UNDRIP), *op. cit.*
9. *See* United Nations Millennium Declaration, UNGA Res. 55/2 (A/55/L.2), Sept. 8, 2000, para. 19, *available at* http://www.un.org/millennium/declaration/ares552e.htm. The 2000 Declaration established eight benchmarks for 2015: (1) reducing extreme poverty and hunger by one-half; (2) achieving universal primary education; (3) promoting gender equity; (4) reducing infant mortality by two-thirds; (5) reducing maternal mortality by three-quarters; (6) combating HIV/AIDS; (7) ensuring environmental sustainability; and, (8) developing a global partnership for development.
10. *See* UNDP *Human Development Report* for 2010 at 227, *available at* http://hdr.undp.org/en/media/HDR_2010_EN_Complete_reprint.pdf.
11. *See* the UNDP *Human Development Report* for 2010 at 227. *See also* UN Office of the High Representative for Least Developed Countries, Landlocked Developing Countries and Small Island Developing States (UNOHRLLS), "Least Developed Countries: Country

Profiles," *available at* http://www.unohrlls.org/en/ldc/related/62/. The UNOHRLLS considers 48 countries to be the least developed, of which 33 are in Africa, 14 are in Asia, and 1 is in Latin America (Haiti). *Id.*

12. For example, in 2004, the United States had a gross domestic product (GDP) of $41,890 per capita, of which 6.9 percent went to public health expenditures. Yet, in Malawi that same year, with $667 GDP per capita, 9.6 percent was devoted to public health. *See* the UNDP *Human Development Report* for 2007/2008 at 229 (US GDP), 247 (US public health expenditures), 232 (Malawi GDP), and 250 (Malawi public health expenditures), *available at* http://hdr.undp.org/en/media/HDR_20072008_EN_complete.pdf. Similarly, in 2004, Sao Tomé and Principe had a GDP of $2178 per capita, of which 9.9 percent was spent on public health. *See* the UNDP *Human Development Report* for 2007/2008 at 230 (Sao Tomé GDP) and 249 (Sao Tomé public health expenditures).

13. *See* UNOHRLLS, *The Criteria for the Identification of the LDC's,* (2003), *available at* http://www.un.org/special-rep/ohrlls/ldc/list.htm.

14. *See* UNDP *Human Development Report* for 2010 at 227.

15. *See* UNDP *Human Development Report* for 2010 at 26 and 224. The *Human Development Report* for 2007/2008 includes a fuller description of the "human development index": "The human development index (HDI) is a composite index that measures the average achievements in a country in three basic dimensions of human development: a long and healthy life; access to knowledge; and a decent standard of living. These basic dimensions are measured by life expectancy at birth, adult literacy and combined gross enrolment in primary, secondary and tertiary level education, and gross domestic product (GDP) per capita in Purchasing Power Parity US dollars (PPP US$), respectively. . . . the HDI offers a powerful alternative to GDP per capita as a summary measure of human well-being." *See* the UNDP *Human Development Report* for 2007/2008 at 225.

16. *See* UNDP *Human Development Report* for 2010 at 146.
    For a critique of the use of gross domestic product (GDP) as a meaningful reflection of the health of an economy, see the work of Eric Zencey, professor of historical and political studies at Empire State College. Zencey points out the GDP is essentially a measure of market-based expenditures which excludes the value of both "natural-capital services," such as the sun-drying of clothes, and noncompensated services, including volunteer work and the unpaid rearing of children. Moreover, GDP does not differentiate between expenditures that constitute benefits, such as spending on education, and those that constitute losses, such as spending on the devastation caused by flooding and hurricanes. Zencey recommends renaming GDP as *gross domestic transactions* and then creating a new measure of *net economic welfare*. "[W]hat we need is not simply a measurement of how much money passes through our hands each quarter, but an indicator that will tell us if we are really and truly gaining ground in the perennial struggle to improve the material conditions of our lives." *See* Eric Zencey, *G.D.P. R.I.P.,* N.Y. TIMES, A15, August 10, 2009.

17. *See* UNDP *Human Development Report* for 2010 at 143, 146. The United States is ranked fourth in the world, with an HDI of 902. *Id.* at 143.

18. *See* UNDP *Human Development Report* for 2010 at 145, 146.

19. UNDP stresses that it is a "user" rather than a "producer" of statistics, combining and presenting data from a variety of UN-affiliated and NGO sources. *See* UNDP *Human Development Report* for 2010 at 137.

20. *See* UNDP *Human Development Report* for 2010 at 146.

21. *See id.*

22. *See id.* By comparison, for the world's richest countries, life expectancy is 80.3 years, average years of schooling are 11.3, and GNI per capita is $37,225. *Id.*

23. *See* UNDP *Human Development Report* for 2010 at 145, 146.

24. *See id.* at 156, 158, 159.
25. John Siebert, *Addressing Armed Violence in Development Programming*, PLOUGHSHARES MONITOR 29, 1: 1 (Spring 2008), *available at* http://www.ploughshares.ca/libraries/monitor/monm08e.pdf, citing Project Ploughshares, *Human Development and Armed Conflicts, 1997–2006 (2007)*, *available at* http://www.ploughshares.ca/imagesarticles/ACR07/humdev06.pdf.
26. *See generally*, Pinstrup-Andersen and Satoru Shimokawa, *Do Poverty and Poor Health and Nutrition Increase the Risk of Armed Conflict Onset?* FOOD POL'Y 33, 6: 513–520 (Dec. 2008) (the authors conclude that government policies that improve access to food and health care enhance stability).
27. In UNDP's 1991 HUMAN DEVELOPMENT REPORT, 127 countries were designated as "developing countries" as opposed to the 33 states identified as "industrial countries." Of the 127 developing countries in 1991, Sierra Leone was ranked 127th, with an HDI of .048, Burundi 106th, with an HDI of .177, and Uganda 101st, with an HDI of .204. For comparative purposes, in 1991, Japan was in 1st place, with an HDI of .993, and the United States was in 7th, with an HDI of .976. *See* United National Development Programme, HUMAN DEVELOPMENT REPORT 1991 (Oxford University Press) at 13, Table 1.1, "HDI ranking for industrial countries" and 16, Table 1.2, "HDI ranking for developing countries," both available at http://www.arab-hdr.org/publications/other/undp/hdr/1991/hdr-e.pdf.
28. In UNDP's 2007/2008 HUMAN DEVELOPMENT REPORT, all 177 countries for which data was available were included in a single ranking. Of the 177, Sierra Leone was 177th, with an HDI of .336, Burundi was 167th, with an HDI of .413, and Uganda was 154th, with an HDI of .505. Again for comparative purposes, Iceland was ranked in 1st place with an HDI of .968, Japan had moved to 7th place, with an HDI of .953, and the United States was in 12th place, with an HDI of .951. *See* UNDP HUMAN DEVELOPMENT REPORT FOR 2007/2008: HUMAN SOLIDARITY IN A DIVIDED WORLD (Oxford University Press) at 229–32, Table 1, "Human Development Index," *available at* http://hdr.undp.org/en/media/HDR_20072008_EN_Complete.pdf.

In compiling its statistics for 2010, UNDP slightly adjusted its HDI calculation methodology, such that countries were ranked out of a total of 169, rather than the previous 177 for 2007/2008. Uganda, Sierra Leone and Burundi retained similar relative positions in 2010, ranked 143rd, 158th, and 166th out of 167 countries, respectively. Notably, all three were assigned lower HDI values in 2010 than they had been two years previous. Sierra Leone went from an HDI for 2007/2008 of .336 to an HDI for 2010 of .317. Uganda dipped from an HDI for 2007/2008 of .505 to an HDI for 2010 of .422. Finally, Burundi descended from an HDI of .413 for 2007/2008 to .282 in 2010. *Compare* UNDP's HUMAN DEVELOPMENT REPORT for 2010 at 145, 146, *with* UNDP's HUMAN DEVELOPMENT REPORT for 2007/2008 at 229–32.
29. *See* http://www.freedomhouse.org/template.cfm?page=351&ana_page354&year=2009.
30. *Id.*
31. *See* http://www.freedomhouse.org/uploads/fiw09/tablesandcharts/Combined%20Average%20Rathings%20(Independent%20Countries)%20FIW%202008.pdf.
32. *See* http://www.freedomhouse.org/template.cfm?page=228&year=2009&country=7725.

Transparency International (TI), a research institution that focuses on anticorruption measures and good government, also ranks countries based on their anti-corruption programs and policies. TI has developed a corruption perception index (CPI), which assigns individual countries a score from 0 to 10, with 10 indicating the highest degree of good government. Uganda received a 2.6 CPI score, and was ranked 126 out of 180 countries surveyed (a position shared with Eritrea, Ethiopia, Guyana, Honduras, Indonesia, Libya, and Mozambique). For comparative purposes, the United States received a 7.3 CPI score, and was ranked 18th out of 180 countries. Denmark, New Zealand, and Sweden shared first place, with a 9.3 CPI. *See* www.transparency.org/policy_research/surveys_indices/cpi/2008.

33. *See* http://www.freedomhouse.org/template.cfm?page=363&year=2009&country=7699. Transparency International assigned Sierra Leone a 1.9 CPI (out of a possible 10) and a rank of 158 of 180 countries surveyed in the area of good governance. *See* www.transparency.org/policy_research/surveys_indices/cpi/2008.
34. *See* http://www.freedomhouse.org/template.cfm?page=22&year=2009&country=7578. Transparency International assigned Burundi a 1.9 corruption perception index score, and a rank of 158 out of 180 countries surveyed, the same score and position assigned to Sierra Leone (as well as Angola, Azerbaijan, Congo Republic, the Gambia, Guinea Bissau, and Venezuela). *See* www.transparency.org/policy_research/surveys_indices/cpi/2008.
35. *See* Chapter 1, Section B(5) on "The Porous Border between Primary and Secondary Sources."
36. *See* UDHR, Preamble.
37. *See* UDHR, art. 2.
38. *See* UN Charter, art. 1(1) and (2).
39. *See* African (Banjul) Charter, *op. cit.*, arts. 19–24.
40. United Nations Declaration on the Rights of Indigenous Peoples (UNDRIP), *adopted* Sept. 13, 2007, G.A. Res. 61/295, U.N. Doc. A/RES/47/1 (2007).
41. *See* UNDRIP, art. 8 (right of indigenous peoples to cultural preservation), 11 (right to revitalization of indigenous cultural traditions), art. 12 (right to practice and teach indigenous spiritual traditions), art. 13 (right to revitalization of indigenous languages), and art. 26 (collective rights to use land and resources that indigenous peoples have traditionally owned or used).
42. *See* UDHR, art. 30.
43. Under US Supreme Court jurisprudence, the state action requirement continues to circumscribe judicial remedies for alleged violations of the equal protection clause of the Fourteenth Amendment. A significant degree of state involvement must be proven before acts of discrimination at the hands of private parties are deemed unconstitutional. *See* Moose Lodge No. 107 v. Irvis, 407 US 163, 173 (1972) ("where the impetus for the discrimination is private, the State must have 'significantly involved itself with the invidious discrimination'"), citing Reitman v. Mulkey, 387 US 269, 380 (1967).
44. Convention on the Prevention and Punishment of the Crime of Genocide, *adopted*, Dec. 9, 1948, *entered into force*, Jan. 12, 1951, 78 UNTS 277.
45. *See* http://www.ohchr.org/EN/NEWSEVENTS/Pges/GenocideConvention.aspx. A plausible reason that at least some of the remaining 54 states failed to ratify the Genocide Convention is the exclusion of political and other social groups from the treaty's definition of genocide, and the concern that this exclusion was calculated to shield agents of the Soviet Union, or certain Allied Powers, from prosecution for the crime of genocide in the aftermath of World War II. *See* ROBERT GELLATELY AND BEN KIEMAN, THE SPECTER OF GENOCIDE: MASS MURDER IN HISTORICAL PERSPECTIVE (Cambridge University Press, 2003) at 267.
46. Accession, like ratification, is a method by which a state may give its consent to be bound by a treaty. For countries that use accession to become party to a treaty, the term signifies that the treaty had already entered into force (because the requisite number of state ratifications had been secured) by the time that the state decided to give its consent to be bound to the treaty. For further discussion of treaty ratification and accession, *see* MARK W. JANIS, AN INTRODUCTION TO INTERNATIONAL LAW, *op. cit.*, at 22.

47. Information on Sierra Leone's signing or ratification of international human rights treaties is available at http://www1.umn.edu/humanrts/research/ratification-sierraleone.html. The Rome Statute of the International Criminal Court is discussed in Chapter 4.
48. *See* Genocide Convention, art. II.
49. Use of the term *genocide* is somewhat controversial in the context of the Khmer Rouge's reign of terror in Cambodia from 1975–1979, in which upwards of 1.5 million Cambodians were killed, many buried in mass graves. Although some victims were non-Khmer, particularly ethnic Karen, most were perceived or actual members of the political opposition. Some scholars argue that genocide charges against Khmer Rouge perpetrators are supported by the language of the treaty. *See generally* Hurst Hannum, "Genocide in Cambodia: The Sounds of Silence," 11 HUM. RTS. Q. 82 (1989). Other scholars insist that the plain meaning of Article II of the treaty requires the intent to destroy an ethnic or religious group "as such." *See* STEVEN R. RATNER AND JASON S. ABRAMS, ACCOUNTABILITY FOR HUMAN RIGHTS ATROCITIES IN INTERNATIONAL LAW: BEYOND THE NUREMBERG LEGACY 285–87 (2nd Ed. 2001).

    The drafters of the Genocide Convention were called to action by the tragedy of the European Holocaust, in which millions of Jewish victims were clearly identified as members of a distinct religious and ethnic community. Nevertheless, large numbers of political opponents of the Nazis were also murdered, including Communists, as well as members of certain disfavored social groups, including gays and gypsies or Roma people. In light of this history, the application of the term *genocide* to political and social groups may be in keeping with the original spirit of the Convention itself.
50. Genocide Convention, art. II (a)–(c).
51. *Id.*, arts. IV (regarding responsibility to punish) and III (punishable acts).
52. *Id.*, art. IV.
53. *Id.*, art. VIII.
54. *See* ICCPR, art. 6(3) (recognizing that the prohibition against genocide is non-derogable) and the ICC Statute, art. 6. The Statute of the International Criminal Court will be further studied in Chapter 4.
55. *See* the Supplementary Convention on the Abolition of Slavery, the Slave Trade, and Institutions and Practices Similar to Slavery, 226 UNTS 3, *adopted*, Sept. 7, 1956, *entered into force*, Apr. 30, 1957; *see also* the International Convention on the Suppression and Punishment of the Crime of Apartheid, 1015 UNTS 243, *adopted*, Nov. 30, 1973, *entered into force*, July 18, 1976.
56. The treaties against apartheid and genocide lack the broad assignation of the 1949 Geneva Conventions. The Apartheid Convention has 107, and the Genocide Convention has 140, compared to the almost universal status of the Geneva Conventions. Treaty ratification information is available at http://www1.umn.edu/humanrts/instree/auox.htm.
57. *See* CASS R. SUNSTEIN, THE SECOND BILL OF RIGHTS: FDR'S UNFINISHED REVOLUTION AND WHY WE NEED IT MORE THAN EVER 100–02 (Basic Books, 2004).
58. Uganda acceded to the ICESCR on January 21, 1987, and to the ICCPR on June 21, 1995. There is an Optional Protocol to the ICCPR, which concerns petitions by individuals alleging violations of their rights under the treaty. Uganda acceded to the Optional Protocol on November 14, 1995. Burundi acceded to both the ICESCR and the ICCPR on May 9, 1990, but has not acceded to the Optional Protocol. Sierra Leone acceded to the two Covenants and the Optional Protocol August 23, 1996.
59. ICESCR, *adopted*, Dec. 19, 1966, *entered into force*, Jan. 3, 1976, 999 UNTS 3.
60. *Id.*, Preamble ("the ideal of free human beings enjoying freedom from fear and want can only be achieved if conditions are created whereby everyone may enjoy his economic, social and cultural rights, as well as his civil and political rights.").

61. *Id.*, Preamble.
62. *Compare* UDHR, arts. 22 and 25, *with* ICESCR, arts. 9 and 11.
63. *See* ICESCR, art. 11(a) and (b).
64. ICESCR, art. 2. The last six articles of the ICESCR (Arts. 26–31) define the ways in which states may become party to the treaty, as well as its entry into force and potential amendment or modification. *Id.*, arts. 26–31.
65. In 2006, the Commission on Human Rights, a subsidiary organ of the UN Economic and Social Council (ECOSOC), was reconfigured into the larger and ideally less politicized Human Rights Council. *See* http://www2.ohchr.org/english/bodies/hrcouncil/.
66. Specialized agencies of the United Nations include the Food and Agricultural Organization (FAO), the UN Children's Program (UNICEF), the UN Development Program (UNDP), the UN Environmental Program (UNEP), the World Food Program (WFP), and the World Health Organization (WHO).
67. The International Covenant on Civil and Political Rights, *adopted*, Dec. 19, 1966, *entered into force*, Mar. 23, 1967, 999 UNTS 171.
68. *Id.* Preamble ("the ideal of free human beings enjoying . . . freedom from fear and want can only be achieved if conditions are created whereby everyone may enjoy his civil and political rights, as well as his economic, social and cultural rights") ("recognition of the inherent dignity and of the equal and inalienable rights of all members of the human family is the foundation of freedom, justice and peace in the world . . .").
69. *Compare*, ICESCR, Art. 2(2) *with*, ICCPR, Art. 2(2) (states party "respect . . . the rights recognized . . . without distinction of any kind . . .).
70. *Id.*, art. 2(1).
71. *Id.*, art. 3.
72. *See* UDHR, art. 14.
73. *See* ICCPR, art. 12.
74. *See id.*, art. 13.
75. *See* Convention relating to the Status of Refugees, *infra*.
76. *Id.* art. 33.
77. *See* Jennifer Moore, *Restoring the Humanitarian Character of U.S. Refugee Law: Lessons from the International Community*, 15 BERKELEY J. INTL. L. 51, 58 (No. 1, 1997) ("under conventional as well as customary international law, all refuges are entitled to the protection of the norm of *non-refoulement*"); *see also* Joan Hartman, *The International Dimension of U.S. Refugee Law*, 15 BERKELEY J INTL. L. 1, 3 ("the United Sates is seriously out of compliance with the single most important and peremptory norm of refugee law—the prohibition on *refoulement*").
78. *See* THIRD RESTATEMENT ON FOREIGN RELATIONS LAW OF THE UNITED STATES, *op. cit.*, section 102, Reporters Note 6. As discussed in Chapter 1 of this text, the Restatement takes a kindred approach to nonderogable human rights as that expressed in the Civil and Political Covenant, including among peremptory norms of international law the prohibitions against genocide, the slave trade and apartheid, among others. *Id.*
79. 1949 Geneva Conventions, art. 3.
80. *See* Optional Protocol to the ICCPR, *adopted*, Dec. 19, 1966, *entered into force*, Mar. 23, 1976, 999 UNTS 302. A second protocol to the ICCPR was adopted 23 years later, promoting abolition of the death penalty. *See* Second Option Protocol to the ICCPR, aiming at the abolition of the death penalty, *adopted*, Dec. 15, 1989, *entered into force*, July 11, 1991, UNGA Res. 44/128, 44 UN GAOR Supp. (No. 49) at 206, UN Doc. A/44/49 (1989).
81. *See* Decision Adopted by the Human Rights Committee, Communication No. 841/198: Sierra Leone. 11/04/2008. CCPR/C/64/D/841/1998, *available at* http://www.unhchr.ch/tbs/doc.nsf/(Symbol)/f00622b37ecd6e4ac1256ad900320779?Opendocument. This case is further discussed in Chapter 8 on Sierra Leone, in the section exploring the Final Report of the Truth and Reconciliation Commission.

82. International Convention on the Elimination of All Forms of Racial Discrimination, *adopted*, Mar. 7, 1966, *entered into force*, Jan. 4, 1969, 660 UNTS 195, Preamble.
83. *Id.*, art. 1.
84. Information about the ratification of international human rights treaties by individual states is available at http://www1.umn.edu/humanrts/treaties.htm.
85. Convention on the Elimination of All Forms of Discrimination Against Women, *adopted*, Dec. 18, 1979, *entered into force*, Sept. 3, 1981, UNGA Res. 34/180, 34 UN GAOR Supp. (No. 46) at 193, UN Doc. A/34/46 (1980), art. 1.
86. *Id.*, art. 3.
87. *Id.*, art. 5(a).
88. Uganda ratified CEDAW on July 22, 1986, Burundi on January 8, 1992, and Sierra Leone on November 11, 1988. Treaty ratification information is available at http://www1.umn.edu/humanrts/treaties.htm.
89. *Id.*, arts. 17 and 18.
90. *Id.*, art. 21.
91. *Id.*, Preamble.
92. *See* González *et al.* ("Cotton Field") Case, Judgment of Nov. 16, 2009, Inter-Am. Ct. H. R. (Ser. C) at 31, n. 64 (reference to the Government of Mexico's 2005 report to the CEDAW Committee), *available at* http://www.corteidh.or.cr/docs/casos/articulos/seriec_205_ing.pdf.
93. *Id.*, at 98, para. 398.
94. *Id.*, at 38, para. 132 and n. 116 (referencing *id.* at 31, n. 64).
95. Chapter 8 on Sierra Leone includes a discussion of the Gender Bills enacted by Sierra Leone's Parliament in 2007.
96. *See* Freedom House, *Freedom in the World* 2009, http://www.freedomhouse.org/template.cfm?page=22&year=2009&country=7725 (re: Uganda), http://www.freedomhouse.org/template.cfm?page=22&year=2009&country=7578 (re: Burundi), http://www.freedomhouse.org/template.cfm?page=22&year=2009&country=7699 (re: Sierra Leone).
97. Convention Against Torture and Other Cruel, Inhuman or Degrading Treatment or Punishment, *adopted*, Dec. 10, 1984, *entered into force*, June 26, 1987, UNGA Res. 39/46, 39 UN GAOR Supp. (No. 51) at 197, UN Doc. A/39/51 (1984), Preamble.
98. *Id.*, art. 1.
99. *Id.*, arts. 2(1) ("effective legislative, administrative, judicial or other measures to prevent acts of torture in any territory under its jurisdiction"), 4 (criminalization of torture), and 15 (exclusion of testimony obtained through torture).
100. *Id.*, art. 3 ("[n]o State Party shall, expel, return (*refouler*) or extradite a person to any other State where there are substantial grounds for believing that he would be in danger of being subjected to torture").
101. *Id.*, art. 10.
102. *Id.*, art. 16.
103. *See*, Convention relating to the Status of Refugees, *infra*, Chapter 5.
104. *See*, CAT, arts. 21 and 22.
105. Under the Racial Convention, signatories "automatically" open themselves up to complaints by other states, but can choose if they would like to do the same with respect to individual petitions. *See*, CERD, arts. 11 and 14. In contrast, under the Civil and Political Covenant, signatories can avoid all complaints, by not making the requisite declaration regarding inter-state communications, and by failing to ratify the First Optional Protocol on individual petitions. *See* ICCPR, art. 41, and First Optional Protocol, art. 1.
106. With 147, the Convention against Torture has fewer parties than the two International Covenants, with 166 for the Civil and Political Covenant, and 160 for the Economic and

Social Covenant. Uganda acceded to the Convention Against Torture on November 3, 1986, Burundi acceded on February 18, 1993, and Sierra Leone ratified on April 25, 2001. Treaty ratification information is available at http://www1.umn.edu/humanrts/treaties.htm.

107. *See* [European] Convention for the Protection of Human Rights and Fundamental Freedoms (as amended by Protocols 3, 5, 8, 9, 10 and 11), *signed*, Nov. 4, 1950, *entered into force*, Sept. 3, 1953, 213 UNTS 222, Europ. TS No. 5.

108. *See* Soering v. United Kingdom, 161 Eur. Ct. H.R. (Ser. B) (1989), para. 82 (a signatory to the European Convention is prohibited under Article 1 from sending an individual to a country in which Convention rights cannot be guaranteed, and not simply from engaging in direct violations of the treaty on its own territory). *See also* European Convention, art. 1 ("[t]he High Contracting Parties shall secure to everyone within their jurisdiction the rights and freedoms defined in Section 1 of this Convention").

109. *Id.*, art. 15.

110. *Id.*, arts. 19 and 24. Until 1998, petitions filed by individuals against states were only valid if the state made a separate declaration opening itself up to individual claims. *Id.*, art. 25.

111. *See* Protocol No. 11 to the [European] Convention of Human Rights and Fundamental Freedoms, which served to restructure the control machinery established under the treaty (ETS No. 155), Strasbourg, 11.V.1994, *adopted*, May 11, 1994, *entered into force*, Nov. 1, 1998.

112. *See* BBC, Profile: European Court of Human Rights, Sept. 11, 2008, http://news.bbc.co.uk/2/hl/europe/country-profiles/4789300.stm.

113. *See* Ireland v. United Kingdom, 2 Eur. Ct. H.R. 25 (1978).

114. *See* BBC, *op. cit.*

115. *See* American Convention on Human Rights, *signed*, Nov. 22, 1969, *entered into force*, July 18, 1978, OAS Treaty Series No. 36, at 1, OAS Off. Rec. OEA/Ser. L/V/II.23 doc. rev. 2.

116. *Id.*, arts. 4 (right to life), 23 (right to participate in government) and 27 (suspension of guarantees).

117. "Every person has the right to seek and be granted asylum in a foreign territory, in accordance with the legislation of the state and international conventions, in the event he is being pursued for political offenses or related common crimes." *See* American Convention, art 22(7). Article 22 is qualified for several reasons. The mention of state "legislation" appears to defer to national rules and procedures for processing asylum claims, which may differ considerably in their eligibility criterion. Moreover, the reference to "being pursued for political offenses" appears to limit the concept of persecution, the heart of the refugee definition, to a narrow set of circumstances that might not include the targeting of members of ethnic, religious or other social groups as well as political dissidents. On the other hand, Article 22 also defers to "international conventions", including such treaties as the 1951 Convention relating to the Status of Refugees, which articulates a much broader concept of persecution. *Compare* American Convention, art. 22(7), and Refugee Convention, art. 1, *infra*. The definition of persecution, and refugee law more generally, will be explored in Chapter 5.

118. *Id.*, art. 26.

119. *Id.*, art. 33.

120. *Id.*, arts. 44 (individual petitions) and 45 (interstate petitions).

121. Velasquez Rodriguez Case, Judgment of July 29, 1988, Inter-Am. Ct. H. R. (Ser. C) Nov. 4 (1988), *available at* http://www1.umn.edu/humanrts/iachr/b_11_12d.htm.

122. *Id.*, at para. 119 (finding of fact that Velasquez Rodriguez was disappeared at the hands of individuals affiliated with the Honduran Armed Forces), para. 186 (legal conclusion of a violation of his right to personal liberty under Article 7 of the American Convention on

Human Rights [ACHR]), para. 187 (legal conclusion of a violation of his right to personal integrity under Article 5) and para. 188 (legal conclusion of a violation of his right to life under Article 4).
123. Santiago Canton, "The Inter-American Commission on Human Rights: 50 years of Advances and the New Challenges," AM. Q., published by the Americas Society and the Council of the Americas, Summer 2009, http://www.americasquarterly.org/Inter-American-Commission-Human-Rights.
124. American Convention, art. 26.
125. Additional Protocol to the American Convention on Human Rights in the Area of Economic, Social and Cultural Rights, *signed*, November 17, 1988, *entered into force*, November 16, 1999, OEA/Ser.L.V/II.82 doc.6 rev.1 at 67 (1992), arts. 11 (healthy environment), 15 (protection of families), 16 (rights of children), and 17 (protection of the elderly).
126. *Id.*, arts. 6–8 (related to labor conditions and organization), 9 (social security), 10 (health), 12 (food), and 13 (education).
127. *Id.*, arts. 15 (families), 16 (children), 17 (elderly), and 18 (handicapped).
128. *See* American Convention, art. 1.
129. *See* Protocol of San Salvador, art. 1.
130. *Id.*, art. 19.
131. González, *et al.* ("Cotton Field") Case, Judgment of November 16, 2009, Inter-Am. Ct. H. R. (Ser. C) at 146 (section X ["Operative Paragraphs], para. 4) ("State violated rights to life, personal integrity and personal liberty recognized in Articles 4(1), 5(1), 5(2) and 7(1) of the American Convention, in connection with the general obligation to guarantee such rights established in Article 1(1) and the obligation to adopt domestic legal procedures established in Article 2 thereof . . . to the detriment of Claudia Ivette González, Laura Berenice Ramos Monarrez and Esmeralda Herrera Monreal . . . "), *available at* http://www.corteidh.or.cr/docs/casos/articulos/seriec_205_ing.pdf.
132. *Id.* at 147, para. 12 (investigations and trial), and 148, paras. 13 and 14 (appropriate sanctions), para. 16 (public acknowledgment of responsibility) and para. 17 (public monument commemorating Juarez femicides).
133. *Id.* at 146, para. 4, referencing the rights to life [American Convention, art. 4(1)], personal integrity [art. 5(1) and (2)], and personal liberty [art. 7(1)].
134. *Id.* at 99, para. 404.
135. *Id.* at 146, paras. 3 (re: "obligation to respect") and 4 (re: "obligation to guarantee").
136. *See* Carson Osberg, *Mexican Congress Approves Reparations Fund for Victims of Human Rights Violations to Comply With Inter-American Court Judgments*, Human Rights Brief (Center for Human Rights and Humanitarian Law, Washington College of Law, American University), March 11, 2011, *available at* http://hrbrief.org/2011/03/mexican-congress-approves-reparations-fund-for-victims-of-human-rights-violations-to-comply-with-inter-american-court-judgments/.
137. *See* African [Banjul] Charter on Human and Peoples' Rights, *adopted*, June 27, 1981, *entered into force*, Oct. 21, 1986, OAU Doc. CAB/LEG/67/3 Rev. 5 (1981).
138. Burundi acceded to the Banjul Charter on July 28, 1989; Sierra Leone ratified the Charter on September 21, 1983, and Uganda on May 10, 1986.
139. *See* Universal Declaration, art. 14, and American Convention, art. 22(7).
140. *See* Banjul Charter, arts. 27–29.
141. *See* Welch, *The African Commission on Human and Peoples' Rights: A Five-Year Report and Assessment*, 14 HUM. RTS. Q. 43, 45–49, 53–47 (1992) (referencing analysis of the Banjul Charter from African scholars such as B. Obinna Okere).
142. *See* Banjul Charter, art. 8 ("[f]reedom of conscience. . . . subject to law and order"), art. 9 ("the right to express and disseminate his opinion within the law"), art. 10 ("the right

to free association provided that he abides by the law"), art. 11 ("the right to assemble freely with others.... [s]ubject only to necessary restrictions provided by for law"), art. 12 ("the right to freedom of movement and residence ... provided he abides by the law"), art. 13 ("the right to participate freely in the government ... in accordance with the provisions of the law"), and art. 14 ("[t]he right to property shall be guaranteed [and].... [m]ay only be encroached upon in the interest of public need ... and in accordance with the provisions of appropriate laws").

143. *Id.*, art. 194.
144. *Id.*, art. 45.
145. *See id.*, arts. 47 and 55.
146. *See id.*, art. 56 (1)–(7).
147. Information about communications heard by the African Commission on Human and People's Rights is available at http://www.achpr.org/english/_info/List_Decision_Communications.html.
148. [African] Commission 157/96, Association Pour la Sauvegarde de la Paix au Burundi/ [vs.] Uganda *et al.*, May 15–29, 2003, *available at* http://www.achpr.org/english/Decison_Communication/Uganda/Comm.157-96.pdf.

   In another case involving military intervention, the Commission found that Uganda, Burundi, and Rwanda were responsible for the human rights abuses carried out by their troops stationed in the Democratic Republic of the Congo in 1998, and recommended the payment of adequate reparations. *See* [African] Commission 227/99, D. R. Congo/ [v.] Burundi, Rwanda and Uganda, May 2003, *available at* http://www.achpr.org/english/Decison_Communication/Burundi/Comm.227-99.pdf.
149. [African] Commission 231/99, Avocats Sans Frontières (on behalf of Gaetan Bwampamye)/ [v.] Burundi, October 23–November 6, 2000, *available at* http://www.achpr.org/english/Decison_Communication/Burundi/Comm.%20231-99.pdf.
150. [African] Commission 223/98, Forum of Conscience/ [v.] Sierra Leone, October 23–November 6, 2000, *available at* http://www.achpr.org/english/Decison_Communication/Sierra%20leone/Comm.223-98.pdf. The African Commission's findings in the Sierra Leone execution case are also discussed in Chapter 8 on Sierra Leone, in the section on the Final Report of the Truth and Reconciliation Commission.
151. Protocol to the African Charter on Human and People's Rights on the Establishment of an African Court on Human and People's Rights [Banjul Protocol], *adopted*, June 9, 1998, *entered into force*, Jan. 25, 2004, OAU Doc. OAU/LEG/EXP/AFCHPR/PROT (III).
152. *See* Protocol on the Statute of the African Court of Justice and Human Rights (ACJHR Protocol), July 1, 2008, 48 I.L.M. 317 (2008), *available at* http://www.africa-union.org/root/au/Documents/Treaties/text/Protocol%20on%20the%20Merged%20Court%20%20EN.pdf. The ACJHR Statute is an annex to the ACJHR Protocol itself. Article 28(b) of the Statute empowers the ACJHR to interpret any and all treaties promulgated by the African Union or its precursor, the Organization of African Unity. Article 28(c) specifically references the African Charter on Human and People's Rights (Banjul Charter) as a treaty which the African Court has jurisdiction to interpret and apply. *See* ACJHR Statute, art. 28(b) and (c).
153. *See* Human Rights Watch, "AU: Press Libya to Obey African Court's Order [in] First Ruling Against a State Sought to End Attacks on Civilians," April 19, 2011, *available at* http://www.hrw.org/en/news/2011/04/19/au-press-libya-obey-african-court-s-order. Human Rights Watch urged the African Union to pressure the Government of Libya to obey the Court order. The Protocol to the Banjul Charter mandates the Executive Council of the African Union to oversee the implementation of Court rulings. *See id.* and ACJHR Protocol.

154. *See*, Arab Charter on Human Rights (Arab Charter), *adopted* Sept. 15, 1994, *entered into force* Mar. 15, 2008, *reprinted in* 12 INT'L. HUM. RTS. REP. 893 (2005). The League of Arab States comprises 22 Arabic-speaking countries, including ten in Africa: Algeria, Comoros, Djibouti, Egypt, Libya, Mauritania, Morocco, Sudan, Somalia, and Tunisia. *See* Pact of the League of Arab States (Arab League Pact), March 22, 1945, UN Doc. A/C. 6/L. III, 70 UNTS 237. Membership in the Arab League is open to "independent Arab states." *See* Arab League Pact, art. 1. The Arab Charter is open for signature by members of the Arab League. *See* Arab Charter, art. 42.
155. *See id.*, Preamble. The paragraph regarding "Islamic Shari'a and the other divinely-revealed religions" suggests an affirmation of religious pluralism among the three Abrahamic religious traditions.
156. *Id.*, art. 2.
157. *Id.*, art. 4(c).
158. *Id.*, art. 37.
159. *Id.*, art. 4(a).
160. *Id.*, arts. 27 ("freedom of belief, thought and opinion except as provided by law") and 29 ("the right to form trade unions and the right to strike within the limits laid down by law.").
161. *See id.*, art. 40.
162. *See id.*, art. 41.
163. *See* The Constitution of the Republic of Uganda, 1995, Chapter Four ("[t]he Protection and Promotion of Fundamental and Other Human Rights and Freedoms"), arts. 20–58, *available at* http://www.ugandaembassy.com/Constitution_of_Uganda.pdf.
164. *Id.*, art. 44.
165. Article 43 of the Ugandan Constitution, regarding "General limitation on fundamental and other human rights and freedoms," provides in subsection (2) that "[p]ublic interest under this article shall not permit . . . (b) detention without trial." *See* Constitution of Uganda, art. 43. In contrast, Article 9 of the Civil and Political Covenant, which protects against arbitrary arrest and detention, is not included among those nonderogable rights enumerated in Article 4. *See* ICCPR, art. 4.
166. *See* The Constitution of Sierra Leone, 1991 (Act No. 6 of 1991), Chapter III (entitled "[t]he Recognition and Protection of Fundamental Human Rights and Freedoms of the Individual"), arts. 15–30.
167. *See* La Constitution de La République du Burundi, Loi No. 1/010 du 18 Mars 2005, Titre II ("De la Charte des Droits et des Devoirs Fondamentaux, de L'Individu et du Citoyen") [The Constitution of the Republic of Burundi, Law No. 1/0101 of March 18, 2005, Title II ("Concerning the Charter of Fundamental Rights and Duties of the Individual and Citizen")], arts. 19–74.
168. "Nul ne peut être soumis a des mesures de sûreté que dans les cas et les forms prévus par la loi notamment pour des raisons d'ordre publique ou de sécurité de L'Etat." *Id.*, art. 42.
169. "Nul ne peut abuser des droits reconnus par la Constitution ou par la loi pour compromettre l'unité nationale, la paix, la démocratie, l'indépendance du Burundi, porter atteinte à la laïcité de L'Etat ou violer de toute autre manière la présente Constitution." *Id.*, art. 61.

CHAPTER 4

International Criminal Law

Accountability for Crimes of War and Crimes Against Humanity

> [In Rwanda] the international community has again recognized and pursued a role in a process that establishes that there are certain crimes that have ramifications beyond the borders of any nation and constitute crimes against humanity. [. . .] Justice assigns responsibility, and few will deny that justice is an essential ingredient of social cohesion. . . . And even as justice is not served by punishing the accused before the establishment of guilt, neither is it served by discharging the guilty without evidence of mitigation—or remorse.
>
> Wole Soyinka[1]

International criminal law seeks to hold individuals accountable for committing offenses that attack the very fabric of our global society. This body of law is most explicitly enforced through trials conducted by transnational judicial bodies, each operating within its own distinctive geographical, temporal, and substantive framework. As examples, the Allied powers established the Nuremburg Tribunal in 1945 to try suspected Nazi war criminals; the United Nations Security Council (Security Council) in 1993 and 1994 mandated the International Criminal Tribunals for the former Yugoslavia and Rwanda to prosecute the leading perpetrators of the genocides in those two countries; the United Nations and the Government of Sierra Leone in 2002 created the Special Court for Sierra Leone to try offenders in that country's civil war; and by 2002, sixty states had ratified and brought into force the Rome Statute of the International Criminal Court (Rome Statute or ICC Statute), whose potential jurisdiction over war crimes and crimes against humanity extends throughout the world.[2]

In addition to judicial bodies operating at the global level, international criminal law is also brought to bear through domestic prosecutions in which state courts apply criminal statutes adopted by their national legislatures for the specific purpose of giving effect to international norms. Some treaties require implementation, including the Convention Against Torture (CAT or Torture Convention), which calls on each signatory to criminalize torture under its domestic law.[3] Subsequent to such domestication, the national court is invoking both national and international law when it tries an individual for specific crimes.[4]

Although legal scholars differ on this point, restorative justice should be considered an essential component of international criminal justice.[5] In reference to the classic philosophical foundations of criminal law—retribution, deterrence, rehabilitation, and moral condemnation[6]—restoration is closest to rehabilitation and adds a collective dimension. Whereas rehabilitation concerns the individual offender's return to society, restorative justice seeks the transformation and healing of the society itself. From this standpoint, international criminal law is vindicated through both traditional and modern institutions at the national and local levels that facilitate amnesty and social reintegration for offenders; economic reparations, social assistance, and political empowerment for victims; and truth-telling and reconciliation for offenders and victims alike.

Restorative justice mechanisms in Uganda, Sierra Leone, and Burundi will be explored in the three final chapters and briefly referenced in this chapter. To begin with, the Acholi communal atonement ceremony of *mato oput* has been held up as an alternative to war crimes prosecutions for at least some offenders in the Ugandan civil war.[7] Ugandan non-governmental organizations (NGOs) are also advocating for the Ugandan parliament to create a truth-telling process at the national level. Sierra Leone, adapting the South African model, established a national Truth and Reconciliation Commission (TRC) to provide assistance to victims and amnesty to offenders who publically confessed to the crimes they committed against civilians. So-called *fambul tok* ("family talk") reconciliation is also occurring at the village level.[8] Burundi's peace accord contemplates a national truth commission to "promote reconciliation, and clarify the national history,"[9] with current plans for such a mechanism to be established in 2012. Some observers suggest that *ubushingantahe*—traditional Burundian dispute resolution by panels of respected community members—may offer an alternative mechanism for trying suspected war criminals in the Burundian civil war.[10]

Alternative justice mechanisms are controversial, given the mainstream criminal law emphasis on the retributive dimension. Nevertheless, community atonement ceremonies, designed to work in tandem with national reconciliation commissions, will foster a deeper popular commitment to the rule of law than would be possible solely by virtue of remote trials conducted at the national and international level.[11] This greater confidence in the criminal and economic justice systems at the grassroots level may also help prevent an eventual return to violence as the social roots of the conflict are more meaningfully addressed.

This chapter will focus on the formally constituted international criminal courts, namely, those tribunals created by international treaty or United Nations resolutions to try suspected perpetrators of crimes against humanity and war crimes. Later chapters will examine in greater depth the role of amnesty, truth-telling and remedial mechanisms in national dialogues on postconflict reconstruction.[12] Nevertheless, this survey and assessment of international criminal justice mechanisms adopts a broader framework that recognizes the basic kinship between national reconciliation and the international rule of law.

International crimes include any wrongful acts defined as such by customary international law or international treaties, from piracy and human trafficking to terrorism and torture. This chapter will focus on offenses that occur in time of armed conflict, meaning war crimes, as well as acts of brutality against whole communities, defined as crimes against humanity. As explored in Chapter 2, war crimes are violations of international humanitarian law, which seeks to regulate the conduct of armed conflict through such rules as the prohibition against military attacks on civilians. As noted in Chapter 3, crimes against humanity constitute large-scale human rights violations that may occur in time of war or peace, including genocide, apartheid, and slavery, as well as rape, torture, and other human rights abuses inflicted wholesale on the members of particular communities.

A. THE NUREMBERG TRIBUNAL

The International Military Tribunal (IMT or Nuremberg Tribunal) was established in 1945 by the Agreement for the Prosecution and Punishment of the Major War Criminals of the European Axis of August 8, 1945 (London Agreement, Nuremberg Statute, or Nuremberg Charter),[13] a treaty between the four World War II victor powers: France, the Union of Soviet Socialist Republics (USSR or Soviet Union), the United Kingdom (UK), and the United States (US). Of the twenty-one Nazi leaders who were tried before the IMT, eleven received death sentences, seven received terms of imprisonment, and three were acquitted.[14] Although both the Nuremberg Tribunal and the International Military Tribunal for the Far East (IMTFE or Tokyo Tribunal) have been criticized as manifestations of "victors' justice,"[15] many of Nuremberg's jurisprudential principles have withstood the tests of time including limitations on the defense of obeying orders[16] and the affirmation of the rule of *nullen crimen sine lege,* or the prohibition against ex post facto criminal liability. In expressing fidelity to the principle of *nullen crimen sine lege,* the Nuremberg Tribunal was asserting that the defendants were aware that international law already forbade the atrocities for which they were convicted.[17]

The London Agreement established three sets of crimes within IMT jurisdiction—crimes against peace, crimes against humanity, and war crimes. Both war crimes and crimes against humanity were considered violations of the *jus in bello* governing the conduct of war. In contrast, crimes against peace were violations of the *jus ad bellum,* signifying that there was no justification for the decision to use military force in the first instance. Notably, the crime of genocide was not enumerated in the IMT Statute.[18] Although the Nuremberg Tribunal was fundamentally an international reckoning with the "final solution," the term *genocide* was not defined by treaty until the adoption of the Convention on the Prevention and Punishment of the Crime of Genocide (Genocide Convention) in 1948.[19]

In Article 6, the Nuremberg Statute provided definitions of the crimes within its jurisdiction. *Crimes against peace* encompassed "planning, preparation, initiation or waging of a war of aggression, or a war in violation of international treaties . . . ."[20] *War crimes* denoted "violations of the laws or customs of war, . . . includ[ing] . . . murder, ill-treatment or deportation to slave labor . . . of civilian population. . ., murder or ill-treatment of prisoners of war . . ., killing of hostages, plunder . . ., wanton destruction of cities . . ., or devastation not justified by military necessity."[21] "*Crimes against humanity,* finally, meant "murder, extermination, enslavement, deportation, and other inhumane acts committed against any civilian population, before or during the war, or persecutions on political, racial or religious grounds. . ."[22]

Crimes against peace constituted the category of Nuremberg crimes most in need of elaboration. It led to a very slow evolution in the definition of aggression.[23] The 2010 Amendments to the Rome Statute of the International Criminal Court on the crime of aggression (Rome Statute or ICC Statute) defines acts of aggression and crimes of aggression, although these definitions will not become operational until at least 2017. The 2010 Amendments to the Rome Statute are further discussed later in this chapter, in Section D. Contrastingly, the definition of *war crimes* set forth in Article 6(b) of the Nuremberg Statute remains an effective distillation of the essential content of customary international humanitarian law.

Nuremberg's enumeration of war crimes was elaborated upon by the 1949 Geneva Conventions and their 1977 Additional Protocols, described in depth in Chapter 2. There is a particularly strong resonance between Nuremberg's Article 6(b) and the Third and Fourth Geneva Conventions dealing, respectively, with the treatment of prisoners of war and civilians. The identification in the Nuremberg Statute of "devastation not justified by military necessity" as a war crime illustrates the customary norms of necessity and proportionality. This language is also consistent with the provision of Additional Protocol I to the Geneva Conventions that prohibits indiscriminate attacks, including those "which may be expected to cause incidental loss of civilian life . . . excessive in relation to the concrete and direct military advantage anticipated."[24] Importantly, both Nuremberg and Protocol I set limits on the legality of so-called collateral damage, in US parlance, in the conduct of military operations.

Finally, crimes against humanity, defined in Article 6(c) of the Nuremberg Charter, have been broadened in one very important respect since 1945. Although the essential understanding of crimes against humanity as attacks on a "civilian population" has endured, Nuremberg's reference to "inhumane acts committed. . . before or during the war" has gradually been eliminated. Crimes against humanity are still defined as wholesale attacks on communities, but the connection to armed conflict is no longer necessary. As we shall see below, when we trace the evolution in international criminal law from the two ad hoc tribunals to the International Criminal Court (ICC), the modern consensus is that genocide and other crimes against humanity will sometimes occur in time of war, but need not.[25]

B. THE AD HOC TRIBUNALS FOR THE FORMER YUGOSLAVIA AND RWANDA

1. The International Criminal Tribunal for the Former Yugoslavia

The International Criminal Tribunal for the former Yugoslavia (ICTY, or Yugoslav Tribunal) was established in 1993 by Resolution 827 of the UN Security Council, acting under Chapter VII of the Charter of the United Nations (UN Charter).[26] Like the Nuremberg Tribunal, the jurisdiction of the ICTY is limited both temporally and geographically, encompassing "the prosecution of persons responsible for serious violations of international humanitarian law committed in the territory of the former Yugoslavia since 1991."[27] But unlike the Nuremberg Tribunal and the ICC, both the ICTY and its sister tribunal for Rwanda lack constitutional treaties, and are instead creatures of the Security Council. As noted in Chapter 1,

Chapter VII Security Council resolutions are primary sources of international law because of explicit terms in the UN Charter that give them this obligatory character.[28] In this sense, the ultimate validity of the so-called ad hoc tribunals ultimately rests upon a multilateral treaty, as is the case for other international courts. Nevertheless, these ad hoc institutions are distinct from other transnational criminal tribunals in that their constitutional structure and powers are defined by resolutions of the Security Council.

Since 1993, over 160 individuals have been charged by the Yugoslav Tribunal, and 60 have been convicted of offenses against international law, including war crimes, genocide, and crimes against humanity, as defined in Articles 2–5 of the ICTY Statute.[29] The conflict in the former Yugoslavia is viewed as having had both international and internal dimensions. Nevertheless, the war crimes provisions of the ICTY Statute apply specifically to interstate conflicts. Thus, Article 2 of the ICTY Statute concerns "Grave breaches of the Geneva Conventions of 1949," and Article 3 relates more generally to "Violations of the Laws and Customs of War." The statute's definitions of war crimes draw in part from corresponding provisions of the 1949 Geneva Conventions and Additional Protocol I of 1977, which governs international armed conflicts. For example, Article 3 of the ICTY Statute prohibits the "wanton destruction of cities... not justified by military necessity... [and the] attack... of undefended towns..."[30] In a similar vein, Protocol I provides that "[t]he civilian population as such... shall not be the subject of attack"[31] and prohibits "an attack which may be expected to cause incidental loss of civilian life... excessive in relation to the concrete and direct military advantage anticipated."[32]

With regard to genocide, the ICTY Statute definition set forth in Article 4 is modeled on that of the Genocide Convention, which includes specific "acts committed with intent to destroy, in whole or in part, a national, ethnical, racial or religious group, as such."[33] Under the ICTY Statute, genocide entails "the *special* intent to destroy, in whole or in part, a national, ethnical, racial or religious group, as such."[34]

Like the Nuremberg Charter, Article 5 of the ICTY Statute links crimes against humanity to armed conflict, but the scope of conflicts under Article 5 is broader than the war crimes provisions in Articles 2 and 3. Listing inhumane acts including murder, enslavement, torture, and rape, the tribunal has jurisdiction to prosecute such crimes "when committed in armed conflict, whether international or internal in character, and directed against the civilian population."[35] Thus, through Articles 2, 3 and 5, the ICTY Statute encompasses wartime atrocities in both interstate and internal conflicts, whether the atrocities are deemed war crimes or crimes against humanity.

2. The International Criminal Tribunal for Rwanda

The International Criminal Tribunal for Rwanda (ICTR, or Rwandan Tribunal) was created by UN Security Council resolution[36] in the aftermath of the 1994 Rwandan Genocide, in which between five-hundred thousand and one million members of the Tutsi minority and alleged Hutu collaborators were massacred by ultranationalist Hutu militants. The tribunal was mandated to prosecute individuals for "serious violations of international humanitarian law" committed in Rwanda and neighboring countries in 1994.[37] As of November 2009, the ICTR had convicted thirty-one individuals of genocide, other crimes against humanity, and war crimes;[38] and acquitted six individuals of similar charges; and ten cases were pending appeal.[39]

In 1998, the Rwandan Tribunal became the first international criminal court to secure a conviction for genocide. The trial of Jean Kambanda, Rwanda's Prime Minister during the 1994 genocide, represented two other precedents as well: the first genocide conviction against a former head of state, and the first guilty plea in a genocide trial. Kambanda is currently serving a life sentence.[40] In 2011, the ICTR became the first international tribunal to find a woman guilty of the crime of genocide. Pauline Nyiramasuhuko, the former Rwandan Minister of Family and Women's Affairs, and her son, Arsène Ntahobali, were convicted of genocide, war crimes, and crimes against humanity. Included among the charges against Minister Nyiramasuhuko was rape as a crime against humanity. The court found that she aided and abetted rapes carried out by her son, and hence had "responsibility as a superior."[41]

Article 2 of the ICTR Statute sets forth an identical definition of genocide to that found in the ICTY Statute.[42] However, in the domain of war crimes and crimes against humanity, the Rwandan Tribunal takes a different approach than that of the Yugoslav Tribunal. Because the violence in Rwanda has been characterized as a civil war, the focus of the statute is on "[v]iolations of Article 3 common to the Geneva Conventions and of Additional Protocol II,"[43] concerning non-international armed conflicts. Perhaps more significantly, crimes against humanity before the Rwandan Tribunal are not limited to the context of armed conflict at all, but entail murder, enslavement, torture, rape, and other offenses "when committed as part of a widespread or systematic attack against any civilian population on national, political, ethnic, racial or religious grounds."[44] Thus the Rwandan Tribunal definitively eliminated the war nexus[45] requirement of both the Nuremberg and Yugoslav Charters for crimes against humanity.

C. THE SPECIAL COURT FOR SIERRA LEONE

Upwards of seventy thousand people are believed to have lost their lives in the civil conflict in Sierra Leone between 1991 and 1999, when the Government of Sierra Leone and the insurgent Revolutionary United Front (RUF) signed the Peace Agreement Between the Government of Sierra Leone and the Revolutionary United Front of Sierra Leone (Lomé Peace Agreement, Lomé Agreement, or Lomé Accord). In response to a request by the Government of Sierra Leone, and with the authorization of the UN Security Council, the UN and the Government of Sierra Leone agreed, in 2002, to establish a Special Court for Sierra Leone (the SCSL or Special Court). The Special Court was mandated to prosecute "persons who bear the greatest responsibility for serious violations of international humanitarian law and Sierra Leonean law committed in the territory of Sierra Leone since November 30, 1996."[46] Subsequent to the entry into force of the bilateral agreement between the UN and the Government of Sierra Leone, in 2002, the parties enacted the Statute of the Special Court for Sierra Leone (Special Court Statute), which further defined the structure and competence of the Special Court, including the substantive crimes falling within its jurisdiction.[47]

Thirteen individuals have been indicted by the SCSL, including five commanders of the RUF, whose rebels first invaded Sierra Leone from Liberia in 1991 under the leadership of Foday Sankoh. The charged parties also included three leaders of the Civil Defense Forces (CDF), progovernment forces organized to combat the RUF; and four high-ranking members of the Armed Forces Revolutionary Council (AFRC), former members of the Sierra Leonean Army, who allied themselves with the RUF after mounting a coup against the Government of Sierra Leone in 1997.[48] The thirteenth indictment by the SCSL was against Charles Taylor, the former president of Liberia, believed to be the primary patron of the RUF.

Of the thirteen defendants, the Special Court has convicted eight individuals of crimes against humanity and war crimes, including three RUF leaders,[49] two CDF officers,[50] and three AFRC members.[51] Foday Sankoh died in custody, one additional RUF commander died in Liberia, one CDF member died while seeking medical care, and one AFRC leader is at large after escaping detention.[52] Charles Taylor's trial entered the defense stage in July of 2009; disposition and sentencing are expected in 2012. The Special Court is notable for its prosecution and conviction of individuals from all sides of the conflict, insurgent and government-affiliated forces alike. As we shall see below, a majority of those indicted by the ICC have been affiliated with rebel movements, and those few government officials who have been indicted are not in ICC custody.

One fascinating aspect of the history and prosecutorial parameters of the Special Court is that the Lomé Accord of 1999 included an extremely broad amnesty for war criminals. RUF Corporal Foday Sankoh himself received an individual pardon.[53] Although the UN Secretary General's Special Representative, in endorsing the Lomé Accord, added a reservation limiting the scope of the amnesty to offenses not rising to the level of war crimes or crimes against humanity, the text of the treaty itself was not qualified.[54] The Lomé Accord broke down in 2000, and fighting resumed, involving the RUF, UN Peacekeepers, and British Special Forces, who arrested Foday Sankoh.[55] Thereafter, the Government of Sierra Leone set in motion the establishment of the Special Court of Sierra Leone, in 2002, and the prosecution of high-ranking members of the CDF, AFRC, and RUF for wartime atrocities, including Corporal Sankoh of the RUF.

The Special Court Statute limits the Special Court's jurisdiction to war crimes, crimes against humanity, and certain violations of Sierra Leonean law.[56] Genocide was not included in the chargeable crimes because of a lack of evidence that the atrocities against civilians in Sierra Leone were motivated by an intention to destroy an ethnic or religious community "in whole or in part," as required by the Genocide Convention.[57] Most commentators point to profound class tensions and political corruption as the primary causes of Sierra Leone's rebel war, rather than ethnic politics. These themes are further explored in Chapter 8.

With regard to violations of humanitarian law, war crimes are referenced in the Special Court Statute principally in terms of violations of Common Article 3 of the 1949 Geneva Conventions and Additional Protocol II, both of which relate to non-international armed conflict.[58] For the same reason, given the internal nature of the Sierra Leonean conflict, "grave breaches" of the Geneva Conventions are not within the jurisdiction of the Special Court.[59] The Special Court may also try "other serious violations of international humanitarian law," such as attacks on humanitarian workers and the conscription of child soldiers.[60]

Although the Special Court's competence does not extend to genocide, it does encompass other wholesale assaults on communities. Moreover, as with the Rwandan Tribunal, there is no requirement of a "war nexus" in the Special Court's definition of crimes against humanity, which the statute defines as occurring in the context of a "widespread or systematic attack against any civilian population."[61] Finally, the Special Court is empowered to try certain violations of Sierra Leonean law, including the abuse or exploitation of girls.[62]

Another unique facet of the mandate and vision of the Special Court is the fact that its jurisdiction is limited to individuals at least fifteen years old at the time that criminal acts allegedly occurred.[63] Moreover, with respect to a young person between fifteen and eighteen years old, the statute requires that he or she:

> shall be treated with dignity and a sense of worth, taking into account his or her young age and the desirability of promoting his or her rehabilitation, reintegration into and assumption of a constructive role in society, and in accordance with international human rights standards, in particular the rights of the child.[64]

Finally, when a young person comes before it, the Special Court is required to order appropriate social service interventions, from foster care to participation in disarmament and reintegration programs.[65] Effectively, Article 7 of the statute signifies that, although the conscription of child soldiers is a humanitarian law violation for which individuals may be charged, child soldiers themselves may not be tried for offenses they committed while under the age of fifteen.

D. THE INTERNATIONAL CRIMINAL COURT

The Rome Statute of the ICC was adopted on July 17, 1998, and came into force on July 1, 2002.[66] In the Preamble, state signatories commit to international cooperation in prosecuting "grave crimes" "that deeply shock the conscience of humanity."[67]

Four crimes or groups of crimes fall within ICC jurisdiction: genocide, crimes against humanity, war crimes, and aggression.[68] Although aggression was not defined in the 1998 Rome Statute,[69] amendments to the statute adopted in 2010 now define an act of aggression as a cross-border military attack, occupation, or annexation carried out by a state's armed forces in violation of the UN Charter; and a crime of aggression as the planning or execution of such an act by an individual in control of the armed forces.[70] Nevertheless, a separate amendment defers the ICC's exercise of jurisdiction over the crime of aggression until at least 2017.[71]

The other three crimes are defined in Articles 6 through 8 of the original ICC Statute. Genocide, according to Article 6, encompasses certain acts "committed with intent to destroy, in whole or in part, a national, ethnical, racial or religious group as such. . . ."[72] This definition tracks the 1948 Genocide Convention. Crimes against humanity, under Article 7, comprise certain acts "committed as part of a widespread or systematic attack directed against any civilian population with knowledge of the attack. . ."[73] The lack of reference to armed conflict in this provision indicates that the "war nexus" has been eliminated in the modern conception of crimes against humanity.

Finally, war crimes take on a very comprehensive character in Article 7 of the Rome Statute, combining grave breaches of the 1949 Geneva Conventions, "[o]ther serious violations of the laws and customs applicable in international armed conflict," Common Article 3 of the Geneva Conventions, and "[o]ther serious violations of the laws and customs applicable in armed conflicts not of an international character...."[74] Unlike the Yugoslav Tribunal, whose war crimes provisions are limited to international armed conflict, and the tribunals of Rwanda and Sierra Leone, both of which address internal conflicts, ICC jurisdiction extends fully to both international and non-international armed conflicts.

Important constraints on the potential impact of the Rome Statute are established in its "preconditions to the exercise of jurisdiction" and "issues of inadmissibility," which are set forth in Articles 12 and 17. In most cases, in order for the ICC to be able to try an individual for one of the enumerated crimes, either the crime must have occurred on the territory of a state party to the statute, or the accused must be a national of a state party.[75] If one of these two prerequisites is met, then the case may be referred to the ICC in either of two ways: referral by a state party, or commencement of an investigation by the ICC Prosecutor acting on his or her own initiative, *propio motu*.[76] There is a third way for a case to be brought to the ICC, and that is a referral by the UN Security Council acting under Chapter VII of the UN Charter. In the case of a Security Council referral, there is no requirement that the offender is a national of a party to the Rome Statue or that the offense occurred on the territory of a state party.[77] This aspect of the treaty was essential in the ICC's ability to take on the case concerning Darfur, addressed below.

Even once preconditions to jurisdiction have been met, referral of the case to the ICC is no guarantee that the court will exercise its jurisdiction. A second winnowing factor is the principle of "complementarity," which serves as an important factor in the determination of whether a case is admissible. Article 17 of the Rome Statute designates a case as *inadmissible* if the state is taking bona fide steps to prosecute domestically, or if the state has decided not to pursue the case for valid reasons not reflecting "the unwillingness or inability of the State genuinely to prosecute."[78] In such cases, the court in effect defers to the state's domestic prosecution as well as its concerted decision not to prosecute. Criminal law scholar Linda Keller argues that the pursuance of alternative justice mechanisms, including truth and reconciliation procedures, may constitute valid reasons for nonprosecution, and hence ICC inadmissibility under Article 17.[79] Article 17 also allows for a determination of inadmissibility if "[t]he case is not of sufficient gravity to justify further action by the Court."[80]

There are three other bases for nonprosecution by the ICC in addition to a finding of inadmissibility. The first is a request for such inaction by the

Security Council, under Article 16; the second is the protection against double jeopardy in cases of prior conviction by a domestic court, under Article 20; and the third is the ICC Prosecutor's discretion to defer a prosecution, which "is not in the interests of justice," under Article 53. As in the context of inadmissibility, Keller reads the interests of justice deferral to encompass situations in which meaningful alternative justice mechanisms are being pursued. She cautions that neither the ICC nor the Office of the Prosecutor "should stretch the language of the statute so far unless the [alternative justice mechanisms] meet the standards of international criminal justice."[81] Nevertheless, Keller suggests that in certain cases, such as Uganda, the "alternative" mechanisms may have a greater likelihood of success in meeting those standards than do the ICC prosecutions themselves:

> the Ugandan truth commission and *mato oput* constitute an improvement over ICC prosecution in advancing victim-conscious retribution, expressivism, and restorative justice while not falling that much farther short that the ICC in furthering [offender-focused] retribution and deterrence.[82]

As of 2011, six states have come within the jurisdiction of the ICC for the alleged occurrence on their territories of genocide, war crimes or crimes against humanity: Uganda, for crimes committed by the Lords' Resistance Army; the Democratic Republic of the Congo (DRC), for crimes committed in the Ituri region; Central African Republic (CAR), for crimes committed on its territory; the Sudan, for crimes committed in the region of Darfur; Kenya, in response to postelection violence in 2007 and 2008; and Libya, for government attacks on civilians in Libya's Arab Spring uprising.[83] The Uganda, DRC, and CAR cases were state referrals; the Security Council initiated the Darfur and Libya cases; and the ICC Office of the Prosecutor opened the Kenya case *propio motu*, or on its own initiative.[84]

Additionally, by late 2009, the ICC had initiated preliminary investigations into possible crimes against humanity in the Republic of Guinea, based on widespread reports that Presidential Guards killed, raped, and wounded hundreds of unarmed protestors inside a stadium in the capital city of Conakry on September 28, 2009.[85] Because the cases involving Kenya, Libya and Guinea are still at the preliminary stage, the discussion below is limited to the initial four ICC cases, addressing Uganda in greatest detail. The Uganda case is also discussed in Chapter 7.

1. Uganda

The civil war in northern Uganda led to the first "self-referral" to the ICC. The Government of Uganda referred the situation on its territory to the

ICC on January 29, 2004, asking the prosecutor to investigate alleged crimes by the Lord's Resistance Army (LRA). To date, the ICC has issued and unsealed one consolidated indictment against LRA leader Joseph Kony and his four top deputies. Kony and two of his deputies remain at large, most likely in a neighboring country,[86] and the other two are deceased.[87] At the time of the referral, a general amnesty for combatants was in force, which the Government intends to amend to allow for the prosecution of LRA leaders.[88] Nevertheless, it remains the policy of the Ugandan government that many LRA members should not be prosecuted, either domestically or internationally. The government's 2004 press release announcing its ICC referral illustrates an important challenge to the concept of complementarity, namely, the extent to which international prosecutions can coexist with and defer to domestic amnesties and national reconciliation efforts, as well as domestic prosecutions:

> Many of the members of the LRA are themselves victims, having been abducted and brutalised by the LRA leadership. The reintegration of these individuals into Ugandan society is key to the future stability of Northern Uganda. This will require the concerted support of the international community—Uganda and the Court cannot do this alone.[89]

The Ugandan case in the ICC has been notable, and criticized, for its exclusive prosecutorial focus on rebel actors in the civil conflict, despite the fact that Ugandan troops also have been widely accused of human rights abuses in the government's military campaign against the Lord's Resistance Army.[90] William Schabas, Director of the Irish Centre of Human Rights at the National University of Ireland, Galway, has written extensively on the work of the ICC and the Special Court for Sierra Leone, in his broader treatment of transitional justice. Schabas has expressed concern that in cases of self-referral, in which a state refers the situation on its own territory to the ICC, the tendency for one-sided prosecutions may be particularly difficult to avoid. Speaking of Uganda's President Yoweri Museveni and the LRA, Schabas writes that "Museveni . . . shrewdly understood that the Court might put decisive pressure upon an adversary he had been unable to defeat on the battlefield."[91]

Although the ICC Office of the Prosecutor justified its exclusive indictment of LRA leaders on the basis of an interpretation of the lesser "gravity" of reported attacks on civilians by Ugandan government troops as compared to alleged LRA attacks on civilians,[92] Schabas urges a different assessment of the relative accountability of the two parties to the Ugandan conflict. Conceding the requirement of "gravity" in the text of of Article 17 of the Rome Statute[93] regarding case admissibility, Schabas nevertheless suggests that a smaller number of civilian deaths attributable to the state may be just as grave as a larger number of deaths at the hands of the LRA:

> Even assuming that the Ugandan People's Defense Forces have killed significantly fewer innocent civilians than the Lord's Resistance Army, is not the fact that the crimes are attributable to the state germane to the gravity of the case?... With respect to the government forces,... we are confronted with the classic impunity paradigm: individuals acting on behalf of a state that shelters them from its own courts.[94]

Schabas remains convinced that the early efforts of the ICC prosecutor, including the LRA indictments, illustrate "a sincere effort to make the Court operational." Nevertheless, he warns of the dangers of an enduring perception that the ICC "might even be counted upon to partner with governments in the pursuit of their adversaries."[95] If the situation in the Republic of Guinea results in ICC indictments against individual members of the Presidential Guard, and if the Kenya case leads to the conviction of government officials, these developments would help defuse the charge that the court is unduly focused on nonstate offenders, as would progress in the war crimes and genocide case against President Al-Bashir of the Sudan.

Domestic Developments in Uganda Related to the ICC Case

The ICC indictments against the top leadership of the LRA have been quite controversial within Ugandan civil society. Criticism of the court has not been limited to its failure to indict officers of the Ugandan People's Defense Forces. An additional concern has been the impact of the LRA arrest warrants on the ongoing civil conflict. Certain NGOs, notably the Beyond Juba Project, based at the Faculty of Law of Makerere University in Kampala, have been outspoken in their criticism of the international prosecutions as, at best, a distraction from progress towards meaningful social and political reform in Uganda and, at worst, a catalyst for continued armed conflict and the perpetuation of ingrained social injustice.[96]

Partly in response to civil society activism, the Government of Uganda called for the suspension of the ICC indictments, and the "domestication" of the Rome Statute through the establishment of a war crimes unit within Uganda's High Court, whose "first objective will be to investigate and prosecute the top leadership of the LRA."[97] In March of 2010, the Ugandan parliament passed legislation implementing the Rome Statute and establishing the International Crimes Division of the Ugandan High Court with jurisdiction to try suspected war criminals domestically.[98]

The Beyond Juba Project (BJP) appears as wary of the Ugandan government's recent commitment to domestic prosecutions of the LRA as it has been to the ICC prosecutions, pointing to the experience of the Special Court of Sierra Leone as a cautionary tale. According to the BJP, the Special Court has expended far more funds—one hundred times the amount—on prosecuting war criminals as it has on restorative justice.[99] The organization asks rhetorically whether "the prosecution of a handful of perpetrators of crimes [will] be at the cost of a broader program of reparations and compensation for the wrongs done to their victims."[100] The BJP is concerned that for the average Ugandan, like the average Sierra Leonean, there may be "something paradoxical about the fact that perpetrators are the object of so much more financial attention than the victims."[101]

Despite calls from civil society for alternatives to ICC prosecutions of the LRA leadership, UN High Commissioner for Human Rights Navi Pillay renewed her endorsement of ICC trials in two reports issued in December 2009. Around the same time, the UN was responding to reports of attacks by the LRA in the neighboring countries of Sudan and the DRC. UN investigations in 2008 and 2009 revealed the rape, mutilation, and murder of scores of civilians, as well as the displacement of hundreds of thousands more.[102]

2. Democratic Republic of the Congo

The civil conflict in the DRC has raged for twelve years, kicked off by the overthrow of Mobutu Sese Seko in 1997. More than five million Congolese people have died. Described as Africa's "First World War," the conflict has been fed by internal politics, competition for mineral resources, and the intervention of six other African countries motivated by shifting loyalties to the governments of Laurent Kabila and his son, Joseph Kabila, president since his father's assassination in 2001. In particular, the mercurial support of Rwanda and Uganda for various Congolese factions has been influenced by the presence of Rwandan insurgents on Congolese territory since the 1994 Rwandan genocide.[103]

The 5.4 million people who have died in the DRC since 1998 include hundreds of thousands of murdered civilians, and many more killed by war-related hunger and disease. In addition to massive loss of life, all factions have systematically tortured and displaced civilians, raped women, and recruited child soldiers. Congolese rebel groups fighting the DRC armed forces include the Union des Patriotes Congolais (UPC) and the Forces Patriotiques pour la Libération du Congo (FPLC).[104]

The Government of the Democratic Republic of the Congo referred the situation occurring on its territory to the ICC on April 19, 2004. Although the DRC communicated with the court several months after the Government of Uganda, the ICC acted on the DRC referral first, initiating the first investigation by the ICC Office of the Prosecutor on May 23, 2004.[105] The ICC Pprosecutor has issued three separate indictments against four individuals in the DRC case, all of whom are rebel leaders, as in the case of Uganda.[106]

The trial of Thomas Lubanga Dyilo commenced in January of 2009. Lubanga, alleged former commander of the FPLC, is charged with the war crime of conscripting children under fifteen into military combat. The trial of Germaine Katanga and Mathieu Ngudjolo Chui commenced in November of 2009. Katanga and Ngudjolo, the alleged commanders of two other rebel organizations, are charged with war crimes for conscripting children and attacking civilians. Their indictment also includes charges of murder, rape, and sexual slavery, characterized as crimes against humanity. A fourth individual is still at large.[107]

The ICC Trial Division has twice interrupted Lubanga's trial for abuse of process by the prosecution, only to have the suspension lifted by the Appeals Chamber.[108] In addition to allegations of overzealous conduct, the prosecution has also been criticized for limiting Lubanga's indictment to child conscription, despite evidence that his troops systematically committed acts of sexual violence against women.[109]

3. Central African Republic

The Government of the Central African Republic (CAR) referred the situation in its country to the ICC on January 7, 2005. To date one individual, Jean-Pierre Bemba Gombo (Bemba), has come within the jurisdiction of the ICC for alleged crimes committed in CAR. Bemba, the former leader of the Movement for the Liberation of Congo, a rebel movement that became a political party in the DRC, had been invited by the CAR government in 2002 to help repress an attempted coup on its territory. He was the second vote-getter in the Congolese presidential election in 2006 and, in 2007, he was elected to the national senate. Bemba was indicted for crimes against humanity and war crimes charges involving murder, rape, and pillaging in CAR. He was arrested in May 27, 2008, his charges were confirmed in 2009, and his trial is pending.[110]

Whether Bemba is a state or nonstate actor is an interesting question. A former Congolese rebel leader turned politician, who once enjoyed state protection in the Central African Republic, Bemba is perhaps best characterized as a hybrid figure. Like the rebel leaders indicted in the Ugandan and DRC cases, Bemba ultimately ran afoul of the government on whose territory he operated, and that government then sought and supported his indictment and prosecution by the ICC.

4. Darfur, Sudan

On March 31, 2005, the UN Security Council referred to the ICC the humanitarian emergency unfolding in the Darfur region of Sudan,[111] unabated since its inception in 2003. The Darfur conflict has been characterized by widespread attacks on civilian communities, particularly in villages populated by Fur, Masalit, and Zarghawa tribespeople. These attacks are widely reported to have been carried out by government-armed militia fighters, called Janjaweed, often riding on horseback, with aerial support and bombardment from Sudanese helicopter gunships.[112] The Darfur case represents the first time that the Security Council has exercised its authority to bring a case to the ICC under Article 13 of its statute. It is also the first case involving genocide charges, in addition to allegations of war crimes and crimes against humanity.

The ICC Trial Chamber has indicted four individuals for their alleged involvement in crimes against humanity and war crimes in Darfur. Of these, three remain at large, namely, Ahmad Harun, the former Sudanese Minister of Humanitarian Affairs; Ali Kushayb, a Janjaweed militia leader; and Sudanese President Omar Hassan Ahmad Al-Bashir. Charges were dropped against the fourth individual, Bahar Idriss Abu Garda, who is the chief of military operations of the United Resistance Front (URF), and the former leader of the Justice and Equality Movement.[113] The URF is a coalition of five Darfur-based rebel movements, including the Justice and Equality Movement, one of two insurgent groups that first mounted armed resistance against Sudanese security forces in 2003.[114] Abu Garda is in custody on war crimes charges for murder, attacks on a peacekeeping mission, and pillaging.[115] It is notable that of the four individuals indicted in the Darfur case before the ICC, all three who remain at large are affiliated with the Government of Sudan; only the insurgent leader has been arrested.

The case of Al-Bashir, the first indictment of a head of state by the ICC, also represents the first time that Prosecutor Luis Moreno-Ocampo has asked the court to issue a warrant for genocide in addition to crimes against humanity and war crimes. In March of 2009, the ICC Trial Chamber made a preliminary determination that the proffered evidence against the President was sufficient only to justify charges on the lesser two types of crimes.[116] Nevertheless, in July 2010, the ICC announced the issuance of a new arrest warrant against Al-Bashir on three counts of genocide.[119]

The ICC's initial rejection of the genocide charge against Al-Bashir was criticized, in part because of the evidentiary standard that was applied. Some observers believed that, in essence, the ICC Trial Chamber required the prosecutor to present the same quantum of proof that would have been necessary to convict the Sudanese president, rather than assigning the lesser burden appropriate to the issuance of an arrest warrant on a particular charge.[120] The subsequent willingness to bring genocide charges against a sitting African president helps to bring ICC jurisprudence in accord with precedents established by the two current ad hoc international criminal tribunals. The ad hoc tribunals for both the former Yugoslavia and Rwanda have secured genocide convictions against various state officials, including Jean Kambanda, the former Rwandan prime minister, whose genocide conviction was upheld by the Appeals Chamber of the International Criminal Tribunal for Rwanda, on October 19, 2000.[121]

Although the ICC case against Al-Bashir remains controversial,[122] it has huge symbolic significance as a stand against state impunity. If the charges lead to the arrest and trial of the Sudanese president, it will represent important progress toward international criminal accountability for state and nonstate actors alike. In the meantime, some humanitarian organizations working in the region suggest that the Al-Bashir indictment is also having a subtle and constructive impact on the peace process in Darfur.[123]

E. THE ONGOING PURSUIT OF INTERNATIONAL CRIMINAL JUSTICE IN UGANDA, SIERRA LEONE, AND BURUNDI

The challenges in achieving the various dimensions of transitional justice in Uganda, Sierra Leone, and Burundi will be further explored in Part II. For now, it seems fitting to conclude this chapter with an overview of the strengths and weaknesses of each country's efforts to implement the norms of international criminal law.

Uganda represents a dynamic illustration of the concept of complementarity, given that international criminal prosecutions of the Lord's Resistance Army in the ICC have inspired the creation of a new war crimes unit within Uganda's High Court that is mandated to conduct domestic prosecutions of midlevel offenders. The International Crimes Division will itself likely defer to *mato oput* and other traditional justice mechanisms in the case of lower level offenders. Ugandan-style complementarity thus weaves together three strands of criminal justice: the international, the national, and the local reconciliative. How well this blending works in practice remains to be seen. Nevertheless, the maturity of civil society organizations in Uganda is evidenced in their capacity to criticize political manipulation of international trials and domestic prosecutions alike, and in their call for social justice and historical reckoning to be part of the criminal justice equation.

In Sierra Leone's approach to transitional justice, complementarity has become an art form. The Special Court for Sierra Leone is hybrid in the classic sense that it is an international court composed of international and national judges. But the very fact that most of its proceedings were conducted in the capital of Freetown makes them simultaneously international and domestic trials. Moreover, criminal justice has been less partisan in Sierra Leone than in the ICC, to the extent that the Special Court has prosecuted and convicted rebel and government-affiliated soldiers alike. As for the restorative dimension, Sierra Leone's Truth and Reconciliation Commission has completed its work, pardoning some offenders and compensating some victims of the civil war. Nevertheless, the Achilles' heel of transitional justice in Sierra Leone is the disproportionality between the modest reparations paid to victims of war crimes and the high cost of war crimes prosecutions. The social justice dimension of post-conflict reconstruction in Sierra Leone is widely recognized and remains a work in progress.

Burundi has not yet established the formal transitional justice mechanisms contemplated by the classic international criminal law paradigm, although both a truth commission and a special tribunal are planned. To date there are no ICC trials, no hybrid or ad hoc courts, no domestic war crimes prosecutions, and no amnesty and reparation panels. Weighing the punitive, reparative, and truth-telling aspects of criminal justice, Burundi has prioritized establishing the historical record, honoring the dead, and empowering the living among all the nation's ethnic communities. An important step will be the establishment of a national truth and reconciliation commission in 2012. Meanwhile, Burundi's greatest preoccupations are lowering youth unemployment, disarming the civilian population, and promoting pluralism in the political process.

International criminal law seeks to hold individuals accountable for grave offenses committed against the international community. Whereas international criminal law prosecutes *fugitives* from justice, international refugee law seeks to protect displaced *victims* of injustice. Thus, in Chapter 5, we turn to international refugee law, and the rights of individuals who flee persecution, in time of war and peace.

NOTES

1. WOLE SOYINKA, THE BURDEN OF MEMORY, THE MUSE OF FORGIVENESS (Oxford University Press, 1999) at 31. In this work, Nigerian Nobel Laureate Soyinka explores

the tensions between truth-telling and reconciliation in the pursuit of social healing after mass atrocities. He emphasizes the importance of restitution, and suggests the possibility of a "healing millennial trilogy: Truth, Reparations, and Reconciliation." *Id.* at 92.

2. The Rome Statute entered into force on July 1, 2002, once the sixtieth state ratification was received, as required by the treaty. Rome Statute of the International Criminal Court, UN Doc. A/CONF. 183/9 (1998), 2187 UNTS 90, art. 126. As of September 2009, the Statute had 109 parties.

3. Article 4 of the Convention Against Torture includes the requirement of domestic criminalization. CAT, art. 4(1).

4. For example, in the United States, torture is a crime under 18 USC sec. 2340a (1994). The US Anti-Torture Statute was enacted by the US Congress to implement the Convention Against Torture, *supra*, after its ratification by the US Senate in 1993. http://treaties.un.org/Pages/ViewDetails.aspx?src=TREATY&mtdsg_no=IV-9&chapter=4&lang=en.

5. Linda Keller identifies the four principal purposes of international criminal law, reflected in the mandate of the International Criminal Court (ICC), as retribution, deterrence, expressivism, and restorative justice. *See* Linda M. Keller, *Achieving Peace With Justice: The International Criminal Court and Ugandan Alternative Justice Mechanisms*, 23 CONNECTICUT J. INT'L. L. 209 (2008) at 260. Retribution and deterrence are the familiar offender-focused elements of criminal justice, while expressivism and restoration focus on the impact of crime and punishment on victims and society as a whole. By *expressivism*, Keller refers to a strong message of condemnation by the official judicial body of the unlawful conduct, which must be received by members of the society impacted by the offense and not merely by the convicted wrongdoer him or herself. Expressivism or moral condemnation requires a public process of truth-telling, which establishes a shared historical record of the conflict and the atrocities that occurred. *Id.* at 273–74. Keller defines restorative justice in terms of reconciliation or reparation, reflected in the tribunal's provision of rehabilitation, essential social services, and monetary compensation to victims. *Id.* at 275–76. Keller's four goals of international criminal law can be reconfigured as three interrelated understandings of justice—retribution and deterrence constituting punitive justice, expressivism as historical justice, and restorative justice as social justice. We will return to these themes throughout our text.

6. *See* Miriam J. Aukerman, *Extraordinary Evil, Ordinary Crime: A Framework for Understanding Transitional Justice*, 15 HARV. HUM. RTS. J. 39, 44 and footnote 23 (2002). Aukerman refers to five theories of punishment underlying domestic criminal law. First is the rationale of *desert*, linked to the idea of retribution or vengeance. Second and third are the goals of *deterrence* and *rehabilitation*, respectively. Fourth is the concept of *communication*, linked to the ideals of condemnation and social solidarity. Aukerman's fifth essential theory of punishment is restorative justice. *Id.* at 44–45.

7. The Acholi people traditionally inhabit Northern Uganda, where the violence of the Ugandan civil war has been concentrated. The Lord's Resistance Army (LRA) has drawn most of its conscripts and most of its victims from the Acholi community. *Mato oput* is a reconciliation process conducted under the auspices of traditional Acholi chiefs, in which offenders acknowledge their crimes, offer reparations to their victims, and finally participate in a cleansing ceremony in which they are received back into the community. We will discuss this practice in greater detail in Chapter 7.

8. *Fambul tok* means "family talk" in Krio, the national language of Sierra Leone. The work of the organization Fambul Tok in facilitating victim-offender reconciliation in Sierra Leone is discussed in Chapter 8.

9. *See* Matthias Goldmann, *Does Peace Follow Justice or Vice Versa? Plans for Postconflict Justice in Burundi*, 30 FLETCHER FORUM OF WORLD AFFAIRS, 137, 142 (Winter 2006), available at http://ssrn.com/abstract=1369121. The Goldmann article references policy

discussions regarding the potential establishment of a Burundian "National Truth and Reconciliation Commission."

10. *See id.* at 147–48. *Ubushingantahe* is further discussed in Chapter 9 on Burundi.
11. Professor Patrick Hoenig suggests that proponents of international war crimes trials increasingly accept traditional justice mechanisms as a component of transitional justice, if a secondary one. "ICC supporters," he writes, "have over time refined their tactics. Open condescension and rejection have given way to more subtle arguments.... The UN High Commissioner for Human Rights, for example, advocates 'different levels of justice processes' to address 'different levels of perpetrators and crimes' .... In plain language, what the UN body means to say is that the ICC will be dealing with the prominent human rights cases, while the national courts, the traditional justice system and the amnesty program are free to divide up the rest among themselves." *See* Patrick Hoenig, *Peace and Justice in Northern Uganda*, 14 E. AFRICAN J. PEACE & HUM. RTS. 333, 374 (2008).

    In addition to the increasing tolerance of traditional justice practices within international criminal law circles, some advocates of grassroots dispute resolution argue persuasively that communal atonement ceremonies are punitive in their own right. When the offender acknowledges guilt, asks forgiveness, and returns to live in the community of those he offended, there is a powerful measure of accountability. As one Acholi leader described the reconciliation process of *mato oput*, "[y]ou are free, but feel the weight of what you've done." *See*, Lucy Hovil and Zachary Lomo, *Whose Justice? Perceptions of Uganda's Amnesty Act 2000: The Potential for Conflict Resolution and Long-Term Reconciliation*, Refugee Law Project Working Paper No. 15, February 15, 2005, *available at* http://www.refugeelawproject.org, at 27.
12. National prosecutions and alternative justice mechanisms are further discussed in Chapter 6, in the sections on courts and communities as arenas for conflict resolution, and in the final three chapters devoted to transitional justice in Uganda, Sierra Leone, and Burundi.
13. The Agreement for the Prosecution and Punishment of the Major War Criminals of the European Axis of August 8, 1945 (London Agreement), 59 Stat. 1544.
14. BETH VAN SCHAACK AND RONALD C. SLYE, INTERNATIONAL CRIMINAL LAW AND ITS ENFORCEMENT: CASES AND MATERIALS at 26–27 (Foundation Press, 2007). Another defendant was tried and sentenced to death in absentia. *Id.*
15. In fact, one member of the International Military Tribunal for the Far East (IMTFE or Tokyo Tribunal), Justice R.B. Pal, stated in his dissenting opinion to the Judgment of 1948 that "there is nothing in [Japan's terms of surrender] ... which ... would authorize the victor nations or the Supreme Commander to legislate for Japan and for the Japanese or in respect of war crimes." The United States of America v. Akaki, Sadao *et al.*, IMTFE, Dissentient Judgement of Justice R.B. Pal (IMTFE), *reprinted in* SCHAACK AND SLYE, *op. cit.*, at 27.
16. *See* Judgment of Nuremberg Tribunal (IMT, Nuremberg, 1946), as reported in 41 AM. J. INT. L. 172, 221 (1947), citing Article 8 of the Nuremberg Charter. ("That a soldier was ordered to kill or torture in violation of the international law of war has never been recognized as a defense to such acts of brutality, though, as the Chamber here provides, the order may be urged in mitigation of punishment.")
17. *See id.* at 217. In mounting their defenses, some of the accused at Nuremberg maintained that they were charged with offenses that had not been recognized as criminal acts at the time of their commission. The IMT squarely rejected these claims: "In the first place, it is to be observed the maxim *nullen crimen sine lege* is not a limitation of sovereignty, but is in general a principle of justice. To assert that it is unjust to punish those who in defiance of treaties and assurances have attacked neighboring states without warning is

obviously untrue, for in such circumstances the attacker must know that he is doing wrong, and so far from it being unjust to punish him, It would be unjust if his wrong were to go unpunished...." *Id.*
18. *See* London Agreement, London, August 8, 1945, art. 6, 59 Stat. 1544, 1547–48, *available at* http://www.icrc.org/ihl.nsf/FULL/350?OpenDocument.
19. The definition of genocide and other aspects of the treaty are explored in Chapter 3.
20. The London Agreement, art. 6(a).
21. *Id.*, art. 6(b).
22. *Id.*, art. 6(c).
23. In 1974, the UN General Assembly passed a resolution defining aggression as "the use of armed force by a State against the sovereignty, territorial integrity or political independence of another State or in any other manner inconsistent with the Charter of the United Nations . . . ." Definition of Aggression, GA Res. 3314 (XXXIX), UN GAOR, 6th Comm., 29th Sess., 2319th plen. mtg. (Dec. 14, 1974). The 1974 definition was consistent with the language of Article 2(4) of the UN Charter, which obligates "Members . . . [to] refrain from . . . the threat or use of force against the territorial integrity or political independence of any state." Nevertheless, this nonbinding resolution of the General Assembly failed to specify which types of military actions would be deemed attacks on territorial sovereignty.
24. Protocol I, art. 51(5) (b).
25. *See* William Schabas, *Prosecutorial Discretion v. Judicial Activism at the International Criminal Court*, 6 J. INT'L. CRIM. JUST. 731, 755 (Sept. 2008). In this article, the author discusses the evolution of the definition of crimes against humanity from Nuremburg to the ICTY.
26. SC Res. 827, UN. Doc S/RES/827 (May 25, 1993).
27. SC Res. 808, UN Doc. S/RES/808 (Feb. 22, 1993).
28. UN Charter, arts. 25 ("Members of the United Nations agree to accept and carry out the decisions of the Security Council in accordance with the present Charter") and 39 ("[t]he Security Council shall . . . decide what measures shall be taken . . . to maintain or restore international peace and security.").
29. The ICTY anticipates that its last four trials will be completed between 2010 and 2012, culminating with the conclusion of the trial of Radovan Karadzic, the former political leader of the Bosnian Serb community. http://www.icty.org/sections/AbouttheICTY.
30. ICTY Statute, SC Res. 827, UN Doc. S/RES/827 (May 25, 1993), art. 3.
31. Protocol I, art. 52(1).
32. *Id.*, art. 52(5) (b).
33. Genocide Convention, art. II.
34. ICTY Statute, art. 4, emphasis added.
35. ICTY Statute, art. 5. It is important to note that despite the reference to armed conflict in Article 5, the ICTY itself has stated that "there is no logical or legal basis for . . . [the war nexus] requirement and it has been abandoned in subsequent State practice with respect to crimes against humanity." Prosecutor v. Tadic, Case No. IT-94-1-1. Decision on the Defense Motion for Interlocutory Appeal on Jurisdiction (Oct. 2, 1995), as excerpted in Van Schaack and Slye, *op. cit.* at 379–80. *See also* William Schabas, "Prosecutorial Discretion v. Judicial Activism at the International Criminal Court," 6 J. INT'L. CRIM. JUST. 731, 755 (Sept. 2008) ("[T]he definition of crimes against humanity [in the Rome Statute] reflected the belief, still common at the time, that customary international law required a *nexus* between crimes against humanity and armed conflict. In the *Tadic* Jurisdictional Decision of October 2, 1995, the majority said such a requirement was inconsistent with customary law.")
36. ICTR Statute, SC Res. 955, UN Doc. S/RES/955 (Nov. 8, 1994).

37. *Id.*, art. 1. The ICTR's competence specifically applies to "individuals" suspected of humanitarian law violations on Rwandan territory, and "Rwandan citizens responsible for such violations in the territory of neighbouring States" as well. *Id.*
38. *See* http://unictr.org/default.htm (the information regarding ICTR individual convictions is found by going to the ICTR default web page, and clicking on "Cases" and then "Status of Cases.")
39. *Id.*
40. *See* Prosecutor v. Kambanda, Case No. ICTR 97-23-S, Judgment and Sentence, 61 (Sept. 4, 1998).
    Further information about the Kambanda judgment is available on the webpage of the American University War Crimes Research Project, at http://www.wcl.american.edu/warcrimes/ictr_judgements.cfm/.
41. Marlise Simons, *Life Sentences in Rwanda Genocide Case*, N.Y. TIMES, June 24, 2011, *available at* http://www.nytimes.com/2011/06/25/world/africa/25rwanda.html.
42. *Compare*, ICTY Statute, art. 4, *with*, ICTR Statute, art. 2.
43. ICTR Statute, art. 4.
44. *Id.*, art. 3.
45. *See generally*, SCHAACK AND SLYE, *op. cit.* at 379–380. *See also* William Schabas, *Prosecutorial Discretion v. Judicial Activism at the International Criminal Court*, 6 J. INT'L. CRIM. JUST. 731, 755 (Sept. 2008) (contemporary understanding that the requirement of "a *nexus* between crimes against humanity and armed conflict.... [is] inconsistent with customary law").
46. Agreement Between the United Nations and the Government of Sierra Leone on the Establishment of a Special Court for Sierra Leone, Jan. 16, 2002, art. 1, *available at* http://www.sc-sl.org/scsl-agreement.html.
    The benchmark year for the jurisdiction of the Special Court is 1996 because of the peace accord signed on November 30 of that year by the Government of Sierra Leone and the RUF in Abidjan, Ivory Coast. The Abidjan Accord broke down when former members of the Sierra Leonean Army mounted a coup against the government. The Abidjan Accord was followed by the Lomé Accord in 1999. *See* Peace Agreement Between the Government of Sierra Leone and the Revolutionary United Front of Sierra Leone [Lomé Accord], July 7, 1999, *available at* http://www.sierra-leone.org/lomeaccord.html. The Preamble to the Lomé Accord cites the 1996 Abidjan Accord. *Id.*
    The temporal jurisdiction of the Special Court was left "open-ended," as acknowledged by the UN Secretary General in his 2000 report to the UN Security Council two years before the establishment of the Court. However, then-Secretary General Kofi Annan clarified that "the lifespan of the Special Court . . ., as distinguished from its temporal jurisdiction, will be determined by a subsequent agreement between the parties upon the completion of its judicial activities . . . ." *See* Report of the Secretary General on the establishment of a Special Court for Sierra Leone, UN Doc. S/2000/915 (4 October 2000) at para. 28, *available at* http://www.afrol.com/Countries/Sierra_Leone/documents/un_sil_court_041000.htm.
47. Statute of the Special Court for Sierra Leone, *available at* http://www.scsl.org/LinkClick.aspx?fileticket=uClnd1MJeEw%3d&tabid=176.
48. On May 25, 1997, under the leadership of Major Johnny Paul Koroma, the Armed Forces Revolutionary Council overthrew the administration of President Ahmad Tejan Kabbah and offered the RUF the opportunity to join the government. *See* Somini Sengupta, *Sierra Leone: Police Seek Ex-Ruler*, N.Y. TIMES, [World Briefing Africa], Jan. 21, 2003, *available at* http://www.nytimes.com/2003/01/21/world/world-briefing-africa-sierra-leone-police-seek-ex-ruler.html?ref=ahmad_tejan_kabbah.

49. RUF commander Issa Hassan Sesay received a 52-year prison sentence; Morris Kallon, 40 years; and Augustine Gbao, 25 years, all for the commission of war crimes and crimes against humanity. More information on the Kallon and Gbao case can be found on the website of the Special Court for Sierra Leone, at http://www.sc-sl.org/CASES/ProsecutorvsSesayKallonandGbaoRUFCase/tabid/105/Default.aspx.

50. CDF leader Moinina Fofana received a 15-year prison sentence, and Allieu Kondewa received twenty years, both for war crimes and crimes against humanity. Prosecutor v. Moinina Fofana and Allieu Kondewa, SCSL-04-14-T, Judgment (Aug. 2, 2007) (Special Court for Sierra Leone, Trial Chamber I).

51. AFRC member Alex Tamba Brima received a 50-year prison sentence; Ibrahim Bazzy Kamara, 45 years; and Santagie Borbor Kanu, 50 years, all for war crimes and crimes against humanity. Prosecutor v. Alex Tamba Brima, Brima Brazzy Kamara, and Santigie Borbor Kanu, SCSL-04-16-T, Judgment (June 20, 2007) (Special Court for Sierra Leone, Trial Chamber II).

52. Sam Bockarie of the RUF died in Liberia; Sam Hinga Norman of the CDF died while seeking medical care; and Johnny Paul Koroma of the AFRC is at large. The website for the SCSL has individual pages for each of the consolidated cases of the RUF, CDF, and AFRC, which provide details about the individual defendants. Sankoh: http://www.sc-sl.org/CASES/FodaySankoh/tabid/187/Default.aspx; Bockarie: http://www.sc-sl.org/CASES/SamBockarie/tabid/189/Default.aspx; Norman: http://www.sc-sl.org/CASES/ProsecutorvsFofanaandKondewaCDFCase/tabid/104/Default.aspx; and Koroma: http://www.sc-sl.org/CASES/JohnnyPaulKoroma/tabid/188/Default.aspx. *See also*, Global Policy Forum, *Taylor, Koroma Frustrate UN Court*, June 27, 2005, *available at* http://www.globalpolicy.org/component/content/article/168/29153.html.

53. Article IX of the Lomé Accord reads:

    1. In order to bring lasting peace to Sierra Leone, the Government of Sierra Leone shall take appropriate legal steps to grant Corporal Foday Sankoh absolute and free pardon.
    2. After the signing of the present Agreement, the Government of Sierra Leone shall also grant absolute and free pardon and reprieve to all combatants and collaborators in respect of anything done by them in pursuit of their objectives, up to the time of the signing of the present Agreement.
    3. To consolidate the peace and promote the cause of national reconciliation, the Government of Sierra Leone shall ensure that no official or judicial action is taken against any member of the RUF/SL, ex-AFRC, ex-SLA or CDF in respect of anything done by them in pursuit of their objectives as members of those organisations, since March 1991, up to the time of the signing of the present Agreement. In addition, legislative and other measures necessary to guarantee immunity to former combatants, exiles and other persons, currently outside the country for reasons related to the armed conflict shall be adopted ensuring the full exercise of their civil and political rights, with a view to their reintegration within a framework of full legality.

    Peace Agreement between the Government of Sierra Leone and the Revolutionary Front of Sierra Leone (Lomé, Togo, July 7, 1999), Art. IX, *available at* http://www.sierraleone.org/lomeaccord.html.

54. *See* VAN SCHAACK AND SLYE, op. cit., pp. 164–65, citing Noah B. Novogrodsky, *Speaking to Africa: The Early Success of the Special Court for Sierra Leone*, 5 SANTA CLARA J. INT'L L. 194, 196–98 (2006) and Seventh *Report of the Secretary-General on the United Nations Observer Mission in Sierra Leone*, Security Council, UN Doc. S/1999/836. *See also* Lomé Accord, Art. IX, *op. cit.*

55. *See* Novogrodsky, *op. cit.*

56. *See* Statute of the Special Court, *op. cit.* at arts. 2–5.

57. *See* Genocide Convention, art. II; *see also* Tom Perriello and Marieke Wierda, *The Special Court for Sierra Leone Under Scrutiny* at 21 (International Center for Transitional Justice, Mar. 2006), *available at* http://www.ictj.org/static/Prosecutions/Sierra.study.pdf.
58. *See* Statute of the Special Court, *op. cit.* at art. 3.
59. *Id.*, art. 3.
60. *Id.*, art. 4.
61. *Id.*, art. 2.
62. *Id.*, art. 5(a); *see also* Perriello and Wierda, *op. cit.* at 15.
63. Statute of the Special Court, art. 7.
64. *Id.*, art. 7(1).
65. Art 7(2) of the Special Court Statute reads: "In the disposition of a case against a juvenile offender, the Special Court shall order any of the following: care guidance and supervision orders, community service orders, counselling, foster care, correctional, educational and vocational training programmes, approved schools and, as appropriate, any programmes of disarmament, demobilization and reintegration or programmes of child protection agencies."
66. Rome Statute of the International Criminal Court (Rome Statute or ICC Statute), 2187 UNT.S 90, art. 126. Although the United States is not a party to the ICC Statute, as of August 2009, the US government committed to "engage" with the court and to attend multilateral conferences on its evolving mandate. Colum Lynch, *U.S. to attend conference held by war crimes court*, WASH. POST, Nov. 17, 2009; http://www.washingtonpost.com/wpdyn/content/article/2009/11/16/AR2009111603662.html.
67. Preamble of the Rome Statute. In the Preamble, the States Parties affirm that they are:

"[c]onscious that all peoples are united by common bonds, their cultures pieced together in a shared heritage, and concerned that this delicate mosaic may be shattered at any time, [m]indful that during this century millions of children, women and men have been victims of unimaginable atrocities that deeply shock the conscience of humanity, [r]ecognizing that such grave crimes threaten the peace, security and well-being of the world, [and]
[a]ffirming that the most serious crimes of concern to the international community as a whole must not go unpunished and their effective prosecution must be ensured by taking measures at the national level and by enhancing international cooperation . . . ."
68. *Id.*, art. 5(1).
69. *Id.*, art. 5(2).
70. Article 8 *bis* (re: the "Crime of Aggression") amends the ICC Statute to define aggression. An *act* of aggression is "[t]he invasion or attack by the armed forces of a State of the territory of another State, or any military occupation, however temporary, resulting from such invasion or attack, or any annexation by the use of the territory of another state." *See* Rome Statute, art. 8 (2) *bis*, Resolution RC/Res. 6, adopted at the 13th plenary meeting [of the parties to the ICC Statute], on June 11, 2010, by consensus, *available at* http://www.icc-cpi.int/iccdocs/asp_docs/Resolutions/RC-Res.6-ENG.pdf. The *crime* of aggression is "the planning, preparation, initiation or execution, by a person in a position effectively to exercise control over or to direct the political or military action of a State, of an act of aggression which, by its character, gravity and scale, constitutes a manifest violation of the Charter of the United Nations." *See* Rome Statute, art. 8(1) *bis*.
71. *See* Rome Statute, art. 15 *bis* ["Exercise of jurisdiction over the crime of aggression"]. Article 15 *bis* provides that jurisdiction over the crime of aggression may not be exercised until thirty or more state parties have ratified the amendments, and in any case no earlier than January 1, 2017, subject to a specific decision by thirty or more state parties to initiate

the exercise of jurisdiction. *See id.*, art. 15(2) and (3) *bis, available at* http://www.icc-cpi.int/iccdocs/asp_docs/Resolutions/RC-Res.6-ENG.pdf.
72. 1998 ICC Statute, art. 6.
73. *Id.*, art. 7.
74. *Id.*, art. 8.
75. *Id.*, art. 12(2)(a) and (b).
76. *Id.*, art. 13(a) and (c). In the case of a state referral under article 13(a), the state may refer to the ICC either the situation in another state, or the situation on its own territory (a so-called "self-referral"). *See id.*, art. 13(a). *See also* ROB CURRIE, *Côte d'Ivoire and the ICC: A New Kind of "Self-Referral"?* (on-line update of Prof. Currie's casebook, INTERNATIONAL AND TRANSNATIONAL CRIMINAL LAW (Irwin Law 2010)), *available at* http://rjcurrie.typepad.com/international-and-transna/2011/05/c%C3%B4te-divoire-and-the-icc-a-new-kind-of-self-referral.html.
77. *Compare* art. 12(2) regarding preconditions to the exercise of ICC jurisdiction, which apply exclusively to state referrals and Prosecutor-initiated investigations under article 13, paragraph (a) and (c) *and* art. 13(b), which concerns referral by the Security Council.
78. *Id.*, art. 17(1)(b).
79. Professor Keller suggests that the [Rome] statute might allow *sub rosa* recognition of amnesty or other alternative justice mechanism (AJM) in exceptional circumstances, including an interpretation of Article 17 by which "the Ugandan AJM render the case inadmissible." Keller, *op. cit.* at 238. Keller clarifies that Article 17(2) negates a finding of inadmissibility when the alternative proceedings were undertaken "for the purpose of shielding the person concerned from criminal responsibility," (art. 17(2)(a)) or "are not being conducted independently or impartially" (art. 17(2)(c)). *See* Keller, *op. cit.* at 257.
80. Rome Statute, art. 17(1)(d).
81. Keller, *op. cit.* at 259.
82. *Id.* at 278. Although Uganda does not yet have a national truth commission, non-governmental organizations (NGOs) including the Beyond Juba Project (BJP) have called for legislation to establish such a process. The work of BJP in promoting transitional justice in Uganda is further discussed in Chapter 7, as are traditional Ugandan conflict resolution practices developed at the local level, including *mato oput*.
83. *See* [US] Congressional Research Service, *International Criminal Court Cases in Africa: Status and Policy Issues,* July 22, 2011, RL 34665, *available at* http://www.fas.org/sgp/crs/row/RL34665.pdf, at summary, p. 8 (Libya), and p. 9 (Kenya).
84. *See* Rome Statute, arts. 13(a), (b) and (c). An overview of the five cases before the ICC is available on the court's website, at http://www.icc-cpi.int/Menus/ICC/Situations+and+Cases/.

On May 3, 2011, the President of Côte d'Ivoire, Alassane Ouattara, wrote to the ICC Prosecutor, asking the prosecutor to initiate a *propio motu* investigation of alleged crimes that have occurred in his country since September 2002. If the letter is acted upon, the prosecutor will be undertaking a *propio motu* investigation of the very state that requested the investigation, although targeting a period that began during a previous government, before that state's accession to the Rome Statute. Professor Currie of the Delhousie University Schulich School of Law in Nova Scotia suggests that this state-initiated *propio motu* under Article 13(c) of the ICC Statute constitutes a "new kind of 'self-referral.'" *See* Currie, *op. cit.*, citing Rome Statute, arts. 13(c) and 14.
85. *See* Neil MacFarquhar, *U.N. Panel Refers Guinea's Leaders to International Court Over Massacre,* N.Y. TIMES, Tuesday, December 22, 2009, at A6. *See also* "No impunity for Guinea massacre, says ICC," BBC NEWS, February 18, 2010, *available at* http://news.bbc.co.uk/2/hi/africa/8521642.stm.

86. Joseph Kony is variously said to be in the Central African Republic (CAR), the Democratic Republic of the Congo (DRC), and the Sudan. In March of 2010, President Museveni speculated that Kony had fled to Darfur. *Ugandan President Says Rebel Chief Likely in Darfur*, AGENCE FRANCE PRESSE, Mar. 11, 2010, http://news.yahoo.com/s/afp/20100312/wl_africa_afp/ugandarebelssudan. When asked about the possibility that the government of Sudan had granted safe haven to Kony, Museveni replied "[i]f the Sudanese want to accommodate him in Darfur, that makes no difference to us." The Ugandan President went on to express confidence that Kony would be captured if he made his way to Uganda, Southern Sudan, the DRC, or CAR, so long as the Ugandan military continued to operate in all those countries. *Id.*
87. This and further information regarding the ICC Uganda case can be found on the ICC website, at http://www.icc-cpi.int/Menus/ICC/Situations+and+Cases/Situations/Situation+ICC+0204/. In recent years, Ugandan troops have killed two LRA commanders on the territory of the CAR, including Bok Abudema, who was killed in January of 2010. In September 2008, Ugandan troops captured Joseph Kony's bodyguard. *See* Justin Moro and Chris Ochowun, *Army Kills Kony's Third in Command*, NEW VISION (Kampala, Uganda), Jan. 2, 2010, *available at* http://allafrica.com/stories/201001030001.html.
88. The original 2004 ICC press release that announced Uganda's referral of the situation in Northern Uganda contains useful information about the evolving state of Ugandan law regarding the domestic prosecution of accused war criminals, and is available at http://www.icc-cpi.int/menus/icc/press%20and%20media/press%20releases/2004/president%20of%20uganda%20refers%20situation%20concerning%20the%20lord_s%20resistance%20army%20_lra_%20to%20the%20icc?lan=en-GB. Ongoing proposals to amend the 2000 Amnesty Acts are discussed in Chapter 7 on Uganda.
89. *Id.*
The ICC Statute provides that a case should be deemed inadmissible if "the [concerned] State has decided not to prosecute the person concerned, unless the decision resulted from the unwillingness or inability of the State genuinely to prosecute." Rome Statute, art. 17(1) (b). The question of when a domestic amnesty program constitutes a valid reason not to prosecute will be further explored in Chapters 7 and 8 on Uganda and Sierra Leone, respectively.
90. *See* William Schabas, *Prosecutorial Discretion v. Judicial Activism at the International Criminal Court*, 6 J. INT'L. CRIM. JUST. 731, 752 (Sept. 2008). Schabas reports that "[w]hen the Ugandan arrest warrants were made public, the Prosecutor was sharply criticized by international non-governmental organizations for being one-sided." *Id.* The prosecutor later clarified to the Government of Uganda his interpretation that the scope of his investigation encompassed all crimes occurring in the context of the conflict with the Lord's Resistance Army, only implying that government soldiers were not immune from prosecution. *See id.* Nevertheless, the ICC has issued no subsequent arrest warrants against state actors in the Uganda case.
91. *Id.*
92. *Id.* at 738 (public statement by ICC Prosecutor that "crimes committed by the LRA were much more numerous and of much higher gravity than alleged crimes committed by the UPDF [Ugandan People's Defense Forces]").
93. ICC Statute, art. 17(1) (d).
94. Schabas, 6 J. INT'L. CRIM. JUST. at 747–48.
95. *Id.* at 759.
96. Chris Dolan, of Makerere University's Beyond Juba Project (BJP), advocates a vision of "justice which has both retributive and restorative elements and which considers the various wrongs committed by all parties to the conflict," insisting that "justice [serve] as the handmaiden of sustainable peace." *See*, Chris Dolan, *Whatever happened to*

comprehensive justice? (Beyond Juba Project, Refugee Law Project, Faculty of Law, Makerere University, June 2007), paras. 2 and 7, *available at* http://www.refugeelawproject.org/press_releases/WhateverHappenedtoTrueJustice.pdf.

See also, Internal Displacement Monitoring Centre, Norwegian Refugee Council, *op. cit.*, para. 5 (statement released by over thirty humanitarian and civil society organizations from within and outside of Uganda, stressing the need to "promote reconciliation across Ugandan society and establish accountability for crimes committed during the war").

97. "Prosecuting Crimes or Righting Wrongs: Where is Uganda heading to?" (Press Release, Beyond Juba [Project]: Building Consensus on a Sustainable Peace Process for Uganda, a transitional justice project of the Faculty of Law, the Refugee Law Project and Human Rights and Peace Centre, University of Makerere, Aug. 17, 2007).
98. Bill Oketch, *Uganda Set for First War Crimes Trial*, ACR Issue 264, Institute for War and Peace Reporting, June 16, 2010, *available at* http://www.iwpr.net/report-news/uganda-set-first-war-crimes-trial.
99. *Id.*
100. *Id.*
101. *Id.*
102. "UN urges countries to bring LRA leaders to face ICC," AFP, Dec. 21, 2009, http://www.google.com/hostednews/afp/article/ALeqM5iC_i-ugBKX988yXtMgi5DsF3mENg.
103. *See* Anup Shah, *The Democratic Republic of the Congo*, GLOBAL ISSUES, Aug. 21, 2010, *available at* http://www.globalissues.org/article/87/the-democratic-republic-of-congo.
104. "The Office of the Prosecutor of the International Criminal Court opens its first investigation" (ICC Press Release), May 23, 2004, available at http://www.icc-cpi.int/menus/icc/press%20and%20media/press%20releases/2004/the%20office%20of%20the%20prosecutor%20of%20the%20international%20criminal%20court%20opens%20its%20first%20investigation?lan=en-GB.
105. *Id.*
106. Schabas, *op. cit.*, at 751.
107. This and further information on the ICC case regarding the Democratic Republic of the Congo can be found on the ICC website at http://www.icc-cpi.int/Menus/ICC/Situations+and+Cases/Situations/Situation+ICC+0104/.
108. *See* "Congolese ex-militia chief can go free unless appeal" (AFP), July 15, 2010, *available at* http://news.yahoo.com/s/afp/20100715/wl_africa_afp/warcrimesiccdrcongolubanga-trial_20100715174730; *see also Thomas Lubanga*, Times Topics, N.Y. TIMES, January 12, 2011, *available at* http://topics.nytimes.com/top/reference/timestopics/people/l/thomas_lubanga/index.html.
109. *See* Marlise Simons, *For International Criminal Court, Frustration and Missteps in its First Trial*, N.Y. TIMES, November 21, 2010, *available at* http://www.nytimes.com/2010/11/22/world/europe/22court.html?_r=1&pagewanted=1.
110. Information on the ICC case regarding the Central African Republic can be found on the ICC website at http://www.icc-cpi.int/Menus/ICC/Situations+and+Cases/Situations/Situation+ICC+0105/.
111. SC Res. 1593, UN Doc. S/RES/1593 (Mar. 31, 2005). The Security Council acted pursuant to Art. 13(b) of the ICC Statute, which permits the Security Council to refer cases involving countries which are nonparties to the statute.
112. *See generally*, Samantha Power, *Dying in Darfur: Can the Ethnic Cleansing in Sudan be Stopped?* NEW YORKER, Aug. 30, 2004, *available at* http://www.newyorker.com/archive/2004/08/30/040830fa_fact1.
113. This and further information regarding the ICC Darfur case can be found on the ICC website, at http://www.icc-cpi.int/Menus/ICC/Situations+and+Cases/Situations/Situation+ICC+0205/.

114. *See* SUDAN TIMES, July 27, 2008, http://www.sudantribune.com/spip.php?article28043. The other Darfur-based insurgency that rose up against the Sudanese government in 2003 was the Sudan Liberation Army (also called the Sudan Liberation Movement). *See* http://www.icc-cpi.int/NR/rdonlyres/AB04D7D8-7AE8-4530-92B0-648DE6EC5E84/282210/HarunKushaybEng.pdf.
115. *See* ICC website regarding the Darfur case, at http://ww.w.icc-cpi.int/Menus/ICC/Situations+and+Cases/Situations/Situation+ICC+0205/.
116. *See* David Stoelting, *In a Controversial Decision, ICC Issues Arrest Warrant for Sudan's President but Rejects Genocide Charge,* INT'L. LAW NEWS, ABA Section of International Law (Summer 2009) at 23. The prosecutor was granted leave to appeal the exclusion of the genocide charge on June 24, 2009. *Id.*

    The Trial Chamber had made an initial determination that evidence of attacks on Fur, Masalit, and Zarghawa communities, even if responsibility could be imputed to the President as an "indirect co-perpetrator," did not imply an intent on Al-Bashir's part to destroy those communities, as the treaty-based definition of genocide requires. *See id.* Instead, the Trial Chamber found "reasonable grounds to believe" that such violence was motivated by his intent to repress the rebel insurgency, rather than to destroy the three ethnic communities as such. *See id.* at 24.

    On February 3, having heard Prosecutor Moreno-Ocampo's appeal of the charges, the Appeal's Chamber directed the Trial Chamber to reconsider the genocide charge against President al-Bashir. *See* "Groups Welcome Appeal of Genocide Charges Against Sudan's Bashir," Voice of America, Feb. 4, 2010, *available at* http://www.publicinternationallaw.org/warcrimeswatch/archives/wcpw_vol04issue23.html#dar1.
117. *See* Marlise Simons, *International Court Adds Genocide to Charges Against Sudan Leader,* N.Y. TIMES, July 13, 2010, *available at* http://www.nytimes.com/2010/07/13/world/africa/13hague.html?_r=1&ref=world.
118. According to Jerry Fowler, President of the Save Darfur Coalition:

    "[t]he statute of the International Criminal Court is pretty clear in saying that at the arrest warant stage, you just have to establish a reasonable basis that the crime was committed. And the Pre-Trial Chamber kind of twisted that standard, and they basically insisted that the only reasonable inference from the evidence would be genocide, which made it that the Prosecutor had to show beyond a reasonable doubt. And I think what the Appeals Chamber did was put it back into perspective that at this stage, you [merely] have to establish a reasonable basis to believe that the crime was committed."

    See id.
119. *See* Prosecutor v. Kambanda, Case No. ICTR 97-23-S, Judgment and Sentence, 61 (Sept. 4, 1998). For more information about the Kambanda decision by the ICTR, see the website of American University's War Crimes Research Office, *available at* http://www.wcl.american.edu/warcrimes/ictr_judgements.cfm.
120. In late 2009, the African Union criticized the ICC's arrest warrant against Al-Bashir indictment on all charges, endorsing instead the creation of a hybrid court to include Sudanese as well as international judges, as recommended by former South African President Thabo Mbeki. *Mbeki Softens Stance on Darfur Hybrid Court Proposal,* SUDAN TRIBUNE, Dec. 17, 2009, WAR CRIMES WATCH, Vol. 4–Issue Dec. 19, 19, 2009, Frederick K. Cox, International Law Center, Case Western Reserve University School of Law, *available at* http://www.publicinternationallaw.org/warcrimeswatch/archives/wcpw_vol04issue19.html#dar3. Although the Khartoum government objected to the AU approach as a violation of its sovereignty, it may ultimately deem prosecution of crimes against humanity by a hybrid court preferable to trials of state officials in the International Criminal Court. *See id.*

121. According to President Jerry Fowler of the Save Darfur Coalition,

> "[t]he experience of the last year and a half since the Prosecutor first requested the arrest warrant, which happened in July of 2008, is that it's not affecting peace negotiations. They're being driven by their own political dynamics, and in fact, peace negotiations picked up steam after the Prosecutor first requested the arrest warrants. So to that extent, they seem to have a positive impact."

See "Groups Welcome Appeal of Genocide Charges Against Sudan's Bashir," Voice of America, Feb. 4, 2010, http://www.publicinternationallaw.org/warcrimeswatch/archives/wcpw_vol04issue23.html#dar1.

CHAPTER 5

International Refugee Law

Protection for Individuals Fleeing Persecution and Armed Conflict

You left your country to seek refugee in another man's land.
You will be confronted by strange dialects.
You will be fed with unusual diets.
You've got to sleep in a tarpaulin house, which is so hot.
You've got to sleep on a tarpaulin mat, which is so cold.
Living like a refugee is not easy.
Reuben M. Koroma[1]

A. REFUGEES, ARMED CONFLICT, AND INTERNAL DISPLACEMENT: AN OVERVIEW

Since 1951, mainstream international law has defined the refugee as someone with a well-founded fear of persecution on account of ethnicity, politics, religion, or social standing who flees her country of origin and seeks asylum in another nation.[2] This definition has promoted an understanding of the refugee as an exceptional individual distinguished from her peers and at risk of harsher treatment, a viewpoint particularly prominent in the industrialized countries of the global North.[3] The classic definition has also inspired a broader vision, prevalent in Africa and elsewhere in the world, emphasizing the commonality of the refugee experience. This perspective acknowledges that most refugees are part of a greater movement of people fleeing pervasive violence—whether armed conflict, endemic persecution, or crushing poverty—in search of safety, shelter, food, medicine, and livelihood.

There were 15.4 million refugees living throughout the world in late 2010, according to the United Nations High Commissioner for Refugees (UNHCR), the agency with primary responsibility for protecting and assisting refugees.[4] This figure encompasses persons with individualized experiences of persecution, as well as those who have fled more generalized conditions of violence and unrest, all of whom have crossed an international boundary.[5] Of that total, 2.2 million, or nearly one-fifth, were living in sub-Saharan Africa.[6] Alongside these cross-border refugees, there are an even larger number of individuals who are also displaced by repression, war, and other catastrophes but never leave their countries of origin. International refugee law is still trying to cope with and incorporate the needs and rights of internally displaced persons (IDPs).

Given the often similar circumstances of refugees and IDPs, UNHCR and other agencies sometimes group them together within the broader category of *forced migrants*. As of late 2010, UNHCR reports that there were 43.7 million people "forcibly displaced." This figure includes the 15.4 million cross-border refugees, as well as 27.5 million IDPs.[7]

This chapter explores the evolution of international refugee law and practice. The initial focus is on the question of legal status for individual exiles fearing targeted persecution. We then consider the claims to protection and assistance of people fleeing the pervasive violence of civil war and widespread deprivations of human rights, both within and across national boundaries. Starting with the international treaties on the status of refugees, proceeding to regional instruments concerning refugees, and considering emergent law on internally displaced persons, we ultimately confront the disproportionate economic burden of assisting refugees and IDPs that falls on the world's poorest countries. The chapter ends with a consideration of the ways refugee law complements and supplements humanitarian, human rights and international criminal law in seeking to resolve the causes, as well as treat the symptoms, of armed conflict and repression.

This chapter concerns refugee law and practice throughout the world, with a special focus on Africa. Individual sections are devoted to the 1969 Convention Governing the Specific Aspects of Refugee Problems in Africa adopted by the Organization of African Unity (OAU Refugee Convention) and the 2009 African Union Convention for the Protection and Assistance of Internally Displaced Persons in Africa (Kampala Convention) addressing the plight of IDPs in Africa. The text also examines the situation of countries within and outside of Africa that are currently coping with the compound responsibility of hosting large numbers of refugees from other countries alongside their own internally displaced citizens.

B. THE REFUGEE IN INTERNATIONAL AND REGIONAL LAW

1. The 1951 Refugee Convention

The 1951 Convention relating to the Status of Refugees (1951 Refugee Convention) is the bedrock of modern refugee law. With its 1967 Protocol, it articulates universal standards for refugee protection in all regions of the world. Considered together, the two treaties had 147 state parties as of April 2011, including Uganda, Sierra Leone, and Burundi.[8] According to Article 1 of the 1951 Refugee Convention, reaffirmed in Article I of the Protocol, a refugee is a person who,

> owing to well-founded fear of being persecuted for reasons of race, religion, nationality, membership of a particular social group or political opinion, is outside the country of his nationality and is unable or, owing to such fear, is unwilling to avail himself of the protection of that country[.][9]

Article 1 of the 1951 Refugee Convention limited eligibility for refugee status to individuals displaced by historical events existing prior to 1951 and gave individual state signatories the option to further restrict the scope of the treaty to events occurring on the European continent.[10] The 1967 Protocol to the 1951 Refugee Convention was drafted to eliminate these geographical and temporal restrictions,[11] reflecting a growing understanding on the part of the international community that refugee flight and exile were not temporary or isolated problems, but persistent facets of the human condition. In addition to adopting and universalizing the well-founded fear definition of a refugee, the 1967 Protocol incorporated all the remaining substantive provisions of the 1951 Refugee Convention.[12]

The Article 1 definition speaks of the refugee as an individual who has crossed an international boundary in fear of persecution linked to specific aspects of his or her identity. Nevertheless, the drafters of the 1951 Refugee Convention, recognizing that the ultimate reach of refugee law should exceed its initial grasp, specifically urged that individuals in need of protection be treated as refugees even if ineligible under an unduly mechanistic application of the treaty provisions:

> The Conference, [e]xpresses the hope that the Convention relating to the Status of Refugees will have value as an example exceeding its contractual scope and that all nations will be guided by it in granting so far as possible to persons in their territory as refugees and who would not be covered by the terms of the Convention, the treatment for which it provides.[13]

One troublesome aspect of international refugee law is the difference between refugee status and asylum, a distinction that is far more than technical. Refugee status signifies that the United Nations (UN) or a state recognizes that the individual has a well-founded fear of persecution. Asylum means that the refugee enjoys the legal right to reside in a particular country. Not all refugees enjoy this privilege. Although individuals who meet the refugee definition certainly are entitled to *seek* asylum, the 1951 Refugee Convention does not require signatories to grant asylum to refugees. The discretionary nature of asylum is reinforced by the fact that the term is nowhere mentioned in the treaty. Moreover, ten substantive provisions of the convention apply explicitly and exclusively to refugees who have been deemed "lawfully in [the] territory," including various employment, social service, and mobility-related rights.[14] As for determining that refugees are "lawfully present" or granting them durable status, Article 34 of the 1951 Refugee Convention merely encourages that "Contracting States shall as far as possible facilitate the assimilation and naturalization of refugees."[15]

The simple reality is that being a refugee does not entitle one to asylum. Put somewhat differently, although states have the right to grant asylum to refugees, refugees do not have the right to receive it. Hence, although Article 14 of the Universal Declaration of Human Rights (UDHR or Universal Declaration) speaks of the right to "seek and enjoy... asylum," this right is still making the journey from soft to hard law.[16]

Despite the nonentitlement to asylum, there are a number of unqualified obligations that state signatories owe to all refugees under the 1951 Refugee Convention. Three are the most significant. Article 3 prohibits discrimination against refugees on account of race, religion, or national origin.[17] Article 31 prohibits states from penalizing refugees' unlawful entry or presence, pending the consideration of their status.[18] Article 33 prohibits a state signatory from forcing a refugee back to the country in which she fears persecution. After the Article 1 refugee definition itself, the so-called norm of *non-refoulement* is the most well-known provision of the 1951 Refugee Convention. Article 33 provides that

> [n]o Contracting State shall expel or return ("*refouler*") a refugee in any manner whatsoever to the frontiers of territories where his life or freedom would be threatened on account of his race, religion, nationality, membership of a particular social group or political opinion.[19]

This prohibition against forced return to threatened persecution is particularly significant, given the refugee's lack of entitlement to asylum.[20]

The UNHCR Executive Committee, an advisory board to the refugee agency composed of state representatives, has reiterated on numerous occasions the fundamental character of the protection against forced return to feared persecution. A 1980 Conclusion of the Executive Committee clarified that "[a]ction where a refugee is obliged to return... to a country where he has reason to fear persecution constitutes a grave violation of the recognized principle of *non-refoulement*."[21] Academics and practitioners continue to affirm the peremptory character of the norm, and the fact that it applies to all refugees.[22] As refugee law scholar Guy Goodwin Gill clarifies, "the protection of *non-refoulement* is conditioned simply upon satisfying the well-founded fear criterion."[23]

To reconcile the refugee's nonentitlement to asylum with the absolute prohibition against *refoulement* of a refugee, Article 33 must imply the refugee's right to temporary protection in the country of would-be asylum. This protection extends through the granting of asylum, or until the refugee enjoys asylum in another country, or can return to her own country in safety and dignity and without fear of persecution.[24]

2. The 1969 Organization of African Unity Refugee Convention

African refugee law is less preoccupied than classic international refugee law with determining an individualized fear of persecution. As we will see in the section below, individual African countries host hundreds of thousands of refugees, and, in such instances, their governments typically extend prima facie refugee status, conferred en masse on groups of similarly situated persons seeking refuge from violence on their territories.[25] This collective approach to refugee protection is supported by the text of the African refugee treaty itself, adopted under the auspices of the Organization of African Unity (OAU), and called the 1969 Convention Governing the Specific Aspects of Refugee Problems in Africa (OAU Refugee Convention).[26] As of 2011, fifty-three African states are parties to the OAU Refugee Convention, including Uganda, Sierra Leone, and Burundi.[27]

The OAU Refugee Convention is notable for incorporating and expanding upon Article 1 of the 1951 Refugee Convention. In addition to individuals with a well-founded fear of persecution on one of the five enumerated grounds, the African definition also embraces individuals displaced by war and other more generalized conditions of social unrest:

> The term refugee shall also apply to every person who, owing to external aggression, occupation, foreign domination or events seriously disturbing public order in either part

or the whole of his country of origin or nationality, is compelled to leave his place of habitual residence in order to seek refuge in another place outside his country of origin or nationality.[28]

Like the 1951 Refugee Convention, the OAU Refugee Convention includes a *non-refoulement* provision, which prohibits states from forcibly returning a refugee to the country she fled if the threat remains:

> [n]o person shall be subjected by a Member State to measures such as rejection at the frontier, return or expulsion, which would compel him to return to or remain in a territory where his life, physical integrity or liberty would be threatened for the reasons set out in Article I, paragraphs 1 and 2 [which encompass a "well-founded fear of persecution" and "events seriously disturbing public order"]...[29]

Thus, just as the OAU definition includes war refugees alongside refugees from targeted persecution, the OAU *non-refoulement* provision prohibits return of refugees to armed conflict as well as persecution.

By encompassing war refugees, the OAU Refugee Convention does more than expand the boundaries of refugee law. It also codifies a norm of humanitarian law governing the conduct of armed conflict. Whereas international humanitarian law seeks to lessen the suffering caused by war, the *non-refoulement* provision of the OAU Refugee Convention stipulates what should happen if that norm is violated and civilians are forced to flee across borders: The country of would-be asylum may not forcibly return a refugee to the conflicted territory from which she fled.

The OAU Refugee Convention is hence an illustration of the interrelationship between humanitarian and refugee law. Together, they protect civilian victims of war, along with individuals who flee violence and persecution. By virtue of the OAU Refugee Convention, *non-refoulement* has attained a new dimension. As the most important limitation on state power in two refugee treaties, one international and one regional, *non-refoulement* is the heart of refugee law and integral to humanitarian law. In protecting civilian victims of war from return to the very violence they flee, the African norm of *non-refoulement* entitles civilians to safe harbor from armed conflict.

3. The 1984 Cartagena Declaration on Refugees

In 1984, ten Latin American states signed the Cartagena Declaration on Refugees (Cartagena Declaration).[30] Like the African Convention, the Cartagena Declaration is notable for building upon and expanding the refugee definition set forth in the 1951 Refugee Convention. Conclusion 3 of the declaration defines refugees as those who meet

> ... the elements of the 1951 Convention and the 1967 Protocol, including among refugees persons who have fled their country because their lives, safety, or freedom have been threatened by generalized violence, foreign aggression, internal conflicts, massive violations of human rights or other circumstances which have seriously disturbed public order.[31]

Although the Cartagena Declaration is not a treaty, at the time of its adoption, it evidenced emerging state practice in the Americas. It is debatable whether the resolution has jelled into a customary norm binding on all American states, including the United States. But at the very least, it constitutes a secondary source of regional international law. The Cartagena Declaration calls upon countries to grant refugee status to individuals who flee "massive violations of human rights," as well as the individualized persecution contemplated by the 1951 Refugee Convention and the insecurity associated with armed conflict spotlighted in the OAU Refugee Convention.

The OAU Refugee Convention was transformative in taking the refugee definition from the 1951 Refugee Convention and making it more responsive to the realities and displacements of armed conflict. The Cartagena Declaration inspires a further expansion in the context of "dirty wars" or "low-intensity conflict," in which state repression is so pervasive that any armed insurgency is effectively neutralized. Just as the OAU Refugee Convention is a source of humanitarian and refugee law, the Cartagena Declaration illustrates the interconnectedness of refugee, humanitarian, and human rights law.

Fundamentally, the 1951 Refugee Convention, the OAU Refugee Convention, and the Cartagena Declaration are all sources of international human rights law. Each recognizes the basic rights of refugees to nondiscriminatory treatment and protection from *refoulement*. Moreover, all three documents recognize eligibility for refugee status on the part of individuals with a well-founded fear of persecution."[32] The 1984 Cartagena Declaration has an additional human rights dimension because it is the only refugee instrument that explicitly refers to widespread human rights abuses as a cause of flight and a basis for asylum.[33]

C. INTERNALLY DISPLACED PERSONS: REFUGEES WITHIN

An important component of the international refugee definition is the requirement that the asylum-seeker have crossed a border into another country. This formal definition excludes those who flee from place to place within their country of origin—so-called *internally displaced persons*—even though IDPs have much in common with refugees in their human and material circumstances and in the causes of their flight. Their vulnerability may even be compounded by their government's role in their displacement, or failure to prevent it. Because IDPs do not come within the ambit of the 1951 Refugee Convention, they also fall outside the formal protection and assistance mandate of the United Nations High Commissioner for Refugees.

Despite the lack of a legal protection regime in their name, IDPs have slowly risen on the international agenda over the past twenty years. Enhanced attention to IDPs is the confluence of two dynamics, one humanitarian and the other political. First, the sheer magnitude of unmet human needs has resulted in a greater willingness on the part of UNHCR and other UN agencies to assist IDPs by stretching their mandates even if the treaty-based refugee definition remains the same. Second, an endorsement by UN members of the "responsibility to protect," discussed in Chapter 2, raises the prospect of humanitarian intervention if states neglect their own displaced citizens in violation of international human rights obligations. States emerging from prolonged civil wars have an added incentive to attend to the needs of the internally displaced, given that the long-term success of post-conflict reconstruction hinges upon the successful political and social reintegration of IDPs into the fabric of the new society. Indeed, a stated commitment to the concerns of IDPs, along with a renewed commitment to the rule of law, is often at the heart of a peace settlement.[34]

In recognition of the related claims to protection on the part of refugees and IDPs, the UN and the African Union have taken a series of graduated steps toward better recognizing and ensuring the rights of IDPs. The first initiatives were within the humanitarian agencies and administrative organs of the UN. Then came the drafting of the first legal instruments setting forth the rights of IDPs and the obligations of states to assist and protect them.

As an initial measure in the early 1990s, UNHCR began providing limited assistance to IDPs under its "extended mandate," particularly in countries in which it was already working with cross-border refugees.[35] In order to raise the profile of IDPs within the UN bureaucracy, the United Nations created the post of Special Representative of the Secretary General for IDPs, first held by former Sudanese Foreign Minister Frances Deng from 1992 to 2004 and, subsequently, by Swiss refugee law scholar Walter Kalin. In 2000, UNHCR spearheaded a UN interagency plan of action. UNHCR resolved to take the lead in overall assistance to IDPs, UNICEF was tasked to handle sanitation, the World Health Organization (WHO) agreed to address IDP health care needs, and the UN Development Programme (UNDP) resolved to incorporate IDPs into its long-term development initiatives.[36]

While UN agencies were broadening their missions, ideally to the benefit of IDPs, the first rumblings of new international norms were heard. Early pronouncements included the 1994 Addis Ababa Document on Refugees and Forced Population Displacement in Africa, and the 1998 United Nations Guiding Principles on Internal Displacement.[37] Then on July 29, 2000, the International Law Association (ILA) met and approved, by consensus, the London Declaration of International Law Principles on Internally Displaced Persons (London Declaration).[38] The London Declaration affirmed the rights of IDPs to protection and humanitarian assistance. To this end, it called upon states to protect IDPs and prohibited them from mounting armed attacks on IDP settlements. It further obligated states to allow IDPs nondiscriminatory access to humanitarian assistance and to refrain from interfering with relief operations organized by other agencies.[39] Though properly characterized as "soft law" rather than a primary source of international law, the London Declaration established important benchmarks and called for further action by the international community on behalf of internally displaced persons.

Nearly a decade after the London Declaration, the African Union (AU) concluded and opened for signature the first treaty on IDPs. The 2009 African Union Convention for the Protection and Assistance of Internally Displaced Persons in Africa (Kampala Convention)[40] was signed on October 23, 2009, by seventeen African states at the conclusion of a conference held in Kampala, Uganda.

The Kampala Convention walks a fine line between two pairs of competing goals and realities, the first between prevention and response, the second between affirming the rights of IDPs and recognizing resource limitations. Addressing the first tradeoff, the Kampala Convention strikes a balance between calling on states to prevent the massive internal displacement of their people, on the one hand, and obligating states to provide assistance and protection to displaced people in light of the reality of such displacements, on the other. The Preamble to the Kampala Convention conveys these competing goals in expressing the signatories' determination:

> to adopt measures aimed at preventing and putting an end to the phenomenon of internal displacement by eradicating the root causes, especially persistent and recurrent conflicts as well as addressing displacement caused by natural disasters, which have a devastating impact on human life, peace, stability, security, and development;

[while at the same time]

> affirming our primary responsibility and commitment to respect, protect and fulfill the rights to which internally displaced persons are entitled, without discrimination of any kind[.][41]

Regarding the second tension, the Kampala Convention calls on states to "bear the primary duty and responsibility for providing protection of and humanitarian assistance to internally displaced persons" in Article 5(1). Yet "where available resources are inadequate to enable them to do so," the convention obligates states to "cooperate in seeking the assistance of international organizations and humanitarian agencies" in Article 5(6).

The detailed and ambitious Kampala Convention comprises 23 articles. They impose obligations on states, international and humanitarian organizations, armed groups, and the AU.[42] The enumerated obligations of state parties to the Kampala Convention are the most extensive and the treaty divides them into categories, including general obligations,[43] obligations regarding the prevention of internal displacement,[44] obligations to assist IDPs in the context of internal displacement,[45] and obligations to respect the nonderogable human rights of IDPs in the context of internal displacement.[46] On February 25, 2010, Uganda became the first country to ratify the Kampala Convention.[47] The treaty will come into force once fifteen African countries have ratified it.[48]

D. THE INTERDEPENDENCE OF PROTECTION AND ASSISTANCE FOR REFUGEES AND IDPS

In addition to protecting refugees through conferring varying types of legal status, the UN and host governments seek to provide basic assistance to persons fleeing persecution who are in need of shelter, food, sanitation, medical care, and education. Although much of UNHCR's annual budget, 2 billion US dollars (USD) in 2009, goes toward the care and maintenance of refugees, the ultimate patrons of refugees are the countries that receive them, some richer and more stable than their neighbors, but most as poor and conflicted as the countries from which refugees flee. Given that it is the poorest nations that host the lion's share of refugees and IDPs worldwide, the assistance component of UNHCR's mandate is essential, and sometimes overshadows legal protection for displaced persons, particularly in situations of flight en masse.

Indeed, an important symbiotic relationship between assistance and protection is revealed, particularly when the refugees' initial welcome by a struggling local community is short-lived and the competition for scarce resources is palpable. Regular shipments of international assistance—from plastic tarpaulins for shelter to bags of grain for registered refugees' monthly food entitlements—have profound and sometimes negative impacts on rural economies and social networks. Granting local people access to refugee food distributions and medical clinics tends to reduce tensions and enhance the economic security of the refugees and their hosts alike. In the words of one UNHCR administrator, "rice buys protection." Sharing humanitarian aid with governments and host populations enhances the de facto protection that refugees enjoy, by helping to ensure that they do not wear out their welcome.[49]

1. Refugee Assistance: Global Burden-Sharing

Many countries host significant cross-border refugee populations, throughout both the developing and industrialized worlds. Nevertheless, the extent of burden-sharing varies considerably, even among the top ten "major refugee hosting countries,"ranging from Pakistan, which shelters almost two million refugees, to the United Kingdom (UK), which hosts slightly less than 300,000.[50] Some of the range in the absolute size of refugee populations is explained by the fact that the majority of refugees come from developing countries and seek asylum in neighboring developing countries.[51] But host nations assume even more disparate burdens in light of the size of their resident populations and the strength of their economies. Because of their limited resources, developing countries are economically impacted by refugee populations to a much greater extent than richer ones.

One way to illustrate and evaluate the relative material impacts of refugee populations on individual countries is to compare the population and economic output of three countries that, in recent years, have hosted three-hundred thousand or more refugees: Germany representing the industrialized world, Tanzania representing the continent of Africa, and Pakistan the continent of Asia. These countries are significant actors on the global refugee stage because, in absolute terms, they care for large numbers of refugees: Germany, the largest number in Europe and the industrialized world overall; Tanzania, the largest number in Africa, in cumulative historical terms; and Pakistan, the largest number in the world, both recently and historically.[52] In order to make a meaningful comparison, we consider each country's gross domestic product adjusted for purchasing power parity (GDP PPP) in USD, and its non-refugee population; and calculate how many refugees are hosted per dollar of adjusted GDP per capita.[53]

Germany, with a population of around 82 million people, a GDP PPP of approximately $2.9 trillion, and the fifth largest economy in the world, hosted nearly six-hundred thousand refugees in 2009. In absolute terms, Germany sheltered the largest number of refugees of any country in Europe and, proportional to its national wealth and population, more than any other major industrial country. Germany hosts 17 refugees for every dollar of its per capita GDP.[54]

Tanzania, with a population of around 41 million people and a much lower adjusted GDP of approximately $54.3 billion, provided asylum in 2008 to three-hundred thousand cross-border refugees. After naturalizing more than 150-thousand Burundian refugees the following year, Tanzania continued to host over one-hundred thousand refugees by the end of 2009. Accounting for its population, national wealth, and local economic conditions, Tanzania hosts 97 refugees for each per capita dollar of adjusted GDP, and thus assumes six times the relative burden borne by Germany.[55]

Finally, Pakistan shelters more refugees than any other country in the world, with a population of around 176 million people and an approximate GDP of $431 billion. Pakistan hosts nearly two million refugees, which amounts to 745 people per dollar of adjusted GDP per capita, and forty-four times the economic burden assumed by Germany.[56]

Given the disparate material impacts of refugee populations on nations throughout the world, various conclusions might be drawn about the responsibilities of wealthier nations to assume greater burdens, whether in opening their borders to more refugees, or in providing more international aid to developing countries of asylum. As we have seen, the 1951 and OAU Refugee Conventions do not require parties to grant asylum to refugees, let alone mandate a certain level of financial support to refugee assistance worldwide. The legal bite of these treaties, and their chief limitations on state power, emanates from their prohibitions against the forced return of refugees to persecution and armed conflict; and their bans on discrimination on the basis of race, religion, or national origin. Nevertheless, additional obligations on industrialized states can be implied from the text of other human rights treaties. The UN Charter states as one of its fundamental purposes "to achieve international co-operation in solving international problems of an economic, social, cultural or humanitarian character."[57] The International Covenant on Economic, Social and Cultural Rights (ICESCR), for its part, calls on states to provide "international assistance" and to participate in international "economic and technical" cooperation.[58] These treaties suggest that providing assistance to states hosting refugees in the global South is one manifestation of a broader duty on the part of Northern states to lessen inequities in material conditions of life between the industrialized and developing worlds.

2. Assisting IDPs Alongside Refugees

Although some of the world's leaders in sheltering refugees offer a stable environment in terms of political and social security, other major refugee-hosting countries are doubly burdened by large movements of internally displaced persons. Germany, currently the largest refugee-receiving country in the industrialized world, hosted six-hundred thousand refugees in 2009, but had no IDPs to contend with. Similarly, Tanzania, the most historically significant country of asylum in Africa, hosted one-hundred thousand refugees in 2009 and no IDPs. In contrast, Pakistan, the world's premier country of asylum for the past twenty years, coped with the internal displacement of nearly two million of its own nationals in 2009, in addition to hosting the same number of refugees.[59] Another 15 to 20 million Pakistanis were rendered homeless as a result of the summer floods of 2010.

In Africa, it is not unusual for the same country that is assisting refugees from neighboring countries to support an even larger population of IDPs. These numbers play out variously in specific countries, depending upon whether the host country for cross-border refugees is experiencing civil strife of its own. By way of example, in 2009, Burundi hosted nearly 25,000 refugees and 100,000 IDPs; in Uganda, there were nearly 130,000 refugees and around 450,000 IDPs.[60] These IDP numbers reflect the recent conflicts in both Burundi and Uganda, and the progress still to be made to restore infrastructure throughout Burundi and in northern Uganda. Sierra Leone, on the other hand, hosted approximately 9,000 refugees and no registered IDPs in 2009, a decade after the signing of the 1999 Lomé Peace Agreement between the Government of Sierra Leone and the Revolutionary United Front.[61]

The realities of protecting IDPs in Africa are particularly daunting in the Darfur region of Sudan, as well as in neighboring Uganda. In Darfur, the humanitarian emergency has been marked by massive internal displacement, as well as loss of civilian life. Estimates of civilian deaths vary widely, ranging, in 2005, from sixty thousand, the most conservative estimate by the US Department of State, to four-hundred thousand, as reported by the Coalition for International Justice.[62] The number of internally displaced in Darfur, at the start of 2009, amounted to 2.7 million people.[63] Similarly, for Uganda, in 2006, after twenty years of civil war, nearly two million northern Ugandans had been displaced from their homes. Beginning with the signing of the first ceasefire agreement between the LRA and the Government of Uganda, in August of that year, IDPs slowly began to return to their communities. In 2008, the IDP population was down to one million, and by December 2010, ninety percent of all IDPs had reportedly returned to their homes in northern Uganda.[64]

Despite improved security in northern Uganda since the end of large-scale military engagements between LRA rebels and government soldiers, in 2008, former IDPs continued to face precarious living conditions. Upon returning to their home areas, many returnees experience food shortages and inadequate access to health care and proper sanitary facilities.[65] The marginal circumstances of IDPs in countries like Uganda, emerging from protracted civil wars, illustrate the need for fuller incorporation of IDPs within the international refugee protection regime.

E. REFUGEE LAW AND ITS SISTER FIELDS OF INTERNATIONAL LAW

The UN and African refugee conventions, like the Cartagena Declaration, have significant human rights and humanitarian dimensions. As instruments of international refugee law, they seek to protect individuals displaced across national borders from further persecution or forced return. In the heat of violence, regional or international, the essential mandate of refugee law is to shelter victims rather than to prosecute perpetrators. Nevertheless, persecutors and combatants may also be vulnerable to international criminal procedures, given evidence that they committed war crimes or crimes against humanity. If such prosecutions have a deterrent effect on future conduct, then the means of criminal law will have served the ends of refugee protection. Thus, while refugee law is importantly defined by the urgency of its protection and assistance mandate, the deliberative procedures of criminal law may also play a vital role in preventing future acts of persecution.

From the broader standpoint of comparative international law, it might be said that refugee law is less about legal enforcement and more about humanitarian assistance, in contrast to international criminal law, which is associated with extensive formal judicial institutions. Similar to humanitarian law, refugee law has a certain rough-and-readiness about it, generated by the drive to provide life-saving shelter and sustenance in the midst of extreme suffering. And like human rights law, refugee law serves as an essential affirmation of human dignity. But these four sister fields of law are inherently interdependent. Refugee law needs humanitarian law to realize the norm of humanitarian action, as the UN High Commissioner for Refugees and the International Committee of the Red Cross (ICRC) share their moral authority to act in favor of victims of war and persecution. Refugee law and humanitarian law look to international criminal law to provide powerful incentives for the demobilization and rehabilitation of combatants, so long as prosecutions do not have the unintended effect of inspiring renewed conflict. And refugee law needs human rights law as a reminder that combating forced displacement will require political participation and socioeconomic transformation as much as emergency relief or legal process.

The heart of refugee law remains guaranteeing freedom from forced return to persecution, and providing the material aid necessary to sustain a dignified way of life. But if refugee law is to live up to its potential as a tool of conflict resolution, it must embrace those living on its margins. Like those who flee persecution across state borders, the internally displaced and all victims of war are human beings who deserve protection and assistance.

Chapter 5 concludes Part I, devoted to the *rules* of international law relevant to conflict resolution. Part II will concentrate on specific *tools* for the practical implementation of international humanitarian law in Uganda, Sierra Leone, and Burundi, three African countries emerging from armed conflict.

NOTES

1. "Living Like a Refugee" is track 1 on Disc One of the Sierra Leone Refugee All Stars' *Living Like a Refugee* album (a two-disc CD set). *Living Like a Refugee* is a Sodasoap Production, 2005, five tracks (including track 1) recorded in Sembakounya Refugee Camp, Guinea (Anti Records 2006).
2. The international refugee definition is found in the 1951 Convention relating to the Status of Refugees (1951 Refugee Convention), July 28, 1951, 189 UNTS 137, art. 1 (A) (2). This definition is further discussed in section B of our text below.
3. In the United States, refugee status determination is done on an individual basis, sometimes through an adversarial process in which the asylum seeker is not guaranteed free legal counsel, and may be detained while her claim is pending. The adversarial process begins before a specialized immigration judge, with two levels of appeal—first to an administrative panel and then to a federal court of appeals—followed by a discretionary appeal to the United States (US) Supreme Court, granted in rare instances. As in other industrialized countries with complex and often daunting status determination regimes, in the United States, administrative and federal judges meticulously analyze the numerous elements of the refugee definition for each asylum-seeker—requiring that the harm suffered or feared rises to the level of persecution, ascertaining that the fear is well-founded, ensuring that the asylum seeker fears persecution on account of one or more of the enumerated grounds, and so forth. In US courts, particular emphasis is placed on proof of the motivation behind the persecutor's mistreatment of the asylum seeker, the so-called "nexus" between the persecution and the claimed basis or ground for that persecution. In a landmark and controversial decision, the US Supreme Court, in 1992, denied asylum to a Guatemalan who received a credible death threat in the context of an attempted forced military conscription by the armed insurgency then fighting the Government of Guatemala. The court required some evidence that the rebel soldier was specifically motivated to persecute Jairo Elias-Zacarias because of Jairo's political opinion opposing the goals of the rebel movement, and not merely because he refused to serve. In the absence of such insight into the mind of the persecutor, Elias-Zacarias was found ineligible for asylum. *See* INS v. Zacarias, 502 US 478, 483 (1992). *See also* Joan Fitzpatrick, *The International Dimension of U.S. Refugee Law*, 15 BERKELEY J. INT'L L. 1, 20 (1997) ("the Court imposed a double burden on asylum applicants . . . and evinced little sensitivity to the international law framework within which the asylum . . . provisions were drafted").
4. *See* United Nations High Commissioner on Refugees (UNHCR), "2010 Global Trends: 60 years and still counting" [UNHCR 2010 Global Trends] at 2, *available at* http://www.unhcr.org/4dfa11499.html.

5. Canadian refugee scholar James Hathaway contrasts the so-called "individualist perspective" on refugee status more prevalent in the West with what he calls the "social perspective" more prevalent in Africa. *See* James Hathaway, *The Law of Refugee Status* (Butterworths, 1991) at 4–6 and 16–19. Hathaway's treatise on refugee law lays out three historical perspectives on the refugee definition: the juridical perspective, which predominated from 1920–1950, and emphasized the state's unwillingness to provide de jure protection to particular groups of people, often for political reasons; the social perspective, predominating from 1935–1939, and emphasizing the state's inability to provide de facto state protection to certain groups of people, often as a result of widespread and tumultuous circumstances; and the individualist perspective, predominating from 1938–1950, which contemplated a case-by-case determination of refugee status based on the particular circumstances and risks associated with the individual asylum seeker. Hathaway at 2–6. The 1951 Convention relating to the Status of Refugees (1951 Refugee Convention), cited above, might be said to reflect an individualist perspective. In contrast, certain regional instruments, including the major treaty of the Organization of African Unity (OAU) dealing with refugees, also cited below, manifest a social, de facto, or group-oriented approach. Within the parameters of the social perspective on refugee status, the individual is not expected to demonstrate the reasons for her flight or to justify her claim to protection. Hathaway at 16–18.

6. UNHCR 2010 Global Trends at 11, 13 (Table 1). UNHCR estimates that 80 percent of all refugees were hosted by developing countries as of the end of 2010. *See id.* at 11.

7. *See id.* at 5. In addition to the 15.4 million refugees and 27.5 million internally displaced people (IDPs) as of late 2010, by UNHCR count, there were .8 million individuals seeking protection as refugees whose claims had yet to be adjudicated. *See id.*

8. *See* UNHCR, "States Parties to the 1951 Convention relating to the Status of Refugees and the 1967 Protocol," *available* at http://www.unhcr.org/3b73b0d63.html.

9. 1951 Convention relating to the Status of Refugees (1951 Refugee Convention), July 28, 1951, 189 UNTS 137, art. 1(A) (2); 1967 Protocol relating to the Status of Refugees (1967 Protocol), Jan. 31, 1967, 606 UNTS 267, art. I (2).

    The Article 1 definition also encompasses certain stateless persons, specifically, an individual "who, not having a nationality and being outside the country of his former habitual residence as a result of such events, is unable or, owing to such fear, is unwilling to return to it." 1951 Refugee Convention, art. 1(A) (2).

10. The Article 1 refugee definition of the 1951 Refugee Convention referenced "events occurring before January 1, 1951" in paragraph (A), and allowed state signatories the option of limiting the substantive definition of refugees to individuals displaced by events occurring in Europe in paragraph (B). 1951 Convention, art. 1(A) (2) and (B) (1).

11. The heart of the Article 1(A) (2) definition was reaffirmed in the 1967 Protocol to the 1951 Refugee Convention, but without the temporal and geographic restrictions. Article 1(A) of the 1951 Refugee Convention was amended slightly by the Protocol to remove the "events occurring before January 1, 1951 clause." 1967 Protocol, art. I (2). Although the Protocol allowed 1951 Refugee Convention signatories to continue to impose geographical restrictions already in place, first-time signatories to the Protocol are required to apply the definition to individuals throughout the world. *Id.*, art. I (3). These revisions to Article 1 in the Protocol served to strengthen the universal character of the refugee definition.

12. Articles 2–34 of the 1951 Refugee Convention are incorporated wholesale in the 1967 Protocol. *See* 1967 Protocol, art. I (1).

13. Final Act of the 1951 United Nations Conference of Plenipotentiaries on the Status of Refugees and Stateless Persons, 189 UNTS 37, para. E (published in excerpted form as Annex I to the 1951 Convention relating to the Status of Refugees, 189 UNTS 37).

14. Ten of the substantive obligations that a state party has toward refugees under the 1951 Refugee Convention are qualified by the requirement that they are "lawfully staying in their territory," meaning that these obligations do not apply to refugees who have not already been granted asylum or some other type of legal status. Specifically, the "lawfully staying" requirement applies to the right of association or membership in trade unions (Art. 15), the right to engage in wage-earning employment (Art. 17), the right to secure self-employment opportunities (Art. 18), the right to work in a professional field for which they have appropriate training (Art. 19), the right to equal access to housing (Art. 21), the right to public benefits (Art. 23), the right to social security (Art. 24), the right to freedom of movement (Art. 26), the right to travel documents (Art. 28) and the right against arbitrary expulsion (Art. 32). *See, id.,* arts. 15, 17, 18, 19, 21, 23, 24, 26, 28 and 32. Importantly, the possibility of arbitrary expulsion of refugees in an informal status is qualified by the norm of *non-refoulement*, discussed below, which signifies that no refugee can be sent back to a situation in which he or she would fear persecution. *Compare, id.,* arts. 32 and 33.
15. 1951 Refugee Convention, art. 34. Article 34 goes on to state that "[contracting states] shall in particular make every effort to expedite naturalization proceedings and to reduce as far as possible the charges and costs of such proceedings." *Id.*
16. Article 14 of the Universal Declaration of Human Rights (UDHR) codifies the right of all persons to "seek and enjoy in other countries asylum from persecution." UDHR, GA Res. 217A (III), UN Doc A/810, at 71 (1948). Nevertheless, the UDHR is a resolution of the UN General Assembly, and thus generically a secondary rather than a primary source of international law, as discussed in Chapter 1 of our text. Although major portions of the UDHR are regarded as having achieved the status of customary international law, we need evidence of state practice and *opinio juris* to conclude that the same is true of Article 14. Unlike the customary norms against torture, inhuman treatment, and arbitrary execution, the right to asylum has not been codified in an international treaty of universal scope. Two regional human rights treaties do recognize the right to asylum: the American Convention and the Banjul Charter. *See* discussion in Chapter 3, sections C.4.b and c.
17. 1951 Refugee Convention, *op. cit.*, art. 3. Other fundamental freedoms are accorded refugees regardless of status: Article 4 protects refugees' freedom of religious practice; Article 16 protects their access to courts of law; and Article 20 protects them from discrimination where the state finds it necessary to establish a system of public rationing of essential consumer products. *Id.*, arts. 4, 16, and 20.
18. *Id.*, art. 31. Related to the non-penalization of unlawful status is the requirement that states issue identity documents to refugees without valid travel documents. *Id.*, art. 27.
19. *Id.*, art. 33.
20. The discretionary nature of asylum paired with the mandatory character of *non-refoulement* is reflected in the implementing legislation of parties to the convention and protocol. For example, in the US, the provision of the Immigration and Nationality Act (INA) that pertains to asylum provides that "[t]he Attorney General *may* grant asylum to an alien who has applied for asylum . . . if the Attorney General determines that such alien is a refugee. . . ." In contrast, the INA provision with respect to *restriction on removal*, the US equivalent of *non-refoulement*, provides that "the Attorney General *may not* remove an alien to a country if the Attorney General decides that the alien's life or freedom would be threatened in such country on account of race, religion, nationality, membership in a particular social group or political opinion." *Compare* INA sec. 208, 8 USC sec. 1158, *with* INA sec. 241(b)(3), 8 U.S.C. sec. 1251(b)(3), emphasis added.
21. *Conclusions Endorsed by the Executive Committee on Refugees Without a Country of Asylum*, UN GAOR, 34th Session, Supp. No. 12A, at 17, UN Doc. A/34/12/Add. 1 (1980).

22. *See* Jennifer Moore, *Restoring the Humanitarian Character of U.S. Refugee Law: Lessons from the International Community*, 15 BERKELEY J. INT'L L. 51, 55–58 (1997) ("all refugees are entitled to the protection of the norm of *non-refoulement*").

    The United States stands alone among the signatories to the 1951 Refugee Convention and 1967 Protocol in declaring that only a select group of refugees are eligible for *non-refoulement*, namely, those who can demonstrate that persecution is more likely than not, a standard thought to require a higher quantum of proof than the well-founded fear of persecution, which is the basis for refugee status under both the 1951 Refugee Convention and applicable US statutory law. *See INS v. Stevic*, 467 US 407 (1984); *see also INS v. Cardoza-Fonseca*, 480 US 420, 440–41 (1987). The US Supreme Court decisions in *Stevic* and *Cardoza* have been criticized with respect to their unprincipled constriction of the norm of *non-refoulement*. *See* Joan Fitzpatrick, *The International Dimension of U.S. Refugee Law*, 15 BERKELEY J. INT'L L. 1, 7–8 (1997) ("nothing in the Convention or Protocol, the interpretive UNHCR Handbook, or other relevant sources of international refugee law suggests that any group of *bona fide* refugees ... is left unprotected by Article 33").

23. GUY GOODWIN-GILL, THE REFUGEE IN INTERNATIONAL LAW at 137 (1996).

24. In addition to protecting and assisting refugees, UNHCR is also mandated to seek durable solutions to their situation, which include voluntary repatriation, settlement in the country of asylum, and third country resettlement. To be voluntary, repatriation requires that refugees have meaningful access to information about conditions in their countries of origin. Voluntary repatriation is a tricky enterprise at best, given the dynamic conditions that exist in countries emerging from armed conflict and repression. Thus, UNHCR should only promote voluntary repatriation if conditions on the ground suggest that refugees may return in safety and dignity. *See* UNHCR, *The State of the World's Refugees: The Challenge of Protection* 169, 172–75 (1993).

25. During the 1992–2005 Burundian civil war, close to half a million Burundians sought refuge in Tanzania, where they were accorded prima facie refugee status by the Government of Tanzania, without the necessity of individualized status determination. As of 2002, 370,000 Burundians living in Tanzanian refugee camps near the Burundian border were subject to this group designation. *See* Jennifer Moore, *The Alchemy of Exile: Strengthening a Culture of Human Rights in the Burundian Refugee Camps in Tanzania*, 27 WASHINGTON U. J. L. & POL. 139 at 142, note 7, and 144.

26. OAU Convention, UNTS 14,691, *entered into force* June 20, 1974, art. I (1).

27. *See* US Committee for Refugees and Immigrants, "Refugee Warehousing International Standards" (2011), *available at* http://www.refugees.org/resources/refugee-warehousing/refugee-warehousing.html. Burundi ratified the OAU Refugee Convention in 1975, and Sierra Leone and Uganda ratified in 1987. *See* University of Minnesota Human Rights Library, "Convention Governing the Specific Aspects of Refugee Problems in Africa," *available at* http://www1.umn.edu/humanrts/instree/z2arcon.htm.

28. OAU Refugee Convention, art. I (2).

29. *Id.* at Art. II (3).

    Article II (3) refers us back to the Article I refugee definition of the OAU Refugee Convention, which includes individuals who fall within the 1951 Refugee Convention definition (referenced in OAU Refugee Convention, Art. I (1)), plus persons "compelled to leave" their countries of origin "owing to . . . events seriously disturbing public order" (OAU Refugee Convention, Art. I (2)). Thus the OAU Refugee Convention's *non-refoulement* provision explicitly protects refugees fleeing individualized persecution as well as those displaced by armed conflict and generalized conditions of unrest. *See id.*, Arts. I (1) and (2), and II (3).

30. *See* Cartagena Declaration on Refugees (Cartagena Declaration), adopted under the auspices of the Government of the Republic of Colombia, Cartagena de Indias,

November 22, 1984, reproduced in *Annual Report of the Inter-American Commission on Human Rights* 1984–85, OEA/Ser.L/II.66, doc. 10, rev. 1, at 190–193.
31. Cartagena Declaration, Conclusion 3, paragraph 3.
32. *See* Office of the UNHCR, *Handbook on Procedures and Criteria for Determining Refugee Status under the 1951 Convention and the 1967 Protocol relating to the Status of Refugees* (Geneva, Jan. 1988).
33. *See* Cartagena Declaration, Conclusion 3, paragraph 3.
34. Uganda's Peace Agreement between the Government of Uganda and the Lord's Resistance Army (LRA), still awaiting final signature by the leadership of the LRA, comprises five documents. Agenda Item 2, the "Agreement on Comprehensive Solutions between the GOU and the LRA," was signed on May 2, 2007, by a government representative and the leader of the LRA delegation. It focuses on the return and reintegration of internally displaced persons. The text of all five Agenda Items is found at http://www.resolveuganda.org/peaceagreement. The Ugandan peace process is further discussed in Chapter 7.
35. *See* UNHCR, *The State of the World's Refugees: A Humanitarian Agenda* 117 (1997).
   In 2009, UNHCR statistics powerfully suggest that the distinction between refugees and IDPs is less significant in practice than in theory. Of the close to 26 million people who were assisted by UNHCR in both those years, 15.6 million were IDPs, and only 10.4 million were refugees. This breakdown reflects the greater number of IDPs relative to refugees worldwide, and the common vulnerability experienced by both communities. *See* UNHCR 2009 Global Trends, *op. cit.*, at 1, *available at* http://www.unhcr.org/4c11f0be9.html.
36. *See* Ray Wilkinson, *The Biggest Failure of the International Community: A New Approach to Help the World's Internally Displaced People*, REFUGEES MAGAZINE, Vol. 4, No. 141, 2006, at 6–10; *see also* Musalo, Moore, and Boswell, *Refugee Law and Policy: A Comparative and International Approach* (4th Edition, Carolina Academic Press 2011) at 1133.
37. The 1994 Addis Ababa Documents and the 1998 UN Guiding Principles are both referenced in the Preamble to the 2009 African Union (AU) Convention for the Protection and Assistance of Internally Displaced Persons in Africa, cited and discussed in our text below.
38. London Declaration of International Law Principles on Internally Displaced Persons, July 29, 2000, 69 ILA, Conference Report (2000), *available at* http://www.ila-hq.org.
39. *See* Luke Lee, *The London Declaration of International law Principles on Internally Displaced Persons*, 95 AJIL 454–58 (2001). The author chaired the International Law Association's International Committee on Internally Displaced Persons, which drafted the declaration.
40. Kampala Convention, *adopted*, Oct. 22, 2009 (not yet in force), *available at* http://www.unhcr.org/refworld/docid/4ae572d82.html. *See, generally,* Won Kidane, *Managing Forced Displacement by Law in Africa: the Role of the New African Union IDPs Convention*, 44 VANDERBILT J. TRAN'L L. (Jan. 2011) 1–85.
41. *See* Kampala Convention, Preamble.
42. *See id.*, arts. 3–5, 9, and 11 (obligations on states), art. 6 (obligations on humanitarian organizations), art. 7 (obligations of armed groups) and art. 8 (AU obligations).
43. General obligations of states under the Kampala Convention include undertaking to "[p]revent political, social, cultural and economic exclusion and marginalization, that are likely to cause displacement or populations" and "incorporate[ing] their obligations under this Convention into domestic law." *See* Kampala Convention, art. 3(1) (b) and art. 3(2) (a).
44. State obligations concerning the prevention of internal displacement include "devising early warning systems" and refraining from arbitrary displacement are set forth in Article 4.

See Kampala Convention, art. 4(2) and (4). Prohibited types of arbitrary displacement include "displacement based on policies of racial discrimination," "mass displacement of civilians in situations of armed conflict, unless the security of the civilians involved or imperative military reasons so demand, in accordance with international humanitarian law," "displacement intentionally used as a method of warfare," and "displacement used as a collective punishment." See Kampala Convention, art. 4(4) (a), (b), (c) and (g).

45. State obligations to protect and assist in the context of internal displacement under Article 5 include bearing "the primary responsibility for providing protection of and humanitarian assistance to internally displaced persons . . . without discrimination of any kind," and "where available resources are inadequate to enable them to do so, . . . cooperat[ing] in seeking the assistance of international organizations and humanitarian agencies, civil society organizations and other relevant actors." See Kampala Convention, art. 5(1) and 5(6).

46. Article 9, like Article 5 of the Kampala Convention, relates to state obligations in the context of internal displacement, but is designed to draw together the most fundamental obligations of states towards the internally displaced, by affirming the nonderogable human rights that IDPs share with all other human beings. These peremptory rules include the norm against discrimination; the absolute prohibitions against genocide, crimes against humanity and war crimes; the *jus cogens* protections against arbitrary killing, torture, and other violations of nonderogable human rights; and protections against sexual and gender-based violence. See Kampala Convention, art. 9(1) (a), (b), (c) and (d). Article 9 also establishes affirmative state obligations to prioritize the special needs of certain IDPs, including unaccompanied children, female heads of household, and victims of sexual violence. See Kampala Convention, art. 9(2) (c) and (d).

47. See "IDP Convention–Now the Hard work Begins," Oct. 26, 2010, *available at* http://allafrica.com/stories/200910261530.html.

48. See Kampala Convention, art. 17.

49. Author's recall of her Associate Protection Officer training session with UNHCR Programme Officer, UNCHR Branch Office in Conakry, Republic of Guinea, circa June 1991.

50. See UNHCR 2009 Global Trends, *op. cit.*, at 7, *available at* http://www.unhcr.org/4c11f0be9.html.
    The five top refugee-hosting countries in 2009, in descending order of importance, were Pakistan, the Islamic Republic of Iran, the Syrian Arab Republic, Germany, and Jordan. The same countries were in the top five in 2008 and 2009. *Id.* Refugee host nations in the second tier for 2009, also in descending order, were Kenya, Chad, China, the US, and the UK. *Id.*

51. UNHCR reports that 80 percent of cross-border refugees have found asylum in developing countries. *See id.* at 1. At the same time, around 83 percent of refugees are believed to remain in their region of origin. *See id.* at 6. Together, these statistics suggest that well over half of all refugees come from the developing world and remain in the developing world.

52. Statistics regarding Germany's 2009 refugee caseload are available in UNHCR 2009 Global Trends, *op. cit.*, at 7, and indicate that Germany hosted more refugees than any other European or major industrial country that year. For its part, Tanzania was the largest refugee-hosting country in Africa from 1997 to 2007, and in 2002, had 700,000 refugees living on its territory. *Id.* at 8. As for Pakistan, in 2007, 2008, and 2009, it was the top refugee hosting country in the world, hosting 1,740,700 refugees in 2009, most of whom were Afghans. *See id.* at 7. Pakistan's assistance to Afghan refugees has endured over several decades. In 1991, Pakistan hosted 3,098,000 Afghans. By 1992, the number of refugees in Pakistan decreased by almost 50 percent to 1,629,200, largely due to the voluntary repatriation of Afghan refugees. See UNHCR, *The State of the World's Refugee: The Challenge of*

Protection (1993) at Annex I.1, "Refugee Populations by Country or Territory of Asylum and by Origin: 1991–1992," and at Annex I.8, "Indicative Numbers of Returnees During 1992."

53. Gross domestic product (GDP) is calculated in US dollars (USD), with an adjustment for purchasing power parity (PPP). Quantifying GDP PPP in US dollars seeks to equalize differences in the price of goods and services between countries. As a result of the conversion, one US dollar of GDP, adjusted for PPP, should have the same purchasing power in the local economy as it would in the US. UNDP, Human Development Report 2009, *op. cit.*, at 212. Author's use of the term *adjusted GDP* refers to the conversion of GDP dollars to reflect PPP.

    In addition to compiling statistics for the number of refugees living in a given country, UNHCR also attempts to measure the impact of refugees on developing countries and their economies by determining the number of refugees hosted by a given country per one US dollar of that country's GDP prorated per capita (1 USD GDP PPP [per capita]). The developing country most economically impacted by refugees is Pakistan, with 745 refugees per 1 USD GDP PPP. The next two most impacted countries are the Democratic Republic of the Congo, at 592 refugees per 1 USD GDP PPP; and Zimbabwe, at 527.

54. Economic statistics on Germany come from the CIA World Factbook, https://www.cia.gov/library/publications/the-world-factbook/geos/gm.html [Germany, "People" page, featuring demographic data, including a July 2009 population figure estimated at 82,829,758 persons; and Germany, "Economy" page, including a GDP calculation of 2.925 trillion USD for 2008, adjusted for PPP (GDP PPP)]. Statistics on the refugee burden assumed by Germany's relative to its population and economic strength come from UNHCR's 2009 Global Trends. Germany's precise refugee caseload in 2009 was 593,800. *See id.* at 7 and 9.

55. Economic statistics on Tanzania come from the CIA World Factbook, *op. cit.*, https://www.cia.gov/library/publications/the-world-factbook/geos/gm.html [Tanzania, "People" page, featuring demographic data, including a July 2009 population figure estimated at 41,048,532 persons; and Tanzania, "Economy" page, including a GDP PPP calculation of 54.38 billion USD for 2008]. Statistics on the refugee burden assumed by Tanzania in 2009, relative to its population and GDP, come from UNHCR's 2009 Global Trends. Tanzania's precise 2009 refugee caseload was 118,700. *Id.* at 8.

    In 2008, the United Republic of Tanzania was in seventh place out of major refugee-hosting countries in, with 262 refugees per 1 USD PPP in 2008. *See* UNHCR 2008 Global Trends at 8, 10, *available at* http://www.unhcr.org/4a375c426.html. In 2009, Tanzania was ranked number twelve among refugee-hosting countries. Tanzania fell off of the top ten refugee hosts that year because it naturalized 155,000 Burundians who had been living as refugees on its territory, and 30,000 refugees from both Burundi and the Democratic Republic of the Congo voluntarily repatriated to their countries of origin. *See* 2009 Global Trends, at 8.

56. Economic statistics on Pakistan come from the CIA World Factbook, *op. cit.*, https://www.cia.gov/library/publications/the-world-factbook/geos/gm.html [Pakistan, "People" page, featuring demographic data, including a July 2009 figure estimated at 176,242,949 persons; and Pakistan, "Economy" page, including a GDP PPP calculation of 431.2 billion USD for 2008]. Pakistan's precise refugee caseload in 2009 was 1,740,700. This statistic, and the refugee burden assumed by Pakistan relative to its population and adjusted GDP per capita, comes from UNHCR's 2009 Global Trends, *op. cit.*, at 7 and 9.

57. *See* UN Charter, *op. cit.*, at art. 1(3).

58. *See also* ICESCR, *op. cit.*, at art. 2(1), which states that "[e]ach state party ... undertakes to take steps individually and through international assistance and co-operation especially

economic and technical . . . with a view to achieving progressively the full realization of the rights recognized in the present Covenant by all appropriate means . . ."

59. UNHCR 2009 Global Trends at 24, 25, 26.
60. Statistics for IDPs in Burundi reflect the fact that a final peace accord between all the parties to the civil war was still being negotiated in 2008. The precise figure for refugees in Burundi in 2008 is 24,967, with 100,000 IDPs. *Id.* at 24. IDP numbers in Uganda are linked to ongoing conflict between the Ugandan armed forces and the LRA in 2008. The precise statistics for forced migrants in Uganda in 2008 are 127,345 refugees and 446,300 IDPs. The number of Ugandan IDPs in 2009 was substantially less than in 2008, given the over 400,000 IDPs who had returned to their homes by 2009. *Id.* at 26.
61. *Id.* at 25. The lack of registered IDPs in Sierra Leone reflects progress in post-conflict reconstruction since the signing of the Lomé Peace Agreement in 1999, the establishment of the Special Court for Sierra Leone in 2002, and the work of its Truth and Reconciliation Commission from 2002–2004. Sierra Leone's 2008 caseload comprised 7,826 refugees, most IDPs having returned to their homes by that time. In contrast, Kenya hosted over 350,000 refugees in 2009, along with nearly 400,000 IDPs. The marked level of popular displacement in Kenya resulted from unrest following the disputed elections in 2007 and the ensuing crackdown on the political opposition. The precise forced migrant statistics for Kenya in 2009 were 358,928 refugees and 399,000 IDPs. *Id.* at 25 and 26.
62. Marc Lacy, "Tallying Darfur terror: Guesswork with a cause," N.Y. TIMES, May 11, 2005, *available at* http://www.nytimes.com/2005/05/10/world/africa/10iht-journal.html?_r=1.
63. Statistics on IDPs in Darfur are kept by the Internal Displacement Monitoring Center. http://www.internal-displacement.org/idmc/website/countries.nsf/(httpEnvelopes)/0026B2F86813855FC1257570006185A0?OpenDocument. The number of IDPs in all parts of the Sudan amounts to 4.9 million people. http://www.internal-displacement.org/8025708F004CE90B/(httpCountries)/F3D3CAA7CBEBE276802570A7004B87E4.
64. *See* Patrick Hoenig, "Peace and Justice in Northern Uganda," 14 E. AF. J. PEACE & H. RTS. 333, 334 (2008). *See also* Norwegian Refugee Council, "Uganda: Difficulties continue for returnees and remaining IDPs as development phase begins," a Profile of the Internal Displacement Situation at 7 (Internal Displacement Monitoring Center, Dec. 28, 2010), *available at* http://www.internal-displacement.org/8025708F004BE3B1/(httpInfoFiles)/AA7A8CB8B06E752DC12578070057B4C6/$file/Uganda+-+December+2010.pdf.
65. The total number of IDPs in Northern Uganda, in February 2009, comprised 710,000 people. At the same time, there were 681,000 formerly displaced individuals who recently had returned to their villages in the Northern Ugandan subregions of Acholi, West Nile, Toro-Bunyoro, and Teso. These figures come from the Internal Displacement Monitoring Centre, based in Geneva. http://www.internal-displacement.org/idmc/website/countries.nsf/(httpEnvelopes)/2439C2AC21E16365C125719C004177C7?OpenDocument. IDMC was established in 1998 by the Norwegian Refugee Council to monitor "conflict-induced internal displacement worldwide." IDMC operates an online database, which it established at the urging of the United Nations. http://www.internal-displacement.org/8025708F004BD0DA/(httpSectionHomepages)/$first?OpenDocument&count=1000.

PART II

Humanitarian Law and Post-conflict Reconstruction in Africa

CHAPTER 6

Tools for Implementing Humanitarian Law

Courts, Troops, the Media, Development, and Communities

There are grave events taking place in Africa.... motherland, nourish me,... protect me,... comfort my childish tears.[1] ...
What is important is that we are all Africans. Whether Black or White is not important. What is crucial is that we respect each other.[2] ...
Victims of war, why so much hatred? ... we must forgive, my generation.[3] ...
My people, oh, Africa—cool your anger, tolerate each other.[4] ...
Sudan, Rwanda, Angola, Malawi, Liberia, Zaire, stop the killing ... war is never good. Reconciliation is the key word.[5]

Papa Wemba, Lourdes Van Dunem,
Youssou N'Dour, Lagbaja, and Jabu Khanyile[6]

A perennial and powerful critique of international law charges that its reach exceeds its grasp. Some philosophers go so far as to suggest that international law is not law because there is no sovereign to enforce it and it is so often honored in the breach.[7] Other scholars point out that all legal and ethical frameworks contain gaps between theory and implementation.[8] Domestic legal systems are rife with illustrations of the disconnects between de jure norms of equal protection and due process, on the one hand, and de facto realities of discrimination, entrenched poverty, and the abuse of power, on the other.

The reality is that all fields of law have aspirational as well as pragmatic strands. The very idea of *humanitarian law in action* envisions a rule of law endowed with a hopeful heart and a courageous spirit.[9] But international law must be effective as well as idealistic for scholars and practitioners to defend the rights of individuals and communities and not merely bear witness to the abuses they suffer.

This chapter lays the foundation for studying the practical implementation of humanitarian law in Uganda, Sierra Leone, and Burundi, by setting forth five tools or mechanisms through which international law responds to armed conflict and widespread abuses of human rights, namely, courts, troops, the media, development, and communities. *Courts* connote international and domestic tribunals that prosecute suspected perpetrators of war crimes and crimes against humanity. *Troops* entail international or regional peacekeeping forces sent in to end armed conflict, monitor a peace treaty, or protect noncombatants and humanitarian aid workers. Human rights *media* encompass organizations devoted to raising awareness of violations of human dignity, building a culture in which human rights norms are ingrained in the community, and demanding protections against violence and repression. *Development* comprises health, sanitation, education, employment, and other social programs designed to improve living conditions, lessen economic inequality, and address the root causes of armed conflict. *Communities* embrace myriad efforts to reestablish conditions of security and respect in societies torn by violence, including the demobilization and reintegration of former combatants, truth-telling and reconciliation among individual offenders and survivors, reparations to individual victims, and the reaffirmation of a shared ethic of pluralism and nonviolence.

The chapter sections below address in turn the five mechanisms for implementing international humanitarian law (IHL). Each section offers examples of the ways in which Uganda, Sierra Leone, and Burundi have utilized the given tool in their own historical contexts. These brief illustrations will help pave the way toward the more focused country studies to follow in Chapters 7, 8, and 9.

There is considerable overlap between courts, troops, the media, development, and communities as mechanisms of conflict resolution. Essential to all five arenas is the notion that humanitarian law in action promotes a culture of accountability, social security, and respect for human dignity by all entities and members of society.

A. COURTS AS ARENAS FOR CONFLICT RESOLUTION

1. Judicial Tribunals and the Enforcement of Humanitarian Law

Courts are often viewed as the most powerful and appropriate mechanisms for implementing international law, given that, in many domestic legal systems, the central role of the judiciary is to interpret and apply laws made by the legislature. The role of international courts as enforcers of the law is particularly compelling in the case of war crimes, crimes against humanity, and genocide. As discussed in Chapter 2, war crimes encompass violations of the basic principles of distinction, humanity, necessity, and proportionality, including attacks on civilians and abuses of wounded combatants and prisoners of war (POWs). Under the Rome Statute of the International Criminal Court (Rome Statute or ICC Statute), crimes against humanity comprise acts "committed as part of a widespread or systematic attack directed against any civilian population."[10] Genocide is a particularly egregious crime against humanity involving the intent to destroy a community defined in ethnic, linguistic, or religious terms. The logic behind international crimes is that military attacks on civilians and campaigns to destroy entire social groups threaten the very fabric of the international community. Criminal prosecutions, at least in theory, vindicate the values and integrity of the international community, by holding individuals accountable for such offenses.

The Special Court for Sierra Leone (SCSL or Special Court), the ad hoc United Nations (UN) Security Council-mandated tribunals for the former Yugoslavia and Rwanda, and the Ugandan High Court's War Crimes Division are other examples of tribunals that explicitly work to implement international humanitarian norms through individual criminal accountability. By implication, these courts and the International Criminal Court (ICC) also apply human rights law, to the extent that war crimes and crimes against humanity entail egregious and widespread human rights violations.

The effectiveness of criminal enforcement of humanitarian law varies depending on the goals and broader impact of individual prosecutions. Popular support for indicting a select group of suspected war criminals in national or transnational courts is essential, in the first instance. The ultimate vindication of criminal procedures, however, depends on the extent to which such trials inspire greater respect for the rule of law, and help break the cycle of violence and recrimination within the society as a whole.

2. Judicial Enforcement of Humanitarian Law in Uganda, Sierra Leone, and Burundi

Determining whether or not courts are fruitful arenas for implementing international humanitarian law is enhanced by considering the experiences of individual countries emerging from prolonged armed conflict.

Uganda

In 2004, the Government of Uganda initiated a self-referral to the International Criminal Court, resulting in the issuance of arrest warrants for the five senior leaders of the insurgent Lord's Resistance Army (LRA). Although two of the five LRA commanders have died and the other three have thus far eluded custody, these prosecutions remain controversial. It is plausible that the indictments have inspired further militancy on the part of the LRA, which is now mounting attacks on civilians in neighboring countries. Moreover, some Ugandans and other observers are concerned that the ICC trials have had a negative impact on the rule of law in Uganda, given the ICC's failure to hold governmental troops accountable for abuses of Ugandan civilians, and because such prosecutions fail to address or ameliorate the root causes of the violence in northern Uganda.[11] Some of the critiques leveled at the ICC may be defused by the new War Crimes Division of Uganda's High Court, especially if it is evident that prosecutorial discretion is being exercised in an even-handed manner.[12]

Nongovernmental organizations (NGOs), particularly Makerere University's Beyond Juba Project (BJP), recommend an approach to criminal accountability in Uganda that serves to strengthen national and local institutions in both the judicial and socioeconomic realms. Traditional dispute resolution practices, including *mato oput* reconciliation ceremonies practiced among the Acholi,[13] are part of this integrated policy. In essence, voices from Ugandan civil society are calling for a vision of national reconstruction that links criminal justice with community reconciliation, and recognizes individual accountability, community healing, and historical honesty as equal attributes of justice.

Sierra Leone

The civil war in Sierra Leone is not before the ICC, nor did it result in the establishment of an ad hoc tribunal by the UN Security Council (Security Council) as in the case of Rwanda. Rather, the UN and the Government of Sierra Leone entered into a bilateral treaty to establish a hybrid tribunal, the Special Court for Sierra Leone (Special Court), composed of both Sierra Leonean and international judges.[14] The Special Court has indicted thirteen individuals, including twelve Sierra Leoneans and the former Liberian President Charles Taylor, eight of whom had been convicted of war crimes and crimes against humanity as of 2011. The Government of Sierra Leone also passed legislation creating a Truth and Reconciliation Commission (TRC), whose formal work finished in October 2004.[15] Thus far, the Special Court and the TRC have been the main components of Sierra Leone's transitional justice program, although grassroots reconciliation efforts are also spreading throughout the country.

Burundi

As of 2011, there have been no war crimes prosecutions stemming from Burundi's civil war.[16] This is in marked contrast to Uganda, with its ICC case against the Lord's Resistance Army, and the recent creation of the Ugandan High Court War Crimes Division; and Sierra Leone, with its Special Court. Burundi's approach to transitional justice is also distinct from that of neighboring Rwanda, where, in addition to domestic prosecutions of suspected *genocidaires* and proceedings before grassroots *gacaca* courts, higher level suspects have been tried by the ad hoc international criminal tribunal based in neighboring Tanzania.[17]

Although Burundi has not been the subject of indictments by the ICC or any specially mandated international criminal court, plans have been in the works for two domestic institutions of transitional justice since the Arusha Peace and Reconciliation Agreement (Arusha Agreement) was first drafted in 2000. Building on the Arusha mandate, the UN Secretary General and the Security Council called in 2005 for the establishment of "a twin mechanism for Burundi," comprising both a national truth commission and a specialized division within the Burundian court system.[18] More recently, in July of 2011, Burundian President Nkurunziza announced that his country's long-awaited Truth and Reconciliation Commission would be established in 2012, with a mandate to conduct its work over a two-year period.[19]

Burundi also has its own traditional dispute resolution mechanisms, including *ubushingantahe*, in which aggrieved community members come before local panels of elders, known as *bashingantahe*. A number of scholars and peace activists believe that *ubushingantahe* has potential value in Burundi's pursuit of transitional justice.[20] Nevertheless, village-level conciliation has not been used extensively to handle criminal offenses under Burundi's domestic or customary law. Adapting the village counsels into an accountability mechanism for civil war-related atrocities would require significant development and further discussion within Burundian civil society.

3. Collaboration between Courts and Other Arenas for Conflict Resolution

The fact that war crimes and crimes against humanity offend all nations, as well as specific civilian populations, does not justify the use of criminal prosecutions as the primary mechanism for global response. The judicial realm, though an important arena for the implementation of international humanitarian law, should not be overemphasized as a means of conflict resolution. Courts may have formal criminal jurisdiction, and states or other bodies, as a political matter, may choose to invoke that jurisdiction. Nevertheless, judicial bodies are seldom equipped to try more than a small sample of suspected offenders in the aftermath of prolonged armed conflict or crimes against humanity. For this reason, the criminal law model—focusing as it does on accountability for individual offenders—should be a complementary rather than an exclusive mechanism for affirming the rule of law in the aftermath of war or genocide. This is particularly the case in the aftermath of war or genocide in which broad sectors of the population were perpetrators or victims of violence, or both.

Putting aside, for the moment, whether courts are the best or most appropriate venue for implementing humanitarian law, the more essential question is how they can become more effective tools of conflict resolution, acting alone or in concert with other mechanisms.[21] The tensions and tradeoffs between criminal prosecutions and community-based reconciliation efforts have been noted already, and will be discussed further below. Nevertheless, it is significant that post-conflict societies choose to utilize both court procedures and communal atonement practices as pathways toward conflict resolution, even though they sometimes appear to work at cross-purposes. The willingness to accept war crimes trials while embracing truth commissions may simply reflect the popular understanding that neither mechanism is capable of achieving national reconstruction on its own.

The very issue of proportionality, discussed above, is one reason *mato oput* and other forms of local conciliation are believed to complement criminal prosecutions. In Sierra Leone and Uganda, criminal prosecutions have targeted but a small percentage of those responsible for wholesale violence and human rights abuses. Moreover, in Uganda, the five individuals originally named in arrest warrants issued by the ICC represent the upper echelon of one party to the conflict, namely, the leader and four top deputies of the LRA. In light of that reality, it would seem particularly important that both governmental actors and members of civil society have the option of pursuing alternative programs that seek to reconcile former adversaries, compensate victims, and reckon honestly with the past.

Contemporary scholarly analysis of conflict resolution tends to focus on apparent or assumed tensions between courts and communities, or criminal prosecutions and alternative justice mechanisms. Along with acknowledging the justice versus peace debate, it is important to highlight and explore the potential synergies between courtroom and community-level pathways toward post-conflict reconciliation. This involves questioning the assumptions that criminal trials always further accountability and communal forgiveness necessarily furthers impunity. In fact, high-level criminal trials held in a foreign country that sentence a handful of suspected war criminals have a limited impact on strengthening the rule of law in the society emerging from civil war. By the same token, truth and reconciliation proceedings may provide a meaningful measure of accountability for both offenders and victims.

As an Acholi leader in northern Uganda told his interviewer, when asked about the meaning of terms such as amnesty, forgiveness, punishment and justice,

> [w]e believe that a wrongdoer will not be punished by death because he will not realise the effect. We want him to be alive to see—let him feel the shame. Let him be blamed and return, and it will teach very many people. . . . So the amnesty. . . . pardons people in the same way the Acholi culture does. You are free, but feel the weight of what you've done.

Moreover, we should not neglect the interactions between courts and the other three arenas of conflict resolution, namely, troops, the media, and development. Peacekeeping troops can certainly prolong armed conflict. Nevertheless, in monitoring ceasefires, they may also help to create a climate of increased security that builds confidence in both criminal trials and victim-centered reparations programs. The media, particularly community-level human rights education programs, can play an important role in informing and engaging with the public about criminal trials, providing members of civil society with a more vested interest in their outcomes. Finally, the establishment and strengthening of development programs and social service provision on an equitable basis throughout the country will help build confidence in government and in the rule of law, including the criminal justice system.

It is important not to view with starry eyes the potential synergies among criminal trials conducted by courts and the interventions and contributions of troops, the media, development, and communities. Justice and peace are ideas that are constantly tested on the ground. Economic realities and popular perceptions may undermine as well as strengthen the prospects for authentic post-conflict reconciliation. Uganda may offer the best example of a situation in which criminal trials backfired, to the extent that the ICC prosecutions are believed to have inspired continued LRA insurgency and attacks on civilians. Nevertheless, in Sierra Leone, members of civil society have embraced elements of both retributive and restorative justice in their path toward post-conflict reconstruction by establishing a high-level hybrid court alongside a national truth commission.

B. TROOPS AS TOOLS OF CONFLICT RESOLUTION

> Excuse me, to say thanks to those who contributed to the peace-building of our lovely nation. Please allow me to praise the workers of peace in my land – ECOMOG, you know what I'm saying. [...] For over ten years, Sierra Leone has been longing for peace. ... Thank you for bringing peace.... Canada, O.A.U.,..., Senegalese, Ugandans, South Africans, the Kenyans, the British, the Americans, Security Council, United Nations, ECOMOG, ECOWAS, A.U. We say thank you everyone.
>
> Reuben M. Koroma[22]

1. Peacekeeping Troops and the Enforcement of Humanitarian Law

When the band members of the Sierra Leone Refugee All Stars praise *ECOMOG* in their song, "Compliments for the Peace," they are referring to the regional peacekeeping force organized by the Economic Community of West African States (ECOWAS) to pacify Liberia and Sierra Leone in the early 1990s. (ECOMOG stands for the Economic Community's Monitoring Observer Group.) The very term *peacekeeping forces* suggests that armed soldiers under responsible command can serve the cause of conflict resolution, ideally preventing violations of humanitarian law. With some frequency, international and regional organizations recruit and authorize peacekeeping troops to monitor ceasefires. Peacekeepers are also called upon to pacify and disarm warring factions. Whether monitoring or disarming, peacekeepers are sometimes specifically mandated to protect civilians and humanitarian relief workers.[23] In recent years, international political and economic entities have constituted peacekeeping missions on the African continent, including the twenty-thousand-strong joint United Nations–African Union peacekeeping force established in the Darfur region of the Sudan.

At the same time, troops are a problematic instrument for the implementation of humanitarian law, if only because the use of force so often evidences a breakdown in peaceful relations and a failure of the rule of law. Beyond the irony of using force to resolve conflicts, we may legitimately question the practical wisdom of sending troops to stop war crimes and crimes against humanity, given the risk that peacekeeping troops will become full-fledged parties to the conflict they have been sent to stop. ECOMOG's combat role in the Liberian and Sierra Leonean wars bears witness to this tendency, as noted in the final report of Sierra Leone's TRC, discussed in Chapter 8. Peacekeeping forces have also been implicated in sexual exploitation and sexual violence against war-affected populations, including the abuse of women, who were living in refugee and displaced persons camps and under the care of those very peacekeepers.[24]

The presence of peacekeeping troops has also been used to justify terrorist attacks on the countries of origin of the troops themselves, as in July of 2010, when al-Shabab, an al-Qaeda-affiliated terrorist organization based in Somalia, took responsibility for two bombings that killed over seventy-five persons in Kampala, Uganda, during the viewing of the final match of the World Cup soccer competition. Al-Shabab cited the participation of Burundian and Ugandan soldiers in the peacekeeping force propping up the transitional government of Somalia as the catalyst for the deadly attacks.[25]

Just as criminal trials may complicate as well as alleviate peace negotiations, military interventions have a tendency to inflame as well as pacify armed conflict. This is particularly true if individual peacekeepers have themselves been accused of targeting civilians, notably in Sierra Leone.[26] If peacekeeping is to be regarded as a legitimate means of implementing humanitarian law, we need to judge military intervention in terms of its impact on the ground, no matter its legal or political justification.

If peacekeeping troops protect civilians and disarm combatants, they will promote greater respect for international humanitarian law. This is especially the case when peacekeeping forces facilitate the provision of humanitarian assistance to noncombatants in the form of food, shelter, health care, and sanitation. A successful peacekeeping operation may also help galvanize local commitment to restoring individual accountability, such that war crimes prosecutions are organized later, whether at the national or international level. Moreover, when commanders of peacekeeping forces carry out international law trainings, they help engender a culture of awareness of and respect for human rights and humanitarian norms.

Finally, peacekeeping operations have an impact on refugee law and refugees' experiences. Peacemaking forces that are engaged in combat with one or more warring factions may cause civilians to flee dangerous areas, thus contributing to greater levels of displacement. Alternatively, peacekeepers may be charged with protecting refugees and internally displaced persons (IDPs) in settlements and on the run. Peacekeepers may force civilians to vacate one area, or confine them to specific refugee or IDP camps. In light of their complex roles in zones of conflict, peacekeeping forces need to be trained in principles of asylum, and safe and dignified return in order to prevent violations of the rights of displaced persons.

2. Military Enforcement of Humanitarian Law in Uganda, Sierra Leone, and Burundi

Uganda

The civil war between the LRA—and its precursor, the Holy Spirit Movement—and the Ugandan People's Defense Forces (UPDF) has lasted over twenty years. Although the LRA is still active in the region, by 2007, its troops had largely withdrawn from Ugandan territory. Nevertheless, the LRA continues to recruit soldiers and attack civilian communities in the neighboring countries of the Democratic Republic of the Congo (DRC), Central African Republic (CAR), and the Sudan.[27]

Throughout the height of the conflict in northern Uganda and today, as it pursues rebel forces in cross-border operations, UPDF soldiers have struggled to pacify the LRA without the assistance of the UN, AfricanUnion (AU), or other transnational entities authorized to use military force in response to specific threats to international peace and security. Although Uganda has not had the benefit of formally mandated peacekeeping troops, foreign governments including the US have pledged to support the disarmament, demobilization, and reintegration of LRA fighters.[28] Nevertheless, the LRA has not been the only perpetrator of humanitarian law violations in northern Uganda. The UPDF has been involved in full-scale combat against the LRA, and also has been accused of unlawful attacks on civilians.[29] Thus, soldiers and police officers throughout Uganda benefit from ongoing humanitarian law trainings, as do military and law enforcement personnel throughout the world.

Sierra Leone

In 1990, the Economic Community of West African States constituted ECOMOG to help bring peace first to Liberia, and then to Sierra Leone, whose rebel insurgency began in 1991. ECOWAS dispatched soldiers to Sierra Leone to engage the warring parties on the ground, in order to change the course of the civil war and help bring an end to the fighting. Thus, ECOMOG troops were more appropriately characterized as a peacemaking or *peace enforcement* force because, in essence, they were mandated to *create* rather than to *keep* the peace. Chapter 8 includes references to the conduct of ECOMOG troops during the rebel war. Only after the Lomé Peace Agreement (Lomé Agreement or Lomé Accord) was signed in 1999 could full-fledged peacekeeping activities begin in earnest. In 2000, the UN established what would become the largest multilateral peacekeeping operation of its time, peaking at eighteen thousand troops from thirty-seven countries, at a cost of 2.6 billion United States dollars (USD) over a several-year period. UNAMSIL (the UN Mission in Sierra Leone) disarmed forty-five thousand combatants in less than eighteen months, such that, in January of 2002, President Kabbah declared the war officially over.[30]

Burundi

In 2003, Burundi hosted the first peacekeeping mission under the auspices of the new AU. Burundi's peacekeepers were characterized as a classic peacekeeping mission, in that the AU forces were not mandated to take offensive action to engage insurgent forces, but rather to monitor and encourage compliance with the terms of Burundi's evolving peace accords. The AU force was absorbed into a UN peacekeeping operation, in 2004.[31] Burundi's peacekeeping force is discussed further in Chapter 9.

3. Collaboration between Troops and Other Mechanisms for Conflict Resolution

Just as international courts are a classic arena for the implementation of international criminal law, peacekeepers are in a unique position to promote respect for humanitarian law. But troops, like courts, have the capacity to inflame conflict and complicate peace negotiations as well. Ideally, peacekeeping forces will help uphold the principles of IHL, in collaboration with courts, the media, development, and communities, through the proper training and disciplining of their soldiers, and by insisting that civilians shall be protected, the wounded and sick cared for, and detained persons treated humanely.[32]

Peacekeeping contingents do not operate in a vacuum, any more than judicial tribunals, advocacy organizations, development agencies, or members of civil society function in isolation. Rather, peacekeeping has the potential to enhance as well as frustrate the work of other mechanisms of conflict resolution.

If troops help prevent or monitor war crimes, they may facilitate international criminal trials; if they participate in such crimes, they may be subjects of such prosecutions. If the commanders of peacekeeping missions conduct trainings on gender-based violence, they will promote respect for human rights law; but they will do damage to those same norms if they encourage or turn a blind eye to sexual assault. If peacekeeping operations are coordinated with humanitarian relief activities and development projects, they will contribute to post-conflict reconstruction; if they displace and impoverish members of the local population, they will intensify the humanitarian emergency they have been called upon to alleviate. If peacekeepers work with grassroots organizations to disarm, rehabilitate, and reintegrate former combatants, they will enhance reconciliation; whereas if they are disdainful of such community voices, they will contribute to ongoing discord.

Peacekeeping missions are an essential arena for the implementation of humanitarian law, not the least because of their troops' capacity to engage in further conflict. In order to implement and promote respect for international humanitarian law, rather than giving mere lip service to the cause of conflict resolution, peacekeeping forces must engage in creative collaborations with criminal tribunals, human rights organizations, development agencies, and grassroots community groups.

C. THE MEDIA AS A MEANS OF CONFLICT RESOLUTION

> For over ten years, Sierra Leone has been longing for peace. But now that peace has returned, some big, big mouths have opened, causing a lot of anxiety and misinformation. When in every bad mouth there is a padlock, there will be the best peace in Sierra Leone.
>
> Reuben M. Koroma[33]

1. The Role of Human Rights Media in Enforcing Humanitarian Law

The songs of the Sierra Leone Refugee All Stars educate their listeners about "living like a refugee," and bear witness to the experiences of Sierra Leoneans who sought refuge in neighboring Guinea, beginning in 1991, at the start of Sierra Leone's rebel war. The Refugee All Stars also use their performances and recordings to draw attention to and raise funds for human rights and development organizations working in other parts of Africa.[34]

The media as a mechanism for the implementation of humanitarian law refers to the spectrum of organizations and communication technologies that work to internalize international law within civil society and popular culture. Human rights media include musicians and artists, advocacy organizations, and peace education programs. Such organizations increasingly use new internet and mobile technologies to disseminate information and build support for human rights campaigns, particularly among youth.

The entertainment field is but one medium for human rights education and advocacy. Other humanitarian action media include human rights monitoring organizations such as Amnesty International (AI), and agencies dedicated to preventing egregious human rights violations, such as the

US-based Genocide Intervention Network. All these organizations share the capacity to raise popular awareness of human rights principles and exert collective pressure on governments, armed groups, and civil society in order to prevent and alleviate violations of human rights and humanitarian law.

The role of international media organizations is more wide-ranging, in comparison to that of either peacekeeping troops, thought to have expertise in military and humanitarian law, or criminal courts, expected to prosecute perpetrators of war crimes and crimes against humanity. Because the media are typically involved in publication and communication activities, as opposed to field operations or legal prosecutions, they can educate, inform, and mobilize international civil society about a broad array of legal and social topics. When the media turn their attention from the commercial to the humanitarian realm, they become powerful tools of conflict resolution.

2. The Media's Role in Implementing Humanitarian Law in Uganda, Sierra Leone, and Burundi

Uganda

Several Ugandan agencies collaborating within a broader coalition of human rights organizations are the Refugee Law Project (RLP) and the Human Rights and Peace Centre (HURIPEC), both based at Makerere University Faculty of Law, and the Beyond Juba Project,[35] which engages civil society in the implementation of Uganda's peace accords. These organizations have served as watchdogs over Uganda's transitional justice process, inspiring dialogue about the relative merits of punitive and restorative models of justice. The work of the Beyond Juba Project will be spotlighted in Chapter 7, in particular for its critique of the ICC case against the Lord's Resistance Army, and its argument that criminal trials weaken respect for the rule of law unless they promote accountability for all parties to the conflict.

Sierra Leone

The Refugee All Stars broadcast its musical advocacy, literally and figuratively, from Sierra Leonean refugee camps in neighboring Guinea during the civil war.[36] A broader spectrum of organizations dedicated to humanitarian and human rights education operates in Sierra Leone today. It includes the International Committee of the Red Cross (ICRC), based in

Geneva, with an office in Freetown; the Centre for Development and Peace Education (CD-Peace), based in Bombali District, Northern Province; the Centre for Accountability and the Rule of Law (CARL), based in Freetown; and Fambul Tok (Family Talk), a grassroots reconciliation organization whose work began in Kailahun District, Eastern Province, and is expanding throughout the country.

Sierra Leonean media organizations also work in a variety of arenas, including socioeconomic development and community reconciliation, in addition to their advocacy activities. Focusing on their human rights education and advocacy activities, ICRC disseminates information and conducts trainings on international humanitarian law, CD-Peace offers classes in conflict prevention, CARL monitors and publicizes the activities of the Special Court for Sierra Leone, and Fambul Tok promotes dialogue on the meaning and potential value of reconciliation.

Burundi

A variety of media organizations have been involved in human rights education and advocacy in Burundi throughout its nearly twelve-year civil war and since the last insurgent movement signed a durable peace accord during the summer of 2009. International agencies such as AI and Human Rights Watch conduct fact-finding missions and report regularly on human rights conditions in Burundi. Moreover, there are growing numbers of Burundian civil society organizations dedicated to violence prevention, and youth and women's empowerment, including le Centre d'Alerte et Prévention de Conflits (CENAP or Conflict Alert and Prevention Center), l'Association des Femmes Entrepreneurs de Burundi (Association of Burundian Women Entrepreneurs), and Moi, Mon Futur et Mon Pays (Me, My Future and My Country), a youth engagement organization.

3. Collaboration between the Media and Other Mechanisms for Conflict Resolution

NGOs involved in human rights education and advocacy appear uniquely positioned to enforce or implement human rights law. It seems fitting to link human rights media with international human rights law, just as it appears appropriate, in the abstract, to link courts with international criminal law, on the one hand, and troops with IHL, on the other. Nevertheless, like the other mechanisms, human rights media are not cabined in one narrow field of international law. They are concerned with humanitarian law, broadly defined.

Just as humanitarian law can be defined in terms of international criminal law and other sister fields of international law, human rights law itself involves significant humanitarian, criminal, and refugee law dimensions. Human rights media organizations, in naming and shaming human rights violators and advocating for the rights of all individuals, also have important roles to play in defending civilian victims of war, under humanitarian law; sheltering displaced persons, under refugee law; and upholding the rule of law in prosecutions of individuals accused of war crimes and crimes against humanity, under international criminal law.

Far from isolated, human rights media interact closely with courts, troops, development agencies, and communities in the cause of post-conflict reconstruction. For example, when human rights organizations publicize the criminal prosecutions of war crimes suspects, residents of a country emerging from conflict are more apt to follow those trials and become vested in their outcomes. This is the case with the public education work of the Centre for Accountability and the Rule of Law in Sierra Leone and the Beyond Juba Project in Uganda. Humanitarian organizations also disseminate materials on the law of war, and conduct trainings for peacekeepers and other members of the armed forces, lessening the likelihood that such troops will commit humanitarian law violations. Such is the work of the International Committee of the Red Cross throughout Africa and around the world. Furthermore, human rights groups can partner with governments and development agencies to support public schools, fund health clinics, and promote agricultural development, as demonstrated by the work of the Centre for Development and Peace Education in Sierra Leone.

Finally, human rights organizations working nationally and internationally can partner with grassroots community groups on specific human rights campaigns and actions. The synergy between international and national human rights agencies is illustrated by the partnership between Interpeace, based in Geneva, and Burundi's CENAP. A similar symbiosis exists between Catalyst for Peace, based in Portland, Maine, and Fambul Tok, a grassroots reconciliation organization based in Freetown, Sierra Leone.

Peace education media have a special opportunity to inspire discussion and debate along the full spectrum of human rights and humanitarian law, from respect for civilians to women's empowerment and youth engagement. For example, during Fambul Tok's Radio Listening Clubs, broadcast to communities in rural Sierra Leone, "Peace Mothers" spread awareness about domestic violence and encourage former child soldiers to return to their communities.[37] Radio programming is but one powerful example of how the media may build on a foundation of mass communication to facilitate dialogue and promote conflict resolution.

D. DEVELOPMENT AS A CATALYST FOR CONFLICT RESOLUTION

1. The Role of Development Programs in Implementing Humanitarian Law

The previous section examined the role of human rights educators and advocates—media organizations—in promoting understanding of and respect for human rights and humanitarian norms. Now comes the role of development in humanitarian law and action. *Development*, as the term is used here, comprises the full range of socioeconomic programs and initiatives seeking to enhance human well-being and lessen economic inequality by improving access to education, income-generation, health care, and sanitation for vulnerable individuals and groups. Development encompasses long-term socioeconomic policies, as well as humanitarian relief programs that offer life-saving assistance to war-affected populations in the short and medium term.

Development programs have the potential to implement human rights law by enhancing socioeconomic well-being. Development also helps realize the fundamental principles of humanitarian and refugee law by facilitating access to humanitarian assistance. Finally, by promoting socioeconomic justice, development programs serve as a bulwark against resurgent armed conflict.

Along with courts, troops, the media, and communities, development is a catalyst for post-conflict reconstruction. At the same time, development programs—just as judicial trials and military operations—may constitute double-edged swords, with the potential to generate as well as resolve armed conflict. Despite their contributions to enhancing human security, emergency relief and development programs may also fuel inequity and armed conflict. Relief and development aid make positive contributions to the economy and the social welfare system, by providing material goods and resources to needy populations, and generating education and employment opportunities for other members of society. By the same token, humanitarian and development inputs may also have negative implications, particularly if they compound class divisions or create new forms of inequality.[38]

In the context of emergency assistance for war-affected populations, humanitarian aid may alleviate the suffering of war, but it may also throw fuel on the fire. Even the material components of humanitarian assistance are fungible and may be converted into currency that enriches some sectors of society at the expense of others, potentially favoring one party to the conflict over another.[39] Just as "rice buys protection,"[40] when food aid encourages governments to protect and assist refugees and the internally displaced, rice also buys weapons, when humanitarian aid is corrupted, and sold or bartered for guns and other materiel of war.

If relief and development programs are to play a more constructive role in conflict resolution, they must be carefully tailored to avoid bankrolling the war economy, or further poisoning an already intense competition for resources. Grassroots organizations involved in long-term sustainable development activities have a vital role to play in ensuring that assistance programs alleviate inequality rather than exacerbate it.

2. Development as a Mechanism for Conflict Resolution in Uganda, Sierra Leone, and Burundi

Uganda

Numerous development projects in Northern Uganda provide social services to war-affected populations, including UN-affiliated, government-sponsored, international NGO-run, and community-based programs. Among the most innovative and successful are those that focus on the reintegration of former child soldiers, and the return and resettlement of former internally displaced persons.

One Ugandan NGO whose track record extends back into the civil war is the Kitgum Concerned Women's Association (KICWA), founded in 1998, and now active throughout the district of Kitgum along the Sudanese border in northern Uganda. KICWA has helped reintegrate over four thousand former child soldiers through its reception centers. More recently, KICWA has expanded its activities to helping former IDPs to resettle in their home communities. Another offshoot is KICWA's Girl Soldiers and Affected Children Project. The Girl Soldiers Project (GSP) serves young women and their children, in recognition of the heightened stigma experienced by female combatants and girls who served as "bush wives" or sex slaves to male commanders. GSP improves access to education and health care for young woman and their children and sponsors income-generation and community reconciliation activities.[41]

An NGO working on kindred issues is the United Movement to End Child Soldiering (UMECS). UMECS has offices in Kampala, Uganda, and Washington, DC, and prioritizes the psychosocial needs of war-affected children, running peace education programs for public secondary schools throughout the districts of northern Uganda. UMECS has also developed reintegration programs to help child soldiers return to their communities.[42]

Sierra Leone

From the UN Peacebuilding Office in Freetown to grassroots community organizations, development organizations have achieved a remarkable degree of consensus around the priorities for post-conflict reconstruction in Sierra Leone. Women's equality and protection from violence, youth engagement and employment, poverty alleviation, and the strengthening of the agricultural, public education, and public health sectors are the chief areas of activity and fund-raising.[43] Two organizations exemplify this integrated approach to social development in Sierra Leone, one a grassroots organization, the other an international NGO.

The Centre for Development and Peace Education is based in the village of Mayagba in the Bombali District of Northern Province. The organization has four program areas, comprising agriculture, education, health, and women's empowerment. Within this framework, CD-Peace encourages youth to develop skills in modern agricultural techniques, provides infrastructure and scholarship support to primary and secondary schools, funds primary health clinics, and prioritizes women in income generation and continuing education opportunities.[44]

The US-based International Rescue Committee (IRC) has defined four areas of concentration in Sierra Leone, building on its own areas of expertise and funding sources, and overlapping with several of the priorities of CD-Peace. In addition to sponsoring income-generating programs for at-risk youth, supporting the government's Free Healthcare Initiative for mothers and children under five, and researching more productive varieties of rice, IRC is increasingly focused on combating gender-based violence throughout Sierra Leone. The IRC advocated for recently-enacted legislation criminalizing domestic violence, prohibiting early marriage, and recognizing women's inheritance rights. With the support of Irish Aid, the development arm of the Irish Foreign Ministry, the IRC is establishing Rainbow Centers in Freetown and the provinces where, for the first time, female survivors of domestic and sexual violence may receive shelter, life-saving medical care, and legal and other assistance.[45]

Burundi

Unlike Sierra Leone, whose rebel war ended, in 2002, and Uganda, whose civil war wound down in 2006, Burundi's last rebel group only signed the

Arusha Peace and Reconciliation Agreement (Arusha Agreement) in late 2008. The Front National de Libération (FNL) then underwent disarmament and registered as a political party in 2009.[46] Even though the majority of the nearly one million Burundians who were internally displaced at the height of the armed conflict in 1999 have returned home, as of late 2009, one-hundred thousand remained displaced.[47] Moreover, out of a total national population of nearly ten million people, six-hundred thousand Burundians required food aid in 2008.[48] Thus, to a greater extent than either Ugandans or Sierra Leoneans, Burundians remain dependent on humanitarian assistance in addition to benefiting from long-term social development programs.[49]

NGOs assisting the internally displaced in Burundi include the Norwegian Refugee Council, Danish Church Aid, the Burundian Red Cross, and the International Committee of the Red Cross.[50] In Sierra Leone, ICRC has substantially scaled back its wartime operations, such that its small suboffice in Freetown now reports to the ICRC delegation in neighboring Guinea. In contrast, ICRC maintains a higher operational profile in Burundi, with a delegation in Bujumbura, and two sub-delegations in Ngozi and Gitega, in northern and central Burundi, respectively.[51] Over the past decade, ICRC has operated approximately fifty sanitation and potable water projects serving over one million people, and these programs continue to be a major focus of its assistance activities in Burundi.[52]

Alongside humanitarian programs, Burundian government ministries and NGOs are working in the longer term to improve the level of health care, education, and employment opportunities enjoyed by the population as a whole. Progressive state policies, including the abolition of school fees for primary school students, enacted in 2005, and free medical care for mothers and children, enacted in 2006, have resulted in overwhelming demand, with swamped health clinics, and children turned away from overcrowded schools.[53]

Partners in Health (PIH), the international NGO founded by Paul Farmer, is one agency working to bridge the gap between need and capacity in Burundi's health care sector. PIH has developed a public–private collaboration model, first implemented in Haiti, whereby the agency funds and provides technical support for community health clinics staffed by local doctors and nurses typically employed by the national health service. In Burundi, PIH supports a local NGO founded by Deogratias Niyizonkiza, the young doctor called Deo, who was profiled in *Strength in What Remains*, Tracy Kidder's memoir of the Burundian genocide.[54] In November of 2007, Deo opened the Village Health Works medical clinic in the district of Kayanza, northern Burundi, over a dozen years after he fled the massacres then occurring in his native region.[55]

3. Collaboration between Development and Other Arenas of Conflict Resolution

Emergency assistance programs serve to implement essential principles of humanitarian and refugee law, by helping to lessen the suffering of individuals impacted and displaced by war. In a similar vein, long-term development programs strengthen an essential dimension of international human rights law, by enhancing socioeconomic welfare. Development programs may also have a direct effect on the enforcement of criminal law. To begin with, contributions from international donors support the establishment, staffing, overhead, and day-to-day functioning of international courts, from the ICC to the Special Court for Sierra Leone. But development assistance for national judicial institutions is likely to have an even deeper impact on the rule of law. Practical improvements in domestic court systems and growing confidence in the equal protection of the laws act as long-term insurance against armed conflict.

Media and development organizations are also prime candidates for collaboration in the cause of conflict resolution. Human rights advocates have an important role to play in educating civil society about development programs that enhance the quality of life for all sectors of society. By the same token, development programs can provide essential financial and institutional support to human rights advocates.

Finally, development agencies and communities offer untapped potential for common cause in the realm of conflict resolution. Local communities are best positioned to evaluate the impact of development assistance on civilian populations, identify the kinds of socioeconomic programs that are most critical, and expose the unintended consequences of aid on regional agricultural markets and other aspects of the local economy and society. In the end, development programs ignore the perspectives and expertise of community members and grassroots organizations at their peril. Without such consultations, development activities are insignificant, at best, and counterproductive, at worst. The final section of this chapter brings communities to the center stage as arenas for conflict resolution.

E. COMMUNITIES AS PLACES FOR CONFLICT RESOLUTION

1. The Role of Communities in Realizing Humanitarian Law

In the previous section we saw that the development sector—comprising emergency relief as well as longer-term socioeconomic development programs—engages various dimensions of international law, from humanitarian principles all the way to human rights norms and the physical security and quality of life enjoyed by individuals and groups on a daily basis. As we turn to the role of communities in implementing international law, common wisdom suggests that civilians are most concerned with peace and human security, and focused on bringing an end to active combat between government troops and insurgents. But the community is as complex and sophisticated an arena for conflict and conflict resolution as the court, troop, media, and development realms already examined.

Broadly speaking, *communities* are interdependent groups of individuals coexisting at national, regional, and especially local levels. More specifically, the term compasses social healing ceremonies and material assistance programs that war survivors embrace and adapt to refortify themselves after prolonged periods of armed conflict. These postwar community efforts are often clustered together under the rubric of reconciliation, restorative justice, or alternative justice programs, and run the gamut from national truth commissions to local and traditional dispute resolution practices. Typical goals of restorative justice are reckoning with the past, reconciling offenders and victims, and assisting war-affected individuals and populations. As we shall see, war-affected communities are also concerned with accountability, and often regard reconciliation and responsibility as mutually inclusive values.

Two typical models for alternative justice institutions are the national truth commission and village-level arbitration, including the practices of *mato oput* in Uganda, *fambul tok* in Sierra Leone, and *ubushingantahe* in Burundi.[56] For both national truth commissions and local dispute resolution procedures, the fundamental goal is to remedy the harm, rather than to punish the offender. The restorative approach is manifested in efforts to record the history of past injustices, uphold the common welfare, and assist individual victims.[57] This contrasts, although not necessarily conflicts, with the objective of criminal trials to convict and sentence perpetrators of war crimes and crimes against humanity.

2. Community Mechanisms for Implementing Humanitarian Law in Uganda, Sierra Leone, and Burundi

In the scholarly debate about transitional societies, restorative mechanisms sometimes get subsumed within a somewhat hackneyed analysis pitting peace against justice, as if local communities want peace, and the international community wants justice. Local communities tend to have rather nuanced outlooks on peace and justice. Rather than peace *or* justice, grassroots community organizations tend to talk about peace *and* justice—and to explore the multiple components of justice itself.

Uganda

Within Ugandan civil society, justice is understood to have social and economic aspects, as well as criminal and legal dimensions. This perspective is expressed with particular clarity by Chris Dolan of Makerere University's Refugee Law Project, who calls for a working definition of "justice which has both retributive and restorative elements," such that justice may serve "as the handmaiden of sustainable peace."[58] In Uganda, a remarkably broad spectrum of civil society, including academics, human rights advocates, and civilians displaced and brutalized by the civil war, have questioned the capacity of ICC trials against leaders of the LRA to further either peace or justice in northern Uganda. Such observers and activists call for transitional justice measures more capable of "addressing the deep political causes of the conflict,"[59] and believe that communal atonement programs may be a better path towards social accountability for war-related crimes.

In 2000, the Ugandan parliament's Amnesty Act offered legal amnesty to former LRA combatants willing to turn in their weapons and renounce violence. In the context of over 400 interviews, authors of a 2005 study by the RLP of Makerere University found that Acholi people of northern Uganda widely concluded that "[a]mnesty. . . rhymes with our cultural system."[60] The RLP study suggests that in embracing the Amnesty Act, the Acholi were doing more than seeking an end to the military conflict.[61] Instead, the widely shared perception was that the Amnesty Act created a viable mechanism for welcoming former combatants, many of whom were abducted as children, back into their communities, and restoring the health of those very communities.[62]

Recognizing the virtues of restorative justice, some observers of post-conflict reconstruction in Uganda believe that communal atonement programs such as *mato oput* must go further than disarmament and forgiveness if they are to repair communities and prevent future conflict. As the RLP's 2005 study concluded, "while amnesty is clearly a good tool for encouraging insurgents to leave the bush, it does not adequately address issues of ensuring that they accept responsibility" or that war-scarred individuals are cared for.[63] Thus, the Ugandan experience suggests that community-based conflict resolution has at least three elements: the welcoming home of former combatants, the admission of guilt by offenders, and the provision of reparations to victims.

Sierra Leone

The 1999 Lomé Peace Agreement called for the creation of the national Truth and Reconciliation Commission. The TRC began its work in 2002, issuing its final report in October of 2004.[64] The TRC held a series of hearings in Freetown and in district capitols throughout the country where victims and offenders testified. The TRC's Final Report documented the war, identified as its primary causes government corruption and the betrayal of public trust, and issued a series of recommendations to the government, including the abolition of the death penalty and the criminalization of rape.

The TRC carried out its work while the Special Court for Sierra Leone was preparing for the trials of thirteen accused war criminals. Although this unusual combination of restorative and retributive justice mechanisms generated some tensions, Sierra Leoneans express a fair amount of pride in their two national institutions devoted to transitional justice. Nevertheless, many observers stress that both the TRC and the Special Court have had a very limited impact on rural communities since the TRC hearings did not extend below the district level and the Special Court only indicted thirteen individuals.

Typically, in villages throughout Sierra Leone, offenders and their victims live side-by-side without ever having acknowledged the crimes that occurred, resulting in repeated opportunities for renewed psychological trauma. In response to this reality, the Fambul Tok organization was founded to carry out the work of reconciliation at the village level through truth-telling and cleansing rituals as well as cooperative development projects.[65] Sierra Leone thus makes an important contribution to our understanding of conflict resolution. Community restoration must occur from the bottom up as well as from the top down.

Burundi

In 2007, the Government of Burundi resolved, with the United Nations High Commissioner for Human Rights, to establish a truth and reconciliation commission and a national war crimes tribunal.[66] In July, 2011, President Pierre Nkurunziza announced that Burundi's TRC would be formally constituted and begin its work in 2012. In addition, certain voices within Burundian civil society call for a return to village-level arbitration as a measure of accountability for perpetrators of crimes against humanity, utilizing traditional Burundian panels of elders trained in dispute resolution.[67] Nevertheless, although *ubushingantahe* panels exist in some communities, they have not yet received broad endorsement as a mechanism for addressing the atrocities of the Burundian civil war.

Burundi's major postwar preoccupations are disarming the civilian population, improving levels of employment, and overcoming electoral fraud and ethnic polarization in party politics. Since independence, the only government many Burundians have been willing to trust has been the one run by members of their ethnicity. Interethnic fear remains a factor in the Burundian political psyche. Indeed, the very term *community* in Burundian French is a euphemism for ethnic group. Burundi's experience with post-conflict reconstruction suggests that community reconciliation must start with a more expansive definition of the *communautée*.

3. Interactions between Communities and Other Arenas for Conflict Resolution

Just as peace and justice are not mutually exclusive concepts or goals, community organizations seeking an integrated vision of peace and justice need not work alone or in opposition to other arenas of conflict resolution. For example, Uganda's Beyond Juba Project has been critical of international criminal prosecutions of a handful of high-ranking military leaders of the LRA, but also has called for even-handed criminal prosecutions of both army and insurgent soldiers for war crimes and crimes against humanity. Thus, Uganda illustrates the potential collaboration between communities and courts in the realm of conflict resolution.

Similarly, although Sierra Leone's TRC was critical of the conduct of ECOMOG peacekeepers during the rebel war, UN peacekeeping troops helped bring the rebel war to a final conclusion. UNAMSIL orchestrated a very successful disarmament process beginning in 2000, creating space for a national transitional justice program including both the TRC and the Special Court. To this extent, Sierra Leone illustrates a potential synergy between community reconciliation and peacekeeping troops.

Further, media organizations may do their most effective work in implementing humanitarian and human rights law at the level of the community. Although international human rights agencies are often best known for their efforts to influence state policy by naming and shaming governments for human rights violations, they also have the capacity to internalize respect for human dignity within local communities. Advocacy organizations serve as tools of community reconciliation when they conduct human rights training programs in primary schools, military academies, and camps for refugees and the internally displaced.[68] CD-Peace brings materials about the TRC to rural chiefdoms in Sierra Leone, talks with primary and secondary students about conflict prevention, and facilitates gender awareness workshops to combat domestic violence. In all these activities, CD-Peace demonstrates the potential role of human rights education in community building.[69]

Finally, even though some international humanitarian organizations have been criticized for compounding civil wars, particularly in Central Africa,[70] other development organizations have worked resolutely at the grassroots level in particular countries to begin addressing the underlying causes of poverty and violence. In Burundi, for example, the NGO Partners in Health has collaborated with local people to improve health services, training community members to work as health care professionals. Thus, Burundi represents the possibility for common cause among communities and development agencies.

When communities call for reconciliation, reparations, amnesties, or depoliticized prosecutions by criminal tribunals, they are not simply seeking a formal end to the civil war. They are seeking a durable peace, with an alleviation of the root causes of the conflict. They want an even-handed justice, strengthening the judicial infrastructure from top to bottom. In appreciating the interconnectivity of criminal and social justice, building upon the interdependence of human rights law and human rights education, and understanding peace in both physical and socioeconomic terms, communities serve the dual causes of conflict resolution and human dignity. At the same time, communities engaged in creative forms of conflict resolution hold international law to one of its most basic tenets, the idea that law is governed by rules and legitimized by the appropriate and humane use of power.

Courts, troops, the media, development, and communities are five tools of post-conflict reconstruction. They each have the capacity to implement various aspects of humanitarian law, but also the potential to impede progress towards durable peace. Criminal courts insist on accountability for wartime atrocities, but may conduct targeted prosecutions and contribute to prolonging the conflict. Troops demand an end to insurgency, but may engage in humanitarian violations of their own. The media educate about human rights and humanitarian principles, but need resources to support their advocacy. Development agencies provide humanitarian relief and opportunities for social advancement, but may exacerbate inequities between various sectors of society. Communities seek reconciliation for their members, but may return to armed conflict without accountability for offenders and social welfare for victims.

To engage humanitarian law in action, these five mechanisms must work collaboratively to reckon with the crimes of the past, prevent the resurgence of violence in the future, and cultivate a culture of peace. Accountability requires criminal justice, conflict prevention requires social justice, and peace education requires historical justice. Courts, troops, and communities can seek individual accountability for the crimes of the war, through a combination of trials for high-level combatants and amnesty and community reintegration for less culpable participants. Development agencies and communities can further social justice, through the improvement of education, health care, and employment opportunities for all members of society. Media organizations and communities further historical justice by facilitating truth-telling about the human rights violations of the past, and insisting on humane governance in the future. It is ultimately the weaving of humanitarian principles into the fabric of society that will fortify the culture of peace.

In the final three chapters of our text, we will compare and evaluate the experiences of Uganda, Sierra Leone, and Burundi as they continue to navigate the transition from war to peace. In pursuing criminal justice, social justice, and historical justice, the three countries utilize and adapt the five mechanisms for implementing humanitarian law set forth in this chapter. Their ongoing efforts and partial successes illustrate the challenges of post-conflict social transformation and offer important lessons to other countries emerging from civil war into reconstruction and reconciliation.

NOTES

1. "So Why?" © 1997 International Committee of the Red Cross (ICRC). This verse of the song, "So Why?" is an English translation of a French translation of lyrics sung in Lingala by Congolese musician Papa Wemba. (The French translation is the work of the album's producers, and the unofficial English translation is the work of the author.)
2. This verse is an English translation, by the album's producers, of lyrics sung in Quimbundo by Angolan musician Lourdes Van Dunem.
3. This verse is an English translation, by the producers, of lyrics sung in French (as well as Wolof and English) by Senegalese musician Youssou N'Dour.
4. These lyrics are sung in English (as well as Yoruba and Ibo) by Nigerian musician Lagbaja.
5. This verse is sung in English (and Zulu) by South African musician Jabu Khanyile.
6. "So Why?" was composed and produced by Wally Badarou, and performed by five African artists who volunteered their time as part of an initiative organized by the ICRC called "Woza Africa (Come on Africa): Music Goes to War." "So Why?" is track one of an album by the same name, distributed by ICRC. With, "So Why?" ICRC seeks to educate civil society around the world about the realities of armed conflict in Africa, in order to build greater awareness of and commitment to the norms of international humanitarian law.
7. *See* JOHN AUSTIN, THE PROVINCE OF JURISPRUDENCE DETERMINED (1st ed. 1832) at 203 ("the law obtaining between nations is not positive law: for every positive law is set by a given sovereign to a person or persons in a state of subjection to its author.")
8. Prof. David Barash, Founder and Director of the University of Washington's Peace and Strategic Studies Program, writes that "the international human rights regime can seem woefully inadequate, based as it is on mere . . . exhortations, and devoid of enforcement mechanisms. But legal systems always have difficulty controlling powerful actors . . . ." David P. Barash, "Human Rights," from AN INTRODUCTION TO PEACE STUDIES

(Wadsworth, 1991), excerpted in *Approaches to Peace: A Reader in Peace Studies* at 155 (ed., D. Barash, Oxford University Press 2000).

9. As Prof. Richard Falk writes, "[l]ooking back on this century of world wars and weaponry of mass destruction, it may well be that the gradual development of a human rights framework will be the centerpiece of a more hopeful narration of the experience of the period." The struggle for human rights and humane governance is "the only responsible basis for positive citizenship at this stage of history." See Richard Falk, "On Humane Governance," from ON HUMAN GOVERNANCE (Pennsylvania State University Press 1995), excerpted in APPROACHES TO PEACE: A READER IN PEACE STUDIES, *op. cit.*, at 248, 249.

10. *See* Rome Statute of the International Criminal Court (Rome Statute or ICC Statute), 2187 UNTS 90, art. 7(1).

11. *See, generally*, Hovil & Lomo, "Whose Justice? Perceptions of Uganda's Amnesty Act 2000: The Potential for Conflict Resolution and Long-Term Reconciliation" (Refugee Law Project Working Paper No. 15, Feb. 2005). *See also*, Amy Ross and Chandra Lekha Siram, "Catch-22 in Uganda: the LRA, the ICC and the Peace Process" (JURIST Legal News & Research, University of Pittsburgh School of Law, July 17, 2006), para. 10 (citing a "recent UN report not[ing] that more than 90% of the fatalities in Northern Uganda are the result of the policy of forced displacement [by the Ugandan military] with 9% attributed to attacks by the LRA"). *See also* William Schabas, *Prosecutorial Discretion v. Judicial Activism at the International Criminal Court*, 6 J. INT'L. CRIM. JUST. 731, 747–48 (Sept. 2008) (even a lesser number of direct civilian deaths at the hands of the Ugandan People's Defense Forces, as compared to the Lord's Resistance Army (LRA), arguably represents a "classic impunity paradigm," given that the killers were "acting on behalf of a state that shelters them from its own courts.")

12. In March 2010, the Ugandan Parliament passed a War Crimes Act, as a legislative basis for implementing Uganda's obligations under the Rome Statute. This legislation and some of its implications for transitional justice in Uganda are discussed more fully in Chapter 7 on post-conflict reconstruction in Uganda.

13. *Mato oput* ceremonies are discussed in Chapter 7 on Uganda.

14. The Special Court for Sierra Leone has concurrent but primary jurisdiction, meaning it does not automatically displace jurisdiction over criminal prosecutions in the domestic courts of Sierra Leone, but may require deferral of such prosecutions under Article 8 of its Statute. See Human Rights First, "The Special Court for Sierra Leone," available at http://www.humanrightsfirst.org/cah/ij/w_context/w_cont_04.aspx, last accessed May 14, 2010. *See also* Agreement [creating] the Special Court for Sierra Leone (signed Jan. 16, 2002, ratified Mar. 2002) and Statute of the Special Court for Sierra Leone (annex to the Agreement), *available at* http://www.sc-sl.org/scsl-agreement.html and http://www.sc-sl.org/scsl-statute.html, Art. 8 (domestic courts must defer prosecution if requested by the Special Court).

15. *See generally* [2004] Final Report of the Truth and Reconciliation Commission of Sierra Leone, *available at* http://www.justiceinperspective.org.za/index.php?option=com_content&task=view&id=30&Itemid=66.

16. *See also* Stef Vandeginste, "Burundi's unturned stones," Radio Netherlands Worldwide, Oct. 4, 2010, *available at* http://www.rnw.nl/international-justice/article/burundis-unturned-stones.

17. *See* Chapter 4, Section B.2, discussion of the International Criminal Tribunal for Rwanda, located in Arusha, Tanzania.

18. *See* "Report of the assessment mission on the establishment of an international judicial commission of inquiry for Burundi," Mar. 11, 2005, S/2005/158, *available at* http://www.ictj.org/static/Africa/Burundi/s2005.158.kalomoh.eng.pdf. The Secretary General

reported to the President of the UN Security Council that the mission "recommends the establishment of a twin mechanism: a non-judicial accountability mechanism in the form of a truth commission and a judicial accountability mechanism in the form of a special chamber within the court system of Burundi" rather than an international judicial commission. *See* Letter dated Mar. 11, 2005, from the Secretary General addressed to the President of the Security Council, *available at* http://www.ictj.org/static/Africa/Burundi/s2005.158.kalomoh.eng.pdf.

19. *See* "Burundi slates truth and reconciliation panel for 2012," AFP, July 27, 2011, *available at* http://www.google.com/hostednews/afp/article/ALeqM5gpzDMrMKfwu2ssHaFktemmMGVPQ?docId=CNG.b8ddcd45fb4de7570a444013d5b8e3ad.311.

20. *See* Matthias Goldmann, *Does Peace Follow Justice or Vice Versa? Plans for Postconflict Justice in Burundi*, 30 FLETCHER FORUM OF WORLD AFFAIRS, 137, 147–48 (Winter 2006), available at http://ssrn.com/abstract=1369121. *See also* Barbara Vi Thien Ho, "Post-conflict Burundi and the Role of Ubushingantahe Council", July 17, 2009, Africa Faith & Justice Network, *available at* http://afjn.org/focus-campaigns/restorative-justice/147-commentary/660-post-conflict-burundi-and-the-role-of-ubushingantahe-council-.html.

21. Soldiers, who have targeted civilians in violation of the laws of war, and other individuals, who have participated in genocide or other orchestrated attacks on civilian populations, can also be called to account through truth commissions or atonement ceremonies. The relationship between punitive and restorative justice is explored in Chapter 4 on international criminal law, as well as in the sections of Chapters 7 and 8 devoted to transitional justice in Uganda and Sierra Leone, respectively.

22. "Compliments for the Peace" is track 10 on Disc Two of the Sierra Leone Refugee All Stars' *Living Like a Refugee* album (a two-disc CD set). *Living Like a Refugee* is a Sodasoap Production, 2005, recorded at Island Studios, Freetown, Sierra Leone.

23. In 1993, the UN Security Council created the UN Observer Mission Uganda-Rwanda (UNOMUR), which was mandated to monitor the border between Uganda and Rwanda and "to verify no military assistance reaches Rwanda." SC Res. 846 (1993), para. 3, S/RES/846 (1993), June 22, 1993. UNOMUR was subsequently reconstituted as the UN Assistance Mission for Rwanda (UNAMIR). In April 1994, in the early weeks of the Rwandan Genocide, while the UN Security Council adjusted the mandate of the UNAMIR peacekeepers, troops were not given an explicit authorization to seize weapons or to protect civilians. Rather, UNAMIR's mandate was limited to facilitating a cease-fire, assisting in the provision of humanitarian relief, and "monitor[ing] . . . the safety and security of the civilians who sought refuge with UNAMIR." SC Res. 912 (1994), para. 8, S/RES/912 (1994), Apr. 21, 1994.

24. As a result of widespread recognition of the prevalence of sexual violence against women by all parties to armed conflicts, including members of peacekeeping forces, the UN Security Council adopted Resolution 1888 in 2009, which called for "specific provisions . . . for the protection of women and children from rape and other sexual violence in the mandates of UN peacekeeping operations." SC Res. 1188 (2009), S/RES/1888 (2009), September 30, 2009.

25. *See* Sudarsan Raghavan, *Arrests made in bomb attacks on World Cup fans in Uganda*, WASH. POST, July 13, 2010, *available at* http://www.washingtonpost.com/wpdyn/content/article/2010/07/13/AR2010071301537.html.

26. *See* Chapter 8 on Sierra Leone.

27. The conduct of the LRA throughout the armed conflict in Northern Uganda is discussed extensively in Chapter 7.

28. In 2009, the United States Congress passed the Lord's Resistance Army Disarmament and Northern Uganda Recovery Act. *See* "Obama Presents Plan to Help Disarm LRA in

Uganda," Voice of America News, Nov. 25, 2010, *available at* http://www.voanews.com/english/news/africa/Obama-Presents-Plan-to-Help-Disarm-LRA-in-Uganda-110613824.html.
29. The conduct of the UPDF in the context of the conflict with the LRA is discussed in Chapter 7.
30. Perriello and Wierda, *op. cit.*, at 7.
31. The AU peacekeeping force was absorbed into the UN peacekeeping mission in Burundi in 2004, creating a hybrid force, which lasted until 2006. At that time, the UN transformed its mission in Burundi from one of peacekeeping to peace-building and post-conflict reconstruction. *See* Tim Murithi, *The African Union's Foray into Peacekeeping: Lessons from the Hybrid Mission in Darfur,* J. PEACE, CONFLICT & DEV., Issue July 14, 2009, *available at* http://www.peacestudiesjournal.org.uk/dl/Issue%2014%20Article%2015%20Revised%20copy%201.pdf.
32. *See* Geneva Conventions of August 12, 1949, art. 3, Common.
33. "Compliments for the Peace" is track 10 on Disc Two of the Sierra Leone Refugee All Stars' *Living Like a Refugee* album (a two-disc CD set). *Living Like a Refugee* is a Soda-soap Production, 2005, recorded at Island Studios, Freetown, Sierra Leone (Anti Records 2006). This song speaks to the challenges inherent in implementing a peace accord, even after "peace has returned." The lyrics illustrate the power of music to educate about politics, culture, and the rule of law.
34. Ana Maria Trujillo, *Concert to fund medical care for African villagers*, SANTA FE NEW MEXICAN, May 4, 2010, *available at* http://www.santafenewmexican.com/mobile/Concert-to-fund-medical-care-for-African-villagers. The article describes the Sierra Leone Refugee All Stars' support of Hope International for Tikar People, an NGO operating a medical clinic in the village of Tikar, in rural Cameroon.
35. *See* http://www.beyondjuba.org/.
36. The Republic of Guinea has served as host to as many as half a million Liberian and Sierra Leonean refugees at any given time over the course of the past two decades.
37. The work of Fambul Tok is discussed in Chapter 8.
38. Peter Uvin has written about the role of development assistance in reproducing hierarchy in some countries, by intensifying the special status that a certain privileged minority in the society already enjoyed. *See generally*, AIDING VIOLENCE: THE DEVELOPMENT ENTERPRISE IN RWANDA (Kumarian Press, 1998). *See also*, TRACY KIDDER, STRENGTH IN WHAT REMAINS: A JOURNEY OF REMEMBRANCE AND FORGIVENESS (New York: Random House, 2009) at 271–72.
39. From 1991—1993, when the author was serving as Associate Protection Officer for the United Nations High Commissioner for Refugees in Conakry, Guinea, the country was hosting over half a million Liberian and Sierra Leonean refugees. On regular shopping sprees to one of several large open-air markets serving the city, it was typical to see vendors' kiosks draped in the tell-tale blue tarpaulins of the United Nations, standard issue in the refugee camps, as well as to find cups of rice ladled from burlap sacks emblazoned with block letters reading: GIFT FROM THE UNITED STATES OF AMERICA. NOT FOR RESALE.
40. The relationship between material assistance for refugees and their legal protection in countries of asylum is further discussed in Chapter 5, Section D.
41. KICWA estimates that of the approximately twenty thousand Ugandan children who were abducted and conscripted from 1986 to 2006, 20–30 percent were girls. More information on the Kitgum Concerned Women's Association is available at http://www.ict-uk.org/uganda_home.html. For a fuller discussion of the challenges faced by young mothers who were associated with the civil wars in Northern Uganda, Sierra Leone, and Liberia, *see* Susan McKay *et al.*, "Community-Based Reintegration of War-Associated

Young Mothers: Participatory Action Research (PAR) in Liberia, Sierra Leone and Northern Uganda" (July 2010), *available at* www.pargirlmothers.com.
42. More information on the United Movement to End Child Soldiering is available at http://www.endchildsoldiering.org/index.htm.
43. *See* the Joint Vision for Sierra Leone of the United Nations Family, Freetown, May 30, 2009, cited and discussed in Chapter 8.
44. The work of CD-Peace is more fully discussed in Chapter 8.
45. *See* notes from interview with Aitor Sanchez Lacomba, International Rescue Committee Representative in Sierra Leone, Oct. 13, 2010, from pp. 45 (a)—(b) of author's field notebook. *See also* notes from interview with Anne-Marie Callan, Chargé d'Affaires, Irish Embassy, Freetown, Sierra Leone, Oct. 14, 2010, from p. 48(a) of author's field notebook. Chapter 8 provides a fuller discussion of the Gender Laws passed by the Sierra Leonean Parliament in 2007.
46. Burundi's peace process and postconflict reconstruction are discussed in depth in Chapter 9.
47. Internal Displacement Monitoring Centre [IDMC], "Burundi: Long-term IDP's need land security" (Oct. 20, 2009) at 3, 4, *available at* www.internal-displacement.org.
48. *Id.* at 6.
49. Like Sierra Leone's Peacebuilding Office, Burundi has a Peacebuilding Fund, which also receives assistance from the UN Peacebuilding Commission. In the case of Burundi, peace-building monies are significantly focused on serving the internally displaced and other war-affected populations. *Id.* at 7.
50. *Id.*
51. ICRC BULLETIN, "The ICRC in Burundi," Jan. 2010 at 1, general information *available at* www.icrc.org.
52. *Id.*
53. IDMC, *op. cit.* at 6.
54. *See generally* TRACY KIDDER, STRENGTH IN WHAT REMAINS: A JOURNEY OF REMEMBRANCE AND FORGIVENESS (New York: Random House, 2009).
55. The Kayanza clinic opened on November 7, 2007, in the village of Kigutu, thanks to the physical and moral support of community members, and under the direction of a US citizen of Burundian origin. Deogratias had survived the 1993 genocide while a medical student, only to return to his native country some twelve years later. *See* KIDDER, *op. cit.* at 252–59. *See also* "Village Health Works/Burundi," *available at* Partners in Health website, http://www.pih.org/pages/burundi/. The experiences of Deogratias Niyizonkiza are further detailed in Chapter 9 on Burundi.
56. The practice of *mato oput* is also discussed in Chapter 4, on international criminal law, and in Chapter 7, on Uganda. *Fambul tok* is discussed in Chapter 8, on Sierra Leone. *Ubushingantahe* is discussed in Chapter 4 and Chapter 9, on Burundi.
57. Direct payments to individual victims can be a powerful facet of restorative justice, even if the compensation is more symbolic than actual. Eritrea and Ethiopia established a Claims Commission, in 2000, in the aftermath of their border war. *See* Eritrea-Ethiopia Claims Commission, Permanent Court of Arbitration home page, http://www.pca.org/showpage.asp?pag_id=1151. In a similar vein, Sierra Leone, in response to specific recommendations of its Truth and Reconciliation Commission, established a Social Action Commission (SAC) in 2008. The SAC has made thousands of one-hundred-dollar payments to civil war victims, including amputees and survivors of sexual violence. Restorative justice in Sierra Leone is further discussed in Chapter 8, Section C.2.f.
58. *See* Dolan, "Whatever happened to comprehensive justice?" (Beyond Justice Project, Faculty of Law, Makerere University, June 2007), paras. 2 and 7, *available at* http://www.refugeelawproject.org/press_releases/WhateverHappenedtoTrueJustice.pdf.

59. Hovil & Lomo, *op. cit.*, *Whose Justice? Perceptions of Uganda's Amnesty Act 2000: the Potential for Conflict Resolution and Long-term Reconciliation* (Refugee Law Project Working Paper No. 15, February 2005), at 22.
60. *Id.* at 10.
61. *See generally*, Hovil & Lomo, op. cit.
62. As one interviewee explained, "[t]he innocent children who were abducted, forced to do many atrocities but against their will, I really welcome them . . . ." *Id.* at 9 and n. 28.
63. *Id.* at 27 and 14 (One interviewee stated that "[t]he communities were hurt when they saw ex-combatants were given iron sheets for building and other assistance while the widows and orphans they victimized are not benefiting in any way.").
64. *See* http://www.justiceinperspective.org.za/index.php?option=com_content&task=view&id=30&Itemid=66.
65. The work of Fambul Tok is discussed in greater detail in Chapter 8.
66. "Burundi, UN agree on truth commission, tribunal," Reuters, May 23, 2007, *available at* http://www.alertnet.org/thenews/newsdesk/L23458718.htm.
67. Barbara Vi Thien Ho, "Post-conflict Burundi and the Role of Ubushingantahe Council," Africa Faith & Justice Network, posted July 17, 2009, available at http://www.afjn.org/focus-campaigns/restorative-justice/147-commentary/660-post-conflict-burundi-and-the-role-of-ubushingantahe-council-.html.
68. *See* Moore, *Alchemy of Exile: Strengthening a Culture of Human Rights in the Burundian Refugee Camps in Tanzania,* 27 WASH. J. L. & POL. (2008) 139, 151–58.
69. The work of CD-Peace is further explored in Chapter 8 on Sierra Leone.
70. *See generally* PETER UVIN, AIDING VIOLENCE, *op. cit.*

CHAPTER 7

Beyond Juba in Uganda

Reconciling Restorative and Retributive Justice[1]

Listen Ocol, my old friend,
The ways of your ancestors
Are good,
Their customs are solid
And not hollow
They are not thin, not easily breakable
They cannot be blown away
By the winds
Because their roots reach deep into the soil.
                    Okot p'Bitek[2]

The Republic of Uganda,[3] whose capital Kampala rests on the shores of Lake Victoria in East Africa, celebrated its independence from Great Britain in 1962. Yoweri Museveni seized power in 1986, and has served three elected terms as president of Uganda since 1996. The people of Uganda endured over two decades of civil war on the northern part of their territory between 1986 and 2008, waged between the Ugandan People's Defense Forces (UPDF) and the rebel soldiers of the Lord's Resistance Army (LRA). Since 2006, the Government of Uganda has engaged in peace talks with the LRA, under the framework of the 2006 Juba Agreement on Cessation of Hostilities between the Government of the Republic of Uganda and the Lord's Resistance Army/Movement (2006 Juba Accord).[4] In the carrot and stick nature of Uganda's peace process, the Ugandan Parliament passed an Amnesty Act in 2000 and a War Crimes Act in 2010.

Uganda helped inaugurate the work of the International Criminal Court (ICC), in 2004, when Museveni asked the court to consider evidence of humanitarian law violations by the LRA. While the ICC case against the LRA is sometimes regarded as the pinnacle of internationally mediated criminal accountability, the merits of the LRA case are frequently called into question by Ugandan human rights activists and international law scholars alike. Ugandan civil society is engaged in a nuanced debate about whether war crimes prosecutions are capable of furthering both peace and justice, and whether international trials exclusively directed at enemies of the state potentially weaken rather than strengthen the rule of law.

In general, what is meant by rule of law is a bit more than the classic liberal notion of a government constrained by the fundamental principles of due process, equal protection, and judicial review of legislative and executive action. Building off this important conception of "a government of laws, not of men" is a common-sense understanding of the rule of law as the heart of a political culture of accountability and the appropriate use of power by officers of the state and nonstate actors alike. The concept embodies *justice*, in all its legal, socioeconomic, and historical manifestations. Although respect for civil liberties is an important component of the rule of law, the concept also encompasses concern for integrity of the society as a whole, and the well-being of all its members. In countries emerging from armed conflict, the establishment of the historical record, and the functioning of public schools and medical clinics are as essential to state legitimacy and social health as legitimate courts and fair elections.

As in other countries, the rule of law in Uganda has a variety of more specific meanings. Since the Juba peace process began to bear fruit in 2006, the broader notion has been given a variety of innovations by individual voices within Uganda civil society and government. For some, justice requires individual accountability for both rebel and government soldiers, and a full exploration of the root causes of the conflict. For others, the rule of law entails deferral to traditional and cultural mechanisms for dispute resolution, an appreciation of the restorative as well as punitive dimensions of justice, the pairing of criminal sanctions for some war crimes perpetrators with economic reparations for civilian victims of war, and increased investment in socioeconomic development in northern Uganda. For another contingent, justice is manifested through prioritizing the psychosocial needs of women and children who experienced sexual and other forms of exploitation during the conflict, and acknowledging that some perpetrators were themselves victims of war crimes. Finally, a characteristically Ugandan perspective maintains that as war victimizes society as a whole, reconciliation will repair the fabric of the society, affirming the humanity of all its members.

A. A BRIEF HISTORY OF UGANDA AND THE UGANDAN CIVIL WAR

1. Independence and the Obote I Era

Uganda achieved its independence in 1962 when Britain ended its 68-year protectorate over Ugandan territory. The core of the Ugandan Protectorate (Protectorate), established in 1894, was the Buganda Kingdom, comprising much of Uganda's Central Province, and ruled since 1500 by a series of Kabakas, or hereditary kings. Although the Protectorate also encompassed tribes of the north, east and west, some of which had previously been at war with the Baganda, the British "designated the Baganda as the 'most advanced tribe' and so used them–and their sophisticated local government structures–to rule other parts of Uganda."[5] As journalist and author Richard Dowden put it, Britain's divide-and-rule approach to the administration of its Ugandan Protectorate "[s]tored up problems for the future." Given that the Baganda constituted a minority of the population of post-independence Uganda, when elections were held in 1962, predictably a northerner, Milton Obote, was elected prime minister, while the ceremonial post of president was given to the Baganda Kabaka, Frederick Mutesa.[6]

Milton Obote served his term as Uganda's Prime Minister from 1962 until 1966, when he seized power from President Mutesa and designated himself Executive President.[7] As chief executive, Obote initially exercised emergency powers until he adopted a new constitution in 1967, establishing the Republic of Uganda and abolishing the traditional tribal kingdoms, including the authority of the Bagandan Kabaka. Obote promoted a socialist program of economic development and by the late 1960s was contemplating the nationalization of British-owned industries in Uganda.[8] Before he could fully realize his vision for Uganda, Obote was overthrown by his Army Chief of Staff Idi Amin Dada in 1971.[9] Amin was "a street kid from West Nile" who grew up in an army camp, and then underwent training, like other young men from Uganda's northern and western tribes, to serve in the King's African Rifles (KAR).[10] The KAR saw action in Burma during World War II and evolved into the Ugandan Army, which then received training from the Israelis during the postindependence period.[11]

2. Amin, Obote II, and the Ethnopolitics of Northern and Western Uganda

An important theme running throughout modern Ugandan history has been the role of the army in Ugandan politics and demographics. Various rebel movements have made their own contributions to the socio-political landscape of dreams, expectations, violence, and changing power dynamics in Uganda. The army and rebel insurgencies alike have served as channels or chimeras of social mobility and political power for members of various tribal communities, as well as outlets for popular dissatisfaction with the reigning head of state. Throughout modern Ugandan history, the military has both repressed and uplifted young people from the North and the West, disappointing as often as encouraging. Field Marshall Idi Amin Dada's biography is but the most infamous illustration of this phenomenon.[12]

Related to the ethno-military dynamic in Uganda has been the mercurial relationship between the central government and the traditional tribal communities. Support for, resistance to, or outright repression of traditional tribal authorities has been a factor in the waxing and waning of Ugandan political leaders. Milton Obote, for example, did not endear himself to the Baganda when he took power from the Kabaka in 1966, but at the same time, he relied heavily upon the Israelis for military training of an army recruited largely from the Acholi community, a northern tribe, and from other communities, including Obote's own Langi ethnic group.[13]

For his part, once Amin came to power in 1971, he enjoyed initially a pro-Baganda reputation "because he had removed the Baganda's archenemy Obote," and for repatriating the remains of the former President and Kabaka Frederick Mutesa, who had died in exile.[14] Yet despite his championing traditional values and feigned respect for both tribal elders and the British who remained in Uganda after independence,[15] some of the first victims of Amin's repressive policies were the Acholi and Langi Army soldiers who were massacred upon his orders during the early months of his rule.[16]

During Amin's eight-year rule, officials of his government murdered between 100,000 and 500,000 Ugandans across ethnic groups.[17] Close to 80,000 Ugandan civilians of South Asian heritage were deported, including nearly 20,000 who were Ugandan citizens.[18] Partly through the military intervention of the Tanzanian armed forces, Amin was overthrown in 1979, and Milton Obote returned to power in presidential elections held in 1980.[19]

During the Obote II period, human rights violations shadowed those of the Amin years, and Yoweri Museveni's National Resistance Army (NRA) mounted an insurgency against the central government.[20] In 1985, Obote was removed from power in a military coup led by a largely ethnic Acholi Army brigade. Tito Okello, also an Acholi, assumed the presidency by negotiating with Museveni's NRA. The NRA seized the capital Kampala and the rest of Uganda in 1986, organizing a government under Museveni. During the same year, several Acholi-dominated rebel movements, including the Holy Spirit Movement, launched an insurgency in northern Uganda.

The Lord's Resistance Army (LRA), led by Joseph Kony and founded in 1987, is the successor to the Holy Spirit Movement.

3. Museveni and the Lord's Resistance Army

After Museveni came to power in 1986, his government established parish-level Resistance Councils, whose members were elected by their local constituents.[21] In 1995, one of the amendments to the Ugandan Constitution restored the legitimacy of certain cultural and traditional authorities, including the Bagandan Kabaka. Museveni was elected president of Uganda in the national elections of 1996 and reelected in 2001, and again in 2006, after the Ugandan Parliament removed previous presidential term limits. He began his fourth term in 2011.[22]

The soldiers of the Ugandan People's Defense Forces (UPDF) have been battling Kony's LRA for most of Museveni's 25 years in power.[23] Throughout the course of the civil war in northern Uganda, LRA soldiers killed thousands of civilians and kidnapped and conscripted upwards of 30,000 children "for use as porters, fighters and sex slaves."[24] For their part, in attempting to defeat the LRA, soldiers of the UPDF killed thousands of civilians and displaced hundreds of thousands more.[25] At the height of the civil war in northern Uganda, upwards of two million people resided in camps for internally displaced persons (IDPs).[26]

Recognizing the staggering human costs of the government's inconclusive military campaign against the LRA, the Ugandan Parliament passed an Amnesty Act in 2000, offering immunity from prosecution to demobilized LRA combatants.[27] That same year, Uganda ratified the Rome Statute of the International Criminal Court (Rome Statute or ICC Statute).[28] These two legislative acts laid the foundation for a carrot-and-stick dance by the Government of Uganda in which negotiations with the LRA are interwoven with threatened prosecutions of LRA senior commanders. This hybrid approach was manifested in Uganda's 2004 referral of the LRA to the ICC and its participation in the yet-to-be finalized 2007 Juba Accord.

Although the LRA was originally styled as an Acholi-nationalist, Christian-revivalist movement, most of the LRA's victims are themselves Acholi villagers[29] and most of the rebel soldiers are Acholi who were forcibly conscripted as children.[30] Most LRA child soldiers were kidnapped and, as part of their induction, forced to engage in murders and mutilations, often of their own relatives or village members.[31] Uganda's 2004 referral to the International Criminal Court (ICC) of the LRA's conduct in northern Uganda was significantly focused on evidence of widespread LRA child conscription, among other criminal offenses. In 2005, the ICC issued indictments against Joseph Kony and his top lieutenants.

Uganda's twenty-year-plus civil war between the rebels of the LRA and the soldiers of the UPDF began to wind down in August 2006, when an initial ceasefire agreement was signed in the city of Juba in Southern Sudan.[32] The preliminary ceasefire was followed in 2007 by the Juba Peace Agreement on Accountability and Reconciliation (2007 Juba Accord).[33] These accords are but two of six agreements signed by the Government of Uganda and the LRA. The other four were devoted respectfully to the resettlement of IDPs,[34] a durable end to hostilities,[35] the disarmament and reintegration of rebel fighters,[36] and a monitoring mechanism.[37] Despite the willingness of the LRA and the Government of Uganda to continue negotiations, a final peace accord for Uganda is still forthcoming. Nevertheless, from the peak in 2006 of 1.8 million IDPs in northern Uganda, by December 2010, 90 percent of IDPs had returned to their homes as the peace process began to bear fruit.[38]

As efforts to finalize the Juba Accords continue, Joseph Kony and his top deputies remain fugitives of arrest warrants issued in 2005 by the ICC. And although hostilities in northern Uganda have ended for all intents and purposes, the same is not true of cross-border regions where LRA soldiers have sought safe haven, including neighboring Central African Republic (CAR), the Democratic Republic of the Congo (DRC), and the Sudan.[39] In recent years, Kony is reputed to have been hiding out in the Darfur region of Sudan,[40] while LRA fighters attacked civilians in the DRC and mounted raids in CAR throughout 2010.[41] The consolidation of the government of the newly independent state of South Sudan will likely create a less hospitable climate for LRA rebels in that region, given historical ties between the Government of Uganda and the people of southern Sudan.[42]

4. The Political Dance between LRA Prosecutions and Ugandan Peace Talks

Even those who challenge the ICC, typically for exclusively prosecuting the top leadership of the LRA,[43] are willing to give the international community credit where credit is due, for helping bring Joseph Kony to the negotiation table.[44] Beyond the impact of war crimes trials on Kony himself, the ICC indictments also influence the conduct of mid-level LRA soldiers. Recently, the media has spotlighted the work of former LRA soldiers assisting the UPDF in the capture of LRA commanders in the DRC, CAR, and Southern Sudan.[45] These military developments will likely continue to play into Kony's own evolving calculus, as suggested by a statement attributed to one of his translators. The LRA leader's self-described "peace interpreter" clarified in 2010 that Kony had not rejected further talks, and merely required additional time to understand the current negotiating terms of the Government of Uganda.[46]

Although there is considerable merit in the concern that outstanding ICC arrest warrants will continue to dampen the rebel leaders' enthusiasm for full disarmament, the relationship between the international judicial realm and *realpolitik* developments on the ground in Uganda is both complex and evolving. The military and political movements of both the LRA and the UPDF are dynamic and will continue to play themselves out in the future. This was particularly the case in 2011, as government and civil society actors began to respond to the implementation of the ICC Act enacted by the Ugandan Parliament in 2010.

B. CLOSING THE ACCOUNTABILITY GAP IN UGANDA FOR ACCUSED PERPETRATORS OF CIVIL WAR ATROCITIES: CRIMINAL TRIALS IN HIGH COURT AND *MATO OPUT* AT THE VILLAGE LEVEL

Certainly the atrocious nature of LRA forced conscriptions, in which children are socialized to violence and combat and alienated from their families and communities, has made the LRA an obvious target for ICC prosecutions in the context of the Ugandan civil war. At the same time, the fact that the LRA is an army largely composed of Acholi children and adolescents profoundly impacts the way that northern Ugandans think about retribution and fairness under the banner of transitional justice.[47] Moreover, human rights organizations based inside and outside of Uganda have gathered evidence of extrajudicial killings and torture by the UPDF,[48] and even more civilian deaths have resulted from the forced relocation of Ugandans into displaced persons camps by the UPDF.[49] Finally, many former child soldiers and slaves have escaped LRA service only to be reconscripted by other armed groups, including "army commanders" in South Sudan allied with the Government of Uganda.[50]

For all these reasons, ICC indictments of LRA leaders without any parallel war crimes indictments of government soldiers in international or domestic Ugandan courts have raised the specter of differential treatment in Uganda's approach to transitional justice,[51] a reality that Uganda's new International Crimes Division (ICD) will be asked to help rectify. But for many Acholi people living with war and its aftermath in northern Uganda, war crimes trials may never address their deepest preoccupation in the search for justice—ending the cycle of violence.

In March of 2010, the Ugandan Parliament passed the ICC Act and, in July 2010, the legislation was signed into law by President Museveni.[52] The ICC Act implements the Rome Statute, to which Uganda is a signatory. As foreseen in the 2007 Juba Peace Accord,[53] the ICC Act empowers the new ICD within the Ugandan High Court to try individuals for war crimes and crimes against humanity, explicitly incorporating the ICC Rome Statute's definitions of these crimes into Ugandan law.[54] The scope of prospective domestic prosecutions under Ugandan law requires further definition, whether from parliament or the ministry of justice, particularly concerning the impact of the new legislation on the Ugandan Amnesty Act, still in force until such time that the Ugandan parliament fails to extend its mandate.[55] Nevertheless, one hope for the role of the Ugandan ICD is that it will help close a considerable gap in the accountability spectrum for individuals believed to have committed war crimes and crimes against humanity during the Ugandan civil war.

Prior to the ICC Act, Ugandans could look to the high-profile ICC prosecutions of a handful of senior LRA, with no apparent plans for similar war crimes prosecutions of mid-level LRA or any government military officers or soldiers whatsoever. On the other end of the accountability continuum, Ugandans have been implementing grassroots conciliation proceedings for low-level perpetrators of war crimes since 2001.[56] These so-called traditional justice proceedings, including *mato oput*, seek to reconcile and welcome offenders back into their home communities, often alongside the surviving kin of their victims.

Mato oput is a reconciliation process conducted under the auspices of traditional Acholi chiefs, in which offenders acknowledge their crimes, offer reparations to their victims, and finally participate in a cleansing ceremony in which they are received back into the community.[57] The ceremony is named for the oput tree, from whose topmost branches leaves are taken to make a brew for the victim and perpetrator, "symbolizing the bitterness in their hearts," and shared in an act of mutual forgiveness.[58] Such alternative dispute resolution procedures have received a measure of official sanction since Uganda's 1995 constitution recognized the authority of cultural leaders in certain contexts, and have since been applied to crimes as serious as homicide.[59] In the context of Uganda's civil war atrocities, *mato oput* has been offered chiefly to less culpable offenders, including those who committed crimes as children, or under other circumstances of duress.

In the middle of the accountability continuum, there has been a certain neglect of mid-level offenders–i.e., perpetrators of serious crimes who acted intentionally, but who were not necessarily in positions of command responsibility over other offenders. It is within this intermediate tier that the Ugandan ICD is likely to concentrate, starting with former LRA combatant Thomas Kwoyelo, whose trial in the ICD commenced on July 11, 2011.[60] Whether war crimes defendants will include members of the UPDF as well as soldiers of the LRA remains to be seen. Nevertheless, some Ugandans view this "middle path" towards domestic prosecutions as an ideal solution to the criminal accountability gap.[61]

C. A TRUTH AND RECONCILIATION COMMISSION FOR UGANDA?

In addition to *mato oput* and other traditional justice practices at the local or village level, and criminal prosecutions at the national and international level, the 2007 Juba Accord contemplated the creation of a National Reconciliation Commission. In 2009, various non-governmental organizations (NGOs) called for the creation of a National Reconciliation Forum.[62] Their draft National Reconciliation Bill has been debated in the public realm but had not been formally tabled in parliament as of 2010. The proposal was prepared by the Coalition for Reconciliation in Uganda, under the leadership of Makerere University's Refugee Law Project (RLP) and the Beyond Juba Project (BJP).[63] If enacted, the legislation would create a Reconciliation Forum empowered to hear testimony by individual offenders and victims, recommend prosecution in appropriate instances, and grant reparations to victims. In the tradition of kindred institutions around the world, including South Africa's Truth and Reconciliation Commission, the Ugandan Reconciliation Forum would be charged with a broader mandate to help Ugandan civil society establish the historical record of what happened during the war and of who was responsible.[64]

Ugandan politicians and academics as well as residents of northern Uganda continue to call for a truth and reconciliation process, whether in addition to or instead of criminal prosecutions. In December of 2010, Norbert Mao, Chairman of the Democratic Party of Uganda, expressed his preference for a truth and reconciliation commission like that in South Africa, "to allow us to decide who did what during the conflict."[65] For his part, Sultan Kasimu Opio, a displaced northern Ugandan who lost many relatives in the LRA war, asserts that "[w]hat we need today is reconciliation between us and the perpetrators, and not the criminal proceedings against them."[66] Building on Opio's perspective, Frederick Golooba of the Makerere Institute of Social Research cautions: "We in the south don't understand the gravity of the LRA war on the northern part of the country. If people in the north are saying a truth and reconciliation commission is what will solve the problem, then why do we insist on the ICC?"[67]

D. CIVIL SOCIETY SPEAKS OUT ON JUSTICE, PEACE, AND TRUTH-TELLING

1. The Heart of Justice and Peace in Northern Uganda: Returning Children and Respecting Women

Before launching into a deeper discussion of retributive and restorative visions of justice in the Ugandan context, it is important to focus on two aspects of the conflict in northern Uganda, the recruitment of children and the sexual abuse of women.

a. Bringing Our Children Home

A crucial fact of life in northern Uganda is that the civil war has been fought primarily by abducted children who come from the very communities that have borne the brunt of LRA violence and UPDF displacement. Thus, in confronting the "torture"[68] suffered by the civilians of northern Uganda over the twenty-year life of the civil war, an unavoidable aspect of their experience is the stark reality of their brutalization at the hands of their own youth.

In the same vein, when academics and human rights advocates weigh punishment against forgiveness, and criminal justice against social justice in Uganda, they must be reminded that these child offenders were Acholi children, belonging to the same Acholi families who have struggled to survive the war and displacement in northern Uganda for these many years. It is impossible to overemphasize this basic truth, as is reflected in interviews of northern Ugandans conducted by the Refugee Law Project of Makerere University in 2005. The results of the RLP study convey "the overwhelming desire for most civilians in northern Uganda to see their children return home safely."[69] Most interviewees, when asked about transitional justice, defined fairness as "any process that allows the vicious cycle of violence to end, and the children to come home..."[70]

When transitional justice proponents speak of "forgiveness" and "reintegration" in northern Uganda, they are speaking in part of Ugandans forgiving their own children, and welcoming them home. In the words of one elder, "[t]he innocent children who were abducted, forced to do many atrocities but against their will, I really welcome them.... this magnitude of suffering means we just want these people back."[71]

In the context of Uganda's 2000 Amnesty Act, whose blanket amnesty terms[72] still need to be reconciled with the 2010 War Crimes Act, amnesty is seen as a pathway to return and reconciliation. But again, return and reconciliation signify an intensely emotional reality—former child soldiers being accepted back into communities that they caused to suffer. Hovil and

Lomo of Makerere University's RLP provide an on-the-ground northern-Ugandan perspective on the amnesty program, which had been supported by local religious and cultural leaders long before it was enacted into law at the national level:[73]

> In northern Uganda, particularly in Gulu, there was widespread awareness about the Amnesty Law.... Many returnees in Gulu said that they heard about it on the radio. For instance, the recent initiative of encouraging senior ex-rebels to speak out in support of the amnesty process on a Mega FM programme, "Dwong Paco" (meaning "come back home") was frequently referred to, and appears to have had a significant impact in building trust in the amnesty process among rebels in the bush.[74]

Despite the overall climate of support for the return of former child soldiers to their communities, there have been instances of returnees being called names by their schoolmates.[75] Nevertheless, in the 2005 study conducted by the RLP, "such intimidation, unkind as it is, has not been translated into violence [and] no incidents were reported to the researchers of returnees being physically harmed by members of the community."[76]

One elder from northern Uganda expressed with particular eloquence the role of amnesty in both encouraging return and ending armed conflict: "We just sympathise with them and welcome them very well [and] that encourages those who are left in the bush to also come out peacefully. I think that is why war has stopped from this place."[77]

b. Respect for Women

The particular experiences of girl children and women who were inducted by the LRA compose a second facet of the reality in northern Uganda requiring attention on a human level. Of those abductees sexually exploited by the LRA, the vast majority have been girls and women.[78] Although it is widely accepted by residents of northern Uganda that these young women would benefit from special social services upon return to their communities, the tragic irony is that they are sometimes stigmatized upon return, as if their very sexual enslavement was a form of privilege. In the words of one female abductee, "[p]eople say that we were wives of rebels, that's why we survived[,] even though my husband and son were killed. My late husband's relatives are very hostile to me."[79]

In addition to verbal intimidation, women, like other former conscripts, face economic challenges upon return to their communities. In on-the-ground interviews in northern Uganda conducted in 2004, "it was apparent that many of those who were abducted and have returned are living in appalling conditions—again, particularly women."[80]

In another aspect of the reality for women in northern Uganda, while the IDP camps are gradually being disbanded, women in and outside of IDP camps continue to experience high levels of domestic violence and rape. Although domestic violence by definition occurs within the home,[81] rape occurs widely both within and outside marriage and is perpetrated by acquaintances and strangers. In the case of stranger rape, the contexts in which women face the threat of forced sexual intercourse are myriad:

> Women in the camps face the threat of rape as they gather firewood, food and water in the hinterlands around their camps or even within the camp itself. They face it as they travel along the roads between their dwelling places and the town centers. They face the threat as they sleep at night in exposed urban areas where no protection is provided and in the IDP camps. They face it when they are abducted or if they are imprisoned by the armed forces.[82]

Other forms of violence in IDP camps that women exclusively or disproportionately experience include wife inheritance[83] and so-called economic violence, in which men "forcefully take the distributed relief items like foodstuff, saucepans, jerry cans, mosquito nets, or tools from home and sell them at a very nominal fee to simply get some petty cash which they can use to buy alcohol or even entice other women."[84]

Although all violence against women in northern Uganda cannot be attributed to the civil war and its aftermath, armed conflict and displacement have influenced the complex social and political relations between men and women in Uganda society, and some of these changes have increased the physical vulnerability of women. On the positive side, women in northern Uganda today are more apt to be engaged in small businesses, including "brewing, selling food stuff [and] running small lodging houses, in order to be able to meet the family needs."[85] On the negative side, "many of the men in the Acholi region are idle, frustrated and have no income base."[86] For women, this changed economic power differential can have dangerous implications, especially in situations where "[m]en use violence, physical or otherwise, to reinstate their lost glory ... [T]his only increases the extent of abuse against women and the continued disregard of the legal regimes governing gender-based violence."[87]

c. Legal Protection and Social Security

One of the messages emerging from the individual experiences of former child soldiers and internally displaced persons, men and women alike, is that the socioeconomic aspects of return and reintegration are often as significant as the legal status of those welcomed home. Some of the tensions and name-calling experienced by former combatants, female and male, are explained by the fact that the communities to which they return are also suffering material deprivations. Thus amnesty and reconciliation for former soldiers cannot be evaluated and supported without concern for the human security of those civilians in northern Uganda whose circumstances remain precarious.[88]

As one woman from Kasese town put it, "[t]he communities were hurt when they saw ex-combatants were given iron sheets for building and other assistance while the widows and orphans they victimized are not benefiting in any way."[89] The willingness of northern Ugandans to forgive those who have attacked their own communities is powerful, but this generosity may be difficult to sustain without reconciliation programs that also include reparations for the communities themselves. Some of the most ambitious and promising socioeconomic development work happening in northern Uganda today focuses on women's social and economic empowerment as the heart of sustainable development in communities emerging from poverty and war.[90]

2. Retributive and Restorative Justice

Ugandan and international human rights advocates have not been reluctant to question the wisdom of the ICC's investigation of the situation in northern Uganda. At worst, the LRA case is viewed as a formula for continued armed conflict and atrocities against civilians, such that some call for the ICC to consider "quietly retracing its steps in northern Uganda."[91] At best, critics characterize the ICC case against the LRA as state-centric justice,[92] given the international community's so-far exclusive indictments of senior rebel leaders. Fidelity to the principle of individual accountability for atrocious crimes against civilians, the logic goes, will require international or domestic trials of lower-level LRA fighters, as well as soldiers of the UPDF.[93] Domestic trials conducted by the Ugandan High Court's ICD may face similar rebuke, if the new court's docket fills with cases against mid-level LRA to the exclusion of government soldiers.[94] Nevertheless, not all Ugandan human rights advocates dismiss the idea of criminal prosecutions out of hand.[95] The dominant call within Ugandan civil society today is for an expansion rather than a wholesale rejection of the penal approach to transitional justice.

The Refugee Law Project of Makerere University School of Law, notably, has offered an alternative vision of transitional justice that combines criminal prosecutions with grassroots reconciliation programs. Chris Dolan,

Director of the RLP,[96] articulates a conception of "justice which has both retributive and restorative elements," where "justice [serves] as the handmaid of sustainable peace."[97] The notion that restorative justice is a component of criminal justice challenges the oppositional vision of peace and justice that continues to permeate much of contemporary international human rights and criminal law discourse. The work of Dolan and his colleagues inspires a rethinking of the accountability–reconciliation continuum, prioritizing the community values inherent in restorative justice, while emphasizing the capacity for grassroots conciliation to *enhance* accountability rather than weaken it.[98]

Blending retributive and restorative models of justice will not always be an easy or self-evident exercise. A primary concern of the restorative approach is to identify those values that the community coming out of conflict deems most crucial to the reconciliation process. While some of those principles will resonate with classic Western conceptions of criminal law— including the right to confront witnesses, and to speak in one's own defense, other values will differ in significant regard. For example, in the *mato oput* village-level conciliation process touched upon earlier,[99] severe criminal penalties are anathema, whether capital punishment or life imprisonment.[100] Contemporary international criminal law has abolished the death penalty, establishing life imprisonment as the maximum penalty, as evidenced in the Treaty of Rome.[101] Uganda's 2010 ICC Act includes a similar stipulation.[102] But life imprisonment is also problematic from a community–reconciliation perspective in northern Uganda, where removing individuals permanently from their communities is not considered to be an ideal solution for a society knitting itself back together in the aftermath of civil war.[103]

Despite potential conflicts between local principles of community reconciliation and international norms of criminal justice, there is reason to believe that combining retributive and restorative elements will result in a better system of justice overall. Ugandans working in the field of post-conflict reconstruction describe an "extractive process" in which the essential components of transitional justice are distilled.[104] Just as "local values" of restorative justice may rein in certain excesses of retributive justice, "global values" of individual accountability may serve to keep restorative justice honest, so to speak, and true to its underlying goal of community reconciliation.

Ugandans appear to find deepest fault in the international community's so-far exclusive drive to prosecute senior LRA fighters, whether in international or domestic criminal tribunals. Thus, Ugandan civil society seems to be demanding a more inclusive approach to transitional justice in at least three respects. First, criminal prosecutions should encompass both higher and lower level offenders. Second, prosecutions should be directed at both rebel and government troops. Finally, criminal process should be linked with efforts to reconcile offenders with their communities. Building upon and supplementing the ICC case against the LRA, a combination of Ugandan war crimes prosecutions and reconciliation ceremonies at the local level has great potential to foster deeper faith in the rule of law on the part of the Ugandan people.

3. Communities of Victims and Perpetrators

Even human rights advocates who urge a hybrid retributive-and-restorative approach to transitional justice sometimes reinforce the notion that criminal accountability is for perpetrators of war crimes whereas restorative justice is for victims in need of reparations. Zahara Nampewo, lecturer in Gender and the Law at the University of Makerere, suggests another way of viewing communities in need of reconciliation. Because "perpetrators are also victims," she argues, we need "a bit of both" criminal trials and restorative programs, particularly when offenders return to their communities after serving sentences or taking part in village-level conciliation procedures.[105] Although the former child soldier might be the most emblematic example of offender-as-victim, many other perpetrators of war crimes also suffered atrocities, both personal attacks and abuses of their loved ones and neighbors.

Transitional justice scholar Patrick Hoenig has interviewed many Ugandans in the context of his study of the peace process in northern Uganda:

> Whenever the news of rebel casualties spread in the villages of northern Uganda, I was told, many a mother's heart skipped a beat: among the dead could be their own child, abducted, forcibly recruited or siding with the rebels for material gain. That today's perpetrator can be tomorrow's victim—and vice versa—is conventional wisdom. What emerges from the analysis of victims' narratives in northern Uganda, however, is a deeper truth. The distinguishing between perpetrator and victim, while being a defining element of the international justice system, runs counter to the cosmology of northern Ugandans who believe that even the perpetrator of the most heinous crimes retains agency to help rebuild peace and restore justice.[106]

Hoenig's insights reveal the shared victimization and common humanity of all survivors of such a prolonged and searing armed conflict. In the interests of rebuilding Uganda, however, his "deeper truth" is that Ugandans simply cannot afford to make an absolute and artificial separation between perpetrators and victims. To do so would deprive Uganda of essential resources its people will need—human capital and human agency—to work together to create a new future on the ashes of the past.

4. Establishing the Historical Record through Truth-telling

In addition to the two criminal-accountability and community-reconciliation strands of transitional justice, a third aspect is emphasized by Dr. J. Oloka-Onyango, Director of Makerere University's Human Rights and Peace Centre. He asks: "What is the place of truth in this discussion? How did we get here?"[107] His questions suggest that peace and justice in their punitive and restorative incarnations are only part of the story. Equally vital to Oloka-Onyango is a collective process, in which the history of the civil war is recorded and the causes of the conflict are exposed and explored.[108] His approach inspires a broader understanding of transitional justice as a stool with three legs—criminal justice, social reconciliation, *and* collective memory. This triad can also be conceived of as retributive justice, restorative justice, and historical justice.

The truth-telling or historical justice leg of post-conflict reconstruction has both its individual and collective components. There is the need for individuals to accept responsibility for their wrongful acts, including atrocities against civilians.[109] But linked to truth-telling by each former combatant is the necessity for collective truth-telling about the roots of the conflict in northern Uganda, including the role of the government. Given the ICC's focus to date on wrongdoing by the LRA, a broad-based amnesty and reconciliation process will be essential in order to "address . . . the deep-rooted political causes of the conflict."[110] As one elder in Kitgum town, northern Uganda, attested, "[i]f you walk around here there are mass graves from government troops, and . . . if you look at history you can see why this whole thing flared up."[111] Truth-telling or historical justice appears to constitute the weakest leg of the transitional justice stool in Uganda, and one that a future truth and reconciliation commission will be asked to strengthen, along with promoting individual accountability and communal reparations.

E. UGANDA'S BLUEPRINT FOR TRANSITIONAL JUSTICE

1. The Justice, Law and Order Sector, and the Transitional Justice Working Group

In addition to ratifying the Rome Statute in 2000, taking part in peace talks with the LRA beginning in 2006, and committing to implement the new War Crimes Act passed by the Ugandan parliament in 2010, the Government of Uganda, since 1999, has been building a comprehensive program to reform the administration of justice, under the auspices of the Justice, Law and Order Sector (JLOS). JLOS is an inter-ministerial collaboration between several cabinet departments, including the Ministry of Justice and Constitutional Affairs. In its first Strategic Investment Plan, adopted in 2001, JLOS focused on equal access to criminal and commercial justice, and in its second, adopted in 2006, the lens was widened to encompass land and family justice, "in order to address the concerns of the poor and marginalized, for example women and children."[112]

Most essential for the Ugandan peace process, in 2008, at its third annual forum, JLOS spotlighted transitional justice and brought together a range of state and civil society stakeholders to discuss how the Ugandan government should most effectively implement its obligations under the Juba Accords. Based on the discussions, JLOS decided to establish a Transitional Justice Working Group and defined its vision for transitional justice as entailing restorative and retributive justice, traditional justice mechanisms, criminal jurisdiction for war crimes in Ugandan courts, truth-telling and reconciliation, and complementarity between formal criminal and alternative justice procedures.[113]

In summarizing the main themes of its 2008 forum, the Ugandan government's JLOS used language that resonated with the hybrid vision of transitional justice explored above. First, the "Government expressed commitment to a transitional justice system that incorporates both the restorative and retributive justice that is also sensitive to the rights of women and children, for a lasting peace in Uganda."[114] JLOS also acknowledged "the crucial role of the traditional justice mechanism in an effective transitional justice system as it promotes truth telling, reconciliation and reintegration," while cautioning that "cultural leaders ... together with JLOS ... need to explore how they can make the cultural processes relevant within the current legal framework."[115]

Third, anticipating parliament's passage of the ICC Act (signed into law in 2010), JLOS identified several challenges in the establishment of a successful framework for domestic war crimes prosecutions. In particular, JLOS emphasized the need to carefully define victims "given that some perpetrators are victims themselves;" the importance of imposing "sentencing which should not be merely punitive;" and the unfinished business of reconciling the "express prohibition of the death penalty for war crimes (now included in the ICC Act) with the provision for it in the Constitution of Uganda."[116] Fourth, with regard to truth-telling and reconciliation, JLOS stated plainly that "[t]ruth telling processes will have to include reparations in terms of compensation, restitution and rehabilitation for victims for it to be credible and effective."[117]

Finally, in thinking about how to establish an integrated system of criminal and alternative justice mechanisms, JLOS noted the complexity of trying "to fuse the traditional justice system . . . [with] the formal justice process particularly for those with command responsibility."[118] Applying the notion of complementarity, in the spirit of the Rome Statute, JLOS suggested that traditional mechanisms would be most appropriate for "lesser offenders" or those who "were children or acting under coercion at the time serious crimes were committed."[119]

2. The Complementarity of International and Ugandan Law in Transition

A wide range of Ugandan observers express the view that retributive and restorative justice are not mutually exclusive, and are even compatible: "We can have both in Uganda" is the dominant sentiment.[120] Nevertheless, there are certain unresolved issues with respect to the implementation of transitional justice in Uganda, particularly concerning the need to reconcile the 2010 ICC Act with other laws and policies in force. First, the ICC Act, which empowers the new ICD within the Ugandan High Court to try individuals for war crimes as defined in the Rome Statute, needs to be squared with Uganda's Amnesty Act of 2000, which would block such prosecutions.[121] If the parliament amends the Amnesty Act as proposed by the Ugandan government in 2010, amnesty will be foreclosed for senior LRA leaders, opening the way for domestic prosecutions.[122]

Second, the proposed National Reconciliation Bill is an example of a fruitful collaboration between parliament, various government ministries, and civil society. In fact, one of the primary drafters of the bill was Makerere's Refugee Law Project. Just as the ICC Act needs to be squared with the Amnesty Act, the National Reconciliation Bill would need to be squared with the ICC Act, in terms of parsing out those individuals who would be immune from prosecution, and those who may be criminally prosecuted. One approach is that individuals with significant command responsibility, whether within the LRA or the UPDF, would be barred from reconciliation procedures. Similarly, the government would need to devise a system for certifying that those who go through alternative justice procedures are not subsequently tried in the International Crimes Division. While explicit instances of double jeopardy would clearly be barred, a related issue that has not been resolved is whether evidence produced in traditional justice proceedings for one individual might be used to try another individual in a war crimes proceeding.[123]

Third, both the Government of Uganda and civil society are beginning to confront the challenge of equal justice for government soldiers and members of the LRA. Even before the ICC Act was enacted by parliament in March of 2010, rebels could be charged by the Ugandan Director of Public Prosecutions for weapons-related crimes.[124] For their part, members of the UPDF may be prosecuted by court martial under the Ugandan Anti-Terrorism Act.[125] Nevertheless, the treatment of rebels and nonrebels is not equivalent. In theory, UPDF soldiers must answer for war-related crimes, but their accountability is difficult to evaluate given that court martial proceedings are largely sheltered from public view.[126]

Finally, Ugandan attorneys speak in constructive terms of the connections between international law and Ugandan law. Rather than lamenting the inconsistencies between the two legal systems, or touting the ascendency of Ugandan domestic law, they allude to a rich and dynamic relationship between the two realms. Rachel Odoi-Musoke works with the Ugandan JLOS. She expressed her appreciation for the opportunity to work in a creative environment in which "international legal principles are coming to life."[127]

F. PEACE AS CULTURAL IDENTITY

Alongside a disciplined scholarly analysis of the legal and political aspects of international law and post-conflict reconstruction in Uganda, the question arises whether peace as a way of life has penetrated to the grassroots, into the marrow of Ugandan civil society. Do ordinary Ugandans believe they are emerging from their collective and prolonged experience of suffering, violence, depravation, social dysfunction, and underdevelopment? Have people across Ugandan society become personally vested in the peace process? Are they ready to "swallow much in the name of peace"?[128] Because significant numbers of people, particularly youth, have taken up arms against their government and their neighbors, "conflict resolution" in Uganda will require a gut sense that there is more to be gained from incremental improvements in material conditions of life than there is from ongoing armed struggle.

Certainly the paradigm shift from war to peace requires many elements—confidence in the rule of law, the evolution of viable criminal justice mechanisms, the provision of reparations and social welfare services, the promise of historical reckoning. Criminal justice, social justice, and historical justice are needed in tandem. In addition, an essential and hard-to-capture component of durable peace is the collective acknowledgment of a profound form of battle fatigue. A society choosing post-conflict reconstruction needs to be sick of conflict, traumatized by it, and ready to let go of it.

Signs that peace has been embraced on a psychosocial level, as an essential aspect of individual and cultural identity, are evident to some observers working in northern Uganda. One humanitarian worker described the situation in early 2010: "Peace is there on the ground," she affirmed. "The call for revenge is not there. Human beings have a great capacity for resilience, and at a certain point they want to move on."[129] Hovil and Lomo concur in the perception that northern Ugandans have affirmatively chosen reconciliation over retribution: "[g]iven the extraordinary level of brutality employed by the LRA, and often carried out by children, the capacity of communities to resist taking revenge is remarkable."[130]

The lack of a spirit of revenge in northern Uganda sheds light on the common preference for communal atonement over criminal sanctions as a mechanism for accounting for the wrongs of the past. Reconciliation values the restoration of community relationships over the punishment of offenders. For those northern Ugandans who have decided they "would rather reconcile than revenge,"[131] it would appear that this willingness to forgive is not a blind or unstudied impulse, but a conscious choice.

In addition to its redemptive qualities, reconciliation has a practical, even survival dimension.[132] Amnesty for perpetrators of war atrocities helps end the violence in the short term, as increasing numbers of rebels lay down their arms.[133] But reconciliation also has a vital role to play in the longer term, as offenders accept responsibility for their wrongful acts and reenter their communities with new commitments to contribute to their well-being. Nevertheless, it is the truth-telling aspect of amnesty and atonement programs in northern Uganda that constitutes the weakest link in the transitional justice chain, particularly with regard to the government's role in the conflict.[134] For reconciliation to contribute to durable peace in Uganda, the truth leg of the criminal-social-historical justice stool must be strengthened, such that "the process of truth telling and public admittance of guilt ... [is] interwoven unequivocally in the process"[135] of transitional justice.

The idea that a civil war is likely to run out of gas when ordinary combatants become tired of the conflict makes sense on an intuitive level. Violence will continue, the logic goes, unless those most engaged in the conflict are convinced that they have more to gain from laying down their arms than by continuing to participate in armed struggle.[136] But while battle fatigue on the part of combatants is essential to conflict resolution, noncombatants must also experience their own war weariness, in order to convince the government and the insurgency alike to stop pursuing politics by military means. This latter element may be more difficult to realize in a large country where the armed conflict has been concentrated in one region of the country, as is true of Uganda, where the war was largely confined to the northern region. One reason that the Ugandan civil war may have lasted for over 22 years, some observers say, is that residents of Central Uganda, Kampala in particular, were able to get on with their lives in practical terms, at times even envisioning northern Uganda as something akin to a separate country.[137] For durable peace to become ingrained in Uganda, civil society, as a whole, must demand it.

Whether Uganda as a country and as a society has irrevocably shifted from civil war to post-conflict reconstruction is for Ugandans to decide and to ensure. The signs point to such a transformation occurring. The LRA is largely neutralized in northern Uganda, although still committing atrocities in the DRC, the CAR, and the Sudan. Displaced persons in northern Uganda are returning to their homes, and displaced persons camps are being dismantled. The Ugandan parliament has passed a War Crimes Act implementing the Rome Statute, and permitting domestic war crimes prosecutions of state and nonstate actors to proceed alongside the ICC's case against senior LRA commanders.

Most important, civil society is actively shaping the course of transitional justice in Uganda. There are calls for a National Reconciliation Commission with truth-telling as well as restorative functions. Individuals and organizations are also participating in and helping to strengthen grassroots atonement, cleansing and community welcoming programs, including *mato oput*, designed to reintegrate offenders into their communities. Finally, Ugandans are calling for reparations, and demanding enhanced expenditures to improve health care, education, public safety, sanitation, and agricultural development programs throughout the country.

Post-conflict reconstruction and transitional justice are beginning to thrive in Uganda, fueled by a growing perception that the war's direct and indirect costs are simply impossible for the country as a whole to sustain. Proponents of criminal, social, and historical justice in Uganda continue to work toward a shared understanding that prosecutions, restorative justice, and truth-telling about the war are interdependent, and vital to the health and revitalization of their society as a whole.

NOTES

1. The title of this chapter is inspired by the Beyond Juba Project (BJP), a civil society organization based at the Makerere University School of Law in Kampala, Uganda. BJP seeks to further sustainable peace through research about and constructive engagement in the transitional justice process in Uganda.
2. From SONG OF LAWINO and SONG OF OCOL, by Okot p'Bitek, combined school edition, with an introduction by G.A. Heron (East African Publishing House, Nairobi, Kenya, 1972) at 48. *Song of Lawino*, written in Acholi and translated into English by the author, was first published in 1966. Ugandan Okot p'Bitek (1931–1982) pioneered the East African Song School of poetry. His signature "comic singing" voice was characteristically expressed through ironic, empathic, and dramatic monologues, as in "Song of Lawino," the lament of an Acholi married woman, and "Song of Ocol," her husband's response, first

published in 1970. *See generally* SAMUEL OLUOCH IMBO, TRADITIONS AS PHILOSOPHY: OKOT P'BITEK'S LEGACY FOR AFRICAN PHILOSOPHY (Lanham Rownan & Littlefield, 2002).

3. Uganda's population is close to 32 million, and its territory is around 240,000 square kilometers, roughly equivalent to that of the United Kingdom (UK). Comparatively speaking, Uganda has around 2 percent of the land mass of the United States, with 10 percent of its population. *See* CIA Factbook, Uganda (under "Geography"), *available at* https://www.cia.gov/library/publications/the-world-factbook/geos/ug.html.

Uganda has a republican form of government, with a unicameral legislature and an executive branch led by the popularly elected president. The president appoints the cabinet from among the national legislators. Roughly two-thirds of the members of parliament are popularly elected. The other members are nominated by "legally established special interest groups" and then elected by electoral colleges. *Id.* (under "Government"). Uganda's current constitution was adopted on October 8, 1995. Amendments enacted in 2005 abolished presidential terms limits and legalized a multiparty system. *Id.* (under "Government" and "Constitution").

As of February 2011, the Ugandan parliament had 374 members, of whom 237 were popularly elected. The remaining 137 seats were filled by representatives nominated by special interest groups comprising the women's caucus (112), the armed forces (10), disabled persons (5), youth (5), and labor (5). *See* Uganda Parliament Report of Last Elections, compiled by the Inter-Parliamentary Union, *available at* http://www.ipu.org/parline/reports/2329_E.htm.

4. Agreement on Cessation of Hostilities between the Government of the Republic of Uganda and the Lord's Resistance Army/Movement, Juba, Sudan, Aug. 26, 2006 (also known as "Juba Agenda Item #1"). The full text is *available at* http://www.beyondjuba.org/peace_agreements/Agreement_on_Cessation_Of_hostilities.pdf.

5. RICHARD DOWDEN, AFRICA: ALTERED STATES, ORDINARY MIRACLES (Public Affairs/Perseus Books Group, 2009) at 40. The Baganda (or Ganda) people make up nearly 17 percent of Uganda's current population. *See* CIA Factbook, Uganda (under "People"), available at https://www.cia.gov/library/publications/the-world-factbook/geos/ug.html.

6. *Id.* at 41.

7. *Id.* at 41.

8. *Id.* at 42.

9. Initial analysis of the Amin coup credited the British with working behind the scenes, given their assumed antipathy to Obote's socialist policies. Nevertheless, the British supported socialist President Julius Nyerere in neighboring Tanzania, and Dowden believes that the better view is that Israel was behind the coup that brought Amin to power in Uganda. *Id.* at 42. Uganda's support for southern Sudanese separatist movements, first the Anya–Nya in the 1960s, and later John Garang's Sudanese People's Liberation Front in subsequent decades, may also be traced to an Israeli source. Israel helped arm the Anya-Nya, partly to punish the Sudan for its Arab nationalist stance in the 1967 war. "Uganda, Sudan's southern neighbor, was the conduit, and Idi Amin was the agent . . ., act[ing] as Israel's arms supplier to the Anya Nya." *Id.*

10. *Id.* at 39.

11. *Id.*

12. The psychosocial development of Idi Amin has been explored and re-imagined in numerous historical and literary works, including Giles Foden's fictional *Last King of Scotland* (Knopf, 1998), adapted into a film of the same name. Journalist Dowden spotlights the young rugby star Idi Amin being treated to beers by British members of the Kampala Rugby Club in preindependence Uganda. The club members passed the bottles to Amin

through the clubhouse fence, because Africans were not allowed at the bar. *See* DOWDEN, *op. cit.*, at 39. As Dowden puts it, "[n]o-one seemed to ask what that might do to a man psychologically." *Id.*

13. *Id.* at 46, 42. Despite Obote's acceptance of Israeli assistance, he was generally a champion of pan-Arab nationalism, and supported the Sudanese government in Khartoum. *Id.*
14. *Id.* at 44.
15. *Id.* at 45.
16. *Id.* at 46.
17. The most conservative estimate of extrajudicial killings in Uganda during the Amin years is 100,000, according to international relations scholar Richard H. Ullman. Ullman, *Human Rights and Economic Power: The United States Versus Idi Amin*, 56 FOREIGN AFFAIRS 529, 529 (April 1978).
18. "Uganda: Flight of the Asians," *Time*, September 11, 1972, *available at* http://www.time.com/time/magazine/article/0,9171,906327-1,00.html.
19. Julian Marshall, *Milton Obote: The first leader of an independent Uganda, he imposed virtual one-man rule, but was twice overthrown* [obituary], THE GUARDIAN, Wednesday, October 12, 2005, *available at* http://www.guardian.co.uk/news/2005/oct/12/guardianobituaries.hearafrica05.
20. Between the extrajudicial killings of civilians and the deaths related to Uganda's Bush War against the rebels of Museveni's National Resistance Army, one-hundred thousand Ugandans are believed to have lost their lives during the Obote II period. According to the Ugandan administration of Yoweri Museveni, another 500,000 Ugandans died in the context of the forced relocation policy of the Obote government during the guerrilla war. *See* CIA, *The World Factbook*, Uganda, available at https://www.cia.gov/library/publications/the-world-factbook/geos/ug.html (last updated April 22, 2010); *see also* Marshall, *op. cit.*
21. *See generally*, Dirk Beke, *Legislation and Decentralization in Uganda: From Resistance Councils to Elected Local Councils with Guaranteed Representation*, in FOBLETS, MARIE CLAIRE AND TRUTZ, VON TROTHA, EDS., HEALING THE WOUNDS: ESSAYS IN THE RECONSTRUCTION OF SOCIETIES AFTER WAR (Hart Publishing, Portland, Oregon, 2004), pp. 145–167.
22. *Id.*
23. As recorded by Hovil and Lomo of Makerere University's Refugee Law Project (RLP), "22 known groups have taken up arms to fight the government since President Museveni's National Resistance Movement (NRM) came into power in 1986." Lucy Hovil and Zachary Lomo, "Whose Justice? Perceptions of Uganda's Amnesty Act 2000: The Potential for Conflict Resolution and Long-term Reconciliation," Refugee Law Project Working Paper No. 15 (February 2005) at 6 and note 11, *available at* http://www.refugeelawproject.org. The LRA is but the "most notorious . . ." *Id.* at 6. This chapter focuses on the civil war between the UPDF and the LRA. Nevertheless, it bears mentioning that Western Uganda and West Nile are two other regions that have dealt with insurgencies in the post-1986 period. Two prominent rebel groups outside of northern Uganda, both of which have been largely demobilized as of 2010, are the Allied Democratic Forces, based in Western Uganda, and the West Nile Bank Front, active in West Nile. *Id.* at 6, note 11 and at 8. Also importantly, the 2000 Ugandan Amnesty Act has applied to all rebel groups, and significant numbers of ADF and WNBF combatants have reported for amnesty under its terms. *Id.*
24. Patrick Hoenig, *Peace and Justice in Northern Uganda*, 14 E. AFRICAN J. PEACE & HUM. RTS. 333, 334 (2008).
25. *Id.* Some in-depth investigations by journalists in northern Uganda indicate that civilian deaths caused by forced displacement by the Ugandan armed forces outstrip the

number of civilians killed by the LRA. *See,* Amy Ross and Chandra Lekha Siram, "Catch-22 in Uganda: the LRA, the ICC and the Peace Process" (JURIST Legal News & Research, University of Pittsburgh School of Law, July 17, 2006). [Ross *et al,* also cited in Chapter 4.]

26. Patricia Atim, "The Legal Regime Governing Sexual and Gender-Based Violence: A Case Study of Pajule Internally Displaced People's Camp, Uganda," 15 E. AFRICAN J. PEACE & HUM. RTS. 186, 188 (2009).

27. *See* Amnesty Act, 2000 ch. 294 (2000) (Uganda), available at www.ulii.org/ug/legis/consol_act/aa2000294120/.

 Observers of northern Uganda stress that the primary impetus behind the Ugandan Amnesty Act 2000 was from civil society, and not the LRA. "The initiative for creating an amnesty came from within this [northern Ugandan] region, spearheaded by the religious and cultural leaders, and was a clear rejection of a failed military approach to ending the war. The fact that the Amnesty Law was in keeping with wishes of the victims of conflict, rather than by perpetrators trying to negotiate their own safety, is a crucial aspect of the Amnesty." *See* Hovil and Lomo, *op. cit.* at 6.

28. The Rome Statute is discussed extensively in Chapter 4, Section D.

29. Minorities at Risk Project, "Assessment for Acholi in Uganda," Dec. 31, 2006, *available at* http://www.cidcm.umd.edu/mar/assessment.asp?groupId=50001. Minorities at Risk, founded in 1986 by Ted Robert Guir, has been based since 1988 at the University of Maryland's Center for International Development and Conflict Management.

30. Hovil and Lomo, *op. cit.* at 9 ("the majority of LRA fighters are abducted children").

31. Hoenig, *op. cit.; see also, generally,* Peter W. Singer, *Children at War* (Pantheon, 2005).

32. Agreement on Cessation of Hostilities between the Government of the Republic of Uganda and the Lord's Resistance Army/Movement, Juba, Sudan, Aug. 26, 2006 (also known as "Juba Agenda Item #1"). The full text is *available at* http://www.beyondjuba.org/peace_agreements/Agreement_on_Cessation_Of_hostilities.pdf.

33. Agreement on Accountability and Reconciliation between the Government of the Republic of Uganda and the Lord's Resistance Army/Movement, Juba, Sudan, June 29, 2007 (also known as "Juba Agenda Item #3"). The full text is *available at* http://www.beyondjuba.org/peace_agreements/Agreement_on_Accountability_And_Reconcilition.pdf, a website maintained by the Beyond Juba Project, a non-governmental organization (NGO) dedicated to building sustainable peace in Uganda. *See also* Stephen Tumwesigye, *The Annexure to the Juba Peace Agreement on Accountability and Reconciliation: Unanswered Legal and Enforcement Questions,* 15 E. AFRICAN. J. PEACE & HUM. RTS. 476 at note 1 (2009), citing the June 2007 Juba Agreement.

34. Agreement on Comprehensive Solutions between the Government of the Republic of Uganda and the Lord's Resistance Army/Movement, Juba, Sudan, May 2, 2007 (also known as "Juba Agenda Item #2"). The full text is *available at* http://www.beyondjuba.org/peace_agreements/Agreement_on_comprehensive_solutions.pdf.

35. Agreement on a Permanent Ceasefire between the Government of the Republic of Uganda and the Lord's Resistance Army/Movement, Juba, Sudan, Feb. 23, 2008 (also known as "Juba Agenda Item #4"). The full text is *available at* http://www.beyondjuba.org/peace_agreements/Agreement%20_on_a_Permanent_ceasefire_Btween_The_GOU_and_LRA.pdf.

36. Agreement on Disarmament, Demobilisation and Reintegration between the Government of the Republic of Uganda and the Lord's Resistance Army/Movement, Juba, Sudan, Feb. 29, 2008 (also known as "Juba Agenda Item #5"). The full text is *available at* http://www.beyondjuba.org/peace_agreements/Agreement_on_Disarmament_Demobilisation_and_Reintergration_btn_The_GOU_and_LRA.pdf.

37. Implementation Protocol to the Agreement on Comprehensive Solutions, Government of the Republic of Uganda and the Lord's Resistance Army/Movement, Juba, Sudan, Feb. 29, 2008 (also known as "Juba Agenda Item #6"). The full text is *available at* http://www.beyondjuba.org/peace_agreements/Implementation_and_monitoring_mechanisms.pdf.
38. Norwegian Refugee Council, "Uganda: Difficulties continue for returnees and remaining IDPs as development phase begins," a Profile of the Internal Displacement Situation at 7 (Internal Displacement Monitoring Center, Dec. 28, 2010), *available at* http://www.internal-displacement.org/8025708F004BE3B1/(httpInfoFiles)/AA7A8CB8B06E752DC12578070057B4C6/$file/Uganda+-+December+2010.pdf.
39. Professor Patrick Hoenig has researched various actual and potential alliances of convenience between the LRA and a range of state-sponsored and insurgent groups in the DRC, the Sudan and the Central African Republic. He cites recent "[m]edia reports [in 2008] . . . that LRA cadres have also been moving into the Central African Republic (CAR) . . ., allegedly exploring the possibility of linking up with rebels fighting the government of CAR under President Francois Bozize." He cautions that "it does not take much imagination to see the whole Great Lakes region tumbling back into war, potentially locking Uganda, DRC, CAR and Sudan in escalating clashes with shifting alliances." Patrick Hoenig, *Peace and Justice in Northern Uganda*, 14 E. AFRICAN J. PEACE & HUM. RTS. 333, 337 (2008).
40. Milton Olupot, "Uganda: I'm Ready to Face Trial–Museveni," *The New Vision* (Kampala, Uganda), Mar. 13, 2010, *available at* http://allafrica.com/stories/201003150369.html.
41. "LRA rebels kill 19 in DR Congo attacks," AFP, *The New Vision* (Kampala, Uganda), Mar. 18, 2010, *available at* http://www.newvision.co.ug/D/1/10/713330.
Over the ten-month period from September 2008 to June 2009, the LRA was on the offensive in the DRC, killing 1,300 people, abducting 1,400, and displacing 230,000 more. *See* UN News Centre, "Ugandan rebels murder, rape, mutilate, displace thousands in DR Congo, Sudan," Dec. 21, 2009, *available at* http://www0.un.org/apps/news/story.asp?NewsID=33310. The LRA reportedly carried out ten raids in the Central African Republic within a six-week period in 2010. *See* Lisa Schlein, "Alarming Increase in LRA Attacks Against Civilians," VOA News, May 14, 2010, *available at* http://www.publicinternationallaw.org/warcrimeswatch/archives/wcpw_vol05issue4.html#car1.
42. "If we have our own country, the government will be able to defend us [from the LRA]," said Yunis Egbaguru, a resident of Southern Sudan who fled an LRA attack on her village in December of 2010. *See* Jason Benham, "South Sudanese see new state as buffer to LRA," Reuters Africa (online news agency), January 11, 2011, *available at* http://af.reuters.com/article/topNews/idAFJOE70A04V20110111?pageNumber=2&virtualBrandChannel=0&sp=true.
43. In June 2010, ICC Chief Prosecutor Luis Moreno-Ocampo announced that the ICC was considering allegations of war crimes by the Ugandan military. Though open to bringing indictments against members of the Ugandan People's Defense Forces (UPDF) in the face of compelling evidence, Moreno-Ocampo maintains that the most serious civil war offenses were committed by the LRA, and not the UPDF. Olara Otunnu, the leader of the opposition Ugandan People's Congress, has called for an ICC investigation of President Museveni, in addition to members of the UPDF. *See* "UGANDA: ICC to investigate allegations of Army atrocities" (United Nations Office for the Coordination of Humanitarian Affairs, Integrated Regional Information Networks, June 3, 2010), *available at* http://www.reliefweb.int/rw/rwb.nsf/db900SID/VVOS-863L85?OpenDocument.
44. *See* notes from roundtable discussion at the Centre for Human Rights and Peace, Makerere University, March 22, 2010, from p. 3(b) of author's field notebook.

45. Jeffrey Gettleman, *Ugandan Enlists Former Rebels to End a War*, NY TIMES, Apr. 10, 2010, http://www.nytimes.com/2010/04/11/world/africa/11lra.html.
46. "Uganda claims capture of LRA peace interpreter, 4 others," *Afrique en ligne*, Kampala–Pana, 07/04/2010, http://www.afriquejet.com/news/africa-news/uganda-claims-capture-of-lra-peace-interpreter,-4-others-2010040747238.html.
47. *See* Hovil and Lomo, *op. cit.* ("[i]t is also a war that is being fought predominantly by abducted children from the side of the LRA") at 9.
48. The London-based NGO Redress, found "thousands of victims of UPDF torture over the past decade," citing Redress, *Torture in Uganda: A Baseline Study on the Situation of Torture Survivors in Uganda* (2007), at 37 & 44. Patrick HOENIG, *op. cit.* at 341.
    In June 2010, United Nations High Commissioner for Human Rights Navi Pillay visited Uganda to investigate reports of three recent attacks by the UPDF on northern Uganda villages in which civilians were killed, two in January and one in April. *See* Robert Evans, "UN rights chief urges inquiry on Uganda army acts," Reuters, June 7, 2010, *available at* http://www.alertnet.org/thenews/newsdesk/LDE6561LU.htm.
49. *See,* Amy Ross and Chandra Lekha Siram, *op. cit.*, at para. 10 (citing a "recent UN report not[ing] that more than 90% of the fatalities in Northern Uganda are the result of the policy of forced displacement [by the Ugandan military] with 9% attributed to attacks by the LRA").
50. The Gulu Support Children's Organization (GUSCO) based in Gulu, northern Uganda, had by 2007 "already documented sixty cases of this new phenomenon of 'double-bondage' which . . . [the director of GUSCO] said, was collectively ignored by the Ugandan government, the diplomatic community, UN agencies and the OTP [the Office of the Prosecutor of the International Criminal Court], presumably for lack of desire to inconvenience the South Sudanese brokers of the Juba talks." HOENIG, *op. cit.* at 336.
51. *See* William Schabas, *Prosecutorial Discretion v. Judicial Activism at the International Criminal Court*, 6 J. INT'L. CRIM. JUST. 731, 747–48 (Sept. 2008) (even a lesser number of direct civilian deaths at the hands of the Ugandan People's Defense Forces, as compared to the LRA, arguably represents a "classic impunity paradigm," given that the killers were "acting on behalf of a state that shelters them from its own courts.") [Schabas also cited in Chapter 4.]
52. *See* International Criminal Court Act No. 11 of 2010, *The Uganda Gazette*, No. 39, Volume CIII, dated June 25, 2010, *assented* May 25, 2010. *See also,* Bill Oketch, "Uganda Set for First War Crimes Trial," Institute for War and Peace Recruiting, July 14, 2010, *available at* http://iwpr.net/report-news/uganda-set-first-war-crimes-trial; *see also* "MPs Pass ICC Bill," *The New Vision*, March 10, 2010, *available at* http://www.newvision.co.ug/D/8/13/712528?highlight&q=ICC%20BILL.
53. *See* [2007] Peace Agreement on Accountability and Reconciliation (also known as "Juba Agenda Item #3"), *supra* note 33.
54. *See* Luke Moffett, "The Ugandan International Criminal Court Act: What does it mean for victims?" Victims' Rights Working Group, Oct. 20, 2010, *available at* http://www.vrwg.org/smartweb/home/home/post/21-the-ugandan-international-criminal-court-act-2010-what-does-it-mean-for-victims/.
55. The term of the Amnesty Act has been extended several times since its passage in 2000. In December 2010, the Government of Uganda announced its intention to amend the Act prior to its extension in 2011. Under the government's proposal, the act will henceforth exclude members of the senior LRA leadership from eligibility for amnesty. *See* "Uganda: New amnesty to exclude top LRA leaders," IRIN Humanitarian News and Analysis (a service of the UN Office for the Coordination of Humanitarian Affairs), December 2, 2010, *available at* http://www.irinnews.org/report.aspx?reportid=47689.

56. Barney Afako, "Reconciliation and Justice: 'Mato oput' and the Amnesty Act," *conciliation resources* (2002), *available at* http://www.c-r.org/our-work/accord/northern-uganda/reconcilation-justice.php.
57. *Id.* It is important to recognize that *mato oput* is only one of several traditional dispute resolution practices that are utilized in northern Uganda. Also referenced in the 2007 Juba Agreement are *culo kwor, kayo cuk, alluc,* and *tona cikoka*. Though *mato oput* is traditionally an Acholi ceremony, practices such as *culo kwor* are associated with other tribes, including the Iteso, Mati, and Langi peoples, who have also been affected by the civil war in northern Uganda. *See* Tumwesigye, *op. cit.*, at 483–84. In note 34 on p. 483, Mr. Tumwesigye cites both Sveker Finnstrom [*Living with Bad Surroundings: War and Existential Uncertainty in Acholi Land in Northern Uganda* (2003)] and "Ritual Abuse: Problems with Traditional Justice in Northern Uganda," [in *Courting Conflict, Justice, Peace and the ICC in Africa* (N. Waddell & P. Clarke eds., 2008) at 47–53].
58. This description of *mato oput* comes from Sultan Kasimu Opio, a survivor of the war in northern Uganda, whose uncle was killed, and whose sister was abducted and raped by LRA soldiers. As Opio explains, "[b]oth parties present a sheep and the blood from these animals is mixed with the top most 'oput' tree leaves and brewed." *See* Leiuh Asuman Wakida and Priscilla Nadunga, *TRC Rather Than ICC for Uganda*, Radio Netherlands Worldwide, Dec. 15, 2010, WAR CRIMES PROSECUTION WATCH (Vol. 5, Issue 19, Dec. 20, 2010), *available at* http://www.publicinternationallaw.org/warcrimeswatch/archives/wcpw_vol05issue19.html#car3.
59. *Id.*
60. Thomas Kwoyelo was originally arrested in 2009, prior to the creation of the International Crimes Division of the Ugandan High Court. *See* Bill Oketch, "Test Case for Ugandan Justice–Kampala puts Former LRA Commander on Trial" (IWPR), Wednesday, July 29, 2009, *available at* http://www.friendsforpeaceinafrica.org/analysis-op-ed/48-analysis/410-test-case-for-ugandan-justice-kampala-puts-former-lra-commander-on-trial-iwpr.html.

When Kwoyelo was indicted by the Ugandan Director of Public Prosecutions in 2008, he was not charged with war crimes. Instead, he was charged with twelve counts of kidnapping with intent to murder, for the disappearance of villagers from Attiak and Pabo, subcounties located in Amuru and Gulu Districts, Uganda. *Id.* Although the Ugandan government received some criticism from civil society quarters for the lack of war crimes counts against Kwoyelo, in fact, as a matter of Ugandan law, until the ICC Act was adopted in 2010, there were no domestic legal mechanisms for war crimes prosecutions in Uganda. *See* Moffett, *op. cit.* Kwoyelo, 37 year of age at the time of his arrest in 2009, had been abducted by the LRA at the age of 15. *See* Oketch, *op. cit.*

Once the Ugandan International Crimes Division was created, Kwoyelo's case was transferred to the ICD, and his trial commenced on July 11, 2011. Human Rights Watch, "Uganda: Update on the Trial of Thomas Kwoyelo, Former LRA Combatant," July 12, 2011, *available at* http://allafrica.com/stories/201107121476.html.
61. *See* notes from roundtable discussion at the Centre for Human Rights and Peace, Makerere University, Mar. 22, 2010, from p. 4(b) of author's field notebook.
62. *See* 2009 National Reconciliation Bill, 2009, *available at* http://www.iccnow.org/documents/TRC_Bill_for_Uganda_2009.pdf. *See also* "Statement on the National Reconciliation Bill of 2009," Uganda Victims Foundation, Nov. 4, 2009, *available at* http://www.coalitionfortheicc.org/documents/UVF_Position_Paper_National_Reconciliation_Bill_of_2009.pdf.
63. *See* Stephen Oola, "The Coalition for Reconciliation in Uganda: Important Lessons for Proactive Civil Society Engagement in Catalysing Transitional Justice Discourse," at 6–7

(August 2010), *available at* http://www.transitionaljustice.org.za/docs/2010workshop/4_Oola.pdf. The author presented this paper at the African Transitional Justice Research Network Workshop on "Advocating Justice: Civil Society and Transitional Justice in Africa," convened Aug. 30–31, 2010 in Johannesburg, South Africa. Oola previously served as staff attorney with the Beyond Juba Project of the Refugee Law Project at Makerere University School of Law.

64. *See* Uganda Victims Foundation, *op. cit.*
This aspect of the mission of the prospective Ugandan National Reconciliation Commission is of great interest to Dr. J. Oloka-Onyango, the Director of the Human Rights and Peace Centre, housed within the School of Law of Makerere University in Kampala. Dr. Oloka-Onyango emphasizes the importance of truth-telling, in addition to reparations and other essential components of restorative justice, as discussed below, in Section D. 4 and footnote 107 of this chapter.

65. *See* Wakida and Nadunga, "TRC Rather Than ICC for Uganda," *op. cit.*
66. *Id.*
67. *Id.*
68. *See* Hovil and Lomo, *op. cit.* at 18. Northern Ugandans and observers of northern Uganda alike use the term *torture* descriptively to describe the reality of war for civilians. For example, a man from Arua interviewed by Makerere's RLP, in referring to the standard economic reintegration "package" provided to LRA soldiers taking advantage of the 2000 Ugandan Amnesty Act, voiced the opinion that civilians should also be compensated for war injuries, stating matter-of-factly that "[t]hose who were tortured should get the package." *Id.* In a similar vein, Chris Dolan, Director of the RRP, refers to the situation in northern Uganda as a shared experience of "Social Torture." Chris Dolan, *Understanding War and its Continuation: The Case of Northern Uganda* (2005) (PhD thesis published by University of London, and owned by the British Library, OCLC: 500315235) at 29–30.
69. *See* Hovil and Lomo, *op. cit.* at 22.
70. *Id.* at 5.
71. *Id.* at 9 and note 28, citing interview with elderly man, community member, Kitgum town, Nov. 20, 2004.
72. *See id.* at 6 (referring to the controversial nature of the blanket amnesty provisions of Uganda's 2000 Amnesty Act).
73. The "initiative of creating an amnesty [was] spearheaded by the religious and cultural leaders." *See* Hovil and Lomo, *op. cit.* at 6. "Many informants referred to the fact that they had been 'doing' amnesty before it had become law, as it was a culturally recognized approach to carrying out justice within the specific context." *Id.* 10.
74. *Id.* at 10 and note 34, citing interview with ex-combatant, Gulu town, Nov. 9, 2004.
James Jacob Okabo, the radio broadcaster of "Dwong Pako," passed away in 2010. At his funeral service in November, Former Vice President Dr. Wandera Kazibwe credited Okabo with contributing to bringing peace to northern Uganda, by inspiring many child abductees to return home. *See* Bill Oketch and Patrick Okino, "Gov[ernmen]t to Support Ex-LRA Abductees," *The New Vision* ["Uganda's Leading Website"], Nov. 7, 2010, *available at* http://allafrica.com/stories/201011070103.html.
75. *See* Hovil and Lomo, *op. cit.* at 12 and note 44 ("[a]t home we have no problems with people, but at school other students finger point at us and give us nicknames like calling you with a rebel commander's name.").
76. *Id.*
77. *Id.* at 14 and note 54 (interview with male elder, Mpondwe town, Nov. 12, 2004).
78. Joy Okech, "Women bear the brunt of LRA insurgents," NewsfromAFRICA, July 2004, *available at* http://www.newsfromafrica.org/newsfromafrica/articles/art_6080.html.
79. Hovil and Lomo at 14 and note 56 (interview in Kasese district, Nov. 11, 2004).

80. *Id.* at 15 and note 66 (interview with female community member, Kiguzu village, Kasese district, Nov. 10, 2004). Hovil and Lomo point out in their study that "[w]omen in particular, appear to carry a stigma and are often referred to as 'Kony's wives.'" *Id.* at 12.
81. In a study of gender-related human rights abuses in Pajule IDP camp in northern Uganda, domestic violence was defined as "any acts of assault or battery against a domestic partner that may cause physical injury or harm to the victim." Patricia Atim, *The Legal Regime Governing Sexual and Gender-Based Violence: A Case Study of Pajule Internally Displaced Peoples' Camp, Uganda*, 15 E. AFRICAN J. PEACE & HUM. RTS. 186, 203 (No. 1, 2009).
82. Atim, *op. cit.*, at 205 and note 51, citing Patrick Sooma, *Despair and Disdain: A Tale of Sexual Abuse Against Internally Displaced Women in Northern Uganda*, in 12 E. AFRICAN J. PEACE & HUMAN RTS. 91, 103 (2006).
83. "Wife inheritance refers to a situation where a woman is forced to marry her deceased husband's brother or his cousin." Atim, *op. cit.*, at 206.
84. *Id.* at 208 and note 62 ("[w]hen I asked him how he could do such a thing yet he knows that the food was meant for feeding the family, he started fighting and beating me up, he chased me from his home and is now liv[ing] with another woman . . . " [from interview with a 30-year woman]).
85. *Id.* at 208.
86. *Id.*
87. *Id.* at 209. Elsewhere in her text, author Patricia Atim references numerous international treaties and declarations, also discussed in Chapter 3 of this book, including the Universal Declaration of Human Rights, the International Covenant on Civil and Political Rights, the African Charter on Human and Peoples' Rights, and the Convention on the Elimination of all Forms of Discrimination against Women. *Id.* at 195–97.
88. *Id.* at 11 and note 37 ("[g]iven that the majority of those living in Gulu, Kitgum and Pader have been forced to leave their homes and are now living in the most appalling conditions, serious questions have to be raised as to the implications of relocating reporters [i.e., those who 'report' or apply for amnesty] into this environment").
89. *Id.* at 14 and note 59 (Nov. 12, 2004 interview).
90. *See* Richard Kavuma, "How can we empower women in Uganda's rural communities?" Katinechronicles Blog, posted May 5, 2010, available at http://www.guardian.co.uk/katine/katine-chronicles-blog/2010/may/05/women-rights-uganda. Katine is a village, categorized as a subcounty, in northern Uganda.
91. Professor Patrick Hoenig has suggested a principled basis for an ICC withdrawal from the case against the LRA, on the grounds that continued prosecution of the LRA is deemed no longer to be "in the interests of justice." Patrick Hoenig, *Peace and Justice in Northern Uganda*, 14 E. AFRICAN J. PEACE & HUM. RTS. 333, 349 (2008), citing Article 53(2) of the ICC Statute. Hoenig concludes that "withdrawal of the ICC from the situation in northern Uganda will save it from further damaging its reputation and allow for fresh debates to unfold on the meaning of justice for people bereft of peace." *Id.*
92. *See* Amy Ross and Chandra Lekha Siram, "Catch-22 in Uganda: the LRA, the ICC and the Peace Process" (JURIST Legal News & Research, University of Pittsburgh School of Law, July 17, 2006), para. 10 (citing a "recent UN report not[ing] that more than 90% of the fatalities in northern Uganda are the result of the policy of forced displacement [by the Ugandan military] with 9% attributed to attacks by the LRA").

See also William Schabas, *Prosecutorial Discretion v. Judicial Activism at the International Criminal Court*, 6 J. INT'L. CRIM. JUST. 731, 747–48 (Sept. 2008) (even a lesser number of direct civilian deaths at the hands of the Ugandan People's Defense Forces, as compared to the LRA, arguably represents a "classic impunity paradigm," given that the killers were "acting on behalf of a state that shelters them from its own courts.")

93. A potential increase in criminal accountability for wartime offenses in Uganda is suggested by the 2010 indictment of Thomas Kwoyelo, a senior LRA commander by the Ugandan Director of Public Prosecutions, even before the enactment of the War Crimes Act by the Ugandan Parliament. Kwoyelo was captured by Ugandan troops in the Democratic Republic of the Congo in March 2009, and arraigned in a regional court in Gulu in August 2009 on twelve counts of kidnapping with intent to murder. *See* Bill Oketch, "Test Case for Ugandan Justice–Kampala Puts Former LRA Commander on Trial—but Not for War Crimes," Institute for War & Peace Reporting (London) *available at* http://allafrica.com/stories/200907290919.html.

94. In fact, Ugandan scholars such as Dr. J. Oloka-Onyango stress that historically the judiciary in Uganda has proved unable "to act as a bastion against executive excess." He exposes an "undercurrent of autocratic behavior" by the executive branch of government, which, in his view, continues to burden the principle of judicial independence in Uganda. J. Oloka-Onyango, *Criminal Justice, the Courts and Human Rights in Contemporary Uganda: A Perspective Analysis,* 1 MAKERERE LAW J. 5, 53 (No. 1, 2006).

95. In fact, some Ugandans credit the ICC with bringing Kony to the bargaining table ("had the ICC not stepped in . . . [and given Kony] pressure to dialogue . . ., it would have been difficult to get here.") *See* notes from roundtable discussion at the Centre for Human Rights and Peace, Makerere University, Mar. 22, 2010, from p. 4(b) of author's field notebook.

96. The Beyond Juba Project is a joint endeavor of the School of Law, the Human Rights & Peace Centre, and the RLP, all within Makerere University.

97. *See* Dolan, "Whatever happened to comprehensive justice?" (Beyond Justice Project, School of Law, Makerere University, June 2007), paras. 2 and 7, *available at* http://www.refugeelawproject.org/press_releases/WhateverHappenedtoTrueJustice.pdf (also cited in Chapters 4 and 6).

98. *See* notes from roundtable discussion at the Centre for Human Rights and Peace, Makerere University, Mar. 22, 2010, from p. 4(b) of author's field notebook.

99. *Mato oput* is described in footnote 59 and related text of this chapter, and referenced in Chapter 4, Section E.

100. A 2005 study by Makerere's RLP casts further light on traditional Acholi views toward physical punishments, including the death penalty, and indicates that there is an important measure of accountability in the Acholi preference for restorative justice practices. As one cultural leader explained, "the Acholi do not have corporal punishment. We believe that a wrongdoer will not be punished by death because he will not realise the effect. We want him to be alive to see—let him feel the shame." Hovil and Lomo, *op. cit.* at 27.

101. Rome Statute of the International Criminal Court, UN Doc. A/CONF/183/9, *entered into force* July 1, 2002, art. 77 (applicable penalties), *available at* http://untreaty.un.org/cod/icc/statute/romefra.htm.

102. *See* Bill Oketch, "Uganda: First War Crimes Trial," Institute for War & Peace Reporting, July 21, 2010, *available at* http://www.africafiles.org/article.asp?ID=24061.

103. *See* notes from roundtable discussion at the Centre for Human Rights and Peace, Makerere University, Mar. 22, 2010, from p. 3(b) of author's field notebook.

104. *See id.*

105. *See* notes from interview with Ms. Zahara Nampewo, Makerere University Human Rights and Peace Centre, Kampala, Uganda, Mar. 22, 2010, from p. 4(b) of author's field notebook. Ms. Nampewo is a Lecturer in the School of Law of Makerere University.

106. HOENIG, *op. cit.* at 349.

107. *See* notes from interview with Dr. J. Oloka-Onyango, Director of the Makerere University Human Rights and Peace Centre (HURIPEC), Kampala, Uganda, Mar. 22, 2010,

from p. 5(a) of author's field notebook. HURIPEC is a project of the Makerere University School of Law.

108. Other scholars, including Dr. Patrick Hoenig, have also called for a forward-looking approach. Hoenig cautions that focusing "on criminal justice and the headhunt for Kony and his close associates has begun to divert attention from identifying the root causes of the conflict and ways of preventing further abuse." Hoenig, *op. cit.* at 340. In a similar vein, Hovil and Lomo, of the University of Makerere's Refugee Law Project, refer to truth-telling as "the missing link" in a process of long-term reconciliation for northern Uganda. *See* Hovil and Lomo, *op. cit.* at 26.

109. Hovil and Lomo emphasize that "the lack of formal mechanisms for the process of truth-telling, or the admittance of guilt on the part of former combatants, is currently hindering the process of reconciliation." *See* Hovil and Lomo, *op. cit.* at 1.

110. *Id.* at 22.

111. *Id.* at 21. In a similar vein, a rebel commander of the Allied Democratic Forces (a largely demobilized rebel movement, which had mounted its armed struggle in Western Uganda) spoke of the roots of that insurgency: "They were arresting us like insects and putting us in prison. That is why we went to the bush." *Id.* at 15 and note 62 (group discussion with eight Ex-ADF combatants, all senior commanders, Kampala, Nov. 17, 2004).

112. "Reform through a Sector Wide Approach," Justice Law and Order Sector Strategic Investment Plan, 2006–2011 ([Government of Uganda] Justice Law and Order Sector, 2007, produced by the JLOS Secretariat), *available at* http://www.jlos.go.ug/index.php.

113. *Theme: Developing and Managing an Effective Transitional Justice System for Uganda*, Report on the Third National JLOS Forum, [Ugandan] Justice, Law and Order Sector (July 30–Aug. 1, 2008, Imperial Resort Beach Hotel, Entebbe), *available at* www.jlos.go.ug.

114. *Id.* at 5.

115. *Id.*

116. *Id.* at 6.

117. *Id.*

118. *Id.* at 7.

119. *Id.* at 25.

120. *See* notes from meeting at the [Ugandan] Ministry of Justice & Constitutional Affairs, Mar. 23, 2010, from p. 6(a) of author's field notebook. *See also* notes from roundtable discussion at the Centre for Human Rights and Peace, Makerere University, Mar. 22, 2010, from p. 4(b) of author's field notebook.

121. *See* Lucy Hovil and Zachary Lomo, *Whose Justice? Perceptions of Uganda's Amnesty Act 2000: The Potential for Conflict Resolution and Long-Term Reconciliation*, Refugee Law Project Working Paper No. 15 (February 2005), *available at* http://www.refugeelawproject.org.

122. *See* "Uganda: New amnesty to exclude top LRA leaders," IRIN Humanitarian News and Analysis (a service of the UN Office for the Coordination of Humanitarian Affairs), Dec. 2, 2010, *available at* http://www.irinnews.org/report.aspx?reportid=47689.

123. *See* notes from meeting at the [Ugandan] Ministry of Justice & Constitutional Affairs, Mar. 23, 2010, from p. 6(a) of author's field notebook.

124. For example, Thomas Kwoyelo, a mid-level combatant within the LRA, was indicted by the Director of Public Prosecutions for war-related offences, in particular kidnapping and attempted murder. *See* Bill Oketch, "Test Case for Ugandan Justice–Kampala puts Former LRA Commander on Trial" (IWPR),Wednesday, July 29, 2009, available at http://www.friendsforpeaceinafrica.org/analysis-op-ed/48-analysis/410-test-case-for-ugandan-justice-kampala-puts-former-lra-commander-on-trial-iwpr.html.

When Kwoyelo was indicted by the Ugandan Director of Public Prosecutions, he was not charged with war crimes. Instead, he was charged with twelve counts of kidnapping

with intent to murder, for the disappearance of villagers from Attiak and Pabo, subcounties located in Amuru and Gulu Districts, Uganda. *Id. See* endnotes 60 and 102, *supra*.
125. *See* notes from meeting at the [Ugandan] Ministry of Justice & Constitutional Affairs, Mar. 23, 2010, from p. 6(a) of author's field notebook.
126. *See id.*, p. 9(a) of author's field notebook.
127. *See* notes from interview with Rachel Odoi-Musoke, [Ugandan] Ministry of Justice & Constitutional Affairs, Mar. 23, 2010, from p. 8(b) of author's field notebook. *NB*: In March 2010, Ms. Odoi-Musoke was serving as Technical Advisor for the Ugandan Ministry of Justice. Currently, she is working with the Justice, Law and Order Sector [JLOS], an inter-agency program of the Ugandan government. JLOS is dedicated to improving access to justice and enhancing the administration of justice across all relevant ministries and agencies. Ms. Odoi-Musoke's title is Technical Advisor, Land and Commercial Justice, JLOS, Government of the Republic of Uganda.
128. *See*, Hovil and Lomo, *op. cit.* at 16 and note 71 (interview with local government official, Arua, Nov. 22, 2004).
129. *See* notes from interview with humanitarian worker, Kampala, Uganda, Mar. 23, 2010, from pp. 10(b) and 12(a) of author's field notebook.
130. Hovil and Lomo, *op. cit.* at 12.
131. *Id.* at 23 and note 110 (from interview with security officer in Kitgum Town, Nov. 24, 2004, who stated that "people would rather reconcile than revenge").
132. One community member in Gulu town, northern Uganda, in an interview conducted in 2004, gave his opinion regarding the prospect of amnesty for LRA leader Joseph Kony: "What we Acholi think is that we want this war to end. So we have to forgive him." Hovil and Lomo, *op. cit.*, at 23 and note 110.
133. *Id.* at 23 ("[i]f we don't forgive the rebels, they will come in and cut off a second leg") and note 111 (interview with community member Kasese town, Nov. 10, 2004).
134. As Hovil and Lomo report, "[w]hile there were some reports of cleansing ceremonies occurring, what is apparent is that dialogue and the admittance of guilt is not happening with any frequency during the reintegration of former combatants.... while amnesty is clearly a good tool for encouraging insurgents to leave the bush, it does not adequately address issues of ensuring that they accept responsibility." *Id.* at 27. *See also id.* at 21 and 15 (regarding government accountability and root causes of the conflict).
135. *Id.* at 28.
136. The importance of "war-weariness" in progress toward resolving the conflict in Northern Ireland has been emphasized and debated in scholarly and policy circles. *See generally*, Michael Cox, Adrian Guelke and Fiona Stephen, A Farewell to Arms?: Beyond the Good Friday Agreement (Manchester University Press, 2nd Edition 2006). An analysis of the Good Friday process may shed light on prospects for the ultimate success of the Juba process, given that both the people of Northern Ireland and the population of northern Uganda suffered deeply in the two civil wars. Nevertheless, scholars of Northern Ireland also emphasize other important factors, including the impact of the end of the Cold War on revolutionary nationalist ideology. *See* Michael Cox, "Rethinking the international and Northern Ireland: a defence," from Cox, Guelke and Stephen (eds.), *op. cit.* at 428.
137. Patrick Hoenig's interviews of Ugandans on the subject of the civil war in northern Uganda reflect a certain split perspective between northerners and southerners. He "learned that Northerners are finding the incumbent government at fault for 'using the LRA to punish the local population for having supported the wrong guy [Tito Okello] in the past,' while Southerners only half-jokingly suggested to 'put the northern tribes in a bottle so that they can go ahead and battle it out among themselves.'" Hoenig, *op. cit.* at 345.

CHAPTER 8

After Lomé in Sierra Leone

The Special Court and National Reconciliation

> War is complete separation, complete destruction,
> Complete waste of resources.
> The Sierra Leonean people *needed* a revolution,
> But not a bloody revolution, not a negative revolution.
> We needed a *positive* revolution.
>
> Reuben Koroma[1]

The Republic of Sierra Leone is nestled on the Western coast of Africa between Guinea to the north and Liberia to the south, home to approximately five million people.[2] Its capital of Freetown was conceived by British abolitionists as a settlement for freed slaves from the Americas, the first of which arrived at the end of the American Revolutionary War.[3] Sierra Leone became a British crown colony in 1808, was designated a British Protectorate in 1896, and attained its independence from Great Britain in 1961. Prime Minister-then-President Siaka Stevens twice transformed the country's governing structure during his term of office. He declared Sierra Leone a republic, in 1971, and a one-party state, in 1978.

Sierra Leone has maintained a strong pluralistic tradition throughout its postcolonial period. It has seen notable tribal and Christian–Muslim integration at the community level as well as a high incidence of interethnic and interfaith marriage. Nevertheless, beginning shortly after independence, successive national governments steadily reduced their investments in the social welfare of the citizenry. Government corruption and systematic weakening of the education, health, and agricultural sectors reached a crescendo under the administration of Siaka Stevens, in power from 1968 to 1985, and continued under his successor, Joseph Momoh. Fueled by a generation of youth bereft of schooling and employment opportunities, Sierra Leone descended into a bloody civil war in 1991.[4]

The Sierra Leonean conflict was launched by insurgent soldiers of the Revolutionary United Front (RUF), armed by Liberia's former rebel leader-then-President Charles Taylor, who attacked a number of villages in the eastern part of country. For much of the next decade, the RUF and various other armed groups traded control of villages and mines in rural Sierra Leone, resulting in extremely high civilian casualties. Other warring parties included reconstituted former members of the armed forces, civil defense militias, and regional peacekeeping troops.

Although Sierra Leone's so-called "rebel war" is often characterized as a conflict between the RUF and the national army, the rebel organization did not easily fit the mold of a classic insurgency with a revolutionary vision.[5] Citizens and observers of Sierra Leone widely agree that, after a few years of conflict, the rebel movement devolved into an opportunistic and vicious criminal organization that inspired competitive waves of brutality and banditry by other armed groups.[6] War tactics by all factions were characterized by the targeted killings of civilians and heavy reliance on child soldiers. The habitual rape of women, as well as amputations and other mutilations of victims, were the special although not exclusive *modus operandi* of the RUF.[7]

Defying a campaign of rebel intimidation, the people of Sierra Leone elected Ahmad Tejan Kabbah president, in 1996. In 1999, Kabbah's government and the RUF signed the Lomé Peace Agreement (Lomé Agreement or Lomé Accord), which included a blanket amnesty for all war-related offenses. After the death of as many as one-hundred thousand Sierra Leoneans,[8] the displacement of two million more, the conscription of thousands of child soldiers, and the rape and sexual enslavement of countless numbers of women,[9] then-President Kabbah declared the war officially over, in 2002. The country emerged from armed conflict, marking the beginning of a process of national reconstruction with the establishment of a Truth and Reconciliation Commission (TRC) to expose the roots of the conflict and address the needs of victims and survivors and a Special Court for Sierra Leone (SCSL or Special Court) to try the most responsible war criminals.

The rule of law is a set of principles that help a functional government function better, and remain faithful to its charge. But, in a nation like Sierra Leone that is emerging from state collapse, pervasive violence, and mind-numbing suffering, the establishment of a credible framework for criminal, social, and historical justice takes on an existential character. Holding offenders accountable, empowering survivors, and telling the truth about the war become gateways to reconstruction, catalysts for reconciliation, and bulwarks against renewed conflict.

Sierra Leone's approach to social reconstruction after armed conflict weaves together the three strands of transitional justice explored in the context of Uganda's postwar transformation. Its war crimes tribunal is composed of both Sierra Leonean and international judges. At the same time, the administration of punitive justice by the Special Court has sought to complement the pursuit of restorative and historical justice by the TRC, and vice versa.

Sierra Leone is unique among contemporary post-conflict societies in Africa for having established a hybrid war crimes tribunal alongside a truth commission. Despite considerable pride in its two national institutions devoted to transitional justice, some Sierra Leoneans contend that punitive and restorative justice work at cross-purposes, particularly given that the Special Court eviscerated the amnesty provision in the Lomé Accord. Others charge that convictions have been too few and narrowly focused, and that much reconciliation work remains to be done, particularly at the village level.[10] A common complaint is that reparations have been too modest, while more resources have gone to reintegrate former combatants than to rehabilitate civilian survivors of the war.

In addition to greater accountability and truth-telling in the aftermath of the civil war, Sierra Leone has a pressing need for improved material conditions of life for the majority of its people. Sierra Leoneans recognize that the alleviation of poverty and the provision of affordable health care and enhanced education and employment opportunities are essential components of long-term peace. Advances in socioeconomic development are vital to addressing both the desperate situation facing disenfranchised youth and the daily violence still experienced by many Sierra Leonean women. At the same time, meaningful improvements in human security will require leaders with integrity, who are committed to government service on behalf of all their constituents. Sierra Leone's fight against corruption is integral to its pursuit of transitional justice.

Sierra Leoneans call for progress in the three classic dimensions of transitional justice—criminal justice, historical justice, and social justice— to avoid a rekindling of armed conflict. But in focusing on the foundation of ethical and pluralistic governance, Sierra Leoneans look past the transitional stage. Criminal accountability, historical honesty, and social welfare are only sustainable, in the long term, to the extent that Sierra Leone rededicates itself as a political community founded on a rule of law applicable to citizens and leaders alike.

A. SIERRA LEONE FROM THE COLONIAL PERIOD TO THE INCEPTION OF THE CIVIL WAR

1. Settlement and Colonial History

The contemporary nation's capital of Freetown was originally established by British abolitionists in 1787 as a settlement for freed African slaves, who had been living on the streets of London after fighting on the British side in the American War of Independence. Most of the first settlers died of starvation and disease within a year. In 1792, the Freetown Colony was established by survivors of the first freedmen's settlement and a larger group of African émigrés from Canada. This new wave of former slaves had earlier been transferred to Nova Scotia by the grateful British, in recognition of their support for the Tory cause. The freedmen veterans and their families were unable to subsist on the Canadian lands the British had granted them, and West Africa appeared the better prospect. Later, these early settlers were joined by Jamaican "maroons," members of a guerrilla-style slave resistance movement who were offered return passage to Africa, in 1800, in exchange for abandoning their revolt against the British. Finally, Freetown became home to Africans of various origins who were liberated from French, Portuguese, and Dutch slaving ships by an antislavery patrol established by the British Royal Navy off the West African coast in the first decade of the nineteenth century.[11]

From the early years of settlement, the Freetown Colony developed a separate identity from the surrounding environs. Initially, Freetown was populated largely by Creoles from the Americas and other parts of Africa, whereas the hinterland of what would become Sierra Leone was inhabited by so-called natives. In 1896, the British formally designated the territory beyond Freetown as the Sierra Leone Protectorate (Protectorate). As political scientist Jimmy Kandeh describes it, there was a firm "political, administrative and legal distinction between the colony and the protectorate... [such that] Creoles were British subjects while natives were British protected persons... [and] Creoles were allowed token representation in colonial institutions" while native Africans were not.[12]

Kandeh speaks of a "political, administrative and legal dualism" between the colony and Protectorate, having social, cultural, and ethnic facets as well. Especially dramatic were the patterns of labor migration. The interior of Sierra Leone "came to constitute the locus of a labor reserve army from whence cheap labor was recruited to work not only in Freetown but in such distant places as the Belgian Congo, German East Africa... and British Honduras."[13] Migrant workers living in Freetown at the turn of the twentieth century were seen as unsophisticated, if not racially inferior by some Creoles. As "aboriginal" or Protectorate people, they were socially and residentially marginalized, even as their numbers grew.[14] Schools, roads, and other services in the Protectorate were inferior to those in Freetown. Within the Protectorate itself, a geographic split began to develop. Roads, rail lines, Christian missions, and schools were more numerous and better endowed in the majority Mende and mainly animist areas of southern Sierra Leone than in the majority Temne and largely Muslim northern areas.[15]

Since the founding of the Freetown colony in 1792, the three largest ethnocultural groups in Sierra Leone have been the settler-descended Creoles or Krios, the Mende, and the Temne. Today, the Krios comprise around 10 percent of the national population, the Mende and the Temne represent 30 percent each, and nearly a dozen indigenous tribal communities make up the other 30 percent.[16] Across ethnic groups, Krio is Sierra Leone's *lingua franca*. As for religious affiliation, the country's overall population is 60 percent Muslim, and 40 percent Christian and animist.

Despite the economic and political stratification of the colonial period, a considerable degree of ethnic pluralism became ingrained in Sierra Leonean culture and society, even before independence. Since the mid-twentieth century, Sierra Leonean society has been characterized by a high degree of intermarriage among ethnic and religious groups and, through the common Krio language, there is a strong pan-Sierra Leonean sense of identity.[17]

2. Independence and Postcolonial Sierra Leonean History

Sir Milton Margai was named the first prime minister of Sierra Leone just prior to sovereignty, in 1961, having led independence talks with the British government as the standard-bearer for the Sierra Leone People's Party (SLPP). He was elected to the post the following year, when the SLPP won a definitive number of parliamentary seats in the nation's first general election based on universal franchise.[18] Although Margai was a member of the Mende tribe, the ethnic community which became most identified with the SLPP,[19] his government was notable for including members of various interest groups and ethnic backgrounds.[20] When Margai died in 1964, he was succeeded as prime minister by his half-brother, Sir Albert Margai. Sir Albert later developed a reputation for corruption and patronage, including limiting opportunities for government service among members of certain groups such as the Krio and Temne communities.[21]

In 1967, the opposition All People's Congress (APC) won a plurality of the parliamentary seats. Siaka Stevens assumed the role of prime minister after campaigning on a socialist platform. Stevens was a Limba and, under his leadership, the APC had significant support from the Temne and Limba tribes.[22] He survived several coup attempts and oversaw Sierra Leone's conversion to a constitutional republic, becoming its first president, in 1971. Corruption and autocratic policies reached catastrophic levels under Steven's leadership, culminating in the 1978 amendment of Sierra Leone's constitution to permit the imposition of a one-party system. In 1985, Stevens retired from the presidency, appointing Major General Joseph Saidu Momoh as his successor.[23]

During the 1970s, Stevens' self-enriching regime provoked a student opposition movement. One of its factions evolved from an intellectual Marxist base in Freetown's Fourah Bay College into an increasingly militant organization. In the 1980s, members of the student opposition and other Sierra Leoneans were recruited to Libyan training camps, reputably established by Mu'ammar al-Qadhafi to encourage the destabilization and overthrow of West African governments. Upon their return to West Africa, the students met Foday Sankoh, an illiterate former corporal and photographer in the Sierra Leonean Army. After some debate, more radical voices prevailed over moderate and intellectual viewpoints. Sankoh took on the leadership of what would become the Revolutionary United Front (RUF) of Sierra Leone.[24]

Sankoh had also spent time in Libya, where he met Charles Taylor, the future leader of the National Patriotic Front of Liberia (NPFL). When Taylor's NPFL entered Liberia from the Ivory Coast on Christmas Day, 1989, Sierra Leone's RUF militants were part of the invading rebel force. When Sankoh's RUF launched its insurrection in Sierra Leone two years later, Charles Taylor returned the favor, supplying the RUF with soldiers and arms. This support would continue throughout the Sierra Leonean conflict, facilitated by the flow of diamonds from RUF-controlled mines into Liberia.[25]

B. THE CAUSES AND CONDUCT OF THE CIVIL WAR

1. Class, Ethnicity, and Politics underlying Sierra Leone's Civil War

A meaningful assessment of the strengths, deficiencies, and challenges of Sierra Leone's path to transitional justice requires an examination of the social roots of the armed conflict. Particularly important are the impacts of state corruption, class polarization, and ethnic identity on Sierra Leonean history. Although ethnicity is often emphasized as a cause of armed conflict, particularly in Africa, ethnic affiliations are dynamic in Sierra Leone, and intermarriage and political collaboration across ethnic and religious group are common. Nevertheless, the country has gone through periods of pronounced ethnic tensions, including frustration in the northern part of the country among Temnes and other groups with Mende dominance of the SLPP in the early years after independence.[26]

Kandeh has written extensively about ethnicity and politics and nation-building in his native Sierra Leone. In a study comparing the ethnic affiliation of presidential cabinet members during the Milton Margai and Albert Margai SLPP administrations, and the Siaka Stevens and Joseph Momoh APC administrations, Kandeh demonstrates that the largest plurality of SLPP cabinet members were Mende, and the largest plurality of APC cabinet members were Temne.[27] According to Kandeh, "the inescapable conclusion that emerges from such comparisons is that the ethnic base of the SLPP regime (under both Milton and Albert Margai) was unquestionably Mende while that of the APC has been Temne or a loose coalition of northern ethnic groups."[28]

While exposing the tribal affiliations of the leadership of Sierra Leone's two dominant political parties, Kandeh also reveals the tendency for ethnic labels to mask underlying political and class dynamics. He explores the ways in which political parties have manipulated ethnic identity in order to concentrate the power of elites within these parties, while sacrificing the interests of the very base for whom they campaigned and on whose support they rely. Sierra Leoneans of Temne and other tribal affiliations grew disappointed with the APC under Stevens and Momoh, the very party that was supposed to be their champion.[29] Kandeh observes that, typically, political ethnicity in sub-Saharan Africa has "functioned more as a mechanism for elite domination than as an emancipatory, mobilizational resource."[30] Such has been the case for Sierra Leone.[31]

A number of Sierra Leone's purported ethnic fault lines—including competing Mende and Temne, Krio versus indigenous tribes, and the factions of Krios of Nova Scotian and Jamaican heritage—break down upon closer examination.[32] The predominantly Mende-identified SLPP was founded by former Prime Minister Milton Margai, who was known for his inclusionary politics.[33] Ahmad Tejan Kabbah, SLPP President of Sierra Leone for most of the period from 1996 to 2007, is of mixed Mandingo and Mende ethnicity. The three leaders of the Temne-affiliated APC, including current President Ernest Bai Koroma, were of Limba or mixed Limba–Temne ethnicity. Even with its Temne base, growing opposition to the APC during the 1980s was broad-based and interethnic.[34] Indeed, it was an initially Temne-majority RUF that rose up against the Temne-dominated APC governments of Presidents Siaka Stevens and Joseph Saidu Momoh.[35] It would thus appear that ethnicity is neither the dominant determinant of power politics in Sierra Leone, nor the primary cause of the civil war.

Sierra Leone's rebel war was born of a complex mosaic of historical and sociological factors, including class tensions, resource competition, and regional politics that fed and channeled the RUF insurgency and the ten-year course of the conflict. Two commonly cited factors underlying the war are Sierra Leone's diamond mines, alongside Charles Taylor's manipulation of the RUF.[36] In addition to his desire to profit from the weapons-for-diamonds trade with the RUF, Taylor was frustrated by the resistance to his military insurrection in Liberia mounted by a regional peacekeeping force, the Economic Community of West African States' Monitoring Observer Group (ECOMOG). He likely wanted to punish Sierra Leone for contributing troops to the ECOMOG contingent in Liberia.[37] Moreover, Taylor knew that opening a "second front" in Sierra Leone would weaken ECOMOG's fighting force.[38]

Although hunger for revenues from Sierra Leone's diamond mines was certainly a catalyst for the civil war, a deeper wellspring of conflict was the gap between privileged and impoverished Sierra Leonean citizens.[39] An important aspect of Sierra Leonean society is the profound sense of cultural separation between the nation's capital and its interior, a legacy of the historical distinction between the Freetown Colony and the up-country Protectorate. The deep chasm between urban elites and rural poor is captured in British journalist Richard Dowden's description of "a nation-wide resentment of Freetown's corruption and domination,"[40] which, in his view, inspired the 1991 launching of the rebel war. American journalist Douglas Farah also touches on this underlying reality, evocatively describing the 1997 looting of Freetown and the murder of its residents by the youthful soldiers of the RUF, "many of whom had never [before] seen electricity or running water."[41]

An essential perspective on the causes of the Sierra Leonean conflict comes from the conclusions of the country's Truth and Reconciliation Commission. The Final Report of the Truth and Reconciliation Commission of Sierra Leone (Final Report) emphasizes the essential similarities between the two opposing political parties of Sierra Leone and their shared responsibility for the brutal insurrection born in 1991:

> Neither the SLPP nor the APC made any genuine effort to attend to the debasement of the post-independence politics and economy of the country. On the contrary, history speaks of a systemic failure, whereby all the members of the political elite belonged to the same failing system. While they claimed to be ideologically different, in reality the two parties shared a brand of politics that was all about power and the benefits it conferred. Tragically these characteristics persist today in Sierra Leone.[42]

While recognizing the role of "external forces," including Charles Taylor and the international diamond trade, the TRC emphasized "internal causes" and "[t]he corrupt, morally bankrupt elite that brought the country to its knees by the end of the 1980's and that set the stage for the rebellion" by disenfranchised and radicalized young people.[43]

2. The Revolutionary United Front—Insurgency or Banditry?

The systemic governmental failure and abject social desperation that characterized Sierra Leonean society by the late 1980s provided an obvious ideological justification for the RUF's armed uprising in 1991. Nevertheless, there is a notable tendency for analysts of the Sierra Leonean conflict to characterize the Revolutionary United Front as a criminal army rather than a militant political movement. Dowden describes the RUF's early evolution from "an idealist Marxist movement" to "a movement of pure terror." Farah depicts the RUF as "an army that had neither a coherent ideology nor a revolutionary credo."[44]

Sierra Leonean historian Ibrahim Abdullah, affirming that "the mutilation, murder and rape of innocent women and children by the RUF are acts that are incompatible with a revolutionary project," explores the genesis of this "revolutionary movement without revolutionaries."[45] Abdullah argues that the RUF's lack of a governing political ideology derived from two historical and social realities. First, he points to Sierra Leone's dominant "conservative orientation" during the postcolonial period, and the country's lack of a strong tradition of labor activism or leftist populism.[46] Second, he emphasizes that the RUF, both leadership and ranks, was largely composed of "lumpens"—"unemployed and unemployable youths, mostly male, who live by their wits. . ., [and are] prone to criminal behavior, petty theft, drugs, drunkenness and gross indiscipline."[47] Given these two factors, the RUF had little choice but to evolve into a "revolutionary movement which slaughters and terrorizes the very people it claims to be liberating."[48]

If there is a significant difference of opinion regarding the ideological framework of the Revolutionary United Front, it concerns whether the RUF was already devoid of political vision when it invaded eastern Sierra Leone on March 23, 1991, or whether the corruption of its goals set in months or years after the violence began. Some Sierra Leoneans argue that members of the RUF were initially motivated by an ideology of social transformation in defiance of Sierra Leone's corrupt, disdainful, and dysfunctional central government. These observers maintain that the RUF enjoyed a degree of popular support during the first two years of the conflict, at least in discrete communities in eastern and southern Sierra Leone.[49] This depiction of the RUF evokes a political movement that lost its way several years into the civil war.

A broad-based Sierra Leonean perspective on the orientation and conduct of the RUF comes from the nation's Truth and Reconciliation Commission, which published its findings on the causes and conduct of the civil war in 2004 after eighteen months of testimony and hearings.[50] The TRC Final Report defines three stages of the conflict: Phase I, 1991–1993, characterized by "conventional" or "target" warfare; Phase II, 1994–1994, the period of "guerrilla warfare"; and Phase III, 1997–2000, comprising increased factionalism and gradually productive peace negotiations.[51]

The TRC Final Report depicts the escalating brutality of the war over time, and the increasing failure of all armed factions to distinguish between military and civilian targets. Nevertheless, the authors state clearly that "the original 'revolutionary' programme [of the RUF] never materialised in the form it was intended to take. It was supplanted by a deviant, militant agenda spearheaded by Foday Sankoh. . ."[52] Moreover, the TRC Final Report concludes that even Phase I of the war was characterized by "the inclusion of civilian settlements within the scope of. . . RUF assaults."[53] The TRC's close examination of the specific military tactics utilized by the RUF and other armed groups reveals that atrocities and targeted attacks on civilian communities were a constant from the war's inception, and only increased in magnitude over the course of the eleven-year civil war.

3. The Evolution of the War: from Kailahun to Lomé and the TRC

In March of 1991, the RUF invaded Sierra Leone's Eastern Province from Liberian territory.[54] During these early days of the war, the RUF called for a popular uprising against APC President Joseph Momoh. At the same time, RUF fighters were attacking civilian settlements, beginning with the town of Bomaru, in the District of Kailahun.[55] This tactic, combined with the recruitment of child soldiers, eventually generated more fear than solidarity for the rebel movement. When Captain Valentine Strasser of the Sierra Leonean Army led a successful and nonviolent young officers' coup against Momoh's government, in 1992, and installed himself as the head of the National Provisional Ruling Council (NPRC), it was the new NPRC government and not the RUF that won popular support and legitimacy.[56]

Richard Dowden describes the brutalizing methodology of child recruitment by the RUF:

> Politically the RUF proclaimed a vague message of liberation and played on the hopelessness of Freetown's street children and village kids up country who had just enough education to understand that they would never see any benefit from the riches around them. But it quickly resorted to forced recruitment, initiating young new members in

horrific ways that prevented them ever returning home. Sometimes they were forced to rape their relatives or kill their own parents. The children became "other," no longer themselves.[57]

Ishmael Beah, who was recruited by government soldiers of Strasser's NPRC in 1993 at the age of thirteen, described the process of psychic desensitization of children by the army. He was forced to participate in a contest with other boy soldiers requiring them to torture and kill RUF captives with their bayonets. He won the competition, and for that he was named a junior lieutenant. After he enrolled in a United Nations Children's Fund (UNICEF) child soldier rehabilitation program and fled to a refugee camp in neighboring Guinea, Beah resettled as a refugee in the United States and enrolled at Oberlin College. He reflected back on the early psychological impact of his experiences: "The idea of death didn't cross my mind at all and killing had become as easy as drinking water. My mind had not only snapped during the first killing, it had also stopped making remorseful records, or so it seemed."[58]

From 1992 to 1994, the RUF and the armed forces of the NPRC fought a relentless but ultimately inconclusive series of battles in the Sierra Leonean countryside, in which civilians made up the great majority of the casualties. Although government soldiers kept the RUF from reaching Freetown during this period, at various times the rebels occupied significant territory in the interior, including diamond and other mining regions. As Perriello and Wierda describe it, the war "rarely involved pitched battles or traditional troop maneuvers, but mainly consisted of factions trading off control over villages, which resulted in massive human rights abuses against civilians."[59]

In response to popular frustration with the inability of the NPRC to protect the civilian population, a number of traditional hunting societies in the chiefdoms of rural Sierra Leone began reconstituting themselves to fight the RUF. In 1994, the NPRC pushed RUF troops back towards the Liberian border, but failed to hold its new territory. That same year, Sam Hinga Norman formed the Civil Defense Forces (CDF) as an umbrella group for the local militias. Norman had served as the regent chief of Telu Bongor, in the Bo district of Sierra Leone's Southern Province.

In 1996, Valentine Strasser was overthrown and succeeded by his defense minister, Brigadier General Julius Maada Bio. Bio agreed under diplomatic pressure to a transition to civilian rule. He held parliamentary and presidential elections in March of that year. Career diplomat Ahmad Tejan Kabbah of the Sierra Leone People's Party was elected, despite widespread public intimidation tactics, including RUF soldiers amputating the limbs of would-be voters.[60] President Kabbah made Chief Norman of the CDF his defense minister, and signed a preliminary peace agreement with the RUF in late 1996.[61]

Kabbah was overthrown the following year by Johnny Paul Koroma of the Armed Forces Revolutionary Council (AFRC) "in an exceptionally violent coup by breakaway army officers. After years of blurring the distinction between soldier and rebel, the AFRC had close relationships with the RUF, and one of Koroma's first acts was to invite the RUF to come to Freetown and join his government."[62] The AFRC-RUF *sobels* (soldier-rebels) brought the full force of civil war violence to Freetown for the first time, looting homes and businesses, and mugging and attacking civilians. Ishmael Beah, demobilized and living in the capital in 1997, recalls that rebels and soldiers on the front lines "started pouring into the city [and] the entire nation crumbled into a state of lawlessness."[63]

After being deposed by the AFRC in 1997, Kabbah went into exile in neighboring Guinea. While the defense minister initially joined the President, Chief Norman later returned to Sierra Leone, likely against Kabbah's advice. Now opposing both the RUF and the ostensible government forces of the AFRC, Norman took the CDF into the bush to fight AFRC and RUF combatants alike.[64]

By 1997, Charles Taylor had been elected President of Liberia, and material support to the RUF increased in several respects, including radio communications equipment for the field, enhanced training, and more sophisticated and destructive weaponry such as rocket-propelled grenades. As in the case of previous support from Liberia, the weapons and supplies were exchanged for diamonds exported from RUF-controlled mines. RUF chief Foday Sankoh was arrested in Nigeria in March of 1997 for attempting to carry a concealed weapon onto a plane. Overall, command of the RUF transferred to Sam Bockerie, who "often said he viewed Taylor as his father [and] ensured the diamonds flowed from Sierra Leone to Liberia in an orderly manner."[65]

The international community was unwilling to let the AFRC coup against Kabbah stand. Since the early 1990s, West African peacekeeping troops had been operating in Liberia and then Sierra Leone under the ECOMOG banner. In March of 1998, ECOMOG troops restored Kabbah to the presidency by driving the AFRC out of the capital. ECOMOG was assisted by CDF forces. Although RUF atrocities may have been the most infamous, particularly those involving sexual violence, all factions were accused of large-scale human rights abuses during this period, including ECOMOG and the CDF.[66]

In January of 1999, RUF and ex-army soldiers returned to Freetown, under the direction of a faction of the AFRC, Johnny Paul Koroma's "West Side Boys." Inside of a week, six thousand people were killed in "Operation

No Living Thing." For a second time, ECOMOG peacekeeping troops drove the sobels out of Freetown, again committing war crimes of their own.[67] In July of 1999, his war-weary populace willing to sacrifice for peace, President Kabbah joined with the RUF in signing the Lomé Peace Agreement (Lomé Agreement or Lomé Accord).[68]

Under the Lomé Accord, all combatants were granted amnesty for all crimes; Foday Sankoh was released from prison and, in a somewhat ironic twist, designated Chairman of the Strategic Mineral Resources Commission; ECOMOG forces were ordered to withdraw from Sierra Leonean territory; and all parties committed to establishing a truth and reconciliation commission.[69] In a diplomatic countermove that would prove significant several years later, the Special Representative of the UN Secretary-General, although not a party to the agreement, "appended a handwritten reservation to the amnesty stating that the UN would not recognize amnesty for 'international crimes of genocide, crimes against humanity, war crimes and other serious violations of international law.'"[70]

The violence of the war was dampened but not fully extinguished with the signing of the Lomé Accord. The withdrawal of ECOMOG troops, in May 2000, and Foday Sankoh's return to Freetown inspired the RUF to capture five hundred UN peacekeepers in the countryside, his bodyguards to shoot peace activists demonstrating outside his compound, and Koroma's West Side Boys to seize eleven British soldiers just outside of Freetown. British special forces attacked Koroma's fighters, and "[t]his demonstration of firepower so impressed the rest of the RUF that they released their hostages."[71] By August 2000, the last hostages were freed, and Foday Sankoh was back in custody.[72] Moreover, as ECOMOG withdrew, the largest international peacekeeping mission in the world was being established, designated the United Nations Mission in Sierra Leone (UNAMSIL). Under UNAMSIL supervision, forty-five thousand combatants were disarmed by mid 2001, such that by January of 2002, Kabbah could declare the war over. In May of 2002, Kabbah was elected for a second five-year term, and the work of political and social reconstruction in Sierra Leone began.[73]

C. TRANSITIONAL JUSTICE IN SIERRA LEONE

The retributive justice facet of Sierra Leone's post-conflict reconstruction process has been centered in a hybrid tribunal called the Special Court for Sierra Leone, established in 2002 with the support of the United Nations, and at the request of former President Kabbah.[74] The restorative and historical justice components were undertaken by the Truth and Reconciliation Commission, which received testimony from witnesses and convened hearings from 2002 to 2003. The TRC finished its work in October 2004, with the submission of a report and recommendations to the Government of Sierra Leone.[75]

Sierra Leone is unique among the three countries explored in this text for having created both a hybrid national/international war crimes tribunal and a national truth commission. Not all observers reach the same assessment of the effectiveness of these two institutions, either considered separately or in concert. However, most Sierra Leoneans agree that, alongside Special Court trials and the Final Report of the TRC, further grassroots reconciliation is required. Moreover, there is widespread consensus that poverty alleviation and economic opportunities are essential ingredients for long-term violence prevention.

A crucial component of Sierra Leone's successful pursuit of transitional justice will be addressing the social, economic, and political inequities in Sierra Leonean society that fueled the civil war. Women remain second-class citizens in Sierra Leone, increasingly victimized by domestic violence: only one-third attend school, nearly two-thirds are married before age eighteen, and nearly 95 percent undergo female genital cutting.[76] Young people remain economically marginalized, with a 60-percent youth unemployment rate.[77] Moreover, the majority of Sierra Leone's people still have limited access to education, health care, and gainful employment; corrupt practices in government continue;[78] and meaningful reforms of the criminal justice system have yet to be implemented. Palpable improvements in these areas will further the process of national reconciliation, and inadequate progress will imperil it.[79]

1. The Special Court for Sierra Leone—The Costs and Benefits of Retributive Justice

a. The Creation and Docket of the Special Court

On June 12, 2000, then-President Kabbah wrote a letter to the UN Secretary General asking for assistance in establishing a tribunal to try high-ranking RUF leaders,[80] despite the broad amnesty provision of the 1999 Lomé Accord. Kabbah was alarmed and emboldened by the spike in RUF violence during the spring and summer of 2000. The resumption of military force by the RUF and the taking of hostages were cited as breaches of the Lomé Accord, in purported justification of international prosecutions of RUF members. Kabbah was also encouraged by the international community's growing rhetoric and action against impunity, evidenced by the creation of the International Criminal Court in 1998, and the understanding of the UN Special Representative that the 1999 Lomé amnesty would not cover war criminals. Moreover, Kabbah was concerned that RUF prosecutions in Sierra Leonean courts would complicate the conflict, and might even provoke another direct attack on Freetown by rebel forces. For this reason, he sought the creation of a tribunal supported by the international community.[81]

The fruit of these negotiations was the adoption, on January 16, 2002, of a treaty between Sierra Leone and the UN creating the hybrid Special Court for Sierra Leone. Despite Kabbah's original vision of prosecuting the RUF, the tribunal was empowered to try suspected war criminals from any armed group. The Special Court was composed of two Trial Chambers, one Appeals Chamber, and a total of eleven judges appointed by the UN Under-Secretary-General, four of whom were nominated by the Government of Sierra Leone.[82] The Special Court sits in Freetown, although it can also conduct proceedings outside of Sierra Leone when security conditions so require, as demonstrated by the decision to hold the trial of Charles Taylor in the Netherlands.

The Government of Sierra Leone and the UN considered various models for the Special Court, and, in fact, there was something of a tug of war between the UN Security Council and the UN Secretariat regarding its structure and scope, in which the Security Council largely prevailed. While the Secretariat had urged the availability of robust enforcement mechanisms, funding based on mandatory contributions from UN members, and jurisdiction to try a wide range of potential defendants, these recommendations were not adopted. Under its statute, the Special Court lacks Security Council enforcement mechanisms, depends on voluntary contributions, and is limited to prosecuting individuals "who bear the greatest responsibility" for war-related crimes.[83] Finally, under Article 10 of the statute, "[a]n amnesty granted to any person falling within the jurisdiction of the Court [based upon charges of crimes against humanity or war crimes]... shall not be a bar to prosecution." The evisceration of the amnesty provisions of the Lomé Accord is one of the more controversial aspects of the Special Court's legacy.

The Special Court issued indictments against thirteen individuals, including members of the insurgent RUF, the CDF militias, and the coup-installed AFRC, as well as former Liberian President Charles Taylor. As of 2011, Taylor's trial is nearing completion,[84] Johnny Paul Koroma of the AFRC is at large, and three indictees are deceased: RUF leader Foday Sankoh, who died in detention; RUF deputy Sam Bockarie, who was killed in a shoot-out in Liberia; and CDF chief Sam Hinga Norman, who died while seeking medical care. The Special Court has handed down convictions of the remaining eight individuals: Issa Hassan Sesay, Morris Kallon, and Augustine Gbao of the RUF;[85] Moinina Fofana and Allieu Kondewa of the CDF;[86] and Alex Tamba Brima, Ibrahim Bazzy Kamara, and Santigie Borbor Kanu of the AFRC.[87] These eight individuals are currently serving their sentences in Rwanda.[88] No Sierra Leonean political leaders have been indicted by the Special Court.

b. Criticism and Praise for the Special Court

One set of challenges to the Special Court has concerned the limited scope of prosecutions, in which thirteen indictments have led to eight convictions. More targeted criticism has been leveled at the prosecutor's failure to charge political leaders. This viewpoint is particularly pronounced among those Sierra Leoneans and foreign observers who emphasize government corruption as the root of the rebel war, in addition to those who seek state accountability for atrocities committed by government-affiliated soldiers.[89] Given the immunity enjoyed by former President Kabbah in particular, many Sierra Leoneans had trouble accepting the prosecution of Sam Hinga Norman, Kabbah's deputy defense minister. Norman had served as commander of the Civil Defense Forces, regarded as the one grassroots movement that rose up to protect the country from lawlessness and brutality.[90] These perspectives are reflected in the Final Report of the Truth and Reconciliation Commission, further explored below.

Another area of criticism of the Special Court concerns its circumscribed temporal jurisdiction, which is limited to the prosecution of crimes occurring after November 30, 1996. Although the court's post-1996 jurisdiction spans the 1997 and 1999 sackings of Freetown by the AFRC and the RUF, as well as the RUF's hostage-taking, it does not cover the early years of the war, nor the crimes committed by the NPRC under Valentine Strasser from 1992 to 1996. As Perriello and Wierda stress, "[t]he worst of the crimes in the provinces were committed earlier, and some have argued that it 'sends the wrong signal' that the crimes under scrutiny [largely] affected the people of Freetown."[91]

Despite concerns regarding the limited scope of its prosecutions, the Special Court is given considerable credit for a number of its rulings, particularly those affirming the human rights of women and children. In 2004, in a preliminary ruling, the Appeals Chamber determined that the recruitment of child soldiers violated international customary law, as of 1996.[92] Later, the Special Court handed down the first convictions by any international criminal court for the crime of recruiting child soldiers and the crime of forced marriage, in 2007 and 2009, respectively.[93]

On the other end of the spectrum from those seeking more penal accountability from the Special Court are those who believe the court's operations should have been more circumscribed, in deference to Sierra Leone's two-lane path to transitional justice. Joseph Sesay of the Centre for Accountability and the Rule of Law argues that prosecutions of accused war criminals likely compromised the restorative justice mandate of the Truth and Reconciliation Commission. While acknowledging the legitimacy of both institutions, Sesay's concern is with their simultaneous operation, resulting in "people being afraid to give true and honest testimony to the TRC for fear of being prosecuted by the SCSL."[94]

Perriello and Wierda also stress concerns about the Special Court by various constituencies within Sierra Leonean society. Two unique aspects of the court's identity are its hybrid nature and its closeness to the Sierra Leonean people. Despite this idealized vision, Sierra Leonean judges have been in the minority, and some Sierra Leonean lawyers were disappointed in their expectation that a significant number of professional posts at the Special Court would go to members of the national Bar. Moreover, the participation of groups representing civilian victims of war has been largely limited to their role in facilitating testimony before the court. Some victims' groups have expressed frustration at the Special Court's inability to award reparations as part of its sentencing power.[95]

Civil society organizations have extended praise as well as criticism at the Special Court. At a 2005 National Victim Commemoration Conference organized by the Special Court in Freetown, delegates stressed the tribunal's role in educating civil society about women's experiences in war and peacetime, their vulnerability to rape and forced marriage, and their rights to participate equally in all sectors of Sierra Leonean society.[96] Working in parallel to the court, although without its direct participation, the Sierra Leonean Parliament began debating draft legislation aimed to increase the rights of women under domestic law. In 2007, these efforts resulted in the unanimous passage of three Gender Bills, including provisions criminalizing domestic violence, raising the marriageable age to eighteen, and ensuring a woman's inheritance rights in the event of her husband's death.[97]

As Beth Dougherty illustrates in her assessment of transitional justice in Sierra Leone, the limited mandate of the Special Court was in some ways a product of lessons learned from the ad hoc tribunals for the former Yugoslavia and Rwanda, discussed in Chapter 4. Those tribunals, possessed of Security Council oversight, mandatory contributions, and broader jurisdiction, grew far beyond expectations. Collectively, by 2000, they amounted to 10 percent of the regular budget of the UN and, by 2003, had racked up combined cumulative expenditures of over one billion dollars. However, Dougherty ends up arguing that the pendulum swung too far in the direction of fiscal and jurisdictional restraint in the mandate of the Special Court, particularly in limiting prosecutions "to the architects and commanders of the violence" and to offenses occurring after 1996.[98] Dougherty concludes that "[w]ith assessed funding, a broader jurisdictional scope, a longer timeframe and Chapter VII powers, the SCSL would be right-sized. The people of Sierra Leone deserve no less."[99]

c. Self-Assessment by the Special Court

The Office of the Registrar of the Special Court has separate sections devoted to public outreach and the legacy of the court. The Outreach Section screens videos on trial proceedings and disseminates literature about the Special Court throughout the country. The Legacy Section works to ensure that the court will strengthen the rule of law in Sierra Leone in the long term.[100] The court has encouraged public monitoring of its proceedings, as well as the establishment of oversight bodies for the judicial system as a whole that are intended to survive its tenure. One example is the establishment of the Sierra Leone Court Monitoring Program, which oversees proceedings in the national tribunals as well as the Special Court.[101]

Staff members of the Legacy Section highlight additional ways in which the court has had a positive impact on Sierra Leone's domestic legal system, beginning with a greater familiarity with international law on the part of Sierra Leonean lawyers who have argued or observed proceedings before the court. The Office of the Registrar is also working with the Sierra Leonean National Police to establish a National Witness Protection Unit. This unit will function after the court has been disbanded, and will provide ongoing security and assistance for witnesses who have testified before the Special Court, while also protecting witnesses in trials conducted in national courts.[102]

In summing up the Special Court's essential legacy, one official stressed that Sierra Leone now has a "never-again culture." She concluded that the Special Court has provided an "opportunity for justice to be imbedded" in Sierra Leonean law.[103]

Notwithstanding the Special Court's forward-looking evaluation of its impact on Sierra Leonean law, no one would contest that eight convictions is a modest accomplishment, even if fully consistent with the court's mandate to try those "most responsible" for violations of humanitarian law. Given that the Special Court will never prosecute the vast majority of Sierra Leoneans who committed atrocities during the rebel war, it is essential that we evaluate the capacity of the Truth and Reconciliation Commission to promote accountability as a facet of community reconciliation. Thus, we turn now to the form and function of the TRC.

2. The Truth and Reconciliation Commission—The Meaning of Restorative Justice

a. The Establishment of the TRC

In 1999, the parties to the Lomé Peace Agreement committed to establishing the Truth and Reconciliation Commission. As conceived in the Lomé Accord, the TRC would be given a broad mandate to investigate and expose the causes of the war; facilitate dialogue, apology, and forgiveness between offenders and survivors; and promote reparations and other forms of assistance to victims. The following year, the Sierra Leonean parliament passed implementing legislation.[104] In 2002, the Statute for the Special Court for Sierra Leone was adopted, and both institutions began their work in tandem.

The TRC was composed of seven commissioners–three women and four men, four of whom were Sierra Leonean and three of other nationalities—and was chaired by Bishop Dr. Joseph Humper.[105] The TRC's work between 2002 and 2004 comprised a testimony phase, followed by the conducting of oral hearings, and the issuance of the Final Report. Over a three-month period from late 2002 to early 2003, a total of 7,706 written testimonies were recorded. The hearings phase occurred between April and August of 2003. National hearings were held in Freetown on overarching themes, including issues of corruption, the abuse of women and girls, and the role of youth in the conflict. In addition, one week of hearings were held in every district capital throughout the four provinces of the country.[106] Although most hearings were open to the public, one day was set aside for closed hearings in each district capital, to permit victims of sexual violence to testify in private if they so desired.[107] After nearly two years of operation, the TRC issued its Final Report in October 2004, while prosecutions at the Special Court remained ongoing.

b. The Historical and Cultural Significance of the TRC

Although the legal basis for the Truth and Reconciliation Commission was the Lomé Accord, the cultural meaning of the TRC is quite complex. Sierra Leone's embrace of reconciliation reflects at least three aspects of its culture and recent history: the importance of social networks, the pervasive nature of the civil war violence, and the belief that reconciliation furthers accountability, rather than destroys it.

With respect to social networks, the Catholic Bishop of Makeni, George Biguzzi, explains:

> [European philosophy] says, "I think, therefore I am." Here, it's "I'm related, therefore I am."... You don't exist if you don't belong, if you are not related to somebody. This is the

centripetal force in the culture that brings people into unity. They find strength in being together. They also find the courage to open up in the group, because somehow they know the group is there for healing.[108]

With respect to the pervasive violence, in the words of a resident of Kailahun District, Eastern Province, where the rebel war was launched: "We don't believe in punishing somebody. Because if we say we're going to punish, there would be so many, we would end up punishing everybody."[109]

Finally, the TRC reflects a particular understanding of the relationship between reconciliation and accountability. The Final Report diplomatically points out that the TRC was envisioned as a *replacement* for retributive justice, consistent with the amnesty provisions of the Lomé Accord, and not as a mere auxiliary to criminal prosecutions: "the Sierra Leone TRC was proposed as a substitute for criminal justice in order *to establish accountability* for the atrocities that had been committed during the conflict."[110] The specific words utilized by the TRC are instructive— reconciliation activities are a replacement for retribution but not a replacement for accountability.[111] Rather, the reconciliation process is an alternative pathway to accountability, nonpunitive in nature, but still entailing the acknowledgment of responsibility for wrongdoing.

The understanding of reconciliation as an alternative form of accountability is shared by John Caulker, former chairman of the Truth and Reconciliation Working Group (TRWG), and founder of Fambul Tok, a grassroots restorative justice organization:

> We have a tradition that forgiveness comes from the whole truth.... to benefit from the forgiveness process, that person would come forward and own up to what he or she did. That is the acknowledgement and that's the basis for reconciliation at the community level.[112]

Related to the concern that the Special Court undermined the alternative pathway to accountability forged by the TRC, is the possibility that perpetrators would be reluctant to testify before the TRC out of suspicion that their statements would become evidence before the Special Court. Despite the prosecutor's statements to the contrary,[113] staff members of the court concede that ongoing prosecutions may have had a slight chilling effect on the work of the TRC.[114] Joseph Sesay of the Center for Accountability and the Rule of Law has analyzed the complex interplay between the two institutions. He concludes that the Special Court should have "finished its work" before the TRC process commenced, thereby defusing any perception of role confusion.[115]

Although the Truth and Reconciliation Commission adapted to the reality of its partnership with the Special Court, important tensions and tradeoffs persisted, notably the impact on future amnesty provisions. In its Final Report, the TRC cautioned that "the international community has signaled to combatants in future wars that peace agreements containing amnesty clauses ought not to be trusted and, in so doing, has undermined the legitimacy of such national and regional peace initiatives."[116]

Despite the significant concerns expressed by the TRC itself, experts on transitional justice emphasize the uniqueness of Sierra Leone's two-pronged institutional approach, and the advantages of combining the Special Court's retributive work with the restorative vision of the TRC.[117] In addition to its work reconciling perpetrators and survivors of wartime atrocities, an essential legacy of the TRC is the extensive historical record it created. The TRC's Final Report has become an essential source of analysis and testimony regarding the roots of the Sierra Leonean conflict, as well as a blueprint for moving the country forward.

c. The Causes and Nature of the War: The TRC's Final Report

As suggested above, the TRC, when it issued its Final Report in 2004, emphasized the profound betrayal of the public trust underlying Sierra Leone's rebel war:

> The Commission finds that the central cause of the war was endemic greed, corruption and nepotism that deprived the nation of its dignity and reduced most people to a state of poverty. Successive political elites plundered the nation's assets, including its mineral riches, at the expense of the national good. Government accountability was non-existent. Institutions meant to uphold human rights, such as the courts and civil society, were thoroughly co-opted by the executive.[118]

As for the nature of atrocities committed during the war, the TRC concluded that responsibility for crimes against civilians was spread across the various factions. As William Schabas writes, the TRC "acknowledges that the majority of atrocities can be laid at the feet of the RUF." Nevertheless, in intensity if not in frequency, atrocities by other armed groups, including the Civil Defense Forces, "were on a par with the worst that the RUF had to offer."[119] The Final Report of the TRC called each party to the conflict to account, noting that:

> The RUF pioneered the concept of forced recruitment, including the enlistment of child combatants. It also bears overwhelming responsibility for the widespread use of drugs

by its members, which precipitated spates of crazed violence and compounded the prevailing general sense of oppression and hopelessness. [. . .] The second highest institutional count was attributed to the AFRC... [which] demonstrated a "specialisation" in the practice of amputations in the period from 1998 to 1999. [...] A defining characteristic of the CDF became its ceremony of "initiation", described to the Commission by many witnesses as entailing physical and psychological torture as well as other gross abuses of human rights.[120]

In addition to its accomplishments in promoting public dialogue on the war and assisting civilian victims, the TRC's Final Report should be remembered for its assignment of blame to all combatant groups, its essential identification of state corruption and collapse as the ultimate cause of the rebel war, and its articulation of recommendations for resolving the root causes of the conflict.

d. Restorative Justice through Ethical Governance and Law Reform: The TRC's Final Recommendations

Building on the foundation of its analysis of the causes and conduct of the civil war, the Truth and Reconciliation Commission did not mince words in pointing out the essential structural changes that would be necessary for Sierra Leone to avoid a resurgence of violence. In its Final Report, the TRC expressed concern that the central causes of the war had not yet been addressed in the four years since former President Kabbah declared an end to the conflict, particularly the deeply entrenched problem of corruption, and the profound sense of moral bankruptcy on the part of the governing elites:

> Today, proper governance is still an imperative, unfulfilled objective in Sierra Leone. Corruption remains rampant and no culture of tolerance or inclusion in political discourse has yet emerged. Many ex-combatants testified that the conditions that caused them to join the conflict persist in the country and, if given the opportunity, they would fight again. Yet, distressingly, the Commission did not detect any sense of urgency among public officials to respond to the myriad challenges facing the country. [...] The state is an abstract concept to most Sierra Leoneans and central government has made itself largely irrelevant to their daily lives. In order to correct this deficit in engagement, an overhaul in the culture of governance is required. The executive needs to prove that it is different from its predecessors in the post-independence period.[121]

At the close of the executive summary of its Final Report, the Truth and Reconciliation Commission presented its blueprint for transforming "the culture of governance" in Sierra Leone. In seventy pages of text, the TRC made an extensive number of specific recommendations, organized into seventeen categories, from the protection of human rights to the establishment of a committee to monitor government implementation of the Final Report.[122] According to the Truth and Reconciliation Act of 2000, and as noted in the Final Report, the Government of Sierra Leone is required to implement recommendations which are specifically addressed to state entities.[123] Examples of the TRC's "imperative" recommendations are the repeal of the death penalty, the release of all prisoners under administrative detention, an end to the practice of corporal punishment in schools, and an end to impunity in cases of sexual violence against women and girls:

> The Commission recommends the abolition of the death penalty and the immediate repeal by Parliament of all laws authorising the use of capital punishment. [. . .]
>
> Several of the detainees have been held in detention without charge or trial since 2000. The detention of such persons constitutes a gross and unjustifiable violation of their human rights. The Commission recommends the immediate release of all persons held in "safe custody detention". The Commission further recommends that such detention never be resorted to again. [. . .]
>
> Children are the future of Sierra Leone. There is no justification for permitting another generation of children to be subjected to brutality, whether this is in the name of education or ideology. The Commission recommends the outlawing of corporal punishment against children, whether this be in schools or the home. This is an imperative recommendation. [. . .]
>
> Women and girls who are sexually violated rarely lay complaints, as the current environment is not conducive to doing so. This has led to a culture of impunity in respect of crimes of a sexual nature. In order to address these inadequacies, the Commission recommends that laws that link the prosecution of sexual offences to the moral character of a complainant should be repealed. This is an imperative recommendation.[124]

In order to involve civil society more fully in the process of national reconciliation, the TRC constituted an advisory body. The Truth and Reconciliation Working Group was mandated to educate the populace about the accomplishments of the TRC, and to encourage the government to implement its recommendations. In carrying out dissemination activities, John Caulker, Chairman of the TRWG, focused on the role of youth:

> The importance of the need for secondary school students and other youths to know about the findings and recommendations in the report cannot be over emphasized. This generation of Sierra Leoneans will sooner than later be in responsible positions that will provide them with numerous opportunities to partake in the implementation of these

recommendations, which – if put in place – would impact positively on the development of the country.[125]

e. Quasi-Judicial Findings by the Truth and Reconciliation Commission

The TRC also weighed in on its relationship to the Special Court for Sierra Leone and the deeper linkages between retributive and restorative justice. Similarly to scholars such as William Schabas, who argues that "post-conflict justice requires a sometimes *complex mix of therapies*,"[126] the Final Report of the TRC emphasized the need for collaboration and equality between courts and truth commissions:

> In future post-conflict societies, there may be compelling reasons to justify the establishment of a body to engender truth and reconciliation. Alternatively, there may be strong grounds to support the creation of a body to address impunity and bring retributive justice. There may even be good cause to have both bodies working side by side. [. . .] The Commission does, however, issue certain cautionary advisements in the event that the parallel option should be adopted. The Commission's recommendations for this eventuality are as follows: [a.] There ought to be recognition from the outset that there is a primary objective shared by both organisations, namely that the processes of both institutions must ultimately lead to the goal of building lasting peace and stability. In the pursuit of this objective, both bodies are equal partners.[127]

One area in which the TRC lacked equal partnership with the Special Court concerned decision making in the prosecution of individual defendants. The Final Report does not belabor this fact, nor explicitly condemn the Special Court's decision to prosecute CDF Commander Sam Hinga Norman while shielding former President Kabbah. Rather, the TRC took upon itself the quasi-judicial role of evaluating the lawfulness of Kabbah's conduct. Having sifted through its voluminous testimony from a wide spectrum of witnesses to the rebel war, the TRC "held" that Kabbah was responsible for any wrongdoing attributed to Norman and the CDF:

> The Commission finds that the SLPP Government was aware of human rights violations and abuses carried out by the CDF, through the role of its Deputy Defence Minister, Chief Sam Hinga Norman, who served as CDF National Coordinator, and through members of the CDF War Council at Base Zero. The Government was further kept informed through its Security Committee briefings and through reports received from ECOMOG. Nevertheless the Government failed to take steps to stop such violations

and abuses. The Commission, accordingly, holds the Government responsible for the violations and abuses of human rights committed by the CDF.[128]

The TRC further determined that President Kabbah was directly responsible for human rights abuses of his own:

> President Kabbah and his government proceeded with the executions of 24 soldiers in 1998, ignoring an appeal from the United Nations Human Rights Committee not to proceed. [. . .] The executions were subsequently declared to have violated both the International Covenant on Civil and Political Rights and the African Charter on Human and Peoples' Rights. The Commission endorses these findings against the Sierra Leone Government by the African Commission [. . . and the Human Rights Committee.][129]

In this part of its report, the TRC speaks in the judicial parlance of a human rights court, weighing the findings of two international human rights bodies. Endorsing the findings of the UN Human Rights Committee and the African Commission on Human and People's Rights (African Commission), Sierra Leone's TRC concluded that Kabbah had imposed arbitrary death sentences on suspected rebels.[130]

Finally, the TRC found that the Special Court should have granted Norman and other indicted persons the right to testify before the TRC itself, despite the fact that they were being tried by the Special Court:

> The Commission [TRC] was effectively blocked by the Special Court from holding any public hearings or confidential interviews with the detainees. The decision to deny Chief Sam Hinga Norman and the other detainees their right to appear before the Commission represents an impairment of basic rights, not only to the detainees but also to the people of Sierra Leone.[131]

In essence, the TRC held that retributive justice and restorative justice are not either-or propositions, and that both mechanisms impose responsibility for the wrongs of the past. In the very judicial tone of its pronouncements, the TRC reinforced the idea that restorative justice furthers accountability, rather than negating it. The fact that the Special Court decided to try Sam Hinga Norman for war crimes and crimes against humanity need not have deprived him and the Sierra Leonean people of a different kind of face-to-face reckoning in the nonadversarial setting of the Truth and Reconciliation Commission. In the end, these debates about the proper contours of transitional justice were academic as far as Sam Hinga Norman was concerned. He died while awaiting medical care, thus depriving the Sierra Leonean people of both retribution and reconciliation in his case.

f. Restorative Justice through Reparations: The TRC Speaks out on Social and Historical Justice

The recommendations section of the TRC's Final Report also addresses reparations to victims and survivors of the war, in the areas of "health, pensions, education, skills training and micro credit, community reparations and symbolic reparations."[132] Some of these recommendations do not mention executive or legislative governmental bodies, and thus it is difficult to argue that they are "imperative" to the same degree as the recommendations grouped under the category of "human rights protections." Nevertheless, this distinction is unlikely to reflect a higher priority accorded civil and political rights over economic and social rights by the TRC, given its identification of endemic poverty and official abuse of power as twin causes of the civil war.

The more qualified nature of the TRC's language with respect to reparations reflects the reality of Sierra Leone's current level of development, and its limited ability to dedicate funds to social service programs. Despite these constraints, the TRC called for the establishment of a national reparations program to provide specific forms of support for war-affected individuals, as these two examples illustrate:

> In relation to war victims who are amputees, the Commission recommends that they be given free physical healthcare for the rest of their lives. Wives who were married to such persons... should be eligible for free primary health care. Children of the eligible adult amputees... should be eligible for free primary health care. [...]
>
> In addition to... [free primary education], there should be free education until senior secondary level for specific groups affected by the conflict. Those eligible include... children who were abducted or conscripted; orphans of the war; and children of amputees, other war wounded... and victims of sexual violence.[133]

In the concluding pages of its Final Report, the TRC discusses some of the guiding principles behind the provision of reparations, and the relationship between reparations and truth-telling itself. In quoting José Zalaquet, a former member of Chile's Truth and Reconciliation Commission, the TRC suggests that creating a historical record is in itself a form of reparation, in that the truth helps "repair" the fabric of society torn by the war: "A nation's unity depends on a shared identity, which in turn depends largely on a shared memory. The truth also brings a measure of healthy social catharsis and helps to prevent the past from reoccurring."[134]

At the same time, the TRC's Final Report recognizes that disabled war survivors cannot live on shared historical memory alone. Rather, Sierra Leoneans struggling with war injuries require a measure of material support to survive. This social and economic assistance is also a means of protecting the society as a whole from returning to the violence of the past. In the words of Tamba Finnoh, a war survivor who testified before the TRC on April 14, 2003:

> The first thing I want to recommend is that most of us are willing to forgive, but to sustain this forgiveness, you can all see that we have lost our dignity because we used to be fit to fend for ourselves but this is not so anymore. That has caused most of us to become beggars in the streets. . . . So I will recommend to the Commission that they should put mechanisms in place, which will ensure that there are provisions for us, which will be sustainable and not something that we can eat in a single day; something that will be sustainable maybe as long as we are alive and even for our children. This is one of the recommendations I will make.[135]

The Kabbah administration's failure to value reparations to survivors of the war as highly as the prosecution of war offenders is one of the most scathing critiques leveled by the TRC. Official neglect of war amputees, along with unemployed youth, reflects disdain for the continued suffering of the people, and risks renewed conflict. Former President Kabbah's government issued a qualified endorsement of the TRC's Final Report in June 2005, without making hard commitments to implement its "imperative" recommendations, in particular regarding the abolishment of the death penalty.[136]

In November 2007, the UN and the Sierra Leone Human Rights Commission urged newly elected President Ernest Bai Koroma to come up with a plan for the speedy implementation of the 2004 recommendations of the TRC. Subsequently, the government established a National Commission for Social Action for this purpose and, in August of 2008, the commission received a three-million dollar grant from the UN Peacebuilding Fund to support its work. As of early 2010, nearly thirty thousand victims had been registered and individual payments of one hundred dollars had been made to eligible amputees, war wounded, and survivors of sexual violence. The National Commission for Social Action is committed to implementing other TRC recommendations, including those in the area of health care and education.[137] In April 2010, President Koroma announced a free health care initiative, waiving fees for pregnant and lactating women and their children.[138] Sierra Leonean civil society continues to press the government of Sierra Leone to more fully realize the historical insights and policy prescriptions of the TRC.[139]

D. CONTINUING THE WORK OF TRUTH AND RECONCILIATION AT THE GRASSROOTS LEVEL

1. Fambul Tok

Even the strongest defenders of the TRC and the Special Court acknowledge their modest impact. War crimes prosecutions by the Special Court targeted a total of thirteen individuals, and have yielded only eight convictions as of 2011. The TRC convened its hearings in Freetown and the district capitals, without penetrating to the section and village levels. Despite concerted media and educational outreach efforts by both entities, many communities throughout the country have not benefited, on a concrete level, from the work of the Special Court or the TRC. Former offenders have returned to live alongside their former victims, without having acknowledged or atoned for their crimes. Given daily reminders of traumatic experiences and fears of renewed violence between neighbors, some participants in the TRC process have called for a deeper and ongoing process of reconciliation in rural communities throughout the country.[140] In the words of a youth leader from Kailahun District, Eastern Province, where the war started, the Special Court:

> is targeting those who bear the greatest responsibility, but what about somebody who has done wrong to somebody in a village, and both of them are living in that community. Dealing with Charles Taylor—will that solve the problem? No. . . . It is good for people living in the community to reconcile first with themselves. You as a perpetrator ask the victim for forgiveness so that will permit a reconciliation process.[141]

A powerful appeal for an ongoing process of reconciliation throughout Sierra Leonean society comes from John Caulker, who served as chairman of the Truth and Reconciliation Working Group. In considering the accomplishments of the TRC, Caulker became convinced that, by the end of the two years of investigations, testimony, and hearings convened between 2002 and 2004 at the national and district levels, a meaningful process of national reconciliation had only barely begun. He decided to found an organization that would facilitate long-term reconciliation activities at the village level involving youth, women, and men in preparing the communities for reconciliation; incorporating local ceremonies for dispute resolution; and initiating long-term development activities.

The goal, as Caulker envisioned it, was to go beyond momentary reconciliations of former perpetrators and victims, to sustained reinforcement of the relationships among all members of the community. In order to realize his plan, Caulker took an NGO he directed called Forum of Conscience, and joined forces with a US-based NGO called Catalyst for Peace. Together, in 2007, the two entities founded a new organization called Fambul Tok (Krio for "family talk"), "built upon Sierra Leone's 'family talk' tradition of discussing and resolving issues within the security of a family circle." The program brings together victims and their offenders in outdoor group settings, utilizing traditional truth-telling and cleansing ceremonies, "practices that many communities have not employed since before the war."[142]

According to Fambul Tok's overarching reconciliation process, an Outreach Committee (OC) is formed at the section level within a particular district, which typically comprises four or five villages. The OC, composed of five young women and five young men, meets with community members to talk about their understanding of the meaning and value of reconciliation. Then a Reconciliation Committee (RC) is formed, composed of five women and five men, including the section chief, a Muslim leader, and a Christian leader. The RC prepares the community for the truth-telling and cleansing ceremonies, including identifying and talking with individual perpetrators and victims who know one another and might be prepared to reconcile.[143]

Several months after the process begins, an evening truth-telling bonfire is organized, to which all members of the community are invited. A central aspect of Fambul Tok's work is compassion toward victims and offenders alike, and this value is expressed throughout the ceremony. During the bonfire, individual perpetrators stand before their neighbors, confess to their offenses, and ask for forgiveness, often specifically speaking out to those they wronged, and then joining them around the circle. The following morning, a cleansing ceremony is held involving worship in the local mosque or church, or a ritual to appease the ancestors, depending upon the practices, customs, and preferences of the particular community.[144]

It is crucial that the bonfire and cleansing ceremonies are the beginning and not the end of the process of reconciliation. Follow-up activities include collective farming projects, reconciliation football leagues, and media outreach. Radio programs focus on preventing violence against women, inviting and welcoming perpetrators back into their communities, and other aspects of peace education.[145]

Agricultural projects are particularly crucial to Fambul Tok's work. Although Sierra Leone was historically the rice basket of West Africa, many rural communities were still importing rice nearly ten years after the conflict had ended. Collaborative farming programs helped close this gap in the region where the war commenced. In 2009, Fambul Tok's second year of operation, 40 villages in Kailahun District held a Peace and Reconciliation Agricultural Show, at which villagers sold surplus stocks of rice, cassava, potatoes, bananas, pepper, and pumpkins.[146] The annual report of the organization for that year notes that "for the first time since before the war, Fambul Tok communities in Kailahun describe not having to buy imported rice."[147]

Fambul Tok is not a cure-all for Sierra Leone as its people struggle with the transition from armed conflict to durable peace. Its accomplishments are local yet powerful, because they can be replicated throughout the country as the process of reconciliation is considered, adopted, and adapted by new communities. Grassroots restorative justice builds on the interlocking relationships between truth-telling, reconciliation, and socioeconomic development. While employment and income generation are essential aspects of long-term conflict resolution, the experience of Fambul Tok suggests that community reconciliation may be a necessary precondition for sustainable resource development and collective survival in a country like Sierra Leone emerging from the trauma of civil war.

The work of Fambul Tok concentrates chiefly on two aspects of transitional justice. Social justice is furthered through its development programs and historical justice through its reconciliation ceremonies. Confronting their victims, civil war offenders accept responsibility for the humanitarian law violations they committed in the presence of their neighbors and relatives. Such face-to-face reckonings implement humanitarian law at the local level, rivaling the impact of remote criminal trials of high-ranking senior combatants.

2. CD-Peace

Another dynamic grass roots organization involved in community building in rural Sierra Leone is the Centre for Development and Peace Education (CD-Peace), based in the village of Mayagba, some 100 miles northeast of Freetown. CD-Peace was founded in the 1990s, principally to support agricultural development activities in Bombali District, located in Sierra Leone's Northern Province. The organization "went to sleep" during the latter years of the rebel war until 2008, when its founders Thomas and Mary Turay revitalized the agency, supported by a two-year grant from the Canadian International Development Agency, and in collaboration with a Canadian NGO called Peaceful Schools International.[148]

Over the past several years, CD-Peace has expanded its activities from agricultural development into the education, health, and women's empowerment sectors. In addition to its consulting and training activities throughout the country and overseas, CD-Peace currently targets its work in two chiefdoms in Bombali District. Through its community projects, the organization expands opportunities for primary, secondary, and tertiary education through school-fee waiver and continuing education programs for children and teachers alike; provides resources to rural health clinics; encourages youth to prepare for careers in agriculture through demonstration projects; and enhances the rights of women through gender equity trainings, teacher training scholarships and micro-enterprise grants.[149]

CD-Peace is primarily a community development and education organization. While Fambul Tok uses reconciliation activities as a springboard for development, CD-Peace uses development activities to support community healing. Fundamentally, both organizations seek to promote healthy relationships at the community level. The integrated and cohesive nature of CD-Peace's staff is a powerful symbol and reinforcement of Sierra Leone's interfaith and pan-tribal traditions.[150] Its efforts to strengthen the social health of communities contribute to conflict prevention and guard against future humanitarian law violations.

Sierra Leone's efforts to implement humanitarian law in the postwar period have been both top-down and bottom-up. From the top, the country created two national institutions with distinct but overlapping visions of transitional justice. The Special Court, a hybrid tribunal to try humanitarian law offenders, was created in the classic retributive tradition of criminal law. The Truth and Reconciliation Commission sought to promote an alternative vehicle for community accountability in the restorative justice tradition, based on truth-telling and reparations, seeking a combination of historical and social justice. The inconsistencies between the Special Court and the TRC have yet to be fully resolved, but the tension is a creative one, requiring and empowering civil society to continue the unfinished business of humanitarian law in action. Civil society organizations, working on the ground and in collaboration with international partners, engage in the grittier aspects of humanitarian transformation, through face-to-face reckonings between perpetrators and survivors of war crimes, and day-by-day improvements in the social wellbeing of Sierra Leonean men, women, and children.

NOTES

1. These spoken words introduce "Monkey Work," originally recorded in Sembakounya refugee camp, Guinea in 2005. "Monkey Work" is Track 15 on Disc One of the Sierra Leone Refugee All Stars' *Living Like a Refugee* album, a Sodasoap Production (Anti Records 2006).

2. Sierra Leone's 2010 population is recorded at 5,132,138 people, occupying a territory of 71,740 square kilometers, nearly the size of the United States (US) state of South Carolina. Comparatively speaking, the land mass is less than one percent of that of the US, with less than 2 percent of its population. *See* CIA Factbook, Sierra Leone (under "Geography" and "People"), *available at* https://www.cia.gov/library/publications/the-world-factbook/geos/sl.html.
3. RICHARD DOWDEN, AFRICA: ALTERED STATES, ORDINARY MIRACLES (Public Affairs 2009) at 290–91.
4. *See* ISHMAEL BEAH, A LONG WAY GONE: MEMOIRS OF A BOY SOLIDER (Farrar, Straus and Giroux 2007) at 220–225 (Chronology). *See also* Jimmy Kandeh, "Politicization of Ethnic Identities in Sierra Leone," AFRICAN STUD. REV., Vol. 35, No. 1 (April 1992), 81–99 at 8–5.
5. *See* DOWDEN, *op. cit.*, at 302 (describing the Revolutionary United Front's (RUF's) evolution from an intellectual movement to a violent criminal organization). *See also* DOUGLAS FARAH, BLOOD FROM STONES: THE SECRET FINANCIAL NETWORK OF TERROR (Broadway Books, 2004) at 10–11 (emphasizing the RUF's lack of a consistent political vision).
6. *Id. See also* The [2004] [Executive Summary of the] Final Report of the Truth & Reconciliation Commission (TRC Final Report) of Sierra Leone [TRC Final Report Executive Summary], © 2004, Sierra Leone Truth and Reconciliation Commission, Chapter 1, para. 14. Chapters 1 and 2 of the Final Report, "Executive Summary" and "Findings," are available at http://www.brandeis.edu/coexistence/linked%20documents/Sierra%20Leone%20TRC%20Report.pdf. (Para. 14 is found on p. 4 of the pdf file.) *See also* Joseph Opala, *What the West Failed to See in Sierra Leone*, WASH. POST at B2, May 14, 2000. The increasing incidence of "entrepreneurial" civil wars, related to the phenomenon of "competitive banditry," is discussed in Chapter 2 on international humanitarian law, Section D.1, footnotes 69 and 70, and related text.
7. *See* Tom Perriello and Marieke Wierda, *The Special Court for Sierra Leone Under Scrutiny* (The International Center for Transitional Justice, March 2006) at 4–9. Perriello and Wierda chronicle the background of the war and the nature of the atrocities committed by the various armed groups. The Armed Forces Revolutionary Council (AFRC) also engaged in intentional mutilations. *Id.* at 9.
8. *See* Perriello and Wierda at 9. Some of these war-related deaths occurred after the signing of the Lomé Peace Agreement (Lomé Agreement or Lomé Accord), in the aftermath of its mandated withdrawal of regional peacekeepers. The peace accord also called for the release of imprisoned RUF leader Foday Sankoh, which inspired violence on the part of some of his rebel fighters. The evolution and conclusion of the rebel war are explored in greater detail below in Section B.3.
9. *See* Beth Dougherty, *Right-sizing international criminal justice: the hybrid experiment at the Special Court for Sierra Leone*, INT'L AFF. 80, 2 (2004), 311–328 at 315. *See also* Perriello and Wierda, *op. cit.* at 8. The authors point to the research of Physicians for Human Rights, whose study concluded that "more than half the women whom came into contact with the RUF suffered some form of sexual violence." *See id.*, citing Physicians for Human Rights, *War-Related Sexual Violence in Sierra Leone: A Population-Based Assessment*, 2002.
10. *See* Perriello and Wierda, *op. cit.*, at 28–29 and 37–38.
11. *See* RICHARD DOWDEN, *op. cit.*, at 290–93, for a good synopsis of the early history of Freetown.
12. *See* Jimmy D. Kandeh, *Politicization of Ethnic Identities in Sierra Leone*, AFRICAN STUDIES REV., Vol. 35, No. 1 (April 1992), 81–99 at 83, *excerpt available at* http://www.jstor.org/pss/524446. The Final Report of Sierra Leone's TRC also notes that "[p]eople in the Colony enjoyed vastly superior social, political and economic development and access to

vital resources such as education." *See* The TRC Final Report, *op. cit.*, chapter 1, para. 11 (found on p. 3 of the pdf file).

The split between the Freetown colony and the Sierra Leone Protectorate is also portrayed in *Allah n'est pas obligé*, a novel written by Ivorian author Ahmadou Kourouma in 2000, and translated into English by Frank Wynne. *Allah is not obliged* was published by William Heinemann Ltd. in 2006.

13. Kandeh, *op. cit.*, at 84–85.
14. Kandeh cites an article from the *Sierra Leone Weekly News* of October 2, 1900 referring to Africans from the Protectorate as "unredeemable savages," calling on the colonial authorities to "zone the city," and suggesting that "to the swarm of Mendis and other aboriginal tribes, who infest this metropolis from end to end, should be apportioned plots of vacant land in one and another of our deserted villages." Kandeh, *op. cit.*, at 85–86.
15. Kandeh, *op. cit.*, at 86. Kandeh explains that Christian missionaries concentrated their activities in the animist areas of the south, which were less resistant to colonial government and Christian evangelism than the majority Muslim north. "The northern Temnes," he explains, "had not only been mostly converted to Islam, their opposition to colonial authority was legendary." *Id.* Moreover, by 1938, fully 80 percent of all Protectorate schools were located in the Mende area of southern Sierra Leone. *Id.*
16. *See* Perriello and Wierda, *op. cit.*, at 4–5, for useful background information on the demographics of Sierra Leone.
17. *See* Joseph Opala, "Sierra Leone: Hard Truths and Hidden Strengths," briefing for newly appointed US Ambassador to Sierra Leone Thomas Hull, Ambassadorial Seminar on Sierra Leone, July 9, 2004, Washington, DC (on file with author).
18. *See* BEAH, *op. cit.*, at 14. Beah provides a good political and historical overview of Sierra Leone in his Chronology on pp. 219–26 at the conclusion of his memoir.
19. *See* Perriello and Wierda, *op. cit.*, at 4.
20. When Sierra Leone attained its independence, *The New York Times* published a profile of Sir Milton Margai, reporting that the 65-year-old prime minister was named a member of the Order of the British Empire in 1943 and knighted by Queen Elizabeth II, in 1959, for his service to the people of Sierra Leone, including over twenty years as a public health doctor. Sir Margai was famously respected by his fellow Sierra Leoneans, from his fellow politicians to rural farmers without access to education, for his "cool administrative head balanced by a warm heart. . . . Sir Margai is credited with knowing where the fountainhead of political power lies, understanding the role of custom and tradition in tribal life and possessing a sixth sense awareness of potential pitfalls." *See Sierra Leone's Leader: Milton Augustus Strieby Margai* ("Man in the News"), N.Y. TIMES, April 28, 1961, *available at* http://query.nytimes.com/mem/archive/pdf?res=F30816FE3B5912738DD DA10A94DC405B818AF1D3.
21. The website of the Sierra Leone People's Party profiles Sir Albert Margai, indicating that he "did not enjoy the reverence which old age had bestowed upon his elder brother. . . . [He] did not enjoy the support and confidence of all factions of his party . . . [and] he openly asked traditional rulers to stay out of politics." By the end of his term in office, and "[r]acked by accusations of corruption in high places and disregard for the interests of significant sectors of the population, Sir Albert lost the 1967 elections to the opposition A.P.C. . . ." *See* "Sir Albert Michael Margai (1920–1980), Second Prime Minister," Sierra Leone People's Party Official web site, *available at* http://www.slpp.ws/browse.asp?page=439. *See also* Jimmy D. Kandeh, "Politicization of Ethnic Identities in Sierra Leone," AFRICAN STUD. REV., Vol. 95, No. 1 (April 1992), who writes that "[t]he death of Milton Margai in 1964 led to a conspicuous erosion in leadership tolerance of the political heterogeneity of society." *Id.* at 93.
22. *Id.* at 4.

23. Sierra Leoneans often refer to Stevens' era as the "17-year plague of locusts." *See* Joseph Opala, *What the West Failed to See in Sierra Leone*, WASH. POST, May 14, 2000, at B2. Memoirist Beah remembers his father telling him that Stevens had inaugurated Sierra Leone's era of "rotten politics" and Beah's Chronology details the presidencies of Stevens and Momoh. *See id.* at 14 and 221–22.
24. DOWDEN, *op. cit.* at 302, discusses the evolution of the RUF movement. Perriello and Wierda, *op. cit.* at 5, discuss the Libyan training camps.
25. Perriello and Wierda, *op. cit.* at 5, discuss the possible motivations for Taylor's support of the RUF. Journalist Douglas Farah describes the first encounter between Sankoh and Taylor, RUF participation in the early days of the Liberian insurgency, and the exchange of Sierra Leonean diamonds for Liberian weapons. *See* FARAH, *op. cit.*, at 24–25 and 28. BEAH, *op. cit.*, at 222, references the participation of Liberian rebels in the RUF's initial attacks on villages in eastern Sierra Leone, near the Liberian border in 1991. Richard Dowden also discusses the diamonds for arms exchange between the RUF and Liberia. DOWDEN, *op. cit.*, at 294.
26. *See* Jimmy D. Kandeh, *Politicization of Ethnic Identities in Sierra Leone*, AFRICAN STUD. REV., Vol. 35, No. 1 (April 1992), 81–99 at 92, *excerpt available at* http://www.jstor.org/pss/524446. Kandeh focuses on the growth of the All People's Congress partly as a reaction to perceived Mende hegemony within the SLPP: "That [John] Karefa-Smart [northern politician seeking to succeed Milton Margai as prime minister] and other northern political leaders were to later resign from the SLPP to join the opposition APC is indicative of the impact of perceptions of Mende domination on the politicization and mobilization of northern ethnoregional identity." *Id.*
27. *See* Kandeh, *op. cit.*, at 93. Specifically, in 1962, under Milton Margai of the SLPP, there were 7 Mende cabinet members and 4 Temne cabinet members, out of a total of 18. In 1964, under Albert Margai, also SLPP, there were 6 Mende and 2 Temne out of a total of 14 cabinet members. In contrast, in 1973, under Siaka Stevens of the APC, there were 10 Temne and 3 Mende out of 24 cabinet members; and, in 1988, under Joseph Momoh, also APC, there were 12 Temne and 5 Mende out of a total of 27 cabinet members. *Id.*
28. *See* Kandeh, *op. cit.*, at 92.
29. Dr. Kandeh writes that "much as the northern province is generally considered an APC ethno-regional stronghold, evidence in the past decade [of the 1980s] suggests widespread popular discontent with the performance of the APC regime that cuts across ethnic and regional lines." Kandeh, *op. cit.*, at 95.
30. *See* Kandeh, *op. cit.*, at 82.
31. "The case of Sierra Leone lends credence to the thesis that although ethnicity may well have effective primacy over class and state, processes of class formation and state formation by and large have structural and dynamic primacy over ethnicity." *See* Kandeh, *op. cit.*, at 98.
32. Perriello and Wierda discuss the various likely sources of the Sierra Leonean conflict, including "a subtle conflict between the Mende-dominated Sierra Leone People's Party (SLPP) and the Temne-dominated All People's Congress (APC). " Their scholarship also points to the corruption of the central government, competition for diamond mine revenues, and the cross-border influence of Liberian rebel-then-president Charles Taylor. *See* Perriello and Wierda, *op. cit.*, at 4. *See also* DOWDEN, *op. cit.*, at 292, who points to abiding "bad feeling between Sierra Leoneans of Nova Scotian and Maroon descent."
33. Kandeh's scholarship points to the relative "leadership tolerance of the political heterogeneity of society" under Sir Milton Margai. *See* Kandeh, *op. cit.*, at 93.
34. *See* Kandeh, *op. cit.*, at 95.

35. *See* Minorities at Risk, "Assessment for Temne in Sierra Leone," *available at* http://www.cidcm.umd.edu/mar/assessment.asp?groupId=45104 (information current as of Dec. 31, 2006).
36. Perriello and Wierda present a nuanced and concise exploration of the enmeshed roots of the Sierra Leonean civil war, including ethnic politics, diamond mines, Charles Taylor, and the role of APC President Siaka Stevens, credited with "transform[ing] a relatively stable country, which some referred to as the 'Athens of West Africa,' into a one-party state of endemic corruption." Perriello and Wierda, *op. cit.*, at 4–5. For a detailed chronology of the succession of Sierra Leonean governments since independence, see BEAH, *op. cit.* at 221–24.
37. Perriello and Wierda, *op. cit.*, at 5. The authors quote Taylor when he "infamously declared in 1990 that 'Sierra Leone would taste the bitterness of war.'" *Id.* ECOMOG (the Economic Community Monitoring Observer Group) was originally established by ECOWAS (the Economic Community of West African States) in the early 1990s to pacify the Liberian civil war.
38. *See* FARAH, *op. cit.*, at 25.
39. As discussed in Chapter 3 on international human rights law, in 1991, Sierra Leone ranked at the bottom of the world's least developed countries based upon the UN's human development index, a position it continued to occupy for nearly two decades more. *See* UNITED NATIONS DEVELOPMENT PROGRAMME (UNDP), HUMAN DEVELOPMENT REPORT FOR 1991 (Oxford University Press) at 16, Table 1.2, "HDI ranking for developing countries," available at http://www.arab-hdr.org/publications/other/undp/hdr/1991/hdr-e.pdf. *Compare* UNDP, HUMAN DEVELOPMENT REPORT FOR 2007/2008: HUMAN SOLIDARITY IN A DIVIDED WORLD (Oxford University Press) at 229–32, Table 1, "Human Development Index," *available at* http://hdr.undp.org/en/media/HDR_20072008_EN_Complete.pdf. In 2010, using a slightly revised methodology, UNDP places Sierra Leone 158th out of 169 countries ranked within its human development index. *See also* UNDP *Human Development Report* for 2010 at 145, *available at* http://hdr.undp.org/en/media/HDR_2010_EN_Complete_reprint.pdf.
40. *See* DOWDEN, *op. cit.*, at 293.
41. *See* FARAH, *op. cit.*, at 31.
42. *See* TRC Final Report Executive Summary, *op. cit.*, Chapter 1, para. 14 (found on p. 4 of the pdf file).
43. *See* Schabas, "The Conjoined Twins of Transitional Justice? The Sierra Leone Truth and Reconciliation Commission and the Special Court," J. CRIM. JUSTICE 2 (2004), 1082, 1085. In his analysis of Sierra Leone's resolute pursuit of transitional justice, William Schabas, Director of the Irish Centre for Human Rights, emphasizes the "introspective" approach of the TRC.
44. *See* DOWDEN, *op. cit.*, at 302. *See also* FARAH, *op. cit.* at 10–11.
45. *See* Ibrahim Abdullah, *Bush path to destruction: the origin and character of the Revolutionary United Front/Sierra Leone*, J. MODERN AFRICAN STUD., 36, 2 (1998, Cambridge University Press), 203–235 at 223, 222.
46. *Id.* at 205–06.
47. *Id.* at 207.
48. *Id.* at 222.
49. *See* notes from meeting at humanitarian aid organization, Freetown, Sierra Leone, Oct. 13, 2010, from p. 47(b) of author's field notebook.
50. The TRC's 2004 Final Report is a multivolume document of more than 5,000 pages, analyzing the causes of the conflict, describing the conduct of the civil war, and making specific recommendations for the implementation of policies essential to durable conflict resolution. *See* TRC Final Report Executive Summary, *op. cit.* Chapters 1 and 2 of the Final Report, "Executive Summary" and "Findings," comprise 244 pages,

and are available at http://www.brandeis.edu/coexistence/linked%20documents/Sierra%20Leone%20TRC%20Report.pdf.

51. See TRC Final Report Executive Summary, *op. cit.*, Chapter 1, para. 23, *available at* http://www.brandeis.edu/coexistence/linked%20documents/Sierra%20Leone%20TRC%20Report.pdf (para. 23 is found on pp. 6 of the pdf file).
52. See TRC Final Report Executive Summary, *op. cit.*, para. 24 (found on pp. 6–7 of the pdf file).
53. See TRC Final Report Executive Summary, *op. cit.*, para. 25 (found on p. 7 of the pdf file).
54. Almost simultaneously, the RUF invaded Pujehun District in Sierra Leone's Southern Province and, for this reason, the first phase of the war is often referred to as the "war on two fronts." See TRC Final Report Executive Summary, *op. cit.*, para. 25 (found on p. 7 of the pdf file). For much more detail on the prosecution of phase I of the conflict, and its two fronts, the [Complete] Final Report of the TRC should be consulted. Volume 3A of the five-volume [Complete] Final Report is available at http://www.sierra-leone.org/Other-Conflict/TRCVolume3A.pdf. The relevant section entitled "Differing Dynamics on the Eastern and Southern Fronts" begins with para. 148 of Volume 3A, found on p. 126 of the pdf file.
55. See TRC Final Report Executive Summary, *op. cit.*, para. 24 (found on pp. 6–7 of the pdf file).
56. Perriello and Wierda, *op. cit.*, at 6.
57. DOWDEN, *op. cit.*, at 302.
58. BEAH, *op. cit.*, at 122, and 124–25.
59. Perriello and Wierda, *op. cit.*, at 6.
60. See DOWDEN, *op. cit.*, at 303; *see also* Perriello and Wierda, *op. cit.*, at 6.
61. See DOWDEN, *op. cit.*, at 303.
62. Perriello and Wierda, *op. cit.* at 6.
63. BEAH, *op. cit.* at 203.
64. *See* notes from meeting at humanitarian aid organization, Freetown, Sierra Leone, Oct. 13, 2010, from p. 46(b) of author's field notebook.
65. FARAH, *op. cit.* at 27–28. In 2003, Bockerie, his wife, and several of his children were killed in Liberia, allegedly because Taylor feared that Bockerie would turn him in to the Special Court for Sierra Leone. *Id.* at 28.
66. Perriello and Wierda, *op. cit.* at 6; *see also* DOWDEN, *op. cit.* at 303.
67. Perriello and Wierda, *op. cit.*, at 7; *see also* FARAH, *op. cit.*, at 68; *see also* DOWDEN, *op. cit.* at 303, for a reference to the West Side Boys. According to one humanitarian worker who observed the sacking of Freetown in 1999, 6,000 people were killed in six days during Operation "No Living Thing." *See* notes from meeting at humanitarian aid organization, Freetown, Sierra Leone, Oct. 13, 2010, from pp. 46(a)–(b) of author's field notebook.
68. Peace Agreement between the Government of Sierra Leone and the Revolutionary United Front of Sierra Leone, Lomé, July 7, 1999, *available at* http://www.sierra-leone.org/lomeaccord.html.
69. Perriello and Wierda, *op. cit.*, at 7. Dowden also comments on Sankoh's appointment as chairman of the mining commission: "[s]ince Sankoh had stolen huge quantities of the country's diamonds on behalf of his ally, Charles Taylor, it was hard to see whether this was a bad joke or a naïve attempt to make Sankoh a responsible member of government." *See id.* at 304. For an extensive discussion of the TRC, *see* William Schabas, *Conjoined Twins of Transitional Justice? The Sierra Leone Truth and Reconciliation Commission and the Special Court*, J. INT'L CRIM. JUST. 2, 4 (2004) at 1082–1099. *See also*, Peace Agreement between the Government of Sierra Leone and the Revolutionary United Front of Sierra Leone, Lomé, July 7, 1999.

70. Perriello and Wierda, *op. cit.*, at 10 and n. 36.
71. *See* DOWDEN, *op. cit.*, at 304; *see also* Perriello and Wierda, *op. cit.*, at 7.
72. *See* Perriello and Wierda, *op. cit.*, at 7 and 10.
73. *See id.*
74. Beth Dougherty, *Rightsizing international criminal justice: the hybrid experiment at the Special Court for Sierra Leone,* INT'L AFF. 80, 2 (2004), 311, 316.
75. *See* Schabas, *op. cit.*, at 1084.
76. *See* UN Integrated Peacebuilding Office, UN Country Team, "Joint Vision for Sierra Leone of the United Nations' Family" at 5, Freetown, May 30, 2009, *available at* http://www.sl.undp.org/unsl.htm.
77. *See id.* at 2–3.
78. *See* TRC Final Report Executive Summary, *op. cit.*, Chapter 1, "Introduction" section, para. 21 (found on p. 6 of the pdf file).
79. In its "Joint Vision for Sierra Leone," the UN Integrated Peacebuilding Office has identified essential priorities and concerns in Sierra Leone's process of post-conflict development, including the consolidation of disarmament and security gains, gender equality, youth integration, development of the agricultural sector, health care promotion, good governance, progress towards the Millennium Development Goals, improvement in socioeconomic human rights, and poverty alleviation. *See generally* UN Integrated Peacebuilding Office, UN Country Team, "Joint Vision for Sierra Leone of the United Nations' Family," Freetown, May 30, 2009, *available at* http://www.sl.undp.org/unsl.htm.
80. *See* Perriello and Wierda, *op. cit.*, at 10.
81. *See id.*
82. *See* Perriello and Wierda, *op. cit.*, at 19; *see also* Statute of the Special Court for Sierra Leone, art. 12 (concerning the composition of the Court), *available at* http://www.sc-sl.org/LinkClick.aspx?fileticket=uClnd1MJeEw%3D&. *See also Report of the Secretary General on the establishment of a Special Court for Sierra Leone* (New York: United Nations, Oct. 4, 2000), UN Doc. S/2000/915, para. 26(c).
83. *See* Perriello and Wierda, *op. cit.*, at 10–11. *See also* Statute of the Special Court, art. 1 ("[t]he Special Court shall . . . have the power to try persons who bear the greatest responsibility for serious violations of international humanitarian law and Sierra Leonean law committed in the territory of Sierra Leone since 30 November 1996 . . .").
84. In Charles Taylor's trial, the defense rested in December 2010, and closing statements were made in March 2011. *See* Stephen Binda, *Special Court Rejects Taylor's Transfer to the U.S.,* LIBERIAN OBSERVER, Dec. 22, 2010 (in War Crimes Prosecution Watch, Vol. 5, Issue 20, Jan. 3, 2011, available at http://www.publicinternationallaw.org/warcrimeswatch/archives/wcpw_vol05issue20.html#sl3).
85. In 2009, RUF commander Issa Hassan Sesay received a 52-year prison sentence, Morris Kallon 40 years, and Augustine Gbao 25 years, all for the commission of war crimes and crimes against humanity. More information on the Kallon and Gbao case can be found on the website of the Special Court for Sierra Leone, at http://www.sc-sl.org/CASES/ProsecutorvsSesayKallonandGbaoRUFCase/tabid/105/Default.aspx.
86. CDF leader Moinina Fofana received a 15-year prison sentence, and Allieu Kondewa received twenty years, both for war crimes and crimes against humanity. *Id. Prosecutor v. Moinina Fofana and Allieu Kondewa,* SCSL-04-14-T, Judgment (Aug. 2, 2007) (Special Court for Sierra Leone, Trial Chamber I).
87. AFRC member Alex Tamba Brima received a 50-year prison sentence, Ibrahim Bazzy Kamara 45 years, and Santagie Borbor Kanu 50 years, all for war crimes and crimes against humanity. *Id. Prosecutor v. Alex Tamba Brima, Brima Brazzy Kamara, and*

Santigie Borbor Kanu, SCSL-04-16-T, Judgment (June 20, 2007) (Special Court for Sierra Leone, Trial Chamber II).
88. See The Seventh Annual Report of the President of the Special Court for Sierra Leone, June 2009 to May 2010 (2010) at 5, *available at* http://www.sc-sl.org/LinkClick.aspx?fileticket=33ryoRsKMjI%3D&tabid=53. The eight men were transported to Mpanga Prison outside of Kigali Rwanda on October 26, 2009.
89. See Perriello and Wierda, *op. cit.*, at 13.
90. *Id.* at 20 ("many Sierra Leoneans view CDF members as war heroes").
91. See *id.* at 16.
92. *Id.* at 18.
93. The June 2007 SCSL convictions against AFRC leaders Alex Tamba Brima, Brima Bazzy Kamara, and Santigie Borbor Kanu "were the first convictions by a UN-backed tribunal for the crime of recruiting and using child soldiers." See Coalition to stop the use of Child Soldiers, "Towards a ban on child soldiers," *available at* http://www.child-soldiers.org/childsoldiers/legal-framework (under "The Special Court for Sierra Leone). In February 2009, the SCSL handed down convictions against RUF leaders Issa Hassan Sesay, Morris Kallon, and August Gbao, "marking the first time a court has convicted on the charge of 'forced marriage.'" See "Sierra Leone: 'Forced Marriage' Conviction a First," IRIN humanitarian news and analysis, Feb. 26, 2009, *available at* http://allafrica.com/stories/200902270910.html.
94. Joseph Sesay is Senior Trial Monitor with the Centre for Accountability and the Rule of Law (CARL). CARL is a Sierra Leonean NGO based in Freetown. See Sesay-Moore electronic correspondence, Nov. 11, 2010, on file with author.
95. Perriello and Wierda, *op. cit.*, at 38.
96. *Id.* at 38.
97. *Id.* at 39. On June 14, 2007, the Sierra Leone Parliament unanimously passed three pieces of legislation, known collectively as the Gender Bills. The Domestic Violence Act made domestic violence a criminal offense. The Registration of Customary Marriages and Divorce Act set the minimum marriageable age at 18. The Devolution of Estates Act made a man's property at his death devolve to his wife and children, rather than his parents and brothers as had been the custom. See "Bold women's rights legislation in Sierra Leone puts women's votes in the spotlight," Media Global, Voice of the Global South, July 6, 2007, *available at* http://www.mediaglobal.org/article/2007-07-06/bold-womens-rights-legislation-in-sierra-leone-puts-womens-votes-in-the-spotlight.
98. See Dougherty, *op. cit.*, at 312 and 320–21.
99. See Dougherty, *op. cit.*, at 320, 328. Dougherty also believes that the Special Court prosecutor may have been shortsighted in his decision to foreclose consideration of any cases against child soldiers aged 15–18 years, although such prosecutions are allowed by the court's statute. See Statute of the SCSL, art. 7 ("Jurisdiction over persons of 15 years of age"). Chief Prosecutor David Crane stated publically, in 2002, that "'[t]he children of Sierra Leone have suffered enough both as victims and as persecutors.'" See Dougherty, *op. cit.*, at 324. Not refuting the tragic exploitation of children in Sierra Leone's civil war, a number of nongovernmental and international organizations have called for narrowly targeted prosecutions of youths for whom there is compelling evidence that they acted voluntarily to direct mass atrocities by other soldiers under their command. To Amnesty International (AI) and others, such cases would have created the opportunity to explore alternative and rehabilitative penalties for child soldiers, including "supervision orders, foster care, correctional, educational and vocational training programs, [and] any programs of disarmament, demobilization and reintegration. . . .."), all of which were allowed under the Special Court's statute). See Dougherty, *op. cit.*, at 323, citing AI, *Sierra Leone: recommendations on the draft statue of the Special Court* (New York: Amnesty

International, Nov. 14, 2000), p. 13. *See also* Statute of the SCSL, art. 7(2), regarding "disposition of a case against a juvenile offender".
100. *See* notes from roundtable discussion with officials of the Special Court's Office of the Registrar, Mar. 14, 2010, from p. 47(a) and (b) of author's field notebook.
101. Perriello and Wierda, *op. cit.* at 40.
102. *See* notes from roundtable discussion with officials of the Special Court's Office of the Registrar, Mar. 14, 2010, from p. 47(a) and (b) of author's field notebook.
103. *Id.* at 47(a).
104. Parliament passed the Truth and Reconciliation Commission Act 2000, Supplement to the Sierra Leone Gazette, Vol. CXXXI, No. 9. *See* Schabas, *op. cit.*, at 1082, n. 3.
105. *See* United States Institute for Peace, "Truth Commission: Sierra Leone," *available at* http://www.usip.org/publications/truth-commission-sierra-leone (accessed Nov. 1, 2010).
106. Volume 1 of the five-volume [Complete] TRC Final Report is available at http://www.sierra-leone.org/Other-Conflict/TRCVolume1.pdf. The relevant material is found in Vol. 1, Chapter 5 on "Methodology and Processes," para. 108, on p. 168 of the pdf file (regarding testimonies) and paras. 196-198, on pp. 184–85 of the pdf file (regarding hearings).
107. Women who had experienced sexual violence in particular were counseled of the option of closed hearings and, though most took advantage of the opportunity, others chose to speak in public hearings. Closed hearings for survivors of sexual violence were held before a women-only panel of commissioners. *See* Vol. 1, Chapter 5 ("Methodology and Processes") of the [Complete] Final Report, *available at* http://www.sierra-leone.org/Other-Conflict/TRCVolume1.pdf. The relevant material is found in para. 197, on p. 184 of the pdf file (re: closed hearings at the district level) and paras. 208–09, on p. 187 of the pdf file (re: procedures and options for victims of sexual violence, including women).
108. *See* "Fambul Tok: Community Healing in Sierra Leone, Our First Year" at 4 (2009, Forum of Conscience and Catalyst for Peace). More information on Fambul Tok is *available at* http://www.fambultok.org/.
109. Musu Swarray, Bunumbu, Kailahun District. *See id.* at 23.
110. *See* TRC Final Report Executive Summary, *op. cit.*, Chapter 1, "Introduction" section, para. 68 (found on p. 15 of the pdf file). Emphasis added.
111. The compatibility of TRC procedures with accountability for wartime offences is further illustrated in this excerpt from the TRC Final Report, which distinguishes between the determination of guilt and the assignment of responsibility: "The standard of proof employed was not that used by criminal courts of law, namely proof beyond a reasonable doubt. The Commission did not make findings on questions of innocence or guilt. It made factual findings in relation to responsibility and accountability. The standard of proof utilised by the Commission was therefore more akin to the preponderance or balance of probabilities." *See* TRC Final Report Executive Summary, *op. cit.*, Chapter 2, "Findings," "Introduction" section, para. 7 (found on p. 21 of the pdf file).
112. John Caulker, Executive Director of Forum of Conscience, and Fambul Tok Program Director. *See* "Fambul Tok: Community Healing in Sierra Leone, Our First Year" at 22 (2009, Forum of Conscience and Catalyst for Peace). More information about Fambul Tok is *available at* http://www.fambultok.org/.
113. Special Court–watchers Perriello and Wierda emphasize that "the scope for conflict [between the Special Court and the TRC] . . . was greatly reduced by the Prosecutor's early commitment that he would not seek information from the TRC." *See* Perriello and Wierda, *op. cit.* at 41.
114. *See* notes from roundtable discussion with officials of the Special Court's Office of the Registrar, Oct. 14, 2010, from p. 47(b) of author's field notebook.

115. *See* notes from author's telephone interview with Joseph Sesay, regarding the compatibility of Special Court and TRC mandates, Oct. 13, 2010, from p. 44(a) of author's field notebook.
116. *See* TRC Final Report Executive Summary, *op. cit.*, Chapter 1, "Introduction" section, para. 69 (found on p. 15 of the pdf file).
117. Despite potential challenges, Perriello and Wierda suggest that this sort of "integrated approach" to transitional justice is the best one. *See* Perriello and Wierda, *op. cit.*, at 43.
118. *See* TRC Final Report Executive Summary, *op. cit.*, Chapter 2, "Primary Findings," paras. 13, 14 and 15 (found on p. 22 of the pdf file).
119. *See* Schabas, *op. cit.*, at 1085.
120. *See* TRC Final Report Executive Summary, *op. cit.*, Chapter 1, "Findings," the subsection, "Primary Findings," paras. 33, 34 and 35 (found on p. 22 of the pdf file).
121. *See* TRC Final Report Executive Summary, *op. cit.*, Chapter 1, "Introduction," paras. 21 and 22 (found on p. 6 of the pdf file).
122. The seventeen categories of TRC Final Report recommendations are: the Protection of Human Rights, Establishing the Rule of Law, the Security Services, Promoting Good Governance, Fighting Corruption, Youth, Women, Children, External Actors, Mineral Resources, the TRC and the Special Court for Sierra Leone, Reparations, Reconciliation, National Vision for Sierra Leone, Archiving of Commission Documentation, Dissemination of the TRC Report, and Follow-Up Committee. *See* TRC Final Report, *op. cit.*, Chapter 2, "Recommendations," the subsection, "Organisation of Recommendations," para. 43 (found on pp. 114–16 of the pdf file).
123. "The Act requires that Government shall faithfully and timeously implement the recommendations of the report that are directed to state bodies and encourage or facilitate the implementation of any recommendations that may be directed to others." TRC Final Report Executive Summary, *op. cit.*, Chapter 2, "Recommendations," para. 5 (found on p. 109 of the pdf file).
124. *See* TRC Final Report Executive Summary, *op. cit.*, Chapter 2, "Recommendations," paras. 54, 61, 92, and 332–33 (found on pp. 117, 118, 124, and 155 of the pdf file).
125. John Caulker, Forward "TRC Report: A Senior Secondary School Version" (2005 TRWG, Sierra Leone).
126. Schabas, *op. cit.* at 1088.
127. *See* TRC Final Report Executive Summary, *op. cit.*, Chapter 2, "Recommendations," paras. 474 and 475 (found on p. 173 of the pdf file).
128. *See* TRC Final Report Executive Summary, *op. cit.*, Chapter 2, "Findings," para. 283 (found on p. 63 of the pdf file).
129. *See* TRC Final Report Executive Summary, *op. cit.*, Chapter 2, "Findings," para. 424, (found on p. 87 of the pdf file).
130. *See id.*
131. *See* TRC Final Report Executive Summary, *op. cit.*, Chapter 2, "Findings," para. 597, (found on p. 107 of the pdf file).
132. *See* TRC Final Report Executive Summary, *op. cit.*, Chapter 2, "Recommendations," para. 484 (found on p. 175 of the pdf file).
133. *See* TRC Final Report Executive Summary, *op. cit.*, Chapter 2, "Recommendations," paras. 486 and 493 (found on p. 175 and 176 of the pdf file).
134. *See* TRC Final Report Executive Summary, *op. cit.*, Chapter 2, "Recommendations," the subsection, "Recommendation Tables/Reparations/Defining Concepts," para. 40 (found on p. 214 of the pdf file), citing José Zalaquet.
135. *See* TRC Final Report Executive Summary, *op. cit.*, Chapter 2, "Recommendations," the subsection, "Recommendation Tables/Reparations/Defining Concepts," para. 45 (found on p. 216 of the pdf file).

Nigerian Nobel Laureate Wole Soyinka also emphasizes the importance of reparations when he calls for "a healing millennial trilogy: Truth, Reparations, and Reconciliation." *See* WOLE SOYINKA, THE BURDEN OF MEMORY, THE MUSE OF FORGIVENESS (Oxford University Press, 1999) at 92.

136. IRIN, "SIERRA LEONE: Civil society criticizes "vague" government plan for post-war reform," July 13, 2005, reprinted in CIVIL SOCIETY OBSERVER (Vol. 2, Issue 4, July–Aug. 2004), a publication of the UN Non-Governmental Liaison Service, *available at* http://www.un-ngls.org/orf/cso/cso9/sierra-leone.htm. (IRIN is the acronym for the Integrated Regional Information Networks, an electronic wire service of the UN Office for the Coordination of Humanitarian Affairs.)

137. *See* The United States Institute for Peace, "Truth Commission: Sierra Leone," *available at* http://www.usip.org/resources/truth-commission-sierra-leone.

138. Issa Davies, "Sierra Leone announces free health care for mothers and children," Apr. 27, 2010, *available at* http://www.unicef.org/childsurvival/sierraleone_53435.html. *See also* Adam Nossiter, "In Sierra Leone, New Hope for Children and Pregnant Women," N.Y. TIMES, July 17, 2011, *available at* http://www.nytimes.com/2011/07/18/world/africa/18sierra.html?_r=1.

139. Sierra Leonean civil society continues to engage with government representatives on the fuller realization of the work of the TRC. In October 2010, a two-day meeting was convened in Freetown for the purpose of assessing progress in implementing TRC recommendations. Participants, including the chairman of the Human Rights Commission of Sierra Leone, stressed the need to prioritize the socioeconomic needs and resources of the women of Sierra Leone, among other unresolved issues. *See* Edward Sam, "TRC Recommendations are pre-requisites for Salone's future of hope—HRCSL boss," *Awoko* [Sierra Leone newspaper], Oct. 13, 2010, *available at* http://www.awoko.org/2010/10/13/%E2%80%9Ctrc-recommendations-are-pre-requisites-for-salones-future-of-hope%E2%80%9D-hrcsl-boss/.

140. Sheku Koroma, of the Sierra Leonean NGO Fambul Tok, describes a continual process of retraumatization that occurs in war-affected communities in which perpetrators and victims reside side-by-side but without acknowledgment of the atrocities that occurred. *See* notes from interview of Sheku Koroma, Program Manager of Fambul Talk, Freetown, Sierra Leone, Oct. 15, 2010, from p. 49(b) of author's field notebook.

141. Satie Banyah, Youth Leader in Kailahun District. This quote comes from the first annual report of Fambul Tok, a grassroots reconciliation program founded and implemented by the Sierra Leonean NGO Forum of Conscience, and the US NGO Catalyst for Peace. *See* "Fambul Tok: Community Healing in Sierra Leone, Our First Year" at 7 (2009, Forum of Conscience and Catalyst for Peace). More information at Fambul Tok is *available at* http://www.fambultok.org/.

142. *See id.* at 4. John Caulker, the Chairman of the TRC Working Group and Executive Director of the Sierra Leonean NGO Forum of Conscience, conceived Fambul Tok as a mechanism to bring grassroots reconciliation to villages throughout rural Sierra Leone. *Id.* at 2. He founded Fambul Tok in 2007 in partnership with Libby Hoffman, president of Catalyst for Peace, a US NGO based in Portland, Maine. *Id.* at 4.

143. *See* notes from interview of Sheku Koroma, Program Manager of Fambul Talk, Freetown, Sierra Leone, Oct. 15, 2010, from p. 49(b) of author's field notebook. *See also* "Fambul Tok: Community Healing in Sierra Leone, Our First Year," *op. cit.*, at 15.

144. *Id.*

145. *See* notes from interview of Sheku Koroma, Program Manager of Fambul Talk, Freetown, Sierra Leone, Oct. 15, 2010, from p. 49(b) of author's field notebook. *See also* "Fambul Tok: Community Healing in Sierra Leone, Our First Year," *op. cit.*, at 27.

146. *See* "Fambul Tok International: Community Healing in Sierra Leone and the World, Our Second Year" (2010, Fambul Tok International) at 18, *available at* FambulTok.org.

147. *Id.* at 16.
148. *See* notes from briefing with CD-Peace staff, including Francis Massaquoi, Financial Officer, Moses Lahai, Program Director, George Korlia, Agricultural Coordinator, Agnes Jattu Carew-Bah, Gender Coordinator, and Mark Fornah, Literacy Coordinator, Mayagba, Bombali Province, Sierra Leone, Oct. 10, 2010, from pp. 38(b)–39(b) of author's field notebook. CD-Peace Executive Director Dr. Thomas Turay participated in the meeting by mobile telephone. *See also,* CD-Peace website, http://www.cdpeace.org/.
149. *See* notes from briefing with CD-Peace staff, *supra,* from pp. 39(b)–40(b) of author's field notebook.
150. *See id.,* from pp. 41(a)–41(b) of author's field notebook.

CHAPTER 9
After Arusha in Burundi
Disarming the Heart to Disarm the Body[1]

Umwami agirwa n'abashingantahe.

The king does not exist without the wise men's council.

Burundian proverb[2]

The culture of *ubushingantahe* offers an opportunity to create a situation where women are complementary to men at home as spouses and equal to men in the workplace as colleagues. Teaching these traditional values, but in a version that recognizes the equality of all, is the best path that I know to bring Burundi to a state in which peace can last. On these virtues, Burundians can build justice as well as peace and turn from the easy resort to the machete.

Agnes Nindorera[3]

The Republic of Burundi,[4] whose capital Bujumbura sits on the shores of Lake Tanganika in Central Africa, won its independence from Belgium on July 1, 1962.[5] For the next thirty years, Burundians were ruled by a series of military dictators. On October 21, 1993, Melchior Ndadaye, the nation's first democratically elected president, was assassinated. The ensuing twelve years were marked by civil war battles and massacres in which some three-hundred thousand Burundians of all ethnicities lost their lives.[6] In 2000, the Arusha Peace and Reconciliation Agreement (Arusha Agreement or Arusha Accord)[7] was signed by the Government of Burundi and numerous political and militant groups. However, the last major rebel movement did not sign a ceasefire agreement until 2005, and only registered as a political party in 2009.

Whereas in Rwanda, upwards of half a million civilians were murdered throughout the country in ten weeks during the summer of 1994, in Burundi, perhaps a third of a million people died in more localized, recurring tragedies spread out over more than ten years. While in Rwanda most victims were Tutsis as well as moderate Hutus, in Burundi, people of Tutsi,

Hutu, and also Twa ethnicity died in significant numbers. All Rwandans speak Kinyarwanda as their national language, and its close linguistic cousin Kirundi is the mother tongue of all Burundians. Yet, while the 1994 Rwandan Genocide is marked annually with official commemorations, in Burundi, the civil war deaths are discussed much more tentatively.

Some Burundians even suggest it is taboo to speak of the many ordinary people who lost their lives during the war, let alone of genocide or crimes against humanity.[8] Yet despite the degree of violence that has occurred in Burundi in the name of ethnicity, or perhaps because of it, the yearning for pluralism is palpable among Burundians today. Indeed, one of the most important outcomes sought in Burundi's post-conflict transition is the creation of a political process that transcends ethnicity.[9]

A. ETHNICITY, VIOLENCE, AND TRANSCENDENCE: AN INTRODUCTION TO THE HISTORY, CULTURE, AND POLITICS OF BURUNDI

Deogratias Niyizonkiza (Deo) is the Burundian doctor whose story is told in Tracy Kidder's memoir of Burundi, *Strength in What Remains: A Journey of Remembrance and Forgiveness*.[10] In October of 1993, Deo was working as a medical intern in a rural hospital staffed and visited by Hutus and Tutsis in the northern Burundian town of Mutaho. On October 22, he narrowly survived an attack by Hutu militants, mounted the day after President Ndadaye's assassination.[11] Fleeing the massacre at Mutaho, Deo made his way on foot across the Burundian countryside and into Rwanda, where he spent a short period of time in the informal Burundian refugee camps cobbled together near the border.[12] Several months later, he fled back into Burundi, soon after the April 1994 double assassination of recently installed President Ntyamira of Burundi and Rwandan President Habyarimana, who were traveling on the same airplane. At the time that Deogratias fled back into Burundi, rumors of mass killings of Tutsi in Rwanda were becoming widespread.[13]

Deo later secured a tourist visa and flew via Entebbe, Cairo, and Moscow, then to New York City, where he lived on the street and worked in the underground economy for several years.[14] With the support of friends from several countries, Deo completed his undergraduate degree in philosophy at Columbia University, received a medical degree from Dartmouth College, and applied for and received asylum in the United States. He returns to Burundi regularly, working to improve the provision of health care in his native country.[15] In 2006, thirteen years after the massacre at Mutaho, Deo returned to his home town of Butanza. He explained to his friend and traveling companion, Tracy Kidder, that in Burundi, "people don't talk about people who died. By their names, anyway. They call it *gusimbura* . . . It's a bad word. You are reminding people . . ." of something "they try to forget."[16]

Deogratias was nearly a teenager in the early 1980s when he first heard the terms *Hutu* and *Tutsi* at school. When he asked to which group his family belonged, his father reluctantly told him they were Tutsi. His grandfather, on the other hand, chastised Deo for referring to a man with many cows as a "great Tutsi," insisting that such language revealed prejudice, and demanded to know, "[w]ho is teaching you this?"[17] In October of 1993, when the young doctor Deogratias fled the massacre at Mutaho, he was aware that the killings in Burundi had an ethnic aspect, as he would later realize that nearly half a million Rwandans were killed in mid-1994 because they were believed to be Tutsis or Hutus who sympathized with Tutsis. In this climate of ethnicized fear and violence, Deo had a transformative experience, in late 1993, as he crept across the Burundian countryside.

Approaching the Rwandan border, Deogratias came upon a procession of fleeing Burundians, all women and children, and apparently Hutu. A middle-aged woman in the line of refugees called out to him, and reassured him even as he reacted in panic and pleaded with her not to kill him, not to torture him. She kept insisting that she wished to help him, until they reached the river crossing into Rwanda, and the Rwandans at the border, armed with guns and knives, mocked and terrorized Deo for having a nose "too thin for a Hutu." Each time he was threatened, she protested that Deo was her son, until finally the armed men allowed them to cross the river together.[18] At one point in their journey together, Deo's palpable fear of the woman prompted her to confront the issue of their different ethnicities. Exposing his assumption that she was a Hutu, she confessed that she was, adding "[b]ut I'm a woman and I'm a mother." Those characteristics, she told Deo, reflected her true *ubokwo*, or ethnicity.[19]

An ongoing theme in this chapter is the meaning of ethnicity. For a country that has experienced, over many decades, successive waves of violence between members of the two largest *communautées ethniques*, a rethinking of ethnicity has particular urgency. Since their nation's independence, deeply entrenched fears, and the countless friends and relatives they have seen killed, have encouraged some Burundians to believe that the only political and military leaders who could protect them were those of their own *communautée*.[20] Yet, at the same time, many Burundians, particularly the young who now make up the great majority of the population,[21] long for a healthier society in which there is equal and ample access to education, employment, and social services, including basic medical care. These members of Burundian civil society are committed to transforming their political culture into one marked by panethnic collaboration rather than inter-ethnic strife.

B. SIMILARITIES AND DIFFERENCES BETWEEN BURUNDI AND ITS NEIGHBOR TO THE NORTH

1. Rwanda-Urundi—Historical Commonalities

Since precolonial times, Burundi and Rwanda have been distinguished from most of their African neighbors because they are united by one language. All Burundians speak Kirundi and all Rwandans speak Kinyarwanda. In linguistic terms, Kirundi and Kinyarwanda are mutually intelligible dialects of the Rwanda-Rundi language.[22]

Like Rwanda, Burundi was colonized only briefly by Germany, which lost its African holdings in military defeat at the close of World War I.[23] Belgium then inherited and administered both Central African colonies from the 1920s through their independence struggles in the 1960s.[24] During the colonial period in both Burundi and Rwanda, various African and European languages were utilized by local administrators, including German, Kiswahili, French, Dutch, Lingala, Kinyarwanda, and Kirundi; and French was taught in secondary schools, alongside Latin and Greek.[25] Upon independence in 1962, Kinyarwanda and Kirundi were formally designated the national languages of the two respective countries. French continues to be spoken by elites in both countries, particularly in Burundi, where it is frequently the language of postsecondary education, and is utilized alongside Kirundi in public administrative settings.[26]

Like their Rwandan neighbors, today, most Burundians are considered members of one of three *communautées ethniques*,[27] Hutus constituting an approximately 85 percent majority, Tutsis the largest minority at around 15 percent, and the indigenous Twa constituting less than one percent.[28] Also similar to Rwanda, Burundian Hutus and Tutsis have intermarried extensively over many generations, facilitated by their common language and the widespread Roman Catholic faith. Finally, as in Rwanda, a Tutsi-dominated aristocracy, under a succession of kings, ruled Burundian territory from the seventeenth to the nineteenth centuries, providing a convenient framework on which the Europeans grafted their colonial governments. Up until independence in 1962, Tutsi elites in both Burundi and Rwanda were favored by the German and then Belgian governors as local administrators, under the model of indirect rule utilized by the European powers in Africa and elsewhere around the globe.

This chapter explores and questions the very notion of *ethnicity* with reference to its common usage in Burundi and Rwanda in order to contribute to a broader understanding of this basic and illusive facet of human identity. Ethnicity comes from the Greek *ethnos*, meaning nation, people, or culture.[29] Benedict Anderson wrote that nations were "imagined communities,"[30] as some scholars and social activists argue that race is socially constructed. But ethnicity may be a less ideologically loaded term than race, given that ethnicity is linked to other culturally descriptive aspects of group identity including common language, religion, and national origin. Nevertheless, ethnicity is often a code word for race, and the two terms share a vulnerability to chauvinistic ideology and violent conduct. At the same time, like linguistic groups and extended family networks, ethnic communities are dynamic, interactive with other communities, and heavily mediated by clan, caste, and social class.[31]

Whether Tutsi and Hutu are predominantly racial, ethnic, or social classifications is a fascinating question. The terms are derived from the names of two originally distinct peoples said to have migrated into Central Africa by the tenth and fifteenth centuries CE, respectively. The Hutu are thought to have arrived first from the area of modern-day Chad, and the Tutsi subsequently from somewhere around southern Ethiopia,[32] although anthropologist Liisa Malkki cautions that the history of the region's settlement "must remain largely hypothetical due to paucity of reliable evidence."[33] In the early centuries after their arrival on the territory of modern Burundi and Rwanda, most Hutu adopted a sedentary agricultural lifestyle, whereas many Tutsi maintained their pastoral way of life. A social hierarchy evolved with Tutsi cattle owners tending to dominate. Nonetheless, there was fluidity among the groups and, in fact, Hutu could become Tutsi if they amassed sufficient livestock, and the reverse could occur if former Tutsi lost their herds and the social prestige and economic power that this entailed.[34] As Kidder explains:

> People who mainly herded cattle were called Tutsis, and "Hutu" had come to designate people who mainly farmed the land. There were many exceptions, and it wasn't as if "Hutu" and "Tutsi" described genetic predispositions for plants and cows, but very broadly speaking the aristocracy was drawn from the population of cow-owning Tutsis, and their inferiors or dependents were predominantly Hutu farmers.[35]

By the seventeenth and eighteenth centuries, the Burundian and Rwandan monarchies had become well established, and the class system that privileged Tutsi clans over Hutu clans became more engrained. In Burundi, as in Rwanda, most Hutu had come to constitute the peasant class, occupying and farming the land of Tutsi aristocrats under a quasifeudal system of patronage and servitude facilitated by the exchange of cattle.[36] Thus, throughout the precolonial period, Hutu and Tutsi remained predominantly caste or occupational categories, rather than denoting distinct groups of common descent.[37]

Only in the late nineteenth and early twentieth centuries did the German and Belgian colonizers embrace and reify *Tutsism* and *Hutuism*, establishing Hutu and Tutsi as increasingly ironclad demographic categories, under an ideology of Tutsi racial supremacy and Hutu racial inferiority.[38] As Kidder interprets the role of the colonial governors in entrenching ethnic identity:

> [t]he Europeans added poison to [the] terminology.... the distinction between Tutsi lords and subject Hutus had been conceived as an indigenous difference, a difference that existed among a single people, among relatives, as it were. The Europeans made the distinction into something it had never been, into a racial difference.[39]

Kidder also draws on the writings of Pierre Ryckmans, one of Burundi's Belgian administrators, to illustrate the racist ideology of the colonial period. Ryckmans expounded in 1931 that:

> [t]he Batutsi were destined to rule; their mere demeanor lends them considerable prestige over the inferior races that surround them.... There is nothing surprising about the fact that the less shrewd, simpler, more spontaneous, and more confiding Bahutu braves let themselves be enslaved.[40]

In addition to the racial terminology and racist attitudes developed and utilized most elaborately by the Belgian colonial masters to describe the local people of Rwanda and Burundi, these concepts had stark, at times brutal, social applications. It mattered deeply at the level of everyday life whether one was called a Tutsi or a Hutu throughout Belgian-controlled Central Africa. Being Tutsi in both colonies opened the door to more opportunities for government service, but also more social mobility, and better access to medical care and secondary and postsecondary education. Being Hutu meant social exclusion and political disadvantage, but also less schooling, worse sickness, and more abject poverty.

Moreover, several decades prior to independence, being labeled Hutu or Tutsi became less a matter of whim on the part of a colonial administrator or a fellow Burundian or Rwandan, and more bureaucratized. Beginning with a census completed in the 1930s, Burundians and Rwandans carried identity cards that specified their ethnicity. As Kidder explains, "[m]ore than ever before, one's chances depended on whether the card read Hutu or Tutsi."[41]

The twentieth century racialization of Tutsi and Hutu identity and the accompanying social and political stratification was a process that occurred during the Burundian and Rwandan colonial and postcolonial periods. Nevertheless, Burundi came to differ from its northern neighbor in several important respects regarding specific attributes of ethnic identity, as social and political interactions within and between Burundi's two principal ethnic communities took on their own complexities.

2. More than "the Other Rwanda"[42]—Burundi's Distinct History and Sociology

Ethnic Dynamism in Burundi

Despite its shared heritage with Rwanda, Burundi has several unique historical and social attributes that are of vital importance in understanding the nature of its civil war, and in thinking about post-conflict reconstruction and reconciliation for its people. To begin with, prior to and after Burundian independence, members of the Tutsi community dominated the government and the army for over thirty years, whereas Hutus were to dominate both sectors in Rwanda from independence in 1962 until after the 1994 Rwandan Genocide.[43] Moreover, whereas in Rwanda, since precolonial times, the chief economic and political divisions have been explained by reference to Tutsi or Hutu identity, in Burundi, class and caste differentiations were and remain more nuanced and dynamic.

According to Burundian human rights scholar Agnes Nindorera, Burundian society into the late nineteenth century was characterized by four *ubokwo*, or categories: the Bahutu, the Batutsi, the Batwa, and the Baganwa.[44] With the important exception of the Twa, members of the various ethnic groups could serve as members of local governing councils of *abashingantahe*, men of integrity trained in community dispute resolution.[45] As explained by humanitarian law scholar Peter Uvin, even though Tutsi people dominated the political and economic spheres in precolonial and colonial Burundi, there were typically Hutu as well as Tutsi administrators among the Baganwa or princely class in the court of the Burundian *Mwami* or king, and the Mwami himself was regarded to be neither Tutsi nor Hutu, but the very embodiment of the Burundian people.[46]

Moreover, the Tutsi social structure in precolonial Burundi was itself differentiated and hierarchical, with various caste-like divisions, some rationalized by clan membership. First, there were the Tutsis who served in the royal court or *Ganwa*, composed of a smaller number of Hutus as well, from which the next *Mwami* would be selected."[47] Ranked below the *Ganwa* were the Tutsi-Banyaruguru, who comprised the Tutsi aristocracy, and then the Tutsi-Hima, who were the nonaristocratic or ordinary pastoralists.[48]

Tutsi-Hima Military Dominance and the 1972 "Selective Genocide"

Similar to the Ugandan Army from the first Obote presidency,[49] beginning in the 1960s the Burundian Army created possibilities for social mobility for members of certain groups within Burundian society. In Uganda, it was primarily young men from the northern and western tribes who attained higher social standing through military service; in Burundi, the armed forces came to be dominated by men from a less elite sector of the overall more privileged Tutsi community. This phenomenon was in marked contrast to the corresponding experience in Rwanda from the 1960s through the 1990s, where Hutu leaders steadily dominated both the political and military realms.[50]

In postindependence Burundi, the army became an important pathway to enhanced political power for a select group of Tutsi-Hima leaders from Bururi province: Michel Micombero, Jean-Baptiste Bagaza, and Pierre Buyoya, each of whom served as President of Burundi, and whose collective rule, from 1966 to 1993, Uvin characterizes as "a low-caste Tutsi dictatorship."[51]

In the first ten years of Burundi's independence, three Hutu uprisings in Burundi led to reprisal massacres in which thousands of Hutus were murdered. The first armed repression was led by then-Captain Micombero in 1965, and the other two occurred in 1968 and 1969, carried out by the Burundian armed forces under the presidency of Micombero.[52] As Malkki interprets the unfolding events, "[t]hese years in some sense provided a precedent for the most massive, large-scale killings in Burundi's history, the massacres beginning in April 1972."[53]

The so-called selective genocide of 1972 was also predicated by a Hutu uprising on April 29 of that year, although the historian Warren Weinstein writes that Burundian security forces had already mounted a surveillance operation over Hutu refugees in Tanzania in March, and established roadblocks throughout much of the country.[54] The immediate catalyst for the violence that ensued appears to have been the return to Burundi of the former King Ntare V, deposed in 1966, and his assassination in Gitega on April 29. Following his execution, Hutu rebel attacks on Burundian Army installations were followed by government reprisals, which began on April 30 and continued over a six-month period.[55] The killings abated for a time, and then there was a second outbreak of violence in 1973, after incursions into Burundi by Hutu militants. All told, 100,000 Hutu fled Burundi in 1972 and 1973, and between 150,000 and 250,000 were killed. Several thousand Tutsi also lost their lives.[56]

Reviewing first-hand accounts of the 1972 massacres, Malkki concludes that, in the weeks after the King's assassination and the Hutu rebel attacks, "it started to appear to many observers that the so-called reprisals for the Hutu uprising had become systematic, genocidal killing."[57] One such observer, then United States Ambassador to Burundi Thomas Melady, recalls that his report to the US State Department on May 10, "indicated for the first time that the embassy felt the period of civil strife was clearly past and the actions now were approaching selective genocide. This opinion was shared by most diplomats."[58]

The phrase *selective genocide* was adopted by political scientist René Lemarchand and journalist David Martin to reflect the disproportionate number of "educated or semi-educated" Burundian Hutus who were murdered in 1972.[59] But Lemarchand and Martin, writing close to the time of the 1972 genocide, went further to link the eradication of the Hutu intelligencia with the establishment of an apartheid-like system in which the remainder of Hutu society "is now systematically excluded from the army, the civil service, the university and secondary schools. . . . Hutu status has become synonymous with an inferior category of beings; only Tutsi are fit to rule. . . ."[60]

"Historical inevitability is a fiction," Tracy Kidder writes in his memoir of Burundi. "But it is hard to read about the colonial past of Rwanda and Burundi and not imagine that it sealed the future."[61] Kidder was speaking of the advent of ethnicity-specific identity cards in Rwanda-Urundi in the 1930s, and the bureaucratized calcification of Tutsi and Hutu identity by the region's Belgian governors. Building on this legacy of racist ideology and colonial oppression is Burundi's more recent experience of ethnic separation and exclusion, syncopated and reinforced by waves of violence and counterviolence. In the face of this searing historical reality, we are humbled by the halting but relentless efforts of Burundians to reconstruct a different kind of society, transethnic and democratic.

Majority Rule in 1993 and the Launching of the Civil War

After twenty years of military rule, President Buyoya, the third Tutsi-Hima Burundian head of state, took modest steps to pluralize Burundian politics and government. In the short term, Buyoya's presidency helped spark the civil war in 1993 but, in the long term, his policies strengthen the call for greater ethnic pluralism in Burundi today. In the late 1980s, President Buyoya created new roles for Hutus in the central government. Although the army, police, and most key ministries remained under Tutsi leadership, Buyoya created a National Commission to Study the Question of National Unity, with twelve Hutu and twelve Tutsi members, and he appointed a Hutu as Prime Minister.[62]

Facilitated by Buyoya's reforms, democratic presidential elections were held for the first time in 1993, resulting in the defeat of Buyoya and the election of Melchior Ndadaye, the first Hutu president of Burundi, with 65 percent of the popular vote to Buyoya's 32 percent. Buyoya had run under the banner of la Union pour le Progrès National (UPRONA), or the Union for National Progress, Burundi's first political party. UPRONA, a party with proud biethnic roots stretching back to the 1950s, had subsequently become Tutsi-dominated.[63] The victor Ndadaye ran on the ticket of le Front pour La Démocratie au Burundi (FRODEBU), or the Burundian Democratic Front. FRODEBU, founded in 1990, was nominally interethnic but Hutu-dominated.[64]

President Ndadaye was assassinated after barely three months in office, along with the president and vice president of the National Assembly, the next two in the line of succession to serve as head of state.[65] A study by an international commission of inquiry, led by Human Rights Watch, concluded, in July of 1994, that "important officers of the Burundian army, including the chief of staff," orchestrated the murders.[66] Although the attempted *coup d'etat* was unsuccessful, the assassinations set into motion mass killings of Tutsis who were blamed for the killing of the president, and retaliatory mass killings of Hutus by the Burundian Army.[67]

The extent to which the killings of Tutsis in the aftermath of Ndadaye's assassination were spontaneous or planned is contested. Some investigators emphasize the role of FRODEBU cadres in organizing the attacks.[68] Others stress the upwelling of popular anger at the killing of a president who, finally, represented the Hutu majority.[69] The Human Rights Watch-led investigative commission concluded that a significant number of local government officials participated in or incited the summary executions of Tutsis.[70]

In Rwanda, the genocide of Tutsis and moderate Hutus was orchestrated by extremist Hutus in the Rwandan armed forces, irregular troops, and Interahamwe militia members;[71] and the killings were concentrated in a three-month period in mid-1994. In contrast, the Burundian civil war involved cyclical massacres by Hutu and Tutsi militants alike over more than a decade, in a continually reigniting conflagration in which "no side managed to acquire the upper hand."[72]

The Arusha Peace Accords: From Rebel Insurgencies to Political Parties

Another distinction between the Rwandan Genocide and Burundi's civil war concerns the organization of the violence and the role of formally constituted insurgent movements in the two conflicts. In Rwanda, the genocide was asymmetric, and carried out by soldiers, government-affiliated militia, including Interahamwe, and other armed groups of civilians, who targeted and killed ordinary Tutsis and their perceived Hutu sympathizers. Only after upwards of half a million Rwandans had been massacred was the Rwandese Patriotic Front (RPF), the central expression of Tutsi militancy against the Hutu nationalist-dominated Rwandan state,[73] able to invade the country from its base in Uganda. At that point, the RPF chased Interahamwe killers and former Rwandan armed forces—as well as many Hutu people who had not taken part in the bloodshed—westward and into the former Zaire. The RPF took the reins of government in Kigali within a matter of weeks, and more gradually transformed itself into the Rwandese Patriotic Forces, now the Rwandan Army.[74]

In Burundi, in contrast, the armed conflict was characterized by significant targeted attacks and massacres of Hutus as well as Tutsis. Moreover, two major rebel insurgencies engaged the Burundian Army[75] and its allied militias throughout the 1993 to 2005 period. Both movements were Hutu ultranationalist in character, and one had a formally constituted political wing by 2000, when the peace process began to bear fruit with the signing of the Arusha Peace and Reconciliation Agreement.[76] The parties to this accord were the Government of Burundi and various minor rebel insurgencies, although neither of the two larger armed movements signed until 2003 and 2008, respectively.[77]

The first rebel movement founded in postindependence Burundi was the Front National de Libération (FNL),[78] or National Liberation Front. The FNL constituted the armed wing of the Parti pour la Libération du Peuple Hutu (PALIPEHUTU), or the Party for the Liberation of the Hutu People. PALIPEHUTU is said to have been founded in the Burundian refugee camps in Tanzania, in 1972.[79] Burundi's second rebel movement was the Conseil National pour la Défense de la Démocratie (CNDD), or the National Council for the Defense of Democracy. CNDD was founded by Léonard Nyangoma in 1994. Nyangoma had previously served as Interior Minister during the short-lived FRODEBU government of President Ndadaye, assassinated in 1993.[80] Both rebel movements participated in the Arusha peace process, but the FNL dropped out for a time, and finally only one faction of CNDD was eligible to participate in the 2005 elections, having signed a security-related protocol to the Arusha Agreement. The elections were organized under Burundi's new constitution, approved by referendum on February 28, 2005.[81]

The FNL has been slower to disarm, signing a ceasefire agreement in 2005 and a security agreement with the new CNDD-led government in September of 2006,[82] only to pull out of peace talks in 2007.[83] Step by step, the FNL has moved back from the brink, returning to the negotiating table in May of 2008, agreeing to disarm and demobilize its combatants on December 4, 2008, and, in January of 2009, changing its official name from PALIPEHUTU-FNL to *FNL*, a precondition to its registration as a political party on May 31, 2009.[84] In its Annual Report for 2009, the International Committee of the Red Cross (ICRC) emphasizes the political import of this change in nomenclature:

> In January, the Forces nationals de libération (FNL) dropped the "Parti pour la libération du peuple Hutu" ("Palipehutu") prefix to its name, paving the way for a revival of the previously stalled peace process with the government of Burundi. Subsequent negotiations led to an agreement on the disarmament, demobilization and reintegration (DDR) of 18,500 FNL members, the allocation of government posts to the FNL, the release of FNL detainees, and the recognition of the FNL as a political party. By year-end, implementation of the agreement had neared completion.[85]

The Arusha peace process was facilitated by a new African peacekeeping model, characterized by regional and international components. Beginning in 2003, the first peacekeeping force of the newly constituted African Union (AU) was dispatched to Burundi to monitor compliance with the Arusha Agreement. This contingent was absorbed into a broader United Nations peacekeeping force in 2004. That UN program then transitioned into a peace-building office in 2006, as it became clear that the Burundian civil war was winding down, and the work of post-conflict reconstruction needed to begin in earnest.[86]

Uvin attributes the relative success of the Arusha peace process to two main factors: First, "most people were sick of an unwinnable war."[87] Second, the high command of the new Forces de Défense Nationale (FDN), or National Defense Forces, was created through the explicit integration of officers from the former Burundian army, the Forces Armées Burundaises (FAB), and officers from one faction of the CNDD, in a 60/40 percentage allocation.[88]

By 2005, CNDD had split into CNDD-Nyangoma and CNDD-FDD, the latter associated with the Forces for the Defense of Democracy (FDD).[89] CNDD-Nyangoma was named for Léonard Nyangoma, the original founder of CNDD, who split off from the party he founded to run for president on his own ticket in 2005. Nyangoma was defeated by Pierre Nkurunziza, the standard bearer for CNDD-FDD, and the former leader of the FDD, the armed insurgent group itself.[90] Nkurunziza won by a landslide, and his party secured twice as many seats in the National Assembly as FRODEBU, the party of the first Hutu president of Burundi, Melchior Ndadaye, elected and assassinated in 1993, twelve years before.[91] Likewise, CNDD-FDD legislators outnumbered four-to-one those of UPRONA, the party which had led Burundi for nearly forty of its forty-three years since independence in 1962.[92] Given Nkurunziza's uncontested reelection as President of Burundi in June 2010, in a campaign marred by charges of strong-arm tactics by the ruling party after its decisive showing in communal and parliamentary elections that same year, CNDD-FDD remains by far the most powerful political party in Burundi.[93]

Ethnic Pluralism after Ethnic Violence

There is a final important respect in which Burundi's historical and social development has been quite distinct from that of Rwanda. This difference relates to the predominant political cultures and the prevailing narratives concerning violence and ethnicity in the two countries in the aftermath of the Rwandan genocide and the Burundian civil war. It is significant that Rwandan leaders, avoiding ethnic labels, speak publically and often about the 1994 genocide. Burundians, on the other hand, have only begun to talk publically about their civil war, the profound loss of life, and the need for national memorials for the victims of the intercommunal violence that occurred throughout the conflict.[94] Nevertheless, their reticence in discussing civil war atrocities does not signify that Burundians are unable to talk about ethnic identity. In fact, Burundians may be freer to do so than their Rwandan neighbors.

In contemporary Rwanda, talk of Hutu and Tutsi is discouraged, and indeed President Paul Kagame's government promotes a policy of reconciliation and pan-Rwandan identity.[95] Although the Rwandan government is widely regarded as Tutsi-dominated, and some believe that the avoidance of ethnic labels hides entrenched Tutsi favoritism throughout the organs of government, such criticism may lead to a charge of "divisionism" or even "genocide ideology."[96] In fact, Rwandans wanting to allude to Hutu or Tutsi affiliation increasingly speak of "linguistic lines" rather than "ethnic groups."[97] The term "English-speakers" generally denotes Tutsis, whereas "French-speakers" is frequently a reference to Hutus, for a variety of historical and geographic reasons that are important to touch upon a bit more deeply.

The anglophone characterization of Rwandan Tutsis derives from the several decades in which large numbers of Rwandan, mostly Tutsi-identified, refugees resided in English-speaking countries. Thousands of Rwandans fleeing the 1959 to 1960 anti-Tutsi pogroms sought refuge in Uganda and to a lesser extent in Tanzania, both Anglophone countries, in addition to those who sought refuge in francophone Zaire, now the Democratic Republic of the Congo (DRC). Importantly, the Rwandese Patriotic Front, the central expression of militant resistance to the Hutu-dominated government in Rwanda from 1987 to 1994, was founded and based in English-speaking Uganda.[98] RPF leader Paul Kagame was born in Uganda to Rwandan refugee parents. Under Kagame's direction, the RPF invaded Rwanda from Uganda in the waning days of the genocide in 1994 and drove the soldiers and Interahamwe militia members implicated in the killings, as well as many Hutu civilians, west into the former Zaire, before taking the reins of government.[99] The RPF eventually converted itself into the new Rwandese Armed Forces, which came to number upwards of forty thousand troops, including several thousand former officers and enlisted soldiers who had served in the Rwandan Armed Forces under former President Habyarimana.[100]

The common use of "francophone" to refer to members of the Rwandan Hutu community, on the other hand, derives from the fact that Hutus dominated the Rwandan government, army, and Interahamwe militias from independence until 1994, during which period French was the language of government in Rwanda. When Kagame's RPF invaded Rwanda from Uganda, in 1994, hundreds of thousands of Hutus fled into francophone former Zaire (now the DRC), as well as francophone Burundi, anglophone Tanzania, and other neighboring countries. Although many of these refugees have since returned to Rwanda,[101] the maintenance of a Hutu-affiliated exile group in the DRC helps reinforce the prevailing francophone identity of the Rwandan Hutu community.

Unlike in Rwanda, it is acceptable to refer to ethnic affiliation in Burundi's political arena today. Indeed, identification as Hutu or Tutsi could not be unlawful, given that the government has a formally pluralistic structure, mandated by law.[102] In addition to the 60/40 percentage allocation between Hutu and Tutsi members of the National Assembly set forth in the 2005 Burundian Constitution,[103] both the Constitution and Protocol II to the Arusha Agreement specify that the presidency itself must have ethnic balance.[104]

Burundi's constitutionally prescribed ethnic balance is illustrated by the aftermath of the 2010 presidential election, in which Pierre Nkurunziza of CNDD-FDD ran unopposed and was decisively elected. Because Nkurunziza is a Hutu, and CNDD-FDD has Hutu-nationalist roots, the first vice president, Thérence Sinunguruza, a Tutsi, was selected from among the ranks of UPRONA, Burundi's biethnic but Tutsi-dominant ruling party for much of the period from independence through 2003. The second vice president, Gervais Rufyikiri, a Hutu, was then selected from CNDD-FDD.[105] Although Burundian political parties must be open to Burundians of all ethnicities,[106] their historical ethnic affiliations are also acknowledged.

Despite the fact that ethnic identity remains an explicit component of Burundi's current political culture, some Burundians regard the ethnic quota system as a double-edged sword.[107] In 2011, 18 years after the civil war began, popular and official attitudes toward ethnicity in Burundi continue to evolve. Increasingly, contemporary Burundian social and political activists regard ethnocentric identity as a trap, a vehicle for violence, or, at the very least, a fierce impediment to grassroots democracy and social progress in their country.[108] Others stress the importance of intercommunal dialogue in overcoming the deep-seated fears still engendered by ethnic differences in Burundi today.[109]

C. DURABLE PEACE FOR BURUNDI–MEMORIALS, ELECTIONS, DISARMAMENT, AND EMPLOYMENT

Chapter 7 on post-conflict reconstruction in Uganda introduced the three-legged stool of transitional justice—individual accountability through criminal trials, social development emphasizing education and employment, and community reconciliation through truth-telling and reparations—i.e., criminal, social, and historical justice. Burundi is exploring all three, although in a manner which would seem to prioritize social and historical justice over criminal justice, in particular the need to incorporate youth into productive economic activities and the desire to memorialize all victims of the civil war. Moreover, Burundian civil society has made a conscious choice to confront two powerful impediments to historical and restorative justice, namely, the ethnic polarization of electoral politics and the prevalence of small arms among the civilian population.

Several years ago, the Burundian civil society organization Centre d'Alerte et Prévention de Conflits, or Conflict Alert and Prevention Center (CENAP), set about organizing focus groups of Burundians around the country to talk about the civil war and how Burundians could best move forward to establish conditions for durable peace in their country.[110] In a series of meetings involving civil, military and religious leaders, youth, women, entrepreneurs, and labor organizations, CENAP identified four Burundian problems that called out for resolution in the aftermath of the civil war: (1) the failure to acknowledge, memorialize, or punish those responsible for the many thousands of civilians of all ethnicities massacred during the civil war; (2) the resurgence of ethnically-charged electoral politics; (3) the widespread illegal possession of small arms by individuals and families; and (4) the extreme levels of unemployment and underemployment among the youth population.[111]

After identifying truth-telling, clean elections, disarmament, and higher employment as the four priorities for durable peace in Burundi, CENAP organized a national meeting in Bujumbura from March 23–25 of 2010. The conference was entitled "Paix durable au Burundi: Quelle solution?"("Durable Peace in Burundi: What Solution?"). CENAP invited over two hundred individuals and representatives of various organizations to identify, discuss, and debate the best policies and programs to make progress on the four identified fronts.[112]

1. Memorializing the Dead

Burundians are beginning to confront, especially in public settings, the searing reality that hundreds of thousands of their fellow countrymen and women have died since 1993 on account of their socially constructed ethnicities. Emblematic of the emotional intensity of speaking collectively about the past is the tenor of discussions on the establishment of public memorials to the victims of civil war massacres. At CENAP's March 2010 peace conference in Bujumbura, much of the discussion regarding transitional justice was devoted to the importance of "speaking the truth about what happened." In particular, participants debated whether individual monuments should be dedicated to Hutu victims, Tutsi victims, or Burundian victims overall. There was a palpable tension among the participants between a longing to establish the historical record in specific ethnic terms, and a desire to affirm the humanity of all Burundians.[113]

An infamous massacre in Burundi's civil war occurred in the commune of Kabimba, near Gitega, Burundi's second largest city. In 1993, approximately seventy Tutsi boys and girls attending Gitega Secondary School were herded into a petrol station and burned to death. There is a memorial near the site of the burned-out petrol station, with a placard that reads *plus jamais ça* (never again).[114] One speaker at the March conference suggested that a monument be constructed in Gitega, Burundi, "in memory of all the victims, without taking into account ethnic groups."[115] Another referred specifically to the students who died in Kibimba. Without invoking the name of Dr. Martin Luther King, Jr., her informal remarks were reminiscent of the powerful and iconic oratory of the African-American civil rights leader who masterfully channeled anger at racial injustice against black Americans into a universal vision of social justice for all:[116]

> I have a vision that there will be a day of going to Kibimba to remember the Tutsi students who were killed—everyone should go and should be there together, so that we

no longer see those divisions between people—Hutu and Tutsi—politicians and civil society. *Everyone*, if you feel that you are Burundian, should participate without distinction.[117]

2. Pluralizing Burundian Politics

The dream of interethnic solidarity manifested in the context of creating national memorials has also been expressed in Burundi's democratic process, notably the 2010 communal, presidential, and legislative elections. Building upon the constitutional requirement of ethnically inclusive political parties and the express prohibition against incitement to ethnic hatred,[118] individual Burundians strive to overcome the deep us-versus-them tradition in their politics. During informal discussions with a group of young Burundians at CENAP's March 2010 peace conference, one recent law graduate pointed to the 2008 election of Barack Obama as President of the United States. Acknowledging the tradition of ethnic-bloc voting in his own country, he said that Burundians look at the election of Obama and "they find it amazing that in the United States white people voted for a black man." Pan-ethnic politics "will happen in Burundi," he affirmed, "but it will take time."[119]

Burundian political activists also point to signs that a democratic culture is slowly but surely maturing in their country. Alexis Sinduhije, former presidential candidate of the Movement for Solidarity and Democracy,[120] emphasizes that many political parties that participated in the 2010 presidential elections put forth an agenda linked to the needs of the Burundian people. This represented a significant advance over appeals to the interests of one particular *communautée* that have characterized Burundian party politics for many decades.[121] The next step, Sinduhije suggests, would be for each candidate to translate his or her party platform into a practical blueprint for realizing the party's goals and values.[122]

In a series of conversations with individual Burundians in the run-up to the 2010 elections, the preparation for disappointment was leavened with hope for change. One human rights worker expressed this perspective with a mixture of political realism and a certain gleeful irony. "Ethnic thinking," he said, "may finally be on the wane. Hutu politicians used to say, 'Vote for me, and I'll take care of you.' But now they're in power, and things remain not so good for Hutus. So maybe people will be more willing to vote across ethnic lines in the coming elections."[123]

Although more Hutus are in power today than in any point in Burundi's history, the socioeconomic status of Hutus, overall, has not meaningfully changed. This sobering reality may continue to inspire a popular rejection of ethnic thinking. Evidence of this trend is the fact that UPRONA, the historically Tutsi-affiliated party, has increasing Hutu membership and support.[124] It also appears that the greatest fear on the part of civil society, after the 2010 elections, may no longer be tensions between Hutu and Tutsi political parties, but competition between different Hutu-affiliated political factions.[125]

High hopes on the part of opposition parties for success in the communal elections in May 2010 were dashed when at the close of the polls CNDD-FDD candidates secured nearly 65 percent of municipal positions. After the Electoral Commission refused to respond to charges of vote-rigging by the ruling party in violation of Burundi's electoral law, all opposition candidates for the presidency pulled out of the race, leaving the CNDD-FDD standard-bearer, President Nkurunziza, as the sole contender. Predictably, on June 28, 2010, Nkurunziza was reelected, receiving 91.6 percent of the vote. During and after the presidential polls, widespread reports of state-sanctioned violence against the opposition resulted in some opposition leaders leaving the country, notably Agathon Rwasa of the FNL.[126]

The concern that civil war-era violence between Hutu and Tutsi militants would give way to intra-Hutu violence may have played itself out in a cross-border attack from the Democratic Republic of the Congo, which occurred in 2011. On September 18, militants stormed a bar in the Burundian town of Gatumba and killed over thirty people. The establishment, owned by a supporter of the Burundian government, was frequented by CNDD-FDD party loyalists. While the evidence is murky, some observers have attributed the attack to FNL militants loyal to Agathon Rwasa.[127]

Evidence of CNDD-FDD interference with the 2010 electoral process coupled with more recent allegations of FNL militancy certainly dampen confidence in a more pluralistic political landscape for Burundi, at least in the short term. Burundians involved in human rights, community organizing, and transitional justice work express significant apprehensions about the prospects for cleaner politics, particularly given the climate of intimidation by the ruling party and feared acts of retribution by the opposition. Nevertheless, as Uvin observes, "the current political situation [in Burundi] favors ethnic reconciliation, or maybe more precisely a letting go of ethnicity."[128]

3. *Désarmer le Coeur pour Désarmer le Corps*: Moral and Physical Disarmament in Burundi

Progress in attaining inter-ethnic solidarity is also closely tied to solving the problem of small arms proliferation throughout Burundian society and within families. During the civil war, both Hutu and Tutsi militias distributed arms among the civilian population for their own "protection" against members of the "other" ethnic community. As of 2005, it was estimated that 80 percent of households in Bujumbura were in possession of small arms.[129] Many of these arms came from the civil conflicts in the DRC and Rwanda.[130] Although the process of disarming rebels and reintegrating former FAB and CNDD-FDD fighters into the new army has been quite successful so far, the disarmament of civilians has only begun. A government-sponsored amnesty period for the relinquishing of arms by private citizens expired after only a nominal percentage of arms were surrendered, in exchange for token financial compensation. Subsequently, over 1,000 weapons were seized by government security forces but, in 2010, it was believed that over 80,000 small arms still remained in circulation.[131]

At the CENAP peace conference held in Bujumbura in March 2010, civilian disarmament was one of the four major topics explored.[132] In addition to holding small group brainstorming sessions on solutions to the problem, the participants explored the roots of civilian arms proliferation. One theme that percolated through the discussion was the decades-old lack of trust that ordinary Burundians have had in their security forces, either because they saw the police and army as their enemies, or because they did not perceive either to be capable of protecting them from violence at the hands of militants associated with the other ethnic community.[133] Burundians have developed an informal or self-help security system because the formal security system has not served them, just as an informal or underground economy arises and flourishes when the legitimate marketplace is dysfunctional.

During the conference, CENAP facilitators screened a documentary entitled "Désarmer le coeur pour désarmer le corps" ("Disarming the Heart to Disarm the Body"). One of the women interviewed on screen was very resistant to the idea of turning in her family's weapons, and she talked with great emotion about the injustice of taking people's weapons away after all they had suffered during the war.[134]

In the discussion after the film, participants identified two important and interdependent challenges, which will have to be met before voluntary disarmament is viable: First, the professionalization of the Burundian security forces must occur, so that security officers are deemed servants of the nation, and not agents of the extremist fringe of a particular ethnic community. Second, the standing-down of the civilian population must take place, so that ordinary Burundians are willing to relinquish not just their arms, but their need to *be* armed, and to defend themselves.[135] These two challenges are symbiotic, the discussion revealed, and progress on one will encourage progress on the other: As civilians see that their government uses its power appropriately, they will be more willing to use their own power appropriately in turn.

One participant working in the field of women's entrepreneurship talked informally about the crucial role of women in civilian disarmament. "Marriage and family are the center of Burundian life," she explained, and "women have experienced many accidents in the home caused by weapons." Women are in a powerful position to appeal to their husbands and children to give up their arms in order to avoid these dangers, she emphasized.[136] Her comments suggest that disarmament is a matter of security in the home as well as public safety. Her perspective also inspires a vision of women as centrally involved in the post-conflict reconstruction of Burundian society.

At the close of the discussion of civilian disarmament, the two-hundred-plus participants were invited to rank four suggested programs or policies based on their considered relative values in promoting disarmament. The CENAP organizers set forth their four suggestions, drawn from focus groups they had conducted countrywide over the previous year: (1) Organize neighborhood watch organizations that would provide security forces with advance information regarding security threats. (2) Establish youth anti-violence groups at the community level. (3) Extend the grace period for civilians to turn in their arms without fear of prosecution. (4) Enhance the professional training of the security forces.[137] Although all four options received favorable reactions during the comment period, the third option concerning the extended weapons amnesty was the subject of most extensive discussion. In addition to the amnesty itself and the element of compensation, participants emphasized that, in order to be successful, such a program would require considerable outreach and consciousness raising, which could be provided by women's groups, youth organizations, faith communities, and local administrators, all working in concert.[138]

The following day, when the results of the vote on civilian disarmament were presented in a plenary session, the extended weapons amnesty received the most support.[139] Even more significantly for the participants, at the formal closing of the CENAP conference on March 25, then First Vice President of Burundi Yves Sahinguvu endorsed the amnesty outreach program on behalf of the Burundian government. He thanked CENAP for organizing a conference whose purpose was "to demonstrate that every Burundian has a role to play in rebuilding our country," and he concluded, "long live peace, reconciliation and truth in Burundi."[140]

Education for Peace in Burundi

Burundians began using human rights education as a tool of conflict resolution during the civil war period. Beginning in the late 1990s, *education for peace* was developed as a program of action in the Burundian refugee camps in Tanzania.[141] Subsequently, in the context of the Arusha peace process, rediscovering and reaffirming Burundi's peace culture became an integral component of post-conflict reconstruction.[142] Through the CENAP peace conference in March of 2010, CENAP infused new life into Burundi's culture of nonviolence. In challenging Burundians to *désarmer le coeur pour désarmer le corps*, meaning "disarm the heart to disarm the body," the conference participants were modeling the creation of a culture of peace at the community level, in which interethnic coexistence becomes the chosen survival mechanism, supplanting interethnic violence.

Chapter 6 identified five realms or arenas in which the principles of international humanitarian and human rights law are applied and tested—courts, peacekeeping troops, the media, development, and communities.[143] In grappling with the challenge of psychic or social disarmament, the CENAP peace conference clearly spotlighted the *community* realm of civil society as the essential proving ground for the implementation of humanitarian law in Burundi.

In addition to its message of ethnic pluralism, peace education in Burundi has an important feminist component. Burundian women have suffered and continue to experience economic deprivations, physical attacks, and sexual violence—before, during and since the civil war.[144] For those very reasons, they have special credibility in advocating for nonviolent responses to poverty, underdevelopment, and ethnic tensions in Burundi.[145]

Nindorera acknowledges that, historically, Burundian women have been excluded from public roles in the formal institutions of dispute resolution, an omission that she deems counterproductive.[146] Because women "play a major role in the education of their children," teaching them the very values that promote nonviolent alternatives, she argues that women should be equal partners with men in conflict resolution at the community level.[147]

4. Employment and Other Components of Social Justice in Burundi

Following close on the heels of historical truth-telling, promoting political pluralism, and further propagating the culture of nonviolence in Burundi is the urgency of improving social conditions of life for all Burundians. The March 2010 CENAP peace conference prioritized tackling the problem of youth unemployment, given that 27 percent of Burundians are between 15 and 29 years of age and youth unemployment is over 50 percent.[148]

Violence and nonviolence are structural and symbolic as well as physical, according to Peace Studies founder Johan Galtung.[149] Living conditions in Burundi vividly illustrate the social nature of violence, as Uvin's field research attests:

> The Burundians we met lived lives of stunning deprivation. Most of them never see any international aid. They die from easily preventable or curable diseases—tetanus, malaria—at scandalous rates. They work, or seek work, for endless hours, and go to sleep tortured by the cries of their hungry babies. The women and girls who have been raped are not treated; the young men who desperately try to survive are not helped; the heroes who quietly fight for change are not recognized.[150]

Recalling the discussion of human security and development in Chapter 3, Burundi is ranked 166 out of 169 countries, ranked from higher to lower levels of human development according to data compiled by the UN Development Programme.[151] For Burundians, average life expectancy is 51.4 years, average schooling is 2.7 years, and $402 is the average gross national income (GNI) per capita. Burundi's *human development index* (HDI), as calculated by the UN, is .282.[152] By way of comparison, in the world's least developed countries, the averages are a life expectancy of 57.7 years, 3.7 years in school, $1,393 GNI per capita, and an HDI of .386.[153]

Despite the coldness of socioeconomic statistics, some calculus of human suffering is an essential catalyst to necessary wealth redistribution between the global North and South, including Burundi. Without meaningful if not radical improvements in nutrition, health care, sanitation, education, and employment for average Burundians, durable peace will be difficult to create or preserve in Burundi. Socioeconomic progress will be essential in avoiding a return to armed conflict.[154]

D. DURABLE PEACE IN BURUNDI: TRANSITIONAL JUSTICE IN A LOCAL CADENCE

As suggested above, a full exploration of "durable peace for Burundi" requires examining and adapting the three-legged stool of transitional justice utilized in Uganda and Sierra Leone today. Such a contextual approach allows us to assess the relative priority being accorded the three dimensions of criminal, social, and historical justice in Burundi, in light of the most pressing concerns facing Burundians as they work towards rebuilding their society after over a decade of civil war. Given that four enormous preoccupations for Burundi are historical amnesia, electoral manipulation, an armed civilian population, and youth unemployment, it makes sense that Burundi has chosen to start with the social and historical legs of the stool. Nevertheless, in the long term, Burundian civil society is also evaluating the more traditional criminal accountability component of transitional justice.[155] What is clear is that for many Burundians, the drive for criminal accountability must accommodate the desire for reconciliation and the demand for governmental authority that transcends ethnic identity.

According to Pie Ntakarutimana, a long-time Burundian civil society activist with two decades of experience working with national and international human rights organizations,[156] the common reluctance to openly discuss the violence of the civil war period will begin to dissipate once a legitimate rule of law gains traction in Burundi. Greater entrenchment of the rule of law will in turn encourage Burundians to trust politicians who are not of their ethnic community, as those leaders demonstrate the capacity to represent all Burundians. Ntakarutimana believes that individual accountability for crimes of war is fully compatible with social development and truth-telling, and is confident that Burundi will ultimately implement a trifocal approach to transitional justice. The first component would be a truth commission, focusing on the exhumation and commemoration of mass graves; second, a hybrid court composed of international and Burundian judges mandated to try high-level civil war offenders; and third, a reparations process facilitating restitution to individual victims and local *communes* or municipalities.[157]

In July of 2011, in fulfillment of Ntakarutimana's first prescription, President Pierre Nkurunziza announced that Burundi's Truth and Reconciliation Commission (TRC) would be established in 2012, with a two-year mandate. The exact structure of the TRC is yet to be defined, but one model would build upon a traditional Burundian approach to dispute resolution.

Truth and Reconciliation, Ubushingantahe, and Women's Equality

Burundi's Arusha Agreement called upon Burundian political leaders, in concert with international partners and civil society, to establish a national truth commission to "promote reconciliation, and clarify the national history."[158] The parties to Arusha agreed to draw on traditional Burundian cultural values in devising such an institution.[159]

Building on the Arusha Agreement, Burundian transitional justice expert Agnes Nindorera suggests that Burundi's traditional method of dispute resolution by panels of respected members of the community, the *bashingantahe*, offers an effective model for the establishment of a truth commission, or a mechanism for trying lower-level offenders charged with wartime offenses in the Burundian civil war.[160] In precolonial days, Nindorera explains, *bashingantahe* were required to possess four fundamental values: *ibanga* or confidentiality, *ubupfasoni* or dignity, *ubuntu* or humanity, and *ubushingantahe* or integrity, which also encompasses the other three.[161] For its part, the UN High Commissioner for Refugees has recommended the reinstitution of the *bashingantahe* panels as a mechanism of dispute resolution in postwar Burundi, given their "fundamentally democratic" character and their purpose in serving "the interest of the people" and "the maintenance of order."[162]

Burundian parliamentarian Terence Nahimana identifies *ubuntu* as the heart of *ubushingantahe* and a necessary component of modernizing his country's justice system:

> The first challenge is restoring and preserving human dignity, Ubuntu, as the fundamental value in our particular countries. By "restoring," is meant the renaissance of our fundamental values while "preserving" means the modernization of the procedures in order to defend these values.[163]

In affirming human dignity as a core value of Burundians, Nahimana does more than accord respect for traditional values and practices. Rather, he seizes upon *ubushingantahe* and *ubuntu* as the missing links capable of "harmonizing and integrating traditional/non-formal systems of justice with the formal/modern judicial process."[164]

Nindorera emphasizes the reality of women's exclusion, exploitation, and brutalization in Burundian society, before, during, and since the civil war period. Traditionally, women were not members of the *bashingantahe*, she clarifies. Nevertheless, Nindorera points out that, during Burundi's precolonial era, even though women were not formal members of the panels, their counsel was often sought as spouses of council members. In a similar vein, she cites the historical precedent of the *umugabekazi*, or Queen Mother of Burundi, who traditionally ruled as regent in lieu of her son until he attained majority, at which time she shared power with the king.[165] Nindorera concludes that the inclusion of women in local dispute resolution panels will be essential if *ubushingantahe* is to realize its democratic potential to serve the common good.

Responsible Sovereignty: The Appropriate or Propre[166] Exercise of Power

Proponents of transitional justice in post-conflict societies cannot avoid reckoning with definitions of sovereignty and the rule of law. National sovereignty—of the sort sought after by many less geopolitically powerful states, but also often taken for granted by more powerful states—is not just a matter of respect in military, economic, or diplomatic terms. Nor is it merely a function of free elections, or the trappings of democratic institutions. Sovereignty also depends on the rule of law, the appropriate use of power, and the confidence which members of civil society accord their government. And in a country such as Burundi, which historically has defined itself in terms of different ethnic communities, its sovereign recognition and respect will grow as its people embrace a pluralistic vision of politics, justice, and social welfare.

Uvin believes that "Burundians genuinely desire to move beyond ethnocentricity." He writes that "even in an ethnically devastated society like Burundi, there exists a social basis for issue-based, nonethnic politics," in short, "an entirely different political practice..."[167]

Alexis Sinduhije cautions that the growth of healthy and enduring political and social institutions in Burundi will require a transformed vision of sovereignty from the grassroots of civil society to the top levels of government. As he explains, many Burundians, in light of their history since 1500, define the kingdom or state as a governing entity that rewards its friends and punishes its enemies, attacking any and all groups deemed to threaten its hold on power. What Burundi is on the brink of, Sinduhije hopes, is the creation of a different sort of political community, one that expects and requires its government to protect the people, all the people, no matter their socioeconomic or political fortunes, and without regard for culture, caste, clan, or ethnicity.[168]

Nindorera writes in a similar vein that power in Burundi "has always been confused with ethnicity, a confusion that has provoked much violence."[169] She calls on Burundians to affirm those individual and collective virtues that transcend cultural differences, and to demand that their elected leaders represent them as a community of Burundians. "[T]he only guarantee for rebuilding Burundi," she declares, "is to enhance human values and merit instead of institutionalizing ethnicity. This is a challenge not only for Burundians but also for local and international leaders."[170]

Sinduhije articulates a vision of sovereignty that builds on the theme introduced in Chapter 7 on Uganda, in which the rule of law derives from the appropriate exercise of power by state and nonstate actors alike.[171] This notion of sovereignty is ambitious, to say the least. It requires the government and its representatives to exercise tolerance and respect for others, deliberateness, and self-restraint, all essential facets of *ubushingantahe*, the tradition of local dispute resolution referenced in Burundi's Arusha Peace Agreement.[172] Sinduhije insists that sovereign integrity, if it is anything more than might-makes-right, requires the state to establish itself as protector and not attacker of its people. In Burundi today, this generous vision of sovereignty and the rule of law will require the government in power to cease manipulating one ethnic community for crass political gain, as has so often been the case historically. Instead, the state will need to self-consciously establish itself as champion of *all* the people, across ethnic *communautées*.

Transforming the reality of a still-polarized, fearful, and armed Burundian populace has to be at the forefront of any efforts to seek legal accountability for war criminals, promote social justice for war-affected populations, and rewrite Burundian history in a way that honors the dead and commits to a new definition of Burundi for the living. For Burundians, survivors of a civil war that has raged throughout the country, strengthening the rule of law will require a definition of sovereignty and the nation that encompasses all ethnic, political, and socioeconomic communities. If Burundians make progress on this front, they will have contributed mightily to a more humane vision of sovereignty and justice under international law for all of us.

NOTES

1. The title of this chapter is inspired by the Burundian civil society organization CENAP (Centre d'Alerte et de Prévention de Conflits, or Conflict Alert and Prevention Center), which promotes post-conflict reconstruction in Burundi by facilitating dialogue and creative problem-solving regarding employment, elections, disarmament, and transitional justice. In March of 2010, CENAP sponsored a national peace conference called "Paix durable au Burundi: Quelle solution?" (Durable Peace in Burundi: What Solution?) During one plenary session on the disarmament of civilians, the presenters aired a documentary film called "Désarmer le coeur, pour désarmer le corps" (Disarming the Heart to Disarm the Body). The film called for a grassroots effort to reform the military and security services, such that the civilian population would be willing to risk relinquishing self-help methods, including their light weapons (*armes légères*"). Additional information on CENAP is available at http://www.interpeace.org/index.php/Latest/Burundi.html.
2. This Kirundi proverb expresses the Burundian understanding of "the king's interdependence with his subordinates" and the traditional role of the wise men's council—the *bashingantahe*—in Burundian governance and dispute resolution. *See* Agnes Nindorera, Fellow, Boston Consortium on Gender, Security and Human Rights, "*Ubushingantahe* as a Base for Political Transformation in Burundi," Working Paper No. 102 (2002–2003) at 19, *available at* http://www.genderandsecurity.umb.edu/Agnes.pdf.
3. *Id.* at 28.
4. Burundi's land mass is approximately 28,000 square kilometers, close to that of its former colonial administrator Belgium, and on its territory reside 9.5 million people. By way of comparison, Burundi is .3 percent the size of the United States (US), with around 3 percent of its population. *See* CIA Factbook, Burundi, *available at* https://www.cia.gov/library/publications/the-world-factbook/geos/by.html (under "Geography" and "People").

Burundi has a republican form of government, with a bicameral legislature and an administration headed by a popularly elected president, who serves for five years, and is eligible to be reelected for a second term, according to the 2005 constitution, adopted on

February 28, 2005. The National Assembly has at least 100 members, popularly elected, of whom 60 percent should be Hutu and 40 percent Tutsi, and at least 30 percent are women. In order to ensure 60/40 ethnic representation, additional legislators may be appointed by the National Independent Electoral Commission. The Senate is composed of 54 senators, 34 elected by indirect vote, and the remaining 20 assigned to ethnic communities and former heads of state. *See id.* (under "Government").

The 2005 Constitution created special rules for the election of the first "post-transition" president by a two-thirds majority of the legislature, and otherwise provides for the election of subsequent presidents by popular vote. The current president, Pierre Nkurunziza, was elected on August 26, 2005, under the "transitional" rules, and then popularly reelected on June 28, 2010. Nkurunziza received 91.6 percent of the vote in a race boycotted by the opposition. *Id.* The other political parties (including the FNL, whose president Agathon Rwasa had fled to the Democratic Republic of the Congo) protested interference by CNDD-FDD, the governing party, as well as alleged violence on the part of the police. *See* "Burundi," July 1, 2010, CrisisWatch Database, a service of the International Crisis Group, *available at* http://www.crisisgroup.org/en/publication-type/crisiswatch/crisiswatch-database.aspx?CountryIDs=%7BAB6C96B1-CBF6-4E94-9B98-2031D4CD6EED%7D. Burundi currently has two vice presidents, First Vice President Therence Sinunguzura and Second Vice President Gervais Rufykiri, both elected on August 29, 2010. *See* CIA Factbook, *op. cit.* (under "Government").

5. Burundi was administrated as a Belgian Trusteeship under the auspices of the United Nations (UN) before its independence. *See id.* Prior to the Second World War, it had been designated a Belgian Mandate by the League of Nations. *See generally*, MICHAEL D. CALLAHAN, A SACRED TRUST: THE LEAGUE OF NATIONS AND AFRICA, 1929–1946 (Sussex Academic Press, 2004).

6. This figure is probably low. Although US government sources put the total at "more than 200,000" civil war deaths from 1993–2005 (*see id.,* Introduction), Peter Uvin writes that 300,000 people were killed during the war in Bujumbura alone. *See* PETER UVIN, *Life After Violence: A People's Story of Burundi* (Zed Books, in association with the International African Institute, the Royal African Society and the Social Science Research Council, 2009) at 15. Peter Uvin is the Henry J. Leir Professor of International Humanitarian Studies and Academic Dean at the Fletcher School of Law and Diplomacy, Tufts University, US. Raïs Neza Boneza, Congolese director of the peace-building Transcend Africa Network, reports a figure of 400,000 victims of the Burundian civil war between 1993 and 2003. *See* Boneza, "Peace by African's Peaceful Means: Obstacles and Resources to Peace," Rapport of the project initiated in the Great Lakes region of Africa, Uganda–Burundi–D.R.Congo, Transcend Africa Network (2005–2006), at section 2, "Baraza: Promoting a Culture of Nonkilling in the Great-lakes Region," *available at* http://www.humiliationstudies.org/documents/BonezaRwandaReport05_6.pdf.

7. Arusha Peace and Reconciliation Agreement for Burundi between the Government of the Republic of Burundi, CNDD, UPRONA et al (Arusha Agreement or Arusha Accord) (the Arusha Agreement had nineteen signatories, including the Burundian Government, the Burundian National Assembly, and seventeen political parties and former rebel movements), Aug. 28, 2000, *available at* http://id.cdint.org/content/documents/Arusha_Peace_and_Reconciliation_Agreement_for_Burundi.pdf.

8. *See* notes from meeting with humanitarian aid worker in Bujumbura, Burundi, Mar. 26, 2010, p. 26(a)–(b) of author's field notebook.

9. Uvin, *op. cit.*, at 188–89.

10. *See* TRACY KIDDER, STRENGTH IN WHAT REMAINS (Random House, 2009) at 264.

11. *Id.* at 111–118.
12. *Id.* at 130.
13. *Id.* at 135–136.
14. *Id.* at 7–14.
15. *See id.* at 226, and 252–259, describing Deo's work establishing and staffing health clinic in Kayanza, Burundi.
16. *Id.* at xvii. Words failed Deo when he tried to explain to Kidder the idea of *gusimbura*. When Kidder suggested that speaking of the dead forces the living to confront what "they try to forget," Deo responded, "Exactly."
17. *Id.* at 36–37. As discussed later in this chapter, Tutsis were traditionally herders of livestock, whereas most Hutus were sedentary agriculturalists. Over time, cattle ownership by Tutsis took on an aristocratic connotation.
18. *Id.* at 127–130. Rwanda has ratified the 1951 UN Convention Relating to the Status of Refugees (1951 Refugee Convention), which prohibits signatories from returning or expulsing a refugee to a country in which his or life or freedom would be threatened on account of race, religion, nationality, membership in a particular social group, or political opinion. The prohibition against forced return, also known as the norm of *non-refoulement*, is codified in Article 33 of the 1951 Refugee Convention, and is also recognized as a customary norm of international law. *See* Chapter 5 of this text, Section B.1 and note 19, discussing and citing the 1951 Refugee Convention, 189 UNTS 137, art. 33 (the norm of *non-refoulement*). Although granting refugees long-term status, whether political asylum or legal permanent residency, is discretionary on the part of state, the norm of *non-refoulement* is mandatory. *See id., and compare* 1951 Refugee Convention, art. 33 (re: *non-refoulement*) *with* art. 34 (re: assimilation and naturalization). Thus, the Rwandan border officials were obligated to grant Deo and the women and children equal access to safety on Rwandan territory, regardless of their ethnicity, and especially because they faced persecution on account of their different ethnicities from various quarters in Burundi. *See also* 1951 Refugee Convention, art. 3 (norm of nondiscrimination).
19. Tracy Kidder, *op. cit.*, at 127.
20. *See* notes from March 28, 2010 interview with Alexis Sinduhije, pp. 32(a)–(b) of author's field notebook.
21. Peter Uvin reports that 73 percent of the Burundian population is below the age of thirty, with 46 percent fourteen years of age or younger. *See* Uvin, *op. cit.*, at 33.
22. *See* R. David Zorc and Louise Nibagwire, Kinyarwanda and Kirundi Comparative Grammar (Dunwoody Press, 2007) at 1, footnote 5, *available at* http://www.dunwoodypress.com/148/PDF/KKCG_sample.pdf.
23. The Burundian King Mwéezi IV Gissabo surrendered to German military forces in 1903, after five years of armed resistance. *See* Lothaire Niyonkuru, "Loan-Words in Kirundi: A Preliminary Study," 7 *African Study Monographs* 81–87 (Mar. 1987) at 83, *available at* http://repository.kulib.kyoto-u.ac.jp/dspace/bitstream/2433/68017/1/ASM_7_81.pdf.
24. *See* Uvin, *op. cit.*, at 8.
    Burundi and Rwanda were designated as a German sphere of influence by the Berlin Conference of 1885. The joint territory of Rwanda–Urundi was then converted into a Belgian mandate by the League of Nations in 1917, and reconfigured as a Belgian trusteeship under UN auspices in 1946, once the League's mandate system was taken over by the UN Trusteeship Council. *See* Liisa H. Malkki, Purity and Exile: Violence Memory, and National Cosmology among Hutu Refugees in Tanzania (University of Chicago Press 1995) at 27, citing Warren Weinstein, *Historical Dictionary of Burundi* (Scarecrow Press, 1976) at 4–5. Only upon independence in 1962 were Burundi and Rwanda internationally recognized as separate states—the Kingdom of Burundi and the Republic of Rwanda. Burundi's First Republic, under the military dictatorship

of Michel Micombero, was declared in 1966, upon the overthrow of the monarchy. *See* MALKKI, *op. cit.*, at 30, citing Reginald Kay, *Burundi Since the Genocide*, The Minority Rights Group, Report No. 20 (London 1984) at 3.

25. The use of Swahili and German by the German administrators largely gave way to the French and Dutch idioms of the Belgian governors of Burundi, although Swahili remains popular as a *lingua franca* across Burundian linguistic communities, particularly given the prominence of Swahili-speaking merchants in urban areas. *Lingala*, one of the major local languages of the former Belgian Congo, then Zaire, now the Democratic Republic of the Congo, is also maintained as a local language in Burundi due to a significant community of Burundians of Congolese heritage. *See* Niyonkuru, *op. cit.*, at 83–84. One historical reference point for this linguistic group is the presence of Lingala-speaking Congolese soldiers within the Belgian-commanded *Force Publique*, which defeated the German military authorities in Burundi in 1916. *Id.*
26. *See* CIA Factbook, Burundi, *op. cit.* (under "People").
27. *Communautées ethniques* is literally translated as "ethnic communities" but, in common usage, corresponds closely to the English term *ethnic groups*.
28. *See* MALKKI, *op. cit.*, at 21 ("[c]onstituting less than 1 percent of the country's population, people of the Twa category are now politically marginal").
29. *See* THE SHORTER OXFORD ENGLISH DICTIONARY ON HISTORICAL PRINCIPLES, Vol. I (Oxford University Press, Fifth Edition, 1993) at 865.
30. *See generally,* Benedict Anderson, *Imagined Communities: Reflections on the Origin and Spread of Nationalism* (Verso, London, 1991 [1983]). Liisa Malkki writes that "the modern system of nation-states requires study, not just as a political system narrowly understood, but as a powerful regime of order and knowledge that is at once politico-economic, historical, cultural, aesthetic and cosmological." *See* MALKKI, *op. cit.*, at 5.
31. In her monograph, *Purity and Exile: Violence, Memory, and National Cosmology among Hutu Refugees in Tanzania, op.cit.*, Liisa Malkki conveys the multiplicity of understandings of ethnicity manifested within the largely Hutu Burundian refugee community that has resided in Tanzania since the early 1970s. In particular, she contrasts the national identity of Hutus living in refugee camps, who she explains "were continually engaged in an impassioned construction and reconstruction of their history as 'a people,'" with the variegated identity of Hutus informally settled in Burundian towns who "were creating not a heroized national identity, but rather a lively cosmopolitanism . . ." *Id.* at 3.
32. *Id.* at 21–23.
33. *Id.* at 20.
34. *See* MALKKI, *op. cit.*, at 26, citing RENÉ LEMARCHAND, RWANDA AND BURUNDI (Praeger, New York, 1970) at 37. Lemarchand, as interpreted by Malkki, emphasizes that in Burundi the caste-type relationships between Tutsi and Hutu were fluid, such that the "roles of client and patron were not mutually exclusive." *Id.* The historical evidence of greater caste polarization in Rwanda and greater social dynamism in Burundi is further explored below in Section B.2 of this chapter.
35. KIDDER, *op. cit.*, at 264.
36. *See id. See also* UVIN, *op. cit.*, at 7. Liisa Malkki further describes the institution of *ubugabire* or cattle clientship, by which cattle were exchanged for agriculture products. *See* MALKKI, *op. cit.*, at 26–27, Lemarchand, *op. cit.*, at 19, 36.
37. Liisa Malkki has extensively reviewed Burundi's historical scholarship, and concludes that "the most frequent designation [for 'Hutu' and 'Tutsi'] has been that of 'caste.'" *Id.* at 24, and note 17, citing Coquery-Vidrovitch and Moniot, Trouwborst, Maquet, Lemarchand, and Vansina. *See generally,* Jan Vansina, *La legend du passé: Traditions orales du Burundi* (Musée Royale de l'Afrique Centrale, Tervuren, Belgium, 1972).
38. *See* KIDDER, *op. cit.*, at 264. *See also* UVIN, *op. cit.*, at 8.

39. KIDDER, *op. cit.*, at 265-66, citing the scholar Mahmood Mamdani.
40. *Id.* at 266, citing Pierre Ryckmans, Belgian administrator of Burundi (1931).
41. *Id.* at 267.
42. One Burundian explains that, during the eighteenth century, while a Tutsi Kingdom was ruling in Rwanda, a neighboring Tutsi Kingdom flourished in what is now Burundi. In fact, the modern country name *Burundi* evolved out of the eighteenth-century term *Urundi Rwanda,* or "the Other Rwanda." Thus, Burundian territory was the site of the second biggest Tutsi Kingdom in Central Africa. *See* notes from March 28, 2010, interview with Alexis Sinduhije, pp. 31(a)-(b) of author's field notebook.
43. *See* KIDDER, *op. cit.*, at 196-97. Burundi and Rwanda achieved their independence from Belgium on the same day, July 1, 1962.
44. *See* Agnes Nindorera, "*Ubushingantahe* as a Base for Political Transformation in Burundi," *op. cit.*, at 3, citing Hâtier, *Histoire du Burundi: des Origines jusqu'a la Fin du 19 ème Siècle* at 96. Nindorera writes that "'Ba' forms the plural in Kirundi, the language of Burundi," and thus "Bahutu" means Hutu *people*, "Batutsi" means Tutsi *people*, and so forth. *Id.*
45. *Id.* at 3, 2.
46. *See* UVIN, *op. cit.*, at 7.
Tracy Kidder writes in a similar vein that Burundian social relations were less rigid than in Rwanda. In Burundi, "power lay less with the king than with the small princely class, descendants of the kings, known as the ganwa. The ganwa and the king stood apart from the ethnic categories, and they ceased to be either Hutu or Tutsi. The various rivalrous groupings of ganwa needed all the support they could get, from Hutus as well as from Tutsis. Hutus occupied important positions, especially in the system of justice. So the oppression of Hutus in Burundi was both less onerous than in Rwanda and not as neatly identified as a Tutsi oppression. And the very complexity of Burundi's social hierarchy also seems to have muted ethnic hostility. Tutsis were divided into at least two different classes, the Tutsi-Hima and the Tutsi-Banyaraguru, and both Hutus and Tutsis belonged to lineages of varying status." *See* KIDDER, *op. cit.*, at 264.
47. *See* UVIN, *op. cit.*, at 7.
Although individuals from Tutsi and Hutu families comprised the Ganwa, Tracy Kidder emphasizes that, like the Mwami himself, once part of the Ganwa, they were regarded as neither Tutsi nor Hutu, but servants of the king, himself the embodiment of the Burundian people. *See* KIDDER, *op. cit.*, at 264.
48. *Id.*
49. *See* Chapter 11 of this text on Uganda, Section A.2 and note 12, especially.
50. *See* KIDDER, *op. cit.*, at 196-97.
51. *See* Uvin, *op. cit.*, at 9. Major Michel Micombero of the Burundian Army came into prominence for successfully repressing an attempted *coup* by members of the Hutu *gendarmerie* or police force, and was appointed to a cabinet position in the Burundian executive. Shortly thereafter, he appointed himself President of the First Republic of Burundi in his own bloodless *coup*. Micombero's decade of presidential rule, from 1966-1976, was followed by two more military presidencies, Bagaza's from 1976-1987, and then Pierre Buyoya's from 1987 until 1993. *Id.*
52. *See* LIISA MALKKI, *op. cit.*, at 31.
53. *Id.* at 32.
54. WARREN WEINSTEIN, HISTORICAL DICTIONARY OF BURUNDI (Scarecrow Press, Metuchen, NJ, 1976) at 35, *cited in* Malkki, *op. cit.*, at 32.
55. *See id.*
56. *See* WEINSTEIN, *op. cit.*, at xi, *cited in* MALKKI, *op. cit.*, at 32.
57. *See* MALKKI, *op. cit.*, at 33.

58. THOMAS MELADY, BURUNDI: THE TRAGIC YEARS (Orbis Books, New York, 1974) at 15, *cited in* MALKKI, *op. cit.*, at 33.
59. René Lemarchand and David Martin, *Selective Genocide in Burundi*, Report No. 20, Minority Rights Group (1974) at 15, 5, and note 1 (Lemarchand and Martin borrowed the phrase from an Intelligence Memorandum circulated within the US State Department and quoted in a special report of the Carnegie Endowment for International Peace, published in 1972).
60. *Id.* at 18, *cited in* Malkki, *op. cit.*, at 34.
61. KIDDER, *op. cit.*, at 267.
62. *Id.* at 11.
63. *Id.* at 12 and 8. Despite its more recent Tutsi-affiliation, UPRONA was originally a multi-ethnic nationalist party when founded in 1958 by Prince Louis Rwagasore. *Id.* at 8.
Prince Rwagasore was the "popular, modern, pro-independence son of a deposed king, with good links to the Hutu community." *Id.* In the parliamentary elections of 1961, organized in preparation for independence in 1962, UPRONA won almost 90 percent of the legislative seats, the other 10 percent going to the PDC (le Parti Démocratie Chrétien–the Christian Democratic Party), which the Belgian administrators in Burundi helped found as a counterbalance to UPRONA. *Id.* at 9. The multiethnic character of UPRONA at its birth is demonstrated by the fact that of its 58 legislators seated in 1961, 25 were Tutsi, 22 were Hutu, 7 were Ganwa (members of the king's or Mwami's court, and hence deemed neither Tutsi nor Hutu), and 4 were of mixed parentage. *Id.*
Prince Rwagasore was assassinated on October 13, 1961, reportedly by agents of the rival PDC. Uvin writes that "[t]he historic significance of Rwagasore's murder is enormous: it is truly a day on which doors were closed for Burundi." *Id.* at 8.
64. *Id.* at 12.
65. *Id.* at 13.
66. *See* KIDDER, *op. cit.*, at 268, citing Rapport Final, Human Rights Watch and others, Commission international d'enquête sur les violations des droits de l'homme au Burundi depuis le 21 octobre 1993 (July 1994). (Final Report of International Commission of Inquiry on Human Rights Violations in Burundi since October 21, 1993.)
67. *See* Uvin, *op. cit.*, at 13.
68. *See id.* at 13, citing Prunier, G., "Burundi: A Manageable Crisis?" (Writenet, Oct. 1994), *available at* http://www.grandslacs.net/doc/2005.pdf.
69. *See* Uvin, *op. cit.*, at 13–15. Uvin cites the research of Reyntjens, who rejects the idea of a "genocidal plan" on the part of Hutu extremists, and in fact suspects that such a theory may have been cynically propagated by Tutsi military leaders to deflect their own involvement in the assassination of Ndadaye and subsequent violence against Hutus. *Id.*, citing Reyntjens, F., *Burundi, Breaking the Cycle of Violence* (Minority Rights Group International, London, 1995).
70. *See* KIDDER, *op. cit.*, at 268, citing Human Rights Watch et al, *op. cit.*
71. *Interahamwe* means "those who work together," and refers to the often spontaneously organized militias that were inspired by extremist Hutu military and political leaders to kill Tutsis during the Rwandan genocide. *See* Kidder, *op. cit.*, at 131. Journalist and writer Philip Gourevitch translates *interahamwe* as "those who attack together," and explains that the original use of the term referred to soccer fan clubs organized in the 1980s by the Hutu nationalist Republican National Movement for Democracy and Development (MRND), and subsequently converted into youth militias trained for "civil defense." As Gourevitch explains, economic hardship and unemployment in the 1980s made youth particularly vulnerable to recruitment by the Interahamwes, which "promoted genocide as a carnival romp." *See* PHILIP GOUREVITCH, *We wish to inform you that tomorrow we will be killed with our families: Stories from Rwanda* (Farrar Straus and Giroux, 1998) at 93.

72. *See* UVIN, *op. cit.*, at 14, 16.
73. Gourevitch, *op. cit.*, at 20–21 (re genesis of Rwandese Patriotic Front (RPF)).
74. *Id.* at 220 (the former RPF becoming "backbone of the post-genocide Rwandan government") and 246 (reference to Rwandese Patriotic Army). *See also* LT. GEN. ROMÉO DALLAIRE, SHAKE HANDS WITH THE DEVIL: THE FAILURE OF HUMANITY IN RWANDA (Carroll & Graf Publishers, 2004) at 467.
75. The former Burundian Army is also referred to as les Forces Armées Burundaises (FAB), or the Burundian Armed Forces. The FAB has since been transformed into the Forces de Défense Nationale (FDN), or National Defense Forces, according to the terms of a 2003 Protocol to the 2000 Arusha Accords. *See* UVIN, *op. cit.*, at 17 (citing the October 2003 Pretoria Protocol on Political, Defense, and Security Power-sharing in Burundi) and 19.
76. *See* UVIN, *op. cit.*, at 16. Under the terms of the 2000 Arusha Accord, President Pierre Buyoya, who had returned to power in a military *coup* in 1996, promised to a peaceful handover of power to his Hutu Vice President Domitien Ndayizeye, which occurred in due course, in 2003. *See id.* at 15, 16.
77. *See id.* at 17.
78. *See id.* at 15.
79. *See id.* at 11. In fact, until January of 2009, the official name for the military organization was Palipehutu-FNL. Although Peter Uvin and others locate PALIPEHUTU's genesis in Tanzania (*id.*), some Burundians attest that the movement was founded in Rwanda around 1980. According to one version, then-Burundian President Jean-Baptiste Bagaza reportedly threatened military action against Rwanda if PALIPEHUTU continued to mount attacks on Burundi from Rwandan territory, at which time PALIPEHUTU made a strategic decision to move its base of support to the Burundian refugee camps in Tanzania. *See* notes from interview with Burundian transitional justice expert, Bujumbura, Burundi, March 27, 2010, p. 27(a) of author's field notebook. *See also* Augustin Gatera, "Challenges of Democratic Succession: Case-Study of the Great Lake Countries Rwanda, Burundi, the Democratic Republic of the Congo" at 51, *available at* http://www.idh-benin.org/eng/idh_eng/Challenges_DSAfrica_Augustin_GATERA_speech.pdf (excerpt from text of presentation delivered at conference on democratic succession held in Cotonou, Benin from Feb. 23–25, 2009). Gatera affirms that PALIPEHUTU was founded in Rwanda in 1980.
80. *See* UVIN, *op. cit.*, at 14–15.
81. CNDD-FDD, the Forces for the Defense of Democracy, signed the Pretoria Protocol on Political, Defense and Security Power-Sharing in Burundi in October of 2003. *See id.* at 17. In the 2005 elections, CNDD won 64 legislative seats to FRODEBU's 30. *See id.* at 20.
82. *See id.* at 17.
83. *See* Jennifer Moore, "The Alchemy of Exile: Strengthening a Culture of Human Rights in the Burundian Refugee Camps in Tanzania," 27 WASHINGTON UNIV. J. L. & POLY. 139 at 143 and note 12.
84. *See* Bureau of African Affairs, U.S. Department of State, Background Note: Burundi, "Government and Political Conditions," December 28, 2009, *available at* http://www.state.gov/r/pa/ei/bgn/2821.htm. The Constitution of Burundi requires that political parties be open to all Burundians, thereby barring parties of explicit ethnic character. *See* Constitution of the Republic of Burundi (Loi No. 1/010 du 18 Mars 2005, portant Promulgation de la Constitution de la République de Burundi), art. 78.
85. *See* International Committee of the Red Cross, Annual Report 2009 at 105 (section on ICRC Operations in Burundi), *available at* http://www.icrc.org/web/eng/siteeng0.nsf/htmlall/section_annual_report_2009.
86. *See* Tim Murithi, *The African Union's Foray into Peacekeeping: Lessons from the Hybrid Mission in Darfur*, JOURNAL OF PEACE, CONFLICT AND DEVELOPMENT, Issue July 14,

2009, *available at* http://www.peacestudiesjournal.org.uk/dl/Issue%2014%20Article%2015%20Revised%20copy%201.pdf.

87. *See* Uvin, *op. cit.*, at 18.
88. *See* Uvin, *op. cit.*, at 19.
89. *See id.* at 15.
90. *See id.* at 15.
91. *See id.* at 21.
92. *See id.* at 15, 16–17. With the exception of Hutu presidents Ndadaye and Ntyamira, elected or appointed and killed in 1993 and 1994, respectively, UPRONA presidents had led Burundi from 1962 until 2003, when Hutu Vice President Ndayizeye took over the presidency from secondtime President Buyoya, according to the terms of the 2000 Arusha Accord. *Id.*
93. *See* "Burundi," July 1, 2010, CrisisWatch Database, a service of the International Crisis Group, *available at* http://www.crisisgroup.org/en/publication-type/crisiswatch/crisiswatch-database.aspx?CountryIDs=%7BAB6C96B1-CBF6-4E94-9B98-2031D4CD6EED%7D. *See also* CIA Factbook, Burundi (under "Government").
94. *See* notes from CENAP conference, March 24–25, Bujumbura, Burundi, author's field notebook, pp. 13(a)–23(b).
95. *See* Josh Kron, *For Rwandan Students, Ethnic Tensions Lurk*, N.Y. TIMES, Monday, May 17, 2010 at A9.
96. *Id.* In fact, some critics charge that Kagame's government hides the fact that Hutus are largely excluded from public office behind the veil of its policy and narrative of "reconciliation." *Id.*

    On May 28, 2010, U.S. law professor Peter Erlinder of William Mitchell College of Law in Minnesota was arrested in Rwanda on charges of denying the Rwandan genocide in the context of his defense of Victoire Ingabire, a Rwandan opposition presidential candidate, who herself is facing charges of "genocidal ideology." *See* Josh Kron and Jeffrey Gettleman, *American Lawyer for Opposition Figure is Arrested in Rwanda*, N.Y. TIMES, May 28, 2010, *available at* http://www.nytimes.com/2010/05/29/world/africa/29rwanda.html?scp=1&sq=%22peter%20erlinder%22&st=cse. On June 17, 2010, Erlinder was released on medical bail, after appeals to the Government of Rwanda by fellow law academics, human rights organizations, US government officials, and state legislators. *See* Edmund Kagire, Associated Press, "Rwandan court grants medical bail to US attorney," June 17, 2010, *available at* http://www.google.com/hostednews/ap/article/ALeqM5glFcY-e8EGur7UNMelrapReMrELgD9GD5OCO1.
97. *Id.*
98. Dallaire, *op. cit.*, at 43.
99. *Id.* at 269 (RPF offensive in April 1994) and 469 (July 1994 RFP attack on Gisenyi, near the border with former Zaire, and movement of Rwandan refugees into Zaire).

    In the enormous refugee camps established in the Lake Kivu region of Eastern Zaire, now the Democratic Republic of the Congo, hundreds of thousands of Rwandan Hutu civilians sought safe haven, including many who had not been involved in the killings of Tutsis and moderate Hutus. By way of example, on a single day, July 14, 1994, over 250,000 people are believed to have crossed from the town of Gisenyi in northwest Rwanda into the town of Goma, Zaire, on the northern banks of Lake Kivu. *See* Dallaire, *op. cit.*, at 469. Nevertheless, these camps became heavily dominated by Interahamwe and former Rwandan Army members. In fact, Hutu civilians wishing to return to Rwanda in late 1994 and 1995, as the new government was establishing itself, were often intimidated by their self-appointed leaders into staying in the camps, as part of a planned reinvasion of Rwanda by militant Hutu nationalists desiring to take back the government. *See Gourevitch, op. cit.*, at 265–66. The militarization of the Zairean refugee camps put humanitarian agencies into a very tight spot, because it was well known that items of relief assistance—including grain, foodstuffs, and building materials—were being seized by Interahamwe and other military leaders, used for their own purposes, and sold for weapons and other military supplies. *Id.* at 266. ("It was bewildering enough that the UN border camps should be allowed to constitute a rump genocidal state.") At the same time, agencies such as UNHCR were struggling to provide food, sanitation, shelter, and medical care to close to a million Hutu refugees. *Id.* at 269–70. Faced with this legal and moral conundrum, agencies made different decisions—Doctors without Borders pulled out of the refugee camps in the former Zaire in November 1994, whereas UNHCR stayed. *See* Médecins sans Frontières, *Deadlock in the Rwandan Refugee Crisis: Repatriation Virtually at a Standstill*, Special Report, July 20, 1995, *available at* http://www.doctorswithoutborders.org/publications/article.cfm?id=1467.

100. *See* Gourevitch, *op. cit.*, at 222.
101. *Id.* at 269 (approximately half a million Rwandan refugees returned from the border camps in former Zaire within one year after the genocide).
102. *See* CIA Factbook, Burundi, *op. cit.*, (According to the 2005 Constitution, legislators in the National Assembly must be 60 percent Hutu and 40 percent Tutsi.)
Moreover, the Francophone and Anglophone analogy for Hutus and Tutsis does not seem to apply to Burundi. Burundian Tutsi refugees were not concentrated in Uganda to the extent that Rwandan Tutsis were, and Burundian Hutu militants in exile found safe havens and bases of operation in both Francophone Democratic Republic of the Congo and Anglophone Tanzania. *See* UVIN, *op. cit.*, at 15.
103. Burundian Constitution (Loi No. 1/010 du 18 Mars 2005, portant Promulgation de la Constitution de la République de Burundi), article 164 ("l'Assemblée nationale est composé d'au moins cent deputés à raison de 60% de Hutu et de 40% de Tutsi, y compris un minimum de 30% de femmes, élus au suffrage universel direct pour un mandat de cinq ans et de trois deputés de l'ethnie Twa cooptés conformément au code électoral.") Protocol II to the 2000 Arusha Peace and Reconciliation Agreement, "Democracy and Good Governance," included equivalent provisions. *See* Uvin, *op. cit.*, at 16. *See also* Arusha Peace and Reconciliation Agreement for Burundi between the Government of the Republic of Burundi, CNDD, UPRONA et al (the Arusha Agreement had 19 signatories, including the Burundian Government, the Burundian National Assembly, and 17 political parties and former rebel movements), Aug. 28, 2000, *available at* http://id.cdint.org/content/documents/Arusha_Peace_and_Reconciliation_Agreement_for_Burundi.pdf.
104. Burundian Constitution, *op. cit.*, art. 124 ("[l]es Vice-Présidents appartiennent à des groups ethniques et des partis politiques différents.") *See also*, Arusha Agreement, *op. cit.*, Protocol II, "Democracy and Good Governance," Chapter 1, art. 7 (4) (requirement that the two Vice Presidents belong to different ethnic groups and political parties).
105. *See* "Burundi: Sinunguruza et Rufyikiri sont les deux nouveaux vice-présidents" (Sinunguruza and Rufyikiri are the two new vice-presidents), AFP, Aug. 28, 2010, *available at* http://www.arib.info/index.php?option=com_context&task=new&id=2461.
106. Burundian Constitution, *op. cit.*, art. 78 ("[l]es partis politiques . . . doive être ouverts à tous les Burundais et leur caractère national doit également être reflété au niveau de leur direction. Ils ne peuvent prôner la violence, l'exclusion et la haine sous toutes leurs formes, notamment celles basées sur appartenance ethnique, régionale, religieuse ou genre").
107. *See* Nindorera, *op. cit.*, at 7 ("[t]he State has failed to serve its different citizens or to ensure continuity in governance because ethnicity has been a mobilizing tool for ambitious politicians who want to dominate. . . . The institutionalization of the ethnic quotas settled in Arusha appears, in the context, as a call for the repetition of the same history and the same horrible events.").

108. *See* notes from Mar. 28, 2010, interview with Alexis Sinduhije, pp. 31(a)–32(b) of author's field notebook.
109. At a peace conference held in Bujumbura in March of 2010, the discussion turned to truth and reconciliation. One participant representing a youth organization emphasized the role of individual agency in the process of truth-telling and the cultivation of Burundian democracy. "This kind of discourse," he said, referring to the peace conference, "can help people think of themselves as independent, ethically-minded actors. If a meeting like this had taken place in 1993, the violence and the war would not have happened," he insisted. *See* notes from 2010 CENAP conference in Bujumbura, Burundi, Mar. 25, 2010, p. 19(b) of author's field notebook.
110. *See* Interpeace, *op. cit., available at* http://www.interpeace.org/index.php/Latest/Burundi.html.
111. *See id.*
112. In March of 2010, the author was invited to observe a national peace conference organized by the Burundian nonprofit CENAP (Centre d'Alerte et de Prévention de Conflits–Conflict Alert and Prevention Center). CENAP is a civil society organization created to promote post-conflict reconstruction in Burundi. CENAP's meeting, entitled "Paix durable au Burundi: Quelle solution?" [Durable Peace in Burundi: What Solution?], was convened in Bujumbura from March 23–25, 2010. *See* notes from 2010 CENAP conference in Bujumbura, Burundi, March 25, 2010, pp. 13(a)–23(b) of author's field notebook. *See also* Interpeace, "Path towards lasting peace in Burundi: Burundians prioritize what's next on the peacebuilding agenda," Bujumbura, Burundi, March 25, 2010 (describing the creation of le Centre d'Alerte et Prévention des Conflits, and its preparation for 2010 CENAP Forum), *available at* http://www.interpeace.org/index.php/Latest/Burundi.html. Interpeace, based in Geneva, Switzerland, is the parent organization of CENAP.
113. *See* notes from 2010 CENAP conference in Bujumbura, Burundi, Mar. 25, 2010, pp. 16(a) and 20(b)–22(a) of author's field notebook.

The CENAP conference participants were asked to rank potential action plans under the rubric of "Transitional Justice." The three options on the ballot were collecting and preserving physical evidence, identifying and protecting mass graves, and recording and institutionalizing collective memory. *See* notes from March 25, 2010 CENAP conference in Bujumbura, Burundi, at pp. 20(b)–22(a), author's field notebook. Out of 1462 votes, 682 votes went to Recommendation A, re: "collecter et protéger les traces du passé" [collecting and protecting traces of the past]. The other votes went, in descending order of popularity, to Recommendation B, re: "identification et protection des fosses communes, physiquement et par une loi" [identifying and protecting common graves, physically and by law] (which received 464 votes); and Recommendation C, re: "identifier et institutionaliser la date et le(s) lieu(x) de mémoire collective" [identifying and institutionalizing the date and place(s) of collective memory] (316 votes). *See id.* and appended Transitional Justice Ballot ("Bulletin de Vote, Justice Transitionelle").

Although the plenary discussions also referenced criminal trials and truth commissions, the focus was decidedly on naming and honoring the dead, interviewing witnesses before they pass on, and creating public memorials on the sites of individual massacres. *See id., especially* at pp. 20(b) and 21(a), author's field notebook.
114. *See* Cathrin Daniel, American Friends Service Committee, Burundi Journal Letter, Nov. 2009, *available at* http://www.quaker.org.uk/burundi-november-2009-journal-letter/.
115. *See* author's notes for Mar. 25, 2010, p. 16(a) of author's field notebook.
116. *See generally,* Dr. Martin Luther King, Jr., "I Have a Dream" Speech, Aug. 28, 1963, transcript *available at* http://www.usconstitution.net/dream.html.

117. *See* notes from CENAP conference, Bujumbura, Burundi, Mar. 25, 2010, p. 16(a) of author's field notebook.

   In 2003, the author conducted human rights workshops in two Burundian refugee camps in Tanzania. In Camp Kanembwa, in the Kibondo District of Western Tanzania, one participant invoked a parable about a bountiful banquet attended by starving people to call for transethnic solidarity: "Why don't Hutu and Tutsi take a spoon and feed each other? Then there will be peace." *See* Jennifer Moore, "The Alchemy of Exile: Strengthening a Culture of Peace in the Burundian Refugee Camps," *op. cit.*, at 158.

118. *See* Burundian Constitution, *op. cit.*, art. 78 ("[l]es partis politiques . . . . doivent être ouverts à tous les Burundais. . . . Ils ne peuvent prôner la violence, l'exclusion et la haine sous toutes leurs formes, notamment celles basées sur l'appartenance ethnique, régionale, religieuse ou genre").

119. *See* notes from March 2010 CENAP conference in Bujumbura, Burundi, p. 20(a) of author's field notebook.

120. MSD is the acronym for le Mouvement de Solidarité et Démocratie (Movement for Solidarity and Democracy). *See* notes from March 28, 2010 interview with Alexis Sinduhije, p. 31(a) of author's field notebook.

121. *See id.*, p. 32(b) of author's field notebook.

122. *Id.*

123. *See* notes from Mar. 26, 2010, conversation with human rights worker, Bujumbura, Burundi, p. 24(b) of author's field notebook.

124. *See id.*

125. Conversation with Burundian-American, Albuquerque, New Mexico, June 4, 2011.

126. *See* CIA Factbook, Burundi, *available at* https://www.cia.gov/library/publications/the-world-factbook/geos/by.html (under "Government"). *See* "Burundi," July 1, 2010, CrisisWatch Database, a service of the International Crisis Group, *available at* http://www.crisisgroup.org/en/publication-type/crisiswatch/crisiswatch-database.aspx?CountryIDs=%7BAB6C96B1-CBF6-4E94-9B98-2031D4CD6EED%7D.

127. *See* Jeffrey Gettleman, "Shooting Exposes Instability in Burundi," N.Y. TIMES, September 20, 2011, at A10.

128. Uvin, *op. cit.*, at 164.

129. *See* Edward B. Rackley, *Armed violence against women in Burundi*, HUMANITARIAN EXCHANGE MAGAZINE (commissioned by the Humanitarian Practice Network at the Overseas Development Institute), Issue Sept. 31, 2005, *available at* http://www.odihpn.org/report.asp?id=2742.

130. *See* notes from March 2010 CENAP conference in Bujumbura, Burundi, p. 13(b) of author's field notebook.

131. *See id.* at p. 13(a), author's field notebook.

132. *See* Interpeace, *op. cit.*, *available at* http://www.interpeace.org/index.php/Latest/Burundi.html.

133. *See id.* at p. 13(b), author's field notebook.

134. *See id.* at p. 14(a), author's field notebook.

135. *See id.* at p. 13(b), author's field notebook.

136. *See id.* at p. 14(b), author's field notebook.

137. *See id.* at pp. 13(a) and 13(b), author's field notebook.

138. *Id.* at pp. 13(a)–14(b), author's field notebook.

139. *Id.* at p. 19(b), author's field notebook. Out of 2403 votes, 686 votes went to Recommendation C, re: extending the grace period for the voluntary relinquishment of arms, and an accompanying outreach program at the community level. The other votes went, in descending order of popularity, to Recommendation A, re: community watch posts (which received 592 votes); Recommendation D, re: professionalizing the security forces (581 votes); and

Recommendation B, re: establishing youth anti-violence groups (544 votes). *See id.*, p. 19(b) and appended Disarmament Ballot (Bulletin de Vote, Désarmement).

140. *Id.* at pp. 22(b)–23(b), author's field notebook.
141. *See* Jennifer Moore, "The Alchemy of Exile: Strengthening a Culture of Human Rights in the Burundian Refugee Camps in Tanzania," *op. cit.*, at 148–50.
142. *See generally,* Raïs Neza Boneza, (Coordinator, TRANSCEND AFRICA), "Peace by Africa's Peaceful Means: Obstacles and Resources to Peace," Rapport of the project initiated in the Great Lakes region of Africa, Uganda-Burundi-D.R.Congo, TRANSCEND AFRICA NETWORK (2005–2006), *available at* http://www.humiliationstudies.org/documents/BonezaRwandaReport05_6.pdf and at 3 ("[t]he Transcend Africa Great-lakes project was launched in Trondheim/Norway in February 2004 with the goal of strengthening the civil society in the Great Lakes using peaceful means of conflicts transformation by establishing a partnership between peace builders, researcher, practitioners on the field, and in the Diaspora.").
143. CENAP's peace conference touched on the first four of these fronts or arenas, by (1) exploring available judicial remedies for civil war atrocities (courts), (2) acknowledging the legacy of the African Union's peacekeeping mission in Burundi (troops), (3) inviting the contributions of human rights monitoring organizations (the media), and (4) emphasizing the importance of job creation in the reconstruction of Burundian society (development).
144. *See* Uvin, *op. cit.*, at 2 ("[t]he women and girls who have been raped are not treated") and 97 ("[i]f they are women, they often have stories of sexual abuse behind them").
145. Another female participant at the CENAP March 2010 peace conference, an academic administrator based in Bujumbura, talked about the potential for music and dance to help young Burundian men and women to "traverser leurs barrières ethniques, emotionelles, politiques" (transcend their ethnic, emotional and political barriers). *See* notes from March 25, 2010, CENAP conference in Bujumbura, Burundi, p. 18(a) and (b) of author's field notebook. *See* Uvin, *op. cit.*, at 33.
146. *See* Agnes Nindorera, *Ubushingantahe as a Base for Political Transformation in Burundi, op. cit.*, at 28.
147. *Id.* at 15.
148. Burundian young people constitute "the new generation, who grew up during the war, committed most of the violence and suffered most from it, and who will be the builders of the future of their country." *See* Uvin, *op. cit.*, at 33. Statistics on unemployment, including youth unemployment, in Burundi are difficult to come by. *See* CIA Factbook, Burundi (2010), *available at* https://www.cia.gov/library/publications/the-world-factbook/geos/by.html (under "Economy") where the unemployment category is left blank. The NGO Youth Entrepreneurship and Sustainability (YES) reported, in 2007, that the unemployment rate of uneducated Burundian youth was 60 percent, and that it was 50 percent among educated youth. *See* Marc Ntunzwenimana, YES Burundi Country Profile (2007), *available at* http://www.yesweb.org/Burundicountry-pop.html.
149. *See* Johan Galtung, *Peace by Peaceful Means: Peace and Conflict, Development and Civilization.* (International Peace Research Institute (PRIO), Oslo, 1996). *See also* discussion of Peace & Conflict Studies in the introductory chapter of this text.
150. *See,* Uvin, *Life after Violence: A People's Story of Burundi, op. cit.*, at 2.
151. *See* UNDP *Human Development Report* for 2010 at 145, 146, *available at* http://hdr.undp.org/en/media/HDR_2010_EN_Complete_reprint.pdf.
152. *See id.*
153. *See* UNDP Human Development Report for 2010 at 146. By comparison, for the world's richest countries, life expectancy is 80.3 years, average years of schooling are 11.3, and GNI per capita is $37,225. *Id.*

154. *See generally*, Peter Uvin, "Structural Causes, Development Cooperation and Conflict Prevention in Burundi and Rwanda," presented at Wilton Park Conference 889—Conflict Prevention and Development in Africa: A Policy Workshop, Nov. 2008, *available at* http://www.wiltonpark.org.uk/documents/conferences/WP889/participants/participants.aspx, and cited in Kidder, *op. cit.*, at 272 ("[i]f one recognizes the condition of structural violence, one can understand the profound racist prejudice and outburst of murderous violence are part of a continuum of ever-present violence in which violence is the answer to violence, and in which victims temporarily become perpetrators and then victims again.")

155. *See* Stef Vandeginste, "Burundi's unturned stones," Radio Netherlands Worldwide, Oct. 4, 2010, *available at* http://www.rnw.nl/international-justice/article/burundis-unturned-stones (Burundi has not yet taken concerted steps to establish accountability mechanisms either through a war crimes court or a truth commission).

156. Pie Ntakarutimana served as president of the Burundian Human Rights League of Iteka (la Ligue Burundaise des Droits de L'Homme Iteka). He is also the former president of the Burundian Forum for Strengthening Civil Society (le Forum pour le Renforcement de la Société Civile Burundaise), and the former vice president of the International Federation of Human Rights Leagues (la Fédération International des Ligues de Droits de l'Homme, based in Paris). *See* notes from March 2010 research visit to Bujumbura, Burundi, p. 28(b) of author's field notebook, Mar. 27, 2010.

157. *Id.*

158. *See* Matthias Goldmann, *Does Peace Follow Justice or Vice Versa? Plans for Post conflict Justice in Burundi*, 30 FLETCHER FORUM OF WORLD AFFAIRS 137, 142 (Winter 2006), *available at* http://ssrn.com/abstract=1369121. *See also* 2000 Arusha Agreement for Burundi, *op. cit.*, Protocol I (re "Nature of the Burundi Conflict . . . and Solutions"), art. 8 ("Principles and measures relating to national reconciliation"), *available at* http://id.cdint.org/content/documents/Arusha_Peace_and_Reconciliation_Agreement_for_Burundi.pdf.

159. *See* Agnes Nindorera, "*Ubushingantahe* as a Base for Political Transformation in Burundi," *op. cit.*, at 18, citing Accord d'Arusha pour la Paix et la Reconciliation au Burundi, Arusha 2000 at 22.

160. *See* Matthias Goldmann, *op. cit.*, at 144. *See generally*, Agnes Nindorera, "*Ubushingantahe* as a Base for Political Transformation in Burundi," *op. cit. See also* Terence Nahimana, former Burundian Member of Parliament, "Modernizing and Integrating Traditional Judicial Systems: The Case of the Burundian Bashingantahe Institution," 8 E. AFRICAN J. PEACE & HUM. RTS. 111–120 (2002). It is important to note that some Burundians are more skeptical about the viability of the *bashingantahe* councils as models for truth commissions, given the fact that the councils have sometimes been prone to financial influence at the local level, despite their ethic of confidentiality and integrity. *See* notes from CENAP conference in Bujumbura, Burundi, March 25, 2010, p. 24(a) of author's field notebook. *See also* Barbara Vi Thien Ho, "Post-conflict Burundi and the Role of Ubushingantahe Council," July 17, 2009, Africa Faith & Justice Network, *available at* http://afjn.org/focus-campaigns/restorative-justice/147-commentary/660-post-conflict-burundi-and-the-role-of-ubushingantahe-council-.html.

161. *See* Nindorera, *op. cit.*, at 2.

162. *Id.* at 12, citing UNHCR, Burundi Core Document (1999) at 8, *available at* www.unhcr.org/refworld/country,,HRI,,BDI,,3ae6ae100,0.html.

163. *See* Nahimana, *op. cit.*, at 111.

164. *Id.* at 118.

165. Nindorera, *op. cit.*, at 17.

166. In this usage, the French word *propre* means "clean," in the sense of honest and law-abiding.

167. *See* UVIN, *Life after Violence: A People's Story of Burundi, op. cit.*, at 188–89.
168. *See* notes from March 2010 CENAP conference in Bujumbura, Burundi, p. 32(a) of author's field notebook, March 28, 2010.
169. Nindorera, *op. cit.*, at 7.
170. *Id.* at 25.
171. *See* introductory passage of Chapter 7 on Uganda, in which the rule of law is defined as "a common sense understanding of the rule of law as the heart of a political culture of accountability and the appropriate use of power by officers of the state and non-state actors alike." There is an appropriately poetic quality to the French idiom regarding the rule of law. Politicians with "clean hands"—"politiciens avec les mains propres"—are those who use their power appropriately, humanely, equitably and honestly. *See also*, Chapter 1, Section C.5, "Rights and Responsibilities," which explores the concepts of sovereignty, power, and rule of law in broad terms: "For this reason, a sense of urgency animates our efforts to define the international rule of law in terms of self-restraint and the appropriate use of power by states, communities, organizations and individuals alike."
172. *See* Nindorera, *op. cit.*, at 18.

Conclusion

HUMANITARIAN LAW IN ACTION

Humanitarian law is the engine that drives transitional justice and social transformation in countries emerging from prolonged civil wars. Among the four fields of international law most concerned with armed conflict, international humanitarian law (IHL) is the first among equals, given its central commitment to protect civilians and to alleviate suffering in time of war. Through collaboration with the other bodies of law, IHL is able to build a more comprehensive framework for resolving armed conflicts. Human rights law recognizes the civil-political and socioeconomic rights of war victims and survivors, in addition to their claims to protection from the most brutal forms of physical attack. Criminal law provides a basis for prosecuting violators of IHL. Refugee law, for its part, facilitates the protection and assistance of people displaced by armed conflict and persecution, both within and across national boundaries. Thus, international humanitarian law depends upon human rights, criminal law, and refugee law to reach its full potential.

Just as humanitarian law provides a focal point for understanding the rules of conflict resolution, IHL helps us better utilize the tools of social transformation. Courts, troops, the media, development, and communities are five essential mechanisms for post-conflict reconstruction. As the conceptual foundation for long-term conflict resolution, international humanitarian law guides the activities that occur in these five arenas. IHL defines the jurisdiction of international criminal courts and governs the conduct of peacekeeping troops. It inspires the advocacy of human rights media and helps focus the resources of development agencies. Lastly, IHL serves a touchstone for communities seeking to reconcile their members and rebuild their institutions.

The effective implementation of humanitarian law depends in large part upon what sort of justice is achieved in post-conflict societies. Survivors of prolonged civil wars tend to speak of transitional justice in terms of three essential components—criminal justice, social justice, and historical justice. Criminal justice emphasizes retribution based upon individual accountability. It is vindicated chiefly by judicial tribunals mandated to apply the rules of IHL to insurgents, government soldiers, and peacekeepers alike. Social justice promotes socioeconomic restoration from agriculture and infrastructure to health and higher education. It is supported mainly by development agencies and local communities, in association with national authorities. Historical justice seeks acknowledgment and reconciliation. It is realized largely by social media, human rights education programs, and truth commissions, all working to cultivate a culture of peace within communities.

Thus, our exploration of humanitarian law in action contributes to a better understanding of the complex and dynamic relationship between law, practice, peace, and justice itself. On a theoretical level, the four fields of international law complement one another under the jurisprudential umbrella of IHL, unified by the humanitarian imperative to alleviate the suffering inflicted by armed conflict. On a tactical level, the five mechanisms of implementation work together to strengthen criminal accountability, social welfare, and historical memory, three dimensions of transitional justice. But, ultimately, humanitarian law reveals itself in the gritty realities—unforeseen events, shifting politics, and widespread poverty—borne by countries emerging from protracted armed conflicts. Their experiences demonstrate the relevance of humanitarian law as well as the challenges of its implementation.

Humanitarian Law in Action in Uganda, Sierra Leone, and Burundi

Uganda, Sierra Leone, and Burundi are engaged in a process of crafting their own unique mosaics of international rules and tools for post-conflict reconstruction in their respective societies. Each country has consulted the varied sources and institutions of international humanitarian law and then sought to apply these norms in specific arenas to bring the law to life. Each has grappled with the meaning of transitional justice and reached a unique ordering among its various facets. Yet, despite their differences, the recent histories of these three countries confirm that durable peace rests on a foundation of individual and state responsibility, socioeconomic security, and restored community relationships. Their ongoing efforts and partial successes offer important lessons to other countries emerging from war into a period of transition and transformation.

Uganda: "Justice as the Handmaid of Sustainable Peace"[1]

As we explored in Chapter 7, Uganda has initiated prosecutions of the Lord's Resistance Army (LRA) in the International Criminal Court (ICC), and its parliament passed an Amnesty Act in 2000 and a War Crimes Act in 2010, which have yet to be fully reconciled. At the local level, certain communities have elected to utilize traditional justice mechanisms, including the Acholi ceremony of *mato oput*. Although civil society organizations have called for the creation of a truth commission, the Ugandan parliament has yet to enact legislation that would mandate a truth and reconciliation process at the national level. With respect to the five tools or mechanisms of humanitarian law implementation, the Ugandan government is focused on the criminal courts, whereas civil society is heavily engaged in human rights advocacy, calling for more progress in socioeconomic development and community reconciliation.

Therefore, Uganda has a made a significant symbolic endorsement of state-centric criminal justice and the beginnings of a long-term commitment to historical justice, but has not created a formal testimonial or reparations process at the national level, and has only begun to prepare for domestic prosecutions of mid-level and lower-level war crimes perpetrators. Uganda's initially ICC-focused prosecutorial approach to transitional justice continues to be punctuated by civil society's calls for more even-handed retributive justice, more restorative justice, and more historical justice. A credible criminal justice system will require better accountability for humanitarian law violators within the Ugandan armed forces, whether through the Ugandan War Crimes Division or court martial proceedings. Enhanced attention to restorative justice will demand better endowed reparations programs, more than token material assistance to former internally displaced persons (IDPs) returning to their home areas, and the commitment of substantial and sustained resources to broad-based socioeconomic development programs throughout northern Uganda. Greater emphasis on the historical element of transitional justice will lead to the creation of a national truth-telling process and a thorough examination of the causes and conduct of Uganda's twenty-year civil war.

Uganda offers powerful insights into the meaning of transitional justice, particularly exposing the limits of state-centric criminal justice, and the consequences of initial reliance on an international court as the central mechanism for the implementation of humanitarian law. The ICC case against Joseph Kony and his top deputies within the LRA reveals that war crimes trials will undermine the principle of individual accountability if prosecutions target rebels to the exclusion of government soldiers and other state actors. High-level indictments may even lead to renewed and cross-border violence if the accused are not readily brought into custody, as demonstrated by the continued mass atrocities and ongoing forced recruitment campaigns carried out by the LRA in the Democratic Republic of the Congo (DRC), Central African Republic (CAR), and the Sudan.

To build enduring confidence in the rule of law in Uganda, justice for war criminals must be even-handed, and fully incorporated into the domestic legal system, whether trials are carried out by the International Criminal Court or the new War Crimes Division of the Ugandan High Court. Moreover, as the Beyond Juba Project and other Ugandan human rights organizations maintain, criminal justice is but one component of a meaningful process of reconciliation and social development in northern Uganda. Truth-telling about the causes of the war will be an essential element of this fuller realization of criminal, social, and historical justice.

Sierra Leone: "If We Don't Come Together, the Country Won't Develop"[2]

The Sierra Leonean experience was examined in Chapter 8. Sierra Leone is situated along the transitional justice/post-conflict reconstruction spectrum somewhere between Uganda's initially ICC-centric prosecutorial approach and Burundi's focus on clean elections and the building of a more pluralistic political process. In Sierra Leone, war crimes trials have been conducted by a hybrid tribunal composed of Sierra Leonean and foreign national judges rather than the ICC or strictly domestic courts. The 1999 Lomé Peace Agreement also led to the creation of the Truth and Reconciliation Commission (TRC) that, in 2004, issued recommendations for far-reaching political reforms, yet to be fully implemented. Thus, at the national level, Sierra Leone has created two transitional justice institutions, one for punishing offenders, and the other for establishing the historical record and assisting victims. In so doing, Sierra Leone has made a concerted commitment to all three dimensions of transitional justice—criminal accountability, restorative justice, and collective memory.

With reference to the specific tools for implementing humanitarian law, Sierra Leone has made use of all five mechanisms, to a greater or lesser extent. The Special Court for Sierra Leone (Special Court) and the TRC operate principally in the judicial and community reconciliation sectors. Both institutions also serve as "media" agencies, playing important roles in human rights outreach and education. For their part, non-governmental organizations such as CD-Peace and Fambul Tok are active in the realm of socioeconomic development and grassroots reconciliation. Finally, both the Economic Community of West African States and the United Nations supplied peacekeeping troops to Sierra Leone during and after the conflict. In particular, the UN Mission in Sierra Leone demobilized 45,000 civil war combatants between 2000 and 2002.

While Sierra Leoneans generally value the symbolic force of the Special Court and the TRC, many find fault with their practical impact. Common critiques include the small number of convictions and the sum spent on prosecuting a handful of top offenders, which is larger than that spent on reparations to the many war victims and survivors. Another concern is that lack of clear separation between the two processes may have threatened the integrity of the TRC, given the understandable reluctance of some offenders to testify before the commission out of a fear for their own vulnerability to prosecution by the Special Court.

In addition to evaluating the past accomplishments of the TRC and the Special Court, Sierra Leonean human rights activists look to the future, demanding fuller implementation of TRC recommendations for urgently-needed social and legal reforms, including the abolition of the death penalty, the release of all administrative detainees, and the establishment of an effective national reparations program. One contingent in particular calls upon civil society to implement sustained grassroots reconciliation efforts throughout the country. Many Sierra Leoneans appreciate that without more social justice—including poverty alleviation and women's empowerment, as well as educational and employment opportunities prioritizing youth—no measure of criminal accountability or historical truth-telling will be sufficient to avoid a return to social strife.

Just as Uganda's post-conflict experience illustrates the limits of a predominantly retributive model for transitional justice that relies heavily on the judicial arena, Sierra Leone's experience reinforces the compatibility of retributive, restorative, and reconciliative justice, and the importance of utilizing the full spectrum of tools for social transformation. In addition to judicial and quasi-judicial procedures at the national level (the TRC and the Special Court), much transitional justice in Sierra Leone remains to be pursued through the mechanisms of human rights education and advocacy, socioeconomic development programs, and community activism.

The modest record of the TRC and the Special Court—whether measured in terms of the low level of reparations, the small number of convictions, or the incomplete implementation of essential political reforms—suggests the limited efficacy of any type of transitional justice that occurs exclusively at the national and international levels. War crimes trials and public dialogue between offenders and victims in Freetown and district capitals must be combined with reconciliation and development activities that percolate up from the chiefdom, section, and village levels, and confront the crushing realities of youth disaffection and women's oppression. Grassroots peace educators and development workers in Sierra Leone offer new insight into the symbiotic relationship between social and historical justice in particular. Just as full reconciliation is not possible without jobs and income generation, cooperative development activities are hobbled until community members reckon individually and collectively with the violence of the past.

Burundi: "We Need to Learn to Fight Together, and Not against One Another"[3]

Burundi's search for durable peace was the subject of Chapter 9. This Central African nation has initiated no international war crimes prosecutions to date, and its long-awaited Truth and Reconciliation Commission will not begin operations until 2012. Nevertheless, Burundian civil society is making concerted efforts to pierce the veil of social alienation, while promoting pan-ethnic party politics, women's empowerment, and job creation, particularly among youth.

In contrast to Uganda and Sierra Leone, Burundi has not yet looked to the courts as a significant mechanism for transitional justice in the postwar period. Apart from an initial period of ceasefire monitoring by African Union (AU) peacekeeping troops, in Burundi humanitarian law has largely been implemented in the arenas of human rights education, socioeconomic development, and community mobilization. More activities are anticipated in each of these domains, particularly restorative justice and reconciliation programs, which will require the further investment of significant human and financial resources.

Ubushingantahe refers to traditional Burundian dispute resolution by panels of elders selected for their demonstrated traits of character, including integrity and compassion. Since the signing of the 2000 Arusha Peace and Reconciliation Agreement (Arusha Agreement), the practice has been promoted but not yet systematically adopted as an institution of transitional justice. Although contemplated in the Arusha Agreement, Burundi has yet to establish a national truth commission or a war crimes tribunal. National dialogues on the peace process have, thus far, emphasized social development, electoral reform, and civilian disarmament over judicial or quasi-judicial institutions. In addition to prioritizing job creation for youth and improved status for women, Burundian human rights activists are confronting abiding problems of ethnic manipulation, fraud, and intimidation within the political process.

The problem of the ready availability of small arms among the civilian population is widely recognized in Burundi. Recent grassroots activism by organizations such as the Centre d'Alerte et Prévention de Conflits (CENAP) resulted in a collaborative commitment on the part of the government and civil society to create an extended amnesty to encourage the voluntary surrender of unregistered weapons by individuals and families. Nevertheless, the long-term demobilization of civilian militias and the dismantling of informal security activities will require increased public trust on the part of a populace confident that they can rely upon state security forces to provide protection to all citizens and inhabitants of Burundi, regardless of ethnic or political affiliation.

Burundi's experience offers a unique perspective on humanitarian law in action because it suggests that underlying the punitive, social, and historical facets of justice is a more pluralistic and transethnic conception of the nation itself. Burundi's political and human rights activists increasingly demand that their government serve all Burundians, regardless of class or ethnicity. These leaders suggest that such a cosmopolitan vision of sovereignty[4] will empower Burundians to end the cycle of inter-communal violence.

Despite tenacious optimism in some quarters of Burundian civil society, widespread reports of fraud and violence on the part of the ruling party in the 2010 municipal elections, and the subsequent boycott of the presidential race by all but the incumbent candidate, reveal that the establishment of a free and fair electoral process is still an unrealized goal for Burundi. Nevertheless, a somewhat encouraging development in Burundi's political landscape is that the most intense political competition appears to be among political parties of the same historical ethnic affiliation, rather than between parties associated with either of the two major ethnocultural communities. The postcivil war proliferation of political parties in Burundi, characterized by increasingly sophisticated and substantive party platforms, suggests that tolerant and pluralistic forms of political expression are both feasible and desired by the Burundian people.

Insights and Lessons Learned

The most important common insight gained from the postwar experiences of Uganda, Sierra Leone, and Burundi is that, to be fully realized, humanitarian law in action requires an integrated approach. To achieve this end, the retributive, restorative, and reconciliative strands of transitional justice must be woven together. Humanitarian law in action is not a zero-sum contest between peace and justice, but rather a creative accommodation among the criminal, social, and historical facets of justice in societies emerging from sustained armed conflict. A three-dimensional process encompassing individual accountability, socioeconomic development, and the healing of community relationships is the best path to post-conflict transformation.

It is difficult if not perilous to generalize about the implementation of humanitarian law based on academic research and intense but short field visits to three individual countries emerging from civil war. Thus, the concluding paragraphs of this book on international law and conflict resolution in Africa are framed as insights and aspirations, rather than a blueprint for post-conflict reconstruction. The five ideas set forth below are intended to provoke further study and application, in the spirit of creating a more durable peace. These principles are inspired by the work of individual Ugandans, Sierra Leoneans, and Burundians, whose countries continue to grapple in creative and instructive ways with the opportunities and challenges of humanitarian law in action.

a. Restorative Justice Must Be Extensive and Well Endowed

It is widely recognized that socioeconomic development programs—particularly in the areas of education, employment, and health care—are essential ingredients of successful conflict resolution. Although restorative justice commences with short-term emergency humanitarian aid, it only reaches fruition through long-term investments in socioeconomic development, at the national and community levels. Given the role of underdevelopment in inflaming conflicts in all three countries, the reengagement of youth and the empowerment of women, in both social and economic terms, are vital ways to defuse future violence and build durable peace. Nevertheless, development programs are expensive, and require a massive reallocation of priorities and resources, both within national budgets and between richer and poorer countries. At a minimum, the resources devoted to social justice programs—including reparations for war survivors, health care provision, education, and job development—need to surpass the millions spent on criminal justice and the prosecution of war crimes suspects.

b. Reconciliative Justice Must Be Grassroots and Long Term

The national truth commission is an important model and tool of reconciliation. It is most fully realized, among the three countries studied, in

Sierra Leone's TRC. Nevertheless, the call for reconciliation is not limited to the national and district or provincial levels, but rather extends out and down into individual villages and rural communities. At the grassroots level, war offenders and their victims often live side-by-side, alienated, angered, or retraumatized by each others' presence, and yet open to dialogue. For this reason, it is in small settlements and gatherings of people that reconciliation is most needed, and has the most potential. Moreover, just as reconciliation must be local as well as national, it must be extended over time. Face-to-face dialogue and forgiveness and cleansing ceremonies, powerful as they are, have limited value as one-time events. When offenders and survivors continue to engage with one another over time, their personal interactions may lead to ongoing cooperative efforts, with opportunities to contribute to the economic and social redevelopment of their communities.

c. Restorative and Reconciliative Justice Are Essential and Interdependent

Peace activists and proponents of transitional justice increasingly recognize that restorative justice is a necessary element in the process of national reconstruction, at both the community and the national level. What is less widely appreciated is the role of reconciliation itself in catalyzing socio-economic development. Particularly in Sierra Leone, anecdotal evidence suggests that without meaningful interactions between survivors and their offenders at the community level, collective farming and other subsistence and income-generating activities are hamstrung. On the other hand, with such reconciliation activities, communities have progressed from a dependence upon agricultural imports to the capacity to export surplus products.[5] Thus, the interaction between restorative and reconciliative justice is best understood as a symbiotic relationship in which development feeds reconciliation, and reconciliation makes development possible.

d. Retributive Justice Must Be Even-Handed and Multi-layered

The principal objectives of criminal justice in post-conflict societies are upholding individual accountability for war crimes, promoting a collective reckoning with the wrongs of the past, and fostering greater respect for the rule of law. Nevertheless, there is considerable debate about the efficacy of retributive justice as a primary component of post-conflict reconstruction, with concern, in some quarters, that the punitive approach is as likely to revitalize as to resolve conflict. In response to this critique of retributive justice, it is vital but still insufficient to acknowledge that criminal justice best works in concert with social justice and historical justice. The proposition that criminal justice cannot function in a vacuum is now uncontroversial, but the fact remains that post-conflict societies need *better* penal justice. Criminal tribunals will not play a productive role in reconstruction if they merely prosecute a handful of mid-level-to-senior-level rebel leaders. In such a scenario, as William Schabas effectively argues, criminal trials become a mechanism by which the government uses the courts to continue challenging an adversary it could not vanquish by force of arms, with the rule of law as the ultimate casualty. Rather, the mandate of war crimes tribunals must extend to all parties to the conflict, state and non-state actors alike. And finally, trials—whether conducted by international, hybrid, or national courts—must be observed and critiqued by the people in whose name and for whose benefit they are conducted.

e. Reconciliative Justice Has the Capacity to Transform Criminal Justice

Criminal justice is often pursued in tandem with social justice and historical justice, with a variety of outcomes. As we have illustrated, the principle of individual accountability sometimes clashes with the goals of restoration and reconciliation. Nevertheless, criminal accountability and historical reconciliation need not work at cross-purposes. In the most creative scenarios, historical justice will help realize an important objective of criminal justice, particularly when reconciliation provides meaningful encounters between offenders and victims. Such historical reckoning furthers accountability for the wrongs of the past, as powerfully as the conviction, sentencing, and imprisonment of the offender. At the same time, community truth-telling cultivates the rule of law organically, from the grassroots.

Transitional Justice, Durable Peace, and Pluralism

Humanitarian law in the theoretical realm is a set of legal rules designed to govern the conduct of armed conflict and lessen the suffering of noncombatants and combatants alike. IHL conventions and customs, in combination with human rights and refugee treaties and the statutes of criminal tribunals, affirm the dignity or *ubuntu* of all individuals injured and displaced by war. Humanitarian law in the practical realm is much more complex. Humanitarian law in action picks up the pieces after armed conflict has ravaged the law, the country, and its inhabitants alike. The legal rules that were insufficient to prevent war crimes need to become tools for helping societies rebuild themselves once the conflict is spent.

Courts, troops, the media, development agencies, and communities in Uganda, Sierra Leone, and Burundi are using criminal law, human rights, and humanitarian law principles to realize the retributive, restorative, and reconciliative components of transitional justice. Criminal accountability, social welfare, and historical truth-telling are each vital to durable peace. Yet the simultaneous pursuit of criminal, social, and historical justice is an ambitious and fragile project. It requires the sustained engagement and financial support of the international community, as well as the moral fiber of the post-conflict societies themselves. The countries capable of undergoing this type of transformation must be characterized by a responsible vision of sovereignty and a genuine embrace of difference. Durable peace requires leaders who seek more than their own self-preservation and a nation defined by more than one class or community. Conflict resolution demands a profound commitment on the part of the country and its people to serve all citizens and inhabitants. Thus, the greatest promise and challenge of humanitarian law in action within Africa and throughout the world is engendering a more inclusive definition of society itself.

NOTES

1. *See* Chris Dolan, "Whatever happened to comprehensive justice?" (Refugee Law Project, Faculty of Law, Makerere University, June 2007), paras. 2 and 7, *available at* http://www.refugeelawproject.org/press_releases/WhateverHappenedtoTrueJustice.pdf (*see* chapters 4 and 6). Dolan speaks of "justice as the handmaid of sustainable peace," and suggests that justice has social as well as legal dimensions. *Id.*
2. Chief Maada Alpha Ndolleh, Kailahun town chief. *See* "Fambul Tok: Community Healing in Sierra Leone, Our First Year" at 29 (2009, Forum of Conscience and Catalyst for Peace). More information about Fambul Tok is available *at* http://www.fambultok.org/.
3. *See* notes from March 28, 2010 interview with Alexis Sinduhije, p. 32(a) of author's field notebook.
4. *Cosmopolitan sovereignty* and *plural nationalism* are concepts inspired by the work of anthropologist Liisa Malkki and Burundian journalist Alexis Sinduhije. Malkki's reference to the cosmopolitanism of Burundians living in urban settings in Tanzania and Sinduhije's vision of government as protector of all the people are discussed in Chapter 9.
5. *See* discussion of cooperative agricultural activities sponsored by Fambul Tok in Chapter 8.

INDEX

Abdullah, Ibrahim, 249
Abu Garda, Bahar Idriss, 139
Accession, 114n46
Accountability for war crimes. *See also* War crimes; Truth telling, 215–17
Acholi Army brigade, 212
Acholi people
　and amnesty, 183, 198
　habitat, 142n7
　and LRA, 213
　physical punishment, views toward, 238n100
　Song of Lawino, 229n2
ACHPR. *See* African Court on Human and Peoples' Rights (ACHPR)
ACHR. *See* American Convention on Human Rights (ACHR)
Addis Ababa Document on Refugees and Forced Population Displacement in Africa, 161
Additional Protocol to the American Convention on Human Rights in the Area of Economic, Social and Cultural Rights, 102
AFRC. *See* Armed Forces Revolutionary Council (AFRC)
African-Americans, civil rights, 198
African Charter on Human and People's Rights (Banjul Charter)
　adoption of, 28
　African Commission on Human and People's Rights. *See* African Commission on Human and People's Rights
　collective life, 85
　generally, 87
　overview, 104–6
　quote from, 75
African Commission on Human and People's Rights
　cases before, 40n52
　creation of, 105–6
　and TRC, 265
African Court on Human and Peoples' Rights (ACHPR), 106
African Court of Justice and Human Rights (ACJHR), 106
African National Congress (ANC), 24, 52
African Slave Trade, 68n29
African Union (AU)
　ceasefire, 329
　criticisms of ICC, 151n120
　peace process, 294
　precursor to, 28
African Union Convention for the Protection and Assistance of Internally Displaced Persons in Africa (Kampala Convention)
　generally, 154
　internally displaced persons (IDPs), 161–62
　states, general obligations of, 171n43
African Union Mission in Burundi (AMIB), 9n17
Aggression
　concept of, 46–48, 67n20
　defenses, 144n23
　defined, 147n70
Agreement for the Prosecution and Punishment of the Major War Criminals of the European Axis of August 8, 1945, 125, 143n13

Agreement on Accountability and Reconciliation between the Government of the Republic of Uganda and the Lord's Resistance Army/Movement, 232n33
Agreement on a Permanent Ceasefire between the Government of the Republic of Uganda and the Lord's Resistance Army/Movement, 232n35
Agreement on Cessation of Hostilities between the Government of the Republic of Uganda and the Lord's Resistance Army/Movement, 209, 230n4, 232n32
Agreement on Comprehensive Solutions between the Government of the Republic of Uganda and the Lord's Resistance Army/Movement. *See also* Implementation Protocol to the Agreement on Comprehensive Solutions, 232n34, 232n37
Agreement on Disarmament, Demobilization and Reintegration between the Government of the Republic of Uganda and the Lord's Resistance, 232n36 Army/Movement, 232n35
AI. *See* Amnesty International (AI)
al-Qadhafi, Mu'ammar, 246
al Qaeda, 62
  al-Shabab, 185
  status of organization, 28
Al-Bashir, Omar Hassan Ahmad, 139–40
Alien Tort Claims Act, 27
Allied Democratic Forces, 239n111
All People's Congress (APC), 245–46
American Convention on Human Rights (ACHR), 39n52, 102–4
American Revolutionary War, 241
AMIB. *See* African Union Mission in Burundi (AMIB)
Amin Dada, Idi
  and British, 230n9
  and ethnopolitics, 212
  extrajudicial killings during years, 231n17
  overthrowing of Obote, 211
  psychological development of, 230–31n12
Amnesty Act of 2000 (Uganda)
  children, return of, 218–19
  impetus behind, 232n27
  legal amnesty, 198
  passage of, 209, 213, 325
  term of, 234n55
  transitional justice, 226
Amnesty International (AI)
  child soldiers, 278n99
  media as means of enforcing humanitarian law, 188
ANC. *See* African National Congress (ANC)
Anglophone, use of term, 295
Annan, Kofi
  "In Larger Freedom" report, 51
  poverty alleviation, 25
Apartheid
  International Convention on the Suppression and Punishment of the Crime of Apartheid, 88
  overview, 88–90
APC. *See* All People's Congress (APC)
Appeals Chamber of the International Criminal Tribunal for Rwanda, 140
Arab Charter on Human Rights, 107–8
Armed conflict. *See also* Force, rules regarding; International humanitarian law
  defined, 6, 59–60
  Geneva Conventions (1949), 57–58, 61–62
  human insecurity in context of, 79–80
  resolution of, 1
Armed Forces Revolutionary Council (AFRC), 130, 255–56, 262
Arusha Peace and Reconciliation Agreement (Burundi)
  and disarmament, 195
  drafting, 181
  generally, 6
  peace process, 294, 329
  Protocol II, 316n103
  responsible sovereignty, 307
  signing of, 283, 293
  transitional justice, 305
Ashburton, Lord, 50
Assaily, Nafez, 45
Association of Burundian Women Entrepreneurs, 190
Asylum
  discretionary nature of, 169n20
  nonentitlement to, 156
  right to seek and be granted, 118n117
AU. *See* African Union (AU)

Bacteriological weapons, outlawing of, 55
Bagaza, Jean-Baptiste, 290
Balance Sheet of Freedom (Freedom House), 80
Banjul Charter. *See* African Charter on Human and People's Rights (Banjul Charter)
Ban Ki-moon
  protection of civilians, 25
  responsibility to protect (R2P), 51–52
Banyah, Satie, 281n141
Bashingantahe, 181, 305-06
Battle of Solferino, 55
Beah, Ishmael, 251, 252, 272n4, 273n18
Bello, Emmanuel, 64
Bemba Gombo, Jean-Pierre (Bemba), 138
Beyond Juba Project (BJP), 229n1
  leader of, 149–50n96
  and media, 189, 191
  transitional justice. *See also* Transitional justice; Retributive justice, 218–27
  Truth and Reconciliation Commission, calling for establishment, 217, 229n1, 235n63
Biguzzi, George, 259–60
Bio, Julius Maada, 251
BJP. *See* Beyond Juba Project (BJP)
Blackstone, William, 33n3
Bockarie, Sam, 146n52, 255
Botswana, independence, 7–8n1
Brima, Alex Tamba, 146n51, 256, 277n87, 278n93
Brockmann, Miguel D'Escoto, 52
Burundi, 283–321
  African Commission on Human and People's Rights, 105–6
  Belgian Trusteeship, 309n5
  Camp Kanembwa, 318n117
  civil war
    deaths, 309n6
    launching of, 291–92
  communities, implementation of humanitarian law, 199–200
  Conflict Alert and Prevention Centre (CENAP)
    disarmament, 301–3, 308n1
    durable peace, 297–99, 329
    peace conference organized by, 317n113, 319n143, 319n145
  Constitution, 296, 309n4
    human rights provisions, 109–10

Convention on the Elimination of All Forms of Discrimination Against Women (CEDAW), 98
Convention on the Elimination of All Forms of Racial Discrimination (CERD), 97
Convention on the Prevention and Punishment of the Crime of Genocide, adoption of, 87
courts, judicial enforcement of humanitarian law, 179–80
development as mechanism for conflict resolution, 194–95
disarmament, 297–98, 300–302
durable peace
  Conflict Alert and Prevention Centre (CENAP), 297–99, 301–3, 308n1, 317n113, 329
  disarmament, 297–98, 300–302
  education, 302–3
  elections, 297–98, 299–300
  employment, 297–98, 303–4
  generally, 328–29
  memorializing the dead, 297–99
  transitional justice, 304–8
education, 302–3
elections, 297–98, 299–300
employment, 297–98, 303–4
ethnic dynamism, 289–91
ethnicity, 284–89
ethnic pluralism, 295–97
Forces Armées Burundaises (FAB), 294, 301, 314n75
Forces de Défense Nationale (FDN), 294, 314n75
and Freedom House, 81
Front for Democracy in Burundi (FRODEBU), 294
Ganwa, 289
genocide, 290–91
Gisenyi, RFP attack on, 315n99
Gitega Secondary School, 298
Gross national income (GNI), 304
human development index (HDI), 304
human insecurity, 79–80
humanitarian law, 283–321. *See also Lines throughout this topic*
Hutuism, generally, 288
Hutu people. *See Lines throughout this topic*
Hutu uprising, 290

Index [337]

Burundi (Cont'd)
    insurgency, 292–95
    internally displaced persons (IDPs), 174n60
    justice, ongoing pursuit of, 140–41
    land mass, 308n4
    life expectancy, 79
    majority rule, 291–92
    media, implementation of humanitarian law, 190
    memorializing the dead, 297–99
    Movement de Solidarité et Démocratie (MSD), 299, 318n120
    Mwami, 289
    National Commission to Study the Question of National Unity, 291
    National Council for the Defense of Democracy (CNDD), 293–95
    National Movement for Democracy and Development (MRND), 313n71
    "new generation," 319n148
    nongovernmental organizations (NGOs)
        communities and conflict resolution, 201
        development as mechanism for conflict resolution, 195
    population, age of, 310n21
    post-conflict reconstruction, 4, 6, 283–321
    refugees, 165, 318n117
    responsible sovereignty, 306–8
    and Rwanda, similarities and differences, 286–97
        ethnic dynamism in Burundi, 289–91
        ethnic pluralism, 295–97
        historical commonalities, 286–89
        history and sociology of Burundi, 289–97
        insurgency, 292–95
        majority rule, 291–92
    selective genocide, 291
    socioeconomic security, 78–79
    transitional justice, 304–8
        responsible sovereignty, 306–8
        women's equality, 305–6
    troops, military enforcement of humanitarian law, 187
    Truth and Reconciliation Commission (of Burundi) (TRC), 199, 305
    Tutsi people. See Lines throughout this topic
    Tutsi-Hima leaders, 290
    Tutsism, generally, 288
    ubushingantahe, 181, 197, 199, 329
    UN Commission on the Status of Women (CSW), 99
    Union for National Progress (UPRONA), 292, 294–96, 313n63
    violence, 284–86
    women
        equality, 305–6
        status of, 99
Burundian Forum for Strengthening Civil Society, 320n156
Burundian Human Rights League of Iteka, 320n156
Burundian Red Cross, 195
Bush, George W., 58
Buyoya, Pierre
    and civil war, 291–92
    installed as president, 106
    political power, 290
Bwampamye, Gaetan, 106

Cairo Declaration on Human Rights in Islam, 107
Cambodia
    "killing fields," 87
    Vietnam's invasion of, 50
Camp Kanembwa, 318n117
Canada
    International Development Agency, 270
    Peaceful Schools International, 270
CAR. See Central African Republic (CAR)
Carew-Bah, Agnes Jattu, 282n148
CARL. See Centre for Accountability and the Rule of Law (CARL)
Caroline Incident, 49–50
Cartagena Declaration on Refugees, 158–59
CAT. See Convention Against Torture (CAT)
Catalyst for Peace, 269
Caulker, John, 260, 263–64, 268–69, 281n142
CDF. See Civil Defense Forces (CDF)
CD-Peace. See Centre for Development and Peace Education (CD-Peace)
CEDAW. See Convention on the Elimination of All Forms of Discrimination Against Women (CEDAW)
CENAP (Centre d'Alerte et Prévention de Conflits) See Conflict Alert and Prevention Centre
Center for Constitutional Rights, 27
Central African Republic (CAR)

International Criminal Court (ICC), 138–39, 149n86
　attacks by Lord's Resistance Army, 186
　as safe haven, 214
Centre d'Alerte et Prévention de Conflits (CENAP). *See also* Conflict Alert and Prevention Centre (CENAP)
Centre for Accountability and the Rule of Law (CARL), 190, 191, 260, 278n94
Centre for Development and Peace Education (CD-Peace), 190, 194, 200, 270–71
CERD. *See* Convention on the Elimination of All Forms of Racial Discrimination (CERD)
Children
　Beyond Juba Project, 218–19
　exploitation, Uganda, 210
　punishment, Sierra Leone, 263
　recruitment of, Revolutionary United Front (RUF), 250–51
　soldiers, 278n93. *See also* United Movement to End Child Soldiering (UMECS)
　cases against, 278n99
Chile, Truth and Reconciliation Commission (TRC), 266
Chinese oil companies, 42n73
Chui, Mathieu Ngudjolo, 138
Civil and Political Covenant. *See* International Covenant on Civil and Political Rights
Civil Defense Forces (CDF), 251–52, 256
Civilian Convention. *See also* Geneva Conventions (1949); Fourth Geneva Convention of 1949, 62
Civilian deaths, Uganda, 231n20, 237n92
CNDD. *See* National Council for the Defense of Democracy (CNDD)
CNDD-FDD, 294, 296, 300–301, 314n81
Coalition for International Justice, 165
Committee of Experts on Human Rights (Arab Charter), 107
Communities. *See also* Conflict resolution, communities as places for
　and humanitarian law, 178
　victims and perpetrators, Uganda, 223
Conflict Alert and Prevention Centre (CENAP), 190
　disarmament, 301–3, 308n1
　durable peace, 297–99, 329

　peace conference organized by, 317n113, 319n143, 319n145
Conflict resolution
　communities as place for, 196–202
　　implementation of humanitarian law, mechanisms for, 197–200
　　interactions with other arenas for conflict resolution, 200–202
　　role of communities, 196–97
　courts as arenas for, 178–83, 187–88
　　collaboration between courts and other arenas, 181–83
　　judicial enforcement of humanitarian law, 179–81
　　judicial tribunals, 178–79
　development as catalyst for, 192–96
　　collaboration with other areas of conflict resolution, 196
　　mechanism for conflict resolution, development as, 193–195
　　role of development programs in implementing humanitarian law, 192–93
　international legal rules for
　　criminal law, 123–152
　　human fundamentals of international law, 13–43
　　human rights law, 75–121
　　international refugee law, 153–74
　　law of armed conflict, 45–74
　　overview, 2–4
　media as means of, 188–92
　　collaboration with other mechanisms for conflict resolution, 190–92
　　enforcement, 188–89
　　implementation of humanitarian law, 189–90
　troops as tools for, 184–88
　　enforcement of humanitarian law, 184–85
　　mechanisms for conflict resolution, collaboration between troops and, 187–88
　　military enforcement of humanitarian law, 186–87
　　peacekeeping troops, 184–85
Conflicts of law, domain of, 34n4
Constitution (US). *See* US Constitution
Convention Against Torture (CAT)
　implementation of, 124
　jus cogens, 16

Index [339]

Convention Against Torture (CAT) (*Cont'd*)
  number of parties, 117–18n106
  overview, 99–100
Convention Governing the Specific Aspects of Refugee Problems in Africa, 154, 157–58
Convention on Human Rights and Fundamental Freedoms. *See* European Convention on Human Rights and Fundamental Freedoms
Convention on the Elimination of All Forms of Discrimination Against Women (CEDAW), 97–99, 117n88
Convention on the Elimination of All Forms of Racial Discrimination (CERD), 96–97, 117n105
Convention on the Prevention and Punishment of the Crime of Genocide, 87–88
  adoption of, 95
  definition of genocide, 132
  drafters of, 115n49
  failure of some states to ratify, 114n45
Convention relating to the Status of Refugees (1951 Refugee Convention)
  articles, 156–57
  citations, 310n18
  definition of refugee, 155
  1967 Protocol, 155, 168n11
  Non-refoulement, right to, 93
  overview, 155–57
  signatories, 170n22
Corporations as makers of international law, 27
"Cosmopolitan sovereignty," 329, 333n4
"Cotton Field Case," 103–4
Council of Europe, 1950 Convention on Human Rights and Fundamental Freedoms. *See* European Convention on Human Rights and Fundamental Freedoms
Counterterrorism as armed conflict, 58–59
Courts and humanitarian law. *See also* Conflict resolution, courts as arenas for, 178
Crane, David, 278n99
Crime rate, international aspects, 2
"Crimes Against Peace," 67n17, 126
Criminal accountability, 180
Criminal justice and reconciliative justice, 332–33

Criminal law. *See* International Criminal Court; International criminal law
CSW. *See* UN Commission on the Status of Women (CSW)
Cultural identity, peace as, 227–29

Danish Church Aid, 195
Darfur, Sudan
  internally displaced persons (IDPs), 174n63
  International Criminal Court (ICC), 139–40
  refugees, 165
  Save Darfur Foundation, 151n118
Davis, Mary McGowan, 41n66
Day, Dorothy, 45
Declaration Against Torture, 19
Democratic Party of Uganda, 217
Democratic Republic of the Congo
  African Commission on Human Rights, 120n148
  International Criminal Court (ICC), 137–38
  attacks by Lord's Resistance Army, 186
  as safe haven, 214
Deng, Frances, 160
Deo. *See* Niyizonkiza, Deogratias
Developing countries
  designation as, 113n27
  gross domestic product (GDP), 78
Development, *See also* Conflict resolution, 178
  and humanitarian law
    Sierra Leone, 326–28
  media and development organizations, 196
  Sierra Leone, 326–28
Devolution of *Estates* Act (Sierra Leone), 278n97
Diamond trade, Sierra Leone, 248, 252, 274n32, 275n36, 276n69
Disarmament, Burundi, 300–302
"Disarming the Heart to Disarm the Body," 301, 308n1
Discrimination. *See specific topic*
Displaced persons. *See also* Internally displaced persons (IDPs)
  Uganda, 229
Distinction, principle of, 54
Doctors Without Borders, 8n2
Dolan, Chris, 198, 221–22

Domestic law
  defined, 34n5
  metaphors for international law, 17–18
  relationship with international law, 29–32
Domestic violence. *See also* Gender-based violence
  Uganda, 220
Domestic Violence Act (Sierra Leone), 278n97
Dowden, Richard, 250
DRC. *See* Democratic Republic of the Congo
Dualism, 29–31
Dumont, Henri, 54–55
Durable peace, 323-24
  Burundi. *See also* Burundi, durable peace, 328–29
"Durable Peace in Burundi: What Solution?", 298. *See also* Burundi
"Dwong Pako" (radio program), 236n74
Dyilo, Thomas Lubanga, 138

ECOMOG. *See* Economic Community's Monitoring Observer Group (ECOMOG)
Economic and Social Council (ECOSOC), 25–26
Economic and Social Covenant. *See* International Covenant on Economic, Social and Cultural Rights
Economic and social rights, 84–85
Economic Community of West African States (ECOWAS), 184
Economic Community's Monitoring Observer Group (ECOMOG)
  criticisms, 200
  Kabbah, Ahmed Tejan, restoring to presidency, 252
  and peacekeeping, 184, 186
  peacekeeping troops, 253
  reports to Government of Sierra Leone, 264
  and Taylor, Charles, 248
ECOSOC. *See* Economic and Social Council (ECOSOC)
ECOWAS. *See* Economic Community of West African States (ECOWAS)
Education
  Burundi, 302–3
  women, secondary education, 79
Egbaguru, Yunis, 233n42

Elections. *See specific country*
Employment, Burundi, 297–98, 303–4
Enforcement. *See also* Conflict resolution
  Burundi
    judicial enforcement of humanitarian law, 179–80
    military enforcement of humanitarian law, 187
  Sierra Leone
    judicial enforcement of humanitarian law, 179–80
    military enforcement of humanitarian law, 186–87
  Uganda
    judicial enforcement of humanitarian law, 179–80
    military enforcement of humanitarian law, 186
  UN Security Council, 48–49
Equality, norm of, 82–83
Erlinder, Peter, 315n96
Ethnic cleansing
  "In Larger Freedom" report, 51
  international aspects, 2
Ethnicity. *See specific country*
Ethnic pluralism
  Burundi, 295–97
  and Rwanda, similarities and differences, 295–97
EU. *See* European Union (EU)
European Convention on Human Rights and Fundamental Freedoms
  overview, 101
  violation of, 39n52
European Union (EU), 30

FAB. *See* Forces Armées Burundaises (FAB)
Fambul tok ("family talk," in Krio), 124, 142n8
Fambul Tok (NGO in Sierra Leone)
  and development, 271
  and media, 190
  and reconciliation, 142n8
  and retraumatization process, 281n140
  and grassroots reconciliation, 268–70
Fambul Tok's Radio Listening Clubs, 191
"Family talk." *See* Fambul tok ("family talk")
Farah, Douglas, 274n25
Farmer, Paul, 195
FDD. *See* Forces for the Defense of Democracy (FDD)

FDN. *See* Forces de Défense Nationale (FDN)
Femicides, Mexico, 98, 103
Finnoh, Tamba, 267
FNL. *See* Front National de Libération (FNL)
Foden, Giles, 230n12
Fofana, Moinina, 146n50, 255, 277n86
Force, rules regarding use of, 46–53
   aggression, concept of, 46–48, 67n20
   "armed attack" and self-defense, 48
   exceptions to general prohibition, 48–53
   general prohibition, 46–48
   humanitarian intervention, 50–51
   language, 66n11
   national liberation, wars of, 52–53
   responsibility to protect (R2P), 51–52
   self-defense, claim of, 49–50
   terrorism, wars against, 52–53
   UN Security Council enforcement, 48–49
Forced migrants, 154
Forced return (refoulement), 100, 310n18
Forces Armées Burundaises (FAB), 294, 314n75
Forces de Défense Nationale (FDN), 294, 314n75
Forces for the Defense of Democracy (FDD), 294, 300
Forces Patrioques pour la Libération du Congo (FPLC), 137
Fornah, Mark, 282n148
Fourah Bay College, 246
"Four Freedoms" speech (Roosevelt), 110n3
Four Geneva Conventions (1949). *See* Geneva Conventions (1949)
Fourteenth Amendment, US Constitution, 114n43
Fowler, Jerry, 151n118
Fox, Henry Stephen, 50
FPLC. *See* Forces Patrioques pour la Libération du Congo (FPLC)
"Francophone," use of term, 296
Freedom House, 80–81
Freedom in the World (Freedom House), 80–81
Freetown Colony. *See* Sierra Leone
French Revolution, 76
FRODEBU. *See* Front for Democracy in Burundi (FRODEBU)
Front for Democracy in Burundi (FRODEBU), 294

Front National de Libération (FNL), 195, 293–94, 300

Galtung, Johan, 10n19, 303, 319n149
Gandhi, Mohandas, 45
Ganwa people, 289
Garang, John, 230n9
Gbao, Augustine, 255, 277n85, 278n93
GDP. *See* Gross domestic product (GDP)
Gender-based violence, 187, 204n24, 237n81
Geneva Conference (1864), 55
Geneva Conventions (1949)
   armed conflict
      defined, 59–60
      described, 61–62
      limiting methods of, 60–64
   Common Article 2, 57, 59
   Common Article 3, 57, 59–62, 100, 133
   Common Article 4, 62
   counterterrorism as armed conflict, 58–59
   defining armed conflict, 57–58
   First Geneva Convention of 1949, 61
   Fourth Geneva Convention of 1949, 62
   International Committee of the Red Cross (ICRC)
      generally, 55
      global survey, results of, 64
      limiting methods of armed conflict, 61
      role in creating, 26–27
   prisoners of war (POWs), 127
   Protocol I (Additional Protocol I), 27, 63–64, 73n105
   Protocol II (Additional Protocol II), 27–28, 63–64, 72n86
   Second Geneva Convention of 1949, 61
   Third Geneva Convention of 1949, Article 13, 61
Geneva Protocol of 1925, 55, 66n10
Geneva Protocols of 1977. *See* Geneva Conventions,
   Protocol I and Protocol II
   armed conflict, defined, 60
   enhanced humanitarian protections, 63–64
   generally, 56, 59–60
   limiting methods of armed conflict, 63–64
Genocide. *See also* Convention on the Prevention and Punishment of the Crime of Genocide
   Burundi, 290–91
   defined, 132
   "In Larger Freedom" report, 51

International Criminal Tribunal for
    Rwanda (ICTR), 129
International Criminal Tribunal for the
    Former Yugoslavia (ICTY), 128
  overview, 88–90
  Rwanda, 289, 292
  use of term, 115n49
Genocide Convention. *See* Convention on
    the Prevention and Punishment of
    the Crime of Genocide
Genocide Intervention Network, 189
Germany
  economic statistics, 173n54
  gross domestic product (GDP), 163
  refugees, 163, 172n52
Ghana, independence, 7n1
Girl Soldiers Project (GSP), 193
Gisenyi, RFP attack on, 315n99
Gissabo, Mwéezi IV (king of Burundi),
    310n23
Gitega Secondary School (Burundi), 298
GNI. *See* Gross national income (GNI)
GNP. *See* Gross national product (GNP)
Goldstone, Richard, 41n66
Golooba, Frederick, 217
Gombo. *See* Bemba Gombo, Jean-Pierre
Gonzalez Case, 103–4
Gonzalez, Claudia Ivette, 103–4
Gourevitch, Philip, 313n71, 314n73,
    315–16n99
Grassroots
  reconciliative justice, 330–31
  transitional justice, 268–71
Gross domestic product (GDP)
  calculation of, 173n53
  Germany, 163
  health of economy, use of in determining,
    112n16
  and least developed countries, 78
  Malawi, 112n12
  Pakistan, 164
  Tanzania, 164
  United States, 112n12
Gross national income (GNI)
  Burundi, 304
  and material well-being, 78–79
Gross national product (GNP), 8n4
Grotius, Hugo, 33n3, 45–46
GSP. *See* Girl Soldiers Project (GSP)
Guantanamo Bay, U.S. Naval Base
  detention, 28, 58, 61

Guir, Ted Robert, 232n29
Gulu Support Children's Organization
    (GUSCO), 234n50
Gusimbura, 310n16

Hague Convention IV (1907), 55, 62
Hague, International Criminal Court. *See*
    International Criminal Court
Hague Law, 67n12, 69n47
Hague Regulations, 61
"Hands-off" rights, 83, 84
Hapsburg Empire, 20
Harun, Ahmad, 139
HDI. *See* Human development index (HDI)
Heron, G. A., 229n2
Historical justice, 224, 266–68, 297–99, 324
Holocaust, 47, 87, 115n49
  war criminals. *See* Agreement for the
    Prosecution and Punishment of the
    Major War Criminals of the
    European Axis of August 8, 1945;
    International criminal law;
    International Military Tribunal
    (IMT); Nuremburg Statute
Holy Spirit Movement, 212–13
Hovil, Lucy and Lomo, Zachary, 218–19,
    237n80
Human development index (HDI), 78–79,
    112n15, 113n28, 304
Human Development Report for 2010
    (UNDP), 79
Human dignity, law of. *See* Human rights law
Human insecurity, 79–80
Humanitarian law. *See also* International
    humanitarian law (IHL); Conflict
    resolution; *specific countries*, 45–74
  Africa, humanitarian law norms
    in, 64–65
  communities, 178, 196–202
    implementation of humanitarian law,
      mechanisms for, 197–200
  courts, 178–83
    judicial enforcement of humanitarian
      law, 179–81
  development, 178, 192–96
    role of development programs in
      implementing humanitarian law,
      192–93
  durable peace, 323–24
  generally, 1
  humanitarian law in action, 323–24

Index [343]

Humanitarian law (Cont'd)
  insights gained, 329–33
  media, 178, 188–92
    enforcement of humanitarian law, 188–89
  Sierra Leone, 253–68. *See also* Sierra Leone *for detailed treatment*
  sister fields of international law, 2–4, 32–33, 323
  tools for implementing, 177–207
  transitional justice
    generally, 323–24
    Sierra Leone, 253–68
    Uganda, 226–27
  troops
    conflict resolution, as tools for, 184–88
    enforcement of humanitarian law, 184–85
    peacekeeping troops, 184–85
  Uganda. *See also* Uganda *for detailed treatment*, 226–27
Humanity, principle of, 54
Human Rights and Peace Centre (HURIPEC), 189, 224, 236n64, 238n105
Human rights law, 75–121
  civil and political rights (basic liberties), 83–84
  collective life, 85–86
  economic and social rights, 84–85
  "hands-off" rights, 83, 84
  human liberty, measuring, 77–82
  interdependence of fundamental rights and freedoms, 82–86
  material needs, fundamental, 84–85
  measuring socioeconomic security and human liberty, 77–82
  national constitutions, human rights provisions in, 108–10
  norm of equality, 82–83
  overview, 3
  political liberty, measuring, 80–82
  "positive rights," 84–85
  UDHR. *See* Universal Declaration of Human Rights (UDHR)
Human rights treaties, 86–108. *See also specific treaties*
  institutionalized human rights abuses, treaties to combat, 87–90
  1966 international covenants, 90–95. *See also specific topic*
  regional human rights treaties, 101–8
  specialized human rights treaties, 96–100
Human trafficking, 42n75
Humper, Joseph, 259
HURIPEC. *See* Human Rights and Peace Centre (HURIPEC)
Hutu people. *See* Burundi; Party for the Liberation of the Hutu People (PALIPEHUTU)

Ibanga, 305–6
ICC. *See* International Criminal Court (ICC)
ICC Act of 2010
  complementarity of international and Ugandan law, 226
  passage of, 216
ICCPR. *See* International Covenant on Civil and Political Rights (ICCPR)
ICD. *See* International Crimes Division (ICD)
ICESCR. *See* International Covenant on Economic, Social and Cultural Rights (ICESCR)
ICJ. *See* International Court of Justice (ICJ)
ICRC. *See* International Committee of the Red Cross (ICRC)
ICTR. *See* International Criminal Tribunal for Rwanda (ICTR)
ICTY. *See* International Criminal Tribunal for the Former Yugoslavia (ICTY)
Idi Amin Dada. *See* Amin Dada, Idi
IDPs. *See* Internally displaced persons (IDPs)
IHL. *See* International humanitarian law (IHL)
ILA. *See* International Law Association (ILA)
Immigration and Nationality Act (INA), 169n20
Implementation Protocol to the Agreement on Comprehensive Solutions. *See also* Agreement on Comprehensive Solutions between the Government of the Republic of Uganda and the Lord's Resistance Army/Movment, 233n37
IMT. *See* International Military Tribunal (IMT)
IMTFE. *See* International Military Tribunal for the Far East (IMTFE)

INA. *See* Immigration and Nationality Act (INA)
Indigenous peoples, 27, 85–86
Industrial countries, designation as, 113n27
Ingabire, Victoire, 315n96
"In Larger Freedom" report, 51
Institute of International Law, 58
Institutionalized human rights abuses, treaties to combat, 87–90
Insurgencies as subjects of international law, 27–28
Interahamwe, 292, 313n71
Inter-American Court of Human Rights, 98
Internal Displacement Monitoring Center, 174n63
Internal disturbance, 72n85
Internally displaced persons (IDPs)
   Addis Ababa Document on Refugees and Forced Population Displacement in Africa, 161
   African Union Convention for the Protection and Assistance of Internally Displaced Persons in Africa (Kampala Convention), 154, 161–62, 171n43
   assisting alongside refugees, 164–66
   Burundi, 165, 174n60
   Darfur, Sudan, 174n63
   generally, 154
   interdependence of protection and assistance, 162–66
   overview, 153–54, 159–62
   Sierra Leone, 165, 174n61
   states, general obligations of, 171n43, 172n46
   Uganda, 165, 174n60, 174n65
   United Nations Guiding Principles on Internal Displacement, 161
International Commission on Intervention and State Sovereignty, 51
International Committee of the Red Cross (ICRC)
   Annual Report, 294
   Burundi, role in, 195
   Geneva Conventions (1949), role in creating, 26–27
   global survey, results of, 64
   humanitarian law, as champion and drafter of, 54–56
   media, implementation of humanitarian law, 189–91

"So Why?" (song), 202n1, 202n6
"Woza Africa," 202n6
International Court of Justice (ICJ)
   Article 38, 18
   Statute, 15, 16, 18
International Covenant on Civil and Political Rights (ICCPR)
   Article 4, 94, 99
   articles, 92–95
   establishment of, 89
   generally, 92–95, 99
   genocide, 127
   Human Rights Committee, 95
   and individuals, 22
   jus cogens, 16
   overview, 92–95
International Covenant on Economic, Social and Cultural Rights (ICESCR)
   articles, 91–92
   generally, 86–87
   overview, 90–92
   states, calling on, 164
International Crimes Division (Uganda) (ICD), 215, 235n60
International Criminal Court (ICC). *See also* ICC Act of 2010
   African Union, criticisms of ICC, 151n120
   Central African Republic (CAR), 138–39, 149n86
   Darfur, Sudan, 139–40
   Democratic Republic of the Congo (DRC), 137–38
   generally, 3
   inauguration of, 209–10
   Lord's Resistance Army (Uganda)
     alleged crimes by, 135–36
     cases against, 223
     and domestic developments, 136–37
     indictment of leaders, 5
     International Crimes Division, 140
     prosecutions, 325
   Office of the Prosecutor, 135
   overview, 132–40
   Review Conference (Kampala, Uganda--2010), 47–48
   Rome Statute, 43n84
     "Crimes Against Peace," 126
     overview, 132–33
     ratification by Burundi, 87
     ratification by Sierra Leone, 87

International Criminal Court (ICC) (*Cont'd*)
    ratification by Sierra Leone, 87, 213
    subject matter jurisdiction, 47
    war criminals, 123
    Rwanda
        Appeals Chamber of the International Criminal Tribunal for Rwanda, 140
    sentencing, 146nn49–52
    Sierra Leone, Human Rights Committee petition against, 95
    Statute, 149n89
    torture, prohibition of, 99
    Trial Division of International Criminal Court, 138, 139, 150n116
    Uganda, 134–37
    inauguration of, 209–10
International criminal law, 123–152. *See also* International Criminal Court (ICC); International Criminal Tribunal for Rwanda (ICTR); International Criminal Tribunal for the Former Yugoslavia (ICTY); International Military Tribunal (IMT)
    alternative justice mechanisms, 124–25s
    Burundi, ongoing pursuit of justice, 140–41
    overview, 3, 123–52
    Sierra Leone, ongoing pursuit of justice, 140–41
    Uganda, ongoing pursuit of justice, 140–41
International Criminal Tribunal for Rwanda (ICTR), 41n66, 123, 129, 140, 144n36
International Criminal Tribunal for the Former Yugoslavia (ICTY), 41n66, 123, 127–28, 144n35
International Federation of Human Rights Leagues, 320n156
International humanitarian law (IHL). *See also* Humanitarian law, 45–74
    Geneva Conventions (1949), 56–60. *See also* Geneva Conventions (1949)
    Geneva Protocols of 1977, 56–60
    armed conflict, defined, 60
    humanitarian law, essence of, 53–56
        distinction, principle of, 54
        foundational principles, 54
        humanity principle of, 54
        necessity, principle of, 54
        proportionality, principle of, 54, 70n48

    methods of, limiting, 60–64
    morality of war, 45–46
    overview, 3
International law
    armed conflict, 45–74. *See also* Law of armed conflict
    overview, 3
    corporations as makers of, 27
    criminal law. *See also* International criminal law *for detailed treatment*, 123–52
    customary international law, 15
    domestic law metaphors for international law, 17–18
    domestic law, relationship with, 29–32
    dualism, 29–31
    essence of international law, 13–15
    human fundamentals of, 13–43
    human rights law. *See also* International human rights law *for detailed treatment*, 75–121
    individuals as makers of international law, 22
    international humanitarian law. *See also* International humanitarian law *for detailed treatment*, 45–74
    international refugee law. *See also* International refugee law *for detailed treatment*, 153–74
    jus ad bellum, 34n6. *See also* Force, rules regarding use of, 34n6
    jus cogens, 16–17
    jus in bello, 34n6
    makers of international law, subjects of, 20–29
        corporations, 27
        indigenous peoples, 27
        individuals, 22
        insurgencies, 27–28
        international organizations, 21, 22
        non-governmental organizations (NGOs), 26–27
        rights and responsibilities, 28–29
        states, 20–22
        terrorist organizations, debate regarding, 28
        United Nations, 22–26
    monism, 29–31
    NGOs. *See* Nongovernmental organizations (NGOs)
    opinio juris vel necessitatis, 15

passive nationality principle, defined, 31
polycentricity, 34n7
primary and secondary sources, border between, 19–20
protective principle, defined, 31
public international law, defined, 34n4
purpose of international law, 13–15
responsibility to protect (R2P), 21
secondary sources, 18–19
soft law, defined, 18
sources of, 15–20
   domestic law metaphors for international law, 17–18
   jus cogens, 16–17
   primary and secondary sources, border between, 19–20
   secondary sources, 18–19
   UN Charter, primary sources, 15–16
   UN Security Council Resolutions, 17
subfields of, 32–33
United Nations as model for international organizations, 22–26
   Economic and Social Council (ECOSOC), 25–26
   International Court of Justice (ICJ), 24–25
   Special Court for Sierra Leone (SCSL), 26
   UN Development Program, 25
   UN Environmental Program, 25–26
   UN General Assembly, 23
   UN High Commissioner for Refugees, 26
   UN Secretariat, 25
   UN Security Council, 23–24
   World Food Program, 26
   World Health Organization, 25
universal jurisdiction, 31
UN Security Council Resolutions, 17
International Law Association (ILA), 161
International legal personality, 21, 28
International Military Tribunal for the Far East (IMTFE), 125, 126n15
International Military Tribunal (IMT)
   "Crimes Against Peace," 67n17, 126
   establishment of, 123
   overview, 125–27
International refugee law, 153–74
   interdependence of protection and assistance for refugees and IDPs, 162–66

   internally displaced persons (IDPs), 154, 159–66
   overview, 153–54
   regional law, 155–59
   sister fields, 166–67
Internally displaced persons. *See* International refugee law
International Rescue Committee (IRC), 194
Iranian Revolution, 24–25
Iran, US v., 24
IRC. *See* International Rescue Committee (IRC)
Irish Centre of Human Rights, 135
Israel, Obote's reliance on for military training, 212, 231n13
Italy, Second War of Independence, 55

Janjaweed, 139
JLOS. *See* Justice, Law and Order Sector (Uganda) (JLOS)
Juba Agreement on Cessation of Hostilities. *See* Agreement on Cessation of Hostilities between the Government of the Republic of Uganda and the Lord's Resistance Army/Movement, 209, 230n4, 232n32
Juba Peace Accords (Uganda), 27, 214, 232–33nn32–37
   implementation of, 27
Juba Peace Agreement on Accountability and Reconciliation. *See* Agreement on Accountability and Reconciliation between the Governmnet of the Republic of Uganda and the Lord's Resistance Army/Movement
Jurisdiction, generally, 30–32
   Rome Statute of the ICC, 47
   Special Court for Sierra Leone (SCSL), 203n14
   universal jurisdiction, 31
Jus ad bellum. *See also* Force, rules regarding use of, 6, 13, 34n6, 46–53, 54
Jus cogens, 16–17
Jus in bello. *See also* International humanitarian law, 46, 34n6, 53–54
Justice
   for children, 218–19
   legal protection, 220–21
   respect for women, 219–20
   restorative justice, 221–23. *See also* Restorative justice

Justice (Cont'd)
   retributive justice, 221–23. *See also* Retributive justice
   transitional justice, 224–27. *See also* Transitional justice
   victims and perpetrators, communities of, 223
     sustainable peace, justice as, 325–26
     transitional justice "as a stool with three legs," criminal, social and historical, 224, 297–99, 324
Justice and Equality Movement, 139
Justice, Law and Order Sector (JLOS)
   generally, 224–25
   and Odoi-Musoke, Rachel, 240n127
   Strategic Investment Plan, 225
   Transitional Justice Working Group, 225

Kabbah, Ahmed Tejan
   election of, 242, 251
   and end to war, 262
   ethnic affiliation, 247
   overthrowing of, 106, 145n48, 252
   reparations, failure to value, 267
   shielding of, 264–65
   and Special Court for Sierra Leone (SCSL), 254–56
   transitional justice, 253
Kabila, Joseph, 137
Kabila, Laurent, 137
Kabimba commune, 298
Kagame, Paul, 295–96
Kalin, Walter, 160
Kallon, Morris, 255, 277n85, 278n93
Kamara, Ibrahim Bazzy, 146n51, 256, 277n87, 278n93
Kambanda, Jean, 129, 140
Kampala Convention. *See* African Union Convention for the Protection and Assistance of Internally Displaced Persons in Africa (Kampala Convention)
Kampala Rugby Club, 230n12
Kamu, Santiago Borbor, 146n51
Kandeh, Jimmy, 244–45, 247, 273n14, 274n26, 274n29, 274n31s
Kandu-Bo, Samuth, 95
Kanu, Santigie Borbor, 256, 277–78n87, 278n93
KAR. *See* King's African Rifles (KAR)
Karefa-Smart, John, 274n26

Katanga, Germaine, 138
Kazibwe, Wandera, 236n74
Kelsey, Francis, 33n3
Khanyile, Jabu, 177
KICWA. *See* Kitgum Concerned Women's Association (KICWA)
Kidder, Tracy, 195, 284–85, 291, 310n16, 312n46
"Killing fields," Cambodia, 87
King, Martin Luther, Jr., 298
King's African Rifles (KAR), 211
Kitgum Concerned Women's Association (KICWA), 205n41
   Girl Soldiers Project (GSP), 193
Kondewa, Allieu, 146n50, 255–56, 277n86
Kony, Joseph
   indictments, 8n10, 214, 326
   Lord's Resistance Army, founding of, 213
   whereabouts of, 149n86
Korlia, George, 282n148
Koroma, Ernest Bai, 267
Koroma, Johnny Paul
   Kabbah, Ahmed Tejan, overthrowing of, 145n48, 252
   and Special Court for Sierra Leone (SCSL), 255
   "West Side Boys," 252, 253
   whereabouts of, 146n52
Koroma, Reuben M.
   on media, 188
   song lyrics, 45, 153, 184, 241
Koroma, Sheku, 281n140, 281n143, 281n145
Kosovo, bombing of, 68n33
Krios (Creoles), 245
Kushayb, Ali, 139
Kweyelo, Thomas, 217, 235n60, 239–40n124

Lagbaja, 177
Last King of Scotland (Foden), 230n12
Law of armed conflict, *See* International humanitarian law; Humanitarian law
Lemarchand, René, 291
Liberia, invasion of Sierra Leone, 130
Life expectancy and material well-being, 78–79
Lomé Peace Agreement (Sierra Leone)
   amnesty provision, 243, 253–55
   Article IX, 146n53
   military enforcement of humanitarian law, 186
   signing of, 242

and Special Court for Sierra Leone, 130–31
Truth and Reconciliation Commission (TRC), 6, 71n69, 326
London Agreement, 126
Lord's Resistance Army (Uganda). *See also* Juba Peace Accords
  alleged crimes by, 135–36, 223
  civil war, 213–14. *See also Lines throughout this topic*
  and domestic developments, 136–37
  generally, 2, 27
  Holy Spirit Movement, as precursor to, 213
  indictment of leaders, 5
  International Criminal Court (ICC)
    alleged crimes by, 135–36
    cases against, 223
    and domestic developments, 136–37
    indictment of leaders, 5
    International Crimes Division, 140
    prosecutions, 180, 181, 325
  and Museveni, Yoweri, 213–14
  prosecutions, Ugandan peace talks and, 214–15
  and refugees, 81
LRA. *See* Lord's Resistance Army (Uganda)
Luck, Edward, 52

Majid, Anouar, 34n7
Makerere University
  Beyond Juba Project. *See* Beyond Juba Project (BJP)
  Faculty of Law, 189
  Gender and the Law, 223
  Human Rights and Peace Centre (HURIPEC), 189, 224, 236n64
  Institute of Social Research, 217
  Refugee Law Project. *See* Refugee Law Project (Makerere University)
Malawi, gross domestic product (GDP), 112n12
Malkki, Liisa, 287, 311n31, 311n34, 311n37, 333n4
Mandela, Nelson, 24
Mao, Norbert, 217
Margai, Albert, 247, 273n20, 274n27
Margai, Milton
  election of, 245
  ethnic affiliation, 247
  profile of, 273n20
  successor, 274n26

Martin, David, 291
Maryland, University of
  Minorities at Risk, 232n29
Massaquoi, Francis, 282n148
Material needs, fundamental, 84–85
Material well-being and life expectancy, 78–79
Mato oput (Uganda)
  accountability, 215–17
  and amnesty, 198
  defined, 216
  generally, 235n57
  origins, 235n58
  practices of, 197
Media and humanitarian law. *See also* Conflict resolution, media as means of, 178
Media agencies, 326–27
Melady, Thomas, 291
Me, My Future and My Country, 190
Meta abuses, 89
Mexico
  femicides, 98, 103
  kidnapping and murder of three individuals (2001), 103–4
Micombero, Michel, 290, 312n37
Military enforcement of humanitarian law, 186–87
Millennium Development Goals. *See* United Nations
Milosevic, Slobodan, 68n33
Minorities at Risk, 232n29
Momoh, Joseph, 247, 250, 274n27
Monarrez, Laura Berenice Ramos, 103–4
Monism, 29–31
"Monkey Work" (song), 271n1
Monreal, Esmeralda Herrera, 103–4
Montevideo Convention on the Rights and Duties of States, 20–21
Morality of war, 45–46
Moreno-Ocampo, Luis, 139, 150n116, 233n43
Movement de Solidarité et Democratie (MSD), 299, 318n120
MRND. *See* National Movement for Democracy and Development (MRND)
MSD. *See* Movement de Solidarité et Democratie (MSD)
Murders of women. *See* Femicide

Museveni, Yoweri
    and Lord's Resistance Army, 135, 213–14
    National Resistance Army (NRA), 135,
        231n20
    seizing of power, 209
Mustard gas, 66n11
Mutesa, Frederick, 211, 212
Mwami (Burundian king), 289

Nahimana, Terence, 306
Nampewo, Zahara, 223, 238n105
National Commission for Social Action
    (Sierra Leone), 267
National Commission to Study the Question
    of National Unity (Burundi), 291
National constitutions, human rights
    provisions in, 108–10
National Council for the Defense of
    Democracy (CNDD), 293–95
National Defense Forces. See Forces de
    Défense Nationale (FDN)
National Liberation Front. See Front
    National de Libération (FNL)
National liberation, wars of, 52–53
National Movement for Democracy and
    Development (MRND), 313n71
National Patriotic Front of Liberia
    (NPFL), 246
National Provisional Ruling Council
    (NPRC), 250
National Reconciliation Bill (proposed),
    226, 236n64
National Resistance Army (NRA), 212,
    231n20
National Resistance Movement (NRM),
    231n23
National University of Ireland
    Irish Centre of Human Rights, 135
National Victim Commemoration
    Conference, 257
Nazis. See Holocaust; International criminal
    law; International Military Tribunal
    (IMT); Nuremburg Statute
Ndadaye, Melchoir
    assassination of, 283, 292
    election of, 292
Ndayizeye, 315n92
Ndollch, Maada Alpha, 333n2
N'Dour, Youssou, 177
Necessity, principle of, 54
Ngoni tribe, 64

NGOs. See Nongovernmental organizations
    (NGOs)
Nindorera, Agnes, 289, 316n107
    quote, 283
    women's equality and ubushingantahe,
        305–6
1949 Geneva Conventions. See Geneva
    Conventions (1949)
1950 Convention on Human Rights and
    Fundamental Freedoms. See
    European Convention on Human
    Rights and Fundamental Freedoms
1951 Refugee Convention. See Convention
    Relating to the Status of Refugees
    (1951 Refugee Convention)
1966 international covenants, 90–95
1969 Convention Governing the Specific
    Aspects of Refugee Problems in
    Africa. See Convention Governing
    the Specific Aspects of Refugee
    Problems in Africa
1984 Cartagena Declaration on Refugees.
    See Cartagena Declaration on
    Refugees
1999 Lomé Peace Agreement. See Lomé
    Peace Agreement
Niyizonkiza, Deogratias, 284–85, 310n16
Nkurunziza, Pierre
    election, 294, 296, 309n4
    and Truth and Reconciliation
        Commission (TRC), 181,
        199, 305
Nonentitlement to asylum, 156
Nongovernmental organizations (NGOs)
    Burundi, 195, 201
    consultative status, 26–27
    and creation of international law,
        18, 56
    international legal personality,
        21, 26–27
    NGO Redress, 234n48
    Peaceful Schools International, 270
    Sierra Leone, 194
        Catalyst for Peace, 269
    Uganda, 148n82, 180, 193–94
        National Reconciliation Forum,
        call for, 217
Non-refoulement, right to, 93, 100
Norman, Sam Hinga
    Civil Defense Forces (CDF), formation
    of, 251–52, 256

death of, 146n52, 255
　prosecution of, 264–65
Norm of equality, 82–83
North Atlantic Treaty Organization (NATO), 68n33
Norwegian Refugee Council, 195, 233n38
NPFL. *See* Taylor, Charles
NRA. *See* National Resistance Army (NRA)
NRM. *See* National Resistance Movement (NRM)
Ntahobali, Arsène, 129
Ntakarutimana, Pie, 305, 320n156
Ntare V (king of Burundi), 290
Nuer people, 64
Nuremburg Charter, 47
Nuremburg Statute
　Article 6, 67n17, 126
　"Crimes Against Peace," 67n17
Nuremburg Tribunal. *See* International Military Tribunal (IMT)
Nyangoma, Léonard, 294–95
Nyiramasuhuko, Pauline, 129
Nyerere, Julius, 230n9

OAS. *See* Organization of American States (OAS)
OAU. *See* Organization of African Unity (OAU)
Obama, Barack, 299
Obote, Milton, 211–13, 231n13
Odoi-Musoke, Rachel, 227, 240n127
Okabo, James Jacob, 236n74
Oloka-Onyango, J., 224, 236n64, 238n94
"Operation No Living Thing," 252–53
Opio, Kasimu, 217, 235n58
Organization of African Unity (OAU)
　African Charter on Human and People's Rights (Banjul Charter)
　　adoption of, 28, 104
　　Protocol to, 106
　Refugee Convention, 154, 157–59
Organization of American States (OAS)
　American Convention on Human Rights (ACHR), 102–4
Ouattara, Alassane, 148n84

Pajule IDP camp, 237n81
Pakistan
　economic statistics, 173n56
　gross domestic product (GDP), 164
　refugees, 164, 165, 172n52

Palestinian Liberation Organization (PLO), 52
PALIPEHUTU. *See* Party for the Liberation of the Hutu People (PALIPEHUTU)
Partners in Health (PIH), 195, 201
Party for the Liberation of the Hutu People (PALIPEHUTU), 293, 314n79
Passive nationality principle, defined, 31
Peace. *See also specific topics*
　as cultural identity, 227–29
　defined, 6, 7
　durable peace. *See* Durable peace
Peace and Reconciliation Agricultural Show (Sierra Leone), 270
Peace education, 188, 302–03
Peaceful Schools International, 270
"Peace Mothers," 191–92
Peace of Westphalia, 20–21
Peace Studies. *See also* Galtung, Johan, 6–7, 10n19, 303
Perriello, Tom and Wierda, Marieke, 256, 257, 274n32, 275n36
PIH. *See* Partners in Health (PIH)
PLO. *See* Palestinian Liberation Organization (PLO)
"Plural nationalism," 311n31, 333n4
Pluralism
　ethnic pluralism, 295–97
　generally, 323–24
Poison gas, outlawing of, 55, 66n10
Political liberty, 80–82
Politics. *See specific country*
Polycentricity, 34n7
"Positive" rights. *See* Economic and social rights
Post-conflict reconstruction, humanitarian law
　Beyond Juba Project, 209–40
　Burundi, 4, 6, 283–321
　overview, 4–6
　Sierra Leone, 4–6, 241–82
　Uganda, 4–5, 209–40
POWs. *See* Prisoners of war (POWs)
p'Bitek, Okot, 209, 229n2
Prisoners of war (POWs)
　Geneva Conventions (1949), 127
　judicial tribunals, 179
　POW Convention, 59, 61–62, 73n97
Proportionality, principle of, 54, 70n48
Protective principle, defined, 31

Index [351]

Protocol of San Salvador. *See* Additional Protocol to the American Convention on Human Rights in the Area of Economic, Social and Cultural Rights

Race discrimination. *See also* Convention on the Elimination of All Forms of Racial Discrimination (CERD)
defined, 96
Racial Convention. *See* Convention on the Elimination of All Forms of Racial Discrimination (CERD)
Radio
Sierra Leone, 191–92
Uganda, 236n74
Rape
Sierra Leone, 263, 279n107
Uganda, 220
Reconciliative justice, 330–33
Red Cross. *See also* International Committee of the Red Cross (ICRC)
modern movement, 65
Refoulement, 100, 310n18
Non-refoulement, right to, 93, 100, 156–59
Refugee All Stars (Sierra Leone), 188, 189
Refugee Convention. *See* Convention Relating to the Status of Refugees (1951 Refugee Convention)
Refugee Convention of the Organization of African Unity (OAU), 154
Refugee Law Project (Makerere University), 27, 189, 217
children, return of, 218–19
justice, definition, 198, 221–22
National Reconciliation Bill (proposed), 226, 236n64
National Resistance Movement (NRM), 231n23
reintegration package, interview, 236n68
Refugees
Burundi, 165
Darfur, Sudan, 165
defined, 153, 155, 167n2, 168n11
discrimination against, prohibition, 156
forced migrants, 154
Germany, 163, 172n52
global burden-sharing, 163–64
nonentitlement to asylum, 156
Pakistan, 164, 165, 172n52

protection, 3. *See also* International refugee law
Sierra Leone, 165
statistics, 154
status, determination of, 167–68nn3–4
Tanzania, 164, 165, 170n25, 172n52
Uganda, 81, 165–66
Regional human rights treaties, 101–8
Registration of Customary Marriages and Divorce Act (Sierra Leone), 278n97
Repression, defined, 6
Republic of Uganda. *See* Uganda
Responsibility to protect (R2P)
force, rules regarding use of, 51–52
generally, 21
Responsible sovereignty, 306-08
Restorative justice
Beyond Juba Project, 221–23
nature of, 330–31
Refugee Law Project (Makerere University), 221–22
Sierra Leone, 259–68
reparations, 266–68
Uganda, 221–23
Retraumatization, 281n140
Retributive justice
Beyond Juba Project, 221–23
nature of, 331–32
Refugee Law Project (Makerere University), 221–22
Sierra Leone, 254–58
Special Court for Sierra Leone (SCSI), self-assessment by, 258
Uganda, 221–23
Revolutionary United Front (RUF), 5
child recruitment, 250–51
civil war, generally, 249–50
leadership, 246
Lomé Peace Agreement, signing of, 242
and Special Court for Sierra Leone, 130–31
RLP. *See* Refugee Law Project (Makerere University)
Rome Statute of the ICC, 43n84
"Crimes Against Peace," 126
overview, 132–33
ratification, 87, 213
subject matter jurisdiction, 47
war criminals, 123
Roosevelt, Eleanor, 90
Roosevelt, Franklin D., 110n3

Royal Dutch Shell, 27
RPF. *See* Rwandese Patriotic Front (RPF)
R2P. *See* Responsibility to protect (R2P)
RUF. *See* Revolutionary United Front (RUF)
Rufyikiri, Gervais, 296, 309n4
Rwagasore, Louis (Prince), 313n63
Rwanda
    Burundi, similarities and differences, 286–97
    Gisenyi, RPF attack, 315n99
    Interahamwe, 292, 313n71
    International Criminal Tribunal for Rwanda (ICTR), 129, 140
Rwandan Tribunal. *See* International Criminal Tribunal for Rwanda (ICTR)
Rwandese Patriotic Front (RPF), 293, 295–96
Rwasa, Agathon, 300

SAC. *See* Social Action Commission (SAC)
Sahinguvu, Yves, 302
Sankoh, Foday
    arrest of, 252
    death of, 255
    invasion of Sierra Leone, 130
    pardon, 131
    RUF leadership, 246, 274n25
    Strategic Mineral Resources Commission, 253, 276n69
Save Darfur Foundation, 151n118
Schabas, William, 135–36, 261, 264, 332
SCSL. *See* Special Court for Sierra Leone (SCSL)
Selective genocide, 291
Self-restraint, 7
Sembakounya refugee camp, Guinea, 167n1, 271n1
September 11, 2001 terrorist attacks, 58
Sesay, Issa Hassan, 146n49, 255, 277n85, 278n93
Sesay, Joseph, 257, 260, 278n94
Sierra Leone, 241–82
    African Commission on Human and People's Rights, 106
    All People's Congress (APC), 245–46
    Armed Forces Revolutionary Council (AFRC), 130, 255–56, 262
    CD-Peace. *See also* Centre for Development and Peace Education (CD-Peace), 270–71
    Centre for Accountability and the Rule of Law, 257
    children, punishment, 263
    Civil Defense Forces (CDF), 130, 251–52, 256
    civil war, 80, 246–53, 256
    class issues underlying civil war, 246–49
    colonial history, 244–45
    communities, implementation of humanitarian law, 198–99
    Constitution, 38n44
    human rights provisions, 109
    Convention on the Elimination of All Forms of Discrimination Against Women (CEDAW), 98
    Convention on the Elimination of All Forms of Racial Discrimination (CERD), 97
    Convention on the Prevention and Punishment of the Crime of Genocide, adoption of, 87
    courts, judicial enforcement of humanitarian law, 179–80
    development, 326–28
    as mechanism for conflict resolution, 194
    Devolution of Estates Act, 278n97
    diamond trade, 248, 252, 274n32, 275n36, 276n69
    Domestic Violence Act, 278n97
    ethnicity and civil war, 246–49
    "family talk." *See* fambul tok ("family talk"). *See also* Fambul Tok (NGO, Sierra Leone)
    Fourah Bay College (Sierra Leone), 246
    Freetown Colony
    Protectorate, distinction between, 248, 273n12
    settlement, history, 244–45
    Geneva Conventions of 1949, ratification of, 70n63
    Government of Sierra Leone, petition against, 95
    grassroots level, transitional justice, 268–71
    health care, 266
    human insecurity, 79–80
    humanitarian law, 241–82. *See also Lines throughout this topic*
    independence, history, 245–46
    justice, ongoing pursuit of, 140–41
    Krios (Creoles), 245

Sierra Leone (*Cont'd*)
  Liberia, invasion by, 130
  life expectancy, 79
  Lomé Peace Agreement. *See* Lomé Peace Agreement
  "lumpens," 249
  media, implementation of humanitarian law, 189–90
  National Commission for Social Action, 267
  National Provisional Ruling Council (NPRC). *See* National Provisional Ruling Council (NPRC)
  National Witness Protection Unit, 258
  "Operation No Living Thing," 252–53
  Outreach Committee (OC), 269
  Peace Agreement Between the Government of Sierra Leone and the Revolutionary United Front (RUF), 130
  Peace and Reconciliation Agricultural Show, 270
  politics underlying civil war, 246–49
  population, 272n2
  postcolonial history, 245–46
  post-conflict reconstruction, 4–6, 241–82
  Protectorate, split with Freetown Colony, 248, 273n12
  radio, 191–92
  "rebel war," 242
  Reconciliation Committee (RC), 269
  Refugee All Stars, 188, 189
  refugees, 165
  Registration of Customary Marriages and Divorce Act, 278n97
  reparations, 266–68
  restorative justice, 259–68
  retributive justice, 254–58
  Revolutionary United Front (RUF). *See* Revolutionary United Front (RUF)
  Rome Statute of the ICC, 87
  settlement, history, 244–45
  socioeconomic security, 78–79
  Special Court for Sierra Leone (SCSI). *See* Special Court for Sierra Leone (SCSI)
  Strategic Mineral Resources Commission, 253
  transitional justice, 253–68
  troops, 184
  military enforcement of humanitarian law, 186–87
  Truth and Reconciliation Commission (TRC). *See* Truth and Reconciliation Commission (TRC)
  United Nations Mission in Sierra Leone (UNAMSIL), 253
  "West Side Boys," 252
  women
    rape, 263, 279n107
    vote, 278n97
Sierra Leonean Army, 246, 250
Sierra Leone Court Monitoring Program, 258
Sierra Leone Human Rights Commission, 267, 281n139
Sierra Leone People's Party (SLPP), 245, 251, 264
Sinduhije, Alexis, 21, 299, 307–08, 312n42, 333n4
Sinunguruza, Thérence, 296, 309n4
Slavery and slave trade
  African Slave Trade, 68n29
  overview, 88–90
  Supplementary Convention on the Abolition of Slavery, the Slave Trade, and Institutions and Practices Similar to Slavery, 88
SLPP. *See* Sierra Leone People's Party (SLPP)
Social Action Commission (SAC), 206n57
Social security, Uganda, 220–21
Socioeconomic security, 77–79
Soft law, defined, 18
Song of Lawino, 229n2
South Africa, Truth and Reconciliation Commission, 217
Sovereignty
  responsible sovereignty, 306–8
  state, 14, 35n15
"So Why?" (song), 202n1, 202n6
Soyinka, Wole, 65, 123, 141–42n1
Special Court for Sierra Leone (SCSL)
  benchmark year, 145n46
  creation of, 254–58
  criticism for, 256–58
  docket of, 254–56
  establishment of, 242–43
  force of, 327
  generally, 123
  hybrid tribunal, 271

judicial enforcement of humanitarian
  law, 180
jurisdiction, 203n14
justice, ongoing pursuit of, 141
  as model for international
    organizations, 26
  National Victim Commemoration
    Conference, 257
  operation of, 326
  overview, 130–32
  praise for, 256–58
  retributive justice, 254–58
    docket of, 254–56
    self-assessment by Special Court, 258
  self-assessment, 258
Standing Committee on Human Rights at
  the Arab League, 107
Stevens, Saika
  accusations, 275n36
  All People's Congress (APC), 245–46
  ethnic affiliation, 247
  re 17-year plague of locusts, 274n23
  structure of country, transformation, 241
Steyn, Johan, 42n78
Strasser, Valentine, 250, 251, 256
Strategic Mineral Resources Commission
  (Sierra Leone), 253
*Strength in What Remains: A Journey of
  Remembrance* (Kidder), 195, 284–85
Sudan. *See also* Darfur, Sudan
  as safe haven, 214
Supplementary Convention on the Abolition
  of Slavery, the Slave Trade, and
  Institutions and Practices Similar to
  Slavery, 88

Tallensi tribe (Ghana), 64
Tanganyika, independence, 7n1
Tanzania
  criminal tribunal, 181
  economic statistics, 173n55
  gross domestic product (GDP), 164
  refugees, 164, 165, 170n25, 172n52,
    318n117
Taylor, Charles
  and diamond mines, 274n32, 275n36
  election of, 252
  indictment and trial, 130, 180, 277n84
  National Patriotic Front of Liberia
    (NPFL), 246
  rebels, support for, 5

and RUF, 248, 274n25
  and Special Court for Sierra Leone
    (SCSL), 255
"Terms of trade," 18
Terrorism. *See also* War on Terror
  counterterrorism as armed conflict, 58–59
  terrorist organizations, 28
  Ugandan Anti-Terrorism Act, 227
  UN General Assembly denouncement,
    69n43
TI. *See* Transparency International (TI)
Tokyo Tribunal. *See* International Military
  Tribunal for the Far East (IMTFE)
Tolstoy, Leo, 45
Torture. *See also* Convention Against Torture
  (CAT); Declaration Against Torture
  as crime, United Nations, 99–100, 124,
    142n4
Torture Convention. *See* Convention Against
  Torture (CAT)
Trafficking, 42n75
Transitional justice
  Burundi, 304–8
    responsible sovereignty, 306–8
    women's equality, 305–6
  Sierra Leone, 253–68
    Centre for Development and Peace
      Education (CD-Peace), 270–71
    Fambul Tok, 268–70
    grassroots level, 268–71
    restorative justice, 259–68
    retributive justice, 254–58
  Uganda, 226–27
Transparency International (TI), 113n32
TRC. *See* Truth and Reconciliation
  Commission (TRC)
Treaty of Rome. *See* Rome Statute of the
  ICC, 222
Troops and humanitarian law. *See also*
  Conflict resolution, troops as
    tools for, 178
  Burundi, 187
  peacekeeping troops, 184–85
  Sierra Leone, 184
Trusteeship Council (United Nations),
  40n54
Truth and Reconciliation Act of 2000 (Sierra
  Leone), 263
Truth and Reconciliation Commission
  (TRC) (Sierra Leone), 6, 71n69
  and accountability, 258, 279n111

Index [355]

Truth and Reconciliation Commission (TRC) (Cont'd)
   Chile, 266
   and communities, 200
   creation of, 217, 326
   cultural significance, 259–61
   establishment of, 242, 259
   Final Report, 199, 259–68, 275n50, 276n54
      causes and nature of war, 248, 250, 261–62
      and Special Court for Sierra Leone (SCSL), 256
      force of, 327
      historical significance, 259–61
      Lomé Peace Agreement, 6, 71n69, 326
      quasi-judicial findings, 264–66
      recommendations, 262–64, 280n122
      reparations, 266–68
      restorative justice, 259–68
         reparations, though, 266–68
      Social Action Commission (SAC), 206n57
   transitional justice, 253–54, 305
Truth and Reconciliation Working Group (Sierra Leone) (TRWG), 260, 263, 268
Truth telling
   and accountability, 224, 229
   accountability for war crimes, 224
TRWG. *See* Truth and Reconciliation Working Group (TRWG)
Turay, Mary, 270
Turay, Thomas, 270, 282n148
Tutsi-Hima leaders, 290
Tutsi people. *See* Burundi
Tutu, Desmond, 45
2006 Juba Agreement on Cessation of Hostilities between the Government of the Republic of Juba and the Lord's Resistance Army/Movement, 209

Ubuntu, 306
Ubupfasoni, 306Ubushingantahe, 181, 197, 199, 305–6
UDHR. *See* Universal Declaration of Human Rights (UDHR)
Uganda, 209–40
   accountability for war crimes, 215–17
      truth telling, establishing historical record through, 224

Acholi Army brigade. *See* Acholi Army brigade
Acholi people. *See* Acholi people
African Commission on Human and People's Rights, 105–6
Amin Dada, Idi. *See* Amin Dada, Idi
Amnesty Act. *See* Amnesty Act of 2000 (Uganda)
Beyond Juba Project (BJP). *See* Beyond Juba Project (BJP)
children
   exploitation of, 210
   return of, 218–19
civilian deaths, 231n20, 237n92
civil war
   ethnopolitics, 211–13
   generally, 209
   history of, 211–15
   Museveni, Yoweri, 213–14
   Obote era, 211
   peace talks and LRA prosecutions, 214–15
communities
   implementation of humanitarian law, 198
   victims and perpetrators, communities of, 223
Constitution, human rights provisions, 108–9, 121n165
Convention on the Elimination of All Forms of Discrimination Against Women (CEDAW), 98, 117n88
Convention on the Elimination of All Forms of Racial Discrimination (CERD), 97
Convention on the Prevention and Punishment of the Crime of Genocide, adoption of, 87
courts, judicial enforcement of humanitarian law, 179–80
criminal justice, 140–41, 180
Democratic Party of Uganda, 217
development as mechanism for conflict resolution, 193–194
Director of Public Prosecutions, 227, 235n60, 239–40n124
displaced persons, 229
domestic developments, 136–37
domestic violence, 220
ethnopolitics, 211–13

[356]   *Index*

extrajudicial killings of civilians, 231n20
and Freedom House, 81
history of, 211–15
Holy Spirit Movement, 212–13
human insecurity, 79–80
humanitarian law. *See Lines throughout this topic*
internally displaced persons (IDPs), 174n65
International Crimes Division (ICD). *See* International Crimes Division (ICD)
International Criminal Court (ICC), 134–37
inauguration of, 209–10
Israel, reliance on for military training, 212, 231n13
justice. *See also* Beyond Juba Project
sustainable peace, justice as, 325–26
Justice, Law and Order Sector (JLOS). *See* Justice, Law and Order Sector (JLOS)
King's African Rifles (KAR), 211
life expectancy, 79
Lord's Resistance Army. *See* Lord's Resistance Army (Uganda)
mato oput. *See* Mato oput (Uganda)
media, implementation of humanitarian law, 189
members of parliament, numbers of, 230n3
Ministry of Justice and Constitutional Affairs, 225
National Reconciliation Bill (proposed), 226, 236n64
National Reconciliation Forum, call for, 217
National Resistance Army (NRA), 212, 231n20
nongovernmental organizations (NGOs), 148n82, 180, 193
Obote era. *See* Obote, Milton
peace talks and LRA prosecutions, 214–15
political liberty, 81
population, 230n3
post-conflict reconstruction, 4–5
radio, 236n74
rape, 220
reconciliation, 217

Refugee Law Project (Makerere University). *See* Refugee Law Project (Makerere University)
refugees, 165–66
restorative justice, 221–23
retributive justice, 221–23
social security, 220–21
socioeconomic security, 78–79
transitional justice, 226–27
troops, military enforcement of humanitarian law, 186
Truth and Reconciliation Commission (TRC). *See* Truth and Reconciliation Commission (TRC)
victims and perpetrators, communities of, 223
War Crimes Act. *See* War Crimes Act of 2010 (Uganda)
War Crimes Division, 325–26
"wife inheritance," 220, 237n83
women
exploitation, 210
respect for, 219–20
status of, 99
Ugandan Anti-Terrorism Act, 227
Ugandan People's Defense Forces (UPDF), 5
allegations of war crimes, 233n43, 234n48
civilian deaths, 237n92
civil war, 209
and Museveni, Yoweri, 213
peace talks and LRA prosecutions, 214–15
Ugandan Protectorate, 211
Ugandan Reconciliation Forum, 217
UMECS. *See* United Movement to End Child Soldiering (UMECS)
Umugabekazi, 306
UNAMISIL. *See* United Nations Mission in Sierra Leone (UNAMISIL)
Unanimous Declaration of the Thirteen United States of America, 37n34
UN Charter
Article 1, 14, 47, 85
Article 2, 14
Article 2(3), 47
Article 2(4), 47
Article 39, 48
Article 42, 48

Index [357]

UN Charter (*Cont'd*)
  Article 51, 48
  Chapter VII, 17, 48–49, 127, +133
  generally, 13
  Preamble, 14, 47
  Security Council, role in regulating use of force, 48
  Statute of International Court of Justice, 15–16
  Trusteeship Council, 40n54
UN Commission on the Status of Women (CSW), 98
UN Declaration on the Rights of Indigenous Peoples (UNDRIP). *See also* United Nations Declaration on the Rights of Indigenous Peoples (UNDRIP), 85–86
UN Development Program (UNDP), 304
  Human Development Report for 2010, 79
  and internally displaced persons (IDPs), 160
  as model for international organizations, 25
  socioeconomic security, 77
UNDP. *See* UN Development Program (UNDP)
UNDRIP. *See* United Nations Declaration on the Rights of Indigenous Peoples (UNDRIP)
UN Environmental Program, 25–26
UN General Assembly
  aggression, resolution defining, 144n23
  Convention on the Prevention and Punishment of the Crime of Genocide, adoption of, 87
  generally, 19
  on inherent dignity, recognition of, 76
  "In Larger Freedom" report, 51
  as model for international organizations, 23
UNHCR. *See* United Nations High Commissioner for Refugees (UNHCR)
UN Human Rights Committee, 265
UN Human Rights Council, 69n47
UNICEF. *See* United National Children's Fund (UNICEF)
Union des Patriotes Congolais (UPC), 137

Union for National Progress (UPRONA), 292, 294–96, 313n63
United Movement to End Child Soldiering (UMECS), 193–94
United National Children's Fund (UNICEF), 251
United Nations. *See also* Other headings beginning UN
  birth of, 47
  Charter. *See* UN Charter
  Millennium Development Goals, 77, 111n9, 277n79
  as model for international organizations, 22–26
    Economic and Social Council (ECOSOC), 25–26
    International Court of Justice (ICJ), 24–25
    Special Court for Sierra Leone (SCSL), 26
    UN Development Program, 25
    UN Environmental Program, 25–26
    UN General Assembly, 23
    UN High Commissioner for Refugees, 26
    UN Secretariat, 25
    UN Security Council, 17, 23–24, 48, 49, 127, 139
    World Food Program, 26
    World Health Organization, 25
  Trusteeship Council, 40n54
United Nations Declaration on the Rights of Indigenous Peoples (UNDRIP), 27, 85–86
United Nations Guiding Principles on Internal Displacement, 161
United Nations High Commissioner for Refugees (UNHCR), 26
  Executive Committee, 157
  and internally displaced persons (IDPs), 160
    interdependence of protection and assistance for refugees and IDPs, 162–63
    statistics, 172n51
  statistics, 154
  voluntary repatriation, 170n24
United Nations Mission in Sierra Leone (UNAMSIL), 186–87, 200, 253

United States
  Gross domestic product (GDP), 112n12
  refugees, determination of status, 167n3
Universal Declaration of Human Rights
    (UDHR), 82–86
  adoption of, 23
  Article 1, 83
  Articles 2-21, 109
  Articles 3-21, 83
  Articles 22-27, 84
  basic liberties, 83–84
  collective life, 85–86
  economic and social rights, 84–85
  impact of, 86
  norm of equality, 82–83
  and political liberty, 81
  quote from, 75
  as soft law, 19–20
Universality, 31
Universal jurisdiction, 31
UN Mission to Sierra Leone (UNAMSIL).
    See United Nations Mission in Sierra
    Leone (UNAMSIL)
UN Peacekeeping Office, 194
UN Security Council. *See* United Nations,
    UN Security Council
UPC. *See* Union des Patriotes Congolais
    (UPC)
UPDF. *See* Ugandan People's Defense Forces
    (UPDF)
Upper Canadian Rebellion of the 1830s,
    49–50
UPRONA. *See* Union for National Progress
    (UPRONA)
US Constitution
  Article VI Supremacy Clause, 30
US Military Commissions Act, 73n97
US v. Iran, 24
Uvin, Peter, 205n38, 289, 294, 304, 309n6,
    314n79, 319n144, 320n154

Van Dunem, Lourdes, 177
VCLOT. *See* Vienna Convention on the Law
    of Treaties (VCLOT)
Velasquez-Rodriguez Case, 102
Victim compensation, 206n57
Vienna Convention on the Law of Treaties
    (VCLOT), 15
Vietnam, invasion of Cambodia, 50
Village Health Works (Burundi), 195

Violence. *See also* Galtung, Johan
  Burundi, 284–86
  defined, 6–7, 303–04
  against women, 2, 204n24
Voluntary repatriation, 170n24

War. *See* International humanitarian law;
    International criminal law
War crimes. *See also* War Crimes Act of 2010
    (Uganda)
  accountability for, 215–17, 238n93,
    279n111
  defined, 126
War Crimes Act of 2010 (Uganda), 203n12,
    209, 218, 224, 325
War criminals. *See* International criminal law;
    International Military Tribunal
    (IMT); Nuremburg Statute
War on Terror, 58
  exception to general prohibition against
    use of force, 52–53
  Guantanamo Bay, U.S. Naval Base, 61
War-weariness, 228, 240n136
Webster-Ashburton Treaty (1842), 50
Webster, Daniel, 50
Wemba, Papa, 177
"West Side Boys," 252, 253
Wierda, Marieke. *See* Pierrello, Tom and
    Wierda, Marieke
"Wife inheritance," Uganda, 220, 237n83
Women
  Burundi, role of women in
    ubushingantahe, 305–6
  femicides, Mexico, 98, 103
  gender-based violence, 187, 204n24,
    237n81
  secondary education, 79
  Sierra Leone
    rape, 263, 279n107
    vote, 278n97
  status of. *See* UN Commission on the
    Status of Women (CSW)
  Uganda
    exploitation, 210
    respect for women, 219–20
Women's Convention. *See* Convention on
    the Elimination of All Forms of
    Discrimination Against Women
    (CEDAW)
Woolman, John, 45

World Cup soccer competition, attacks during, 185
World Food Program, 26
World Health Organization, 25
World War I, 66n11
World War II
   aggression, concept of, 47
   bombing runs, 66n11
   Holocaust, 47, 87, 115n49
"Woza Africa," 202n6

Yugoslavia. *See also* International Criminal Tribunal for the Former Yugoslavia (ICTY)
   International Criminal Tribunals, 123
Yugoslav Tribunal. *See* International Criminal Tribunal for the Former Yugoslavia (ICTY)

Zalaquet, José, 266